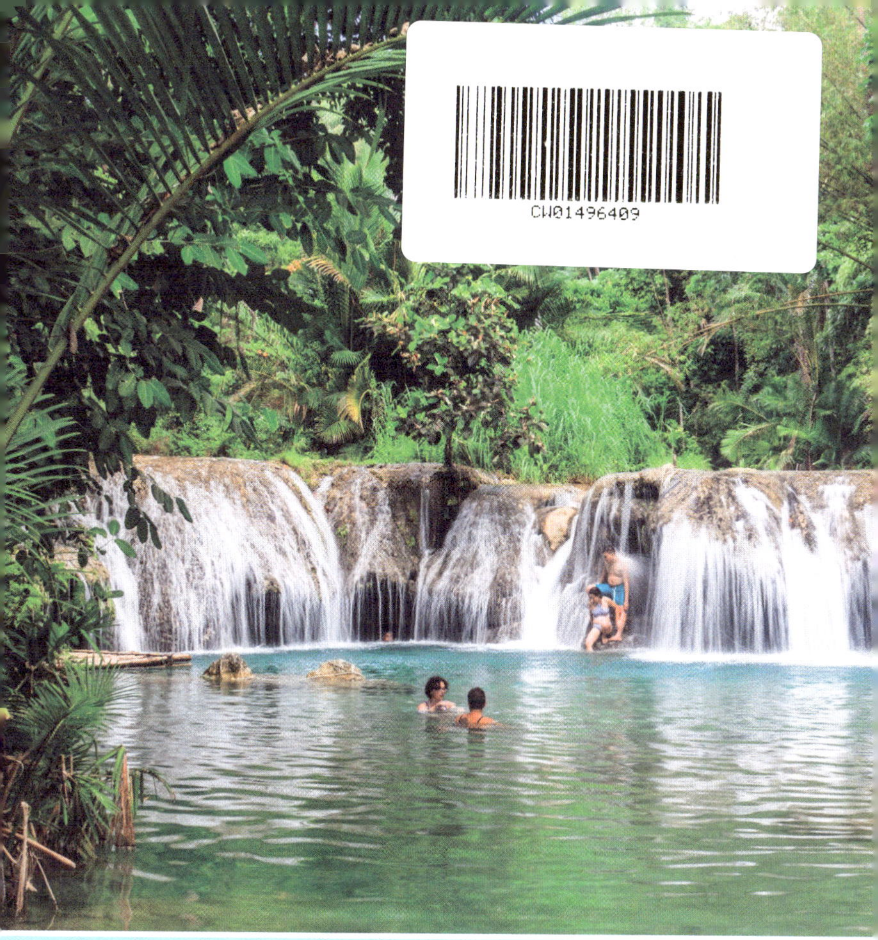

PHILIPPINES

This seventh edition updated by
Martin Zatko

Contents

We've flagged up our favourite places
– a perfectly sited hotel, an atmospheric
café, a special restaurant – throughout
the Guide with the ★ symbol

Introduction to
Philippines

Separated from its Southeast Asian neighbours by the South China Sea, the Philippines have always been a little different. As the only Asian nation colonized by the Spanish, this lush archipelago of dazzling beaches, year-round sun and warm, turquoise waters remains predominantly Roman Catholic, and culturally – a blend of Islamic, Malay, Spanish and American influences – it often feels light years away from its neighbours, with a string of elegant colonial towns that have more in common with Latin America than the rest of Asia. It's an enticing mix: all over the archipelago you'll discover tantalizing food, friendly people and exuberant festivals. And the variety is truly astonishing: you can surf, island-hop or dive pristine coral reefs in the morning, and in the same day visit Indigenous villages, ancient rice terraces and lush, jungle-smothered peaks.

Indeed, the Philippines is often underrated and misunderstood by travellers and its Asian neighbours, casually dismissed as a supplier of maids, tribute bands, mail-order brides and corrupt politicians, epitomized by the gaudy excesses of Imelda Marcos. Don't be put off: while poverty and corruption remain serious problems, the Philippines are far more complex – and culturally rich – than the stereotypes suggest.

The **Filipino people** are variously descended from early Malay settlers, Muslim Sufis from the Middle East, Spanish conquistadors and friars, and later, from Chinese traders. It's an old cliché, but largely true: Filipinos take pride in making visitors welcome, even in the most rustic barangay home. Equally important is the culture of entertaining, evident in the hundreds of colourful **fiestas** that are held throughout the country, many tied to the Roman Catholic calendar. Never far behind partying is eating, and eating well. Filipino **food** is heavily influenced by Spanish and native traditions – expect plenty of fresh fish caught locally, roasted meats (pork and chicken) and a plethora of addictively sweet desserts, many utilizing the vast array of tropical fruits on offer.

THE PHILIPPINES

0 — 200
kilometres

N

Metres
2000
1000
500
200
100
0

Batanes
Islands

Luzon Strait

Babuyan
Islands

Laoag

Vigan

Sagada · Bontoc
Banaue

San Fernando

▲ Mt Pulag

Baguio

Dagupan

Luzon

S
I
E
R
R
A

M
A
D
R
E

PHILIPPINE SEA

Angeles
▲ Mt Pinatubo · San Fernando
Olongapo

MANILA

Corregidor

Daet

Anilao · Lucena
Puerto Galera · Batangas
Calapan City

Naga
▲ Mt Mayon
Legazpi
Sorsogon Town

Catanduanes

Marinduque

Donsol

Mindoro

Apo Reef

Romblon

Masbate

Catarman

Samar

Catbalogan

Busuanga

Boracay

Masbate

*Calamian
Islands*

Kalibo
Roxas

V I S A Y A S

El Nido

*Cuyo
Islands*

Panay

Cebu

Tacloban

*Taytay
Bay*

Iloilo City

Ormoc

Leyte

Bacolod ▲
Mt Kanlaon

Cebu City

Dinagat

Palawan

Puerto Princesa

Negros

Bohol

Siargao

Dumaguete

Surigao

SULU SEA

Siquijor

**BOHOL
SEA**

Camiguin

Butuan

Brooke's Point

*Tubbataha
Reef*

Dipolog

Cagayan
de Oro

Balabac

Zamboanga City

Cotabato

Mindanao

▲ Mt Apo

Davao

**MALAYSIA
(SABAH)**

Sandakan

Jolo

Basilan

General
Santos

Tawi-Tawi

Sulu Archipelago

CELEBES SEA

FACT FILE

- The **population** of the Philippines is estimated to be around 115 million (the 12th highest on earth); around half reside on the island of Luzon.
- The Philippines officially comprises 7641 islands, though the actual figure varies depending on the definition of "island"; reef tips and shoals number in the tens of thousands.
- The Philippines has one of the largest **diasporas** in the world; 11–12 million Filipinos live and work overseas, mostly as nurses, maids or on cruise ships.
- The richest individual in the Philippines is thought to be real estate tycoon and former politician Manuel B. Villar Jr, with a US$17.2 billion net worth – in a country where the average wage isn't much more than US$300/month.
- **Tanduay rum** dates back to 1854, and today remains the nation's spirit of choice. Made with sugar cane milled in Negros, it's frequently cheaper than bottled water.
- Many Filipinos have at least one **uncle or aunt** named Boy, Girlie or Baby.
- Filipino and English are the **official languages** of the Philippines (Filipino is a standardized version of Tagalog), but there are at least 171 languages spoken throughout the archipelago, with Cebuano following Filipino in popularity.

Even the **politics** in Asia's first democracy is rich in showmanship and pizzazz. From Ferdinand Marcos to the "housewife President" Cory Aquino to the controversial President Duterte, the country's leaders have never been short on charisma. But despite impressive economic gains in the last twenty years, all have conspicuously failed to rid the country of its grinding **poverty**, visible everywhere you go in shanty towns and rickety barangay. Ordinary people somehow remain stoical in the face of these problems, infectiously optimistic and upbeat. This determination to enjoy life is a national characteristic, encapsulated in the common Filipino phrase *bahala na* – "what will be will be".

Where to go

Most flights to the Philippines arrive in **Manila**, the crazy, chaotic capital which, despite first impressions, is worth at least a day or two of your time. The city's major historical attraction is the old Spanish walled city of **Intramuros**, while the best museums in the country can be found in nearby **Rizal Park** and skyscraper-smothered **Makati**. There are also some worthwhile day-trips from the city; top of the list is the island of **Corregidor** in Manila Bay, which was fought over bitterly during World War II and, with its now-silent guns and ruins, is a poignant place to soak up the history of the conflict.

Within easy striking distance of Manila – about two hours south by road – a highlight of the province of Batangas is the city of **Tagaytay** and its mesmerizing views over **Lake Taal**, the picture-perfect crater lake with **Taal Volcano** in the middle. Around the small coastal town of **Anilao** you'll find the best scuba diving near Manila, while the adjacent agricultural province of **Laguna** is known for its therapeutic hot springs and luscious *buko* (coconut) pies. North of Manila instead are the theme parks, beaches and wreck-dives of **Subic Bay**.

Subic Bay makes a tempting break before the long ride to the extraordinary attractions and spell-binding mountain scenery of **northern Luzon**. From the mountain city of **Baguio**, it's a rough but memorable trip north along winding roads to

JEEPNEYS

Millions of Filipinos depend on **jeepneys** – a kind of informal minibus service – to get to school and the office, or to transport livestock to market. Jeepneys are able to operate where roads are too narrow for regular buses, and as a result most travellers end up using them at least once. Despite the discomfort, for many it's one of the highlights of their trip – a genuine slice of Filipino life.

The original jeepneys, cannibalized from vehicles left behind by departing Americans at the end of World War II, have evolved over the past six decades into the mass-produced versions that you see on the streets today, decorated with chrome trinkets, blinking fairy lights and images of celebrities. Others sport religious mottos, crucifixes and images of saints, perhaps understandable given the high accident rates they rack up.

Indigenous communities such as **Sagada**, known for its hanging coffins, and **Banaue**, where you can trek through awe-inspiring rice-terrace countryside. Off Luzon's northern tip are the alluring islands of **Batanes**, one of the country's greatest secrets, while along Luzon's west coast you can surf around **San Fernando** or explore the ravishing colonial town of **Vigan**, a UNESCO World Heritage Site.

Head south from Manila through the **Bicol** region and you'll reach perhaps the best-known of Philippine volcanoes, **Mayon**, an almost perfect cone that towers over the city of Legazpi and is a strenuous four- or five-day climb. Around **Donsol** you can swim with whale sharks, and in **Bulusan Volcano National Park** trek through lush rainforest to waterfalls, hot springs and volcanic craters. Even further off the tourist trail, **Catanduanes** offers excellent surfing, while **Marinduque** is a pastoral island backwater that only gets touristy for the annual **Moriones festival**, held at Easter.

If you're looking for some serious diving, head for **Puerto Galera** on the northern coast of **Mindoro Island** – south of Manila, and the closest major Philippine island to the capital, it also boasts some excellent beaches, plus trekking through the jungles of the interior to tribal communities. There's more world-class diving off the west coast of Mindoro at **Apo Reef**, although it can be pricey to get here.

For most visitors, however, the myriad islands and islets of the **Visayas**, right at the heart of the archipelago, are top of the agenda. In the **Western Visayas**, the captivating little island of **Boracay**, with its pristine beach, is on almost everyone's itinerary, but if

DIVE PARADISE

The Philippines is blessed by a dazzling richness and diversity of marine life and **diving** is one of the most popular activities in the archipelago. Under the waves lies an underwater wonderland of stupefying **coral gardens** teeming with brilliantly coloured reef fish, turtles, giant clams and starfish, while at depth there are giant rays and prowling sharks. Indeed, this vast tropical archipelago is at the heart of Southeast Asia's "coral triangle", the most biologically diverse marine ecosystem on earth, with over 300 types of coral and 350 fish species. Diving here is affordable and, thanks to warm waters, can be enjoyed year-round. If you're serious about your diving, booking a trip on a **liveaboard** (see page 40) can be a memorable experience, giving you the opportunity to get away from the more popular dive resorts and explore the wilderness.

Boracay is too touristy for you, try laidback Siquijor or tiny Apo Island near Negros, a marine reserve where the only accommodation is in rustic cottages.

For even less developed spots, head over to the **Eastern Visayas** for Panglao Island off Bohol, or the tantalizing beaches and waters of Malapascua off the northern tip of Cebu Island. For trekking and climbing make for **Mount Kanlaon National Park** on Negros, one of the country's finest wilderness areas. The largest city in the Visayas is **Cebu City**, the arrival point for a limited number of international flights – as well as a major hub for domestic airlines – making it a good alternative base to Manila. It's friendly, affordable and has a buzzing nightlife scene, with great restaurants and live music.

To the west of the archipelago, out in the northern Sulu Sea, is the bewitching province of **Palawan**, most of it still wild and unspoilt. Many visitors come for the superb scuba diving, especially on the sunken World War II wrecks around **Coron Town** in the **Calamian Islands** to the north of Palawan proper. Palawan itself is home to the seaside town of **El Nido** and the **Bacuit archipelago**, hundreds of gem-like limestone islands with sugar-white beaches and lagoons. From **Puerto Princesa**, Palawan's likeable capital, strike out for the laidback beach town of **Port Barton** or the **Underground River**, an entrancing cavern system only accessible by boat.

AVERAGE TEMPERATURES AND RAINFALL

	Jan	Feb	Mar	Apr	May	Jun	Jul	Aug	Sep	Oct	Nov	Dec
MANILA												
°C	25	27	28.5	31.5	31	29	28.5	28	28	28.5	28	27
°F	77	81	83	89	88	84	83	82	82	83	82	81
Rainfall (mm)	0.74	0.46	0.58	1.1	4.2	8.5	13.9	13.6	11.8	6.2	4.8	2.1
BAGUIO (NORTHERN LUZON)												
°C	17	19	20.5	23.5	23	21	20.5	19.5	20	20.5	20	18.5
°F	63	66	69	74	73	70	69	67	68	69	68	65
Rainfall (mm)	0.74	1.2	1.1	1.4	4.8	10.2	14.8	14.2	12.6	8.4	6.6	3.2
SIARGAO (MINDANAO)												
°C	25.5	26	26	27	27	27	27	27	27	27	26	26.5
°F	78	79	79	81	81	81	81	81	81	81	79	80
Rainfall (mm)	17.5	13.4	16.3	8.4	5	4.2	5.7	4.1	5.6	8.8	14.2	20

In the far south, the vast island of **Mindanao** has long been the Muslim heartland of the Philippines, an enticing yet sadly troubled region (see box, page 385). The two offshore islands that are regarded as completely safe and still see large numbers of visitors are **Siargao**, which boasts surf beaches and secret lagoons, and wonderfully friendly and scenic **Camiguin**. You should check the security situation very carefully before considering a visit to the pristine waters of the **Enchanted River**, the durian capital and largest city of **Davao** or nearby **Mount Apo**. Note that at the time this book went to print, western Mindanao, including the **Sulu archipelago**, was definitely too dangerous to visit due to continuing separatist unrest.

When to go

The Philippines has a hot and humid tropical climate with a **wet season** (southwest monsoon, or *habagat*) from May to October and a **dry season** (northeast monsoon, or *amihan*) from November to April. The **best time to visit** is during the dry season, although some regions get quite a lot of rain till February, and even the wet season sees many sunny days with short, intense downpours at dusk. January and February are the coolest months and good for travelling, while March, April and May are very hot: expect sunshine all day and temperatures to peak at a broiling 36°C. As well as higher humidity, the wet season also brings **typhoons** (see box, page 49), with flights sometimes cancelled and roads impassable. The first typhoon can hit as early as May, although typically it is June or July before the rains really start, with July to September the wettest (and stormiest) months. The Palawan, Mindanao and the southern Visayas are less prone to typhoons, and Mindanao sees less rain during the wet season.

Author picks

Scaling the heights of its awe-inspiring volcanoes, enduring sweltering jungle heat and traversing some of Asia's most isolated roads, our hard-travelling authors have visited every corner of this vast, magnificent archipelago – from the rice terraces of Luzon to the beaches of the Visayas. Here are their personal favourites:

Best beach hideaway You don't have to travel for days by bangka to find a slice of serenity in the Philippines; *Amami Beach Resort* in Talipanan, Mindoro (see page 232) is a perfect place to relax and unwind surrounded by nature with dolphins off the beach and monkeys lounging in the trees.

Eat like a Filipino The best fried chicken in the Philippines? For purists, it's still knocked out by *Aristocrat* in Manila (see page 88). The *halo-halo* here is amazing also, but *Aling Taleng's* (see page 105) in Pagsanjan is sublime. For *buko* pie it's a close call, but the options Los Baños (see page 104) are hard to beat.

Go wild Tackle the pristine jungle wilderness of Mindoro with an epic climb up Mount Halcon (see page 235), or conquer Mount Kanlaon on Negros (see page 281); trekking through the UNESCO World Heritage rice terraces in northern Luzon remains an enchanting experience (see page 163), while seeing (or even snorkelling with) whale sharks, the world's largest fish, in Donsol (see page 212) is truly magical.

Best stash of gold One of many reasons to resist the desire to flee Manila as soon as possible, the Ayala Museum (see page 76) is an intriguing introduction to the history and lavish pre-Hispanic culture of the Philippines.

Go paddling Soak up the beauty of southern Luzon by taking a boat through the crystal-clear waters and exploring the awe-inspiring limestone cliffs of the Caramoan Peninsula (see page 201).

Our author recommendations don't end here. We've flagged up our favourite places – a perfectly sited hotel, an atmospheric café, a special restaurant – throughout the Guide, highlighted with the ★ symbol.

AYALA MUSEUM

MOUNT HALCON

20

things not to miss

It's not possible to see everything that the Philippines has to offer in one trip – and we don't suggest you try. What follows, in no particular order, is a selective taste of the country's highlights: exciting diving destinations, remote islands, towering mountains and underground rivers. Each entry has a page reference to take you straight into the Guide, where you can find out more.

1

1 BORACAY
See page 246
You'll never be short of things to do on picture-postcard Boracay Island, with its busy but stunning White Beach.

2 SURFING AT SIARGAO
See page 397
Avid surfers will find several locations where they can catch some decent waves, but Siargao, off the tip of Mindanao, is one of the best.

3 APO REEF MARINE NATURAL PARK
See page 241
The gin-clear waters of Apo Reef, off the west coast of Mindoro, are a scuba diver's dream.

4 CHOCOLATE HILLS
See page 332
Soak up the bizarre landscape of Bohol's iconic Chocolate Hills, conical brown-green mounds said to be the calcified tears of a broken-hearted giant.

5 VIGAN
See page 135
Wonderfully preserved slice of Spanish-era Philippines, with cobblestone streets and gorgeous Baroque architecture.

6 WHALE SHARKS
See page 212
Getting up close to these gentle giants off the coast of Donsol, in southern Luzon, is an unforgettable experience.

7 MOUNT MAYON
See page 207
An almost perfectly symmetrical volcanic cone, which makes for a challenging but thrilling climb when plate tectonics allow.

8 ATI-ATIHAN FESTIVAL
See page 271
At this lively annual festival in Kalibo, on Panay Island, everyone wears Indigenous dress and learns local dances.

9 BATANES
See page 175
Blissfully remote islands halfway between Luzon and Taiwan, home to rolling hills and wild stretches of coast.

10 MALAPASCUA
See page 318
Gorgeous and isolated island hideaway, with bone-white Bounty Beach and superb diving.

11 CORON ISLAND BY BANGKA
See page 377
Tour the jagged, gasp-inducing coast of Coron Island by bangka, taking in hidden coves, secret beaches and two pristine mountain lakes fed by springs.

12 MOUNT PINATUBO
See page 117
The lower slopes of Mount Pinatubo feature canyons formed after the massive 1991 eruption, while the crater is filled by a sulphuric mountain lake.

13 UNDERGROUND RIVER
See page 364
Near Puerto Princesa, Palawan, this is one of the longest subterranean rivers in the world, with eerie stalactites, vast caverns and hidden chambers.

14 RICE TERRACES
See page 175
The mind-boggling rice terraces around Banaue stand as one of Asia's greatest sights, and offer superb trekking.

15 TARSIERS
See page 331
Admire these tiny primates with the enormous, sorrowful eyes at their protected sanctuary in Bohol.

13

14

15

16 SAN AGUSTIN CHURCH

See page 66

This elegantly weathered Spanish pile in the heart of old Manila is the archipelago's oldest stone church.

17 HALO-HALO

See page 33

Nothing beats a tall glass of this icy Filipino treat on a hot day, a concoction of syrups, beans, fruits and ice cream.

18 EL NIDO

See page 368

The strikingly beautiful limestone islands around El Nido in Palawan offer exceptional exploring and adventure.

19 PADRE BURGOS

See page 349

Explore the rich marine life in this exciting dive destination.

20 SAGADA

See page 165

Head to this remote mountain village, home to the Igorots (Cordillera Indigenous peoples) and famed for its hanging coffins.

Itineraries

The following itineraries span the entire length of this incredibly diverse archipelago, from the historic cities of Luzon to the idyllic islands of the Visayas and the remote jungles of Mindanao. Given the time involved moving from place to place, you may not be able to cover everything, but even picking a few highlights will give you a deeper insight into the natural and cultural wonders of the Philippines.

THE GRAND TOUR

This three- to four-week tour gives a taster of the Philippines' iconic landscapes and islands from the nation's chaotic capital to the pristine sands of Boracay.

❶ **Manila** The nation's initially chaotic capital is a vast, boiling blend of history, high culture and wild nightlife. See page 56

❷ **Banaue rice terraces** It's worth taking the journey north to see one of the world's great man-made wonders. See page 172

❸ **Sagada** Extend your stay in northern Luzon with a trip to this rambling old town, home of the famed hanging coffins. See page 165

❹ **Puerto Princesa** Backtrack to Manila for the flight to Palawan's sleepy capital and the trip along the Underground River. See page 354

❺ **El Nido** Continue along the Palawan coast to the spectacular limestone scenery of the Bacuit archipelago. See page 368

❻ **Coron** Take the bangka across to Coron, where wreck-diving and dazzling coves await. See page 374

❼ **Cebu City** Fly to the nation's third city, home of Magellan's Cross and a host of historic attractions. See page 301

❽ **Bohol** Take the ferry to this historic island, home of the Chocolate Hills and the loveable tarsier. See page 324

❾ **Boracay** Backtrack to Cebu for the short flight to this famed resort island, where you can end your tour on a sugary white-sand beach. See page 246

ISLAND-HOPPING: THE WESTERN ROUTE

This tour takes in popular Mindoro en route to the western side of the Visayas, the physical and historic heart of the nation. This is perhaps the most alluring region of the Philippines, a sun-bleached concentration of islands littered with beaches, crumbling churches, sugar plantations

---

Create your own itinerary with Rough Guides. Whether you're after adventure or a family-friendly holiday, we have a trip for you, with all the activities you enjoy doing and the sights you want to see. All our trips are devised by local experts who get the most out of the destination. Visit **www.roughguides.com/trips** to chat with one of our travel agents.

and untouched reefs. This itinerary needs at least three weeks to complete in comfort, though you could race through it quicker.

❶ Puerto Galera Begin your tour at this accessible and congenial beach on the tip of Mindoro, which is also a prime dive resort. See page 226

❷ Romblon Ferries link Mindoro to the more remote Romblon archipelago, three main islands offering a laidback capital, challenging mountain and some splendid beaches. See page 256

❸ Boracay A short boat ride south via Caticlan is the jewel of Philippine beach resorts, justly renowned for its mesmerizing (if crowded) white sands and its party scene. See page 246

❹ Guimaras Bus across from Caticlan to Iloilo City on the south side of Panay, from where it's another short boat ride to this island of mangoes, mountain bikes and handsome Spanish chapels. See page 271

❺ Silay After arriving on Negros by boat, connect via busy Bacolod to this delightful small town, where you can stay in the converted mansion of a sugar baron. See page 279

❻ Dumaguete Traverse Negros and spend some time in the pleasant city of Dumaguete, which has a lovely seafront promenade and is well placed for diving around Dauin and Apo Island. See page 284

❼ Siquijor Take another swift ferry ride across to the island of witches, rich in legend, culture and rugged beauty, as well as a growing number of relaxing resorts. See page 291

ISLAND HOPPING: THE EASTERN LOOP

Skip Manila altogether by beginning and ending your trip in Cebu City, and taking in the wonderful variety of the Eastern Visayas. This route includes everything from urban nightlife, through remote islands and beaches with superb marine life, to inland natural wonders. This itinerary needs at least three weeks to do it justice.

❶ Cebu City Start off in the Philippines' surprisingly cosmopolitan second city, which has great dining, nightlife and shopping, as well as cultural sights and nearby Mactan Island for swimming. See page 301

❷ Moalboal Bus across to Cebu's west coast, where you can lounge on lovely Panagsama Beach, near the quiet town of Moalboal, or take a diving trip to tiny Pescador Island. See page 322

❸ Oslob Several hours south by bus from Moalbal is the small town of Oslob, famous for its friendly whale sharks. See page 325

❹ Bohol Travel by sea via Dumaguete to this fascinating island, which offers the charms of offshore Panglao Island, the Chocolate Hills and those adorable tarsiers. See page 324

❺ Padre Burgos Take a boat from Ubay in eastern Bohol across to Bato on Leyte and on to the up-and-coming scuba centre of the southern Philippines. See page 349

❻ Sohoton Natural Bridge National Park Travel by bus north to Tacloban and nip across to the island of Samar to experience this jungle-clad, limestone wilderness. See page 340

❼ Camotes Islands Double-back to Leyte via Tacloban and take a ferry from Ormoc to

THE GRAND TOUR

ISLAND-HOPPING: THE WESTERN ROUTE

ISLAND HOPPING: THE EASTERN LOOP

PHILIPPINE SEA

SULU SEA

MALAYSIA

CELEBES SEA

this tranquil, picture-perfect island chain, with excellent diving and snorkelling. See page 320

❽ Siargao Island Return to Cebu for the short flight to Siargao, best known for surfing but also rich in empty, wild, sandy beaches and offshore islands. See page 397

THE DIVE MASTER

Millions of visitors come to the Philippines primarily for what's below sea level – the waters surrounding the island chain harbour some of the world's richest marine life. The following tour would ideally take at least three weeks – and lots of advance planning – to complete.

❶ Puerto Galera This easy-to-reach resort makes a great introduction to the local dive scene, with plenty of resorts and operators to choose from. See page 232

❷ Apo Reef Take a day or two to explore this protected reef off the west coast of Mindoro, home to sharks, turtles and rays. See page 241

❸ Coron Try to take the bangka across to Coron for some spectacular wreck-diving, primarily Japanese ships from World War II. See page 374

❹ El Nido Continue on to the Palawan mainland where the numerous dive schools at El Nido can help arrange trips to stunning Tubbataha. See page 368

❺ Apo Island From Puerto Princesa fly to Cebu City then head south to Dumaguete and Apo Island, another dive hot spot. See page 289

❻ Panglao Island From Dumaguete it's a short boat ride to this languid island, home to congenial resorts, beaches and dive sights. See page 328

❼ Padre Burgos Cross over to Leyte to experience this exciting dive location, home to whale sharks, dolphins and manta rays. See page 349

THE BEST OF THE BEACH

The appeal of hiking volcanoes or trudging city streets can wilt (especially in the tropical heat), when compared to the dazzling white beaches on offer in the Philippines. This tour takes in the best of the nation's strips of sand. This itinerary needs a minimum of three weeks, but given the focus on beaches, this route could obviously be extended into

a much longer trip, especially as you will need to break up some of these journeys.

❶ Marinduque Take the short flight from Manila to this lesser-visited island and seek out some of the sandy beaches off its eastern coast. See page 189

❷ Caramoan Peninsula Hop on a ferry back to the Luzon mainland and head east to this rugged promontory, which harbours blue-water coves and enticing resorts. See page 201

❸ Malapascua Island Fly from Legazpi to Cebu City, where it's a four-hour bus and boat ride to this tiny islet ringed by chalky white sands. See page 318

❹ Panglao Island Double back the same way to Cebu City, then jump on a ferry to Taglibaran on Bohol, where the offshore Panglao Island boasts several glorious stretches of sand and great diving. See page 328

❺ Camiguin Island A sporadic bangka service from Jagna on Bohol connects with the compact, easy-to-explore Camiguin Island

THE DIVE MASTER

THE BEST OF THE BEACH

THE TIME TRAVELLER

PHILIPPINE SEA

SULU SEA

MALAYSIA

CELEBES SEA

off the Mindanao coast, boasting gorgeous beaches, hot springs and hikes. See page 390

❻ **Sugar Beach** Travel back via Bohol to Dumaguete on Negros, then on via Sipalay to Sugar Beach, an ultra-laidback budget spot, close to idyllic Danjugan Island. See page 282

❼ **Boracay** After another long haul through Negros and across Panay to Caticlan, you'll be ready to flop out on legendary White Beach in Boracay, then join in the partying when you've got your energy back. See page 246

THE TIME TRAVELLER

Evidence of the Philippines' long and complex history is sprinkled all over the archipelago, but northern Luzon is the most evocative of its Indigenous and colonial past, with handsome old cities and enigmatic remains. This itinerary could be completed in a fortnight, especially if you take some flights, but you'll get a lot more out of it over a good three weeks.

❶ **Intramuros, Manila** The oldest part of Manila drips with history, from Spanish churches and forts to illuminating museums. See page 65

❷ **Taal** Take a tour of this beautiful old town, home to the biggest church in Southeast Asia and bahay na bato architecture still redolent of colonial Spain. See page 110

❸ **Paete** The nation's woodcarving capital makes for an intriguing detour, sprinkled with the stores of local craftsmen. See page 105

❹ **Malolos** The oft-overlooked capital of Bulacan province is crammed with colonial remnants, from the elegant Barasoain Church to a smattering of sixteenth-century Spanish homes. See page 114

❺ **Vigan** The best-preserved colonial town in the Philippines is a treasure-trove of tiny museums, chapels and crumbling villas. See page 135

❻ **Laoag** The capital of Ilocos Norte boasts plenty of historic attractions of its own, while the Malacañang of the north, former holiday residence of the Marcoses, is a short ride away. See page 141

❼ **Sagada** Head into the mountainous heart of Luzon, where Sagada is a focus for the Igorots (Cordillera Indigenous peoples) and the enigmatic hanging coffins. See page 165

❽ **Banaue and Batad** You'd be remiss to travel up here and not spend time among the legendary rice terraces, fantastical ridges in the mountains often shrouded in mist. See pages 171 and 173

TRADITIONAL FISHING BOAT

Basics

Getting there

There are many options for non-stop flights to the Philippines from North America and from Australia; from Europe, the only non-stop flights are from Istanbul with Turkish Airlines. Otherwise, reaching the Philippines from outside Asia usually involves a stopover in Hong Kong, Singapore or Dubai. Most major airlines in the region have regular connecting flights to Manila; a few also fly direct to Cebu.

High season for Philippines travel is November to April, though airfares vary relatively little through the year. This is because the low season for the Philippines (May–Oct) is the peak season in Europe and the US, so flights heading out of these regions to various hub airports are often full.

If the Philippines is only one stop on a longer journey, you might want to consider buying a **Round-the-World** (RTW) ticket. Some agents and airline alliances also offer **Circle Pacific tickets**, which cover Australia, New Zealand, the west coast of North America and destinations in the Pacific; you can include Manila and/or Cebu on some itineraries.

From the UK and Ireland

There are currently no non-stop flights to the Philippines from the UK or Ireland. The second-fastest option is either to fly to Istanbul and pick up the Turkish Airlines flight to Manila, or to fly via Hong Kong, from where there are numerous onward daily flights to Manila and Cebu. Plenty of airlines offer connecting flights to Manila from UK airports, with the cheapest options often Middle Eastern carries such as Emirates, via Dubai; Qatar Airways, via Doha; or Saudia, via either Jeddah or Riyadh (and often both on a return trip). Coming from Ireland, your options are similar. The trip will take between 16 and 24 hours, depending on layover time.

From the US and Canada

Philippine Airlines operates non-stop flights to Manila from **Los Angeles**, New York, **San Francisco**, Seattle and **Vancouver**. However, other airlines offer alternative routes for lower prices, such as **Korean Air** via Seoul, Eva Air via Taiwan, and **Japan Airlines** via Tokyo.

From Los Angeles or San Francisco, the flying time to Manila is around eleven hours. From the east coast of North America, flying via the Pacific, the journey will take around 17 hours excluding any layover (allow at least 2hr extra) along the way.

From Australia, New Zealand and South Africa

Australia is well connected with the Philippines, with Philippines Airlines, Cebu Pacific, and Qantas all offering regular routes, the latter being the most expensive. Flights go daily from Sydney (8-9 hours), near daily from Melbourne (8-9 hours), and several times a week from Brisbane (9-10 hours). They generally have a price leap in December. A cheaper option from Sydney, Melbourne and Perth is to fly via Singapore with Scoot Airlines. If you want to get to **Cebu City**, you can fly via Hong Kong or Kuala Lumpur, although it's probably easiest simply to change in Manila.

From **New Zealand** there are no non-stop flights to the Philippines, so you'll have to go via Australia or a Southeast Asian hub such as Singapore or Hong Kong (15–20hr).

From **South Africa** you'll always make at least one stop en route to Manila, and often two. Depending on the length of the stop, the trip will take from 16 to 26 hours.

From elsewhere in Asia

You can fly direct to the Philippines from almost every major city in Asia, with several budget airlines offering cheap fares. Many of these fly to **Clark International Airport** (see page 116), 80km northwest of Manila, so make sure you factor in additional travel time if necessary. Numerous flights make the two-hour trip **from Hong Kong** to Manila.

AirAsia zips between Manila and Kota Kinabalu, Kuala Lumpur, Macau, Taipei, Tokyo and Seoul. **Cebu Pacific** also offers cheap flights from Bangkok, Brunei, Chiang Mai, Dubai, Hanoi, Ho Chi Minh City, Jakarta, Kuala Lumpur, Seoul and Taipei to Manila, and several routes direct to Cebu City. The **Singapore–Manila** route (3hr 30min) is very competitive, served by Philippine Airlines, Singapore Airlines, Scott and Cebu Pacific.

Handy **regional flights** include: Scoot from Singapore, and Cabu Pacific from Bangkok and Hong Kong, to **Davao** on Mindanao (3hr 50min), and flights from major cities all over Asia to Metro Manila's second airport in Clark/Angeles; **Kalibo International Airport**, serving Boracay, has non-stop flights to Taipei, and charters to several Chinese cities.

By boat

Many unlicensed boats ply back and forth between the Malaysian state of Sabah and the southern Philippines, but these are considered unsafe for tourists. At the time of writing even the primary licensed ferry

A BETTER KIND OF TRAVEL

At Rough Guides we are passionately committed to travel. We believe it helps us understand the world we live in and the people we share it with – and of course tourism is vital to many developing economies. But the scale of modern tourism has also damaged some places irreparably, and climate change is accelerated by most forms of transport, especially flying. We encourage all our authors to consider the carbon footprint of the journeys they make in the course of researching our guides.

route linking **Zamboanga City** with **Sandakan**, Sabah (non-stop) was not advised because of the security situation in Zamboanga (see page 410).

AIRLINES

AirAsia Ⓦ airasia.com
Cathay Pacific Ⓦ cathaypacific.com
Cebu Pacific Ⓦ cebupacificair.com
China Airlines Ⓦ china-airlines.com
Delta Airlines Ⓦ delta.com
Emirates Air Ⓦ emirates.com
KLM Ⓦ klm.com
Korean Air Ⓦ koreanair.com
Philippine Airlines Ⓦ philippineairlines.com
Qantas Ⓦ qantas.com
Scoot Ⓦ flyscoot.com
Singapore Airlines Ⓦ singaporeair.com
Turkish Airlines Ⓦ turkishairlines.com

AGENTS AND OPERATORS

Absolute Travel Ⓦ absolutetravel.com. Luxury tours to the Philippines that can be combined with other destinations in Southeast Asia. The fourteen-day Highlights of the Philippines tour includes Manila, Banaue, Sagada, Baguio, Bohol and Cebu City.
Always Dive Expeditions Ⓦ allwaysdive.com.au. All-inclusive dive packages to prime locations in the Philippines and Southeast Asia. Destinations in the Philippines include Coron, Dumaguete, Malapascua, Moalboal, Donsol and Puerto Galera. Also liveaboards to Cebu, Dauin, Tubbataha and Apo reefs, Coron wrecks and Anilao.
Art of Bicycle Trips Ⓦ artofbicycletrips.com. Bicycle and guided tour specialists, with a variety of bike tours all over Asia and a nine-day "Essential Philippines" tour, plus a longer 14-day odyssey.
Dive Worldwide Ⓦ diveworldwide.com. Specialist dive operator offering trips to a number of destinations in the Philippines. A typical fourteen-day trip to Donsol to see the whale sharks includes flights, domestic transfers and accommodation.
Trailfinders Ⓦ trailfinders.com. One of the best-informed and most efficient agents for independent travellers.

Getting around

The large number of budget airlines and ferry services between major destinations makes it easy to cover the Philippine archipelago, even on a tight budget, though the main drawback is that almost everything longer-distance routes through Manila and Cebu. Long-distance road transport largely comprises buses and jeepneys – the utilitarian passenger vehicles modelled on World War II American jeeps. Throughout the provinces, and in some areas of cities, tricycles – motorbikes with steel sidecars – are commonly used for short journeys.

Note that **holiday weekends** are bad times to travel, with buses full and roads jammed, particularly heading out of big cities to the provinces. Cities start to empty on Friday afternoon and the exodus continues into the night, with a mass return on Sunday evening and Monday morning; Metro Manila is especially gridlocked. Travelling is a particular hassle at Christmas, New Year and Easter with buses and ferries full, airports chaotic and resorts charging more than usual. If you have to travel at these times, book tickets in advance or turn up at bus stations and ferry piers early and be prepared to wait.

By plane

Air travel is a godsend for island-hoppers in the Philippines, with a number of airlines linking Manila with most of the country's major destinations; you will usually, however, have to backtrack to a major hub when jumping from one region to another. **Philippine Airlines** (PAL; Ⓦ philippineairlines.com) has a comprehensive domestic schedule, while **Cebu Pacific** (Ⓦ cebupacificair.com) offers even more routes and very cheap fares, particularly if you book some way in advance. There are several smaller budget airlines, including **AirAsia** (Ⓦ airasia.com), and **PAL Express**, a subsidiary of the national flag-carrier.

Cebu Pacific runs numerous flights out of its hub in **Cebu City**, saving you the effort of backtracking to Manila – you can, for instance, fly straight from Cebu City to Caticlan (for Boracay) and Siargao. **Davao** on Mindanao is a less-developed third hub, with connections to Cebu City, Cagayan de Oro, Iloilo and Zamboanga, but you'll have to transfer in Manila and Cebu for other destinations.

By ferry

Ferries and **bangkas** – wooden outrigger boats – were once the bread and butter of Philippine travel. Though still important, especially in the **Visayas**, most of the longer routes have been made redundant by the growth of budget air travel. Not only are flights faster and as cheap (or cheaper) than cabins on longer ferry routes (Manila to Mindanao for example), they are invariably safer. Indeed, despite some improvements in recent years, ferry accidents remain common in the Philippines and even in the dry season the open ocean can get surprisingly rough. The smaller bangkas are often poorly equipped, with little shelter from the elements, while even many of the larger vessels have been bought secondhand from Japan or Europe and are well past their prime. Ferries of all sizes are frequently crowded.

That said, for many shorter inter-island trips, ferries remain the only form of transport available, and – especially in the Visayas – island-hopping by boat can be an enjoyable and rewarding part of your trip.

There's a hierarchy of vessels, with proper ferries at the top; so-called big bangkas, taking around fifty passengers, in the middle; and ordinary bangkas at the bottom.

Filipino **ferry companies** (see below) operate ships of varying sizes on fixed schedules between major ports, while the timings of bangkas are usually more flexible. The major operator is **2GO**, with SuperCat part of the same group; the other key players are **Montenegro Shipping Lines**, **Cokaliong Shipping Lines**, **Oceanjet** and **Trans-Asia Shipping Lines**. These companies have regular sailings on routes between Manila, Batangas or Cebu and major cities throughout the Visayas and Mindanao, and on secondary routes within the Visayas.

FERRY COMPANIES

2GO Ⓦ travel.2go.com.ph
Aleson Shipping Ⓦ alesonshipping.com
Besta Shipping Lines ☎ 02 345 5568
Cokaliong Shipping Lines Ⓦ cokaliongshipping.com
Montenegro Shipping Lines Ⓦ montenegrolines.com.ph
Moreta Shipping Ⓦ moretashipping.com
Oceanjet Ⓦ oceanjet.net
Roble Shipping ☎ 032 416 6256
Si-Kat Ⓦ sikatferrybus.com
Starlite Ferries Ⓦ starliteferries.com
Super Shuttle Ⓦ supershuttleroro.com
Trans-Asia Shipping Lines Ⓦ transasiashipping.com

Fares and tickets

Ferry **fares** are very low by Western standards, especially if booked in advance; budget for a bit extra for a private cabin. **Tickets** can be bought at the pier up until departure, though it's often more convenient to avoid the long queues and buy in advance: **travel agents** sell ferry tickets, and the larger ferry companies have ticket offices in cities and towns. 2GO and some other companies also offer online ticketing, and for these and other routes you may have luck on agglomerate sites such as Ⓦ 12go.asia (which sounds similar to 2GO, but is unconnected), Ⓦ phferry.com or Ⓦ booktickets.ph.

Accommodation and facilities

The cheapest ferry **accommodation** is in bunk beds in cavernous dorms either below deck or on a semi-open deck, with shared toilets and showers. Older ships might have just a handful of cramped cabins sharing a tiny shower and toilet. The major operators generally have newer ships with a range of accommodation that includes dorms, straw mats in an air-conditioned area and shared cabins (usually for four) with bathrooms. These ferries usually also have a bar, karaoke lounge and a canteen serving basic meals.

By bus

Bus travel can be relatively uncomfortable and slow, but you'll get a real glimpse of rural Philippines from the window, and meet Filipinos from all walks of life. Buses are also incredibly convenient: hundreds of routes spread out like a web from major cities, and even the most isolated barangay will have a service of some sort. You won't go hungry either. Local vendors will often jump onto some services and offer you various snacks and drinks, while on the longer hauls, even express buses stop every three or four hours to give passengers a chance to stretch their legs, use the loo and buy some food.

There are some downsides. Though the largest bus companies have fleets of reasonably new air-conditioned buses for longer routes, they rarely have toilets. On shorter routes buses can be dilapidated contraptions with no air conditioning and, in some cases, no glass in the windows. You'll also need to develop a high tolerance to loud music or Tagalog movies played at full blast throughout the trip.

Bus fares and frequencies

Fares are low. Beyond Manila roads can be poor, and even when the distances involved aren't great, the buses will make numerous stops along the way. Some bus companies advertise express services, but in reality a bus that goes from A to B without stopping is unheard of. Buses that have a "derecho" sign (meaning "straight" or "direct") in the window usually make the fewest stops.

Published **timetables** for most bus companies are non-existent, but departures on popular routes such as Manila to Baguio or Manila to Vigan usually happen every hour or half-hour. The larger operators – such as Victory Liner (Ⓦvictoryliner.com) and Philtranco (Ⓦphiltranco.net) – allow you to book seats in advance on some routes, either online, by telephone (often engaged) or at the terminal. Happily, it's now possible to book many tickets online using agglomerate websites, such as Ⓦ12go.asia, Ⓦbustickets.ph or Ⓦbooktickets.ph; often you'll still need to print out a physical ticket at the terminal. A list of bus destinations and the companies that cover them is given in the Manila chapter (see page 81), and details of bus routes, with local contact details, appear throughout the Guide. Note, however, that there are so many bus companies (many of which go in and out of business on a regular basis, or have permits suspended), and so much variation in routes and journey times, that the information we give in the Guide is just a guideline and always subject to change.

By jeepney

The **jeepney** is the ultimate Philippine icon (see box, page 7), and remains an important form of transport, particularly in Manila, Cebu City, Davao and Baguio, where there are frequent services between key locations in each city. In the provinces, jeepneys connect isolated barangays to nearby towns and towns to cities, but they might run only two or three times a day, depending on demand (they often only leave when full), the weather and the mood of the driver. There are absolutely no timetables.

Routes are painted on the side or on a signboard in the window. Even so, using jeepneys takes a little local knowledge because they make numerous stops and deviations to drop off and pick up passengers. There's no such thing as a designated jeepney stop, so people wait in the shade at the side of the road and flag one down. The vehicles are cramped and incredibly uncomfortable (good luck if you're tall), usually holding at least twenty passengers inside and any number of extras clinging to the back or sitting precariously on top. It can be a hassle to get luggage on and off – small items might end up on the floor, but larger items often go on the roof.

Fares are very low: particularly in the provinces, but even in the cities you won't be bankrupted by this mode of travel. To pay, hand your money to the passenger next to you and say "*bayad po*" ("pay please"). If you're not sitting close to the driver, the fare will be passed down the line of passengers until it reaches him; he will then pass back any change; alternatively, you can run round to the front when you get off.

By UV express, city taxi and van

Not unlike jeepneys in the way they operate, **UV express vans** are air-conditioned vehicles (a bit like Range Rovers, but often Japanese), with signs in the window indicating their destination. They made their debut in Manila in the late 1990s, then known as FX taxis, and now operate in other cities and on some popular inter-city routes. However, routes are often not set, so it takes a little local knowledge to know where to catch the right vehicle. They can be a little claustrophobic – the driver won't even think about moving until he's got ten people on board, three more than the vehicle is designed for.

Elsewhere in the Philippines you may encounter vans (often labelled "GT Express" meaning "Garage to Terminal") that follow fixed routes. They're usually a little more expensive than buses but they're much faster, as, unlike buses, they don't stop off every few hundred metres. In Luzon, vans often have their own terminals in major towns, and operate in competition with bus companies and jeepneys over long distances. Destinations are usually clearly marked on the windscreen.

City taxis generally fall into two categories: yellow airport taxis and regular white taxis, of which the latter is cheaper. The app-based taxi service **Grab** is available in most major cities, often with a cheaper (and usually faster, though more dangerous) **motorbike** option.

By tricycle

The cheapest form of shared transport, **tricycles** are ubiquitous in the provinces. In Manila and Cebu City they are prohibited from using certain roads, but almost everywhere else they go where they like, when they like and at speeds as high as their small engines are capable of. The sidecars are usually designed for four passengers – two facing forwards and two backwards – but it's not uncommon to see extras clinging on wherever they can, the only limiting factor being whether or not the machine can actually move under the weight of the extra bodies. Tricycles never follow fixed routes, so it's usually a question of flagging one down and telling the driver your destination.

Many tricycles charge a set rate per person for trips within town or city boundaries. If you want to use the tricycle as a private taxi you'll have to negotiate a price. You'll need expert bargaining skills but you'll generally find them cheaper than most transportation options; you can also book trikes using the Grab app in some cities, which eliminates problems with negotiation or addresses.

By car

It's possible to **rent a car** in the Philippines but you may not want to. Not only is traffic in cities often gridlocked, but most Filipino drivers have a very relaxed attitude towards the rules of the road. Swerving is common, as is changing lanes suddenly and driving with one hand permanently on the horn, particularly if you're a bus or jeepney driver. That said, if you're used to driving in big cities this might not faze you too much, and in any case, once you reach more rural areas – northern Luzon for example – travelling by car can be incredibly convenient and open up a whole range of otherwise hard-to-reach destinations. Many travellers also rent **motorbikes**, but this is only recommended for experienced riders – the chances of having an accident are statistically fairly high. It's best to avoid driving at night altogether.

If you do drive, you'll need your **driving licence**; be prepared to show it if you get stopped. Rentals are allowed for up to ninety days – longer stays will require a Philippine license. Vehicles in the Philippines drive on the right side of the road and distances and car speeds are in kilometres. The highways usually have a nominal speed limit of 100kph, but anywhere else you'll rarely be going faster than 30kph due to congestion.

Always **drive defensively** – cars, animals and pedestrians will pull out in front of you without warning (in many rural areas people are still not used to traffic), and always give way to jeepneys, which will happily drive you off the road. When passing anything, sound your horn twice as a warning (horns are rarely used in anger).

Note that **police** and "traffic enforcers" – uniformed men and women employed by local authorities to supplement the police – might try to elicit a bribe from you. If this happens it's best to play the dumb foreigner and hand over the "on-the-spot fine" of a few hundred pesos (make sure you have cash with you). If you take the moral high ground and refuse to play along, you'll probably end up having your licence confiscated or, in the worst case, your car towed away and impounded until you pay a fine to eventually get it back.

CAR RENTAL AGENCIES

Alamo Ⓦ alamo.com.
Avalon Transport Services Ⓦ avalonrentacar.com.
Avis Ⓦ avis.com.ph.
ECLPI Ⓦ eclpi.com.ph.
Europcar Ⓦ europcar.com.ph.
Hertz Ⓦ hertzphilippines.com.
Philippine Rent a Car Ⓦ philippinerentacar.org.
Rent A Car Manila Ⓦ rentacarmanila.com.
Thrifty Ⓦ thrifty.com.ph.

Hiring a driver

For a pretty reasonable cost (plus fuel, driver's food and parking/toll fees) you can hire a small car and driver from some car rental agencies for up to eight hours, the extra expense more than justified by the peace of mind a local driver brings. Try the Chauffeur Drive packages at Europcar Philippines.

Beyond Metro Manila, it can be much cheaper to strike a private deal with a car or van owner looking for extra work - you'll need to negotiate to reach an acceptable price. A good way to find someone with a vehicle is to ask at your accommodation; alternatively, locals with cars wait at many airports and ferry ports in the hope of making a bit of money driving arriving passengers into town. You can ask these drivers if they're available to be hired by the day.

By bike

Given the volume of traffic (and driving standards) on most major roads, cycling around the Philippines can be a dangerous idea, but plenty of locals and travellers do use bikes in rural areas. Outfits such as **Art of Bicycle Trips** (Ⓦ artofbicycletrips.com) occasionally run longer excursions by mountain bike.

Accommodation

The Philippines has accommodation to suit everyone, from international five-star hotels and swanky beach resorts to simple rooms – sometimes no more than a bamboo hut on a beach – and budget hotels.

It's generally not necessary to book in advance unless you are visiting at the peak times of Easter, Christmas, New Year or during a major local festival (see page 37). By and large, you'll find the cheapest rates online, but if you do want to book by phone, note that some hotels in out-of-the-way areas won't have a landline telephone on site, in which case they may have a mobile number and/or a booking office in a city (often Manila); details are given in the text as appropriate.

ACCOMMODATION ALTERNATIVES

The following websites are worth checking for useful alternatives to standard hotel and resort accommodation.

Airbnb ⓦ airbnb.com.
CouchSurfing ⓦ couchsurfing.org.
Vacation Rentals by Owner ⓦ vrbo.com.

Hotels and beach resorts

The terms **hotel** and **beach resort** cover a multitude of options in the Philippines. A hotel can mean anything from the most luxurious five-star establishment down to dingy budget pensions or guesthouses with bars on the windows. Beach resorts in turn range from sybaritic affairs on private atolls, with butlers and health spas, to dirt-cheap, rickety one-room cottages on a deserted island. "Resort hotels" are a mid-range or top-range hybrid of the two, sometimes with their own area of private beach.

Many hotels and beach resorts accept credit cards, although there are exceptions, such as in rural areas where electricity supply is not dependable and also in the cheapest budget accommodation, where you must pay cash. It can be worth checking that the air conditioner, where available, isn't noisy. Rooms on lower floors overlooking main roads are best avoided as they can be hellishly noisy; always try to go for something high up or at the back (or both).

Note that in smaller towns and cities beyond Manila, hotels often use the English term "single" room to mean one double bed, and "double/twin" to mean a room with two double beds; in these cases "single" rooms will obviously be big enough for two people – you will rarely find a room that can only sleep one. In the Guide, prices quoted are always based on the **cheapest room for two people sharing** (a "double" in the Western sense), regardless of what the hotel calls it.

Budget

Budget hotels offer little more than a bed, four walls and a fan or small air-conditioning unit, although if you're by the beach, with a pleasant sea breeze blowing and the windows open, air conditioning isn't really necessary. If you do get a private bathroom it will probably only have cold water, and the "shower" is sometimes little more than a tap sticking out of the wall producing a mere trickle of water. Breakfast is unlikely to be included in the rate, though there may be a canteen or coffee shop on the premises where you can buy food. At the higher end of the budget range, rooms are usually simple but can be reasonably spacious, perhaps – if they are on or near a beach – with a small balcony.

Mid-range

There are plenty of **mid-range hotels**, mostly in towns and cities. The rooms typically have air conditioning and a private bathroom with hot water, and usually basic cable TV. Beach cottages in this bracket tend to be quite spacious and will often have a decent-

ACCOMMODATION PRICE CODES

All accommodation prices published in the Guide represent the cost of the **cheapest room for two people sharing** – or beach hut sleeping two – **in high season**, namely November to April. Prices during the May–October rainy season are usually about twenty percent lower. Conversely, during Christmas, New Year and Easter, rates in the popular beach resorts such as Boracay can spike by around twenty percent. In some cases hotels will include **breakfast** in the price but it's worth asking about this when you book. You'll also find that as a "walk-in" guest you'll usually be able to get a cheaper rate than the rack rate listed on hotel websites, especially in the off-season and in less touristy areas.

Value Added Tax of twelve percent and an additional service charge is often included in the published rates, but not always. If you see a room advertised at P1000++ ("**plus plus**") it means you'll pay P1000 plus VAT plus service charge – always ask for clarification if you aren't sure which charge is which. These additional charges have been factored into all our rates.

Accommodation prices, for a standard double room, are marked in this book with the following guide:

P̱ = under P1000
P̱P = P1001–2500
P̱PP = P2501–6000
P̱PPP = over P6000

WI-FI

Most hotels and guesthouses in the Philippines offer free **wi-fi**, although connections can be slow and unreliable in remote locations. If there is a charge for usage or you can only get online in restricted parts of the establishment, this is noted in our accommodation reviews.

sized veranda too. Most mid-range accommodation will feature a small coffee shop or restaurant with a choice of Filipino and Western breakfasts that may be included in the rate.

Top end

In Manila and Cebu, as well as the most popular beach destinations such as Boracay, you can splash out on extremely comfortable accommodation. **Five-star comfort** is offered by some hotels and beach resorts, many of them owned and operated by international chains. Cottages at the most expensive resorts are more like chic apartments, often with a separate living area. Many of these establishments include a lavish buffet breakfast in the rate, and sports facilities and outdoor activities are on offer, though you'll have to pay extra for those.

Campsites, hostels and homestays

Campsites are almost unknown in the Philippines. A small number of resorts allow you to pitch tents in their grounds for a negligible charge, but otherwise the only camping you're likely to do is if you go trekking or climbing and need to camp overnight in the wilderness or on a mountaintop. Note that rental outlets for equipment are few and far between, so you might need to bring your own gear from home.

There are very few **official youth hostels** in the country, most of them in university cities where they may be booked up by students throughout term time. A Hostelling International (HI) card can in theory give you a tiny saving at the handful of YMCAs and YWCAs in the big cities. The problem is that few staff have any idea what an HI card is. On the other hand, **private hostels** can be found in many cities and touristic areas, plus it is quite common for budget hotels and resorts to have **dormitories**.

There's no official **homestay** programme in the Philippines, but in rural areas where there may be no formal accommodation, you'll often find people willing to put you up in their home and provide an evening meal for a small charge. If you enjoy the stay, it's best to offer some sort of tip when you leave, or a gift of soft drinks and treats for the children. You can ask around at town halls if you're interested.

Food and drink

The high esteem in which Filipinos hold their food is encapsulated by the common greeting "Let's eat!" Though Filipino food has a reputation for being one of Asia's less adventurous cuisines, there is a lot more to it than adobo (see box, page 32), and young, entrepreneurial restaurateurs and internationally trained chefs returning to the country and beginning to give native dishes an increasingly sophisticated touch.

In the Philippines snacks – **merienda** – are eaten in between the three main meals, and not to partake when offered can be considered rude. It's not unusual for breakfast to be eaten early, followed by merienda at 10am, lunch as early as 11am (especially in the provinces where many people are up at sunrise), more merienda at 2pm and 4pm, and dinner at 7pm. Meals are substantial, and even busy office workers prefer to sit down at a table and make the meal last. Never be afraid to ask for a doggy bag – everyone does. At smarter restaurants, the final bill you get usually includes VAT of twelve percent and a service charge of ten percent, adding 22 percent to the price shown on the menu. Simple establishments do not add these surcharges.

Don't be confused by the absence of a knife from most table settings. It's normal to use just a fork and spoon, cutting any meat with the fork and using the spoon to put the food in your mouth. This isn't as eccentric as it first seems. Most meat is served in small chunks, not steak-like slabs, so you usually don't have to cut it at all. Fish can be skewered with your fork and cut with the side of your spoon. And a spoon is so much easier for the local staple, steamed rice, than a knife and fork. That said, in some "native-style" restaurants food is served on banana leaves and you're expected to eat with your hands, combining the rice and food into mouthful-sized balls with your fingers – if you don't feel up to this it's fine to ask for cutlery.

Filipino cuisine

Filipino food is a delicious and exotic blend of Malay, Spanish, Chinese and American traditions. Dishes range from the very simple, like grilled fish and rice, to more complex stews, paellas and artfully barbecued

ADOBO HEAVEN

It might seem simple – stewed pork and chicken – but it's hard to resist the justly revered national dish of the Philippines. **Adobo** originally meant "sauce" or "seasoning" in Spanish, but its use has morphed throughout Spain's former colonies – the Filipino version is actually indigenous to the islands, dating back to a dish cooked up here long before Magellan's arrival. Philippine adobo consists of pork, chicken or a combination of both slowly stewed in soy sauce, vinegar, crushed garlic, bay leaf and black peppercorns – it's the latter two ingredients that gives true adobo its distinctive flavour and bite. No two adobos are exactly alike, however – you'll discover different versions all over the country.

meats, many using local fruits such as calamansi, coconuts and mangoes. **Seafood** is especially rich – expect anything from meaty crabs and milkfish to grouper and stingray on the menu. Most meals are served with San Miguel, the local beer, and are followed by sumptuous tropical fruits and decadent desserts.

The staples

Rice is the key Filipino staple, often accompanied by little more than freshly caught fish with a vinegar sauce. **Lapu-lapu** (grouper) and **bangus** (milkfish) are commonly served, while squid, crab and prawns are especially good and cheap in the Philippines. **Chicken** is another key staple – competition for the best fried or barbecued chicken (lechon manok) is fierce. Popular dishes on virtually every menu include **sinigang**, a refreshing tamarind-based sour soup; **kare-kare**, a stew made from delicious peanut sauce with vegetables and usually beef; and sizzling **sisig**, fried pig's head and liver, seasoned with calamansi and chilli peppers. Filipino Chinese dishes such as **pancit** (noodles) and **lumpia** (spring rolls) are common. Probably the most popular meat is **pork**, transformed into dishes such as crispy pata, **adobo** (see box, above) and **lechon**, roasted pig cooked whole on a spit over a charcoal or wood fire. In the Philippines, lechon is usually served with vinegar or special sauce (unique to each lechon shop but normally made from fruits or liver pâté, garlic and pepper). The meat is deliciously fragrant and juicy,

but the real highlight is the crispy smoked skin, a fatty, sumptuous treat sold by the kilo. Pork is also the basis of **Bicol Express**, the best known of very few spicy local dishes, which consists of pork cooked in coconut milk, soy and vinegar, with chillies.

Vegetables are not considered an integral part of Filipino meals, but may well be mixed in with the meat or offered as a side dish. In restaurants serving Filipino food, some of the most common vegetable dishes include pinakbet, an Ilocano dish (usually bitter melon, squash, okra, aubergine and string beans cooked in bagoong, a fermented fish sauce), and a version of Bicol Express with leafy vegetables such as pechay (aka pak choy) and camote tops (sweet potato leaves) in place of pork.

Breakfast

At many hotels and resorts you'll be offered a Filipino breakfast, which typically consists of **longganisa** (garlic sausage), **tocino** (cured pork), fried bangus fish, corned beef or **beef tapa** (beef marinated in vinegar); you'll usually be offered **tapsilog**, a contraction formed from tapa (fried beef), sinangag (garlic fried rice) and itlog (egg), which is exactly what you get: a bowl of garlic rice with tapa and a fried egg on top. Other "combo" dishes include tosilog and longsilog (you get the idea), while there even exists a particularly haute cuisine version called spamsilog (take a wild guess).

If this sounds too much for you, there's usually fresh fruit and toast, though note that local **bread**, either of the sliced variety or in rolls known as pan de sal, is often slightly sweet (wholegrain or rye breads are unusual in all but a few big hotels). Another option is to ask for a couple of hot pan de sal with corned-beef filling; the beef takes away some of the bread's sweetness.

Street food

Though not as common as it is in Thailand or India, **street food** still has a special place in the hearts (and stomachs) of Filipinos as much for its plain weirdness as for its culinary virtues. Hawkers with portable stoves tend to appear towards the end of the working day from 5pm to 8pm and at lunchtime in bigger cities. Much of the food is grilled over charcoal and served on sticks kebab-style, or deep fried in a wok with oil that is poured into an old jam jar and re-used day after day. Highlights include deep-fried **fishballs** and **squidballs** (mashed fish or squid blended with wheat flour), grilled **pig intestines** and adidas – **chicken's feet**, named after the sports-shoe manufacturer. Prices start from a few pesos a stick.

Street vendors also supply the king of Filipino aphrodisiacs: balut, a half-formed **duck embryo**

VEGETARIAN AND VEGAN FOOD

Committed **vegetarians and vegans** face a difficult mission to find suitable food in the Philippines. It's a poor country, and many Filipinos have grown up on a diet of what's available locally: usually chicken and pork. If you ask for a plate of stir-fried vegetables it might come with slices of pork in it, or be served in meat gravy. Fried rice almost always contains egg and meat. That said, most Filipinos will be familiar with the concept of vegetarian food and will try to accommodate you where possible.

Chinese and Japanese restaurants offer the best range of vegetable-based dishes, though you'll have to emphasize that you want absolutely no bits of meat added. In Manila, and to some extent in other cities, and in Boracay, pizzas are an option, or you could head to an upmarket restaurant and ask the chef to prepare something special. At least breakfast is straightforward – even in the most rural resorts, you can ask for toast or pancakes and, if you're not vegan, an omelette or scrambled eggs.

eaten with beak, feathers and all; sellers advertise their proximity with a distinctive baying cry.

Carinderias and seafood buffets

Carinderias are usually humble eateries that allow you to choose from a number of dishes placed on a counter in big aluminium pots. Carinderia fare is usually a blend of Filipino and Asian dishes; typical choices might be adobo, pancit, *pinakbet*, chicken curry, grilled pork, sweet and sour fish, fried chicken and hotdogs. The only problem with carinderias is that the food has usually been standing around a while and is often served lukewarm.

In urban areas and some beach resorts you'll also find **seafood** restaurants displaying a range of seafood on ice; order by pointing at what you want and telling the waiter how you would like it cooked.

Desserts and snacks

Filipinos adore **sweets** and **desserts**. Sold all over the Philippines, **halo-halo** (from the Tagalog word *halo*, meaning "mix") is a mouthwatering blend of shaved ice, evaporated milk and various toppings such as sweetened beans, fruits and taro, served in a tall glass or bowl – the "special" version usually has taro ice cream on top. A speciality of Laguna province (see page 103), **buko pie** is made by layering strips of young coconut and cake mix into a crispy pie crust – the addictive dessert has cult status in the Philippines and an intense rivalry exists between many pie-makers. The most popular traditional Filipino sweet is **polvorón**, a sort of short-bread made with flour, sugar and milk, and often sold in flavours such as cashew nut, chocolate and *pinipig* (crispy rice). Sold on every street corner, **turon** is a crispy deep-fried banana in a spring roll wrapper, while **leche flan** (caramel custard) is a staple on every restaurant menu. Filipinos also eat a huge amount of **ice cream** in an

unorthodox range of flavours, including *ube* (purple yam), jackfruit, corn, avocado and even cheese.

For a snack in a packet, try salted dried fish like **dilis**, which can be bought in supermarkets and convenience stores. *Dilis* are a little like anchovies and are eaten whole, sometimes with a vinegar and garlic dip. They're often served along with other savouries (under the collective name *pulutan*) during drinking sessions. Salted dried **pusit** (squid) is also common.

Fast food

You'll find McDonald's in almost every big town, but the Philippines has its own successful **fast-food chains** fashioned after the US giant. There are hundreds of branches of Jollibee (chicken, burgers and spaghetti), Chowking (noodle soups, dim sum), Mang Inasal (barbecue and unlimited rice) and Max's (fried chicken) throughout the country. Western-style **sandwich bars** have appeared in recent years too.

Most shopping malls also have **food courts**, indoor marketplaces that bring together dozens of small stalls serving Filipino, Western, Japanese, Chinese, Thai and Korean food. Here you can easily get a decent lunch for a very low price.

In many provincial cities, look out also for **ihaw-ihaw** (grill) restaurants, usually native-style

EATING PRICE CODES

Prices for **a two-course meal, including a drink**, are marked in this book with the following guide:

$\bar{P}$ = under P500
$\overline{PP}$ = P501–2000
$\overline{PPP}$ = P501–1000
$\overline{PPPP}$ = over P2000

bamboo structures where meat and fish are cooked over charcoal and served with hot rice and soup.

International cuisine

There are some excellent French, Spanish and Italian restaurants in Manila and Cebu City, and dozens of **European** restaurants in Boracay. Prices depend on where you are, with the highest to be found in the higher-end areas of Manila. However, European cuisine on the coast tends to be a little less sophisticated, simply because it's hard to guarantee supplies of the necessary ingredients.

There are **Chinese** restaurants in every city and in many provincial towns. Don't expect modish Oriental cuisine though; most Chinese restaurants are inexpensive places offering straightforward, tasty food designed to be ordered in large portions and shared by a group. Note that many Chinese restaurants offer shark's fin, which is extremely environmentally destructive – hunters cut off just the fin and leave the shark to die – so you may want to check menus and avoid places that support this practice.

Another of the Philippines' favourite cuisines is **Japanese**, ranging from fast-food noodle parlours to expensive restaurants serving sushi and tempura.

If you are looking for **halal-friendly** restaurants, Metro Manila and Cebu have plenty of options on offer.

Drinks

Bottled **water** is cheap; good local brands such as Viva and Hidden Spring can be picked up easily in convenience stores. Note, however, that many hotels and restaurants have huge bottles of **mineral water** for guests and customers, which save you money and cut down on plastic waste. You can also purify your own water; chemical sterilization using chlorine is effective, fast and inexpensive, and you can remove the nasty taste it leaves with neutralizing tablets or lemon juice. Alternatively, you could invest in a purifying filter incorporating chemical sterilization to kill even the smallest viruses. Fizzy **soft drinks** such as Coca-Cola and Pepsi are available everywhere.

At resorts and hotels, the "**juice**" which usually comes with breakfast is – irritatingly, in a country rich in fresh fruit – often made from powder or concentrate. Good fresh juices, usually available only in the more expensive restaurants, include watermelon, ripe mango, sour mango and papaya. Fresh *buko* (coconut) juice is a refreshing choice, especially on a hot day. In general, sugar is added to fresh juices and shakes unless you specify otherwise, though you might well want sugar with the delightful drink made from calamansi, a small native lime.

Filipinos aren't big **tea** drinkers and, except in the best hotels, the only tea on offer is usually made from Lipton's tea bags. **Coffee** is popular and can be ordered anywhere, but the quality varies widely. It's usually instant, served in "three-in-one" packets, and dominated by Nescafé, although local, Malaysian and Indonesian brands are also available. Where real brewed coffee is served, it's often local and very good. Latte-addicts may be tempted by Starbucks, which has scores of branches across Manila and is popping up in provincial towns such as Bacolod, though there are an increasing number of good private operations, and not just in Manila, plus Bo's Coffee, a Starbucks-like chain that uses local beans (and is actually pretty good; way better than Starbucks in any case). Fresh milk is not always available outside the cities, so you'll sometimes find yourself being offered tinned or powdered milk with coffee or tea.

Alcohol

The **beer** of choice in the Philippines is **San Miguel**, a local pilsner established in 1890 and still dominating ninety percent of the domestic market. San Miguel also produces Red Horse Extra Strong lager, and good apple- and lychee-flavoured beers; they now have 14 different offerings, of which the Pale Pilsen is most popular among foreigners. The only major pan-national competition comes from Asia Brewery, which produces the uninspiring Beer na Beer and Colt 45 brands. Only a few foreign beers are available in bars and supermarkets, notably Heineken, Budweiser and Japanese brands. The worldwide fad for **craft ales** is gradually making its presence felt, however, with a number of decent Filipino microbreweries, especially in Metro Manila; supermarkets and convenience stores here and in Cebu should have a few local canned craft options. For something stronger there are plenty of Philippine-made **spirits** such as Tanduay rum (actually quite good; try sloshing some into a freshly-opened coconut for a fantastic DIY cocktail), San Miguel Ginebra (gin) and Fundador brandy (originally from Spain). Wine can be found in liquor stores in the larger cities, though the range is usually limited to Australian or New Zealand mass-market brands and it tends to be pricey.

Almost all restaurants, fast-food places excepted, serve alcohol, but **wine** is rarely drunk; a cold beer or fresh fruit juice is much preferred. European restaurants usually have a limited wine list. For something authentically native, try the strong and pungent **tapuy** (rice wine), or a speciality called **lambanog**, made from almost anything that can be fermented, including fruit. In the provinces both can be difficult

FILIPINO FRUITS

The Philippines is justly celebrated for its variety and quality of fresh fruit, especially its mangoes, which are ubiquitous throughout the islands and always juicy and delicious. The list below is just a selection.

Atis (custard apple or sugar-apple) This fruit is pine-cone shaped, and about 10cm long with green, scaly skin. Its ripe flesh is gloriously sweet and soft; it might look a bit like custard but it tastes like a combination of banana, papaya and strawberry – or, more prosaically, bubble gum. With its black pips scattered throughout, it can be messy to eat. The main season is late summer to October.

Balimbing (starfruit, aka *carambola*) Crunchy, juicy fruit, with a slightly sweet flavour that tastes a bit like a blend of apple, pear and grape.

Bayabas (guava) Fruit with a tough green skin and distinctive deep-pink pulp that has a sweet flavour, like a lighter, more fibrous version of strawberry.

Buko (coconut) Another Philippine staple grown throughout the archipelago year-round, harvested casually by villagers as much as by commercial plantations for its refreshing juice and nutty white flesh. Used to make *buko* pie and a variety of desserts.

Calamansi Little green lime that is squeezed into juices, hot tea, over noodles, fish and *kinilaw* (raw fish salad) and into numerous dipping sauces.

Chico (sapodilla) Roughly the size of an egg, with brown skin and sticky, soft flesh that has a malty, exceedingly sweet flavour.

Durian The "king" of tropical fruit is spiky, heavy and smells like a drain blocked with rubbish – but its creamy inner flesh tastes like heaven. Rich in protein, minerals and fat, durian is one of the more expensive fruits in the Philippines; they're cheapest in Davao, the centre of production.

Guayabano (soursop) A large, oval fruit with knobbly spines outside and fragrant flesh inside.

Kaimito (star apple) Plum-coloured and round, about the size of a tennis ball, with leathery skin and soft white pulp inside that tastes a bit like grape.

Langka (jackfruit) The largest tree-borne fruit in the world (it can reach 40kg) is also one of the most delicious, with an interior of large, yellow bulbs of sweet flesh that taste like flowery bananas.

Lanzones Small, round fruit grown mostly on southern Luzon, especially in Laguna, and available October to December. It's also grown in northern Mindanao and especially Camiguin, where there is a festival in its honour (see page 390). It tastes a bit like a combination of grape and sweet grapefruit.

Mangga (mango) Eat as much mango as you can in the Philippines – you won't taste any better. Most grown on the islands turn from green to yellow as they ripen, and are always very sweet. The main season runs June to August.

Mangosteen Nothing like a mango, this sumptuous fruit – the size of a tangerine – has a thick, purplish skin and creamy white flesh. The season runs June to August.

Marang If you travel to Mindanao, look out for this special fruit. A bit like a breadfruit, it's a cross between jackfruit and *atis* but with a taste all its own.

Pakwan (watermelon) Usually available year-round, but best between April and June.

Papaya You'll see papaya plants growing in gardens and along roadsides all over the Philippines and it's one of the cheapest fruits. Some 98 percent of the annual crop is consumed locally, and it's extremely nutritious; they're also great in smoothie or shake form.

Piña (pineapple) The Spanish introduced the pineapple to the Philippines and, thanks to huge plantations run by Del Monte and Dole (both in Mindanao), it's one of the nation's biggest export earners.

Saging (banana) A staple crop in the Philippines, with a remarkable range of size and types grown in Mindanao and the Western Visayas throughout the year; the country is one of the largest exporters of bananas in the world.

Santol The *santol* is an apple-sized fruit, with a white, juicy pulp often eaten sour with some salt. It's also popular as a jam or a bitter marmalade.

to find because they're usually brewed privately for local consumption, though *lambanog* is now being bottled and branded, and can be found on some supermarket shelves in Manila and other cities.

Health

As long as you're careful about what you eat and drink and how long you spend in the sun, you shouldn't have any major health problems in the Philippines. Hospitals in cities and even in small towns are generally of a good standard, although health care is rudimentary in the remotest barangays and anything potentially serious is best dealt with in Manila or Cebu. Doctors and nurses almost always speak English, and doctors in major cities are likely to have received some training in the US or the UK, where many attend medical school.

We've listed **hospitals** in the accounts of cities and major towns in the Guide;. There are **pharmacies** on almost every street corner, where you can buy local and international brand medicines. Branches of Mercury Drug, the country's biggest chain of pharmacies, are listed on Ⓦ mercurydrug.com, and you'll also find branches of Hong Kong chain Watsons all over the place.

If you are hospitalized, you'll have to pay a deposit on your way in and settle the bill – either in person or through your insurance company (see page 50).

We strongly recommend you are up to date with tetanus, typhoid and hepatitis A **vaccinations**.

Stomach upsets

Food- and waterborne diseases are the most likely cause of illness in the Philippines. Travellers' **diarrhoea** can be caused by viruses, bacteria or parasites, which can contaminate food or water. There's also a risk of typhoid or cholera – occasional cases are reported in the Philippines, mostly in poor areas without adequate sanitation. Another potential threat is that of hepatitis A. The authorities in Manila claim that **tap water** in the capital and most cities is safe for drinking, but it's not worth taking the chance – unless you filter it yourself, stick to bottled or mineral water (see page 34).

Mosquito-borne diseases

Dengue fever, a debilitating and occasionally fatal viral disease, is on the increase across tropical Asia. Many cases are reported in the Philippines each year,

mostly during or just after the wet season when the day-biting mosquito that carries the disease is most active. There is no vaccine against dengue. Initial symptoms – which develop five to eight days after being bitten – include a fever that subsides after a few days, often leaving the patient with a bad rash all over their body, headaches and fierce joint pain. The only treatment is rest, liquids and paracetamol or any other acetaminophen painkiller (not aspirin). Dengue can result in death, usually among the very young or very old, and serious cases call for hospitalization.

In the Philippines, **malaria** is found only in isolated areas of southern Palawan and the Sulu archipelago (Basilan, Jolo and Tawi-Tawi), and few travellers bother with anti-malarials if they are sticking to the tourist trail. If you are unsure of your itinerary it's best to err on the safe side and consult your doctor about malaria medication. Anti-malarials must be taken before you enter a malarial zone. As resistance to chloroquin-based drugs increases, mefloquin, which goes under the brand name of Lariam, has become the recommended prophylactic for most travellers to the Philippines. This has very strong side effects, and its use is controversial; alternatives are atovaquone-proguanil (malarone) and doxycycline.

To avoid mosquito bites, wear long-sleeved shirts, long trousers and a hat. Use an insect repellent that contains DEET (diethylmethyltoluamide) and – unless you are staying in air-conditioned or well-screened accommodation – you could even pick up a mosquito net treated with the insecticide permethrin or deltamethrin. Mosquito nets are hard to find In the Philippines, so buy one before you go. If you are unable to find a pre-treated mosquito net you can buy one and spray it yourself.

Leeches and rabies

If you're trekking through rainforest, especially in the rainy season, there's a good chance you'll encounter **leeches** (known locally as *limatik*), blood-sucking freshwater worms that attach themselves to your skin and can be tricky to remove (the bite doesn't hurt though). If you find a leech on your skin it's important not to pull it off, as the jaw could be left behind, leading to the risk of infection. Repeatedly flick its head end with your fingernail, or rub salt, tiger balm or tobacco juice onto the leech, then treat the wound with antiseptic. You can guard against leeches in the first place by securing cuffs and trouser bottoms. Climbers in the Philippines say that rubbing detergent soap with a little water on your skin and clothes helps keep leeches at bay. Though leeches might seem unpleasant, they actually present a negligible risk to healthy hikers, and it's fine to let them drop off of their own accord.

Stray and badly cared for dogs are everywhere in the Philippines and are far more dangerous than leeches: **rabies** claims about eight hundred lives a year. The stereotype of rabid animals being deranged and foaming at the mouth is just that; some infected animals become lethargic and sleepy, so don't presume that a docile dog is a safe one. If you are bitten or scratched, wash the wound immediately with soap and running water for five minutes and apply alcohol or iodine. Seek treatment immediately – rabies is fatal once symptoms appear. You should also consider getting a rabies shot before arrival in the Philippines.

MEDICAL RESOURCES

Canadian Society for Global Health ⓦ cagh-acsm.org.
Extensive list of travel health centres.
CDC ⓦ wwwnc.cdc.gov/travel. Official US government travel health site.
Hospital for Tropical Diseases Travel Clinic ⓦ uclh.nhs.uk.
International Society for Travel Medicine ⓦ istm.org. Has a full list of travel health clinics worldwide.
MASTA (Medical Advisory Service for Travellers Abroad) ⓦ masta-travel-health.com. For the nearest clinic in the UK.
South African Society of Travel Medicine ⓦ sastm.org.za.
Offers latest medical advice for travellers and a directory of travel medicine practitioners in South Africa.
Travel Doctor ⓦ traveldoctor.com.au. Lists travel clinics in Australia.
Tropical Medical Bureau Republic of Ireland ⓦ tmb.ie.
Worldwise ⓦ worldwise.co.nz. Travel health advice and list of clinics in New Zealand.

The media

Filipinos are inordinately proud of their nation's historic status as the first democracy in Asia, a fact reflected in their love of a free press.

There is a dark and apparently contradictory side to this, however – the Philippines is also one of the most dangerous places in the world to be a journalist, with many killed every year. Though **press freedoms** are enshrined in the Philippine constitution, paramilitary groups, privately owned militias and even politicians (especially in Mindanao) who have been targeted by the press often seek violent retribution. Due to corruption, few are brought to justice.

Newspapers

Major English-language daily broadsheet **newspapers** include the *Philippine Daily Inquirer* (ⓦ inquirer. net), the *Philippine Star* (ⓦ philstar.com), *Manila Bulletin* (ⓦ mb.com.ph) and the *Manila Times* (ⓦ manilatimes.net).

There are dozens of tabloids on the market, and most of them are in Filipino. Whether tabloid or broadsheet, you'll often find that what's considered major news in the West – wars, and suchlike – usually plays second fiddle here to endless stories about local corruption, and the machinations of various layers of governance.

Television and radio

Terrestrial **television networks** include GMA (ⓦ gmanetwork.com) and ABS-CBN (ⓦ abs-cbn.com), offering a diet of histrionic soaps, chat shows and daytime game shows with sexy dancers. Cable TV is now widely available in the Philippines, with the exception of some of the most undeveloped rural areas. Most providers carry BBC World, CNN and Australian ABC. During the season, there's American football, baseball and most of all basketball on various channels, though outside of Manila it's very hard to find the Be-in channel that carries Premier League football. Movie channels include HBO, Cinemax and Star Movies, though these days you may instead get a smart TV, loaded (but not usually signed into) the regular apps; sometimes you'll also be able to access TV channels with these, too.

There are over 350 **radio** stations in the Philippines, and between them they present a mind-boggling mix of news, sport, music and chitchat. Radio news channels such as DZBB and RMN News AM tend to broadcast in Filipino, but there are dozens of FM pop stations that use English with a smattering of Filipino. The music they play tends towards mellow jazz and pop ballads by mainstream artists. Among the most popular FM stations are All-Radio FM (103.5MHz) and Crossover (105.1 MHz).

Festivals

Every community in the Philippines – from small barangay to crammed metropolis – has at least a couple of festivals a year in honour of a patron saint, to give thanks for a good harvest, or to pay respects to a biblical character. It's well worth timing your visit to see one of the major events: the beer flows, pigs are roasted, and there's dancing in the streets for days on end.

The main fiesta months are from January to May; exact dates often vary. Major mardi-gras-style festivals

ALL SAINTS' DAY

It's the day for Catholic Filipinos to honour their dead, but **All Saints' Day** on **November 1** is nothing to get maudlin about. Sometimes called All Souls' Day, it's when clans reunite at family graves and memorials, turning cemeteries throughout the country into fairgrounds. You don't pay your respects in the Philippines by being miserable, so All Saints' Day is a chance to show those who have gone before how much those who have been left behind are prospering. Filipinos approach All Saints' Day with the same gusto as Christmas, running from shop to shop at the last minute looking for candles to burn, food and offerings. The grave is painted, flowers are arranged and rosaries fervently prayed over, but once the ceremonial preliminaries are over, the fun begins. Guitars appear, capacious picnic hampers are opened and alcohol flows freely. Many families gather the night before and sleep in the cemetery. With many family graves in the provinces, Manila empties fast the day before All Saints' Day, as people leave the city by anything on wheels. Needless to say, it's a bad time to travel.

include the **Ati-Atihan** in January in Kalibo (see box, page 271) and the **Sinulog** in January in Cebu (see box, page 303). One of the biggest nationwide festivals is the **Flores de Mayo**, a religious parade held across the country throughout May in honour of the Virgin Mary.

A festival calendar

Listing all Filipino festivals is impossible. Those included here are larger ones that you might consider making a special trip for, at least if you happen to be in the area.

JANUARY AND FEBRUARY

Feast of the Black Nazarene (Jan 9) Quiapo, Manila. Devotees gather in the plaza outside Quiapo Church to touch a miraculous image of Christ. See page 64.

Ati-Atihan (variable, culminating on third Sun in Jan) Kalibo, Aklan. Street dancing and wild costumes at arguably the biggest festival in the country, held to celebrate an ancient land pact between settlers and Indigenous Atis. See box, page 271.

Sinulog (third Sun in Jan) Cebu City, Cebu. Cebu's biggest annual event, in honour of the Santo Niño (an image of Jesus as a child). Huge street parade, live music and plenty of food and drink. See box, page 303.

Dinagyang (fourth week of Jan) Iloilo, Panay Island ⓦ facebook. com/iloilodinagyangofficial. Relatively modern festival modelled after the Ati-Atihan; includes a parade on the Iloilo River.

Philippine Hot Air Balloon Fiesta (Feb) Clark, Pampanga ⓦ instagram.com/philballoonfest. Balloon rides, microlight flying, skydiving and aerobatics displays.

Pamulinawen (first two weeks in Feb) Laoag City, Ilocos Norte. Citywide fiesta in honour of St William the Hermit. Events include street parties, beauty pageants, concerts and religious parades.

Panagbenga (Baguio Flower Festival; third week in Feb) Baguio City, Benguet ⓦ panagbengaflowerfestival.com. The summer capital's largest annual event includes parades of floats beautifully decorated with flowers from the Cordillera region. There are also flower-related lectures and exhibitions.

Suman Festival (third week in Feb) Baler, Aurora. Another mardi-gras-style extravaganza featuring street parades, dancing and floats decorated with the native delicacy *suman* – sticky rice cake rolled in banana leaves.

MARCH AND APRIL

Moriones (Easter weekend) Marinduque. A celebration of the life of the Roman centurion Longinus, who was blind in one eye. Legend says that when he pierced Christ's side with his spear, blood spurted into his eye and cured him. See box, page 191.

Arya! Abra (first or second week of March) Bangued, Abra. Highlights include hair-raising bamboo-raft races along the frisky Abra River and gatherings of northern Indigenous people.

Bangkero Festival (first or second week of March) Pagsanjan, Laguna. Parade along the Pagsanjan River.

Kaamulan (first week of March) Malaybalay City, Bukidnon, Mindanao. Showcase of Indigenous culture and arts.

Pasayaw (third week of March) Canlaon City, Negros Oriental. Thanksgiving festival to God and St Joseph, with twelve barangays competing for honours in an outdoor dancing competition. The final "dance-off" is held in the city gym.

Boracay International Dragon Boat Festival (April) Boracay, Aklan. A local version of Hong Kong's dragon-boat races, featuring domestic and international teams competing in long wooden canoes on a course off White Beach.

Allaw Ta Apo Sandawa (second week of April) Kidapawan City, Cotabato. Gathering of highland Indigenous people to pay respects to the sacred Mount Apo.

Turumba Festival (April & May) Pakil, Laguna. Religious festival commemorating the seven sorrows of the Virgin Mary. The festival consists of seven novenas, one for each sorrow, held at weekends.

MAY

Flores de Mayo (throughout May) Countrywide. Religious procession celebrating the coming of the rains, with girls dressed as the various "Accolades of our Lady", including Faith, Hope and

Charity. Processions are sometimes held after dark and lit by candles – a lovely sight.

Carabao Carroza (May 3–4) Iloilo, Panay Island. Races held to celebrate the humble carabao (water buffalo), beast of burden for many a provincial farmer.

Pahiyas (May 15) Lucban, Quezon; also in the nearby towns of Candelaria, Tayabas, Sariaya, Tiaong and Lucena. Colourful harvest festival which sees houses gaily decorated with fruits and vegetables. It's held in honour of San Isidro Labrador, the patron saint of farmers.

Obando Fertility Rites (May 17–19) Obando, Bulacan. On the feast day of San Pascual, women gather in the churchyard to chant prayers asking for children, an intriguing combination of traditional dance, Catholicism and far older animist beliefs.

AUGUST AND SEPTEMBER

Kadayawan sa Davao (third week of Aug) Davao City, Mindanao. Week-long harvest festival with civic and military parades and street dances.

Peñafrancia Fluvial Festival (third Sat in Sept) Naga, Camarines Sur. A sacred statue of Our Lady of Peñafrancia, the patron saint of Bicol, is paraded through the streets, then sailed down the Bicol River back to its shrine.

OCTOBER AND NOVEMBER

Kansilay (Oct 19 or closest weekend) Silay, Negros Occidental. Modern festival commemorating Silay's charter day. Eating and drinking contests, beauty pageants and an elaborate street parade.

Ibalong (third week of Oct) Legaspi, Albay and throughout Bicol region. Epic dances and street presentations portraying Bicol's mythical superheroes and gods.

Lanzones Festival (third week of Oct) Lambajao, Camiguin. Vibrant and good-natured outdoor party giving thanks for the island's crop of lanzones (a tropical fruit). See page 390.

Masskara Festival (third week of Oct) Bacolod, Negros Occidental. Festivities kick off with food fairs, mask-making contests, brass-band competitions and beauty pageants, followed by the climax – a mardi gras parade where revellers don elaborate masks and costumes and dance to Latin rhythms Rio de Janeiro-style. See page 275.

MIMAROPA Festival (November) Mindoro, Marinduque, Romblon and Palawan. An annual celebration of different Filipino cultures, featuring impressive street parades and dancing. Held in a different city each year.

DECEMBER

Christmas (December 25). The Christmas season officially starts Dec 16 and lasts until Epiphany on Jan 9. Churches are full for Midnight Mass on Christmas Eve, and some towns hold a Panunulúyan pageant in the days leading up to it, commemorating the journey of Joseph and the pregnant Virgin Mary to Bethlehem. Though Christmas is primarily a family festival, celebrated in the home, without the pageantry on show at other festivals, you'll still see groups of children singing carols all over the archipelago. Christmas Day itself is spent with family and friends – the country largely shuts down for the day.

Outdoor activities

For a sizeable proportion of the tourists who visit every year, one of the main attractions of the Philippines is the fantastic scuba diving opportunities. The abundance of exceptional dive sites and the high standard of diving instruction available have made the archipelago one of the world's foremost diving destinations.

It's not all about getting underwater though: there are some superb wilderness areas in the Philippines and dozens of volcanoes and mountains to be **climbed**, from the tallest in the country, Mount Apo (2954m), to more manageable peaks close to Manila in Batangas and Rizal provinces, some of which can be tackled in a day-trip. The country also offers opportunities for **caving, whitewater rafting, surfing** and **sailing**.

DIVING DOS AND DON'TS

Divers can cause damage to reefs, sometimes inadvertently. Be aware of your fins as they can break off coral heads that take years to regrow. Don't grab coral to steady yourself, and always maintain good buoyancy control – colliding with a reef can be destructive. Don't kick up sediment, which can choke and kill corals. Below is a list of additional dos and don'ts:

- **Collecting aquatic life** Don't take home corals or shells, and never take souvenirs from wreck-dives or remove anything dead or alive – except rubbish – from the sea.
- **Touching and handling aquatic life** For many organisms this is a terrifying and injurious experience – it's best left to people who have experience with the creatures concerned.
- **Riding aquatic life** Hard to credit, but some divers still think it's a great lark to hang onto the back of a turtle or manta ray. Simply put, there are no circumstances in which this is right.
- **Spear-fishing** This has been outlawed in the Philippines, and environmental groups are increasingly reporting spear-fishers to the authorities for prosecution.

Scuba diving

Diving is possible **year-round** in the Philippines, with surface water temperatures in the 25–28°C range, the warmest conditions being from February to June. On deeper dives temperatures can drop to 22°C due to the upwelling of deeper, cooler water, so a light (3mm) wet suit is essential. During the typhoon season from June to November, be prepared for your plans to be disrupted if a major storm hits and dive boats are unable to venture out. **Visibility** depends on water temperature, the strength of the current and wind direction, but generally lies in the 10–30m range.

There are several **recompression chambers** (aka hyperbaric chambers) in the Philippines to treat recompression sickness (see page 41), including a mobile ship-based unit. All ostensibly offer a 24-hour emergency service, but note that facilities do close for maintenance and/or because there are no staff qualified to run them. You might want to check that your dive operator is aware of the nearest operational facility. If it's not, go somewhere else.

Dive trips

Most dive **costs** include rental of the boat and equipment such as mask, booties, wet suit, fins, weight belt and air tanks. For night dives and more demanding technical dives, expect to pay a bit extra. If you've booked a package that includes accommodation at a dive resort, two dives a day will normally be included in the cost.

Courses

All PADI-accredited resorts offer a range of courses run by qualified professional instructors. If you haven't been diving before and aren't sure if you'll take to it, try a gentle twenty-minute "**discovery dive**", guided by an instructor, or the longer PADI **Discover Scuba Diving** course. The main course for beginners is the PADI **Open Water Diver Course** which will allow you to dive at depths up to 18m. You might want to consider doing the pool sessions and written tests before you travel, then doing the check-out dives at a PADI resort in the Philippines. It saves time and means that you don't have to slave over homework in the tropical heat. If you choose this option, make sure that you bring your PADI referral documents with you.

Once you've passed the course and been given your certification card, you are free to dive anywhere in the world. You might also want to take another step up the diving ladder by enrolling in a more advanced course. There are many to choose from, including **Advanced Open Water Diver**, Emergency First Response, which is also suitable for non-divers, and **Rescue Diver**.

Liveaboards

There are two great advantages to diving from a **liveaboard** (a boat that acts as a mobile hotel) – you can get to places that are inaccessible by bangka and once you're there you can linger for a night or two. Liveaboards allow you to explore terrific destinations such as Apo Reef off the coast of Mindoro and

TOP 10 DIVE SITES

Anilao Closest dive site to Manila, teeming with soft coral and tropical fish. See box, page 113.

Apo Island Not to be confused with the reef (see below), this island off Negros is swamped with fish and forests of coral. See page 289.

Apo Reef Few divers and lots of big fish, two hours off the coast of Mindoro. See page 241.

Coron The best wreck-diving in the country, possibly in the world. There are 24 charted wrecks, Japanese ships sunk in one massive attack by US aircraft in 1944. See box, page 378.

Puerto Galera Unrivalled all-round destination with something for everyone, from novices to old hands. See box, page 232.

Padre Burgos Out of the way in undeveloped southern Leyte and a prime spot for discovering new dive sites. See page 349.

Panglao Island The dive sites close to the congenial Alona Beach resorts offer an exceptional range of marine life. See box, page 329.

Samal Island This sleepy island just off the coast of Davao, Mindanao, harbours numerous dive sites. See page 407.

Subic Bay The former US Navy base is an exceptional location for wreck-dives, with the USS *New York* one of the highlights. See box, page 121.

Tubbataha Reef You'll need to book a liveaboard trip but it's worth it, with guaranteed sightings of sharks and a good chance of mantas and whale sharks. See page 358.

MARINE LIFE

The beauty of diving in the Philippines is that you don't have to dive deep to see some incredible marine life. Among the commonest are the exotic and brightly coloured **angelfish**, **damselfish** and eye-catching **humbugs**, striped black-and-white like the sweet. In shallow coral gardens you'll see inquisitive **clownfish** defending their coral nests either singly or in pairs, perhaps with minuscule juveniles at their sides. Also unmissable are the frenetic shoals of **dragonets** and **dottybacks**, with their psychedelic colouring. **Moray eels** take shelter in crevices in the reef and it's not unusual to see one, even in the shallows. Even **turtles** can be seen at this depth.

Where the coral plunges away steeply into an inky darkness, at depths of five or six metres, you'll see bright-green **parrot fish** and mesmerizing **batfish**, who patrol the reef edge in family shoals. These slopes and fore reefs are also home to **snappers**, **goatfish** and **wrasses**, the largest of which – the Napoleon wrasse – can dwarf a person. Deeper still, but usually in the more isolated dive sites such as Tubbataha, it's possible to see sharks, including **white tip reef sharks** and **grey reef sharks**, while if you're lucky an immense but gentle **manta ray** or **whale shark** might drift lazily past.

Poisonous species include the beautifully hypnotic **lionfish** (also called the flamefish), which hunts at night and has spines along its back that can deliver a nasty dose of venom, while shoals of **jellyfish** are common at certain times of year.

Tubbataha in the Sulu Sea, arguably the best dive spot in the country. Packages include all meals and dives, but vary significantly according to destination. Most of the boats used have air-conditioned en-suite cabins for two. Packages often include unlimited diving and are always full board.

LIVEABOARD OPERATORS

There are plenty of liveaboard options in the Philippines, but few ships or agencies run their own websites; it's better to investigate on individual engines such as Ⓦ liveaboard.com.
Atlantis Dive Resorts Ⓦ atlantishotel.com. Operates the 32m-long *Atlantis Azores*, which has eight luxurious cabins with private bathrooms. Trips to Puerto Galera and Apo Reef (Oct–Dec), Tubbataha (mid-March to early June), Dumaguete (June–Sept) and southern Leyte for the whale sharks (Jan–March).
Expedition Fleet Ⓦ stellamarisliveaboard.com. Trips to Tubbataha, and elsewhere, on the ten-cabin *MV Stella Maris Explorer*.

RECOMPRESSION CHAMBERS

Batangas City St Patrick's Hospital, Lopez Jaena St ☏ 043 723 0750.
Cavite City St Paul Hospital, Dasmariñas ☏ 0927 793 1152.
Cebu City Cebu Recompression Chamber, Viscom Station Hospital, Military Camp Lapu-Lapu, Lahug ☏ 032 232 2464.
Makati City Makati Medical Center, 2 Amorsolo St, Makati City ☏ 02 8888 8999.
Manila Asian Hyperbaric Healthcare, Shaw Blvd, Mandaluyong City ☏ 02 920 7183.
Roving Chamber Royal Coast Guard Action Center (two ships based in Cebu) ☏ 0917 186 2488.

DIVING RESOURCES

Asia Divers Ⓦ asiadivers.com. Thoroughly professional dive outfit with an office in Manila and a dive centre and accommodation in Puerto Galera. Good people to learn with.
Divephil Ⓦ divephil.com. Useful guide to scuba diving in the Philippines, plus information about destinations and accommodation.
SeaQuest Ⓦ seaquestdivecenter.net. Long-established operator with centres in Bohol and Cebu, offering general diving advice, safaris, courses and accommodation.
Underwater 360° Ⓦ uw360.asia. Online diving portal for several organizations.

Trekking and climbing

The Philippines offers plenty of opportunities to explore pristine **wilderness** areas. Luzon, for example, has the Sierra Madre (see page 149), rarely visited by tourists and offering exhilarating trekking through dense rainforest and across dizzying peaks. In Bicol there are some terrific volcano climbs (Mt Mayon and Mt Isarog, for instance; see page 207 and page 201), while Mindoro, Palawan and the Visayas between them have dozens of national parks, heritage areas, wildlife sanctuaries and volcanoes. Mount Kanlaon (see page 281), an active volcano in Negros, is one of the country's more risky climbs, while Mount Halcon (see page 235) on Mindoro offers a raw, mesmerizing landscape of peaks, waterfalls and jungle, typical of wilderness areas throughout the archipelago.

The country actually has more than sixty **national parks** and protected areas, but because funds for their management are scarce, you won't find the kind of infrastructure that exists in national parks in the West. While the most popular climbs – Mount Apo in Mindanao (see page 410) and Mount Pulag in Mountain province (see page 161), for example – have trails that are relatively easy to find and follow, it's important to realize that for the most part trails are generally poorly maintained and hardly marked, if they're marked at all. There are seldom more than a few (badly paid) wardens or rangers responsible for huge tracts of land, and where accommodation exists, it will be extremely basic. Some national parks have administrative buildings where you might be able to get a bed in a dorm for the night, or where you can roll out a mattress or sleeping bag on the floor. They may also have basic cooking facilities, but the closest you'll get to a shower is filling a bucket and washing outside. Deep within park territory, the best you can hope for is a wooden shack to shelter in for the night.

This lack of facilities means you'll need to hire a reliable **guide**. Often, the place to make contact with guides is the municipal hall in the barangay or town closest to the trailhead. Make sure you bring food and water with you as it's unlikely that you'll come across anywhere to buy anything once you're on the trail.

There are some **outdoor shops** in big cities – mainly Manila – where you can buy a basic frame-tent and a sleeping bag. Other essentials such as cooking equipment, lanterns and backpacks are also available, and you may be able to rent some items, though the range of gear on offer is limited even in the best shops.

TREKKING AND CLIMBING RESOURCES

Mountaineering Federation of the Philippines Ⓦ mfpi.org. An umbrella group that can offer general information about routes and practicalities.

Pinoy Mountaineer Ⓦ pinoymountaineer.com. This detailed and well-maintained site is a good place to read up about trekking and climbing, with sample itineraries for major climbs and a long list of climbing clubs in the country.

Caving

It's hardly surprising that **caving** – spelunking – is a growth industry, as there are huge caves to explore throughout the country. The largest cave systems are in northern Luzon – in Sagada (see page 167) and in Cagayan province near Tuguegarao, where the Peñablanca Protected Area (see page 149) has three hundred caves, many deep, dangerous and not yet fully explored. The other exciting caving area is the Sohoton Natural Bridge National Park in Samar (see page 340).

Whitewater rafting and ziplining

Whitewater rafting is becoming more popular in the Philippines, notably along the Cagayan River and Chico River in northern Luzon (see page 167) and Cagayan de Oro River in Mindanao (see box, page 387). **Ziplines** have mushroomed all over the islands, but some are much tamer than others – some of the best are near Cagayan de Oro (see page 387) and Tibiao (see page 252).

Surfing and other watersports

Surfing is now well established in the Philippines in eastern Bicol (see box, page 196), Catanduanes (see page 220), eastern Mindanao (especially Siargao Island; see page 399), and around San Fernando in La Union (see page 134). There are also any number of hard-to-reach areas in the archipelago that are visited only by a handful of die-hard surfers, such as Baler in northern Luzon (see box, page 151), or around Borongan (see page 341) in eastern Samar.

Other sea-based watersports such as **kitesurfing**, **waterskiing, wakeboarding** and **ocean kayaking** are also growing in popularity, especially in major tourist destinations such as Boracay.

Spectator sports

When it comes to spectator sports, basket-ball and boxing are among the biggest passions in the Philippines. Pool – or what Filipinos call "billiards" – is also popular. Televised football (soccer) has some fans, though it is difficult to find in most of the country. Cockfighting is one of the few popular pastimes that harks back to the pre-Hispanic era.

Basketball

The Filipinos embraced **basketball** as they did everything else American, from pizza to popcorn. Every barangay and town has a basketball court, even if all it consists of are a couple of makeshift baskets nailed to wooden poles in the church plaza. The major league – the equivalent of the NBA – is the **Philippine Basketball Association** (PBA; Ⓦ pba.ph), founded in 1975. Twelve teams – plus often a guest team from aborad – compete for honours, all of them sponsored by a major corporation and taking their sponsor's name. You might find yourself watching Meralco Bolts play San Miguel Beermen, or NLEX take on Rain or Shine Elasto Painters (good luck working that last one into a chant). PBA games are all played in Manila (see box, page 95).

The San Miguel-Petron franchise (under the name Beermen) is the most successful, while Barangay Ginebra San Miguel is the most popular. The star players are household names to most Filipinos.

Boxing

Boxing has been big business in the Philippines since the Americans introduced the sport in the early twentieth century. In recent years, one name stands out in particular: **Manny "the Pacman" Pacquiao**, the poor boy from Mindanao who became world champion (see box, page 423). Fights are held almost every week, often at major venues in Caloocan (Manila), Cebu City, Mandaluyong (Manila), Tagaytay City, Victoria (Negros) and Taytay in the Luzon province of Rizal. Tickets are cheap and often sell out; whenever there's a bout of any significance Filipinos gather around every available television set. You can check schedules for fights at W philboxing.com.

Pool

Every town and city in the country has some sort of **billiards hall** (for **pool**, not traditional English billiards), even if it's just a few old tables on the pavement where games are played by kerosene lamps between locals for the price of a few San Miguels.

The sport has always been popular – it's cheap and reasonably accessible – but has boomed over the last thirty years or so because of the success of **Efren Reyes** and **Francisco Bustamante**. Reyes, sometimes called "The Magician", is one of the pool world's great cue-wielding characters; a diminutive fellow with a toothy grin, he picked up the nickname "Bata" ("The Kid") while helping out in his uncle's pool halls in Manila as a child. He was born in Pampanga province, to the north of Manila, and has found renown among professional cueists in the UK, US and beyond as one of the most talented players the world has ever seen – you can see plenty of this humble fella's table magic on YouTube.

In 2006, Reyes and Francisco "Django" Bustamante represented their country as Team Philippines and won the inaugural **World Cup of Pool** by defeating Team USA – a victory of major significance for a country with few global sporting heroes. They repeated the feat in 2009, on home turf. Countrymen Dennis Orcollo and Roberto Gomez then won the title in London in 2013, though the accolade has subsequently gone to various other countries; the Philippines were walloped by Austria in the 2019 final, but clinched their fourth title in 2023.

Cockfighting

Cockfighting is the Filipino passion few foreigners get to see – or understand, for obvious reasons. It's a brutal blood sport where fighting cocks literally peck and jab each other to death as onlookers make bets on the outcome. The fight begins when the two roosters are presented to each other in the pit. Both have a razor-sharp curved blade three inches long strapped to their leg. The fight is over in a burst of feathers in no more than a few minutes, when one rooster is too bloodied and wounded, or simply too dead, to peck back at its opponent when provoked. To make the evening last, most major cockfights feature seven contests. Anyone who likes animals should definitely stay well away.

If you do attend a cockfight (*sabong* in Tagalog), you'll be experiencing Filipino culture at its rawest

---

COCKFIGHTING AND THE FILIPINO

Cockfighting has a long history in the Philippines. National hero José Rizal, martyred by the Spanish in 1896, once pointed out that the average Filipino loves his rooster more than he does his children.

Contrary to received wisdom, cockfighting was not introduced to the country by the Spanish. When conquistadors landed in Palawan shortly after the death of Magellan, they discovered native men already breeding domestic roosters to fight, putting them in shared cages and letting them scrap over small amounts of food.

Social scientists say cockfighting is popular in the Philippines because it reflects the national passion for brevity or a quick payoff, the trait of **ningas cogon** (*cogon* being a wild grass that burns ferociously and quickly). Part of the appeal is the **prize money**. For a modest entrance fee, a struggling farmer from the backwoods could finish the day with an annual wage in his pocket, all thanks to a trusty rooster he has groomed and trained assiduously for months. As with all gambling, of course, this is outweighed by the sum total of those who fail to win.

– at the very least it might make you think again about how much "American influence" dominates the culture. It's best to start at one of the main cockpits in Manila, or ask your hotel for the nearest place to see one. Entrance fees are minimal, but you'll rarely see women attending – the cockpit is the exclusive preserve of men, who see it as an egalitarian refuge from the world's woes, a place where class differences are temporarily put to one side and everyone wears flip-flops and vests. In Manila, foreign women should be OK at the main venues, but in the provinces you'll probably feel more comfortable with a male companion.

Culture and etiquette

For many travellers the Philippines seems less immediately "exotic" than other countries in Asia. English is spoken almost everywhere, people wear Western clothes and visit malls and the main religion is Catholicism. Combined with the approachability and sunny disposition of your average Filipino, this appears to make for a trouble-free assimilation into the ways and values of the Philippines.

STREET KIDS

Despite the very real economic progress made in the last twenty years, millions of Filipinos still live in poverty. **Street children** (many orphaned) are one of the saddest consequences of this – some reports estimate that around quarter of a million kids are living rough. In Manila and other large cities you'll see very small children begging for money in the street or dancing in front of cars at dangerous interchanges for tips. You'll also come across kids aggressively begging for change; sometimes they are known as "**rugby boys**" – nothing to do with the sport, but a famous brand of glue that they sniff. Many locals refuse to give them money for fear of encouraging dangerous behaviour – others give a few pesos out of pity. If you want to help, a good place to start is the Cavite-based Life Child (🌐lifechild.org).

However, this can lead to a false sense of security, which over time – as differences begin to surface – can give way to bewilderment and confusion. There are complex rules of engagement that govern behaviour among Filipinos, and failure to be sensitive to them can cast you unwittingly in the role of the ugly foreigner, ranting and raving with frustration at everyone you interact with.

Filipino etiquette

One of the major controlling elements in Filipino society – undetected by most visitors – is **hiya**, a difficult word to define, though essentially it means a sense of shame. *Hiya* is a factor in almost all social situations. It is a sense of *hiya* that prevents someone asking a question, for fear he may look foolish. It is *hiya* that sees many Filipinos refuse to disagree openly, for fear they may cause offence. Not to have *hiya* is a grave social sin; to be accused of being *walang-hiya* (to be shameless) is the ultimate insult. *Hiya* goes hand in hand with the preservation of **amor-propio** (the term literally means "love of self"), in other words to avoid losing face. If you ever wonder why a Filipino fails to broach awkward subjects with you, or to point out that your flies are undone, it is because *hiya* and *amor-propio* are at work.

If you are ever in doubt about how to behave in the Philippines, bring to mind the value of **pakikisama**, which in rough translation means "to get along". For example, don't confront the waiter or bark insults if he gets your order wrong. This offends his sense of *amor-propio* and marks you out as being an obnoxious *walang-hiya* foreigner. Talk to him quietly and ask that the order be changed. The same rules apply with government officials, police, ticket agents, hotel receptionists and cashiers. If there's a problem, sort it out quietly and patiently. A sense of **delicadeza** is also important to Filipinos. This might be translated as "propriety", a simple sense of good behaviour, particularly in the presence of elders or women.

Yes, no, maybe…

One of the root causes of frustration during social intercourse is the use of the word **yes**. In their desire to please, many Filipinos find it difficult to say no. So they say yes instead. Yes (actually *oo* in Tagalog, pronounced oh-oh, though most Filipinos would use the English word when talking to foreigners) can mean one of a great many things, from a plain and simple "yes" to "I'm not sure", "perhaps", "if you say so", or "sorry, I don't understand". A casual yes is never taken as binding.

The concepts of *hiya* and *amor-propio* also filter through to the language in the form of a great many

SEX WORK AND SEX TOURISM

The Philippines, like some other Southeast Asian countries, has an unfortunate reputation for **sex work** and **sex tourism**. It's a huge industry domestically with an estimated 800,000 men, women and, sadly, children working in the trade. The country's international image as a sex destination came about largely as a result of the US military presence here during and after World War II, when "go-go" or "girlie" bars flourished around the bases at Clark and Subic Bay.

While it's illegal to sell or procure sex, the trade still operates under the guise of entertainment: sex workers are employed as singers, dancers, waitresses or "guest relations officers" in clubs and bars where they are expected to leave with any client who pays a fee (the "bar fine"). Then there's what are euphemistically dubbed "freelancers", prostitutes who independently cruise bars looking for paying customers. In the Philippines it's common (because it's so cheap) to hire these girls for several days or weeks to have what's called a GFE ("girlfriend experience").

Men from East Asia, Australia and beyond visit Angeles, north of Manila, in their tens of thousands each year on sex tours. Koreans, Taiwanese and Chinese have developed their own networks, usually based in karaoke bars and restaurants. Manila, Cebu City, Subic Bay and Pasay City are also major sex destinations.

DATING WEBSITES

Though you will often see older Western men accompanied by young, attractive Filipina women all over the Philippines, don't assume that these women are prostitutes. The situation is confused by the legal and equally popular phenomenon of **online dating websites** that exclusively pair Filipinas with foreigners – plenty of the men you'll see have been matched with their Filipina "girlfriend" and intend to seriously date or even marry them (or already have), however dubious this might seem.

CHILD PROSTITUTION

The Philippine government estimates that almost half the sex workers in the country are **underage**, many of them street children lured from the provinces by the promise of work or simply food and water. In recent years, cyberporn has become a major problem – in 2014 the British-led Operation Endeavour uncovered a global network of paedophiles streaming live child abuse by video from the Philippines. If you suspect someone of being a paedophile or engaging in any abusive behaviour towards minors, report it to the police.

euphemisms for the word no (*hindi* in Tagalog). Instead of replying in the negative, in order not to upset you a Filipino will typically say "maybe" (*siguro nga*), "whatever" (*bahala na*) or "if you say so" (*kung sinabi mo ba e*).

These subtleties of language are symptomatic of the unseen ebbs and flows of the tides that govern all social behaviour in the Philippines, few foreigners ever fully coming to terms with the eddies and whirls underneath.

Questions and greetings

Filipinos are outgoing people who don't consider it rude to ask **personal questions**. Prepare to be pleasantly interrogated by everyone you meet. Filipinos will want to know where you are from, why you are in the Philippines, how old you are, whether you are married, if not why not, and so on and so forth. They

pride themselves on their hospitality and are always ready to share a meal or a few drinks. Don't offend them by refusing outright.

In rural areas it's still common for foreign men to be greeted by passers-by with calls of "Hey Joe!" This harks back to the GI Joes of World War II and American occupation.

Filipino time

Why do you never ask a Filipino to do something by the end of the week? He might think you're being pushy. That's an exaggeration of course, but beyond the cities, the old joke still resonates for long-time residents of the Philippines.

In recent years, perhaps due to the number of young Filipinos returning home after an overseas education, the attitude towards **punctuality** has begun to change. For medical or work-related appointments you'll need to be on time, but for social gatherings turn up half an hour late: it is considered impolite to be on time for a party, for instance, simply because it makes you look like a glutton who wants to grab the food before anyone else does. The speed of service in restaurants in the Philippines has also improved, but you should still expect your patience to occasionally be tested.

Women travellers

Women travellers rarely experience problems in the Philippines, either travelling alone or as part of a group. The culture, however, is a **macho** one and, especially in the provinces, foreign women may experience being stared at or the occasional catcall or lewd comment in Tagalog. In the barangays, Filipino men hold dear the oft-regurgitated image of themselves in local movies as gifted romancers, able to reduce any lady to jelly with a few choice words and the wink of an eye. Reacting to this attention is the worst thing you can do. If you smile and remain good-natured but distant, your potential suitors will get the message and leave you alone. To shout back or to poke fun, particularly if Romeo is with his friends, will cause him serious loss of face and lead to resentment and the possibility that they will try to get back at you.

Modesty is essential to the behaviour of young Filipinas, especially in the provinces, and this should also be the case with visitors. Shorts and T-shirts are fine for women anywhere (except sometimes for immigration offices), but bikinis are only for the beach, and even then it's considered bad form to wander through a resort's restaurant or souvenir shop without covering up first (a sarong is perfect for this). Topless sunbathing is unheard of among Filipinas, and tourists in popular resorts such as Boracay who remove their clothes are likely to attract an amazed, gossiping crowd of locals.

Shopping

The Philippines is a great place to buy Indigenous art, woodwork, masks and religious artefacts, mostly at rock-bottom prices. Manila also contains a number of shiny malls with stores offering much the same designer gear you can find in London or New York. The country's two main department-store chains are Rustan's and SM. Both are good for clothes and shoes, at slightly lower prices than in Europe; children's clothes are especially inexpensive.

Souvenirs

Typical souvenirs include **models of jeepneys**, wooden **salad bowls**, cotton **linen** and small items such as **fridge magnets** made of coconut shell or carabao horn, and in department stores you can find **cutlery sets** made from carabao horn and bamboo. **Woven place mats** and coasters are inexpensive and easy to pack to take home. Filipino **picture frames** are eye-catching and affordable. Made from raw materials such as carabao horn and Manila hemp, they are available in most good department stores. Pretty much all towns have markets that sell cheap local goods such as **sleeping mats** (*banig*) that make colourful wall hangings, and earthenware water jars or **cooking pots** that make attractive additions to a kitchen.

For serious souvenir-hunting, you'll have to rummage around in small **antique shops**. There aren't many of these, and they're often tucked away in low-rent areas. The better shops in big cities are listed in the Guide; elsewhere, ask around at your hotel. Many of the items in these shops are religious artefacts (see page 47), although you'll also find furniture, decorative vases, lamps, old paintings, mirrors and brassware.

Some souvenir stores and antique shops will ship goods home for you for an extra charge. Otherwise you could send bulky items home by regular post (see page 52). Note that the trade in coral and seashells as souvenirs in beach areas is decidedly unsound environmentally, as is the manufacture of decorative objects and jewellery from seashells.

VIDEOKE CRAZY

"Videoke" – **video karaoke** – is a major fad in the Philippines, with cheap videoke bars in almost every town and neighbourhood. While it can be fun to participate in a Filipino singing session, being regaled by drunken wailings wafting through your hotel window in the early hours isn't so amusing. Adding to the mix, most Filipino families own one or more karaoke machines that they use throughout the week, and always on special occasions, birthdays and weddings. Incidentally, a Filipino inventor (Roberto del Rosario) actually holds the patent for the karaoke machine (though it had been invented several years previously, in Japan).

Indigenous and religious artefacts

Not all Indigenous and religious artefacts are genuine, but even the imitations make good gifts. **Woven baskets and trays** of the kind used by Cordillera peoples are a bargain, starting from only a few hundred pesos. They come in a range of sizes and shapes, including circular trays woven from grass that are still used to sift rice, and baskets worn like a backpack for carrying provisions. The best are the original baskets, which cost a little more than the reproductions, but have an appealing nut-brown tone as a result of the many times they have been oiled. You can find them in antique shops around the country and also in markets in Banaue and Sagada.

Rice gods (*bulol*; see page 95), carved wooden deities sometimes with nightmarish facial expressions, are available largely in Manila and the Cordilleras. In Manila, they cost anything from a few hundred pesos for a small reproduction to tens of thousands for a genuine figurine of modest size; they're much cheaper if you haggle for them in Banaue or Sagada. At markets in the Cordilleras, look out also for **wooden bowls**, various wooden wall carvings and fabric **wall hangings**.

The best place to look for Catholic **religious art** is in Manila (see page 95), though antique shops in other towns also have a selection. Wooden Catholic statues called santos and large wooden crucifixes are common. Cheaper religious souvenirs such as rosaries and icons of saints are sold by street vendors outside many of the more high-profile pilgrimage cathedrals and churches such as Quiapo in Manila and Santo Niño in Cebu.

Textiles

In market areas such as Divisoria in Manila and Colon in Cebu you can find colourful raw cloth and finished **batik products**. Another native textile is **Manila hemp**, which comes from the trunk of a particular type of banana tree. Both *piña* and Manila hemp are used to make attractive home accessories sold in department stores, such as laundry baskets, lampshades and vases. The versatile and pliable native grass, **sikat**, is woven into everything from place mats to rugs.

Department stores everywhere have a good selection of Philippine **linen products** with delicate embroidery and lace flourishes. Some of these are handmade in Taal (see page 112) but some are not; it's easy to find a good set of pillow-cases and

BARGAINING

Prices are fixed in department stores and most retail outlets in malls, but in many antique shops and in markets, you're expected to **haggle**. Bargaining is always amicable and relaxed, never confrontational. Filipinos see it as something of a polite game, interjecting their offers and counter offers with friendly chitchat about the weather, the state of the nation or, if you're a foreigner, where you come from and what you're doing in the Philippines.

Never play hardball and make a brusque "take it or leave it" offer because that's likely to cause embarrassment and offence. Start by offering **fifty to sixty percent** of the initial asking price and work your way up from there. Note that foreigners tend to get less of a discount than Filipinos.

SARI-SARI STORES

A Philippine institution, the humble **sari-sari store** – *sari-sari* means "various" or "a variety" – is often no more than a barangay shack or a hole in the wall selling an eclectic but practical range of goods. If you're short of shampoo, body lotion, cigarettes, rum, beer or you've got a headache and need a painkiller, the local sari-sari store is the answer, especially in areas without supermarkets. All items are sold in the smallest quantities possible: shampoo comes in packets half the size of a credit card, medicine can be bought by the pill and cigarettes are sold individually. Buy a soft drink or beer and you may be perplexed to see the store holder pour it into a plastic bag, from which you're expected to drink it through a straw. This is so that they can keep the bottle and return it for the deposit of a few centavos. Most sari-sari stores are fiercely **familial**, their names – the Three Sisters, the Four Brothers or Emily and Jon-Jon's – reflecting their ownership.

The sari-sari store is also held dear by Filipinos as an unofficial community centre. Many sari-sari stores, especially in the provinces, have crude sitting areas outside, encouraging folk to linger in the shade and gossip or talk basketball and cockfighting.

bedsheets in Taal's market, though they're often half the price in Rustan's or SM. In beach areas you'll find a good range of cotton sarongs, cheap, colourful and versatile.

Jewellery

The malls are full of stalls selling cheap jewellery, but you'll also find silver-plated earrings, replica Indigenous-style jewellery made with tin or brass, and attractive necklaces made from bone or polished coconut shell. In Mindanao – as well as in some malls in Manila, Cebu City and at souvenir stalls in Boracay – **pearl jewellery** is a bargain. Most of the pearls are cultivated on pearl farms in Mindanao and Palawan. White pearls are the most common, but you can also find pink and dove grey. They are made into earrings, necklaces and bracelets.

Musical instruments

In Cebu, and increasingly on the streets of Manila and Davao, you can pick up a locally made hand-crafted guitar, *bandurria* (mandolin) or ukelele. Though the acoustic quality is nothing special, the finish may include mother-of-pearl inlays, and prices are low. Mindanao's markets – such as Aldevinco in Davao – are a good place to rummage for decorative drums and Muslim gongs.

Travel essentials

Accessible travel

Facilities for people with disabilities are rare except in the major cities. Most vehicles (especially jeepneys, and the more basic buses) are cramped, while bangkas are notoriously tricky even for the able-bodied. For wheelchair users, the pavements represent a serious obstacle in themselves. Often dilapidated and potholed, they are frustrating at the best of times and simply impassable at the worst, when pedestrians are forced to pick their way along the gutter in the road, dodging cars and motorcycles.

In Manila, Cebu City, Davao and some other big cities, the most upmarket hotels cater to the disabled, as do malls, cinemas and some restaurants. Elsewhere, the good news for people with disabilites is that Filipinos are generous when it comes to offering assistance. Even in the remotest barangay, people will go out of their way to help you board a boat or lift you up the stairs of a rickety pier. However, once you're on board a ferry, for example, ramps and disabled toilets are almost certain to be non-existent.

The government-run **National Council on Disability Affairs** or NCDA (🌐ncda.gov.ph) is mandated to formulate policies and coordinate the activities of all agencies concerning disability issues, but it doesn't have much practical advice for travellers with disabilites. Staff at the group's Quezon City office can give general pointers on transport and where to stay.

Addresses

In the Philippines it is common to give an address as, for example, 122 Legaspi corner Velasco Streets, meaning the junction of Legaspi and Velasco streets (in the Guide this is written "122 Legaspi St at Velasco St"). G/F denotes street level, after which come 2/F, 3/F and so on; "first floor" or 1/F isn't used. Some addresses include the name of a **barangay**, which is officially an electoral division for local elections, but is generally used to mean a village or, when mentioned in connection with a town, a neighbourhood or suburb. The word barangay isn't always written out in the address, although it's sometimes included in official correspondence and signposts, often abbreviated to "Brgy" or "Bgy".

The term "**National Highway**" in an address doesn't necessarily refer to a vast motorway – on the smaller islands or in provincial areas, it just means the coastal road or the main street in town.

When it comes to **islands**, Filipinos generally talk loosely in terms of the main island in the vicinity – so, for example, they would talk about visiting Panay when they actually mean offshore Pan de Azucar. We've adopted a similar approach in parts of the Guide, implicitly including small islands in coverage of the nearest large island.

Costs

While upmarket resorts in the Philippines can be as expensive as anywhere else in the world, for anyone with modest spending habits and tastes the country is inexpensive. Outside of Metro Manila you can get by on a frugal **budget** of under P1500 per person a day, but you might need to avoid the most popular tourist destinations such as Boracay (or visit during the off-season), and you'll be limited to bare-bones cottages and pokey rooms in basic hotels, usually without air conditioning or hot water. On this budget you'd also have to confine your meals to local restaurants and carinderias, with little leeway for slap-up feasts in nice restaurants. You'd also have to plan any flights carefully, only buying the very cheapest tickets online or limiting yourself to buses and ferries.

A budget of P2000–3000 a day will take your standard of living up a few notches, allowing you to find reasonable beach cottage and hotel rooms and have enough left for modest eating out, drinking and budget flights. On P4000 a day, you can afford to stay in solid, reasonably spacious cottages on the beach, usually with a veranda and air conditioning, and have plenty left over for domestic flights, good meals in local restaurants and some shopping. After that, of course, the sky's the limit.

Crime and personal safety

The Philippines is a safe place to travel especially if you exercise discretion and common sense. **Insurgency** rarely has an impact on tourists, but you should avoid trouble spots. Updated travel advisories are available on foreign office or state department websites, including Ⓦstate.gov in the US and Ⓦgov.uk in the UK.

There are occasional reports of **thieves** holding up vehicles at traffic lights and removing mobiles and cash from passengers. If you're in a taxi, keep the windows closed and the doors locked, just to be safe. In the Malate area of Manila and Angeles City, the so-called **Ativan Gang** used the drug Lorazepam (Ativan is one of its proprietary names) to make their victims drowsy or put them to sleep – the gang has since disbanded but similar attacks still occur, so it's best to be on your guard in these areas if you're approached by people who seem unusually keen to offer you assistance, especially in bars.

Drug laws in the Philippines are stringent and the police are enthusiastic about catching offenders. No one, foreigner or otherwise, caught in possession of hard or recreational drugs is likely to get much

sympathy from the authorities. Carrying 500g or more of marijuana carried the death penalty until 2006; it's now merely life imprisonment, while lower amounts can result in a prison sentence.

Customs

Visitors are allowed to bring in four hundred cigarettes (or fifty cigars or 250g of pipe tobacco) and two bottles of wine and spirits not exceeding one litre each. If you arrive with more than US$10,000 in cash (unlikely) you are meant to declare it, and you won't be allowed to take out more than this sum in foreign currency on leaving. Note that not more than P10,000 in local currency may be taken out of the country.

Electricity

Wall sockets in the Philippines usually operate at 220 volts (similar to Australia, Europe and most of Asia), although you may come across 110 volts in some rural areas – it's best to ask before plugging in appliances. Most mobile phones, cameras, MP3 players and laptops are dual voltage (older hair-dryers are the biggest problem for North American travellers). **Plugs** have two flat, rectangular pins, as in the US and Canada.

Power cuts (known locally as "brown-outs") are less common than they used to be, but can still occur

THE TYPHOON THREAT

Typhoons regularly rip across the Philippines – typically between July and November – and as **Typhoons Yolanda** and Odette proved in 2013 and 2021 respectively, the effects can be catastrophic and deadly. Though you should always take typhoon warnings seriously (and check weather reports during typhoon season), there's no need to be unduly neurotic about your own safety: the sad truth is that in the Philippines it's mainly poor neighbourhoods that bear the brunt of storms. Most modern hotels and buildings are built to withstand fierce typhoons, and you'll usually be given plenty of notice if a typhoon is heading your way – if it's a big one, go somewhere else and make sure you're nowhere near a ferry or boat when it hits. Though strong winds can be dangerous, flooding, ocean storm surges and landslides are the main cause of most damage and fatalities – if you are not in areas usually affected by any of these you should be fine. Note also that the aftermath of storms can dramatically affect transportation and the services in smaller villages and towns, though Filipinos are a resilient bunch and tourist services are often up and running remarkably quickly post-storm.

For **weather warnings** visit Ⓦpagasa.dost.gov.ph. If you want to volunteer or help in the aftermath of a typhoon, approach official charities such as Care (Ⓦcare.org), Save The Children (Ⓦsavethechildren.org) and the Philippine Red Cross (Ⓦredcross.org.ph).

sometimes in the provinces. If you are worried about using valuable electrical equipment in the Philippines – a laptop computer, for instance – you should plug it into an automatic voltage regulator (AVR), a small appliance that ensures the voltage remains constant even if there is a sudden fluctuation or surge in the mains.

Entry requirements and visas

Most foreign nationals do not need a visa to stay in the Philippines for up to **thirty days**, though a passport valid for at least six months and an onward plane or ship ticket to another country are required, and you must register before being allowed into the country (**W** etravel.gov.ph); it's usually possible to do this on arrival, but some airlines won't let you on the plane without seeing your confirmation.

Your thirty days can be extended by 29 days (giving a total stay of **59 days**) online (e-services.immigration. gov.ph), or at **immigration offices** in Manila or around the country. Note that it pays to be presentably dressed at immigration offices, as staff might refuse to serve you if you turn up wearing a vest, shorts or flip-flops. This extension can itself be extended for a monthly fee.

If you **overstay** your initial thirty days (but have not stayed beyond 59 days) you'll incur a fine which increases per day; overstay longer and you'll be sent to the nearest office of the Bureau of Immigration for a whole lot of trouble.

Temporary Visitor's Visa

If you know you want to spend longer than thirty days in the Philippines, you can apply for a 59-day **Temporary Visitor's Visa** at a Philippine embassy or consulate before you travel. Depending on your plans, you can apply for either a single-entry visa (with which you must enter the Philippines within three months of the issue date) or a multiple-entry visa, valid for one year from the date of issue (but with stays of a maximum 59 days within that year). Apart from a valid passport and a completed application form (downloadable from some Philippine embassy websites), you will have to present proof that you have enough money for the duration of your stay in the Philippines.

Longer stays

Regardless of how you entered the Philippines, to stay longer than 59 days you must apply for **visa extensions** at immigration bureaus every two months. There is also a **Long Stay Visitor Visa Extension** (LSVVE) programme, which allows visitors to extend stays for six months in one go after their first thirty days, but this comes with a hefty price tag.

Note that if you have been in the Philippines continuously for six months, you must have an **Emigration Clearance Certificate** to pass through immigration at the airport. After six months you must also apply for an **ACR-I card** or "Alien Certificate of Registration", and after sixteen months you need approval from the Chief of the Immigration Regulation Division. When you have been in the Philippines for **two years** you really will have to leave, though some have found success doing so and then returning the following day.

PHILIPPINE EMBASSIES AND CONSULATES ABROAD

For a full list of the Philippines' embassies and consulates, check the government's Department of Foreign Affairs website at **W** dfa.gov.ph. **Australia** Canberra **W** philembassy.org.au; Sydney **W** sydneypcg. org; Melbourne **W** melbournepcg.org.
Canada Ottawa **W** ottawape.dfa.gov.ph; Toronto **W** philcongen-toronto.com.
New Zealand Wellington **W** philembassy.org.nz.
South Africa Pretoria **W** pretoriape.dfa.gov.ph.
UK London **W** londonpe.dfa.gov.ph.
US Washington DC **W** philippineembassy-dc.org; San Francisco **W** pcgsanfrancisco.org; Los Angeles **W** philippineslosangeles. org; New York **W** philippinesnewyork.org; Chicago **W** philippineschicago.org. **Consulates also in Honolulu and Agada, Guam.**

Insurance

A typical travel **insurance** policy usually provides cover for the loss of baggage, tickets and cash, as well as cancellation or curtailment of your journey. When securing baggage cover, make sure that the per-article limit will cover your most valuable possession. Most policies exclude so-called dangerous sports unless an extra premium is paid: in the Philippines this can mean scuba diving, whitewater rafting, windsurfing, kitesurfing, trekking and kayaking.

If you need to make a claim, you should keep receipts for medicines and medical treatment, and in the event you have anything stolen, you must obtain an official statement from the police. In the Philippines this is sometimes a slow process that involves the police officer copying, by hand, the details of your loss into what is known as the police "blotter", or file. Once this has been signed by a superior officer you'll get an authorized copy.

Internet

In general **wi-fi** is common in cafés and hotels throughout the country. However, **connections** are often temperamental and speeds slow.

Laundry

There are coin-operated **launderettes** in the Philippines, as well as cheap laundries all over the place offering serviced washes, and most of these places will iron clothes for you for an extra charge. It's also possible to get clothes washed at pretty much any guesthouse, resort or hotel; the pricier the establishment the more it will cost.

LGBTQ+ travellers

Few Filipinos, even the most pious, pay much heed to the Catholic Church regarding homosexuality, and the prevailing attitude is that people can carry on doing what's right for them. **Gay culture** in the Philippines is strong and largely unimpeded by narrow-mindedness, with the possible exceptions within politics and the military, where heterosexuality is still considered correct.

The word **bakla** is used generically by many Filipinos and visitors to the Philippines to refer to gay people, but that would be inaccurate. A *bakla* considers himself a male with a female heart – a *pusong babae*. Most are not interested in a sex-change operation and consider themselves a "third sex", cross-dressing and becoming more "female" than many women. Another category of male homosexual is known as **tunay ne lalake**, men who identify themselves publicly as heterosexual but have sex with other men. Homosexuals who aren't out permeate every stratum of Philippine society; rumours circulate almost daily of this-or-that tycoon or politician who is *tunay ne lalake*.

Lesbians are much more reticent about outing themselves than gay men, no doubt because there is still societal pressure for young women to become the quintessential Filipina lady – gracious, alluring and fulfilled by motherhood and the home. Indeed, some Filipina lesbians complain that the more outspoken **tomboys** – lesbians are often referred to as tomboys – make the fight for women's rights even harder.

The **gay scene** is centred on the bars and clubs of Manila (see box, page 93), though there are also smaller scenes in other major cities such as Cebu, Davao and Cagayan de Oro. The websites Ⓦutopia-asia.com and Ⓦfridae.asia are useful sources of info on local gay life.

Living and working in the Philippines

Opportunities to **work** in the Philippines are limited. Most jobs require specialist qualifications or experience and, unlike other parts of Asia, there's not really a market for foreigners teaching English as a foreign language in paid posts. One possibility is to work for a diving outfit as a dive master or instructor. Rates of pay are low, but board and lodging may be provided if you work for a good operator or resort in a busy area (Boracay or Puerto Galera, for instance). Some international organizations also offer **voluntary placements** in the Philippines. If you do manage to secure work, it's important to secure a work visa beforehand.

VOLUNTEERING ORGANIZATIONS

AVI Ⓦavi.org.au. Well-established Australian organization (AVI is an abbreviation of its old name, Australian Volunteers International), offering short- and long-term postings for professionals interested in working in the developing world. Volunteers in the Philippines have helped introduce sustainable fishing and marine conservation programmes and campaigned for the rights of minority groups.

Coral Cay Conservation Ⓦcoralcay.org. Non-profit organization that trains volunteers to collect scientific data to aid conservation in sensitive environments around the world, particularly coral reefs and tropical forests. Their Philippine base is in southern Leyte.

Peace Corps Ⓦpeacecorps.gov. Places people with specialist qualifications or skills in two-year postings in many developing countries, including the Philippines.

Projects Abroad Ⓦprojects-abroad.org. Worldwide organization that lodges people with host families while they work on projects

ROUGH GUIDES TRAVEL INSURANCE

Looking for travel insurance? Rough Guides partners with top providers worldwide to offer you the best coverage. Policies are available to residents of anywhere in the world, with a range of options whether you are looking for single-trip, multi-country or long-stay insurance. There's coverage for a wide range of adventure sports, 24-hour emergency assistance, high levels of medical and evacuation cover and a stream of travel safety information. Even better, roughguides.com users can take advantage of these policies online 24/7, from anywhere in the world – even if you're already travelling. To make the most of your travels and ensure a smoother experience, it's always good to be prepared for when things don't go according to plan. For more information go to Ⓦroughguides.com/bookings/insurance.

from teaching English and building to jobs requiring more specialist knowledge such as medicine. Their programme in the Philippines is based on Cebu.

VSO (Voluntary Service Overseas) ⓦ vsointernational.org. Charity that sends qualified professionals to work on projects beneficial to developing countries.

Post

Airmail **letters** from the Philippines (ⓦ phlpost.gov. ph) take at least five days to reach other countries, though in many cases it's a lot longer. **Post offices** are generally open from 8am to 5pm, Monday to Friday.

If you have to post anything valuable, use registered mail or pay extra for a **courier**. DHL (ⓦ dhl.com. ph), Fedex (ⓦ fedex.com/ph) and the locally based LBC (ⓦ lbcexpress.com) and 2GO (ⓦ 2go.com.ph) have offices throughout the country (listed on their websites), and can deliver internationally.

Money

The Philippine currency is the **peso**, with polymer notes in denominations of 50, 100, 200, 500 and 1000. Coins come in values of P1, P5, P10 and P20; smaller ones exist, but are rarely seen.

It's best to arrive with some local currency (or at least some dollars), though you can easily get cash from **ATMs** or **exchange booths** at the airport. ATMs are found in cities and tourist destinations all over the country, but not so much in less visited areas such as the interior of Mindanao, the northern mountains, parts of Palawan (outside Puerto Princesa and Coron Town), and in remote areas of the Visayas. It's best to use ATMs at major banks, and preferably in big cities, because these machines tend to be more reliable than provincial ones, which are often out of service. **Credit cards** – and, increasingly, other forms of contactless payment – are accepted by most hotels, restaurants, cafés and shops in cities and tourist areas, though smaller establishments may levy a surcharge if you pay by card, and real budget places operate solely in cash. You'll have to carry at least a little cash around at all times, mainly for small-fry payments such as jeepney and van rides, street food, and most grocery shops and convenience stores.

Banks are normally open 9am–3pm Monday to Friday, and all major branches have ATMs and currency

exchange. The best-established local banks include BPI (Bank of the Philippine Islands), DBP (Development Bank of the Philippines), Metro-bank and BDO (aka Banco de Oro); Citibank and HSBC also have branches in major cities, and at the time of writing the latter did not charge a fee for international withdrawals (though your own bank might). Most banks only change US dollars, and though many hotels will change other currencies, they offer poor rates. It's easy to change dollars in Manila, where there are dozens of small **moneychangers' kiosks** in Malate and P. Burgos Street, Makati, offering better rates than the banks; ask around at a few places and compare. In rural areas there are few moneychangers, and banks don't always change money, so if you're heading off the beaten track, be sure to take enough pesos to last the trip.

Opening hours and public holidays

Most **government offices** are open Monday to Friday 8.30am–5.30pm, but some close for an hour-long lunch break, usually starting at noon, so it's best to avoid the middle of the day. **Businesses** generally keep the same hours, with some also open on Saturday 9am–noon. **Banks** are open Monday to Friday 9am–3pm and do not close for lunch, except for some of the smallest branches in rural areas. **Shops** in major malls open daily 10am–8pm or 9pm, later during the Christmas rush or "Midnight Madness" sales; the latter take place every two weeks on the first Friday after each payday. **Churches** are almost always open most of the day for worshippers and tourists alike. Typically, the first Mass of the day is at around 6am, the last at 6pm or 7pm.

Government offices and private businesses close on **public holidays**, though shops and most restaurants remain open except on Good Friday and Christmas Day. Holidays are often moved to the closest Friday or Monday to their original date (see box below), so that people in the cities can use the long weekend to get back to the provinces to spend a few days with their families. This moving of public holidays is done on an ad hoc basis and is announced in the press just a few weeks – sometimes only a few days – beforehand.

Phones

If you want to use a **mobile phone** bought abroad in the Philippines, it will need to have global roaming activated. For local calls it may work out cheaper to buy an eSIM, or a local **SIM card**, available at dozens of mobile-phone outlets in malls and convenience stores, for any of the country's major mobile

---

EXCHANGE RATES

At the time of writing the **exchange rate** was around P57 to US$1, P77 to £1 and P66 to €1.

networks: Smart (Ⓦsmart.com.ph), Globe Telecom (Ⓦglobe.com.ph) and DITO (Ⓦdito.ph).

Basic mobiles in the Philippines are very inexpensive, so it can be worth buying one if you plan to stay for any length of time. You'll need to pay for your calls with pre-paid cards.

Time

The Philippines is eight hours ahead of Universal Time (GMT) all year round.

Tipping

Keep your purse or wallet well stocked with P10 coins and P20 notes for **tips**. In cafés, bars, hotel coffee shops and basic restaurants, many Filipinos simply leave whatever coins they get in their change. For good service in average restaurants you should leave a tip of about **ten percent**. In more expensive restaurants where the bill could be a couple of thousand pesos, it's okay to leave a somewhat smaller tip in percentage terms, though increasingly a set rate is tacked on to the bill. Bellhops and porters get a coin or two each, and taxi drivers usually expect to keep the loose change; ten percent is a fair tip on Grab and other apps, where possible.

Tourist information

The **Philippine Department of Tourism** (DoT; Ⓦtourism.gov.ph) has a small number of overseas offices where you can pick up glossy brochures and get answers to general pre-trip questions about destinations, major hotels and domestic travel. These offices are not so helpful, however, when it comes to information about places off the beaten track. The DoT has offices throughout the Philippines, but most of them have small budgets and very little in the way of reliable information or brochures. The best source of up-to-date information on travelling in the Philippines is guesthouses and hotels that cater to travellers, most of which have **notice boards** where you can swap tips and ideas.

Another helpful source of information is **Travel Philippines** (Ⓦthephilippines.online) which has lots of helpful info about to get around, where to stay and what to do. They also have a very handy app.

Travelling with children

Filipinos are extravagant in their generosity towards **children**, but because so much of the country lacks infrastructure, specific attractions for them are often

---

PUBLIC HOLIDAYS

January 1 New Year's Day
Jan/Feb (variable) Chinese New Year
March/April (variable) Maundy Thursday, Good Friday, Black Saturday
April 9 Bataan Day
May 1 Labor Day
May/June Eid ul Fitr, the end of Ramadan
June 12 Independence Day
August 21 Ninoy Aquino Day
Last Monday in August National Heroes' Day
November 1 All Saints' Day (see box, page 38)
December 25 Christmas Day; the following day is also a holiday
December 30 Rizal Day, in honour of José Rizal (see page 415)

---

hard to find. Major hotels in big cities such as Manila and Cebu City have playrooms and babysitting services, but even in popular tourist destinations such as Boracay there are few special provisions in all but the most expensive resorts.

This doesn't mean that travelling with children in the Philippines is a nightmare – far from it. Filipinos are very tolerant of children, so you can take little ones almost anywhere without restriction, and they help to break the ice with strangers. They'll be fussed over, befriended and looked after every step of the way.

Supermarkets in towns and cities throughout the Philippines have well-stocked children's sections that sell fresh and formula milk, nappies and baby food. **Department stores** such as Rustan's and SM sell baby clothes, bottles, sterilizing equipment and toys. And travelling with children in the Philippines needn't be a burden on your budget. Domestic **airlines** give a discount of around fifty percent for children under twelve and hotels and resorts offer **family rooms**, extra beds for a minimal charge, or don't charge at all for a small child sharing the parents' bed. Most **restaurants** with buffet spreads will let a small child eat for free if he or she is simply taking nibbles from a parent's plate. Otherwise, try asking for a special portion – the staff are usually happy to oblige.

One potential problem for young ones is the **climate**. You'll need to go to extra lengths to protect them from the sun and to make sure they are hydrated. A hat and good sunblock are essential. As for **medical attention** in the Philippines, there are good paediatricians at most major hospitals, in five-star hotels and many resorts.

Manila

TIMES PLAZA

UM · ARTS ·

NATIONAL MUSEUM OF FINE ARTS, MANILA

1 Manila

If you like big cities you'll love Manila: it's a high-speed, frenetic place, where you can eat, drink and shop 24 hours a day and where the Filipino heritage of native, Spanish, Chinese and American cultures is at its most mixed up. Like many capital cities, Manila bears little resemblance to the rest of the country – something to remember if this is your first taste of the Philippines. With 13.5 million residents, plus the same again in the wider urban area, much of it is chronically overcrowded, polluted and suffers from appalling traffic jams, yet in between the chaos lie tranquil gate-guarded "subdivisions" that resemble affluent parts of the US. There's extreme poverty here, with young children cleaning car windows, dancing or just begging for food at practically every interchange, while middle-class Manileños populate a seemingly limitless number of enormous shopping malls.

Technically sixteen cities and one municipality make up what is officially known as **Metro Manila**, covering a vast 636 square kilometres. Travelling around the city takes some effort; its reputation as an intimidating place stems mainly from its size, apparent disorder and pollution, exacerbated by the equally fierce heat and humidity. To see the sights you will have to sweat it out in traffic and be prepared for delays, but the good news is that the main attractions are essentially confined to Manila proper: the old walled city of **Intramuros**; **Binondo** – Manila's Chinatown – north of the Pasig River; and the museums and parks grouped along the crescent sweep of **Manila Bay** and Roxas Boulevard. **Makati** and **Ortigas** to the east are glossy business districts best known for their malls and restaurants, though the **Ayala Museum** in Makati should not be missed. **Quezon City** on the city's northern edge is a little out of the way for most visitors, but it does boast some lively nightlife, most of it fuelled by students from the nearby **University of the Philippines**. Indeed, Manila prides itself on the quality of its restaurant, bar and club scene and the ability of its residents to whip up a good time – for many tourists, this will be their enduring memory of the place. The city is also a great place to pick up bargains, from the latest goods cranked out by Chinese factories to intricate native handicrafts.

Brief history

Malay settlements along the Pasig River delta go back at least one thousand years, with the **Kingdom of Tondo** most prominent, benefiting from a profitable trade with Ming-era China. After coming under the sway of the Sultanate of Brunei in the fifteenth century, the area was converted to Islam.

Spanish Manila

The village of **Maynila** fell under **Spanish rule** in 1571, when Miguel López de Legazpi defeated the local ruler Rajah Sulaiman II and established the colony of Manila. Spanish Augustinian and Franciscan **missionaries** subsequently established themselves in villages around the city. The Jesuits arrived in 1581 and set up more missions, forming outlying centres of population – embryonic settlements that became the sixteen cities of today. Manila's central location on the nation's biggest island, Luzon, made it the obvious choice as the **colonial capital**, and it became the hub from which the Spaniards effected the political, cultural and religious transformation of Philippine society. From 1571 until 1815 (when it was ended by the Mexican War of Independence), Manila prospered from the **galleon trade** while the rest of the country

SAN AGUSTIN CHURCH

Highlights

❶ Intramuros The atmospheric old Spanish city, with cobbled streets, the elegant San Agustin Church and poignant Rizal Shrine inside Fort Santiago. See page 65

❷ The national museums Two neighbouring museums housing the paintings of Filipino masters, relics from sunken ships and fascinating anthropology displays. See page 69

❸ Manila Hotel The grand old dame of Philippine hotels. Even if you're not staying here, come to enjoy a drink in the sparkling *Lobby Lounge*. See pages 70, 84 and 91

❹ Ayala Museum One of the best museums in the Philippines, an enlightening and innovative

introduction to the history of the islands. See page 76

❺ Aristocrat Manila's most famous restaurant still knocks out the best barbecued chicken, along with a full roster of Filipino favourites. See page 88

❻ Night out in Makati From megaclubs to pubs, there's a good night out to suit everyone in Makati. See page 91

❼ Manila markets Whether you're looking for local crafts or pearl jewellery, Manila's vibrant and chaotic street markets offer the best bargains. See page 96

HIGHLIGHTS ARE MARKED ON THE MAP ON PAGE 60

MANILA

remained economically stagnant. At 7pm on June 3, 1863, a catastrophic **earthquake** struck and large areas of the city crumbled, burying hundreds of people in the ruins. The new Manila that grew in its stead was thoroughly modern, with streetcars, steam trains and US-style public architecture, a trend that continued under **American rule** in the early twentieth century.

World War II
Manila suffered again during World War II. The **Japanese** occupied the city from 1942 until it was liberated by the US at the **Battle of Manila** in 1945. The battle lasted 29 days and claimed 1000 American lives, 16,000 Japanese soldiers and some 100,000 Filipinos, many of them civilians killed deliberately by the Japanese or accidentally by crossfire. Once again, Manila was a city in ruins, having undergone relentless shelling from American howitzers and been set alight by retreating Japanese troops. **Rebuilding** was slow and plagued by corruption and government inertia.

The Marcos era
In 1976, realizing that Manila was growing too rapidly for government to be contained in the old Manila area, **President Marcos** decreed that while the area around Intramuros would remain the capital city, the permanent seat of the national government would be Metro Manila – including new areas such as Makati and Quezon cities. It was tacit recognition of Manila's expansion and the problems it was bringing. **Imelda Marcos**, meanwhile, had been declared governor of Metro Manila in 1975 and was busy exercising her "edifice complex", building a golden-domed mosque in Quiapo, the Cultural Center of the Philippines on Manila Bay and a number of five-star hotels. Her spending spree was finally ended by the **EDSA Revolution** in 1986 (see page 420).

Manila today
In the 1990s, popular police officer **Alfredo Lim** won two terms as Manila mayor – his crime-fighting efforts certainly improved security in the city and he was elected a third time in 2007. He immediately and controversially set about undoing much of the work of his predecessor **Lito Atienza** (mayor 1998–2007), who had spent millions

MANILA ORIENTATION
The key tourist district is the lengthy area fronting **Manila Bay** along **Roxas Boulevard**. The zone of interest starts up north with the areas of **Binondo and Quiapo**, the former often referred to as Manila's Chinatown. Heading over the Pasig River you'll immediately hit the old walled city of **Intramuros**, before heading south across Rizal Park to the busy, characterful neighbourhoods of **Ermita** and **Malate**, parts of which are often referred to as Koreatown. You can walk this whole area in a day if you're in a rush; obviously a little longer would be better, and you can also get from A to B more quickly by using the LRT line, or the numerous jeepneys that course through and along this busy tract of cityscape.

Once you're done with Manila proper, you can head out to see some of the outlying cities, the most prominent of which are linked by the artery of Epifaño de los Santos Avenue, or EDSA for short. South of Malate is **Pasay City**, most notable as a transport hub but also boasting some good malls. East is **Makati City**, 8km southeast of Manila Bay; the city's central business district, built around the main thoroughfare of Ayala Avenue, it's home to banks, insurance companies and five-star hotels, and is great for nightlife. Just to the east of Makati (and almost an extension of it, though technically in Taguig City), lies the city's newest business and retail hub, **Bonifacio Global City** (BGC). Further north along EDSA is the commercial district of **Ortigas**, which is trying to outdo Makati with its hotels, malls and air-conditioned, themed restaurants. Beyond that is **Quezon City**, where many bus routes from the north terminate, though otherwise it's largely off the tourist map.

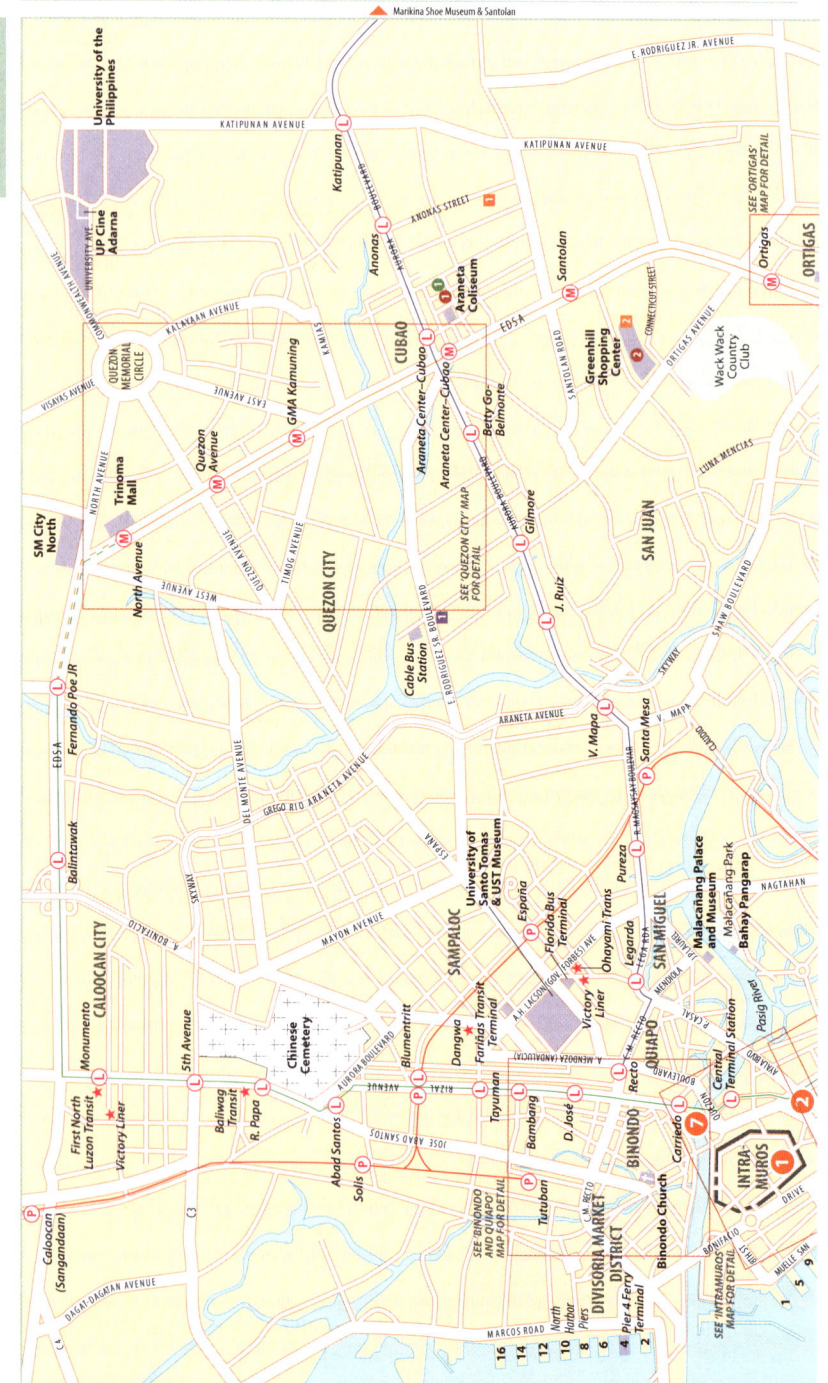

Marikina Shoe Museum & Santolan

University of the Philippines

E. RODRIGUEZ JR. AVENUE

KATIPUNAN AVENUE

KATIPUNAN AVENUE

ANONAS STREET

Katipunan

ORTIGAS

SEE 'ORTIGAS' MAP FOR DETAIL

UP Cine Adarna

Anonas

Santolan

Ortigas

Araneta Coliseum

CUBAO

EDSA

KALAKAAN AVENUE

KAMIAS

Araneta Center–Cubao

Betty Go-Belmonte

CONNECTICUT STREET

Greenhill Shopping Center

Wack Wack Country Club

GMA Kamuning

Araneta Center–Cubao

QUEZON MEMORIAL CIRCLE

SANTOLAN ROAD

ORTIGAS AVENUE

VISAYAS AVENUE

EAST AVENUE

SEE QUEZON CITY MAP FOR DETAIL

Gilmore

LUNA MENCIAS

Quezon Avenue

Trinoma Mall

Quezon Avenue

SAN JUAN

SHAW BOULEVARD

NORTH AVENUE

QUEZON AVENUE

TIMOG AVENUE

J. Ruiz

SM City North

North Avenue

WEST AVENUE

QUEZON CITY

SKYWAY

Fernando Poe JR

E. RODRIGUEZ JR. BOULEVARD

Cable Bus Station

ARANETA AVENUE

V. Mapa

Santa Mesa

V. MAPA

EDSA

DEL MONTE AVENUE

GREGO RIO ARANETA AVENUE

ESPAÑA

Balintawak

A. BONIFACIO

SKYWAY

University of Santo Tomas & UST Museum

Malacañang Palace and Museum

Malacañang Park

Bahay Pangarap

CALOOCAN CITY

MAYON AVENUE

España

Florida Bus Terminal

Legarda

Pureza

SAN MIGUEL

NAGTAHAN

Monumento

5th Avenue

Chinese Cemetery

Blumentritt

Ohayami Trans

A.H. LACSON

GOV FORBES AVE.

MENDOZA

Pasig River

MENDIOLA

P. CASAL

AURORA BOULEVARD

Dangwa

Fariñas Transit Terminal

Victory Liner

QUIAPO

Central Terminal Station

MAGSAYSAY

First North Luzon Transit

Baliwag Transit

R. Papa

RIZAL

Tayuman

A. MENDOZA (ANDALUCIA)

Recto

BONIFACIO DRIVE

INTRA-MUROS

Victory Liner

Abad Santos

Bambang

JOSE ABAD SANTOS

D. José

BINONDO

Carriedo

M. RECTO

DRIVE

Caloocan (Sangandaan)

Solis

Tutuban

DIVISORIA MARKET DISTRICT

Binondo Church

SEE BINONDO AND QUIAPO MAP FOR DETAIL

SEE INTRAMUROS MAP FOR DETAIL

MUELLE SAN

C4

DAGAT DAGATAN AVENUE

C3

MARCOS ROAD

North Harbor Piers

Pier 4 Ferry Terminal

16 14 12 10 8 6 4 2

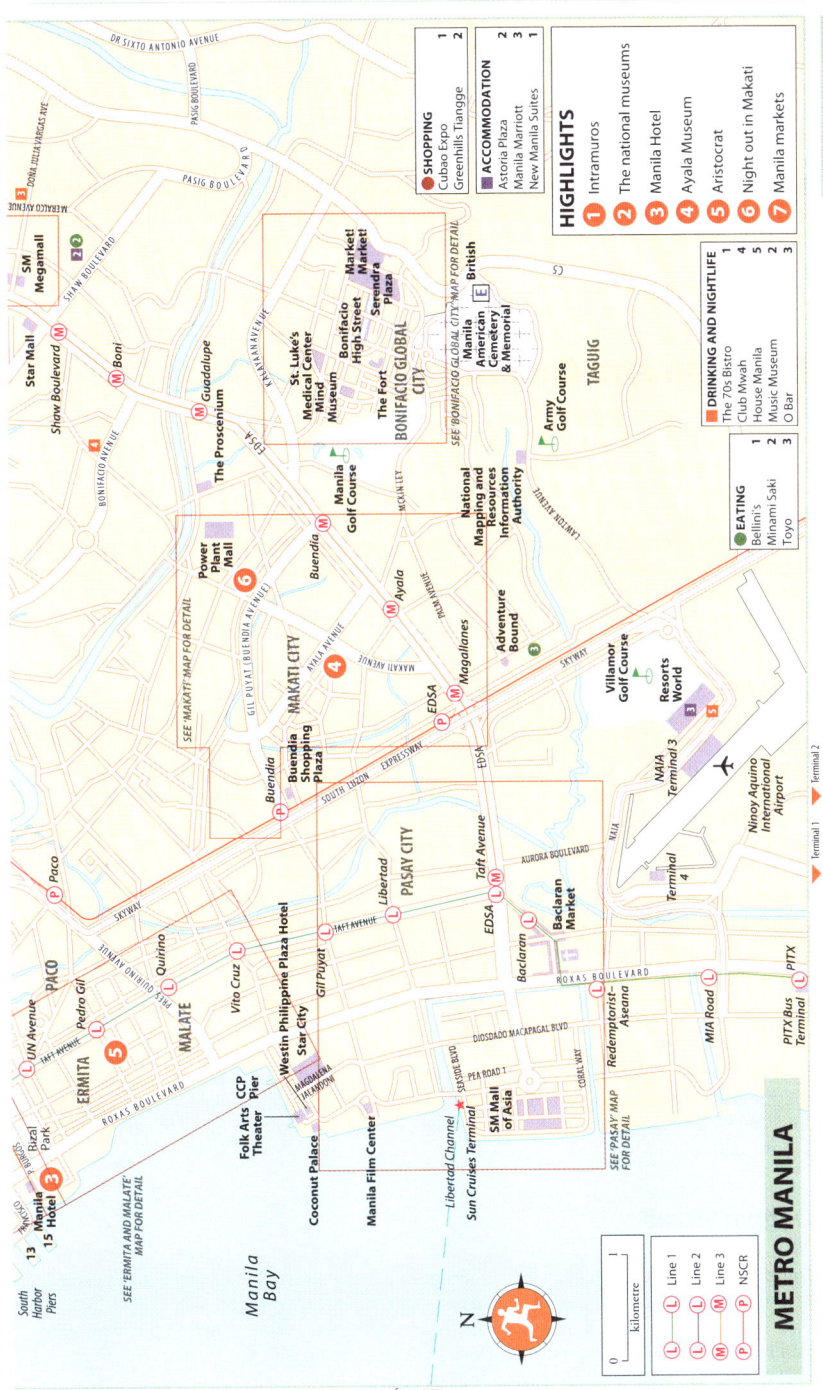

METRO MANILA

1

on city beautification projects. Though congestion and pollution remained huge and apparently intractable problems, Lim presided over a booming economy, removed squatters in Quiapo and cleaned up the Baywalk area. Manileños rewarded him with a fourth term as mayor in 2010, just months before the **Manila bus hostage crisis**, when a dismissed police officer hijacked a bus of Hong Kong tourists, killing eight of them; the mayor's handling of the tragedy was highly criticized in the subsequent inquiry. In a remarkable twist, ex-president **Joseph Estrada** (see page 421) was elected mayor in 2013, a position to which he was re-elected in 2016 but relinquished after losing in 2019 to Isko Moreno, who initiated further city-wide clean-ups. Moreno ran for president in 2022, after which his former running mate Honey Lacuna was elected mayor of Manila, becoming the first ever woman to hold the position.

Binondo and Quiapo

Manila's Chinatown, **Binondo** exercises a curious, magnetic pull. This is city life *in extremis*, a rambunctious ghetto of people on the make, the streets full of merchants and middlemen flogging fake watches and herbs, sandalwood incense and gaudy jewellery. You can lose yourself for an afternoon wandering through its mercantile centre, snacking on dim sum at one of its many fan-cooled teahouses, and exploring the busiest thoroughfare, **Ongpin Street**. A visit to the sepulchral **Binondo Church** will give you some idea of the area's historical significance. Southeast of Binondo lies **Quiapo**, a labyrinth of crowded streets and cheap market stalls a universe away from the city's plush megamalls. The **Quiapo Church** here is said to be the most visited in the Philippines.

Binondo Church

Plaza San Lorenzo Ruiz, Ongpin St • ⓦ facebook.com/binondochurch1596 • LRT to Carriedo; Divisoria jeepneys go past the church

The always-buzzing Minor Basilica of San Lorenzo Ruiz is more commonly known as **Binondo Church**. It stands on the spot where Dominican priests established their church when they first came to Binondo in the late sixteenth century, though the original building was destroyed by shelling in 1762 when the British invaded Manila. The Dominicans promptly left, but returned in 1842 and completed the church you see today, a solid granite structure with an octagonal bell tower and elaborate retablo (altarpiece), in 1854.

The church was badly damaged by bombing during World War II and new features include the canopy at the entrance and the strikingly colourful murals on the ceilings. Depicting the life of Christ and the Assumption of the Virgin, these murals were not actually painted on the ceiling but were executed at ground level, then hoisted up.

The church is well known in the Philippines because it was where **Saint Lorenzo Ruiz**, the Philippines' first saint, served as a sacristan. Of Filipino and Chinese parentage, Ruiz was falsely accused of killing a Spaniard in 1636. It was probably because of this that he was encouraged to go to Japan, where he was arrested in Nagasaki in 1637 for spreading Christianity, and was executed for refusing to renounce his faith. The Vatican canonized him in 1987.

Ongpin Street

LRT to Carriedo

Ongpin Street, Binondo's principal thoroughfare, is about 2km long and runs eastwards through the heart of Chinatown to Santa Cruz Church. It was originally called Calle Sacristia but was renamed in 1915 after Roman Ongpin, a fervent nationalist who was said to be the first Chinese-Filipino to wear the *barong tagalog*, the formal shirt that became the national dress for men. Ongpin Street is now chock-full of restaurants,

BINONDO AND QUIAPO

L—L Line 1
L—L Line 2

Caloocan & Chinese Cemetery

MORIONES

Tutuban Station
MAYHALIGUE

Tutuban Mall

QUIAPO

Manila City Jail

168 Shopping Mall

DIVISORIA MARKET DISTRICT

Divisoria Mall

D. José
Bataan Transit

Philippine Rabbit

Recto

SOLER STREET

BINONDO

Binondo Church

First United Building

Plaza Santa Cruz

Santa Cruz Church

Buses, Jeepways & FX taxis to Makati, Ermita and Malate

Carriedo

Quiapo Church

Regina Building

Escolta Museum

Ilalim ng Tulay

Pasig River

Fort Santiago

Intramuros

● EATING

Chuan Kee	5
Eng Bee Tin	6
Ho-Land Hopia & Bakery	3
Mei Sum Tea House	2
New Po Heng Lumpia House	7
Salazar Bakery	1
Tasty Dumplings	4

● SHOPPING

168 Shopping Mall	1
Divisoria Market District	2
Ilalim ng Tulay	3

University of Santo Tomas & Quezon City

noodle parlours, apothecaries and shops selling goods imported from China, though it tends to shut down early; you'll find **Benavidez Street**, to the north of Ongpin, more lively at night.

Santa Cruz Church

Plaza Santa Cruz • ☎ 02 8733 0246 • LRT to Carriedo

An immense white Baroque structure, **Santa Cruz Church** was originally completed in the seventeenth century for the swelling ranks of Chinese in the area, but was most recently rebuilt in 1957 after damage from earthquakes and war. The most revered image inside is a 250-year-old replica of the **Nuestra Señora del Pilar**, an apparition of Mary (the original of which is in Zaragoza, Spain), but the interior is otherwise unexceptional.

Escolta Street

LRT to Carriedo

The shopping thoroughfare **Escolta Street**, which leads southwest off Plaza Santa Cruz, was named after the horse-mounted military escorts of the British commander-in-chief during the British occupation of 1762. In the nineteenth century this was where Manila's elite promenaded and shopped, but its dizzy days as a Champs-Élysées of the

1

Orient are long gone. Only a few examples of the street's former glory remain; just across the river on the right is the **First United Building**, a pink and white Art Deco gem designed in 1928 by Andres Luna de San Pedro, the son of painter Juan Luna. Opposite is another of his buildings, the all-white **Regina Building** of 1934, with its Art Nouveau cupolas. Both buildings are occupied by shops and small businesses today.

Escolta Museum

2/F, Calvo Building, 266 Escolta St

The beaux-arts Calvo Building, completed in 1933, contains the quirky **Escolta Museum**. The main attraction is an extensive collection of multicoloured vintage bottles, but there are also scale models of Escolta's handsome buildings, old photos and paper advertisements from the 1930s. Unfortunately, it was closed temporarily in 2023, and at the time of writing no date had been set for its reopening.

Quiapo Church

910 Plaza Miranda • ⓦ quiapochurch.com.ph • LRT to Carriedo

Officially called the Minor Basilica of St John the Baptist, **Quiapo Church** – as everyone in Manila calls it – is the home of the **Black Nazarene**, a wooden icon, said to be miraculous, that came to the country on board a galleon from Spain in 1606 and was enshrined here in 1787. The life-size image, bearing a cross, presides over the church from behind the altar.

The church burnt down in 1928, and the new building was expanded in the 1980s to accommodate the crowds that gather every year on January 9 for the **Feast of the Black Nazarene**, when 200,000 barefoot Catholic faithful from all over the Philippines come together to worship before the image.

Ilalim ng Tulay

LRT to Carriedo

The area around Quiapo Church is a good area for bargain-hunters (see page 96). Several stores that sell **handicrafts** at local prices are squeezed beneath the underpass leading to Quezon Bridge (aka Quiapo Bridge) on Quezon Boulevard, a place known as **Ilalim ng Tulay** ("under the bridge" or just Quiapo Ilalim).

Further afield

If you've got some time, there are a few sights close to Quiapo that deserve a look, and are best accessed from this part of Manila. Within walking distance to the east is grand **Malacañang Palace**, which is a fun look at nineteenth-century Manila, as is the **University of Santo Tomas Museum** further north; the extravagant **Chinese Cemetery** sits further north again, on the border of Caloocan City.

University of Santo Tomas Museum

3rd floor, Main Building, University of Santo Tomas (UST), España Blvd • Charge • ⓦ ustmuseum.ust.edu.ph • 20min walk (or a short ride on any jeepney marked UST) from Recto LRT station

The **University of Santo Tomas Museum** is a marvellous throwback to the nineteenth century, an old-fashioned but fascinating private collection of historic documents, rare books and dusty displays on ethnology, natural history, archeology and arts. The collection dates back to 1871 and includes a stuffed orang-utan, a chair used by Pope John Paul II and a macabre two-headed calf. There are also some medieval coins, an assemblage of religious statues, a rather incongruous collection of Chinese porcelain, and some decent art, including *Pounding Rice* (1940) by Vicente Manansala, who also created the stunning, Cubist-influenced *History of Medicine* murals adorning the lobby of UST's medicine faculty in 1958.

UST itself has an interesting history. It was founded in Intramuros in 1611, making it the oldest university in Asia, with the current campus established in the 1920s. It served as an internment camp during World War II, and the old campus was virtually destroyed in 1944.

Today the university is much larger than it seems from the entrance, its **Main Building** an impressive Spanish Revival pile completed in 1927, and the elegant **Arch of the Centuries** above the main entrance on España Boulevard combining the ruins of the original arch of 1611 and its 1950s replica.

The Chinese Cemetery
South Gate entrance off Aurora Blvd, 4km north of Binondo • Free • LRT to Abad Santos

The monumental **Chinese Cemetery** was established by affluent Chinese merchants in the 1850s because the Spanish would not allow foreigners to be buried in Spanish cemeteries. Entire streets are laid out to honour the dead and to underline the status of their surviving relatives. Several of the tombs resemble houses, with fountains, balconies and, in at least one case, a small swimming pool. Many even have air conditioning for the relatives who visit on All Saints' Day, when lavish feasts are laid on around the graves, with empty chairs for the departed. It has become a sobering joke in the Philippines that this "accommodation" is among the best in the city. Just across the way is Manila North Cemetery, which is just as large but less interesting.

Malacañang Palace and Museum
1000 J.P. Laurel St, San Miguel • Free • ⓦ museums.gov.ph • Reservation requests need to be made online at least 3 working days in advance • No shorts, sleeveless tops or flip-flops; taking videos not allowed • A short taxi ride east of Intramuros and Quiapo

Home of the governor-generals and presidents of the Philippines since the 1860s, the **Malacañang Palace** (also "Malacañan" Palace) is a fittingly grand and intriguing edifice, well worth the minor hassle involved in arranging a visit (you can also join a tour). Much of the palace is permanently off limits to the public, but you can visit the wing that houses the **Malacañang Museum**. Housed in the beautifully restored Kalayaan Hall, completed in 1921, the museum traces the history of the palace and of the presidency from Emilio Aguinaldo to the present day. The origins of the Malacañang go back to a smaller stone house dating from 1750, which was bought in 1825 by the Spanish government and, in 1849, made into the summer residence of the governor-general of the Philippines. After the governors' palace in Intramuros was destroyed in the earthquake of 1863, the move to Malacañang was made permanent and the property was extended several times over the years. The president actually resides in **Bahay Pangarap**, across the river in **Malacañang Park**, and maintains his office in Bonifacio Hall within the palace.

Intramuros

The old Spanish heart of Manila, **Intramuros** is the one part of the metropolis where you get a real sense of history. It was established in the 1570s and remains a monumental, if partially ruined, colonial relic – a city within a city, separated from the rest of Manila by its overgrown walls, not to mention a golf course now located in the "moat" area (surely one of the world's most interesting places to play the sport). Central Intramuros is, however, not a museum; plenty of government offices are still located here, and many of Manila's poorest call the backstreets home. The main drag is **General Luna Street**, also known as Calle Real del Palacio. A good way to see the area is by arranging a **walking tour** with Old Manila Walks (see page 84).

The area south of Intramuros is dominated by **Rizal Park** (see page 70), on the northern fringes of which you'll find the **National Museums of Anthropology** and **Fine**

1

Arts; on the other side of Roxas Boulevard, facing the bay, the **Manila Hotel** harks back to the city's golden age.

San Agustin Church and Museum

General Luna St • Charge • ⓦ facebook.com/0904LaConsolacion • LRT to Central Terminal

Dominating the southern section of Intramuros, **San Agustin Church** boasts a magnificent Baroque interior, *trompe l'oeil* murals and a vaulted ceiling and dome. Built between 1586 and 1606, it's the oldest stone church in the Philippines, and contains the modest **tomb of Miguel López de Legazpi** (1502–72), the founder of Manila (see page 414), to the left of the altar. The church was the only structure in Intramuros to survive the devastation of World War II, an indication of just how badly the city suffered.

Access to the church is via the adjacent **San Agustin Museum**, a former Augustinian monastery that houses a surprisingly extensive collection of icons and artefacts, including rare porcelain, church vestments and a special exhibition on Fray Andrés Urdaneta (who led the second voyage to circumnavigate the world in 1528, and pioneered the Manila–Acapulco sea route), though the handsome two-storey building itself and the tranquil central cloisters are just as appealing. The old vestry is where Governor-General Fermín Jáudenes drafted the terms of Spanish surrender to the Americans in 1898, while the oratorio upstairs provides an alternative perspective of the church interior.

Light & Sound Museum

Victoria St at Santa Lucia St • LRT to Central Terminal

One of the city's more unusual attractions, the **Light & Sound Museum** contains a series of dioramas enlivened by animatronic manikins acting out all the key moments in Philippine history (especially the heroic life of José Rizal) – it's a little cheesy, but fun nonetheless. The church-like museum building is a replica of the structure destroyed during World War II, originally the home of the Beaterio de la Compañia de Jesus, a religious school for girls founded in 1684. At time of writing, the Light & Sound Museum was closed for renovations, and no reopening date has been announced.

Silahis Center

744 General Luna St • Free • ⓦ silahis.com • LRT to Central Terminal

Established in 1966, the intriguing **Silahis Center** is a museum-like emporium selling arts, antiques and cultural publications from all over the Philippines. Across a pretty courtyard reached through the back door are the elegant *Ilustrado* restaurant (see page 88) and the atmospheric *Kuatro Kantos* café (see page 88).

Casa Manila

Plaza San Luis Complex, General Luna St at Real St • Charge • ⓣ 02 8527 4084 • LRT to Central Terminal

The splendid **Casa Manila**, a sympathetic replica of an 1850s colonial mansion, offers a window into the lives of rich Filipinos in the nineteenth century. Redolent of a grander age, the house contains an impressive *sala* (living room) where *tertulias* (soirees) and *bailes* (dances) were held. The upstairs family latrine is a two-seater, which allowed husband and wife to gossip out of earshot of the servants while simultaneously going about their business. Though it's a faithful reproduction of period Spanish styles, Imelda Marcos commissioned the house in the early 1980s, during her "edifice complex".

Memorare Manila

Plazuela de Santa Isabel, General Luna and Anda streets • LRT to Central Terminal

Much of Intramuros was reduced to rubble during the Battle of Manila (1945) in World War II, a catastrophe commemorated by the **Memorare Manila**, a series of moving sculptures surrounding a woman weeping as she cradles a dead child. Over a hundred thousand Filipinos are thought to have died in the fighting.

Bahay Tsinoy

32 Anda St at Cabildo St • Charge • ⓦ facebook.com/bahaytsinoy • LRT to Central Terminal

A small but enlightening museum, **Bahay Tsinoy** is a tribute to Manila's influential Chinese population. The name means "**house of the Filipino Chinese**", and the museum traces the crucial role of the Chinese in Philippine history from their first trade contact with the archipelago in the tenth century to the Spanish colonial period. Besides assorted artefacts and multimedia presentations, the displays include life-sized figures and authentic reproductions of objects related to Tsinoy (or "Chinoy") history. Among the items of interest are a large hologram representing the achievements of the Tsinoys and a charming diorama of the Parian ghetto, the area outside the city walls where Chinese were forced to live during Spanish rule. There's also a gallery of rare photographs and a Martyrs Hall dedicated to Tsinoys who formed guerrilla units against Japanese occupation.

Manila Cathedral

Plaza de Roma, Cabildo St at Beaterio St • Free • ⓦ manilacathedral.com.ph • LRT to Central Terminal

Originally just a nipa and bamboo structure, **Manila Cathedral** was officially raised in 1581 but destroyed numerous times down the centuries by a combination of fire,

1

typhoon, earthquake and war. The seventh version was comprehensively flattened during World War II but the Vatican contributed funds to have it rebuilt. The present Byzantine-Romanesque inspired structure was completed in 1958 from a design by Fernando Ocampo, one of the nation's finest architects, and is similar in style to the cathedral that stood here in the nineteenth century.

The cathedral lacks the rich historical ambience of San Agustin, but the interior is impressive in its simplicity, with a long aisle flanked by marble pillars, stained-glass rose windows and a soaring central dome. **Exhibitions** in chapels around the nave throw light on the tumultuous history of the cathedral, and even tackle weighty theological questions such as "what is a cathedral?" and the meaning of the Immaculate Conception, inspired by the cathedral's 1981 award of the title of "Basilica of the Immaculate Conception". Check out also the faithful reproduction of Michelangelo's *La Pietà* in a special chapel to the left of the entrance.

Fort Santiago

General Luna St at Santa Clara St · Charge · Ⓦ visitfortsantiago.com · LRT to Central Terminal

The remains of **Fort Santiago** stand at the northwestern end of Intramuros. The first log fortress was built by Spanish conquistador Miguel López de Legazpi in 1571 on the ruins of Rajah Sulaiman's base, but was rebuilt in stone twenty years later. The seat of the colonial power of both Spain and the US, Fort Santiago was also a prison and torture chamber under the Spanish regime and the scene of countless military police atrocities during the Japanese occupation (1942–45).

Just past the entrance to the site, on the left, is the Baluartillo de San Francisco Javier, fortifications built in 1663 which now house the **Intramuros Visitors Center** (see page 69), a shop and a café. From here you can stroll through the gardens of **Plaza Moriones** to the fort proper, marked by a stone gate, walls and a moat – most of what you see today has been rebuilt in stages since the 1950s, after being virtually destroyed in 1945. Once through the walls, **Plaza de Armas** forms a pleasant green square inside the old fort, with a noble-looking **statue of José Rizal** in the middle.

Rizal Shrine

Entry included with fort ticket

For most visitors the real highlight of Fort Santiago lies on the left side of Plaza de Armas, where the **Rizal Shrine** occupies a reconstruction of the old Spanish barracks (the brick ruins of the original are next door). The site is dedicated to **José Rizal** (see page 415), the writer and national hero who was imprisoned here before being executed in what became Rizal Park in 1896. On the ground floor, the Chamber of Texts preserves some original copies of Rizal's work, while excerpts are artfully displayed on iron girders. You can also peer into a reproduction of the room where he spent the hours before his execution. Upstairs the Reliquary Room displays some of Rizal's clothing and personal effects, while a larger hall houses the original copy of his valedictory poem, *Mi Último Adiós*, the greatest, most poignant work of Filipino literature. The poem was secreted in an oil lamp and smuggled out to his family; here it is displayed in various languages around the walls (the original was written in Spanish). While even the best English translations fail to capture the felicity of the original, they do give a sense of the sacrifice Rizal was about to make and of his love of the country:

Farewell, my adored country, region beloved of the sun,
Pearl of the Orient Sea, our Eden lost,
Departing in happiness, to you I give the sad, withered remains of my life;
And had it been a life more brilliant, more fine, more fulfilled
I would have given it, willingly to you.

Rizaliana Furniture Exhibition
Baluarte de Santa Barbara • Donations requested

1

The eighteenth-century **Baluarte de Santa Barbara** overlooking the Pasig River now houses the mildly interesting **Rizaliana Furniture Exhibition**, showing off Rizal's Spanish colonial writing tables, four-poster bed and the like. More significantly, the exhibit lies above the infamous **dungeon** where around six hundred American and Filipino POWs were incarcerated and left to drown by the rising tide in 1945. There is a cross and **memorial** outside to mark their final resting place.

INFORMATION AND GETTING AROUND INTRAMUROS

Intramuros Visitors Center Baluartillo de San Francisco Javier, Fort Santiago (daily 8am–5pm; ⓦintramuros.gov.ph) offers information and maps, and can also arrange a guide if you need one.

Kalesas Inside Intramuros, for something a bit different you can hire a kalesa (horse-drawn carriage) – their drivers compete with Intramuros tricycles in pestering tourists for business. Rates depend on how hard you bargain.

National Museum of Fine Arts
Taft Ave at Padre Burgos Ave • Free • ⓦ nationalmuseum.gov.ph • LRT to UN Avenue

Just to the north of Rizal Park is the **National Museum of Fine Arts**, the foremost art museum in the Philippines, housed in the grand old Legislative Building (completed in 1926 and home of the Senate till 1996) on the northern edge of Rizal Park. Galleries are laid out thematically in rather desultory fashion over two floors, but each one is relatively small and easy to digest. The highlights are paintings by Filipino masters including **Juan Luna** (1859–99), **Félix Hidalgo** (1855–1913), **José Joya** (1931–95) and **Fernando Amorsolo** (1892–1972), with the most famous works displayed in the Hall of the Masters near the entrance; Luna's vast and magnificent *Spolarium* (1884) is here, a thinly veiled attack in oils on the atrocities of the Spanish regime, portraying fallen gladiators being dragged onto a pile of corpses.

Other galleries are dedicated to National Artist award winners (Amorsolo was the first in 1972), showcasing Joya's *Origins* and Amorsolo's *Portrait of President Manuel Roxas*. There's also a section on architect **Juan Arellano** (1888–1960), who designed the building, and a special gallery dedicated to the large Juan Luna collection; look out for his haunting *Mother in Bed* and the simple naturalism of *Study for Rice Harvesting*. The second floor contains mostly minor works from modern Filipino artists, and also a **Bones Gallery** where a huge sperm whale skeleton takes pride of place.

National Museum of Anthropology
Finance Rd at Padre Burgos Ave • Free • ⓦ nationalmuseum.gov.ph • LRT to UN Avenue

The absorbing **National Museum of Anthropology** occupies what used to be the Department of Finance Building, a stately Greek Revival edifice completed in 1940. Much of the priceless collection of artefacts on display has been retrieved from **shipwrecks**, most notably the *San Diego*, a Spanish galleon that sank off Fortune Island in Batangas after a battle with the Dutch in 1600. Recovered in 1992, the ship yielded over five thousand objects, not all intrinsically valuable: you'll see chicken bones and hazelnuts from the ship's store, as well as tons of Chinese porcelain, storage jars, rosaries and silver goblets. Other rooms contain objects from wrecked Chinese junks going back to the early eleventh century – compelling evidence of trade links that existed long before the Spanish arrived.

The well-labelled **anthropology section** on the third floor is equally engrossing, with displays from almost every region and tribal group in the Philippines, including the enigmatic anthropomorphic jars discovered in Ayub Cave (Mindanao) that date back to 5 BC. These jars were used to hold the bones of ancestors.

Manila Hotel

1 Rizal Park, just east of Manila Ocean Park • ⓦ manila-hotel.com.ph • 1km north up Roxas Boulevard from Malate

The **Manila Hotel**, just northwest of Rizal Park, is the most historic of the city's luxury hotels, though now a little careworn. It's still the best place to get a sense of early twentieth-century Manila, those halcyon days when the city was at its cultural and social zenith; you can even stay (see page 84) in the **General Douglas MacArthur Suite**, residence from 1936 to 1941 of the man Filipinos called the Caesar of America. If staying the night is beyond your means, you can at least sip a coffee or martini in the lobby, while listening to a string quartet and watching the capital's elite strut by.

When the hotel opened in 1912 it represented the epitome of colonial class and luxury. Lavish dances known as rigodon balls were held every month in the **Grand Ballroom**, with high-society guests dancing the quadrille in traditional *ternos* (formal evening dresses) and dinner jackets. Today staff glide around in similarly elegant attire.

The hotel has its own historical **archive**, containing signed photographs of illustrious guests, from Marlon Brando, looking young and slender in a native *barong* (formal shirt), to Ricky Martin and Jon Bon Jovi. The archive is available to guests only, but if you eat or drink at the hotel, one of the guest relations officers should be able to show it to you. South of the hotel is the **Quirino Grandstand** where various official functions take place, including a military parade on Independence Day.

Ermita and Malate

Two of the city's oldest neighbourhoods, **Ermita** and **Malate** nestle behind Roxas Boulevard, facing Manila Bay. Ermita was infamous for its go-go bars and massage parlours up until the late 1980s, when tough-guy mayor Alfredo Lim closed most of them, alleging that they were fronts for **prostitution**. But the massages and KTV hostess bars have gradually slipped back, this time to serve busloads of Japanese and Korean high-spenders, and there has been a resurgence of prostitution in Ermita; after Angeles City, it is now the second-largest centre for paid sex in the Philippines.

Ermita and Malate otherwise remain in most part a ragbag of budget hotels, choked streets, fast-food outlets and bars, with street children all too prevalent on every corner, though the area does look to be changing; several high-end residential developments and hotels have already jazzed up some streets. The big one is still to come: the mammoth Horizon Manila land reclamation project, which will presumably see the bayfront area become a huge mess for years on end (spoiling Ermita's sunsets somewhat), started construction in 2025.

The area begins to the north with **Rizal Park**, Manila's primary green space and the city's favourite meeting place since the Spanish era. You should spend some time here, though most of the sights in this area lie along Manila Bay in the form of the **Cultural Center of the Philippines**, though **Paco Park**, to the east, is also worth a look if you have time.

Rizal Park

Roxas Blvd • Daily 24hr • Free • **Nayong Pilipino** Charge • **Japanese garden** Charge • **Chinese garden** Charge • **Auditorium concerts** Free • LRT to UN Avenue

Still referred to by its old Spanish name of "Luneta", **Rizal Park** is a ten-minute walk south of Intramuros. In a city notoriously short of greenery, the park was where the colonial-era glitterati used to promenade after church every Sunday. These days, Rizal Park is an early morning jogging circuit, a weekend playground for children and a refuge for couples and families escaping the clamour of the city. **Hawkers** sell everything from balloons and mangoes to plastic bags full of *chicharon*, deep-fried pigskin served with a little container of vinegar and chilli for dipping. The park is often busy, with

1

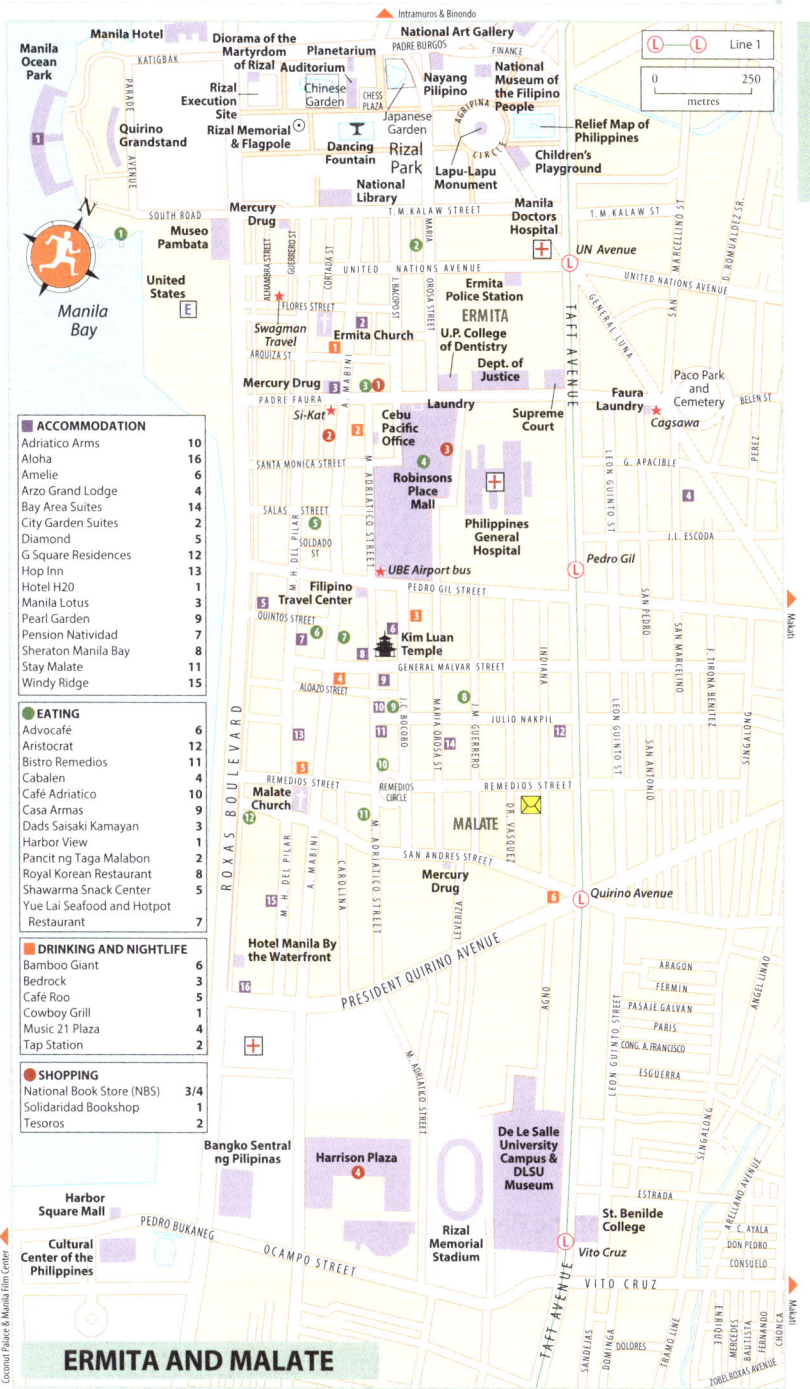

L — L Line 1

0 — 250
metres

ACCOMMODATION

Adriatico Arms	10
Aloha	16
Amelie	6
Arzo Grand Lodge	4
Bay Area Suites	14
City Garden Suites	2
Diamond	5
G Square Residences	12
Hop Inn	13
Hotel H20	1
Manila Lotus	3
Pearl Garden	9
Pension Natividad	7
Sheraton Manila Bay	8
Stay Malate	11
Windy Ridge	15

EATING

Advocafé	6
Aristocrat	12
Bistro Remedios	11
Cabalen	4
Café Adriatico	10
Casa Armas	9
Dads Saisaki Kamayan	3
Harbor View	1
Pancit ng Taga Malabon	2
Royal Korean Restaurant	8
Shawarma Snack Center	5
Yue Lai Seafood and Hotpot Restaurant	7

DRINKING AND NIGHTLIFE

Bamboo Giant	6
Bedrock	3
Café Roo	5
Cowboy Grill	1
Music 21 Plaza	4
Tap Station	2

SHOPPING

National Book Store (NBS)	3/4
Solidaridad Bookshop	1
Tesoros	2

ERMITA AND MALATE

1

many distractions and activities, but few visitors report any problems with hustlers, pickpockets or what Filipinos generally refer to as "snatchers". Renovation of the whole park is underway under an ambitious plan that will take years to complete.

At the far eastern end of the park is an impressive Marcos-era giant **Relief Map of the Philippines**, though it could do with some renovation. In contrast, at the centre lies the lagoon, where the flashy "dancing fountain" entertains crowds every morning and evening. The park's other sundry attractions include: the **Nayong Pilipino**, a flower garden that's a tranquil haven from the hustle outside; a traditional **Chinese Garden**; a fairly bare **Japanese Garden**; the **Chess Plaza**, where amiable seniors challenge each other to board games; an open-air **auditorium** where free concerts are held at weekends; and a **Planetarium**, with regular shows.

Rizal memorials

Diorama of the Martyrdom of Rizal Charge · **Light show** Charge, min 15 people (in English or Tagalog) · LRT to UN Avenue

The western end of Rizal Park is most associated with its namesake, **José Rizal**. The main focus is the stolid-looking **Rizal Memorial**, raised in 1912, where Rizal is entombed, and the 31m flagpole where Manuel Roxas, first President of the Republic, was sworn in on July 4, 1946. Just to the north is the site of **Rizal's execution** in 1896, marked by a memorial that also commemorates the execution of three priests garrotted by the Spanish for alleged complicity in the uprising in Cavite in 1872 – despite the carnival-like atmosphere around it, this is a very poignant site for most Filipinos.

Nearby is the **Diorama of the Martyrdom of Rizal**, containing a series of eight life-size sculptures dramatizing the hero's final days. If the gatekeeper is about you should be able to wander around, but to run the **light-and-sound presentation** they need at least fifteen people.

Manila Ocean Park

Parade Ave, off Roxas Blvd (behind Quirino Grandstand) · Charge · ⓦ manilaoceanpark.com · Taxi, bus or 15–20min walk from UN Avenue LRT station

At the far western end of Rizal Park, along the bayfront, lies **Manila Ocean Park**, one of the city's most popular attractions. The undoubted highlight is the **Oceanarium**, a huge saltwater tank viewed via a 25m-long walkway, packed with some twenty thousand sea creatures. Depending on what entry package you choose, it may include spectacular light shows, musical fountains, sea lion shows, a birds of prey exhibit, a trippy jellyfish installation and a penguin park.

Museo Pambata

Roxas Blvd at South Drive · Charge · ⓦ museopambata.com.ph · LRT to UN Avenue

The entertaining **Museo Pambata** (Children's Museum) has several hands-on exhibitions designed to excite young children; at the Maynila Noon exhibit they can get a feel for history using interactive displays – replicas of ships, churches and native Filipino homes – and there's also a simulated rainforest and seabed. Once a month there's a shadow puppetry show.

Cultural Center of the Philippines (CCP)

Pedro Bukaneg (off Roxas Blvd) · Free · **Museo ng Kalinangang Pilipino** Charge · ⓦ culturalcenter.gov.ph · LRT to Vito Cruz, then an orange CCP jeepney along Pablo Ocampo St to Roxas Blvd

The monumental **Cultural Center of the Philippines (CCP)** was one of Imelda Marcos's grand plans for bringing world-class arts to the Philippines. Conceived during the early, promising years of her husband's presidency and opened on a night of great splendour in 1966, it's a slab-like construction typical of those built on Imelda's orders when she was suffering from her so-called "edifice complex". Various productions by **Ballet Philippines** (see page 94) and Broadway-style **musicals** are staged in the **Main Theater**, and there is a decent **contemporary art gallery** on the third floor (free), showing temporary exhibits from Filipino artists. Upstairs on the fourth floor the **Museo ng Kalinangang Pilipino** holds small but engaging temporary exhibitions on various aspects of Filipino native cultures, as well as housing the permanent Asian traditional musical instruments collection.

The CCP also encompasses several other properties beyond the main complex, further along Pedro Bukaneg, such as the **Folk Arts Theater**, which is the venue for occasional pop concerts, jazz and drama (see page 94), and the **Manila Film Center** (see box, page 73). Note that ferries to the island of Corregidor leave from near the CCP.

Coconut Palace

F. Ma. Guerrero St, next to CCP • Get latest info on ☎ 02 832 6791

Built between 1978 and 1981 on the orders of Imelda Marcos for the visit of Pope John Paul II, the **Coconut Palace** is one of Manila's more bizarre monuments, an outrageous but strangely compelling edifice, seventy percent of it constructed from coconut materials. The pope rightly gave Imelda short shrift when he arrived, saying he wouldn't stay in such an egregious establishment while there was so much poverty on the streets of Manila, and suggested she spend taxpayers' money (the equivalent of some P37 million) more wisely. In 2011 the palace became the residence and office of the **vice president**. Sadly, guided tours have been suspended since 2016, and there's no indication as to whether resume in the future.

The Museum at De La Salle University

2401 Taft Ave • Charge; register at the main entrance first (bring photo ID), then pay at accounting before heading to the gallery in Yuchengco Hall • ⓦ facebook.com/TheMuseumAtDeLaSalleUniversity • LRT to Vito Cruz

Established in 1911, **De La Salle University**, at the southern end of Malate, remains one of the most prestigious private Catholic colleges in the Philippines. The **DLSU Museum** hosts rotating exhibitions showing work from its substantial collection of modern Filipino artists such as Diosdado Lorenzo and Araceli Dans. It's really just a

---

THE MANILA FILM CENTER

If bricks could talk, those at the **Manila Film Center** in Pasay (map page 74) would have a sinister story to tell. Back in the 1970s, **Imelda Marcos** wanted to stage an annual film festival that would rival Cannes and put Manila on the international cultural map. But the centre she commissioned for the purpose was jerry-built and a floor collapsed in 1981, allegedly burying workers under rubble and killing many. No one knows exactly how many (some claim around 170) because most were poor labourers from the provinces, and records were not kept of their names. Police were told to throw a cordon round the building so the press couldn't get to it, and work continued round the clock. The centre was completed in 1982, some say with dead workers still entombed inside, in time for the opening night of the **Manila International Film Festival**. Imelda celebrated by walking onto the stage to greet the audience in a black and emerald green *terno* (a formal gown) thick with layer upon layer of peacock feathers that were shipped specially from India. The centre staged just one more film festival – some say it's haunted, and Imelda herself had it exorcized – and it soon had to make ends meet by showing *bomba* (soft porn) films for the masses. It was briefly rehabilitated in the late 1980s when it was used as a centre for experimental film-making, but after an earthquake hit Manila in 1990 it was abandoned. In 2001 it was partially renovated and now hosts transvestite song and dance extravaganzas dubbed the "Amazing Show" (see page 94).

1

small gallery but even if you're not an art fan, it's worth a quick look just to get a pass to wander the elegant neoclassical DLSU campus, far more redolent of classical Spain than the city outside.

Paco Park and Cemetery

General Luna St at Padre Faura St • Charge; concerts free • ☏ 02 302 7182 • LRT to Pedro Gil or UN Avenue

A circular walled cemetery with an aged and beautiful garden dominated by a classical rotunda, **Paco Park and Cemetery** was built in 1820 just in time for victims of a cholera epidemic. After his execution in 1896, **José Rizal** (see page 415) was buried here in an unmarked grave. The story goes that his sister, Narcisa Rizal-Lopez, saw a group of guards standing beside a mound of freshly turned earth the length of a man; guessing this must be her brother's grave, she convinced the cemetery guardian to mark the site. Two years later Rizal's remains were exhumed and left in the custody of his family until 1912, when they were deposited beneath the Rizal Memorial (see page 72). A monument marks the location of the original grave.

The park's serenity has made it a favourite spot every Friday for "Paco Park Presents" – highly enjoyable **open-air concerts**, usually classical recitals by artists or students.

Pasay

Although it's an easy walk south of Malate, few travellers get to see much of **Pasay City**, except for two highly notable exceptions. First, and foremost, those destined for the gargantuan **SM Mall of Asia** (see page 96), one of greater Manila's most prominent shrines to shopping, and fronted to its west by a bayfront esplanade – great for sunsets, when the weather agrees, though another part of the city threatened by the Horizon Manila land reclamation project, which started in 2025. Secondly, Pasay is also the

departure point for ferries to **Corregidor island**. Other than that, you most likely won't see too much of Pasay, save for quick glances out of the car window on your way to or from the airport.

Makati

Some 5km east of Manila Bay, **Makati City** was a vast expanse of malarial swampland until the Ayala family, one of the country's most influential business dynasties, started developing it in the 1950s. It is now Manila's premier business and financial district, chock-full of plush hotels, international restaurant chains, expensive condominiums and monolithic air-conditioned malls.

Opposite the station, the biggest mall is **Glorietta**, which has a central section and side halls numbered 1–5, and heaves with people seeking refuge from the traffic and heat. A short walk from Glorietta to the other side of Makati Avenue is **Greenbelt Park**, a landscaped garden with the pleasant, modern, white-domed **Santo Niño de Paz Chapel** in the centre. The park forms part of Makati's other main mall, **Greenbelt**, which, like Glorietta, is divided into various numbered halls; on the north side is the excellent **Ayala Museum** (see page 76). Just to the north is the pleasant green swathe of **Ayala Triangle**, bordered by Ayala Avenue, Paseo de Roxas and Makati Avenue. Further along

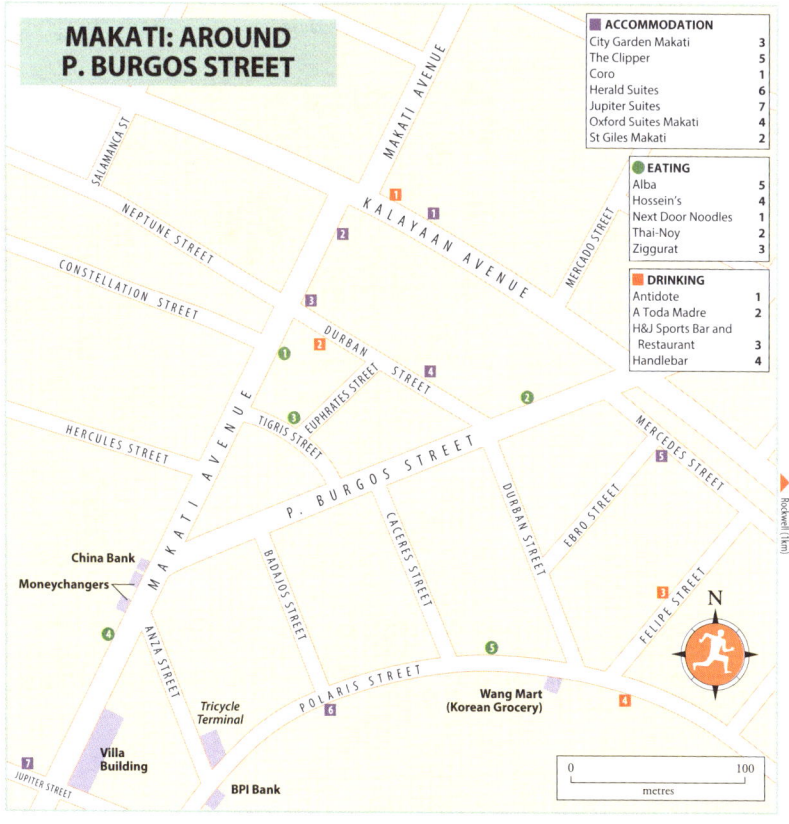

MAKATI: AROUND P. BURGOS STREET

■ ACCOMMODATION	
City Garden Makati	3
The Clipper	5
Coro	1
Herald Suites	6
Jupiter Suites	7
Oxford Suites Makati	4
St Giles Makati	2

● EATING	
Alba	5
Hossein's	4
Next Door Noodles	1
Thai-Noy	2
Ziggurat	3

■ DRINKING	
Antidote	1
A Toda Madre	2
H&J Sports Bar and Restaurant	3
Handlebar	4

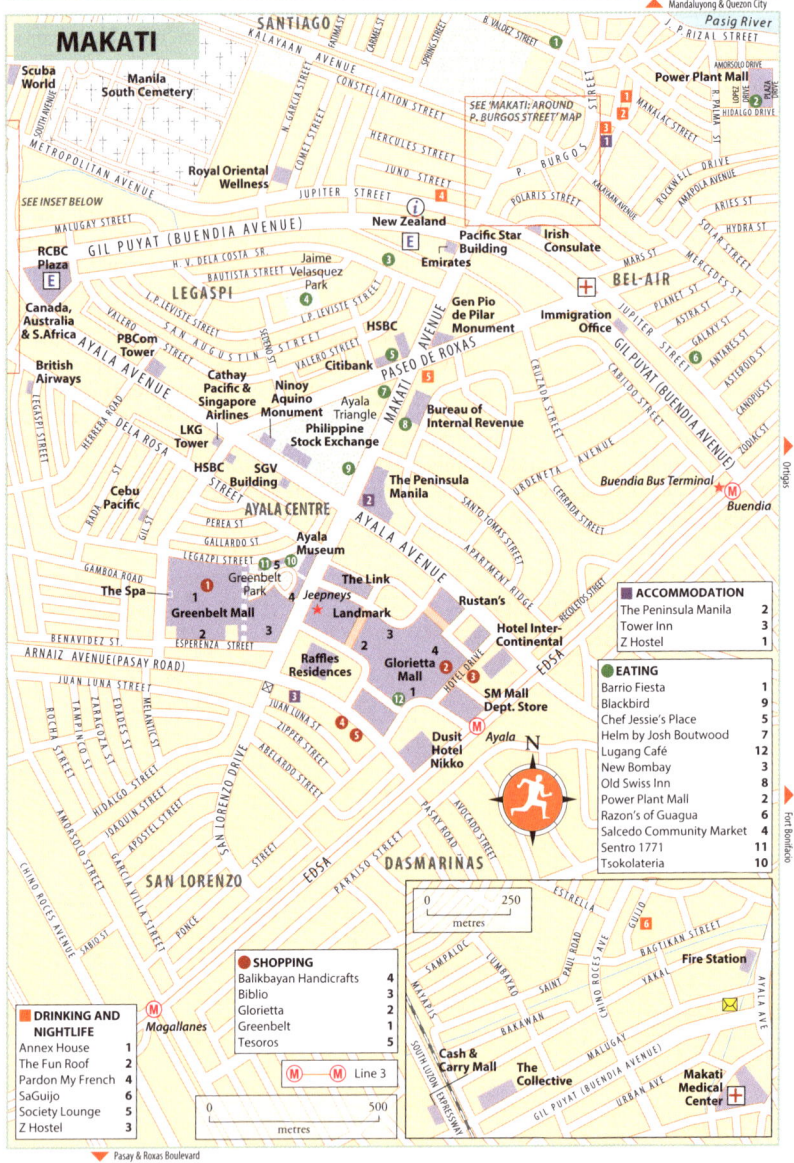

Ayala Avenue, at the junction with Paseo de Roxas, is the **Ninoy Aquino Monument**, built in honour of the senator who was assassinated in 1983, while a block further on is the shimmering **PBCom Tower** (259m), at 6795 Ayala Avenue, the tallest building in the Philippines (closed to the public).

Ayala Museum

Makati Ave at De La Rosa St • Charge • ⓦ ayalamuseum.org • MRT to Ayala

Makati's one must-see attraction is the **Ayala Museum**, by far the best place in the Philippines to get to grips with the nation's complex history. The mighty Ayala family donated much of the initial collection in 1967, and this modern building was completed in 2004. There are no dreary exhibits here, or ponderous chronological approach – the permanent exhibitions just highlight the key aspects of Philippine history beginning on the **fourth floor** with an extraordinary collection of pre-Hispanic goldware, created by the islands' often overlooked Indigenous cultures between the tenth and thirteenth centuries. Over one thousand gold objects are on display, much of it from the Butuan area in Mindanao, including the "**Surigao Treasure**" (see page 414). Don't miss the astonishing Gold Regalia, a huge 4kg chain of pure gold thought to have been worn by a *datu* (chief). Other displays emphasize pre-Hispanic trade links with Asia, especially Song dynasty China, with a huge collection of porcelain and ceramics. On the **third floor** the "Pioneers of Philippine Art" showcases the museum's particularly strong collections of Juan Luna Realism, Fernando Amorsolo Impressionism and Fernando Zobel's more abstract work. On the **second floor** an extensive display of sixty exquisitely detailed dioramas dramatizes all the important key events in Philippine history from prehistory to independence, while three interesting audiovisual presentations tackle the postwar period, the Marcos years and People Power in 1986.

Bonifacio Global City (Fort Bonifacio)

Bonifacio Global City (or **Fort Bonifacio**, after the army camp around which it is located) sits on the eastern fringes of Makati but is rapidly developing a separate identity of its own, with skyscrapers, posh condos and shopping malls developed by Ayala Corp. Other than the **Manila American Cemetery and Memorial**, there's little in the way of traditional sights, though the shops, bars and restaurants of Market! Market! show off Manila's ambitious, affluent side.

Metropolitan Museum

30th St • Charge • ⓦ metmuseum.ph • LRT to Vito Cruz, then an orange CCP jeepney along Pablo Ocampo St to Roxas Bvd

The **Metropolitan Museum** moved to this new, more modern location in 2022, and in the process completely changed tack – once best known for its astounding collection of **pre-colonial gold**, a stunning ensemble of magnificent jewellery, amulets, necklaces and intricate gold-work dating from long before the Spanish Conquest, it now hosts rotating exhibitions focusing on anything from Banksy to Korean knot-making, via local fashion legends – usually well worth a look, especially if you're in BGC already. The facilities are very spacious, and accessibility has been improved greatly; expect to see an intriguing mix of murals, installations and creative collaborations.

Manila American Cemetery and Memorial

McKinley Rd, Global City, Taguig • Free • ⓦ abmc.gov • MRT to Ayala – walk across EDSA near its junction with Ayala Ave and then along McKinley Rd, passing Manila Polo Club on your right, and the cemetery entrance is at the roundabout 1km beyond the polo club; taxi from central Makati usually very cheap

On the southeastern edge of Makati, 3km away from Glorietta mall, lies the serene **Manila American Cemetery and Memorial**, containing 17,201 graves of American military personnel killed in World War II, most of whom lost their lives in operations in New Guinea and the Philippines. The headstones are aligned in eleven plots forming a generally circular pattern, and set among a wide variety of tropical trees and shrubbery. There is also a chapel and two curved granite walkways whose walls contain mosaic maps depicting the battles fought in the Pacific, along with the names of the

1

36,285 American servicemen whose bodies were not recovered (rosettes mark the names of those since found and identified).

Ortigas and around

MRT to Shaw Blvd or Ortigas

A dense huddle of malls and offices, **Ortigas** lies 5km north of Makati on EDSA. The district began to come to life in the early 1980s, when a number of corporations left the bustle of Makati for its relatively open spaces; the Asian Development Bank moved here in 1991 and the Manila Stock Exchange followed one year later. Today its biggest draw for Manileños is the **SM Megamall**, one of Asia's largest shopping malls.

Lopez Memorial Museum

G/F Benpres Building, Exchange Rd at Meralco Ave • Closed for relocation at time of writing • ⓦ lml.org.ph

The one genuine cultural attraction in Ortigas is the **Lopez Memorial Museum**, founded in 1960 by tycoon Eugenio Lopez to provide scholars and students with access to his personal collection of rare books and since expanded to contain other treasures. The oldest is a priceless 1524 copy of the account of Magellan's circumnavigation of the world by one Maximilianus Transylvanus. The museum's art collection includes important paintings by nineteenth-century Filipino masters Juan Luna and Félix

Hidalgo, as well as selected works by Fernando Amorsolo, who gained prominence during the early 1930s and 1940s for popularizing images of Philippine landscapes and beautiful rural Filipinas. The museum's Rizaliana includes some ninety letters written by José Rizal to his mother and sisters in the 1890s, along with the national hero's wallet and paintbrushes, his flute and his personal papers. Exhibits rotate every six months, as there's not enough space to display everything at once, but the library section always contains some of the best rare books, artwork and letters. At time of writing, the museum was closed in advance of its relocation, though the new address has not yet been announced. Check the website for latest information.

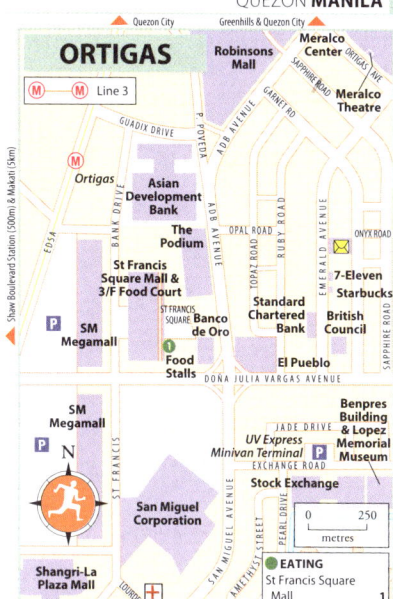

Marikina Shoe Museum

J.P. Rizal St, Marikina, 16km east of Rizal Park • Charge • ☎ 02 8646 2360 • LRT to Katipunan, then taxi

Nothing symbolizes the vanity of **Imelda Marcos** more than her collection of shoes, which numbered in the thousands on the eve of the EDSA revolution in 1986 (it's not known how many she owns today). This ghastly but admittedly stylish legacy is preserved at the **Marikina Shoe Museum** way out in the eastern suburbs, where 749 pairs belonging to the former first lady are displayed under her giant portrait, along with pairs owned by each president of the Philippines (the worn-out-looking shoes owned by Ferdinand Marcos make quite a contrast) and several other local celebrities. The history of shoemaking is explained upstairs. The museum is out in Marikina because the area was dubbed the "**shoe capital of the Philippines**" back in 1956; the industry's heyday was the 1970s and 1980s, though there are still several factories in the neighbourhood.

Quezon

Once viewed as Metro Manila's modern side – a role since taken on by Makati and Bonifacio Global City – **Quezon City** sits to the northeast of Manila proper. While still home to several notable places to eat, drink and sleep, its fortunes were on the wane even before the **shutdown of ABS-CBN broadcasting** in 2020. While this might sound like small beer to foreign visitors, it came about as the result of friction between incoming and departing presidential administrations, which made it a very big deal indeed for locals of pretty much all political stripes. Upon the expiry of their broadcasting franchise, ABS-CBN immediately shut down all of their television and radio channels; the resultant loss of employment was most keenly felt in Quezon, especially the area surrounding the broadcasting centre, where a large television mask still stands sentry, seemingly in memoriam of better times. The colourful "Pinoy Big Brother" house still sees the odd crowd of photo-snappers, but with decreased demand, many local businesses have shut down, and central Quezon City now feels rather ho-hum; the malls in the wider area, however, still do brisk business.

1

University of the Philippines (1km)

TriNoma Mall

NORTH AVENUE

QUEZON MEMORIAL CIRCLE

L — L Line 2
M — M Line 3

M North Avenue

0 — 400 metres

■ **ACCOMMODATION**
Camelot 1
Stone House 2

■ **DRINKING AND NIGHTLIFE**
Big Sky Mind 3
Café 80s 1
Quattro 2
Smart Araneta Coliseum 4

AGHAM ROAD

QUEZON AVENUE

ELLIPTICAL ROAD

KALAYAAN AVENUE

EDSA

MARKIT STREET

Zoological & Botanical Garden

MAYAMAN STREET
MAKATARUNGAN STREET

MATALINO STREET

HSBC

BIR ROAD

MASIGLA STREET

WEST AVENUE

BULLETIN STREET

TIMES STREET

EXAMINER STREET

Quezon
M Avenue

NIA ROAD

EAST AVENUE (CARLOS P. GARCIA AVENUE)

MATAPANG STREET

QUEZON AVENUE

BONG AVENUE

ABS-CBN

MALAKAS STREET

MATIAG STREET

V. LUNA AVENUE

SCOUT SANTIAGO

Mercury
Drug

MOTHER IGNACIA AVENUE

PANAY

SGT. ESGUERRA AVENUE

SAMAR AVENUE

EUGENIO LOPEZ

1

1

SCOUT BAYORAN

AFP
Medical
Center

TIMOG AVENUE (SOUTH AVENUE)

SCOUT BOROMEO

SCOUT MADRINAN

Imperial Palace
Suites Hotel

SCOUT LIMBAGA

SCOUT RALLOS

TIMOG AVENUE (SOUTH AVENUE)

GMA Kamuning
M Victory Liner

SCOUT
TOBIAS

SCOUT FERNANDEZ
FUENTEBELLA

SCOUT RALLOS

Lucena

MAPAGMAHAL

KAMIAS ROAD

SCOUT GANDIA

3

SCOUT LIMBAGA

JAM ★

Jac Liner

SCOUT DE GUIA

SCOUT TUPAZON

5

T. MORATO AVENUE

SCOUT LAZCANO
SCOUT DELGADO

K - 6TH STREET

DON A. ROCES AVE

6

SCOUT TORILLO

JUDGE D. JIMENEZ

EDSA

N

KAMUNING ROAD

Dilliman Creek

ERMIN GARCIA AVENUE

WEST POINT STREET

NEW YORK STREET

CAMBRIDGE

★ DLTB

ALPS &
N. Dela Rosa ★

MARYLAND STREET

ERMIN GARCIA AVENUE

Dominion
Dagupan Bus ★

★ Genesis Transport,
Saulog Transit & Joy Buses

FELIX MANALO STREET

Baliwag Transit ★

St Luke's
✚ Medical Center

E. RODRIGUEZ SR. AVENUE

Victory Liner ★
Five Star ★
Coda Lines ★
Superlines ★

Araneta
Center–
Cubao

L

2

LANTANA STREET

Gateway
Mall

● **EATING**
Behrouz 3
Frazzled Cook 5
Gerry's Grill 1
Greens 6
High Grounds 2
Lydia's Lechon 4

DLTB Araneta ★

Partas ★

AURORA BOULEVARD

MAYA STREET

Dimple Star
Transport

M

Araneta
Coliseum

Betty Go-
Belmonte
L

Araneta
Center–
Cubao

Philtranco ★

4

QUEZON CITY

BY PLANE

NINOY AQUINO INTERNATIONAL AIRPORT (NAIA)

Almost everyone visiting the Philippines arrives at Ninoy Aquino International Airport (NAIA; ⊛ manila-airport.net), on the southern fringes of Manila, named after the anti-Marcos politician who was assassinated here in 1983.

Terminals The airport has four separate and unconnected terminals, making it seem, confusingly, as if there are several different airports (you may hear locals refer to them this way). Most international flights arrive at Terminals 1 and 3, which are on different sides of the airport footprint entirely; Terminal 2, within walking distance of Terminal 1, serves only domestic flights, as does tiny Domestic Terminal

4 a little to the north. An "airport loop" shuttle bus connects all the terminals, running frequently throughout the day, but traffic congestion means transfers can take over an hour in some cases – leave plenty of time. If you're transferring planes here, even between different airlines and on different tickets, you may be able to make use of a faster inter-terminal shuttle system running within the airport compound.

Tourist information Terminals 1, 2 and 3 have small Department of Tourism reception desks, open to meet all flights, where you can pick up maps and current information. Terminal 2 has an airport information desk that sometimes has city maps.

Services There are banks and ATMs at all terminals, but no left-luggage (baggage deposit) facilities. Free wi-fi is available inside the terminals.

GETTING INTO TOWN

The roads around the airport quickly become gridlocked in heavy rain or at rush hour; it can take anything from 20min to 1hr to travel the 7km to the main tourist and budget accommodation area of Manila Bay.

Airport taxis To head into the centre, the best thing to do is to take a cab. Yellow airport taxis charge slightly higher rates than normal white taxis (see page 83). These are not expensive and should be on the meter, though you will need to be on the alert for scam artists – if you are being ripped off, take the taxi number and report the driver.

App taxis App-based taxi services such as Grab are usually very cheap, even with the inevitable airport mark-up, though there are (also inevitably) occasional problems determining pick-up points when you're still at the airport.

Pre-paid taxis The alternative to yellow taxis is to buy a ticket for a pre-paid "coupon" taxi at desks outside the terminals. Unless you have a large group, these big vans are expensive, but they do avoid any hassle.

Jeepneys It's possible to flag down a jeepney from the main roads near any of the terminals, but if you have bulky baggage it can be hard, and sometimes impossible, to drag it on board.

Bus and LRT If you really want to do it on the cheap, Terminal 1 is a 15min walk (or a short jeepney ride) from Ninoy Aquino station, and Terminal 4 the same distance from MIA station, which are both on the green LRT line; Terminal 2 is a 30min walk from the same stations, though the route can be tedious. Terminal 3 isn't yet near any stations, though you could cross the footbridge from the terminal and take a bus.

DOMESTIC FLIGHTS DESTINATIONS

Domestic carriers are covered in Basics (see page 26).

Northern Luzon Batanes (1–2 daily; 1hr 45min); Laoag (1–3 daily; 1hr); Tuguegarao (1–3 daily; 1hr 10min).

Southern Luzon Legazpi (6–7 daily; 1hr 10min); Naga (3–4 daily; 1hr); Virac (1–3 daily; 1hr 10min).

Mindoro San José (1–2 daily; 1hr).

The Visayas Bacolod (1–2 hourly; 1hr 15min); Caticlan (9–11 daily; 1hr); Cebu City (1–3 hourly; 1hr 15min); Dumaguete (4–7 daily; 1hr 25min); Iloilo (1–2 hourly; 1hr 10min); Kalibo (1–2 hourly; 1hr 10min); Tablas Island (2 weekly; 1hr); Tacloban (9–10 daily; 1hr 25min); Tagbilaran (8–9 daily; 1hr 25min).

Palawan Busuanga Island (8–9 daily; 1hr); Puerto Princesa (1–2 hourly; 1hr 20min).

Mindanao Butuan (5 daily; 1hr 35min); Cagayan de Oro (1–2 hourly; 1hr 30min); Cotabato (2–3 daily; 1hr 45min); Davao (1–3 hourly; 1hr 50min); Dipolog (2 daily; 1hr 25min); General Santos (5–6 daily; 1hr 50min); Ozamiz (2 daily; 1hr 30min); Siargao (2 daily; 2hr); Surigao (1 daily; 1hr 40min); Zamboanga (6–7 daily; 1hr 40min).

BY FERRY

2GO Travel ferries (incorporating Negros Navigation, SuperFerry, Cebu Ferries and SuperCat; ⬤ travel.2go. ph) use the passenger terminal at Pier 4, North Harbor (along Marcos Rd, a few kilometres north of Intramuros), from where you can catch a taxi to Ermita.

Departures Bacolod (4 weekly; 20hr); Butuan (1 weekly; 23hr); Cagayan de Oro (4 weekly; 34hr); Cebu City (4 weekly; 23hr); Coron (1 weekly; 15hr); Dipolog (1 weekly; 32hr); Dumaguete (1 weekly; 26hr); Iligan (1 weekly; 42hr); Iloilo (3 weekly; 28hr); Ozamiz (1 weekly; 35hr); Puerto Princesa (1 weekly; 32hr); Zamboanga (1 weekly; 42hr).

BY BUS

Hundreds and hundreds of buses link Manila with the provinces – that's the good news. The bad news is that there are also dozens of companies, each with their own depots, meaning that leaving Manila can often prove a confusing and frustrating affair (see box page 82), though there's now one actual bus terminal (gasp!), and another to come – happier times ahead, especially for first-time visitors. Departures given here are frequent (one or more per hour) unless otherwise stated; this is a basic run-down, and there will often be options with other lines, or from other depots or terminals.

AROUND MANILA

Balanga (3hr 15min–4hr). Bataan Transit (⬤ facebook. com/bataantransit), Cubao.

Batangas (1hr 30min–2hr). ALPS (⬤ alpsthebus.com), Cubao; Ceres Transport (⬤ ceresbuses.com), Buendia and PITX; JAM (⬤ jamlinerbus.com), Cubao and Buendia.

Clark/Angeles City/Dau (bus terminal) (1hr 30min–2hr). Philippine Rabbit (⬤ facebook.com/philippinerabbit), Rizal; Philtranco (⬤ philtranco.net; 5 daily), Pasay; Genesis (⬤ genesisjoybus.com), NAIA.

Laguna JAC Liner (⬤ jacliner.com), Buendia for Pagsanjan

1

LEAVING MANILA BY BUS

Leaving Manila by bus has long been tricky, thanks to the fact that each of the dozens of bus companies used their own depot – and in some cases, more than one. However, things are changing – 2018 saw the opening of the city's first actual bus terminal, the **Parañaque Integrated Terminal Exchange** (**PITX** to its friends, and handily served by an LRT station of the same name). Although it can get cramped and stuffy during busy periods, the terminal has air-con and fans, toilets and plenty of places to eat – and, of course, provides shelter from the rain. The buses using this terminal are, as a general rule (and to avoid extra time negotiating Manila's gridlock) destined for points south, but some head north.

PITX was set to be followed in 2023 by a northern version, though its completion has been delayed, with no set date yet known; not even the name of the terminal is a done deal, with options being bandied about including Unified Grand Central, **North Triangle Common** and various combinations of the salient words. When complete, it's likely to absorb many of the companies currently based in the **Cubao** area of Quezon City, all lined up towards the northern end of EDSA (and usually a short walk from Cubao MRT station).

Even more annoyingly, some buses stop at both PITX and Cubao, and there are also bus-depot clusters around LRT Buendia (gizen as **Buendia** in the listings) the junction of Taft Ave with EDSA (given as **Pasay**), and on Rizal Ave in Quiapo (given as **Rizal**). Generally, for now, if heading south you should aim for PITX, and if heading north you should head for Cubao (until the new bus terminal opens). Your accommodation should be able to advise, but even better is buying your own ticket online with sites such as ⓦ12go.asia or ⓦbooktickets.ph, which will *usually* tell you where to go to get your bus (sometimes even with a map), potentially saving a hot slog walking around trying to find a depot, or a bus with spare seats.

(2hr 30min) via Calamba (1hr 30min) and Los Baños (2hr).

Malolos (1hr). First North Luzon Transit (ⓦfacebook. com/FirstNorthLuzonTransit), Monumento LRT; also vans and taxis from there and from SM City North mall, at the northern end of EDSA.

Mariveles (3–4hr). Bataan Transit (ⓦfacebook.com/ bataantransit), Cubao; Genesis Transport (ⓦgenesisjoybus. com), Pasay.

Nasugbu (3hr). San Agustin, PITX and Pasay.

Subic Bay/Olongapo (3–5hr). Victory Liner (ⓦvictory liner.com), Cubao and Pasay.

Taal/Lemery (2hr 30min–3hr). JAM (ⓦjamlinerbus. com), PITX and Cubao.

Tagaytay (1hr 30min). San Agustin, PITX and Pasay.

NORTHERN LUZON

Alaminos (6–8hr). Victory Liner (ⓦvictoryliner.com), Cubao.

Baguio (5–7hr). Genesis Transport (ⓦgenesisjoybus. com), Cubao; Victory Liner (ⓦvictoryliner.com), Pasay and Cubao.

Baler (5–6hr). Genesis Transport (ⓦgenesisjoybus.com), Cubao.

Banaue (8–9hr, all around 9pm daily). Ohayami Trans (ⓦohayamitrans.com), Buendia; Coda Lines (ⓦfacebook. com/codalinescorporation), Cubao.

Bontoc (12hr). Coda Lines (ⓦfacebook.com/codalines

corporation), Cubao (9pm nightly).

Kiangan/Lagawe (8hr). Ohayami Trans (ⓦohayamitrans. com) Buendia (daily 9.30pm).

Laoag (12–14hr). Fariñas Transit (ⓦfarinastrans.com; 12 daily), Buendia; Partas (ⓦpartas-online; 5 daily), Cubao.

San Fernando (La Union; 6–8hr). Dominion Bus Lines (☎02 741 4146), Cubao; Partas (ⓦpartas-online.com), Cubao.

Sagada (12hr). Coda Lines (ⓦfacebook.com/codalines corporation), Cubao (2 nightly).

Tuguegarao (10–12hr). Victory Liner (ⓦvictoryliner. com), Cubao; Five Star (ⓦ5starbus.com), Cubao.

Vigan (7–9hr). Partas (ⓦpartas-online), Cubao.

SOUTHERN LUZON

Daet (7–8hr). DLTB (ⓦdltbterminal.com), Buendia (15 daily); Philtranco (ⓦphiltrancobus.com), Pasay (6 daily).

Legazpi (11–12hr). DLTB (ⓦdltbterminal.com), Buendia (6 daily); ALPS (ⓦalpsthebus.com), Cubao (6 daily).

Lucena (3hr 30min). JAC Liner (ⓦjacliner.com), Buendia; JAM Liner (ⓦjamlinerbus.com) Buendia.

Naga (8–10hr). Philtranco (ⓦphiltrancobus.com; 2 daily), Pasay; DLTB (ⓦdltbterminal.com; 8 daily), Buendia; ALPS (ⓦalpsthebus.com, 4 daily) Cubao.

Sorsogon City (12hr). DLTB (ⓦdltbterminal.com, 4 daily), Buendia (4 daily); Philtranco (ⓦphiltrancobus.com, 10 daily), Pasay.

MINDORO
Puerto Galera (**Sabang & Muelle pier**; 4hr). Si-Kat (ⓦ sikatferrybus.com, daily 9.30am), City State Tower, Ermita.

THE VISAYAS
Panay Philtranco (ⓦ philtrancobus.com), Pasay to Iloilo (1 daily; 17hr), via Mindoro.

Samar/Leyte Philtranco (ⓦ philtrancobus.com), Pasay to Ormoc (1 daily; 28hr).

MINDANAO
Cagayan de Oro (2 days) Philtranco (ⓦ philtrancobus. com, 1 daily), Pasay.
Cagayan de Oro (2–3 days) Philtranco (ⓦ philtrancobus. com, 1 daily), Pasay.

GETTING AROUND

There are so many vehicles fighting for every inch of road space in Manila that at peak times it can be a sweaty battle of nerves just to move a few hundred metres. **Buses** and **jeepneys** belch smoke with impunity, turning the air around major thoroughfares into a poisonous miasma, but Manila's **taxis** are inexpensive and are mostly air-conditioned, and many visitors use them extensively – especially Grab cabs, which are a regional alternative to Uber. Manila's two light railway lines, the Manila Light Rail Transit (**LRT**) and the MetroStar Express (**MRT**). Trains are best avoided during rush hour (Mon–Fri 7–9.30am & 5–8pm) when you may have to line up just to get into the stations, and carriages will be jam-packed.

BY RAIL/METRO

There are currently three lines in use – Line 1 (also known as LRT-1, coloured green on maps) and Line 2 (LRT-2, coloured purple), and Line 3 (MRT-3, coloured yellow). These are cheap and reliable, but badly integrated – interchanges are poorly designed, and there are no through-fares, so you need to buy a new ticket (or tap your Beep card again), and often even leave the station entirely when changing lines. The vintage national railway line (PNR) shut in 2023, but is being upgraded to become the North–South Commuter Railway (NSCR), with partial service set to commence in 2027.
Fares You can buy a single-journey ticket, or purchase a stored-value Beep card (ⓦ beeptopay.com): these are available from station ticket offices (though they sometimes run out), and from machines at the main entrances of stations (usually faster, because locals seem adverse to them). The Beep cards are also valid on the LRT. If you plan to use the MRT and LRT a lot, you'll save a great deal of time by buying one; you'll still have to line up for a bag check before entering the station, but will avoid having to line up again for a ticket.
Safety Security guards patrol stations (and the first carriage is usually reserved for women), but watch out for pickpockets and the more brazen "snatchers", who rip phones, bags and wallets from your hand and make a run for it.

JEEPNEYS AND FX TAXIS

While sometimes useful (linking SM Mall of Asia and Baclaran station, for example), jeepneys and UV taxis can be incredibly cramped, and traffic congestion can make even short journeys last hours.
Jeepneys are the cheapest way to get around, and they run back and forth all over the city. There'll be a standard fare for the first 4km, which increases every km thereafter. Destinations are written on signboards at the front.
UV taxis You'll also see tiny minivans or "UV taxis" that zip between fixed points, usually without stopping.

BUSES

Local buses in Manila bump and grind their way along all major thoroughfares, such as Taft, EDSA and Gil Puyat (Buendia) Avenue, but are not allowed on most side streets. The destination is written on a sign in the front window. Most vehicles are ageing contraptions bought secondhand from Japan or Taiwan, and feature no particular colour scheme; it's a matter of luck whether a bus has air conditioning.
Fares Most buses charge a set fare for the first 5km, increasing per km thereafter. As with jeepneys, traffic congestion will add travel time and even larger buses will often be packed.

TAXIS

Most Manila taxi drivers are honest these days and use the meter, though some may still try to set prices in advance or "forget" to switch it on (insist on the meter). Taxis come in a confusing mix of models, colours and shapes; most metered taxis are white (and often called "white taxis" to differentiate them from the yellow airport taxis that have higher fares). Fares are good value and you'll save time using taxis over other road transport. Grab is the local ride-hailing app of choice (ⓦ grab.com), and can also be used to get motorbike rides – even cheaper, a lot better at cutting through traffic, though obviously a little unsafe too.

INFORMATION AND TOURS

Tourist information The Tourist Information Center is in the Department of Tourism Building, 351 Sen Gil Puyat

(Buendia) Ave, Makati (Mon–Fri 7am–6pm, Sat 8am–5pm; ⓦ tourism.gov.ph). There are also information desks in the

1

AIRBNB IN MANILA

If you're wondering, yes, there's plenty of choice on **Airbnb** (🌐 airbnb.com), and the various options on offer can work out best for many visitors, especially those looking to stay in town for a while. Two particularly recommended towers are **Milano Residences** and **Knightsbridge Residences** in Makati, which are super-tall luxury towers filled with Airbnb-able rooms; views can be astonishing for the prices on offer, and the lofty swimming pools are quite superb too. Other good options can be found in Bonifacio Global City, Ortigas and Quezon City.

airport arrivals sections.

Tours Filipino Travel Center, G/F *Palm Plaza Hotel*, 524 Pedro Gil St at M. Adriatico St, Ermita (🌐 filipinotravel.com.ph). Old Manila Walks offer walking tours around Intramuros

(see page 65; 🌐 oldmanilawalks.com).

Dive operators Asia Divers, 1741 Dian St, Abimir Place, Palanan, Makati (🌐 asiadivers.com).

ACCOMMODATION

Most of Manila's budget accommodation is in the Manila Bay area, specifically in **Ermita** and **Malate**, which also have a high density of cheap restaurants, bars and tourist services. In recent years a number of reasonably priced mid-range hotels have sprung up, as well as several five-star places along Manila Bay, joining the historic *Manila Hotel*. In the business district of **Makati**, there's some mid-range accommodation in and around P. Burgos St at the northern end of Makati Ave, beyond the *Mandarin Oriental Manila*. This is close to the red-light district, so if you want somewhere else in Makati try the somewhat anaemic but comfortable chain hotels in Arnaiz Ave (formerly Pasay Rd), behind the Greenbelt mall. The hotels in **Quezon City** are almost all around Timog Ave and Tomas Morato Ave, close to the nightlife; if you're planning to catch an early bus from Cubao, it might be worth staying here. If you have an early flight and a bit more cash to spend, try one of the convenient upmarket options close to the airport.

INTRAMUROS, SEE MAP PAGE 66

HOTELS

The Bayleaf Muralla St at Victoria St 🌐 thebayleaf.com. ph. Swish boutique hotel in the historic heart of the city, with spacious, light, modern rooms, roof deck bar and restaurant with great views, and buffet breakfast included. ‾P‾P‾P‾

The Manila Hotel 1 Rizal Park 🌐 manila-hotel.com. ph. Esteemed establishment that reeks of history (see page 70), at least in the old wing where General Douglas MacArthur stayed during World War II; if you've got a small fortune to spare you can stay a night in his suite. The lobby is a grand affair with black-and-white-tiled flooring and oxblood velvet sofas. The rooms, many in need of a revamp, remain stubbornly traditional, with dark wood and four-poster beds. A great Chinese restaurant and a nice pool out back (well, sort of around the side) round up a pleasing picture. ‾P‾P‾P‾P‾

White Knight Hotel Intramuros Cabildo St at Urdaneta St, Plaza San Luis Complex 🌐 whiteknighthotel-intramuros.com. Nineteenth-century building with heaps of character and 29 simple but spacious rooms tastefully furnished in period style, with bathroom, a/c and flatscreen TV. The cheapest decent option in Intramuros. ‾P‾P‾

ERMITA AND MALATE, SEE MAP PAGE 71

HOTELS

Adriatico Arms 561 J. Nakpil St, Malate 🌐 facebook. com/adriaticoarmshotel. A pleasant, no-frills hotel in an unbeatable location. The 23 a/c rooms are smallish, but well kept and functional, and there's a good bar, but no breakfast. ‾P‾P‾

Aloha 2150 Roxas Blvd, Malate ☎ 02 8248 7369. A Manila Bay stalwart, the *Aloha* boasts a fine location with views of the bay from the front (5/F or above). The corridors are a bit scuffed, but the rooms are fine and spacious, and breakfast is included. There's a small café and a Chinese restaurant. ‾P‾P‾

Amelie 1667 Jorge Bocobo St, Malate 🌐 ameliehotel manila.com. Amelie Hotel offers comfortable and clean rooms in a convenient location at the heart of Malate, though the downside of its position is that the neighbourhood can be a little noisy at night – it might be best to ask for a room at the back. There's a small pool, and a nice bar. ‾P‾P‾P‾

Bay Area Suites 1820 Maria Orosa St, Malate 🌐 bay areasuitesmanila.com. The rooms at Bay Area Suites won't win any prizes for innovation, but they're clean and comfortable, and the hotel is well-situated in the thick of things. There's a small pool and gym. ‾P‾P‾

City Garden Suites 1158 A. Mabini St, Ermita 🌐 citygardensuites.com. Standard hotel with sparsely furnished but clean a/c rooms and a reasonable coffee shop in the lobby. ‾P‾P‾

1

Diamond Roxas Bld at J. Quintos St ⓦ diamondhotel. com. A higher-end choice, this well-located skyscraper hotel offers comfortable if fairly unexciting rooms, a gym, sauna and pool, and great views across the bay. There's also a good Japanese restaurant on-site. PPP

Hotel H2O Manila Ocean Park (behind the Quirino Grandstand), Ermita ⓦ hotelh2o.com. The most original boutique hotel in Manila, with a chic "aqua" theme and fabulous views of the bay or Ocean World pool (for the nightly fountain shows). Rooms sport a trendy minimalist design; some even have wall-sized in-room aquariums. The only (slight) downside is that the hotel is a bit cut off from the rest of the city. Rates include breakfast. PPPP

Manila Lotus 1227 A. Mabini St at Padre Faura St, Ermita ⓦ manilalotus.com. Snazzy modern rooms with cable TV and room service, as well as a gym, a spa, an excellent location and decent buffet breakfast (included) make this chain hotel a good deal – book online for the best rates. PP

Pearl Garden 1700 M. Adriatico St at General Malvar St, Malate ⓦ pearlgardenhotel.net. One of the best mid-range hotels on the block, with 83 small but clean and elegant boutique-style rooms. Note that the hotel is smoker friendly apart from one non-smoking floor, and the wi-fi can be a bit iffy. PP

★ **Pension Natividad** 1690 M.H. del Pilar St, Malate ⓦ facebook.com/pensionnatividad. One of the best budget places to stay in the area, this place has spacious, impeccably clean rooms (some en suite and with a/c) in a large old family house. Popular with Peace Corps volunteers, it's safe, quiet and friendly; free wi-fi in the lobby only. PP

Sheraton Manila Bay M. Adriatico St at General Malvar St, Malate ⓦ marriott.com. This is the top choice in Malate for superlative service (each room comes with 24hr butler facility), luxurious rooms and a buffet breakfast that could feed an army. Passing from the street chaos to the soothing outdoor swimming pool and jacuzzi is a surreal but not unpleasant experience. PPPP

Windy Ridge 2033 M.H. del Pilar St, Malate ⓦ facebook. com/windymanila. Dwarfed by the surrounding high-rises, this six-floor hotel is a sweet little place to stay, with a/c, free breakfast, and discounts on three nights or more. PP

HOSTELS, MOTELS AND GUESTHOUSES

Arzo Grand Lodge 1032-1034 Belen, Paco ⓦ arzo hotels.com. Not exactly as grand as the name suggestions, this chain hotel is set in a curved building in a quiet location near Paco Park. It looks a little shabby from outside but the interior is a perfectly serviceable budget hotel, offering a pool, decent breakfasts, and irritatingly noisy a/c. PP

G Square Residences Nakpil St, Malate ⓦ gresidences. com.ph. Tall block that's usually one of the cheapest options you'll find in this area; nothing special, but with

large rooms (mostly featuring a couple of bunk beds, rather than singles or doubles) and a location right in the thick of things. The rooms are yours for 24hr after you check in – ideal for those arriving on late flights, since you can get over your jetlag, eat and sightsee at your leisure, and then even head somewhere else the next evening if you so desire. P

Hop Inn 1850 M.H. Del Pilar St, Malate ⓦ hopinnhotel. com. A perfectly decent budget choice, the Hop Inn offers spotless white rooms inside a tower block painted with bright primary colours. There are several branches across Manila, as well as one in Cebu City, all offering similar quality of room. P

Stay Malate 1750 M. Adriatico St at Nakpil St, Malate ⓦ reddoorz.com. The chilled-out balcony bar, bird's-eye view over Malate and low prices at this backpackers' hostel make it a firm favourite, and a great place to hang out. Fan and a/c rooms are available, some with shared bathrooms. P

PASAY, SEE MAPS PAGES 60 AND 74

HOTELS

The Henry Hotel 2680 F.B. Harrison St, Pasay ⓦ manila. thehenryhotel.com. One of Manila's quirkier choices, the Henry is a beautifully stylish place with gorgeous tiled floors, a marvellous library, and a lovely relaxing garden with a small pool. Bedrooms don't quite match up to the elegance of the common areas, but are still extremely comfortable. The only downside of the Henry Hotel is its distance from the centre. PPP

Manila Marriott 10 Newport Blvd, Newport City Complex ⓦ marriott.com. Fabulous luxury hotel, right across from Terminal 3 (with free shuttle bus to all terminals). Stylish rooms come with flatscreen TVs and snazzy bathrooms with glass walls (with shades for the modest) and big tubs. The pool is a great place to chill out during the day. Walk-in rates are high; you should be able to get rooms for rather less if you book ahead or online. PPPP

HOSTELS, MOTELS AND GUESTHOUSES

Aurora Suites 2235 Aurora Blvd ⓦ 0917 132 0630. Handy for the airport – you can even walk it from three terminals, with light luggage – and also ideally placed for many buses out of Manila, this isn't a bad little spot to spend your first or last night in the city. Rooms are pretty tiny, so's the pool, and so's breakfast, but they'll suffice. P

MAKATI, SEE MAPS PAGES 75 AND 76

HOTELS

City Garden Makati 7870 Makati Ave at Kalayaan Ave ⓦ citygardenhotelmakati.com. A comfortable, modern boutique hotel with spacious and well-maintained a/c rooms, small rooftop swimming pool and giddy views from the rooftop café. Good location, the staff are efficient and

1

you can negotiate a discount off season. **PPP**

Coro 8436 Kalayaan Ave ⓦcorohotel.com. Not really a looker from outside, the Coro Hotel offers attractive, if a little corporate, bedrooms, a relaxing bar, and a very pleasant rooftop pool. Breakfasts, including made-to-order waffles and pancakes, are very good. **PPP**

Herald Suites 45 Polaris St ⓦheraldsuites.com. Step over the threshold into the lobby and you'll feel transported to a different era – the stylish tiled interior just oozes colonial charm. Most bedrooms are similarly impressive, though a few look a little dowdy so it's worth checking out a few before settling. The on-site restaurant is excellent. **PP**

Jupiter Suites 102 Jupiter St at Makati Ave ☏02 8890 5044. Offers spacious a/c singles and doubles, all en suite and with cable TV. If you want quiet, ask for a room at the back – those at the front overlook the busy street and you'll wake to the sound of jeepneys honking their horns at 5am. Breakfast included. **PP**

Oxford Suites Makati 518 P. Burgos St at Durban St ⓦoxfordsuitesmakati.com. Although it's beginning to show its age a little, this is still one of the best hotels on the P. Burgos strip, with 232 spacious rooms and suites, gym, coffee shop and third-floor restaurant. Some rooms have kitchenette, living room and terrace. Buffet breakfast included. **PP**

The Peninsula Manila Ayala Ave at Makati Ave ⓦpeninsula.com/Manila. Ostentatious five-star that takes up a city block and has a superbly elegant lobby where people go to drink coffee and to see and be seen. There are no fewer than seven restaurants, running the gamut from Asian to French. Rooms are as you'd expect at this price, with luxurious furnishings and all mod cons. **PPPP**

St Giles Makati Makati Ave at Kalayaan Ave ⓦstgiles hotels.com. Snazzy hotel, close to all the action. There's a pool and gym, and the rooms are elegantly furnished in light neutral tones. Despite all this, rates can plummet to levels that are almost within backpacker reach, at which times it's an utter bargain. **PPP**

Tower Inn 1002 Arnaiz Ave (Pasay Rd) ⓦtowerinn makati.net. Mid-range hotel that, unlike many of its neighbours, isn't in a tower at all – we can only count four levels. Said floors are filled with 48 rooms, , a business centre and a restaurant, and topped with a roof terrace, all within easy walking distance of Makati's shops and restaurants. Breakfast usually included. **PPP**

HOSTELS, MOTELS AND GUESTHOUSES

★ **The Clipper** 5766 Ebro St ⓦtheclipperhotel.com. An atmospheric little gem, and also known as *Clipper House*, this Art Deco motel is more South Beach than south Manila. Rooms are simple but spacious, and have cable TV. The only catch is its relative proximity to the main drag, which can be a little bit noisy at night. **P**

★ **Z Hostel** 5660 Don Pedro ⓦzhostel.com. The coolest hostel in the area, with good socialising opportunities in the lobby area, and the awesome rooftop bar. The rooms themselves can often feel by-the-way to guests, who use them to sleep and not much more, but they're fine. **P**

BONIFACIO GLOBAL CITY AND AROUND, SEE MAP PAGE 78

HOSTELS, MOTELS AND GUESTHOUSES

★ **Mytown New York** Jacinto St ⓦoyorooms.com. Part of India's *OYO* chain, which seems hell-bent on adding every "just about acceptable" cheap hotel in the world as a franchisee, this is excellent value if you'd like to stay near the fancy BGC area – it's actually across the "border" in Makati (and a short walk , though not an easy one), but close enough to see the high-rise from the rooftop pool, which is a lovely view by night. Rooms are basic, but they do the job, and there's a convenient convenience store on ground level. **P**

ORTIGAS AND AROUND, SEE MAP PAGE 60

HOTELS

★ **Astoria Plaza** 15 Escriva Dr ⓦastoriaplaza.com. Excellent aparthotel within easy walking distance of the Ortigas action. Rooms are both well-appointed and absolutely colossal, and most of them boast wonderful views; breakfast is decent but there's a surprisingly good Japanese restaurant on site, as well as a pool and fitness centre on the third floor. **PPP**

QUEZON CITY, SEE MAPS PAGES 60 AND 80

HOTELS

Camelot 35 Mother Ignacia Ave ☏02 8373 2101. You can't miss it: look for the mock-Arthurian spires. The rooms (all en suite with bathtubs) have a very slight medieval touch about their decor, but not as much as the public spaces, where there are suits of armour and Excalibur swords, a coffee shop called the *Winchester*, and a bar called the *Dungeon*. Breakfast is available, but usually costs extra. **PP**

New Manila Suites 11 Sta. Cecilla ⓦfacebook.com/ NewManilaSuites. Boasting clean rooms, friendly staff and a quiet location, New Manila is a great choice for a stay in Quezon. The peaceful garden to relax in is icing on the cake. **PP**

★ **Stone House** 1315 E. Rodriguez Snr Ave ⓦstone househotelquezoncity.com. A great-value, beautifully kept hotel – if in a slightly remote location – with cable TV, en-suite rooms and a tasty breakfast (included). The budget rooms are in the basement and lack windows, but are otherwise as comfortable as the standard rooms. Take a jeepney from Cubao MRT, heading west down E. Rodriguez Snr Ave. P̄P̄

EATING

Eating in Manila is a real treat; there's a full range of international and Filipino cuisine on offer, and budget eats available on every street corner and in every mall in the form of vast food courts. Everywhere you go, you'll see evidence of the Filipino love of fast-food franchises (see box below).

BINONDO AND QUIAPO, SEE MAP PAGE 63

Binondo has no fancy restaurants, and no bistros or wine bars; people come here for cheap, nourishing Chinese food in one of the area's countless Chinese restaurants or hole-in-the-wall noodle bars. Binondo and Quiapo also have a number of bakeries that are known in the Philippines for their *hopia*, a sweet cake-like snack with a soft pastry coating and thick yam paste in the middle.

RESTAURANTS

Mei Sum Tea House 965 Ongpin St ☎02 8733 6495. Despite its name, this is a restaurant rather than a teahouse. It's known for its excellent dim sums, and in particular *siapao* (steamed stuffed buns), although they'll happily do you a full meal too. P̄P̄

STREET FOOD AND MARKETS

Chuan Kee 650 Ongpin St ☎02 242 5195. This hugely popular place – here since 1940 – looks like the kind of hawker stall you might come across in Singapore or Malaysia, and serves largely the same kinds of food, too. The volunteer firemans' café upstairs is also worth a look. P̄
New Po Heng Lumpia House 621 Carvajal St. Tucked away down a side alley crammed with market stalls and Chinese eateries, this is as basic as things come, but it

doesn't get better than this for cheap *lumpia* (jumbo-size spring rolls). P̄
Tasty Dumplings Norberto Ty St ☎02 8242 5195. With its pretty basic décor, it doesn't look promising, but this little place does – as advertised – serve up very tasty dumplings. It's also highly regarded for its delicious pork chops. P̄P̄

CAFÉS AND DESSERTS

★ **Eng Bee Tin** 628 Ongpin St ⓦengbeetin.com. Filipinos often come to Binondo just to make a pilgrimage to this well-known bakery, which has specialized in various kinds of sweet, sticky mooncake and *hopia* since 1912. The bakers here invented *ube hopia*, made with sweet purple yam and now imitated throughout the country, and you can also buy *tikoy*, the sweet rice cake that is traditionally served during Chinese New Year. P̄
Ho-Land Hopia & Bakery 650 Yuchengco St ⓦholand hopia.com. Classic bakery (and *Eng Bee Tin* rival) serving *hopia* rolls, but also savoury treats such as chicken, beef curry or mushroom pies. P̄
Salazar Bakery 783 Ongpin St ⓦfacebook.com/salazar bakeryph. This bakery dates from 1947 and does a tasty *hopia*, but is also great for savoury *asado* rolls (pork-stuffed buns) and small chicken pies – the hefty mooncakes are worth a try too. P̄

INTRAMUROS, SEE MAP PAGE 66

The old walled city of Intramuros doesn't have many restaurants, but those it does have are mostly in old colonial buildings and are significantly more atmospheric than anything beyond the walls. For cheap eats, try the stalls just within the walls on the eastern edge of Intramuros, or in nearby San Francisco St, in an area known as Puerta Isabel II.

MANILA'S FAST-FOOD CHAINS

Further evidence of the Americanisation of Filipino culture can be found in Manila's myriad fast-food chains – American ones abound, of course, but there are some interesting local ones, a few of which have become part of the national fabric. Then there are also the Asian chains – *Marugame Udon* from Japan, *Mister Donut* from the US (via Japan), *Bonchon* chicken from Korea (via the US), and *Bread Talk* bakery from Singapore.

Chowking ⓦchowking.ph. Cheap Filipino Chinese cuisine; "filling" is probably the best description, but it's actually not that bad.
Bo's Coffee ⓦboscoffee.com. Though this café chain actually started life in Cebu, it's easy to track one down in Manila; they always have a good variety of local beans, and the coffees are generally great.
Goldilocks ⓦgoldilocks.com.ph. Purveyors of the best *polvoron* (peanut candy) and cakes since 1966.

Jolibee ⓦjolibee.com.ph. The undisputed national favourite – Filipinos living overseas will always be able to tell you exactly how many Jolibees there are in their adopted city. Fried chicken is the main draw, particularly the signature Chickenjoy.
Mang Inasal ⓦmanginasal.ph. You'll see this chain's yellow signs anywhere that has lots of people around – malls, intersections, etc. Grilled chicken is the name of the game here.

1

RESTAURANTS

Barbara's Plaza San Luis Complex, General Luna St ⓦbarbaras.ph. Elegant dining in a colonial setting, with woody interiors and rich Filipino and Spanish food pioneered by founder Barbara de los Reyes in the 1970s. Best known for its touristy buffets, and the nightly Kultura Filipina traditional music and dance shows. **PPP**

★ **Ilustrado** 744 General Luna St at the back of Silahis Center, facing Cabildo St ⓦfacebook.com/ ilustradorestaurant. Nothing compares to *Ilustrado* if you're looking for the ambience of colonial Manila. The floors are polished wood, the tables are set with starched linen, ceiling fans whirr quietly and the cuisine is grand. Signature dishes include paella, creamy *bagnet* (deep-fried pork) and tender *lengua con setas* (ox tongue with brown sauce). **PPPP**

Patio de Conchita 681 Beaterio St ⓦfacebook.com/ patio.d.conchita. This great find is off the beaten path but an excellent place to have lunch, offering tasty budget menus. Food is served buffet style, with a range of top-notch Filipino dishes; try the *sinigang na baboy* (sour soup with pork) and freshly barbecued squid. **PP**

CAFÉS AND DESSERTS

Kuatro Kantos 744 General Luna St ☎02 527 2345. This charming little bar and café in the same old building (with same owners) as *Ilustrado* (see page 88) serves all-days breakfasts and other light meals – perfect for a good cup of coffee or a bite to eat while you're wandering around Intramuros. The hot *ensaymada* (a bun with grated cheese on top) makes for a modest treat, and is served with a cup of deliciously thick hot chocolate. **PP**

ERMITA AND MALATE, SEE MAP PAGE 71

RESTAURANTS

★ **Aristocrat** 432 San Andres St, facing Roxas Blvd ⓦaristocratph.com. Established out of an old van in 1936, and now a sizeable restaurant, *Aristocrat* is an institution among Filipinos for its justly lauded barbecued chicken and pork, as well as the whole spread of Filipino comfort food. The special *halo-halo* here is an extravagant concoction of taro ice cream, sliced banana, beans, *nata de coco*, ice and evaporated milk. **PPP**

Bistro Remedios 1911 M. Adriatico St, just off Remedios Circle ☎02 8523 9153. Informal and homely restaurant with pretty Filipiniana interior and charming staff. The food is exclusively Filipino, with cholesterol-filled *pata* (fried pigs' knuckles) and *lechon kawali sa gata* (beef stew and fried pork in coconut milk). There's also good fish and prawns, but not a great deal for vegetarians. **PPP**

Cabalen Robinsons Place (G/F, Padre Faura Wing), Pedro Gil St at M. Adriatico ☎02 536 7987. Hugely popular chain of restaurants famed for their gut-busting buffets of traditional dishes from the province of Pampanga, including *camaru* (rice-field crickets), *batute* (fried pig's trotters), *kuhol* (escargots), *sinigang tiyan ng bangus* (milkfish belly) and desserts such as *halayang ube* (purple yam pudding). You'll find a branch in most malls. **PP**

Café Adriatico 1790 M. Adriatico St ⓦfacebook.com/ CafeAdriatico. This chic but casual stalwart of the Malate nightlife scene opened back in 1979, and was at the forefront of the area's revival. Light Spanish-Mediterranean themed meals include salads, omelettes and fondues. Try the authentic *chocolate-eh*, a thick chocolatey drink served as an anytime "snack". **PPP**

Casa Armas 573 J. Nakpil St at J. Bocobo St ⓦfacebook. com/casaarmasmalate. This Spanish restaurant and tapas bar serves big plates of prawns sautéed in olive oil and garlic and Galician-style octopus, as well as more substantial dishes such as a full paella (serves 2–3 people). **PPP**

Dads Saisaki Kamayan 523 Padre Faura St at Adriatico St ⓦfacebook.com/dadsworldbuffet. Excellent-value buffet restaurant with three sections: a traditional selection of Filipino dishes such as grilled fish, spicy crab, roast chicken and local vegetables; a Western section with more conventional roast beef and the like; and a Japanese area with sushi, tempura and noodles. The staff are dressed in elegant Filipino costumes and strolling minstrels work the tables doing requests. **PPP**

Harbor View South Gate A, Rizal Park ⓦfacebook. com/harborviewrestaurantmanila. Located right on the harbour, between the US Embassy and *Manila Hotel*, this place is perfect for sunset viewing, with cool breezes, fresh seafood from the tank and all the classic Filipino dishes. It's a bit like a posh beach bar. **PPP**

Royal Korean Restaurant Guerrero St, Malate ⓦfacebook.com/royalkoreanrestaurant. One of a number of excellent Korean restaurants in the area, in part serving the growing number of Koreans here on nights out. The large menu includes some good dishes to share, such as fried beef, chicken or fish, and various side dishes including a truly excellent tangy *kimchi*. **PPP**

Yue Lai Seafood and Hotpot Restaurant 1668 A. Mabini St, Ermita ⓦfacebook.com/NewYue LaiSeafoodandHotpotRestaurant. Well-established and extremely popular restaurant, serving up tasty portions of authentic Chinese dishes – expect all the classics, as well as a few unexpectedly options such as sizzling frog's legs and crispy pork with raspberry sauce. **PPP**

STREET FOOD AND MARKETS

Pancit ng Taga Malabon 1025 Maria Orosa St ⓦpancitngtagamalabon.com. The chain that claims descent from the original *Pancit Malabon* stall in the 1890s, when the addictive concoction of oysters, squid, shrimp, smoked fish (*tinapa*), deep-fried pigskin (*chicharon*), crab and duck eggs over thick rice noodles and golden sauce became known as "*pancit bame*". Malabon was the location of the stall, and the name has since been applied to noodle dishes nationwide. P̱

Shawarma Snack Center 484 Salas St ⓦfacebook.com/SSCPhilippines. This unprepossessing place with plastic tables and chairs offers superb and plentiful Middle Eastern dishes, with possibly the best falafels and kebabs in the city, and certainly the hottest chilli sauce. Located in a small Muslim enclave in Malate, replete with halal food and a small mosque just off the road. P̱P̱

CAFÉS AND DESSERTS

Advocafé G/F, Ramon Magsaysay Complex, Dr F. Quintos St ⓦadvocafe.com. Excellent Filipino-grown arabica coffee, home-made cookies and light meals at this cool little café, where you can also buy coffee beans and organic herbal teas. Profits go to the coffee-bean farmers and their Indigenous communities up in the bundoks. P̱

MAKATI, SEE MAPS PAGES 60, 75 AND 76

Makati is the best place in the city when it comes to quality and variety of restaurants, especially around P. Burgos St. Bonifacio Global City, to the east, is an emerging destination for mostly high-end restaurants.

RESTAURANTS

Alba 38-B Polaris St, Bel-Air ⓦalba.com.ph. Cosy Spanish restaurant with faux adobe walls and a wandering guitarist who croons at your table. Dishes include tasty tapas, a large menu of paellas (most serve two), and plenty of fish and seafood. There's also a deli counter selling Spanish-style cold cuts. P̱P̱P̱P̱

Barrio Fiesta Makati Ave at Valdez St ☎0917 328 5805. There are various branches of this colourful Filipino chain restaurant dotted around the city, serving favourites such as crispy *pata*, *kare kare*, barbecued pork and *lechon*, with hefty portions of rice and daily buffet options. P̱P̱

★ **Blackbird** 1229 Makati Ave ⓦblackbird.com.ph. Set in an Art Deco building of 1937 vintage (with its own interesting history, detailed on a plaque outside), this fancy restaurant provides a mix of European and South East Asian dishes, all exquisitely prepared. It's better to dress up a bit for dinner, though lunchtimes are more casual. P̱P̱P̱P̱

★ **Chef Jessie's Place** Rockwell Center, Amorsolo Dr ⓦchefjessie.com. Mingle with Manila's upper class in this temple to fine dining. Top chef Jessie Sincioco (who made a meal for Pope Francis during his visit in 2015) crafts modern Filipino cuisine such as crunchy pork *sisig* (pig's ear) with mayonnaise, Japanese dishes, pasta, steaks and her famous dessert soufflés (the chocolate flavour is hard to beat). One of the top foodie places in the city. P̱P̱P̱P̱

Helm by Josh Boutwood 3/F, Ayala Triangle Gardens, Makati Ave ⓦjoshboutwood.net. An intimate restaurant in one of the area's swankier malls (though one still largely empty at the time of writing), Helm offers a high-end tasting menu with unique and delicious courses, paired with impeccable service and great wine choices. One for a special occasion. P̱P̱P̱P̱

Hossein's 2/F, LKV Building, Makati Ave ⓦhosseins.com. This glitzy take on a kebab house has froufrou decor and prices to match. If you're not in the mood for a brain sandwich, you can choose from dozens of Persian, Arabian and Indian dishes (with a huge range of curry and kebabs). P̱P̱

Lugang Café G/F Glorietta 2, Ayala Center ⓦlugangcafe.com.ph. This renowned Chinese restaurant offers magnificent Taiwanese food, pork buns and *xiaolong bao* (pork dumplings); you'll find branches in malls citywide, of which this is the most central. Others can be found in SM Mall of Asia in Pasay and SM North EDSA at the northern end of Quezon. P̱P̱P̱

New Bombay G/F, Sagittarius Building III, 312 H.V. Dela Costa St ☎02 8804 3788. Speak to Indian residents in Manila and most will tell you that this functional little restaurant is peerless for authentic Indian food. The menu is extensive and includes snacks such as mixed pakora, samosas, curries and freshly prepared naan, roti and chapati. Cheap, cheerful and very tasty. P̱P̱

Old Swiss Inn 7912 Makati Ave at Olympia Towers ⓦoldswissinn.com. Traditional food (including a heavenly Gruyère fondue), jolly alpine decor and waitresses in

MANILA'S FOOD MARKETS

Food markets are scattered throughout the city, from no-frills street stalls to air-conditioned food courts in Manila's poshest malls – cuisine runs the gamut from Filipino snacks to high-end sushi. In general, you'll be spending a lot less here than at sit-down restaurants, with small portions meaning plenty of scope for sampling different vendors. At the more salubrious end of the scale, you can try the Power Plant Mall (see page 90) on the edge of Makati; the St Francis Square Mall (see page 91) in Ortigas lies at the more budget end of the spectrum, and Fiesta Market (see page 90) in Bonifacio Global City somewhere in the middle. On Saturdays, there's also the Salcedo Community Market (see page 90) in Makati.

milkmaids' costumes – this place is as Swiss as it comes. The 24hr menu also includes the classic *gnagi* (pork knuckles) and Zurich *geschnetzeltes* (shredded pork). PPP

Sentro 1771 G/F Greenbelt 5 ⓦsentro1771.com. Modern Filipino restaurant that's packed with office workers at lunchtime, and the pre-cinema crowd in the evenings. The menu includes modern variations of classics such as pork adobo, pancit and Bicol Express (spicy stew); the speciality is *sinigang na* corned beef (sour stew with corned beef). PPP

Thai-Noy 5022 P. Burgos St ⓦthai-noy.com. Attractive Thai restaurant with a youthful vibe, and appropriately a few fusion items among its roster of Thai staples – burgers, tacos, wantons and the like. A fun evening spot, and they serve plenty of alcohol too. PPP

Toyo 2316 Chino Roces Avenue ⓦfacebook.com/toyoeatery. An outstanding Filipino restaurant, owned by the high-profile chef Jordy Navarra, this fantastic place is well worth the splurge. The eight course tasting menu, complete with paired drinks, is a genuine treat. Book ahead. PPPP

Ziggurat G/F Sunette Tower Building, Euphrates St at Tigris St ⓦzigguratcuisine.com. A seemingly endless menu featuring exotic dishes from the Middle East, Mediterranean and East Africa (try the meze combos, or the dangling grilled meat fantastically named the "Hanging Gardens of Ke-Babylon"), with flavoured hookahs to round things off. PP

STREET FOOD AND MARKETS

Next Door Noodles 7876 Makati Ave ⓦfacebook.com/NextDoorNoodlesPH. Cheap-and-cheerful Chinese restaurant, whose dishes (not just noodles, but that's what most go for) are fantastic value. It's a sister restaurant of *North Park Noodles* down the road, which has a similar menu at the same low prices. P

Power Plant Mall Rockwell Drive at Estrella St ⓦfacebook.com/PowerPlantMall. For a large and slightly upmarket selection of restaurants and stalls, check out this plush mall on the edge of Makati. There's also a huge Rustan's supermarket (same hours), a good choice for self-catering. P

Razon's of Guagua 22 Jupiter St ☏02 8897 2481. Lauded Pampanga-style *halo-halo* and *pancit luglug* (fried noodles) chain, with chicken or pork *asado*. PP

Salcedo Community Market Jaime Velasquez Park, Bel-Air ⓦfacebook.com/SalcedoCommunityMarket. One of Manila's culinary highlights, featuring a dazzling display of gastronomic delights from all corners of the Philippines to take away or enjoy at one of the communal tables. Saturdays only. P

CAFÉS AND DESSERTS

★**Tsokolateria** 2/F Greenbelt 5 ⓦinstagram.com/tsokolateria. Part of a local chain, though surely with the best location, looking at the trees of the Greenbelt

parkland in a relatively calm part of the complex. There's a wide menu of modern Filipino food, but most are here for the chocolate – they have no fewer than nine different options for hot chocolate, including bitter, served-into-ice-cream, and (oddly) poured-through-chocolate-disk-onto-fried-pork-belly. Everything's beautifully served, with the receptacles also gorgeous; coffees, shakes and desserts (not *all* chocolate) round out a pleasing picture. PP

BONIFACIO GLOBAL CITY, SEE MAP PAGE 78

RESTAURANTS

Abe Serendra Plaza, Bonifacio Global City ⓦfacebook.com/AbePhilippines. Most taxi drivers will know this much-loved Filipino restaurant (Pampanga-style), where the two highlights are Abe's chicken supreme (chicken stuffed with *galapong* rice, chestnuts and raisins) and mutton adobo with popped garlic. Other dishes utilize forest ferns, banana plant, tiny crabs and fabulous pork knuckle. PPP

★**Brotzeit** G/F Shangri-La, 30th St ⓦbrotzeit.ph. A really good German restaurant catering to Europeans missing their bread – hence the name – and an increasing number of locals. The menu is pan-German but with a slight Bavarian skew; dishes are mostly rather filling, but if you're only peckish try sausage soup with a warm pretzel, or a goulash. Plenty of beer, too. PPP

Gallery by Chele 5/F Clipp Center, 11th Ave at 39th St ⓦgallerybychele.com. For a splurge, try one of the fabulous tasting menus at this stylishly minimalist restaurant, where each of the delicious courses is expertly paired with outstanding cocktails. There's also an a la carte menu available. It's wise to book in advance; the place is also kind of hidden, located as it is on the fifth floor of an ordinary-looking office building. PPPP

★**Manam** 9th Ave, Uptown Mall ⓦmanam.momentfood.com. This increasingly popular chain offers classic and well-loved dishes as well as twists on old favourites; you'll have to queue to get into most branches, but this BGC one generally has seats free, despite being the most attractive *Manam* in the city. The pork *sisig* with garlic rice, the *pancit palabok* and the watermelon sinigang are particularly recommended; for dessert, have a go at their *ube champorado* (sweet potato porridge, which looks infinitely more attractive than it may sound!), or a tall *halo-halo*. PPP

STREET FOOD AND MARKETS

Fiesta Market Mabini Ave at McKinley Parkway, Bonifacio Global City. The spotless, high-end *Market! Market!* mall has tempting fresh-fruit stalls and a massive, covered food court on its southern side. P

CAFÉS AND DESSERTS

Elephant Grounds G/F One Bonifacio High St

w facebook.com/ElephantGroundsPH. One of the area's most attractive cafés, and popular with moneyed young locals; all of their coffee servings are double-shot, while they also have masala chai, matcha latte and other options, plus good cakes. PP

ORTIGAS, SEE MAPS PAGES 60 AND 79

RESTAURANTS
Minami Saki Julia 15 Escriva Dr w astoriaplaza.com. Next door to – but effectively part of – Astoria Plaza hotel (see page 86), this stylish spot serves Japanese food that's surprisingly good, and pleasingly cheap, for a hotel restaurant. Their kara-age (fried chicken) is excellent, as are the tofu steaks, rice bowls and California rolls, while there's a full roster of sushi to choose from. PPP

STREET FOOD AND MARKETS
St Francis Square Mall Julia Vargas Ave at Bank Drive w stfrancissquare.com.ph. The alley along the east side of this budget mall is cheap-eats paradise at lunchtime, with huge pots of delicious Filipino food dolled out for a few pesos. Inside St Francis Mall itself, the 3/F Food Court is another excellent place for local food (with a/c). P

QUEZON CITY, SEE MAPS PAGES 60 AND 80

Quezon City is a burgeoning alternative to Makati and the Manila Bay area for restaurants and nightlife. To get to Quezon from the south of the city (Malate and Makati, for example), you can take the MRT to Kamuning or Quezon Avenue.

RESTAURANTS
Bellini's 3 General Romulo Ave t 02 8913 2550. For excellent, no-nonsense Italian food, Bellini's is the leader of the pack. The pasta dishes are particularly delicious, but the

pizzas aren't half bad either, and there's a good wine list. The place is decorated floor to ceiling with remarkable murals, some of them executed with considerable more skill than others. PPP

Frazzled Cook 78 Gandia St at Tomas Morato w the frazzledcook.net. Set in a relatively urbane part of Quezon, this shabby-chic purveyor of legendary paella negra (serves two people) serves an otherwise eclectic menu including squash soup, spicy lamb stew and scampi pizza. PPP

Gerry's Grill 24 Tomas Morato Ave at Eugenio Lopez Drive w gerrysgrill.com. This is the original outlet of the now popular chain, serving provincial Filipino dishes such as crispy pata (pig's knuckle) and sisig (fried pig's ear and pig's face). They also make a mean halo-halo. PP

Greens 104 Scout Lozano St w greensresto.com. Bargain-priced vegan and vegetarian food, from soups and salads to wraps, pasta and shepherd's pie with neither shepherd nor sheep. PP

STREET FOOD AND MARKETS
Behrouz 50 Scout Tobias St w behrouzpersian.shop. Great late-night hole-in-the-wall snack place, run by a family of Iranians who cook authentic food. The lamb kebabs, beef kobideh (ground-beef kebabs) and aubergine-based moutabal (baba ghanoush) are all superb. No alcohol. PP

★ **Lydia's Lechon** 116 Timog Ave w lydias-lechon.com. The lechon at this local favourite is delicious (especially the boneless variety with paella), but the secret is the sauce – a sweet, barbecue concoction that will have you hooked. The meat is priced per quarter kilo, though you can get chunks of it in smaller lunchbox-style dishes (which are actually pretty big). PP

CAFÉS AND DESSERTS
High Grounds 67 Sct Rallos St w facebook.com/high groundsofficial. Large, decent café in an area without too much to choose from in the coffee department. PP

DRINKING AND NIGHTLIFE

Few visitors to Manila are disappointed by the buoyant, gregarious nature of its **bars** and **clubs**. This is a city that rarely sleeps and one that offers a full range of fun, from the offbeat watering holes of Malate to the chic wine bars of Makati. Manila also has a thriving **live music** scene, with dozens of bars hosting very popular and accomplished local bands almost every night. Clubs are especially prone to open, close and change names with frequency, so check before you head out.

BARS

INTRAMUROS, SEE MAP PAGE 66
Lobby Lounge Manila Hotel, 1 Rizal Park w manila-

hotel.com.ph. It's worth grabbing a coffee or artfully constructed cocktail in this elegant lobby bar, even if you're not staying at the Manila Hotel – it's one of the few places redolent of the city's golden age, with capiz chandeliers, narra wood ceiling and marble floors.

ERMITA AND MALATE, SEE MAP PAGE 71
Nightlife in Ermita and Malate comprises a somewhat confusing mixture of budget restaurants, genuine pubs and a once again flourishing go-go bar scene. Don't make the mistake of arriving early – most places don't even warm up until after 10pm and are still thumping when the sun comes up, with crowds in summer spilling out onto the streets. Friday, as always, is the big night; many places are closed

1

on Sunday.

Café Roo 465 Remedios St, Malate ⓦfacebook.com/ caferooph. Popular rooftop bar which gets pretty lively in the evenings; beer and cocktails are available, and they churn out some decent food, too.

Music 21 Plaza 514 General Malvar St ⓦmusic21plaza. ph. The enduring popularity of karaoke bars means that you should consider dropping in on one, even if only once. Music 21 Plaza is as good a choice as any, with bright, almost psychedelic, colours in the lobby and a selection of private rooms where you can unleash your inner P-Pop star.

Tap Station 1313 Adriatico St ☎02 5310 2174. A microbrewery bar with a big selection of their own beers, including IPAs, brown ales and stouts. The brews are interesting, but a bit hit-and-miss; ask for a sample before you plump for one. They also show English football on the TV.

MAKATI, SEE MAPS PAGES 76 AND 75

Makati nightlife used to revolve around office workers spilling out of the nearby banks and skyscrapers, but these days much of middle-class Manila parties in the bars and clubs here, with plenty of expats and travellers thrown in – it's generally smarter, safer and more fashionable than Malate. The area around P. Burgos St is a bit seedier, though the go-go bar scene here is being driven more by Korean and Japanese KTV-style joints these days, and there are several genuine pubs in between offering cheap beers and snacks.

Annex House 5638 Don Pedro ⓦannex-house.com. Speakeasy-style bar with a youthful vibe, occasional DJ nights – and, if you're in luck, cheap "bottomless" deals.

Antidote Roofdeck, I'M Hotel, 7862 Ave ⓦimhotel. com. There are fantastic views over the city from this rooftop bar – even from the bathroom. The bar staff mix excellent cocktails, served with a performative flourish. There's also decent if not outstanding food, and the place prides itself on being the city's first "jellyfish bar" – you'll probably see why quite quickly.

A Toda Madre G/F Sunette Tower, Durban St ⓦatoda madretequila.com. A lively little tequila bar-cum-mezcaleria with proper, quality tequilas (such as Herradura and Don Julio), as well as, for your mixing-grade spirit, the promise of "not your typical margarita". In case that isn't enough, there are tacos and quesadillas too. ¡Ándele!

★ **The Fun Roof** 4/F Mateus Building, 5382 General Luna ⓦthefunroof.com. Fun Roof by name, fun roof by nature – this bar allows guests to enjoy activities such as baseball and mini golf while they're drinking, which often results in chaos.

H&J Sports Bar and Restaurant Felipe St ⓦfacebook. com/HjSportsBarAndRestaurantMakati. For many years this bar has boasted the same laidback vibe that's popular with expats, live blues and rock bands (nightly), Indian food, pool tables and TVs showing live English Premier League football.

Handlebar 31 Polaris St ⓦhandlebar.com.ph. Hospitable biker bar owned by a group of Harley fanatics. It's primarily for drinkers (with lots of sport on the TVs) but the food also makes it worth a visit. The menu is nothing exotic, just solid, satisfying pizzas, burgers and pasta.

Society Lounge G/F Atrium Building, Makati Ave at Paseo de Roxas ⓦfacebook.com/societylounge makatiavenue. Plush French-Asian fusion restaurant that morphs into trendy lounge bar every night, with plenty of fine wines and champagnes on offer. DJs spin house music at the weekends, when it becomes more like a club.

★ **Z Hostel** 5660 Don Pedro ⓦzhostel.com. Even if you've taken the lift as far as it goes, you'll still have to scurry the remaining way up to this excellent hostel's rooftop bar (see page 86). The views of Makati, and across the BGC, are pretty jaw-dropping even though the place isn't all that high up; drinks are cheap, there's no entry fee, and there are regular DJ nights.

QUEZON CITY, SEE MAP PAGE 80

Quezon City's entertainment district is focused on Tomas Morato and Timog avenues, which intersect at the roundabout in front of *Imperial Palace Suites* hotel. The area has a reputation for quality live music (see page 92), while for more mainstream nightlife there are plenty of chic bars and franchised hangouts at the southern end of Tomas Morato Ave, near the junction with Don A. Roces Ave.

Big Sky Mind 66 Broadway Ave ⓦfacebook.com/ Bigskymind. A dive bar that has been servicing Quezon's low-key types for decades; occasional live music.

Quattro 96 Timog Ave ☎02 8928 1681. Boisterous beer hall chain that serves very average Filipino food, although most guests are too drunk to care. One of Quezon City's most enjoyable places for a drink.

LIVE MUSIC BARS AND VENUES

Quezon City in particular has a reputation for live music, especially from up-and-coming bands formed by students from the nearby University of the Philippines, with an eclectic range of music, from pure Western pop to grunge, reggae and Indigenous styles. Many of the venues in this area are dark, sweaty places that open late and don't close until the last guest leaves. Note that the venues listed here are known primarily for live music, but in Makati and Malate you're never far from a bar or club with a live band, especially at weekends.

ERMITA AND MALATE, SEE MAP PAGE 71

Bamboo Giant 802a San Andres St at Quirino and Taft Ave ☎02 8528 4558. Acoustic bands play most nights in this beach-bar-style bamboo shack. It's easy going, with a chilled vibe, reasonably cold beers, and food if you want it.

Bedrock Unit B, Bellagio Square, J Bacobo St ☎ 02 8256 5586. A rather nondescript little bar for most of the week, but on Fri and Sat evenings it takes over this little square, with live music on stage.

Cowboy Grill 1140 A. Mabini St ⓦ cowboygrill.ph. This place with a Wild West theme has regular musical performances from live bands – it's loud, raucous and great fun, even if the quality of the bands is sometimes a little suspect. The food and beer are surprisingly decent.

MAKATI, SEE MAP PAGE 76

Pardon My French 110 Jupiter St, Makati ⓦ facebook. com/pardonmyfrenchmanila. A party-like atmosphere greets nightly bands at this Makati restaurant, which puts on mostly pop and 70s/80s nights, but also old-school jazz from time to time.

SaGuijo 7612 Guijo St, San Antonio, Makati ⓦ facebook. com/SaGuijo.Cafe.Bar.Events. This hip, arty bar is the best indie venue in Manila, with both its live music (most nights) and art gallery supporting up-and-coming talents. Effortlessly cool, but not pretentious with it.

QUEZON CITY, SEE MAPS PAGES 60 AND 80

The 70s Bistro 46 Anonas St, Quezon City ⓦ facebook. com/The70sBistro. Legendary (in the Philippines) live music venue that plays host to some of the country's best-known bands as well as to impromptu jam sessions with big local names who happen to turn up – a great Manila experience. The only problem is it's a bit tricky to find: Anonas St is off Aurora Blvd on the eastern side of EDSA.

Music Museum Service Rd, Greenhills, San Juan ⓦ musicmuseum.com.ph. This "leisure-entertainment hub" hosts concerts, comedy shows, ballet, theatre and poetry readings, but the music is still the main attraction;

performers are mostly popular Filipino pop and rock acts.

Smart Araneta Coliseum Gen. Araneta at Gen. McArthur, Quezon City ⓦ aranetacoliseum.com. This huge stadium (aka "Big Dome") is the usual venue for large-scale events and concerts, everything from Taylor Swift and Bryan Adams to Disney on Ice.

CLUBS

PASAY, SEE MAP PAGE 74

House Manila 20 Newport Blvd, Pasay ⓦ facebook. com/HouseManilaOfficial. With regular appearances from both local and international DJs, House Manila is one of the city's leading clubs for those hoping to spend the night grooving to EDM and Top 40 hits. If you're not up for dancing, the pool tables might provide an alternative distraction.

BONIFACIO GLOBAL CITY, SEE MAP PAGE 78

XYLO The Palace, 11th Ave at 38th St, Fort Bonifacio ⓦ facebook.com/XYLOatThePalace. This huge dance club – the city's biggest and glitziest – is just one part of a huge clubbing complex that includes a more mature lounge club, a daytime pool club and more. All of them aim for elegance and attract a well-heeled clientele, so leave your trainers at home and dress to impress, but don't forget your wallet.

QUEZON CITY, SEE MAP PAGE 80

Café 80s Sgt. Esguerra Ave, Diliman, Quezon City ⓦ facebook.com/Cafe80sBarandResto. If you've packed your shoulder pads and legwarmers, head straight to Café 80s to relive the glory days. By day, this café serves up decent but unremarkable food; after nightfall, the glitter ball comes out and it's a non-stop 80s disco.

ENTERTAINMENT

For **listings**, try newspapers such as the *Philippine Daily Inquirer* (ⓦ inquirer.net) and the *Philippine Star* (ⓦ philstar. com), which have entertainment sections with details of movies, concerts and arts events in Manila. Daily shows

LGBTQ+ NIGHTLIFE IN MANILA

The **LGBTQ+ scene** in Manila has been vibrant for many years. Even bars and clubs that aren't obviously gay are unreservedly welcoming and the LGBTQ+ community mixes easily and boisterously in the same nightclubs and bars. Traditionally, the gay nightlife scene centred on Malate, but that's by and large no longer the case. Other LGBTQ+ resources are covered in Basics (see page 51).

Club Mwah 3/F The Venue Tower, 652 Bonifacio Ave, Mandaluyong City ⓦ facebook.com/Club MwahOfficial; see map page 60. Club, bar and theatre featuring a burlesque trans show dubbed "Folliespiniana", based on traditional dances and "Las Vegas-Moulin Rouge" inspired acts.

O Bar Ortigas Home Depot, Doña Julia Vargas Ave,

Ortigas ⓦ instagram.com/OBarPhilippines; see map page 60. Its claim to be the home of Asia's finest dancing drag queens may be a slight exaggeration, but you get the idea: drag shows, male go-go dancers and male pole dancers. It's very popular and always crowded, especially on weekends.

1

of **traditional performing arts** (see box, page 94) are hosted at the Cultural Center of the Philippines and a handful of other venues. As for **films**, every mall seems to have half a dozen screens, and international movies are rarely dubbed. Good resources for checking upcoming events include Ticketworld (ⓦticketworld.com.ph) and TicketNet (ⓦticketnet.com.ph), on both of which you can buy tickets in advance, as well as listings websites such as ⓦclickthecity.com.

CABARET AND BURLESQUE

Amazing Show Manila Film Center, Jose W. Diokno Blvd, Pasay ⓦamazingshow.net. Fun transvestite musical variety show in the Manila Film Center (see box, page 73), involving singing, dancing and comedy skits, especially popular with Korean tourists.

THEATRE, DANCE AND CLASSICAL MUSIC

Cultural Center of the Philippines Roxas Blvd, Malate ⓦculturalcenter.gov.ph. Events here range from art exhibitions to Broadway musicals, pop concerts, classical concerts by the Philippine Philharmonic Orchestra, *tinikling* and *kundiman* (see box, below). The CCP is also home to the Tanghalang Aurelio Tolentino (CCP Little Theater), where smaller dramatic productions are staged and films shown; Ballet Philippines; Bayanihan, the National Folk Dance Company; and the CCP's resident theatre group, Tanghalang Pilipino, dedicated to the production of original Filipino

plays. Nearby is the Folk Arts Theater (Tanghalang Francisco Balagtas), built for the Miss Universe Pageant in 1974 and now staging occasional rock concerts and drama.

Meralco Theater Meralco Ave, Ortigas ☎02 631 2222. Stages everything from ballet and musicals by overseas companies to pantomimes with local celebs. Check websites such as ⓦticketworld.com.ph for the latest shows.

Paco Park/Rizal Park "Paco Park Presents" hosts free classical concerts every Fri evening, performed under the stars in the historic cemetery (see page 74); Rizal Park (see page 70) stages similar free "Concerts at the Park" every Sun.

CINEMAS

Arthouse cinema A venue for arthouse and independent films is the UP Cine Adarna (ⓦfilminstitute.upd.edu. ph), UPFI Film Center building at Magsaysay and Osmeña avenues to the northeast of Quezon Memorial Circle, but screenings don't take place every day, so check before you head out there.

Multiplex cinemas Most shopping malls in Manila house multiplex cinemas that show all the Hollywood and Asian blockbusters in the original languages, including The Podium mall (12 ADB Ave, Ortigas; ☎02 633 8976), Greenbelt 3 in Makati (☎02 729 7777) and Power Plant Mall, Rockwell Drive, Makati (ⓦpowerplantcinema.com). In the Malate area, try Robinsons Place in M. Adriatico St (☎02 397 7020). Tickets for cinemas in the Greenbelt and Glorietta malls can be reserved online at ⓦsureseats.com.

SPORTS

BOWLING

Playdium Bowling Center Gregorio Araneta Ave, Quezon City ⓦfacebook.com/bowling.playdium. Also has billiards tables.

Superbowl 3/F Makati Square, Chino Roces Ave, Makati ⓦfacebook.com/SuperbowlOfficial.

GOLF

There are a few golf courses in Manila where non-members

can turn up and pay for a round – it's usually first come, first served (which means waits of 1–2hr at weekends). You can book ahead on ⓦgolfph.com.

Army Golf Club (Kagitingan) Bayani Rd, Fort Bonifacio, south of Makati ☎02 8812 7431. Boasts some of the lowest green fees in the country.

Club Intramuros Bonifacio Drive at Soriano St (formerly Aduana St), Intramuros ⓦclubintramurosgolfcourse.com. This has basic facilities, and a short eighteen-hole course

FILIPINO FOLK ARTS

The Philippines has a rich folk arts heritage, but a scarcity of funds and committed audiences with money to spend on tickets means it's in danger of being forgotten. Folk dances such as **tinikling**, which sees participants hopping at increasing speed between heavy bamboo poles that are struck together at shin height, are seen in cultural performances for tourists, but are only performed occasionally in theatres. The same goes for **kundiman**, a genre of music that reached its zenith at the beginning of the twentieth century, and combines elements of tribal music with contemporary lovelorn lyrics to produce epic songs of love and loss. To see if anything is on, check out websites like ⓦticketworld.com.ph. The CCP sometimes puts on shows (see page 72); otherwise your best bet is to join the tourists at restaurants such as *Barbara's* (see page 88).

1

SPECTATOR SPORTS

Because the PBA (Philippine Basketball Association) teams are owned by corporations, and do not play in a home stadium, most **basketball** games are played at the Smart Araneta Coliseum in Cubao (see page 93) and the Mall of Asia Arena at SM Mall of Asia in Pasay (ⓦ www.mallofasia-arena.com); games usually run on Wednesday, Friday and Sunday from October to July. Tickets are available from ⓦ ticketnet.com.ph or ⓦ pba.inquirer.net.

that runs along the walls of the old city – rather unique.
Villamor Golf Course Jesus Villamor Air Base, Pasay ☎ 02

853 4978. Home of the Philippine Masters.

SHOPPING

The combination of intense heat and dense traffic means many Manileños forsake the pleasures of the outdoors at weekends for the computer-controlled climate of their local **mall** – there can be few cities that have as many malls per head as this one. Note that the developers rarely pay as much attention to the surrounding roads as they do to their precious real estate, which means that traffic is especially gridlocked in these areas. Despite the growth of malls, there are still plenty of earthy outdoor **markets** in Manila, where you can buy food, antiques and gifts at rock-bottom prices, as well as some decent bookshops and fashion boutiques.

BOOKS

Biblio Level 3, Ayala Malls One, Makati ⓦ powerbooks. com.ph; see map page 76. A good range of second-hand books, sometimes available in very cheap bundles.
National Book Store (NBS) G/F Harrison Plaza, M. Adriatico St; Level 1 Robinsons Place, Ermita; and in malls citywide ⓦ nationalbookstore.com; see map page 71. The country's major bookshop chain, concentrating on contemporary thrillers, literary classics and *New York Times* bestsellers, with much of what's on offer stocked specifically for students.
★ **Solidaridad Bookshop** 531 Padre Faura St, Ermita ⓦ facebook.com/solidaridadbookshop; see map page 71. The bookshop with the best literary section in town, with a small selection of highbrow fiction and lots of material on the Philippines.

HANDICRAFTS AND SOUVENIRS

There are touristy shops all over Manila selling reproduction tribal art, especially *bulol* (sometimes spelt *bulul*) – depictions of rice gods, worshipped by northern Indigenous people because they are said to keep evil spirits from the home and bless farmers with a good harvest. Genuine *bulol* are made from *narra* wood and are dark and stained from the soot of tribal fires and from blood poured over them during sacrifices. Good places to pick up souvenirs are markets (see page 96) and the Silahis Center (see page 67).
Balikbayan Handicrafts 1010 Arnaiz Ave (Pasay Rd),

Makati ⓦ balikbayanhandicrafts.com; see map page 76. The first stop for tourists looking for Indigenous gifts and handicrafts is this large store, which sells a mind-boggling array of souvenirs, knick-knacks, home decorations, reproduction native-style carvings and jewellery, plus some larger items such as tribal chairs, drums and musical instruments. Staff can arrange to ship your purchases if requested.
Tesoros 1325 A. Mabini St, Ermita, see map page 71; 1016 Arnaiz Ave (Pasay Rd), Makati, see map page 76; ⓦ tesoros.ph. A handicraft chain selling woven tablecloths, fabrics, *barongs* and reproduction tribal crafts such as *bulol*. Not as big as Balikbayan, but more convenient from budget hotels in Ermita.

MALLS

Cubao Expo 33 Cubao Expo Dr, Quezon City; see map page 60. Megamalls haven't completely taken over Manila, and this active hub of independent retailers, a short walk from Cubao MRT station, has a slew of interesting shops selling vintage toys, skateboarding gear, vinyl records, guitars and bric-a-brac.
Glorietta Ayala Center, Ayala Ave, Makati ⓦ www. ayalamalls.com.ph; see map page 76. A maze of passageways spanning out from a central atrium, Glorietta has five sections, a large annex branch of Rustan's department store, and heaps of clothes and household goods. At the Makati Ave end of the complex is Landmark, a big, functional department store that sells inexpensive clothes and has a whole floor dedicated to children's goods. There's a food court on the third floor.
Greenbelt Ayala Center, Paseo de Roxas at Legaspi St, Makati ⓦ www.ayalamalls.com.ph; see map page 76. A huge, sprawling mall with five sections: Greenbelt 3 and 4 on Makati Ave are the most comfortable for a stroll and a spot of people watching. Most of the stores are well-known chains – Greenbelt 3 has the affordable stuff (including Nike and Adidas) and Greenbelt 4 is full of expensive big names such as Armani and Jimmy Choo. There are some excellent restaurants in Greenbelt 3 for all budgets and more designers in Greenbelt 5 (DKNY, Hilfiger).

1

DE-STRESSING MANILA: SPAS, STEAM AND SHIATSU

After a day sweating it out on Manila's congested streets, a couple of hours in a spa can be extremely tempting. Note also that many of the five-star hotels listed in "Accommodation" (see page 84) have excellent spas.

I'm Onsen Spa Kalayaan Ave, Makati ⓦimonsenspa. com. Good value – come when it's quiet on a weekday afternoon and it's a dreamy, tranquil place with a huge roster of massages. Banana-leaf massages (warm leaves are swept over the body) are particularly relaxing.

Royal Oriental Wellness 233 Nicanor Garcia, Makati ⓦroyalorientalwellness.com. Serene modern spa offering massages using a combination of Chinese and Swedish techniques, including hot stone massages, foot reflexology, and a Chinese mud paste medicinal treatment.

SM Mall of Asia J.W. Diokno Blvd (facing Manila Bay) ⓦsmsupermalls.com; see map page 74. This vast complex, the biggest in the Philippines, contains Manila's first IMAX, a seafront promenade, bowling alley, ice rink and hypermarket, as well as numerous restaurants and stores that appeal to a younger crowd. Any bus or minibus heading west on EDSA showing "MOA" or "Mall of Asia" will get you here.

MARKETS

Taking a taxi from one of Manila's opulent malls to a more traditional market district such as Quiapo or Divisoria is like going from New York to Guatemala in thirty minutes – the difference between the two worlds is shocking. Needless to say, prices in Manila's markets are a lot cheaper than in the malls.

168 Shopping Mall Santa Elena and Soler sts, Binondo ⓦ168shoppingmall.com; see map page 63. Technically a two-section mall but more like a market, with over a thousand stalls flooded with mostly Chinese-made leather hand-bags, jackets, T-shirts, wallets, caps, toys, shoes and clothes for incredibly low prices. Forms part of the Divisoria market district (see below). Daily 8am–8pm.

Baclaran market Pasay City; see map page 74. This labyrinthine street market is spread tentacle-like around the Baclaran LRT station; little stalls huddle under the LRT line as far as the EDSA station, and fill Dr Gabriel St as far west as Roxas Blvd. The focus throughout is cheap clothes and shoes of every hue, size and style, though you'll also come across fake designer watches and the like. The market is a big, noisy, pungent place, and often incredibly crowded,

but lots of fun. It's open all week but especially crowded every Wed, the so-called Baclaran Day, when devotees of Our Mother of Perpetual Help crowd into the Redemptorist Church on Dr Gabriel St for the weekly novena. Daily 24hr.

Divisoria Market District Claro M. Recto Ave, North Binondo; see map page 63. For a range of bargain goods, from fabric and Christmas decorations to clothes, candles, bags and hair accessories, try fighting your way through the crowds at the immense market district. The pretty lanterns (*parols*) made from capiz seashells that you see all over the country at Christmas cost half what you would pay in a mall. The actual Divisoria Mall is at Tabora and Santo Cristo streets, but it's the warren of streets around it that are good for bargains – especially Juan Luna, Ylaya, Tabora, Santo Cristo and Soler. Daily 24hr.

Greenhills Tiangge Greenhills Shopping Center, Ortigas Ave, San Juan ⓦgreenhills.com.ph; see map page 60. Sprawling market inside this mall north of Makati. There's attractive costume jewellery on sale, and an area full of stalls selling jewellery made with pearls from China and Mindanao. Other sections of the mall offer cheap mobile phones (some secondhand), household goods and home decor. Mon–Thurs 11am–9pm, Fri–Sun 10am–10pm.

Ilalim ng Tulay Quezon Blvd, Quiapo; see map page 63. Hunt down the cheapest woodcarvings, capiz-shell items, *buri* bags and embroidery in Manila among the ramshackle stalls beneath the underpass leading to Quezon Bridge in Quiapo (literally "under the bridge"); tell drivers "Quiapo Ilalim". Daily 24hr.

DIRECTORY

Banks and exchange Most major bank branches have 24hr ATMs for Visa and MasterCard cash advances. The moneychangers around Mabini St in Ermita, P. Burgos St in Makati, and in some malls offer better rates than the banks (but shop around as rates vary; moneychangers that display their rates are likely to give better ones than those that don't).

Embassies and consulates Australia, Level 23, Tower 2, RCBC Plaza, 6819 Ayala Ave, Makati ⓦphilippines.embassy.

gov.au; Canada, Levels 6–8, Tower 2, RCBC Plaza, 6819 Ayala Ave, Makati ⓦcanadainternational.gc.ca; Ireland, 3/F, 70 Jupiter St, Bel-Air 1, Makati ☎02 896 4668 ⓦdfa. ie; New Zealand, 35/F, Zuellig Building, Makati Ave at Paseo de Roxas, Makati ⓦmfat.govt.nz; UK, 120 Upper McKinley Rd, McKinley Hill, Taguig City ⓦgov.uk; US, 1201 Roxas Blvd ⓦph.usembassy.gov.

Emergencies ☎911, police ☎117.

Hospitals and clinics Makati Medical Center, 2 Amorsolo

St, Makati (☎ 02 888 8999, ⓦ makatimed.net.ph) is one of the largest and most modern hospitals in wider Manila. Others include: Manila Doctors Hospital, 667 United Nations Ave, Ermita (☎ 02 558 0888, ⓦ maniladoctors.com.ph); St Luke's Medical Center, 279 E. Rodriguez Sr Blvd, Quezon City (☎ 02 723 0101, ⓦ stlukes.com.ph).

Immigration For visa extensions, the Immigration Building is on Magellanes Drive, Intramuros (Mon–Fri 8am–noon & 1–5pm; ☎ 02 527 3257). There's a smaller office (same hours) in Makati at 385 Gil Puyat Ave ☎ 02 899 3831, where it's often faster and easier.

Laundry There are laundrettes absolutely all over the place – even if your accommodation doesn't offer the facility (or if it's absurdly expensive), they'll be able to let you know where to go.

Pharmacies You're never far from a Mercury Drug (ⓦ mercurydrug.com) outlet in Metro Manila – at the last count there were two hundred of them.

Around Manila

TAAL VOLCANO

Around Manila

Despite the proximity of the big city, the provinces that cluster around Metro Manila contain a surprisingly rich array of natural attractions. To the south lies stunning Lake Taal and its volcano, best approached from the refreshingly breezy city of Tagaytay, while further south, on the coast, Anilao offers outstanding scuba diving. North of Lake Taal, Los Baños is best known for its delicious *buko* (coconut) pie, hot springs and mountain pools, and sits not far from the churning waters of the Pagsanjan Falls, where you can take a thrilling – and soaking – raft ride downriver across a series of rapids. North of Manila you can climb the lush slopes of Mount Pinatubo, explore remote Bataan province, or enjoy the beaches and activities on offer at Subic Bay.

The region was also the scene of some of the nation's most important historical events. The island of **Corregidor**, out in Manila Bay, is littered with thought-provoking monuments to World War II, while **Malolos**, north of Manila, was where the Revolutionary Congress was convened in 1898. National heroes **Emilio Aguinaldo** and **José Rizal** were both born in the region, and their family homes are preserved as museums.

South of Manila

The provinces to the south of Manila – **Cavite**, **Laguna** and **Batangas** – are prime day-trip territory, being easy to get to and rich in attractions. The star is **Lake Taal**, a mesmerizing volcanic lake with its own mini volcanic island in the centre, but there are plenty of less-visited natural wonders that provide a break from the city; you can ride down the river to the **Pagsanjan Falls**, soak in the **Laguna hot springs** or clamber up forested **Mount Makiling** for scintillating views. Divers should check out **Anilao** for the best reef action near the capital.

The region also serves up a healthy dose of history. **Paete** has retained its woodworking heritage and **Taal** itself is one of the most beautiful colonial towns in the Philippines. Lastly, many Manileños come here just to eat; *buko* **pie** is an especially prized treat made in Laguna.

GETTING AROUND	SOUTH OF MANILA
By bus and jeepney Without a car, the easiest places to reach by public transport are the attractions to the south of Laguna de Bay, though Batangas City and Tagaytay are also well served by buses. The lakeside town of Santa Cruz is the main transport hub for the area. All the attractions between Calamba and Santa Cruz are served by JAC Liner	buses from Pasay in Manila. Note that the Santa Cruz bus terminals line the National Highway outside the town itself, in the barangay of Pagsawitan. Jeepneys ply the Calamba–Santa Cruz route. From Santa Cruz you can catch jeepneys on to Paete and Pagsanjan.

The Emilio Aguinaldo Shrine and Museum

Tirona Hwy, Kawit · Free · Take a Cavite-bound jeepney or FX taxi from Baclaran LRT station in Manila, but make sure it will stop at Kawit

For most Filipinos, the province of Cavite ("ka-vee-tay") will forever be associated with the Philippine Revolution: in 1872 the Cavite Mutiny precipitated the national revolt against the colonial authorities (see page 415), and the province was the birthplace of independence hero **Emilio Aguinaldo**, the first President of the Republic. The **Emilio**

PACIFIC WAR MEMORIAL MUSEUM

Highlights

❶ Pagsanjan Falls Home to rough rapids and a towering cascade, with the best *buko* pie in the Philippines in nearby Los Baños. See page 104

❷ Tagaytay Clinging to a high volcanic ridge, this town offers mesmerizing views of Lake Taal, and some of the tastiest food in Luzon. See page 106

❸ Lake Taal Gaze across this gorgeous lake towards the top of one of the world's smallest volcanoes. See page 109

❹ Taal Wonderfully preserved colonial town, with *bahay na bato* houses, ivy-clad churches and vibrant markets. See page 110

❺ Anilao A scenic stretch of coast with some choice resorts and excellent scuba diving. See page 113

❻ Mount Pinatubo Enticing volcanic peak, accessible by 4WD and on foot, with a beautiful crater lake at the summit. See page 117

❼ Corregidor Take the fast ferry to this idyllic, jungle-covered island at the mouth of Manila Bay, a poignant monument to World War II. See page 119

HIGHLIGHTS ARE MARKED ON THE MAP ON PAGE 102

Aguinaldo Shrine and Museum in **KAWIT**, 23km south of Manila, is the house in which he was born in 1869. He's also buried here, in a simple marble tomb in the back garden on the bank of the river. Philippine independence was proclaimed here and the Philippine flag first raised by Aguinaldo on June 12, 1898, is commemorated on that day every year, with the president waving the flag from the balcony.

With its secret passages and hidden compartments, the house is testimony to the revolutionary fervour that surrounded Aguinaldo and his men. A number of the original chairs and cabinets have secret compartments that were used to conceal documents and weapons, while the kitchen has a secret passage that he could use to escape if the Spanish came calling. In the general's bedroom, one of the floorboards opens up to reveal a staircase that led to his private one-lane bowling alley under the house and an adjoining hidden swimming pool. Downstairs, the museum displays various Aguinaldo

HIGHLIGHTS

1. Pagsanjan Falls
2. Tagaytay
3. Lake Taal
4. Taal
5. Anilao
6. Mount Pinatubo
7. Corregidor

AROUND MANILA

LAGUNA HOT SPRINGS

Just east of Calamba on the National Highway (accessible by the buses and jeepneys to Santa Cruz), the barangay of **Pansol** touts heavily on tourist custom on the health properties of its **hot springs**, which bubble from the lower slopes of Mount Makiling. There are dozens of resorts of varying quality that use the hot springs to fill their swimming pools, many catering to tour groups, day-trippers, company outings and conferences. It's best to visit on a weekday when the best ones can make for a relaxing few hours.

RESORTS AND SPAS
Monte Vista Hot Springs & Conference Resort National Highway, Pansol ☎049 545 7777. This attractive resort offers eighteen hot mineral pools, assorted giant slides and enough room for 1500 day visitors. Rates entitle you to a room and a 24hr stay. P̲P̲

Sol Y Viento Mountain Hot Springs and Resort Makiling Heights, Pansol, ⓦsyvhotelsandresorts. com. A very popular resort with lovely comfortable and clean rooms, numerous hot water pools, water slides, and a rather silly artificial waterfall feature. There are also a number of good restaurants on site. P̲P̲P̲

memorabilia including clothes, journals and his sword, while upstairs there is the general's bedroom, a grand hall, a dining room and a conference room.

Calamba

The city of **CALAMBA**, just 54km from the capital, is best known today as the birthplace of national hero and revolutionary **José Rizal**. Once a rural backwater, Calamba is now the largest city in Laguna province and effectively a choked extension of Manila – there's nothing to see in the modern section, but the old barangay of **San Juan**, built in Spanish colonial style around the handsome **St John the Baptist Church** (1859), is worth a visit. A marker inside the church indicates that Rizal was baptized here by Fray Rufino Collantes on June 22, 1861. Calamba can be reached on commuter train services from Manila's Tutuban station.

Rizal Shrine
J.P. Rizal St at F. Mercado St • Free

The site where José Rizal was born in 1861 is now the **Rizal Shrine**, though the building here is a late 1940s replica of a typical nineteenth-century Philippine *bahay na bato* – it features lower walls of stone and upper walls of wood, *narra*-wood floors and windows made from capiz shell. All the rooms contain period furniture and the adjacent gallery has displays of Rizal's belongings, including the clothes in which he was christened and a fragment of the suit he was wearing when he was executed. In the garden is a *bahay kubo* (wooden) playhouse, a replica of the one in which Rizal used to spend his days as a child.

Los Baños and around

The lakeside town of **LOS BAÑOS**, around 60km south of Manila, attracts a steady stream of domestic tourists, who primarily come to gorge on its delectable **buko pies** (stuffed with young coconut), said to have first been cooked up here in the 1960s by a food technologist from the local university. Its campus has an interesting **Riceworld Museum**, while the looming volcano cone of **Mount Makiling** makes an enticing target for a day-hike.

Mount Makiling
Trail begins at Makiling Center monitoring station, College of Forestry, Maliking Trail, southwestern end of UPLB campus (ⓦ facebook. com/makilingcenter) • Charge • Jeepneys to the College of Forestry run from Lopez Ave at El Danda St (near Robinsons Mall, just off the National Highway)

2

The dormant volcano of **Mount Makiling** (1090m) is identifiable by its unusual shape, resembling a reclining woman. The mountain is named after Mariang Makiling (aka "Mary of Makiling"), a young woman whose spirit is said to protect the mountain. On quiet nights, so the legend goes, you can hear her playing the harp. The music is rarely heard any more, possibly because Makiling is angry about the scant regard paid to the environment by the authorities, but the University of the Philippines at Los Baños UPLB now manages the **Mount Makiling Forest Reserve** that blankets the mountain and is hoping to develop its ecotourism potential.

From the Makiling Center monitoring station, a well-established but strenuous 8.7km trail leads up to the summit (4–5hr). It's safe and easy to follow, and indeed much of it is a decidedly non-natural road rather than a trail, but be prepared for leeches, sudden downpours and flash floods (the trail was closed for three months after two hikers drowned in 2012). **Guides** are not required. Most climbers start early (go after 9am and you won't be allowed to do the full walk) and complete the hike in one day; you can pitch tents at the Malaboo and Tayabak campsites on the way up, but not near the summit.

ARRIVAL AND DEPARTURE   LOS BAÑOS AND AROUND

By bus and jeepney Los Baños is accessible via Jac Liner buses from Manila (jacliner.com; 2hr), or jeepneys from

Calamba. To head back to Manila from Los Baños, note that the last bus departs around 8.30pm.

EATING

Numerous brands and stalls along the National Highway outside Los Baños sell *buko* pie, though at a standard 9 inches in diameter, these are a little large for solo travellers to enjoy – perhaps even couples; very few places, if any, sell by the slice. Note that shops will close early if they run out of pies. As well as those listed here, other specialist snack stores have set up to cash in on the crowds.

Lety's Buko Pie LBP Building, National Highway, Brgy Anos ⓦletysbukopie.com. Established by Leticia "Lety" Belarmino in 1976, this is a local favourite (next door to *Orient*). Also sells cassava cake, pineapple pie and banana bread. P̄

★ **Orient – the Original Buko Pie Bakeshop** National Highway, Brgy Anos ☎049 536 3783. The best *buko* pies are still baked at this venerable store (note the double-parked cars and buses blocking the road, though also note that the word "Orient" on the shop's sign is very, very small), with young, tender coconut slices in a crispy, well-made crust. Be aware, however, that they do tend to sell out pretty much as fast as they can bake them, although they'll take reservations on weekdays. From Calamba, the shop is on the left just before you reach the town centre; they have another branch at Silang on the Santa Rosa–Tagaytay road. P̄

Pagsanjan

Serving as the capital of Laguna province from 1688 to 1858, the town of **PAGSANJAN** lies 100km southeast of Manila and is home to a few old wooden houses, an unusually ornamental stone gate – or **Puerta Real** – and a pretty Romanesque church. The

SHOOTING THE RAPIDS AT PAGSANJAN

The fourteen **rapids** of the Bumbungan River (bangkas daily 7am–5pm; charge) are at their most thrilling in the wet season (June–Sept); during the dry season the "shooting the rapids" ride is more sedate. You don't need to be especially daring to do the trip, though you will get wet, so be prepared. **Ticket sales** are supervised by the local tourism office (see above), so go there first, and ignore touts offering tickets on the street. The trip includes a raft ride under the falls – make sure to protect your phone and camera. It's customary to tip the boatman.

It usually takes around an hour to climb just over 5km, up through the dramatic gorge in bangkas; when you get closer to the actual 30m-high **Pagsanjan Falls**, you can float on a bamboo raft (*balsa*) to go directly below the cascade into the cavern known as **Devil's Cave** for a swim, another thirty minutes or so. This is an additional charge if not already negotiated as part of your boat trip.

gate sits on the road to Santa Cruz (Rizal Street) and was completed in 1880, while **Our Lady of Guadalupe Church**, dating from 1690 but remodelled in the nineteenth century, is at the other end of Rizal. The town's main claim to fame these days is as the staging point for the dazzling **Pagsanjan Falls**, chosen by Francis Ford Coppola as the location for the final scenes in *Apocalypse Now* in 1975. Most tourists come not for the Hollywood nostalgia value, however, but to take one of the popular "**shooting the rapids**" trips along the Bumbungan River to the falls and back (see box, page 104).

ARRIVAL AND INFORMATION   PAGSANJAN

By bus It can take up to 4hr to get to Pagsanjan from Manila if you hit bad traffic (around 2hr normally) – avoid weekends and public holidays. Jeepneys run frequently from Santa Cruz (see page 100) to Pagsanjan.

Tourist information The tourist office is in the municipal building (daily 8am–5pm; ⊚ pagsanjan.gov.ph) in the centre of town, opposite the main church.

ACCOMMODATION AND EATING

★ **Aling Taleng's** 169 General Luna St (just south of the Balanac Bridge) ⊚ facebook.com/taleng1933. This popular shop has been serving refreshing seven-ingredient *halo-halo* since 1933. Also serves all-day Filipino breakfast, burgers and great noodles. P̲P̲

Calle Arco 57 Rizal St (National Hwy) ⊚ facebook.com/callearcopagsanjan. This old-fashioned restaurant, set in a whimsical wooden house, serves quality Filipino food such as *sinigang na baka sa langka* (beef tamarind soup with jackfruit). Buy the sweet calamansi and tomatoes in jars to take away. Cash only. P̲P̲

Casa del Rio Resort R. Lava St, off Pagsanjan-Cavinti

Rd ☎ 049 501 1948. Offering comfortable rooms in a characterful building, with a decent pool in the garden, the Casa del Rio Resort is a good place to base yourself for your trip to shoot the rapids. The staff can arrange boat rides, as well as providing good quality meals. P̲P̲

Pagsanjan Falls Lodge Pagsanjan-Cavinti Rd ⊚ pagsanjanfallslodge.com.ph. Cheesy but fun resort with plenty of swimming opportunities – the pool facing the river is a real highlight. Rooms are modest, rather plain-looking affairs (presumably because the place is popular with families, and kids will occasionally be kids). P̲P̲

Paete

Sleepy **PAETE** ("pa-e-te"), is Luzon's **woodcarving capital**, packed with stores selling woodcarvings, oil paintings, wooden clogs (*bakya*) and gaily painted papier-mâché masks used in fiestas. Most of the stores are on **Quesada Street** in the centre of town. During the second week of January Paete holds its **Salibanda festival**, the feast of the Santo Niño (Holy Child), which includes a rowdy procession along the main street in which participants and spectators splash water over each other. Paete is also well known for its sweet **lanzones** (harvested Oct–Dec). There is very limited accommodation, but you can visit the town easily in a day.

Santiago Apostol Parish Church

Quesada St at Roces St • ⊚ facebook.com/churchofpaete.official

The town's crumbling but atmospheric Baroque **Santiago Apostol Parish Church** dates from 1646, but like many old Philippine churches it has been reduced to rubble by earthquakes on a number of occasions and rebuilt. The present structure dates from 1939, and has an ornate carved facade, weathered bell tower and a beautifully sculpted altar finished in gold leaf. The wonderfully vivid mural paintings near the main entrance date from the 1850s.

ARRIVAL AND DEPARTURE   PAETE

By jeepney Paete is 10km north of Pagsanjan, just off the main highway that hugs the east coast of Laguna de Bay. It's

best approached by jeepney from Pagsanjan or Santa Cruz (take any one going to Siniloan).

EATING

★ **Kape Kesada Art Gallery** Quesada St ⊚ facebook.com/kapekesada. Café and gallery (selling paintings and

books) that looks like a wooden Japanese house and serves brewed coffee and decent sandwiches. P̲

2

Tagaytay

The compact and breezy city of **TAGAYTAY**, 55km south of Manila, sits on a dramatic 600m-high ridge overlooking **Lake Taal** and its volcano, to which it serves as the gateway. Tagaytay also regularly serves as something of an escape from Manila, for city-dwellers and visitors alike – the city's higher elevation means that its air is markedly cooler, while its far lower population density means that it's markedly cleaner too. There isn't all that much to do here bar admire the stupendous lake views, but it's a pleasant, friendly place, and some visitors end up staying on for longer than they'd intended to – in fact, an increasing number of Manileños are purchasing second homes here, or decamping entirely, a shift most evident in the ever-growing number of surprisingly tall apartment blocks mushrooming from this once-humble town.

Tagaytay is very spread out, which can make it hard to get your bearings. The centre of town is a Rotunda (roundabout), where the ridge road, running east to west, meets the Aguinaldo Highway, running north towards Manila. The town's main transport "hub" is a 200m-long stretch between the Rotunda and Olivarez Plaza, just to the north; the various sights given here are ordered from west to east.

Sky Ranch

Tagaytay–Nasugbu Hwy, 3km west of the Rotunda near *Taal Vista Hotel* • Charge, plus extra for most rides • ⓦ skyranch.com.ph

Visitors with kids may enjoy the **Sky Fun Amusement Park**, which contains the "Sky Eye", the tallest Ferris wheel in the Philippines (at 63m), as well as thrill-filled rides such as the "Super Viking" (a giant boat swing), the "Nessi Coaster" mini rollercoaster and "Wonder Flight", a roundabout for young kids.

Pink Sisters' Convent

East of Aguinaldo Hwy (signposted), 1km north of the Rotunda • Free

A pleasingly tranquil religious institution, the **Pink Sisters' Convent** was said to have been popular with late president Cory Aquino. Watching the nuns at prayertime can be quite uplifting even if you're not a praying type yourself, and their singing is more delightful still; dressed in fuschia-coloured habits, they're rather photogenic too, but do follow the sensible rules of decorum. Also notable is the stand selling home-baked food from a tiny gift shop to the left of the entrance; keep your eyes out for the nuns' home-made "angel" cookies (tasty oat biscuits, originally made from communion wafer leftovers).

Museo Orlina

Tagaytay–Calamba Hwy, 3km east of the Rotunda • Charge

The modern **Museo Orlina** showcases the glass creations of sculptor Ramon Orlina, and is worth a look if you're passing by; everything's beautifully displayed, though for many visitors the main draw is the chance to take photos out in the garden, or of the lake from the rooftop.

Tagaytay Picnic Grove

Tagaytay–Calamba Hwy, 5km east of the Rotunda • **Grove** Charge • **Zipline and cable car** charge

You can take in the views from the **Tagaytay Picnic Grove**, a shabby ridgetop park popular with day-trippers, and one that has huts available to rent. Inside the grove, the **Tagaytay Ridge Zipline & cable car** boasts a 250m-long zipline and a cable-car ride, and there's also a ferris wheel.

People's Park in the Sky

Tagaytay–Calamba Hwy, 8.5km east of the Rotunda • Charge • ☏ 0939 902 7936

The **People's Park in the Sky** is the highest point in the area (750m) offering magnificent panoramas of the lake, the sea, Laguna de Bay – and the smog that hangs over Manila to the north. The other attraction up here is the modest **Shrine of our Lady, Mother of Fair Love**, constructed in 2003.

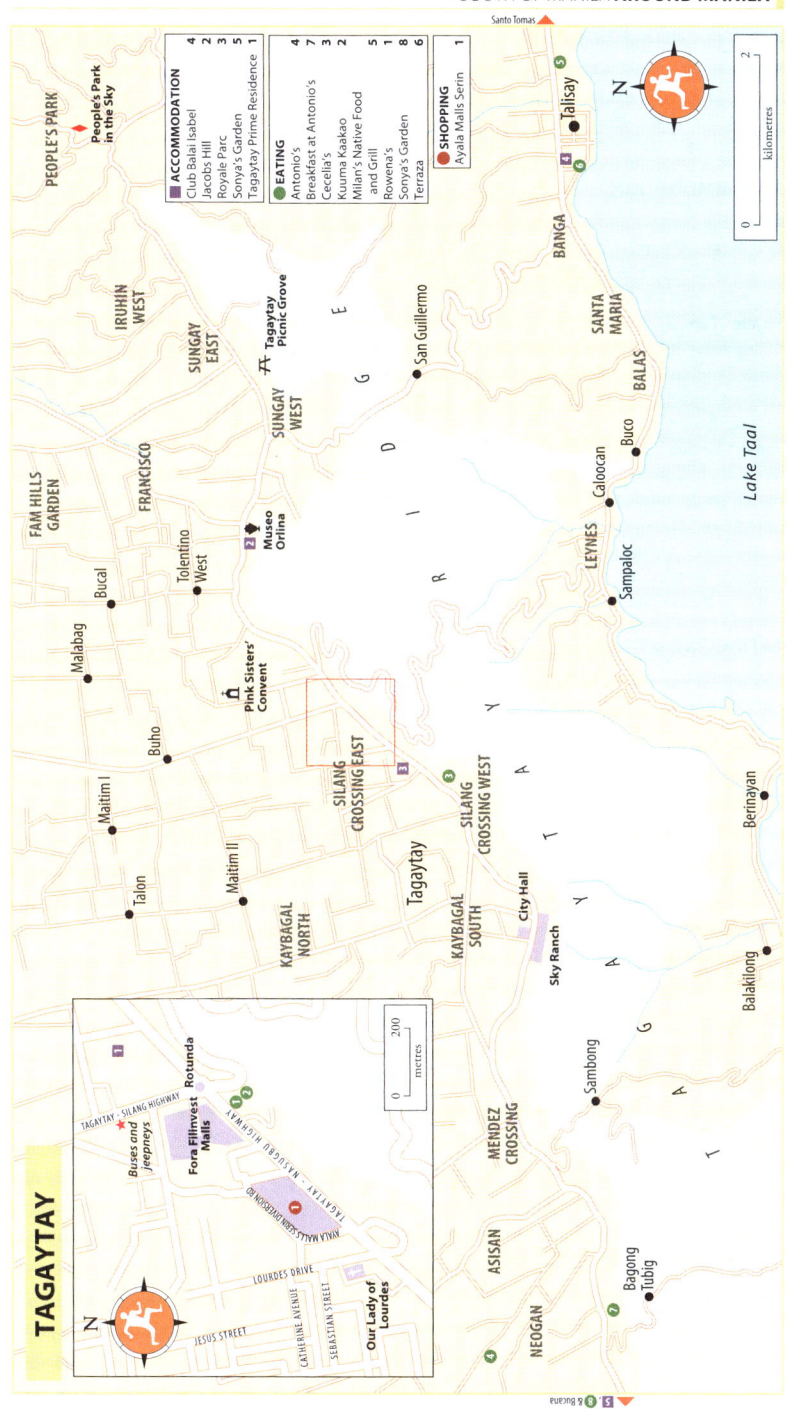

2

Santo Tomas

TAGAYTAY

ACCOMMODATION	
Club Balai Isabel	4
Jacobs Hill	2
Royale Parc	3
Sonya's Garden	5
Tagaytay Prime Residence	1

EATING	
Antonio's	4
Breakfast at Antonio's	7
Cecelia's	3
Kuuma Kaakao	2
Milan's Native Food and Grill	5
Rowena's	1
Sonya's Garden	8
Terraza	6

SHOPPING	
Ayala Malls Serin	1

PEOPLE'S PARK

People's Park in the Sky

IRUHIN WEST

SUNGAY EAST

SUNGAY WEST

Tagaytay Picnic Grove

San Guillermo

FAM HILLS GARDEN

FRANCISCO

Tolentino West

Museo Orlina

Bucal

Malabag

Buho

Maitim I

Maitim II

Talon

KAYBAGAL NORTH

Pink Sisters' Convent

SILANG CROSSING EAST

SILANG CROSSING WEST

Tagaytay

KAYBAGAL SOUTH

City Hall

Sky Ranch

MENDEZ CROSSING

ASISAN

NEOGAN

Sambong

Bagong Tubig

Balakilong

Berinayan

Lake Taal

BANGA

SANTA MARIA

BALAS

Buco

Caloocan

LEYNES

Sampaloc

Talisay

N

0   kilometres   2

Buses and jeepneys

Rotunda

Fora Filinvest Malls

TAGAYTAY – SILANG HIGHWAY

TAGAYTAY – NASUGBU HIGHWAY

AYALA MALLS SERIN AURORA RD

LOURDES DRIVE

Our Lady of Lourdes

JESUS STREET

SEBASTIAN STREET

CATHERINE AVENUE

N

0   metres   200

Santo Tomas

& Bucana

2

ARRIVAL AND INFORMATION

By bus Frequent San Agustin and BSC buses run every 15min from MRT-Taft (Pasay) on EDSA (see page 81) to Tagaytay (1hr 30min). Jeepneys from the Rotunda head north, east and west to most points in Tagaytay.

Tourist information Tagaytay City Tourism Office is in the City Hall (3km west of Tagaytay's central Rotunda; daily 8am–5pm; ☎ 046 413 1220). The local police have a small tourist information post on the south side of the Rotunda.

ACCOMMODATION

SEE MAP PAGE 107

Jacobs Hill Tagaytay-Calamba Hwy ☎ 0917 632 6920. Basic but perfectly serviceable rooms in an attractive villa, some with balconies offering pleasant views. A good value choice if you're on a budget. **PP**

Royale Parc Tagaytay-Nasugbu Hwy ⓦ facebook. com/itsmeroyaleparc. One of a small chain of hotels, the Royale Parc offers simple but attractive rooms set around a courtyard containing a lovely relaxing pool. There's a decent, if not outstanding, restaurant on site. **PPP**

Sonya's Garden Barangay Buck Estate, Alfonso (15km west of Tagaytay) ⓦ sonyasgarden.com. Romantic cottage accommodation in a blossom-filled garden. Cottages are *bahay na bato*-style, with antique beds, lots of carved wood and shuttered windows. The rate includes a delicious breakfast and either lunch or supper. *Sonya's* is quite a distance west of Tagaytay, so is tricky to reach

without private transport: turn north-west once you're past Splendido golf course and then look out for the signs. **PPP**

Tagaytay Prime Residence Off Tagaytay-Calamba Rd, 500m east of the Rotunda. Not a standalone accommodation option, but a whole bunch of them – plenty of rooms in this tall tower (which can be seen from clean across Lake Taal) are of the Airbnb type, though also bookable on Booking.com and other engines. They tend to be a little small but very cheap, and beyond the lower floors, all have fantastic views (though, occasionally, miniscule windows). There's a swimming pool on the third floor, though tower staff are rather officious about what you bring or don't bring there – you'll need a full change of clothes, as well as a towel, just to be allowed in, though there's nowhere to actually change comfortably. **P**

EATING AND DRINKING

SEE MAP PAGE 107

In addition to the following, there are plenty of restaurants and cafés in Ayala Malls Serin, just west of the Rotunda; and Fora Mall, immediately to the Rotunda's north.

★ **Antonio's** Purok 138, 10km northwest of the Rotunda ⓦ antoniosrestaurant.ph. Super-posh restaurant – occasionally voted among the top 50 restaurants in Asia – serving the best Filipino food not just in town, but for many a mile around. Highlights include the huge pots of richly stewed *bulalo* – a meal for two people – plates of fried *tawalis* (anchovy-sized lake fish), a fine adobo and the barbecue chicken. **PPPP**

★ **Breakfast at Antonio's** Tagaytay–Nasugbu Hwy, 8km west of the Rotunda ⓦ antoniosrestaurant.ph. If you can't afford to eat at *Antonio's* proper – or you're sticking to public transport – then their sister offering is well worth a look. It's also exceptionally pretty, with bonus lake views from some tables, but the menu is far more down-to-earth, and centred on all-day breakfasts and brunches both Western and local; indeed, some simply pop by for a cup of coffee, something from their bakery (try their delectable *kouign-amann*), or a scoop or three of home-made ice cream. **PPP**

Cecelia's Tagaytay–Nasugbu Hwy, 2km west of the Rotunda ⓦ facebook.com/CeceliasAllDayBreakfastand Restaurant. The stunning lake views are almost reason enough to visit this simple restaurant, which is one of the better places around town for fish from Taal Lake – in fact, from many a table you can see the fishing boats and farms themselves, all lined up way down below. Good *buko* pie, too. **PP**

Kuuma Kaakao Hillcrest Plaza, Tagaytay–Santa Rosa Hwy, just west of the Rotunda ⓦ facebook.com/ KuumaKaakaoKaffe. Modest café with one of the best possible views of Lake Taal; their coffee is quite the treat of a Tagaytay morning, and they also whip up surprisingly good food, including a highly tasty *longansilog* (sausages and egg on rice). **PP**

Rowena's Hillcrest Plaza, Tagaytay–Santa Rosa Hwy, just west of the Rotunda ☎ 046 483 0129. Delicious pies and tarts: stop by for blueberry or strawberry cheese tarts, or the classic *buko* pie (*buko* tarts are also available, if you can't stomach a full pie), plus excellent coffee and decent meals. **PP**

THE TASTES OF LAKE TAAL

Lake Taal is famed for its delicious **fresh fish**, especially *tawilis* (a freshwater sardine only found here), tilapia and increasingly rare *maliputo* (a larger fish, also only found in Lake Taal, which is featured on the back of the P50 note). The other speciality is *bulalo* – rich beef **bone-marrow soup**. You'll find all of these in abundance in Tagaytay's restaurants.

Sonya's Garden Barangay Buck Estate, Alfonso (15km west of Tagaytay) ⓦ sonyasgarden.com. If you're not staying the night (see page 108), drop by for lunch or dinner: daily unlimited buffets include delights such as pasta with sun-dried tomatoes and banana rolls with sesame and jackfruit for dessert. Book ahead. PPP

SHOPPING   SEE MAP PAGE 107

Ayala Malls Serin Tagaytay-Calamba Hwy, 500m west of Rotunda ⓦ ayalamalls.com. The newer and more attractive of two mall complexes around the Rotunda, with plenty of chain restaurants and shops lining several levels around an open-air, park-like centre. The WalterMart supermarket here is also good for sundries if you're self-catering.

2

Lake Taal and Talisay

The country's third-largest lake, awe-inspiring **Lake Taal** sits in a caldera below Tagaytay, and was formed by huge eruptions between 500,000 and 100,000 years ago. The active **Taal Volcano**, which is responsible for the lake's sulphuric content, lies in the centre of the lake, on **Volcano Island**. The volcano erupted several times between 2020 and 2022, causing 39 casualties, inflicting severe damage on crops and disrupting air traffic. When it blew its top in 1754, however, thousands died and the town of Taal was destroyed; it was rebuilt in a new location on safer ground an hour by road from Tagaytay to the southwest of the lake (see page 110). Before 1754 the lake was actually part of Balayan Bay, but the eruption sealed it from the sea, eventually leading to its waters becoming non-saline. The volcano remains very active, and at time of writing the **island was closed** – check the **Philippine Institute of Volcanology and Seismology** website (PHIVOLCS; ⓦ phivolcs.dost.gov.ph) for the latest updates.

When possible, the departure point for trips across the lake to the volcano (see box below) is the small town of **TALISAY** on the lake's northern shore, some 4km southeast of Tagaytay. This is a much more typical Filipino settlement, with a bustling market, fishermen doubling as tourist guides and nary a fast-food chain in sight.

ARRIVAL AND DEPARTURE   LAKE TAAL AND TALISAY

From Manila you can approach Lake Taal from two directions: from the north via Tagaytay, or via Tanauan, east of the lake. Once in Talisay **tricycles** should take you to nearby hotels or bangka operators.

Via Tagaytay From Tagaytay you can get a tricycle down to Talisay, or get a "People's Park" jeepney to the Talisay turn-off (Tagaytay–Calamba Hwy, 5km east of the Rotunda) and a tricycle or occasional jeepney from there.

Via Tanauan JAM buses from Manila to Batangas stop at Tanauan; from here, take a tricycle to the Talisay jeepney terminal, then pick up one of the frequent jeepneys head to Talisay town from there (40min).

ACCOMMODATION AND EATING   SEE MAP PAGE 107

Most of the lakeside **resorts** are between Talisay, and the village of Laurel a few kilometres to its south. **Hotels** are busiest from Sept to Feb (the coolest months) so book ahead if travelling at these times. Weekdays are always much cheaper year-round. Down by the lakeshore in and around Talisay, simple **eating places** sell barbecued meat and fish, but quality can be hit and miss; the numerous bakeries in Talisay are a safer bet for a snack.

★ **Club Balai Isabel** Brgy Banga ⓦ balaiisabel.com. This fashionable lakeside boutique resort is built around a century-old coconut and mango plantation just east of the town. Rates for the cosy hotel rooms and suites include breakfast, while the luxurious lakeshore suites and villas are self-catering (all have kitchens) and can accommodate up to six people. There's a swimming pool, and a variety of watersports and even a lake cruise can be laid on for guests. The *Terraza* restaurant (see below) is your best bet for a decent meal in Talisay. PPP

Milan's Native Food and Grill East of Talisay ☏ 043 774 4932. Very popular spot on the main road through Talisay offering a great selection of well-priced local dishes, which you can enjoy in the pleasant garden. The grilled chicken is particularly good. PP

Terraza Club Balai Isabel, Brgy Banga ⓦ balaiisabel. com. An attractive hotel restaurant, which isn't actually all that dear – the menu is very wide-ranging, and includes various fish options (including some victims hauled from the adjacent lake), meaty mains, salads, and more snacky options. They also have plenty of alcohol to choose from, and decent coffee. PP

2

VOLCANO ISLAND

Visits to **Volcano Island** were prohibited at the time of writing, and had been for several years – unaware of this, foreigners turn up in Talisay most days hoping to make the trip across, and each one gets turned down, though of course things could change at any time. When the island is open, those who make it across often get ripped off by local "guides", but it's easy to avoid making the same mistake; the only price you need to negotiate is the **bangka** to take you out to the island and back (plus the tricycle/taxi fare to the dock). They can be arranged at the waterfront market in Talisay, or at any of the resorts (see page 109); *Taal Lake Yacht Club* (see below) is also a dependable choice. There will also be a charge for a **guide** to take you up to the main crater (and even to cross on the boat with you), though the trail is easy to follow and you do not need one. On the island is a small information office where you must pay a tourist tax plus a landing fee for the boat. There's a basic restaurant, with vendors selling overpriced drinks.

The principal highlight on the island is the walk up to the rim of the 1.9km-diameter **Main Crater Lake**, where you can look down onto tiny Vulcan Point island ("the island on an island"); the lake itself is usually off limits, depending on current PHIVOLCS warnings (see page 109). You can ride a **horse** up to the top of the crater for an additional charge – most tourists do this because of the heat, but the trail is not difficult for anyone in reasonable fitness (and the condition of the horses is pretty appalling). The trail can be dusty, however, so bring a scarf for your mouth or buy a mask on arrival. If you're staying the night by the lake, your hotel can arrange all this for you, with food and refreshments included. There isn't much shade on the island, so don't go without sunblock, a good hat and plenty of water.

With an early start (boats usually run from 7am), you can climb to the Main Crater Lake and be back in Talisay in time for lunch (the hike takes around 30min depending on fitness level; the trail is around 2.3km with a height gain of 200m). If you want to spend more time on the water, make for the **Taal Lake Yacht Club**, about 1km east of Talisay (ⓦtlyc.com), where you can rent sailing dinghies and kayaks.

Taal

The town of **TAAL**, 130km south of Manila and a further 10km southwest of its namesake lake, is one of the best-preserved colonial enclaves in the Philippines and one of the few places you can get a real sense of its Spanish past. Founded in 1572 by Augustinians, it was moved to this location (and away from the deadly Taal volcano) in 1755 and today boasts a superb collection of endearingly weathered Spanish colonial architecture and *bahay na bato*-style homes, as well as one of the finest basilicas in Luzon. Several of the town's Spanish-era buildings are open to the public.

Basilica de St Martin de Tours
M. Agoncillo St • Free; charge for belfry tower

On the east side of Taal's central plaza lies the elegantly weathered bulk of the **Basilica de St Martin de Tours**, said to be the biggest church in Southeast Asia, its facade visibly cracked, peeling and studded with clumps of weeds. The present church, begun in 1856, has a magnificent interior and is often jam-packed for masses throughout the day. The church (and Taal) is a major pilgrimage site thanks to an aged pinewood image of the Virgin Mary known as **Our Lady of Caysasay**, only 20cm high, which is moved to a shrine on the edge of town each week (see page 111). The statue is said to have been fished out of the Pansipit River in 1603; it was lost then found again in a freshwater spring.

Galleria Taal
60 M. Agoncillo St • Charge • ⓦfacebook.com/galleriataal

This fine old house has been turned into the **Galleria Taal**, a museum of vintage cameras collected over the years by the president of the local camera club (whose family home this was). The cameras will only appeal to enthusiasts, but the house itself, and the collection of old photographs, both dating back to the 1870s, are of more general interest.

Leon Apacible Historic Landmark

59 M. Agoncillo St • Free • ☎ 0917 852 1652

The **Leon Apacible Historic Landmark** is the ancestral home of **Leon Apacible** (1861–1901), lawyer and Filipino revolutionary. Built in the eighteenth century, it has the best-preserved interior in Taal: though it was renovated in 1870 and again in 1940, the wide, highly buffed *narra* floorboards, as well as the wide sweeping staircase (with its curved balustrade) are still original. The sliding doors and oriel windows betray American Art Deco influence while the transom filigree, featuring swirling chrysanthemums, is Chinese style.

Marcela Agoncillo Historical Landmark

14 M. Agoncillo St • Free • ☎ 0917 656 4170

The **Marcela Agoncillo Historical Landmark** is the most evocative and visibly ageing house in Taal, with creaky wooden floors, a dusty library and old-fashioned *sala* upstairs. The eighteenth-century house is the ancestral home of **Marcela Mariño de Agoncillo** (1860–1946), creator of the first Philippine flag in 1898 (she was in exile in Hong Kong at the time). An exhibit of flags from the days of the Philippine Revolution adorns the lower half of the structure, and her statue (holding the flag) graces the garden.

Chapel of Caysasay

Calle Vicente Noble • Free

The **Chapel of Caysasay**, located on the banks of the Pansipit River on the edge of town, is a beautiful coral-hewn chapel where the Our Lady of Caysasay image is transferred from its shrine in the basilica every Thursday and returned on Saturday afternoon. The ruined **Twin Wishing Wells of Santa Lucia**, a short walk from the chapel, are still reputed to have miraculous healing powers.

ARRIVAL AND INFORMATION TAAL

By bus and jeepney Jeepneys between Lemery and Batangas (both accessible by bus from Manila) pass through Taal. To get here from Tagaytay involves taking a Nasugbu-bound bus or jeepney to Boundry, just past Alfonso (15–30min), then a jeepney to Lemery (1hr), and finally a jeepney or tricycle (or a 15–30min walk, mostly slightly uphill) from there to Taal. There are direct buses between Lemery and Manila (2hr 30min–3hr), which can also be boarded or disembarked from in Taal, though some prefer to take a jeepney to Batangas (1hr) and a more comfortable bus from there (2hr).

By tricycle Taal's compact centre is easy to explore on foot, but if it's too hot you can easily hire a tricycle to whisk you around.

Tourist information You can get a town map and basic information at the tourist information office in the square in front of the Basilica (daily 8am–5pm; ⓦ taal.ph).

ACCOMMODATION

Casa Cecilia Diversion Rd (3km east of the centre) ⓦ bit. ly/casa-cecilia. Modern, cosy seven-room hotel sporting Spanish-style architecture and a patio overlooking the garden. Rooms are all en-suite doubles or twins, with parquet floors, tiled bathrooms and cable TV, and on the ground floor there's a good restaurant serving typical Batangueño food (such as *bulalo*). Rates include breakfast. **PPP**

★ **Casa Conchita** Antonio de las Alas ⓦ 0927 722 8463. Almost across the road from the Basilica you'll see this charming hotel – simple in its own way, but decorated (especially in the upstairs lounge) so beautifully that you might not feel the need to see Taal's other heritage homes.

The rooms are almost as pretty (one has a four-poster bed) and fairly comfortable, though with the creaking floors and rattly windows inevitable in a place of such vintage; the English-speaking owner loves to chat with guests, and a delightful breakfast is included with most online bookings. **PP**

Paradores del Castillo C. H. del Castillo ⓦ paradores detaal.com. A central choice in an attractive early twentieth century building, Paradores offers plenty of period charm combined with modern comfort. The entrance hall is beautifully atmospheric, and the bedrooms – some with four-poster beds – are a lovely place to relax. **PPP**

2

EATING

There are a few really good places to eat in Taal, though things close up earlier than you might expect; if stuck for sustenance there are a couple of all-hours convenience stores, including a 7-Eleven right by the Basilica. Downhill in Lemery there are a few fast food chain options.

Café G Calle Ananias Diokno ⓦfacebook.com/cafegtaal. Simple but popular café on Taal's main drag, offering decent coffee and tea, as well as basic meals, though the cakes and desserts are better than the mains. P̄

★ **Cuchara y Tenedor** Graziano Punzalan ⓦparadores detaal.com. The fanciest restaurant in town by far, with stone walls rising up to lofty wooden beams, from which chandeliers dangle – the place looks particularly charming of an evening. They rustle up a winning mix of Spanish food (the paella dishes are particularly popular) and tapas, mixed

up with some Taal-area specialities, including tawilis (a kind of freshwater sardine) breaded or fried. As you'd expect of such a place, there's booze available too. P̄P̄P̄

Cucina de Jardin Paradores del Castillo, C. H. del Castillo ⓦparadoresdetaal.com. The charming *Paradores del Castillo* hotel (see page 111) has a decent restaurant in the garden out back (hence its name), and non-guests are very welcome. The food here is a mix between simple – but well done – Filipino fare such as "sizzler" platters, and Italian pizza, pasta and antipasti. P̄P̄P̄

Don Juan Boodle House Jose W. Diokno ☏043 740 1828. Basic restaurant specialising in "boodles", which are vast spreads of local food feeding five to six people – they do also offer "boodlelitos", which feed two, and a few options for solo diners. P̄P̄

SHOPPING

Taal Public Market Calle Ananias Diokno. The market in the centre of Taal is a good place to eat and to look for local embroidery (*burdang Taal*), including cotton sheets,

pillowcases, tablemats and *barong tagalog* and *saya*, the national costumes. Daily 5am–7pm.

Mount Maculot

Charge, payable at the Registration Point • Guides can be organized at the trailhead • From Manila, take a Lemery-bound bus from Pasay (2hr 30min) and get off in Cuenca, from where it's a 2km walk or tricycle ride to the trailhead

Close to the town of **Cuenca**, on the southeastern side of Lake Taal, some 50km east of Taal itself, **Mount Maculot** (930m) affords mind-blowing views across the lake, surrounding jungle and puffy clouds to the horizon from its summit, yet is relatively undeveloped and (weekends excepted) tourist-free. If you set out from Manila very early – as most local climbers do – you can climb its lush slopes and be in Taal (or back in the capital) for dinner. One reason for Maculot's popularity is an area of sheer rock near the summit known as the **Rockies** (starting at 706m), which rises vertically up from the jungle and has a platform at the top, from where you can see across to Lake Taal. A steep but walkable path around the Rockies takes you to the platform.

The 2km walk or tricycle ride from Cuenca to the trailhead goes via the **Barangay No. 7 Outpost**, a small hut marked by a barrier across the road. Stop off along the way at the Registration Point near the Cuenca barangay administration hall, where you are supposed to register and pay. Though you can organize guides at the trailhead, they're not necessary – the trail is easy to follow (well marked by white arrows and signs), with steps and handrails most of the way. From the trailhead (behind the little sari-sari store known as the "mountaineer's store") it takes about two hours to reach the summit, depending on your fitness level, via the **Grotto of the Blessed Virgin Mary**, a small shrine.

Nasugbu and around

Some of the finest white-sand beaches near Manila lie along the Batangas coastline around **NASUGBU**, 37km west of Tagaytay. The coast here is pitted with resorts, mostly clearly signposted from the main road and grouped in three areas: to the north of Nasugbu on the chalky sands stretching to Fuego Point; around Nasugbu itself on Nasugbu Beach, which has darker sand and is more crowded; and about 12km south of Nasugbu by road along the similarly darker sands of **Matabungkay Beach**, which is often marred by the *balsas* (rafts rented by resorts) that line the shore. Other than the beach, the only real sight is the **Nasugbu Landing Memorial**, consisting of a steel

> ### DIVING AT ANILAO
>
> The **reef** at Anilao is thriving, mainly because this is a protected marine sanctuary, with huge numbers of reef fish, small squid, cuttlefish, colourful nudibranchs (sea slugs) and all sorts of hard and soft coral. There are at least forty dive sites within thirty minutes of most resorts; the most highly rated are Twin Rocks, Basura, Mainit Muck (Secret Bay), Kirby's and Bethlehem. It's justly celebrated for Cathedral Rock, a marine park sanctuary at 20–30m; originally barren, the site comprises two large rock formations inside a natural amphitheatre, topped with a man-made cross and seeded with corals. The resorts are the easiest places to arrange dive trips. March to June is the best time for diving.

landing craft and statues of soldiers coming ashore, which commemorates the second landing of American forces in the Philippines in 1945, at the end of World War II.

ARRIVAL AND DEPARTURE

NASUGBU AND AROUND

By bus From Manila, there are frequent San Agustin buses to Nasugbu (3hr) from Pasay and the PITX terminal. There are jeepneys every few minutes between Nasugbu and Matabungkay (20min).

ACCOMMODATION

Coral Beach Club Matabungkay Beach ⓦcoralbeach. ph. A quiet, attractive hotel with restaurant (which is a bit overpriced), bar, pool tables, beachside pool and a/c rooms, all with cable TV and hot showers. Chauffeur-driven transfer to Manila available. P̄P̄P̄

Lago de Oro National Highway, Balibago, Calatagan (20km south of Nasugbu) ⓦlago-de-oro.com. Modern hacienda-style resort, notable for the cable wakeboard system in its lagoon; a cable drags you around the lake rather than a boat. There's also good food in the European-style restaurant and a pool for lounging, and discounts are usually available outside public holidays. P̄P̄P̄

Matabungkay Beach Resort Matabungkay Beach ⓦmatabungkaybeachhotel.com. Not, perhaps, the most imaginatively named place, but otherwise there's little to quibble with here: clean, well-sized rooms, an attractive pool, and easy access to the beach. The on-site restaurant offers a variety of cuisines, ranging from Italian to Japanese. P̄P̄P̄

Anilao

Some 140km south of Manila, the resort of **ANILAO** (the name refers both to the village and the 13km peninsula beyond it) is primarily a diving destination, popular with city folk at weekends (when the area can get a little busy). During the week it's much more peaceful and you can often negotiate a discount on your accommodation, though there's little point in coming just for the beach.

ARRIVAL AND DEPARTURE

ANILAO

To reach Anilao by public transport, take a bus to Batangas City (2hr from Manila; see page 114), then a jeepney west to Mabini or the wharf at Anilao village (1hr), and continue by tricycle (fares depend on the resort, and may vary widely) along the coastal road to your resort.

ACCOMMODATION

Altamare Dive & Leisure Resort Brgy San Teodoro ⓦaltamare.com.ph. Preferred hideaway for both divers and non-divers, with hotel-like rooms clustered across an intriguingly-designed compound; most stare straight at the beach (and local reef), and so does the little infinity pool. Pool of the table variety is possible in the games room, and elsewhere there's a bar-restaurant and a spa centre. P̄P̄P̄

Aquaventure Reef Club Brgy Bagalangit ⓦaqua-venture.com. Comfortable, unpretentious resort 3km along the coastal road beyond Anilao. Operated by Manila-based dive outfit Aqua One, it's primarily a scuba resort, though it also offers island-hopping and snorkelling trips in rented bangkas. Double rooms come with fan or a/c and bath; buffet-style meals are served in a nice open restaurant overlooking the sea. P̄P̄P̄

★ **Dive Solana** Brgy San Teodoro ⓦdivesolana.com. Along the coastal road beyond the *Aquaventure Reef Club*, this is a slightly bohemian little retreat popular with divers and started by Filipina film-maker Marilou Diaz-Abaya. All rooms (some right on the beach) come with a/c and cable

TV, and the rate includes four buffet meals a day. It's always full at weekends, so book in advance. **PPPP**

Vivere Azure Brgy Aguada Km 108, San Teodoro ⓦ viverazure.com. Elegant (but expensive) boutique resort with the best views in Anilao and fourteen luxurious suites, each featuring earthy tones, stone and wood furnishings. Rates include all meals, use of the pool, kayaks and snorkelling gear, and promotional discounts are usually available. **PPPP**

Batangas City

Lying on the other side of Batangas Bay from Anilao, **BATANGAS CITY** has one of the fastest-growing populations in the Philippines, but offers little to see. Its significance for most visitors is as a transit point on the journey to Puerto Galera on Mindoro.

ARRIVAL AND DEPARTURE BATANGAS CITY

By ferry Batangas Port lies 2km west of the city centre; from here, various ferries head to Puerto Galera (around 2hr). Montenegro Lines operate ferries to Calapan, 44km southeast of Galera (hourly; 2hr 30min), and Fast Cat (8 daily) do the same run in just 1hr 30min. Montenegro and Besta sail to Abra de Ilog, 30km west (16 daily; 2hr 30min). Montenegro, Navios and CSGA also run ferries to Odiongan (1 daily; 7–10hr) and Romblon (10 weekly; 11–13hr), Navios sail to Cajidiocan (3 weekly; 16hr), and Super Shuttle have boats for Culasi (3 weekly; 14hr). 2GO and Starlite Ferries serve Caticlan (2–3 daily; 10hr). You need to pay an additional terminal fee before boarding; departures for Galera also incur an "Environmental User Fee".

By bus Batangas City is usually a 2hr bus ride from Manila via the tollway (potentially double that on the regular road), depending on road congestion. The city has a bus terminal (grandly named the "Grand Terminal"), and the usual array of bus-company depot-stations, though some companies, including Ceres Transport, either or also run services from the port instead – the vast majority of travellers will want to exercise this option. Jeepneys make the run from the port to the city centre, though it's quite walkable if you've light luggage. You'll need a jeepney or taxi to get to the Grand Terminal.

Destinations Manila (2–3hr); Nasugbu (2hr); Santa Cruz (3hr); Taal (1hr); Tagaytay (1hr 30min).

ACCOMMODATION AND EATING

★**A&M Restaurant** Hilltop Ave, 400m off National Rd ☎043 723 1118. This restaurant near the University of Batangas is best known for sumptuous native cuisine such as *bulalo*, *kare kare* and *leche* flan. It's 3km from the port; most taxi or tricycle drivers should know it. **PP**

Hungry Hippo UB Hilltop Arcade, National Rd ☎043 300 2323. Another store with a cult following, right next to the University of Batangas, this small local chain is beloved for its juicy hamburgers. **PP**

RGR Traveler's Hotel DJPMM Access Rd (off Rizal Ave between the city and the port) ☎043 723 6021. A handy place if you need to spend the night in Batangas: nothing fancy, but clean and friendly, and conveniently located between the city centre and the port. Marginally better than the similarly-named *RGR Traveler's Inn*, just south of the main road. **PP**

North of Manila

Most travellers zip through the provinces **north of Manila** – Pampanga, Bulacan and Bataan – to the justly famed attractions of northern Luzon, but there are a few reasons to break the journey. **Malolos** has some historic distractions, while **Mount Pintatubo** provides energetic hikes and gasp-inducing scenery. **Bataan** is a surprisingly wild province, with some excellent beaches and World War II monuments, while **Subic Bay** is turning into an appealing beach, dive and outdoor activity centre. Buses connect all the main attractions with Manila, though fast ferries would be much quicker to Bataan – if they are running (see page 118).

Malolos

The capital of Bulacan province, **MALOLOS** lies some 45km north of Manila, a relatively historic city of 250,000 best known as the location of the **Malolos Convention** of 1898, the meeting of patriots led by Emilio Aguinaldo that led to the establishment of the

SAN PEDRO CUTUD LENTEN RITES

Heading north through Pampanga province, you might be tempted by the rather voyeuristic prospect of watching a dozen or so Catholic devotees being voluntarily **crucified**, a gruesome tradition that started in 1962 and is euphemistically known as the **San Pedro Cutud Lenten Rites**. Every year on Good Friday at San Pedro Cutud, 3km west of **San Fernando**, a dozen or so penitents – mostly men but the occasional woman (and sometimes even the odd foreigner) – are taken to a rice field and nailed to a cross by men dressed as Roman soldiers, using 5cm stainless steel nails that have been soaked in alcohol to disinfect them. The penitents are taken down seconds later. In total some two thousand penitents walk to the site, flagellating themselves using bamboo sticks tied to a rope or shards of glass buried in wooden sticks. The blood – and the cries of pain – are real, but the motivation is questionable to some (one "regular" has been crucified at least 27 times). The Catholic Church does not approve of the crucifixions and does not endorse them, and the media have also turned against the rites, calling them pagan and barbaric – but always managing despite these reservations to allot copious front-page space to photographs of bloodied penitents.

In 2010 the local authorities banned tourists from attending for the first time, and the whole thing was banned during Covid, but in practice this is virtually impossible to enforce and every year some fifty thousand foreigners and locals attend the spectacle – you'll need to get here early to grab a good view (it's normal and accepted that folks jostle to get close-ups of the nails going in). Partas and Dominion Lines buses leave every hour for San Fernando from their terminals in Cubao.

First Philippine Republic – the city served as the capital of the short-lived independent nation until 1899. Today, the location of the convention – **Barasoain Church** – is the city's biggest attraction.

Barasoain Church

Paseo del Congreso • Free • ⓦ barasoainchurch.org

The current incarnation of **Barasoain Church** dates back to 1885, its handsome colonial facade and tower best known as the place where the Revolutionary Congress convened in 1898 (ever the showman, Joseph Estrada chose to be inaugurated president here in 1998). The church also houses the **Ecclesiastical Museum** on the upper floor, which displays religious relics such as antique prayer cards and a bone fragment of San Vicente Ferrer encased in glass, and puts on a light-and-sound presentation depicting events leading to the Philippine Revolution and the Philippine–American War.

Malolos Cathedral

Paseo del Congreso • Free • ⓦ dioceseofmalolos.ph

In 1898, Aguinaldo made his headquarters at the grand **Malolos Cathedral**, also known as the Basilica Minore de la Nuestra Señora de Inmaculada Concepcion. The cathedral's Spanish origins lie in the sixteenth century, but Aguinaldo ordered its destruction in 1899, part of his "scorched-earth policy" to hamper the Americans. What you see today was primarily rebuilt in the 1930s, though work has continued to the present. Don't miss the venerable tree in front of the cathedral, known as the **Kalayaan Tree** (Tree of Freedom), said to have been planted by Aguinaldo himself.

Casa Real

Paseo del Congreso • ☎ 044 662 6135

A gorgeous Spanish house with origins in 1580 and serving many functions over the years, the **Casa Real** is primarily a small museum and shrine dedicated to the "**twenty women of Malolos**". These pioneers began a daring campaign for a school for women

2

in 1888, and the museum has various displays on other barrier-breaking Filipinas from around the country.

ARRIVAL AND INFORMATION   MALOLOS

By van First North Luzon Transit (⊕ facebook.com/FirstNorth LuzonTransit) run buses (1hr) from Monumento LRT station in Manila. Vans and FX taxis run to Malolos from Monumento and from SM City North, at the northern end of EDSA, 400m beyond North Avenue MRT station. There are also vans and UV taxis from there, and also from SM City North EDSA Mall (a short walk north of North Avenue MRT station).

By train The North–South Commuter Railway is under construction from Manila along (actually, mostly above) the old Philippine National Rail line, but is not expected to be in operation until 2027 at the earliest.

Tourist information The helpful provincial tourist office is in the Capitol Building (Mon–Fri 8am–5pm; ⊕ bulacan. gov.ph).

EATING

Enlin's Bakeshop Estrella St ⊕ facebook.com/Enlins Bakeshop2001. Malolos is famed throughout the Philippines for its *ensaymada*, a sweet, buttery bread treat, often crowned

with grated cheese and sliced salted egg. *Enlin's*, opposite the church, sells boxes of the delicacy, as well as *ube* (purple yam) flavour and popular *pastel de leche*. ₱

Clark and Angeles City

Some 80km north of Metro Manila, **CLARK** (or, more formally, Clark Freeport and Special Economic Zone) is an odd mix of converted barracks, unappealing duty-free malls, IT industrial zones, golf courses and prostitution. Indeed, Clark and adjacent **ANGELES CITY** remain one of the Philippines' most notorious sun and sex destinations. Clark was the site of an American military base between 1903 and 1991, and like Subic Bay (see page 120) has been transformed into a "freeport zone" (a tax- and duty-free zone) since the departure of the US Air Force. It's been far less successful in shedding its sleazy image, however; the **airport** has proven popular with budget airlines, though the majority of flights are coming from other cities in East and South East Asia, and the majority of passengers on them are (for some wild reason) male. If you are travelling to the airport or aiming to climb **Pinatubo** or **Arayat**, you may end up spending some time here, but otherwise there's little reason to linger. If you have to overnight in Clark, keep in mind that the hotels are almost universally geared to prostitution.

The name "Clark" is generally used to refer to the former base and the tourist area of Angeles City around it, particularly **Fields Avenue** on the south side where most of the bars are.

ARRIVAL AND DEPARTURE   CLARK AND ANGELES CITY

By plane Several budget carriers connect Clark International Airport (⊕ clarkinternationalairport.com) with Singapore, Taipei, Seoul, Kuala Lumpur, Macau and other regional destinations; there are also lots of domestic services. Outside the terminal are a small convenience store and an ATM. Plenty of fixed-rate taxis meet each flight, but these are expensive, and drivers will try to charge more if they can. Jeepneys run from the airport when full (minimum eight people) to anywhere in Clark, or to the Dau bus terminal. Philtranco (⊕ philtranco.net) runs expensive but direct buses to Manila (3 daily).
Destinations Cebu (1–2 daily; 1hr 25min); Davao (1–2 daily; 2hr); El Nido (1 daily; 1hr 25min); Iloilo (3 weekly; 1hr

20min); Puerto Princesa (5 weekly; 1hr 30min).

By bus For most destinations, head to the Dau bus terminal (pronounced "Da-oo") in nearby Mabalacat, served by almost continual buses from the capital and less frequently to and from Northern Luzon.
Destinations Aliminos (4hr 30min); Baguio (4hr 30min); La Union (4–6hr); Manila (1hr 30min–2hr); Vigan (9–10hr).

By train Angeles, Clark and the airport are all due to become stations on the North–South Commuter Railway, under construction from Manila, but not expected to be in operation until 2027 at the earliest – and quite possibly later for the Clark/Angeles section.

ACCOMMODATION AND EATING

Aling Lucing Sisig G. Valdez St ⊕ facebook.com/ lucingcunanan. Angeles City is known as the *sisig* capital

of the Philippines, after the popular Filipino dish (made from pig's cheek and liver with calamansi and chilli) that

2

PINATUBO BLOWS ITS TOP

On 2 April 1991, people from the village of Patal Pinto on the lower slopes of **Mount Pinatubo** witnessed small explosions followed by steaming, and smelt rotten egg fumes escaping from the upper slopes of the supposedly dormant volcano (the last-known eruption was six hundred years before). On June 12, the first of several major explosions took place. The eruption was so violent that shockwaves were felt in the Visayas and nearly twenty million tons of sulphur dioxide gas were blasted into the atmosphere, causing red skies to appear for months afterwards. A giant ash cloud rose 35km into the sky and red-hot blasts seared the countryside. Ash paralysed Manila, closing the airport for days and turning the capital's streets into an eerie, grey, post-apocalyptic landscape. By June 16, when the dust had settled, the top of the volcano was gone, replaced by a 2km-wide caldera containing a lake. Lava deposits had filled valleys, buildings had collapsed, and over eight hundred people were dead.

The eruption virtually destroyed the traditional way of life of the **Aeta people**, who had lived on the slopes of the volcano. Over thirty years later, many Aeta have re-established small villages near the mountain, but more than seven hundred continue live in poorly maintained bamboo houses on a special relocation site in Sitio Gala near Subic Bay dubbed the Aeta Resettlement and Rehabilitation Center, where they're almost entirely dependent on charitable organizations for their survival.

was first cooked up at this unassuming restaurant in 1974. It's still the best place to sample it but ask how much it'll cost before you order, as the restaurant notoriously does not publish prices. The dish's inventor, *sisig* queen Lucia Cunanan, ran the place until 2008 when, at the age of 80, she was murdered by her gambling-addicted husband for refusing to give him money to bet with. $\overline{\text{PPP}}$

Gill's Buko Sherbet & Ice Cream Booth 6, M&M's Lane, Nepo Mart ⓦ facebook.com/gillssherbert1. Much-loved local sweet treat supplier, where the signature *buko* sherbet (also served with lychees) is the best choice. $\overline{\text{P}}$

Red Planet Don Juico Ave, Angeles City ⓦ redplanet hotels.com. Your best bet for accommodation in Angeles is this generic but efficient, modern and reasonably priced chain hotel, located just off Roxas Highway between Clark and Angeles. $\overline{\text{P}}$

Mount Pinatubo

All visitors must pay a conservation fee

Nothing has quite been the same around **Mount Pinatubo** (1485m), 25km east of Clark, since 1991, when the volcano exploded in one of the largest eruptions of the twentieth century worldwide (see box, above). Today, visits to the resultant moon-like lahar landscape and lake is one of the country's top activities, though independent hikes to the top are not permitted. The local people, the **Aetas**, though devastated by the eruption, have legal ownership over the mountain.

Organized trips to the volcano leave from the small town of **Santa Juliana**, about 40km from Clark, where you register. From here, a 4WD takes you for an hour or so across flat lahar beds and over dusty foothills to the start of a gentle hike to **Lake Pinatubo** (around 5.5km, with a height gain of 300m; 2–3hr); some tour companies will take you closer (via the Korean-built "Skyway"), within ten minutes of the crater (allow 1–2hr for the circuit trail). The lake itself is stunning, with emerald-green waters and spectacular surrounding views. Bring a packed lunch. Swimming and boating on the lake are banned.

ARRIVAL AND DEPARTURE

MOUNT PINATUBO

By bus and jeepney The North Luzon and SCTEX expressways make getting to Pinatubo easy enough, and it's feasible to visit as a day-trip from Manila. Coming from Manila (2–3hr) or Clark on any Tarlac- or Baguio-bound bus, ask to be let off in Capas, where you can catch a jeepney or tricycle to Paitlin, and then a tricycle to the barangay of Santa Juliana. From Santa Juliana, the first 4WD trips depart at around 5.30–6am from Capas Tourism Satellite Office (ⓦ capastarlac.gov.ph/tourism), and you won't be able to do the climb if you arrive in Santa Juliana later than 10am; it's best to arrive by 7am at the latest if possible.

ACCOMMODATION AND TOURS

Several companies run Pinatubo trips, though none will volunteer the information that the longer treks are closed, so question them carefully about what's open to trekkers at present. Prices are dependent on group size. **Hiking** all the way is not really feasible, as it would take at least 8hr, and camping is not allowed.

Alvin's Mount Pinatubo Guesthouse Santa Juliana Ⓦ mt-pinatubo.weebly.com. This little homestay offers accommodation, 4WD rental and trekking packages, as well as tours to local Aeta villages. The Mount Pinatubo trek (including Botolan Zambales mayor's fee, as well as

packed lunch and use of toilet and shower facilities at the guesthouse) offers great value if you are in a group of five; if there are just one or two of you, they can help you form a larger group to lower costs. $\overline{\text{PP}}$

Trekking Mt. Pinatubo Ⓦ trekkingpinatubo.com. Popular tours from Manila, beginning with a minibus ride to the Crow Valley (2hr 30min), where you transfer to 4WD jeep. Guides are good, but this is a long day-trip (pick up at 3–4am), and you won't get much time on the mountain. Trips are best value if you are in a group of ten or more.

Bataan

With 85 percent of it covered in mountainous jungle, the **Bataan** peninsula is one of the most rugged places in the country. The province, forming the western side of Manila Bay, will always be associated with one of the bloodiest episodes of World War II. For four months in 1942, 65,000 Filipinos and 15,000 Americans – "the battling bastards of Bataan" – held out here against the superior arms and equipment of the Japanese. After their surrender in April 1942, the Filipino and American soldiers, weakened by months of deprivation, were forced to walk to detention camps in Tarlac province. About 10,000 men died along the way. **Balanga** is the provincial capital, and there are some picturesque **beaches** on Bataan's southwest coast between **Mariveles**, some 50km south of Balanga, and **Bagac**.

Shrine of Valor

Daily 8am–5pm • Charge, extra fee for elevator up crucifix (closed for repairs at time of writing) • Jeepneys between Balanga, Cabog and Bagac stop at the Mount Samat/Diwa intersection (20min); from here tricycles run to the top (30min each way) or it's a sweaty 7km hike; it's also possible to hire a van from Balanga

A poignant memorial to the American and Filipino soldiers who fought and died here in World War II, the "Dambana ng Kagitingan" or **Shrine of Valor** occupies the summit of **Mount Samat** (564m), 16km inland from Balanga. The shrine has a chapel and a small museum of weapons captured from the Japanese, but the centrepiece is a 92m **crucifix** with an elevator inside (commissioned by Ferdinand Marcos in 1966); it hasn't operated since 2016, but when functioning, it takes you to a gallery at the top with views across the peninsula and, on a clear day, to Manila.

Mount Mariveles

Take a tricycle from Mariveles to the barangay of Alasasin, where you need to register at the barangay hall (charge) and can engage a guide

From Mariveles you can strike out for the ridge of dormant volcano, **Mount Mariveles** (1130m), a tricky overnight climb or a very long day for fit hikers. Apart from food and water, you'll need a good tent or bivouac, a sleeping bag and warm jacket – it can be surprisingly chilly when night falls. The caldera of Mariveles is huge; the ridge runs for 22km and includes several peaks – Tarak Ridge (the most accessible, from Alasasin), Banayan Peak and Mariveles Ridge.

ARRIVAL AND DEPARTURE   BATAAN

By bus Bataan Transit (Ⓦ facebook.com/bataantransit) runs frequent a/c services from Manila, originating both at Five Star Terminal, Cubao, and from Avenida Terminal. Genesis Transport (Ⓦ genesistransportserviceinc.com) runs a similar service from Pasay and Avenida to Balanga, and Pasay and Cubao to Mariveles, and also between Mariveles

and Baguio. Victory Liner (Ⓦ victoryliner.com) connects Balanga with Subic Bay. Jeepneys ply the mountain highway between Balanga, Cabog and Bagac when full.

Destinations from Balanga: Baguio (7–9hr); Manila (2–3hr); Olongapo (for Subic Bay; 1hr 15min).

Destinations from Marivales: Baguio (8–10hr); Manila

(3–4hr).

By boat From Manila, Baatan is a convenient 1hr 30min zip across the bay to Orion (near Balanga), with daily services from the CCP Pier in Pasay.

ACCOMMODATION

Montemar Beach Club Brgy Pasinay, Bagac ⓦ montemar.com.ph. This large, well-established hotel is the best of a number of resorts along Bataan's southwest coast used mostly by Filipinos for weekend breaks. It's on a 500m stretch of clean sandy beach, and has watersports facilities and a swimming pool. The rooms have a/c and a private balcony overlooking either the beach or the gardens. <u>PPP</u>

2

Corregidor

The tadpole-shaped island of **CORREGIDOR**, less than 5km long and 3km wide at its broadest point, is a living museum to the horrors of war. Lying 40km southwest of Manila, it was originally used by the Spanish as a customs post. In 1942 it was defended bravely by an ill-equipped US and Filipino contingent under continual bombardment from **Japanese** guns and aircraft. Some nine hundred Japanese and eight hundred American and Filipino troops died in the fighting, and when the Americans retook the island in 1945, virtually the entire Japanese garrison of over six thousand men was annihilated: little wonder Corregidor is said to be haunted. The island was abandoned after the war, and was gradually reclaimed by thick jungle vegetation – it wasn't until the late 1980s that the Corregidor Foundation began to transform it into a national shrine.

If you visit Corregidor on a day-trip, you'll be restricted to a **guided tour**. Perhaps understandably, the tours tend to focus on the heroism, bravery and sacrifice of the men who fought here, rather than the grisly nature of the fighting itself, but they are still a moving experience. Japanese tourists also come here to pay their respects to the dead of both sides. However, there's no accommodation on the island, and Covid put paid to the ferry operators heading there, and as such it's now only possible to visit on a day-trip with a private boat.

Away from the reminders of one of the war's most horrific battles, Corregidor is unspoilt, peaceful and a great break from the city: you can walk marked **trails** that meander through the hilly interior (look out for the monkeys and monitor lizards). Some boat operators will find a way for you to rent a kayak, or circle the island and do some fishing.

The war memorials

Tours begin near the ferry dock, with the statue of **General Douglas MacArthur**, who was reluctantly spirited away from the island before its capitulation in 1942. His famous words "I shall return" adorn the statue's base, though he actually made the pronouncement in Darwin, Australia. From here tours take in all the main sights on the island, including the **Filipino Heroes Monument**, commemorating Philippine struggles from the Battle of Mactan in 1521 to the EDSA Revolution of 1986, and the **Japanese Garden of Peace**, where the Japanese war dead were buried in 1945. Overgrown and lost, it was discovered in the 1980s, when the remains were cremated and brought back to Japan. A statue of the Buddhist bodhisattva Guanyin (or "Kannon" in Japanese) watches over the site. Eventually you'll reach the **Malinta Tunnel**, a 253m-long chamber and network of damp underground bunkers where MacArthur (and President Manuel Quezon) set up temporary headquarters. These are usually out of bounds; in the past they have been accessible on a **sound and light show** that dramatized the events of 1942, but this is also on hiatus.

Elsewhere you'll see the ruined concrete shells of the once vast barracks that dotted the island, and the remains of various gun batteries, peppered with bullet and shell holes. You can also visit the **Pacific War Memorial** and its small **museum** containing weapons, old photos and uniforms that were left behind. Finally, clamber the 57 steps to the top of the old **Spanish Lighthouse** at the island's highest point (191m), for stupendous views across to Bataan and Mount Mariveles.

2

By boat The only way to the island is by boat, but scheduled services from Manila bit the dust during Covid, and as of the time of research, nothing had returned. Instead the only option was to an outrigger boat (25min) from Mariveles (a 3hr drive from Manila) in Bataan (see page 118); some agencies will get you there and back on a day-trip, though this makes for a very long day (and a very early start), so you may wish to consider staying in or near to Mariveles instead. One agency that regularly gets people to Corregidor is Guia del Mar (⟍guiadelmartoursph.com); it's even possible to book things with them via Facebook. At one time, it was possible to overnight on the island at the *Corregidor Inn*, but the hotel has been closed for refurbishment since 2017 and shows no signs of reopening.

Subic Bay

Since the closure of US Naval Base Subic Bay in 1992, **SUBIC BAY** has been reinvented as a gate-guarded playground for the rich, with golf courses and plush hotels. For most foreign visitors, the main appeal is the wide range of watersports, diving and tranquil beaches.

The Subic Bay area is vast, most lying in Zambales province, an hour southwest of Clark via the SCTEX highway, and some 110km northwest of Manila. The old base

SUBIC BAY

ACCOMMODATION

By the Sea Resort	1
Court Meridian	6
The Lighthouse Marina Resort	4
Mangrove Resort	3
Subic Bay Travelers Hotel	5
Wild Orchid	2

EATING

The Coffee Shop	2
Gerry's Grill	5
Mango's	1
Veranda by Coco Lime	4
Xtremely Xpresso Café	3

DIVE SUBIC BAY

Subic Bay is a popular **diving** site, boasting fifteen shipwrecks in still waters, all no more than fifteen minutes by speedboat from the shore. The **USS New York** is the star attraction of Subic's underwater world, a battle cruiser launched in the US in 1891. When World War II broke out, she was virtually retired, and when the Japanese swept the US Marines out of the Philippines, the Americans had no choice but to scuttle her as they departed from Subic in early 1942. The ship now lies on her port side in 27m of water between Alava Pier in the CBD and the northern end of Cubi Point runway at the airport. For experienced divers, the 120m-long hull presents excellent opportunities for what scuba divers call a "swim-through" – an exploration of the inside of the wreck from one end to the other.

2

The **El Capitan**, a Spanish-era wreck lying 20m down in a pretty inlet on the east coast of Subic Bay is a much easier wreck dive, suitable for novices. The **San Quentin** (16m) is the oldest-known wreck in Subic, a wooden gunboat scuttled by the Spanish in 1898 in a futile attempt to block the channel between Grande and Chiquita islands against invading Americans. Other Subic wrecks include the Japanese POW ship *Oryoku Maru* and the *Seian Maru*, a Japanese cargo vessel sunk by the American Navy in 1945.

DIVE OPERATORS
Arizona Dive Shop Right on the shore at Baloy Long Beach ⓦ arizonadivesubic.com.

Mango's Dive Center 116A National Hwy, Barrio Baretto ⓦ mangosdivecenter.com.

itself is now the **Subic Bay Freeport Zone** (a tax- and duty-free zone), accessed by "gates" manned by security guards, and comprising two parts: most of the banks, restaurants, shops and hotels are located on a small island known as the **Central Business District (CBD)**, while on the **mainland** to the south lie the beaches and most of the outdoor activities, theme parks and attractions.

To the north of the CBD, linked by gates and bridges across the drainage channel (the main gate, at the end of Magsaysay Drive, is known as the **Magsaysay Gate**), **OLONGAPO CITY** – outside the Freeport Zone but considered part of the Subic Bay area – is a typical Philippine provincial town, and is where the bus terminals are located. Around 5km north of Olongapo along the coast (also outside the Freeport Zone), **Barrio Barretto** is gradually shaking off its go-go bar days, though it still attracts its share of the ageing expat/Filipina "girlfriend" scene. Nearby **Baloy Long Beach**, a laidback row of bars and hotels right on the sand, is a better place to crash.

Most visitors come to Subic Bay for the **wreck diving**, which is superb (see box, above), but there are plenty of peaceful, clean **beaches** inside the former base if you just want to chill out (see box, page 122).

Ocean Adventure
Camayan Wharf, Ilanin Rd, West Ilanin Forest Area • Charge • ⓦ oceanadventure.ph

Next to Camayan Beach (see box, page 122), **Ocean Adventure** is one of Subic's major tourist draws, comprising a small aquarium and arena for dolphin and sea lion shows. You can also swim and dive (includes dive gear; bring your certification). It's also possible to have a brief encounter on the beach with the park's dolphins, though the ethics of such practices is debatable.

Zoobic Safari
Ilanin Rd, West Ilanin Forest Area • Charge • ⓦ zoomanity.com.ph • Best reached by taxi

Subic Bay has its own zoo experience, the **Zoobic Safari**, which is popular with Manileños. However, though the animals are reasonably well treated, if you don't like zoos you're unlikely to enjoy this. Among the rather dubious attractions include a tiger safari via jeep (where the guides feed chicken to the "wild" tigers); a serpentarium with iguanas, snakes and lizards; and "croco loco", where crocodiles leap for dangling chickens.

Bat Kingdom

Zambales Hwy, Crown Peak, Cubi • Best reached by taxi from Olopango or the CBD

Other than a few groups of monkeys, the most visible wildlife in the hills around Subic is a colony of around ten thousand bamboo bats, fruit bats and giant flying foxes – the so-called **Bat Kingdom**. The colony tends to move around within the Cubi, Crown Peak area, so ask locals where they are; during the day bats hang from trees asleep, but at dusk thousands take to the air to look for food.

ARRIVAL AND DEPARTURE   SUBIC BAY

By bus Most buses (see page 81) arrive in Olongapo City at the Victory Liner terminal (☎ 047 222 2241) or the Saulog terminal, off Rizal Ave either side of the junction with W 18th St (the Olangapo–Bugalon road).
Destinations Angeles City/Dau (1hr, via SCTEX); Baguio (8hr); Manila Cubao (3–4hr); Manila, Cubao or Pasay (4–5hr).

INFORMATION

Tourist information 2/F, Subic Bay Exhibition & Convention Center, 18 Efficiency Ave (just off the main Manila highway, at the edge of the Zone; daily 8am–5pm; ☎ 047 252 4149); staff can help book tours, hotels and arrange hikes (see box, page 123).

GETTING AROUND

SUBIC BAY FREEPORT ZONE
By taxi Jeepneys and tricycles are banned within Subic Bay Freeport Zone, so transport is best by taxi; there are a couple of local firms/individuals, but using the Grab app works best, and avoids the need to haggle.

OLONGAPO
By jeepney In Olongapo all jeepneys are colour-coded; from West 18th St by the Victory Liner bus terminal you can take frequent blue jeepneys (direction "Castillejos") via Kalklan

Gate (the western CBD entrance) to Barrio Barretto and Baloy, or you can take a yellow jeepney to Magsaysay Gate.
By taxi and tricycle From the bus terminals to Magsaysay Gate, taxis and tricycles are easy to pick up. From Olongapo to the Freeport, you'll have to walk across the Main Gate as the two systems are mutually exclusive (see page 122).
By car To rent a car contact Avis (daily 8am–5pm; ☎ 047 250 0357) at Unit 116, Charlie Building, Subic International Hotel Compound.

ACCOMMODATION   SEE MAP PAGE 120

Places in the Freeport Zone tend to be plush and expensive. Barrio Barretto is dominated by resort complexes, but some of the bars (including *Johan's* and *Mango's*; see opposite) have low-priced rooms available.

SUBIC BAY FREEPORT ZONE
Court Meridian Lot B, Waterfront Rd at Rojas St ☺ court

meridian.com. Modern hotel, very clean with comfortable rooms, cable TV and breakfast included. The location is good, close to restaurants in the Central Business District. PPP
★ **The Lighthouse Marina Resort** Moonbay Marina Complex, Waterfront Rd ☺ lighthousesubic.com. Lavish boutique hotel topped with a replica of a lighthouse (not working). The room theme is "aqua", with soothing blue and

---

SUBIC BAY BEACHES

All Hands Beach San Bernardino Rd ☺ allhandsbeach.com. On the north side of the airport and closest to the CBD, this is a tranquil stretch of sand and beach huts shaded by trees. Though it's been developed into a resort, during most weekdays you'll have it to yourself. Entry fees apply.
Camayan Beach Ilanin Rd (off Corregidor Rd) ☺ camayanbeachresort.ph. South of All Hands, the

best beach in the Freeport Zone is Camayan Beach (formerly Miracle Beach) and now part of the *Camayan Beach Resort*; there are charges to access the resort, and you can rent snorkelling equipment, or go diving or kayaking.
Baloy Long Beach After Barrio Barretto's scrappy beach, this is one of the better strips of sand in Luzon; locals charge a nominal entry fee.

2

HIKING AROUND SUBIC

If you're feeling energetic, you can try numerous hiking trails around Subic Bay, though you'll need to contact the tourism department in advance (see page 122) to arrange mandatory guides, which come with a standard feeper hike. The **Apaliin Trail** runs along the banks of the Apaliin River to the coast (2hr), while visits to the rainforest trails within the **Pamulaklakin Nature Park** (daily 9am–4.30pm) can include an optional three-hour tour from members of the **Aeta** ("eye-ta") Indigenous people, who will take you deep into the forest. The Aeta are "Negritos" (they have dark skin and look quite African), and their ancestors are thought to have been the first people to reach the Philippines. They get no cultural support or recognition from the government, but were generally well treated under US rule, and were one of the few groups sad to see the Americans leave. Aeta warriors later trained US Marines here for service in Vietnam. Taxis to Pamulaklakin from the CBD (15min) are easy to arrange.

green tones, contemporary furnishings and a glass-walled bathroom, some with an old-fashioned tub. PPPP

Subic Bay Travelers Hotel Corner Aguinaldo and Raymundo St, ⓦsubicbaytravelershotel.com. The Subic Bay Travelers Hotel offers glossy and attractive, if a tad corporate, rooms at a reasonable price. There's a pool, and the staff can arrange excursions to local attractions. PPP

BARRIO BARRETTO AND BALOY LONG BEACH

By the Sea Resort 99 National Hwy, Barrio Barretto ⓦbythesea.com.ph. Fifty a/c rooms with cable TV either right on the beach or set back around a quiet garden. There's a convivial restaurant and bar overlooking the sea, and live music Fri. PP

Mangrove Resort Baloy Beach Rd, Baloy Long Beach, ⓦmangroveresortsubic.com. Peaceful resort hotel in an unbeatable location right on the water. The on-site restaurant – mostly centred on fish dishes, though also including a selection of Indian and Thai options – is very good, and you can also arrange to do watersports here. PPP

Wild Orchid Baloy Beach Rd, Baloy Long Beach ⓦwild orchidsubic.com. Justly popular choice, with standard "deluxe" rooms equipped with king-size beds, flatscreen TVs and DVD players. Welcome extras include *Captain Rob's Steakhouse* and *Barefoot Bar* on the beach, and an enormous pool (with jacuzzis and *Scalliwags* swim-up bar). PP

EATING
SEE MAP PAGE 120

The best places to **eat** and **drink** line the CBD waterfront. Cheaper places are in Olongapo City on Magsaysay Drive and Rizal Ave. In Barrio Barretto, some of the **nightlife** still has a seedier side, but certainly not all of it.

of coffee – they have an absolutely bewildering number of options on the menu, including pizzas, pasta, schnitzels, currywurst, sandwiches, meat dishes, waffles, and basically anything else you could think of. PP

SUBIC BAY FREEPORT ZONE

Gerry's Grill Waterfront Rd, near Labitan St ⓦgerrys grill.com. Big, brash chain restaurant that sells local food in immense portions; think fried chicken, *lechon kawali* and crab rice. PPP

Veranda by Coco Lime Dewey Ave ☎047 251 4024. The original Coco Lime restaurant – just north in the Harbor Point Mall – has long provided decent Philippine, Thai and Malay dishes that taste good, if not always totally authentic. This newer offering is much more attractive; have a go at their adobo rice and *pancit canton*. PP

Xtremely Xpresso Café 1 Dewey Ave ⓦxtremely xpresso.com. Not just a café, although it does serve mugs

BARRIO BARRETTO AND BALOY LONG BEACH

The Coffee Shop 2 Rizal St at the National Hwy, Barrio Barretto ⓦcoffeeshophotel.com. Late-night pit stop locally renowned since 1984 for its "jumbo tacos", packed with various meats and veggies in a soft taco shell. Also does decent fried noodles. There are also decent and well-priced rooms here. PP

Mango's 116A National Hwy, Barrio Barretto ☎047 223 4139. Beach bar, restaurant, cheap inn and local landmark (look out for the neon sign), serving both Filipino and Western cuisine. PP

DIRECTORY

Banks and exchange There are a handful of moneychangers on Magsaysay Drive near the junction with Rizal Ave, and ATMs all over the place.

Northern Luzon

CALLE CRISOLOGO

Northern Luzon

North of Manila, Northern Luzon harbours some of the archipelago's least-visited wildernesses, and offers thrilling outdoor adventures including whitewater rafting, trekking, surfing, spelunking and mountain biking. As well as its wonderful mountainous areas and volcanic landscapes, the region is home to some of the country's best surf breaks, along with wild stretches of coast peppered with virgin beaches and emerald-green waters. It is also rich in culture, with a handful of beautifully preserved Spanish colonial towns lining the west coast. Inland are the heartlands of the central Cordilleras mountain range, where spectacular rice terraces lie enveloped in clouds of mist. Further east is the Northern Sierra Madre National Park, the largest protected area in the country, offering exceptional trekking opportunities. More than 100km off the northern coast of Luzon, and closer to Taiwan than the Philippine mainland, lie the remote, scattered islands of Batanes province with their unforgettable hills and wild rugged cliffs.

Along the west coast north of Subic, the **Zambales coast** is dotted with laidback resorts, while the Lingayen Gulf is the location of the **Hundred Islands National Park** – a favourite weekend trip from Manila. The neighbouring stretch of coast at **Bolinao** offers wonderful virgin beaches at times flanked by dramatic rock formations. Further along the coast, the province of **La Union** draws visitors particularly for its surfing. North of here is Ilocos Sur, known primarily for the old colonial city of **Vigan**, where horse-drawn carriages bounce down narrow cobblestone streets. The area around the capital of Ilocos Norte province, **Laoag**, features a number of sites related to former dictator Ferdinand Marcos, who was born in the nearby village of Sarrat. On the northwestern edge of Luzon are excellent beaches around **Pagudpud**. Northern Luzon's east coast offers excellent surfing at **Baler**, while further north **Palanan** is the jump-off point for the barely explored **Northern Sierra Madre National Park**.

Despite the obvious appeal of the coast, for many visitors the prime attraction in Northern Luzon is the mountainous inland **Cordillera** region, where highlights include the mountain village of **Sagada** with its caves and hanging coffins, and the stunning rice terraces – designated by UNESCO as a World Heritage Site – around **Banaue**. In the village of **Kabayan** in Benguet province, it's possible to hike up to a couple of mountaintop caves to see ancient mummies. Kabayan also provides access to **Mount Pulag**, the highest mountain in Luzon.

The Zambales coast

Zambales is an undeveloped rural province – known for its succulent mangoes – that is still largely undiscovered by foreign tourists. It is, however, worth a stop for its scenic **beaches**, good surfing and relaxing resorts. For a break from beaches you can head inland to **Lake Mapanuepe**, formed after Mount Pinatubo erupted in 1991.

Zambales beaches

The **beaches** along the Zambales coast benefit from wonderful sunsets and views of the South China Sea. One lovely long stretch of white sand lies close to the fishing village

Highlights

❶ Surfing in San Juan The sweeping beach in the surf capital of the north has big breakers, magical sunsets and resorts for every budget. See page 134

❷ Vigan Atmospheric old Spanish outpost with cobbled streets, horse-drawn carriages and lively festivals. See page 135

❸ Ilocos Norte A province full of appeal, from sleepy towns such as Sarrat to a number of important Marcos-related sites. See page 144

❹ Trekking in the Cordillera The Cordillera offers wonderful walks through tribal villages and UNESCO World Heritage rice terrace scenery. See page 152

❺ Kabayan A remote village home to centuries-old human mummies interred in caves and burial niches dug out of solid rock. See page 159

❻ Sagada Celebrated mountain Shangri-La with hanging coffins, caves to explore, whitewater rafting, exceptional trekking and very cheap lodgings. See page 165

❼ Batanes Enchanting group of little-visited rural islands off the northern tip of Luzon, offering unforgettable scenery and terrific trekking. See page 175

HIGHLIGHTS ARE MARKED ON THE MAP ON PAGE 128

Batanes Islands (100km) ▲ Babuyan

N

Babuyan Channel

Palaui

Itbayat ● Mayan
⑦
Batanes Islands
Basco ● ● Batan
● Sabtang

Calayan

Dalupiri   *Babuyan Islands*

Fuga   *Camiguin*

0 ─────── 50
kilometres

Claveria
San Vicente
Santa Ana
Aparri

Pagudpud
Burgos ● Bangui
**ILOCOS
NORTE**   **APAYAO**
Calanasan
Luna
Laoag ● **③**
La Paz ● Sarrat
Paoay ● Batac   Scisona
Kabugao   Piat

CAGAYAN

Badoc Island
Badoc
ABRA
Sinait
Bantay
Vigan ● **②** ● Bangued
Santa Maria
Lubuagan   Tabuk
KALINGA
Tinglayan
Iguig
Peñablanca
Tuguegarao ✈

Santa Cruz
**ILOCOS
SUR**   **⑥** ● Bontoc
Cervantes   Sagada
Tagudin   Abatan   **④**
Bauko   Batad
Mt Data   Banaue
(2310m)   Lagawe
**LA
UNION**   **IFUGAO**
Kiangan
San Juan ● **①**
San Fernando ✈   Kabayan
Bauang   **⑤**
BENGUET   Mt Pulag
(2922m)   Bayombong
Agoo   Baguio ✈
Santiago   Rosario   **NUEVA
VIZCAYA**
Bolinao   San Fabian   Santa Fe
Bolinao Falls   Lucap   Dagupan
Alaminos   Lingayen   Urdaneta
**HUNDRED
ISLANDS
NATIONAL
PARK**
Lingayen
Gulf

**MOUNTAIN
PROVINCE**

Lubuagan
Tinglayan

Maconacon

**NORTHERN
SIERRA
MADRE
NATIONAL
PARK**

Ilagan
ISABELA
Cauayan   Palanan
San
Mariano

Santiago

QUIRINO
Dilasag
Dinalungan

*Dasol
Bay*
Santiago
Hermana Mayor
*Hermana
Minor*   Santa Cruz
Uacon
Potipot   Candelaria
Masinloc
ZAMBALES   **TARLAC**
Iba
Botolan   Tarlac
Mt Pinatubo   Dau
(1780m)   Clark
San Narciso   Aglao   Angeles
San Antonio   Lake
Camara   San Marcelino   Mapaniepe
Capones   Subic
San Antonio-Pundaquit   Subic   Olongapo
Bay

PANGASINAN

**NUEVA
ECIJA**
San Jose
Cabanatuan

AURORA
Baler
Digisit
Beach

Mt Arayat
(1030m)
PAMPANGA
San Fernando

Pollilo

HIGHLIGHTS

① Surfing in San Juan

② Vigan

③ Ilocos Norte

④ Trekking in the Cordillera

⑤ Kabayan

⑥ Sagada

⑦ Batanes

NORTHERN LUZON

of **San Antonio** and its popular barangay of **Pundaquit** (sometimes spelled Pundakit), which is also the access point for **Camara** and **Capones islands** – the latter a great place to camp. If your passion is for surfing, make a beeline for *Crystal Beach Resort* just north of the town of **San Narciso**; the best surf is between September and February. Some 35km further north, **Botolan** offers a couple of sleepy but well-run resorts on a nice wide beach in the barangay of Binoclutan, and there's another attractive (brown sand) beach just 8km north of here in the provincial capital **Iba**; the tourist office can arrange tours focusing on mango production, or activities such as mangrove planting. Another 40km further north, the towns of **Candelaria** and **Santa Cruz** serve as jumping-off points to the **islands** of Potipot, Hermana Mayor and Hermana Menor.

Potipot Island
You can hire a bangka from Candelaria (5min; accommodating up to six people)

Tiny **Potipot Island** is an idyllic little white-sand getaway that you can walk around in well under thirty minutes. At times you may have the island to yourself, although it can get busy at weekends and during school summer holidays (mid-March to early June).

3

The Hermana islands
SeaSun Beach Resort in Santa Cruz (see page 130) can arrange a day-trip to the Hermana islands

Close to the border with Pangasinan province, **Santa Cruz** is the main access point for two privately owned islands in Dasol Bay: **Hermana Mayor** and **Hermana Menor**. Neither island has accommodation for visitors, but both have some picturesque coves of fine white sand and good snorkelling.

ARRIVAL AND INFORMATION

By bus Victory Liner (victoryliner.com) have services straight up the coast from Manila, stopping at major towns like Iba (5–6hr from Manila) and Santa Cruz (6 –7hr) but able to drop you en route on request, and they can often even stop right by your resort – make sure to tell the driver where you're going. For Pundaquit, buses stop at San Antonio, a short tricycle ride away (10min), while to get to the Botolan resorts you'll have to catch a tricycle or jeepney (5min) from the spot on the main highway where buses drop you off. Regular local buses also connect all the towns

ZAMBALES BEACHES

along the coast.

By jeepney A number of jeepneys connect the towns along the coast.

By bangka Bangkas connect the Zambales towns with small islands off the coast – Pundaquit to Capones Island, for example (20min). Hotels can often help organize bangka hire.

Tourist information Iba has a tourist office on the second floor of the town's Capitol building (Mon–Fri 8am–5pm; 0930 421 4244). Tours can be arranged from here.

ACCOMMODATION

SAN ANTIONIO-PUNDAQUIT
Megan's Paradiso Beach Resort 0919 480 8520. This basic, welcoming place has simple rooms on two levels, all with minuscule balconies. The resort rents out bangkas, which are handy for exploring nearby Camara and Capones islands, as well as Anawangin Cove where there's good snorkelling. P̄
Punta de Uian facebook.com/PDUofficial. The most upmarket place to stay along the Zambales coast, this large resort offers a selection of rooms from a/c doubles to family villas. Facilities include two pools, basketball and tennis courts, and a playground. P̄P̄P̄

SAN NARCISO
Crystal Beach Resort crystalbeachresortzambales. com. Set on a pine tree-lined beach, this surfers' hangout

is a large place with a few tiki huts and native houses along the sand, as well as a variety of neat a/c rooms, mostly built with native materials. The vibe is laidback, with hammocks slung between the trees and live acoustic bands playing by the bonfire on weekend nights. Surfboard rental and surfing lessons (including board rental) are also on offer. Budget travellers can pitch a tent. P̄P̄

BOTOLAN
C & J Sunset Resort Km 189, National Rd, Brgy Binoclutan cjsunsetview.com. Friendly and welcoming, but slightly overpriced resort, with comfortable if a little bland bedrooms, as well as a decent pool and restaurant. It's ideal for its vicinity to a gorgeous stretch of beach – and as the name suggests, it is a good spot for sunset. P̄P̄P̄

3

Rama International Beach Resort Km 189, National Rd, Brgy Binoclutan ⓦ ramabeach.com. This Aussie-run resort, with a nice stretch of beach right at the doorstep and a fish pond and chirping birds in the leafy grounds, has a selection of family rooms as well as doubles a stone's throw away from the sea. They can also arrange trips to limestone caves near Santa Cruz, the old hilltop gold-mining town of Acoe or nearby Mount Binoclutan. P̄P̄

IBA

Funtasea Beach Resort Iba ⓦ funtaseabeachresort. com. The self-proclaimed best beach resort in Iba offers attractively decorated rooms set around a large pool, with easy access to a lovely stretch of sand. There's a good restaurant with an unexpectedly decent wine list, and there are spa treatments available. P̄P̄P̄

CANDELARIA

Dawal Beach Resort Brgy Uacón ⓦ dawal.com.ph. Large concrete-block resort offering clean, good-value poolside accommodation; some of the rooms at the back are a bit dated. There's a barbecue area for guests, and occasionally live music. The resort arranges trips to Potipot but has no snorkelling equipment for rent. P̄P̄

SANTA CRUZ

SeaSun Beach Resort ⓦ facebook.com/seasunbeach resort. Most of the rooms here have pretty blue tiles, private bath and a/c, while the five simple nipa rooms have fan and shared bath. There's a cluster of shaded open-fronted huts to while away the afternoon, an indoor bar with pool table and a coral reef perfect for snorkelling just 50m away. P̄

The Lingayen Gulf

Much of the western stretch of the **Lingayen Gulf**, between Bolinao and Dagupan, is taken up by working beaches where people fish in the gulf's rich waters and mend their nets. The gulf's primary attraction, the **Hundred Islands National Park** is home to some lovely beaches, while at the western end of the gulf around Bolinao you'll find wild stretches of coast and good **snorkelling**. At the northeastern end of the gulf, the capital of La Union province, **San Fernando**, provides access to more beaches and resorts as well as opportunities for trekking and climbing. There is also excellent **surfing** if you time it right, with surfers congregating in the resorts of **San Juan**.

Hundred Islands National Park

The tiny islands of **Hundred Islands National Park** – there are actually 123, but that doesn't have quite the same ring to it – cover almost twenty square kilometres. Some islands have beaches, but many are no more than coral outcrops crowned by scrub. Sadly, much of the underwater **coral** in the park has been damaged by a devastating combination of cyanide fishing (dripping cyanide in the water to stun the fish) and dynamite fishing (exploding dynamite in the water to kill the fish with shockwaves, then scooping them up when they float to the surface – of course this also kills the coral) along with typhoons and the El Niño weather phenomenon. The authorities are, however, going all out to protect what coral is left and help it regenerate, meaning you can only snorkel in approved areas.

Unless you want to camp, the closest base is the small town of **Lucap**, accessible from Alaminos, where day-trips set off; the town, however, is pretty dull and not recommended as a place to stay. It's far nicer to base yourself at one of the resorts near Bolinao (see page 131).

ARRIVAL AND DEPARTURE   HUNDRED ISLANDS NATIONAL PARK

By bus The closest bus station to the Hundred Islands National Park is at Alaminos, 4km south of Lucap, accessible from Lucap by tricycle (see page 130). Victory Liner (ⓦ victoryliner.com) and Five Star (ⓦ 5starbus.com) serve Manila (roughly every 40min–1hr; 4–8hr) and Santa Cruz (every 30min; 2hr). Victory Liner buses from Manila continue to Bolinao (45min), and there are services to

Dagupan (every 30min; 1hr 30min) from where you can change for Baguio or San Fernando La Union.
By tricycle Tricycles connect Alaminos with Lucap (15min) and can drop you at your hotel or at the national park office at the nearby pier.
By van From Alaminos, a/c vans serve Dagupan (1hr 30min).

INFORMATION AND ACTIVITIES

National park office You can pay your park entrance fee (and additional "environmental fee" and insurance) and arrange camping permits at the tourist office by the Lucap jetty (daily 24hr; ⊕ alaminoscity.gov.ph). They also rent out snorkelling equipment and camping gear, although you should check on availability of the latter before arrival. The office has a handy ATM. It's also possible to visit the islands by kayak; contact the tourist office or the Hundred Islands Eco-Tours Association (☎ 075 552 0773).

ACCOMMODATION AND EATING

The accommodation options in **Lucap** are largely uninspiring, so if you're staying in the area for a few days,

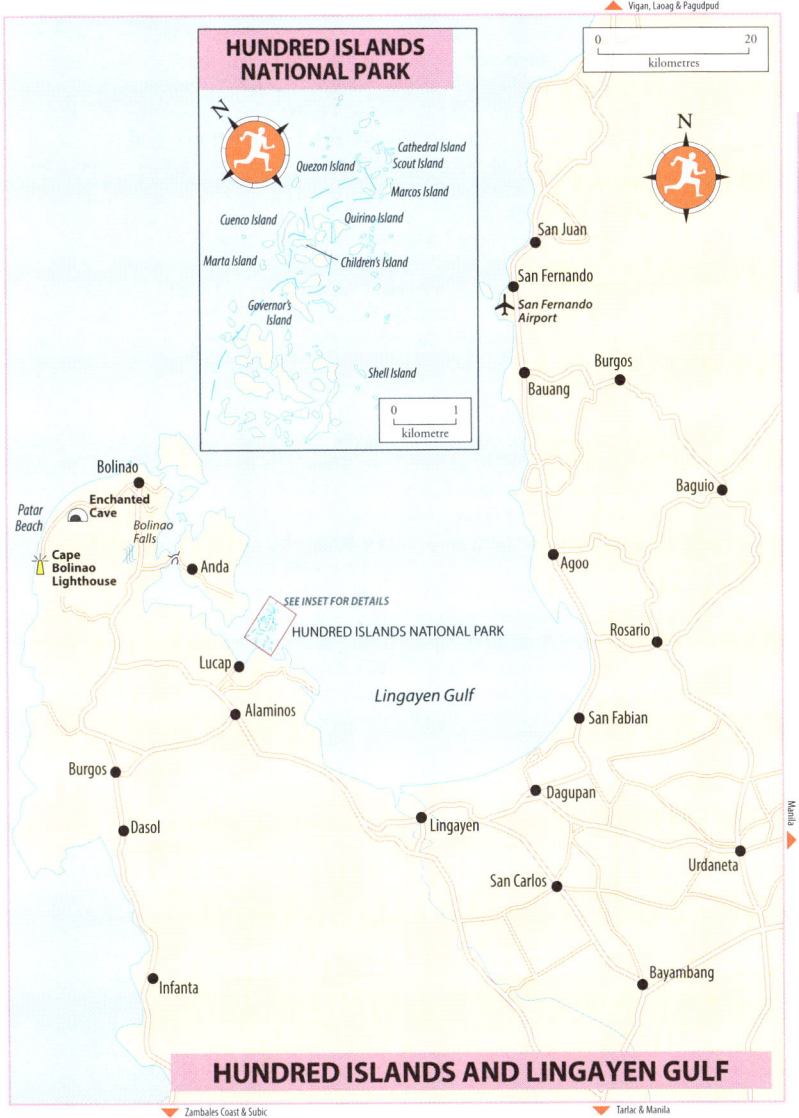

HUNDRED ISLANDS AND LINGAYEN GULF

3

ISLAND-HOPPING IN THE HUNDRED ISLANDS NATIONAL PARK

The best way to visit the pretty cluster of islets that form part of the One Hundred Islands National Park is through an island-hopping trip. The only three islands with any form of development are **Governor's Island**, **Children's Island** and **Quezon Island**. A day-trip to all three in a small boat for five people from Lucap is easy to arrange, and you'll need to choose one island on which you will spend most of your time – the boatman will leave you there for a few hours then return, and you'll visit the other two more briefly.

A much more appealing option is to pay for a "service boat" allowing you to visit the more interesting undeveloped islands. Some of these dots of land are so small and rocky that it's impossible to land on them, while others are big enough to allow for some exploring on foot, with tiny, sandy coves where you can picnic in the shade and swim. One of the prettiest islands is **Marta**, actually two tiny islets connected by a thin strip of bright white sand that almost disappears at high tide. **Marcos Island** has a blowhole and a vertical shaft of rock; you can clamber to the top and then dive into a seawater pool about 20m below. A number of islands, including **Scout Island** and **Quirino Island**, have caves; on **Cuenco Island** there's a cave that goes right through the island to the other side. Shell Island has a lagoon in which you can swim at high tide, while birdwatchers should ask to stop beside **Cathedral Island**.

Boats are available from 6am and will return to Lucap no later than 5.30pm; if you are planning to stay overnight on one of the islands then you need to leave Lucap by 5pm, and you will be charged extra for a service boat to drop you off and pick you up next day. Whatever your plans, the park office (see page 131) may be able to arrange for you to join another group if you do not have enough people to fill a boat and want to save some money.

consider basing yourself in **Bolinao** (see page 133). The hotels listed here are on Lucap's main strip and are within walking distance of one another. You can **camp** overnight on Governor's Island, Children's Island and Quezon Island. Eating options are limited, although most hotels have their own restaurant.

Island Tropic Guest House Lucap ⓦ islandtropichotel. com. In a super convenient location opposite the pier from which Hundred Islands trips depart, the rather brash Island Tropic Guest House is a reasonable enough choice for an overnight. There's a pool and a decent restaurant, and they can arrange island-hopping trips. The hotel can be a bit noisy, so you may need your earplugs. P̄P̄

Maxine By the Sea Lucap ⓦ maxinebythesea.com. Simply furnished rooms with a/c, cable TV and private bath. There's wi-fi in the public areas and a popular open-fronted restaurant serving fresh seafood – try the calamari. P̄P̄

Sea Urchin Lucap ⓦ facebook.com/SeaUrchinHotel.ph. This hotel's very smart – if overly yellow – exterior hides slightly shabby rooms that are a little past their prime. Even so, it's clean, staff are friendly, and the price is low, so it isn't a bad option for a stay in Lucap. P̄

Villa Antolin Lucap ☎ 075 696 9227. This is one of Lucap's best options, with clean rooms spread across two storeys and kitsch knick-knacks dotting the hallways. Not all rooms have hot water, so check first. P̄P̄

Bolinao and around

The landscape around the town of **BOLINAO** is one of cascading waterfalls, rolling hills and white beaches, including the popular **Patar Beach** and the inviting **Bolinao Falls**. The **Church of St James** in the main square was built by the Augustinians in 1609 and boasts a good collection of wooden santos figures.

Patar Beach

The best-known beach in the Bolinao area is **Patar Beach**, 19km west of town, which has fine white sand and good surf. On the road to Patar there are a number of pleasant, relaxed beaches and resorts, which can arrange trips to a large **barrier reef** offshore, near **Santiago Island**, where there is some wonderful solitary snorkelling.

Bolinao Falls

21km south of Bolinao • Charge for each waterfall (though fees are not always collected off-season), plus extra to hire a lifejacket • The falls are not signposted; if driving, make sure to ask for directions, or catch a tricycle from Bolinao (45min)

The **Bolinao Falls** are three emerald waterfalls perfect for a refreshing dip. Bolinao Falls 1 has a cascading fall with a small pool, while the larger Bolinao Falls 2 has a series of inviting pools where you can easily while away an afternoon. Further up is Bolinao Falls 3, which is a short, basin-like affair – not as spectacular, but perfect for a jump and a swim. You can rent open-fronted huts here for the day – there are only two basic stalls selling water and snacks so make sure to bring your own food for a picnic.

Enchanted Cave

Patar Rd • Charge

A popular attraction in the area is the **Enchanted Cave**, where you can descend a short flight of steep and slippery steps to swim in an underground pool of exceptionally clear water. It can get very busy on weekends; it's best to visit on a weekday.

Cape Bolinao Lighthouse

Close to Patar Beach, some 20km from Bolinao, stands the old **Cape Bolinao Lighthouse** (1905), which, sitting on a hill, rises 107m above sea level. There's an easy path to the base of the building; climbing up here from the main road is rewarded by great views across the South China Sea. Though you can't see them, not far offshore lie a number of submerged Spanish galleons and Chinese junks that, according to local lore, still contain treasure.

ARRIVAL AND INFORMATION

BOLINAO AND AROUND

By bus There are regular services from Manila (6hr) to Bolinao with Victory Liner (victoryliner.com) and Five Star (5starbus.com), with stops at Alaminos (45min from Bolinao). For Baguio or San Fernando La Union, take a bus to Dagupan (every 30min; 2hr) and change there.

By jeepney Jeepneys connect Bolinao with Alaminos, although they take much longer than the buses (leave when full; 1hr 30min).

By tricycle Tricycles connect Bolinao town to the resorts along the nearby beach (15min) and to Patar Beach (25min).

Tourist information The tourist office in Bolinao is on Rizal St (Alaminos–Bolinao Rd), opposite the High School (Mon–Fri 8am–5pm; ☎ 075 632 4479 or ☎ 0948 702 5629).

ACCOMMODATION AND EATING

There are only a few recommendable **hotels** and essentially no good **restaurants** in Bolinao proper; it's better to stay, and eat, at one of the nearby beach resorts.

BOLINAO

El Pescador San Andres St, Brgy Germinal ⓦ elpescador. ph. This large well-kept resort has more than fifty warm and welcoming rooms set in the "grand hotel" building by the beach, or in the less expensive "twin building" by the pool. There are also seven clean and cosy a/c kubo cottage huts, all with shared bath, decorated with pretty local materials, as well as a large inviting pool for adults, and a smaller one for children. PP

THE ROAD FROM BOLINAO TO PATAR BEACH

Casa Almarenzo 313 Patar Rd ⓦ casaalmarenzo.com. A smart and well-maintained resort with a lovely infinity pool overlooking the sea, the rooms at this place are attractively decorated, many with a vaguely nautical theme, and several have sea view balconies. There are a variety of entertainment options, including table tennis, a billiards table, and karaoke, the latter of which may be an advantage or disadvantage depending on your point of view. PPP

Puerto del Sol Brgy Ilog Malino ⓦ puertodelsol. com.ph. Bolinao's most upmarket resort offers spacious, tastefully decorated a/c rooms in well-tended grounds, with dark wooden furniture, fridges, cable TV, private verandas and tea and coffee amenities. There's a pool, spa, open-air jacuzzi and a restaurant overlooking a pretty stretch of beach with shallow clear water. PPP

★ **Punta Riviera Resort** Brgy Ilog Malino ⓦ punta rivieraresort.com. The best resort in the area, eco-friendly, with well-tended grounds, palm trees, infinity pool and a colourful dragon-fruit orchard. The tiled a/c rooms are clean and spacious, breakfast is included and the sauna and open-air jacuzzi are perfect spots to unwind after a kayaking trip through the resort's mangroves. Breakfast included. PPPP

Rock View Beach Brgy Patar ⓦ facebook.com/rockview beachresort14.net. The perfect choice for budget travellers, with closed nipa huts and simple a/c rooms (P2000), on a spectacular stretch of wild coastline overlooking rock formations. There isn't a restaurant, but guests can cook in the open-fronted kitchen. PP

Villa Soledad Brgy Ilog Malino ⓦfacebook.com/ VillaSoledadBeachResort. Good-value rooms, although some of the family rooms can be a bit of a squeeze. Accommodation is set around a leafy tropical garden with basketball court and two palm-shaded pools. There's table tennis and billiards, too. Breakfast included. PP

PATAR BEACH

Treasures of Bolinao Patar Beach ⓦfacebook.com/ treasureofbolinao. Overloooking Patar Beach, this resort has a variety of a/c rooms, most with private terraces, and you don't pay much more for the superior suites. There's a pleasant pool area and a deck overlooking the (rather rocky) beach, though some guests end up complaining about the resort's general air of decay, and iffy service. PP

San Fernando and around

The capital of La Union province and site of a former US air base, **SAN FERNANDO** has little of interest to tourists. It is, however, the access point for the popular **San Juan** surfing beach, 8km north.

Chinese-Filipino Friendship Pagoda

Take Zigzag Rd or use the steps up Hero's Hill from Quezon Ave

If you have a few hours to spare in San Fernando, take a walk uphill to Freedom Park and the **Chinese-Filipino Friendship Pagoda**. The pagoda boasts great views across the rooftops and out to the South China Sea. There is more evidence of the Chinese influence in the area at the impressive **Ma-Cho temple**, along Quezon Avenue on the northern outskirts of the city.

San Juan

A dramatic crescent with big breakers that roll in from the South China Sea, the coast just north of **SAN JUAN** in the barangay of Urbiztondo is a prime **surfing beach**. Most of its resorts have surfboards to rent and offer tuition for an additional charge. For experienced surfers there are two breaks in **Urbiztondo**, one a beach break in front of the main huddle of resorts and the other the **Monaliza** point break at the northern end of the beach. The best spot for beginners is the **Cement Factory** break in the nearby barangay of Bacnotan. The peak season is September to March; at other times there may be no waves but you can get significant discounts on accommodation.

ARRIVAL AND DEPARTURE

SAN FERNANDO AND AROUND

By bus The Partas (ⓦpartas.online) terminal is almost 2km north of San Fernando's plaza on Quezon Ave, though some other buses run from the plaza itself.

Destinations Baguio (1hr 30min); Laoag (6hr); Manila (6–8hr); Vigan (3hr 30min).

Transport to San Juan Jeepneys (every 30min; 15min)

run from the old market in San Fernando to San Juan, and tricycles are available too; alternatively, buses travelling between San Fernando and Laoag, Vigan or Abra province pass through San Juan – ask the driver to let you off at one of the resorts.

INFORMATION AND ACTIVITIES

Tourist information San Fernando's city tourist office is in the city hall on F. Ortega Hwy, just north of the plaza (Mon–Fri 8am–5pm; ☎072 888 6922); the regional tourism office (Mon–Fri 8am–5pm; ⓦbit.ly/san-fernando-reg) is at *Oasis Country Resort*, 3km south of San Fernando.

Services Quezon Ave, San Fernando's main drag, has a number of banks with ATMs, as well as a police station in the city hall (☎072 888 6911).

Scuba diving Ocean Deep Diver Training Centre, on Poro Point just west of the airport (☎072 619 3045).

ACCOMMODATION AND EATING

Unless you're staying the night in San Fernando before moving on, you're better off heading for the **San Juan resorts**. All the resorts listed are right on the beach and

within walking distance of each other, and most of them have **restaurants**, but tend to get booked up in high season (Oct–March), so reserve ahead.

SAN FERNANDO

Halo Halo de Iloko 12 Balay Mercado, Zandueta St ☎ 072 700 2030. A restaurant and café with eclectic decor, including zebra-print walls and colourful window panes. The main draw here is the *halo-halo* (shaved ice with evaporated milk and toppings including fruit and purple yam). P̄

Sunset Bay Brgy Canaoay ⓦ sunsetbayphilippines. com. Just south of San Fernando, this welcoming resort overlooking the South China Sea has nicely decorated rooms giving onto a well-tended garden with potted plants and local crafts. There's a pool and a coral reef 90m off the shore where you can snorkel. P̄P̄

SAN JUAN

Angel and Marie's Place ☎ 0917 723 3253. The favourite surfers' restaurant in San Juan offers serious fish dishes such as tuna steak or squid adobo, with banana chocolate crêpes for afters, and Filipino breakfasts at the weekend. It also has rooms (including breakfast) and a smoothie shack on the beach. P̄

★ **The Circle Hostel** ⓦ thecirclehostel.com. Hip budget surf hostel, very sociable, and with breakfasts usually included with the booking. You can stay in a dorm bed with your own mozzie net, or in a hammock. P̄

Gefseis Greek Grill ⓦ facebook.com/GefseisGreekGrill.

A great place for a Greek meal made with fresh local ingredients. Starters include succulent grilled octopus; try with a souvlaki platter for main course. P̄P̄

Kahuna Beach Resort and Spa ⓦ kahunaresort.com. It may not be entirely in keeping with San Juan's laidback surfer vibe, but this upmarket resort certainly has verve. The rooms are stylish and comfortable, and the infinity pool is a great place to sip cocktails. P̄P̄P̄P̄

Little Surfmaid ⓦ surfmaid.wixsite.com. At the northern end of the string of resorts, close to the Mona Liza point break, this Danish-owned place offers spacious a/c rooms with fridge, and there are nice touches such as colourful bedspreads from the Cordilleras. The more expensive rooms have little balconies, and there's a restaurant serving good food. P̄P̄

San Juan Surf Resort ⓦ sanjuansurfresort.ph. Squarely aimed at surfers: there's a shop selling kit, and surf conditions are posted by the bar. It's worth paying a bit extra for a deluxe room with free breakfast and more reliable wi-fi. P̄P̄P̄

Sebay Surf Resort ⓦ sebaysurfcentral.com. The nicely decorated rooms here give onto a leafy pathway and are set in a thatched building adorned with nipa. There's also a larger wooden structure slightly further back from the beach that has more spacious family rooms. P̄P̄

Ilocos

Long and narrow, **Ilocos Sur** province is sandwiched by the sea on one side and the Cordillera Mountains on the other. For most tourists the highlight is undoubtedly the once important trading town of **Vigan**, one of the most atmospheric and enjoyable cities in the country. **Ilocos Norte**, meanwhile, is still strongly associated in Filipino minds with former president Ferdinand Marcos, and his family continues to wield considerable political power in the province. Sites related to the Marcos family include Ferdinand's **birthplace** in Sarrat, his **mausoleum** in Batac, and the mansion known as the **Malacañang of the North** beside Paoay Lake. On the northern coast, the town of **Pagudpud** draws visitors from across Luzon with some of the best beaches on the island.

Vigan

An unmissable part of any North Luzon itinerary, **VIGAN** is one of the oldest towns in the Philippines. Lying on the western bank of the Mestizo River, it was in Spanish times an important political, military, cultural and religious centre. The **old town** is characterized by its cobbled streets and some of the finest **colonial architecture** in the country, mixing Mexican, Chinese and Filipino features. Many of the old buildings are still lived in, others are used as curio shops, and a few have been converted into museums or hotels. The attractions are within walking distance of one another, with **Plaza Burgos** the most obvious reference point, and, adding to the old-world atmosphere, some streets are open only to pedestrians – unusual in the Philippines – and romantic horse-drawn **kalesas**. Vigan sustained damage in the July 2022 earthquake, forcing many sites in the historic centre – including the cathedral – to close for repair work.

VIGAN'S FESTIVALS

The biggest secular festival is the week-long **Vigan Town Fiesta**, involving carnivals, parades, musical extravaganzas, beauty contests and nightly cultural shows. It culminates on January 25 with the celebration of the conversion of St Paul the Apostle, the town's patron saint. Almost straight after that, at the end of January, comes the **Kannawidan Ilocos**, a relatively recent addition to the festival calendar celebrating the culture of Ilocos Sur. It includes a "battle of the bands" and a beauty contest.

The **Viva Vigan Binatbatan Festival of Arts**, held in the first week of May, includes dancing and music; the highlight is the religious celebration on **May 3** (Tres de Mayo), which starts with a Mass at Vigan's cemetery chapel and continues with dancing in Crisologo Street and a kalesa parade. **Holy Week** is also a special time in Vigan, with candlelit processions through the old streets and a *visita iglesia* that sees devotees doing the rounds of churches and cathedrals.

3

Brief history

In pre-colonial times, long before Spanish galleons arrived, **Chinese** junks came to Vigan and helped it to become a major trading port. They arrived with silk and porcelain, and left with gold, beeswax and mountain products brought down by inhabitants of the Cordillera. Stories of Vigan's riches spread and before long immigrants from China arrived to settle and trade here, intermarrying with locals and beginning the multicultural bloodline that Biguenos – the people of Vigan – are known for.

Spanish domination

The **Spanish** arrived in 1572. Captain Juan de Salcedo conquered the town and named it Villa Fernandina de Vigan in honour of King Philip's son, Prince Ferdinand, who died at the age of 4. Salcedo then rounded the tip of Luzon and proceeded to pacify Camarines, Albay and Catanduanes. In January 1574 he returned to Vigan, bringing with him **Augustinian missionaries**, and setting about the task of creating a township his king would be proud of, with grand plazas, municipal buildings and mansions.

One of the potentially incendiary results of this Spanish political domination was the rise of a *mestizo* (mixed ethnicity) master class, whose wealth and stature began to cause resentment among landless natives. In 1763 things came to a head when revolutionary **Diego Silang** and his men assaulted and captured Vigan, proclaiming it capital of the free province of Ilocos. When Silang was assassinated by two traitors in the pay of the Spanish, his wife, Maria Josefa Gabriela Silang, assumed leadership of the uprising. She was captured and publicly hanged in the town square.

The modern day

Unlike in Manila, many of Vigan's fine **old buildings** managed to survive World War II, though the humidity and their wooden construction makes preservation difficult. Many wealthy inhabitants left town in favour of a new life in Manila, allowing their ancestral homes to fall into partial ruin, though Vigan's 1999 inclusion on the **World Heritage Site** list at least guarantees it some level of protection and funding – something it found itself sorely needing after the earthquake hit in 2022.

The old town

Most of the beautiful ancestral houses are in Vigan's **old town**. Also known as the Mestizo District or Kasanglayan ("where the Chinese live"), the old town runs roughly from Plaza Burgos in the north to **Liberation Boulevard** in the south. The most important thoroughfare is elegant old **Crisologo Street**, which is closed to traffic. Architecturally, the houses are fundamentally Chinese or Mexican, influenced either by the immigrant architects from China's eastern seaboard who prepared the plans, or by ideas picked up by the Spanish in their South American colony. Local artisans, meanwhile, added flourishes such as sliding capiz-shell windows. A few homes are open to the public, offering an intimate view of ilustrado (educated middle class) life at the turn of the nineteenth and twentieth centuries.

Crisologo Museum

Liberation Blvd • Donations welcome

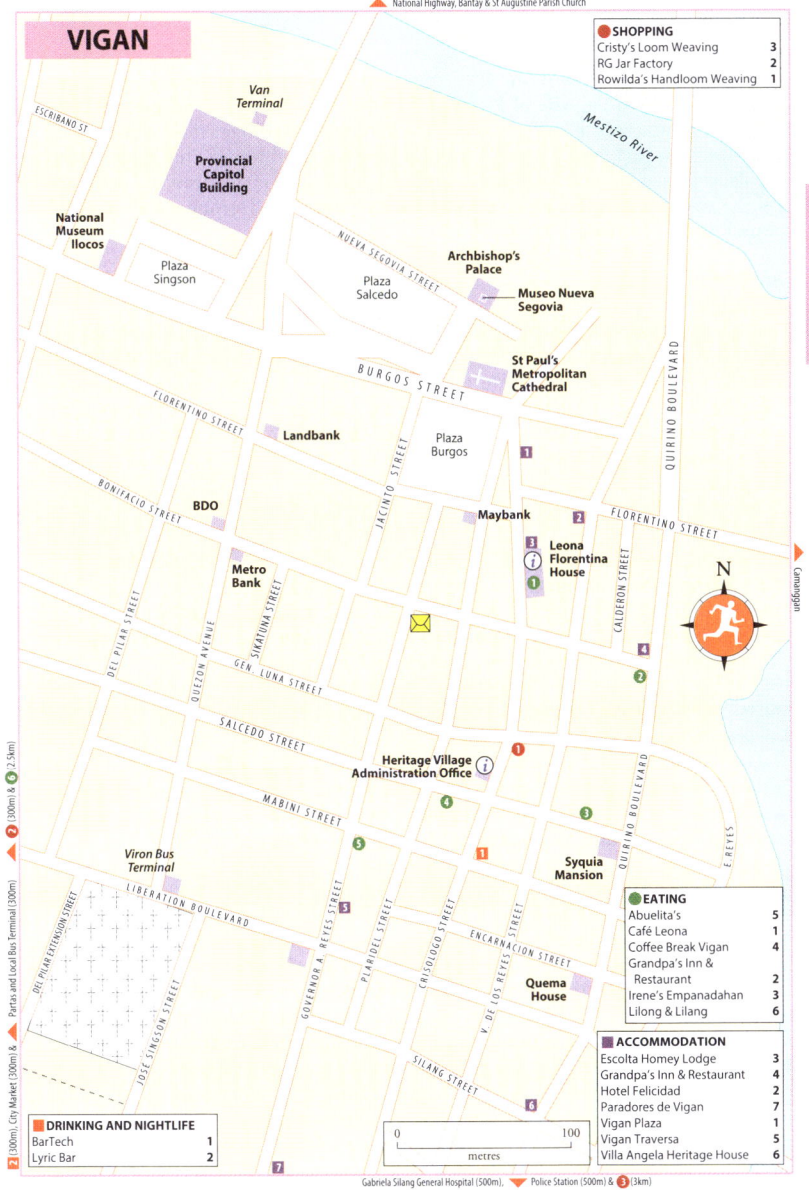

The **Crisologo Museum**, former home of the influential – and sometimes controversial – Crisologo family, displays photographs, mementos and personal memorabilia, including the bright pink Chevrolet in which Governor Carmeling was ambushed in 1961. She survived the attack, unlike her husband, congressman Floro Crisologo, who was shot twice in the head in October 1970 while attending Mass inside Vigan Cathedral. There's a macabre selection of photographs from the death scene, along with the bloodied trousers he was wearing at the time.

Syquia Mansion
Quirino Blvd at Salcedo St • Charge

Built in 1830, **Syquia Mansion**, the former family mansion and holiday home of Doña Alicia Syquia, wife of President Elpidio Quirino, has been restored and furnished in nineteenth-century style. The various furnishings reflect the Chinese roots of the Syquia family, wealthy traders who migrated to the Philippines from mainland China to trade with the Spaniards. Look out for the beautiful 1910 piano and the wooden camphor chest that to this day emanates a strong smell that is a natural insect repellent.

Quema House
8 Encarnacion St

The beautiful **Quema House**, built in the 1820s, was home to Don Mariano Quema, one of the city's wealthiest merchants. The mansion is unique in Vigan in that it contains virtually all the original furnishings and decor, from the Vienna chairs in the living room to the intricately painted vines on the ceiling. The house is not regularly open to the public, but you may be able to persuade the caretaker to let you in if you have a special interest.

St Paul's Metropolitan Cathedral
Burgos St

Built by the Augustinians in 1641, but much battered and repaired since then, **St Paul's Metropolitan Cathedral** was designed in "earthquake Baroque" style, with thick ramparts and a belfry built 15m away so that it stood a chance of surviving if the church itself collapsed. Given Vigan's history, it's not surprising that there's some Chinese influence; see, for example, the brass communion handrails.

Museo Nueva Segovia
Nueva Segovia St • Charge

The **Archbishop's Palace** (*Arzobispado*), completed in 1783, is still the official residence of the Archbishop of Nueva Segovia (the old Spanish name for what is now Ilocos Sur). Inside, the tiny **Museo Nueva Segovia** showcases ecclesiastical artefacts, antique portraits of bishops and religious paraphernalia from all over Ilocos Sur.

National Museum Ilocos
6 Burgos St • Free • Ⓦ nationalmuseum.gov.ph

The **National Museum Ilocos**, still sometimes known as the Burgos House, was once home to one of the town's most famous residents, Padre José Burgos, whose martyrdom in 1872 galvanized the revolutionary movement. Between 1972 and 1975, the building became a branch of PNB bank – you can still see the teller windows on the ground floor. The first couple of rooms introduce Ilocano culture and traditions, with displays including farming and fishing tools, wooden coffins and a nose flute. The third room contains the chamber used to execute Burgos and his two companions, as well as an informative miniature model shedding light on the Spanish tobacco monopoly in the early eighteenth century. Furniture and other Burgos family memorabilia is displayed on the first floor.

ARRIVAL AND DEPARTURE

VIGAN

By plane The small Vigan Airport, about 4km southwest of the centre, has in the past been served by infrequent flights to Manila and Basco; check online to see if these have resumed.

By bus The Partas terminal (ⓦpartas.online) is by the city market, about 300m south of the old town. From Laoag, local buses arrive at the local bus terminal near the city market, but will usually drop passengers in town on their

way through. If travelling to Vigan from Lingayen, Dagupan or Alaminos in the Lingayen Gulf, head to Urdaneta and catch a northbound bus from there (6hr). Buses from Vigan to Manila and Baguio stop in San Fernando (2hr).

Destinations Baguio (5hr); Laoag (2hr); Manila (9–10hr).

By van The van terminal is just by the Provincial Capitol Building. There are regular vans to Santa Maria throughout the day (leave when full; 45min).

INFORMATION AND TOURS

Tourist office The provincial tourist office is at Leona Florentino House, 1 Crisologo St (daily 8am–5pm; ☎ 0927 918 8882). The municipal tourist office on Crisologo St ("Heritage Village Administration Office"; supposedly open daily 8am–5pm) is less helpful and often left unstaffed.

Tours A nice way to get around town, the kalesas, or horse-drawn carriages, also offer tours; you can find them on Burgos St by the cathedral, or on Salcedo St at V. de los Reyes

St. You can ask the *kutchero* (driver) to suggest a route that will take in the main sights; they normally include a visit to the pretty St Augustine Parish Church in the nearby town of Bantay. The grandiosely named "Vigan heritage river cruise" is a 45min boat trip with crackly recorded commentary (hourly 8.30–11.30am & 1.30–4.30pm; charge) that starts at Celedonia Garden in Beddeng Laud.

3

ACCOMMODATION

SEE MAP PAGE 137

Note that the mosquitoes can be particularly ferocious around the riverside; if you're staying in one of the properties nearby, it helps a little to have a room set back from the river-facing side.

Escolta's Homey Lodge 1-14 Crisologo St ⓦfacebook. com/escoltashomeyvigan1572. Housed in a gorgeous old colonial building in a central spot, the Escolta Homey Lodge offers an authentic slice of Vigan life. The rooms are simple but attractive; beds in a ten-person dorm are also available. P̄

Grandpa's Inn & Restaurant 1 Bonifacio St ⓦfacebook. com/grandpasinnvigan. This ancestral house with bare brick walls and parquet flooring has been converted into a lovely inn full of old curios. There are a range of rooms, of which most are a/c and en suite, but the very cheapest are fan-cooled with a shared bathroom. Room 7 is a uniquely furnished twin room where you can sleep in a kalesa (carriage). P̄P̄

Hotel Felicidad 9 V. de los Reyes St ⓦfacebook.com/ hotelfelicidadvigan. A charming option in a beautiful colonial mansion offering tastefully decorated rooms with beautiful hardwood floors and high ceilings. The delightful maestro suite features a solid ironwood king bed and a splendid antique dresser. P̄P̄

Paradores de Vigan Gov. A Reyes St ⓦvigan.paradores. ph. This hotel slightly to the south of the historic centre

manages to capture a degree of the old character of Vigan, despite being housed in a modern building. The rooms, decked out with stylish dark wood furniture, are comfortable and welcoming, and there's a restaurant and gym on-site. P̄P̄P̄

Vigan Plaza Plaza Burgos ⓦviganplazahotel.com.ph. In an excellent location on Plaza Burgos, and just a stone's throw away from the cathedral, this colonial hotel featuring beautiful tiled floors has rooms on three floors. The first- and second-floor options are in a better overall condition than those on the ground floor, most of which give onto a wall and are quite dark. P̄P̄

Vigan Traversa Gov. A. Reyes St ⓦfacebook.com/ ViganTraversaHotel. There are no surprises at the Vigan Traversa – the rooms are comfortable and clean but lack any particular character. That said, the hotel is in an excellent central location and its extremely good value, so it's by no means a bad choice. P̄P̄

★ **Villa Angela Heritage House** 26 Quirino Blvd ⓦfacebook.com/VillaAngela. The most charming of all the colonial hotels, this is a beautiful old museum of a place, wonderful value, and the top choice if you want to wallow in history. You can ask to be given the room Tom Cruise slept in: he had an overnight stay here when *Born on the Fourth of July* was being filmed on the sand dunes near Laoag. P̄P̄

EATING

SEE MAP PAGE 137

Vigan doesn't offer much in terms of **restaurants**, although make sure to try some local specialities, including the town's famous crispy **empanadas**.

Abuelita's 39 Governor A. Reyes St ☎ 077 722 2368. This popular restaurant has some interesting old curios up on its shelf, including radios, rusty number plates and an old sewing machine. The speciality is regional Ilocano cuisine,

and food is displayed in pots at both lunch and dinner – just take your pick and pay accordingly. P̄

Café Leona 1 Crisologo St ⓦfacebook.com/CafeLeona Resturant. Travellers are drawn to the outdoor tables that spill out on the street in the evening, although you can also dine in the tavern-style interior. The menu lists Ilocano and Japanese fusion dishes such as *longganisa maki*, as

> ## VIGAN'S CRISPY EMPANADA
>
> Don't leave Vigan without trying the local **empanada** – a crispy deep-fried tortilla of rice-flour dough containing cabbage and green papaya. Some empanadas – sometimes known as "special" – also contain an egg and *longganisa* (garlic sausage). Either way, eaten with sugar-cane vinegar and chopped shallots, they are delicious. The stalls on the western side of Plaza Burgos, known collectively as **empanadaan**, sell empanadas, *okoy* (egg, prawn, tomato and onion frittata, again eaten sprinkled with sugar-cane vinegar) and other street food.

well as pizza and Vigan specialities – try *daing na bangus*, marinated milkfish. $\overline{\text{PP}}$

Coffee Break Vigan 3 Salcedo St ⓦfacebook.com/coffeebreakvigan. Slightly cheesy-looking place serving good espresso-based coffees, as well as ginger tea, and shakes including soursop and calamansi. There's fierce a/c, and they also whip up simple dishes – toast, bacon and bread, cream-covered waffles and the like. $\overline{\text{P}}$

Grandpa's Inn & Restaurant 1 Bonifacio St ⓦfacebook.com/grandpasinnvigan. Courtyard restaurant with an open kitchen where you can tuck into Ilocano specialities such as *bagnet poqui poqui*, Chinese dishes such as mandarin pork stew, or an extensive selection of noodle and pasta dishes. Seasonal specials include wind-dried wild boar meat, elvers, and eggs scrambled with the roe of a local fish. $\overline{\text{PP}}$

Irene's Empanadahan 13 Salcedo St ⓦfacebook.com/irenesviganempanada. This multi-generation empanada place has been going strong since the 1930s – locals say it's the best place in town to savour the Vigan speciality, which comes in several varieties, including pork, beef, chicken, (canned) tuna and, if you're lucky, crab. $\overline{\text{P}}$

Lilong & Lilang Brgy Bulala, 2.5km west of Vigan ⓦfacebook.com/hiddengardenvigan. This leafy "hidden garden" restaurant is located in a plant nursery, and serves traditional Ilocano dishes, including *poqui poqui*, mashed grilled aubergine sautéed with onions and tomatoes with egg. For dessert try the colourful *halo-halo*, beautifully presented in a coconut husk bowl. You may want to take a tricycle to get here. $\overline{\text{PP}}$

DRINKING AND NIGHTLIFE　　　　　　　　　　SEE MAP PAGE 137

Nightlife is generally very low-key, with limited options – things quieten down substantially at 9pm.

BarTech Crisologo St ⓦfacebook.com/ViganBarTech. Though primarily a restaurant offering a decent buffet, BarTech becomes a bit of a night spot later in the evening, with locals and tourists alike popping in to grab a cold beers

and enjoy the live bands that occasionally take to the small stage. $\overline{\text{P}}$

Lyric Bar Alcantara St, by Partas bus terminal ☎077 722 2988. Lively bar, in an old cinema south of the centre, with a dark interior featuring hexagonal mirrors and glitzy chandeliers. Live bands play several times weekly. $\overline{\text{P}}$

SHOPPING　　　　　　　　　　　　　　　　SEE MAP PAGE 137

Cristy's Loom Weaving Camangaan, 3km southeast of the city centre ☎0916 491 9320. Here you can watch women weaving at old rickety looms, and buy the finished products, including sheets, pillowcases, tablemats and runners, in the small nearby shop. To get here catch a tricycle from town (15min).

RG Jar Factory 48 Gomez St ⓦinstagram.com/rgpottery. The massive wood-fired kilns here produce

burnay – huge jars used by northerners for storing everything from vinegar to fish paste. Broken jars, called *gibak*, are used as a bed to dry salt. You can get involved too: staff are happy to let you have a go at making your own jar.

Rowilda's Handloom Weaving Crisologo St at General Luna St ☎077 722 1482. This souvenir shop, with a workshop in nearby Camangaan, offers a selection of handwoven fabrics including place mats, table runners, napkins and blankets.

DIRECTORY

Banks and exchange You'll find several banks with ATMs on Quezon Ave, including BDO and Metro Bank, a Landbank on Florentino St by Quezon Ave, and a Maybank at the corner of Plaridel and Florentino streets.

Hospital Gabriela Silang General Hospital (☎077 674 1309), south of the centre on Quirino Blvd.

Police station Rivero St, Brgy 8, south of the city centre (☎077 722 0890).

Santa Maria Church and around

38km south of Vigan • From Vigan, take any Manila-bound bus (1hr), or catch a van to Santa Maria (leave when full; 45min); tricycles to Pinsal Falls leave from Santa Maria town (45min)

JUAN LUNA

Born in the mid-nineteenth century Juan Luna enjoyed a colourful career: after initially training as a sailor, he soon discovered a talent for painting and travelled to Europe, where his reputation as an artist grew, and his works *La Batella de Lepanto* and *Rendición de Granada* won the 1887 Exposition. In 1892, he shot and killed his wife Maria de la Paz Pardo de Tavera and mother-in-law owing to a suspicion that Maria was having an extra-marital affair; though arrested and charged with murder, Juan was acquitted on the basis that the killing was a crime of passion. He was arrested in 1896 again, this time for involvement in the Philippine independence movement, and subsequently became a member of the Philippine revolutionary government's delegation to Paris. He died in 1899.

The UNESCO World Heritage-listed **Santa Maria Church**, dating from 1769, is a solid structure with a brick facade, set on a hill and reached via 83 steps; unsurprisingly, it was used as a fortress during the Philippine Revolution. The interior is quite plain with the exception of its geometric floor tiles, and it's inhabited by birds and bats. While you're in the area it's worth travelling 8km to **Pinsal Falls**, a spectacular set of waterfalls with two large emerald-green pools. Make sure to bring snacks and refreshments, as there are no shops.

Badoc

Juan Luna Shrine • Free • ⓦ nhcp.gov.ph

The coastal road north of Vigan to Laoag is sealed all the way, and the journey time is only two hours, but if you want to break the journey you could stop at **BADOC**, the birthplace of the Filipino painter Juan Luna. His reconstructed house, known as the **Juan Luna Shrine**, stands in a side street close to the seventeenth-century Virgen Milagrosa de Badoc church. About 1km off the coast, **Badoc Island** is gaining a reputation for good surfing (late Oct to early March & late June to early Sept) – get there by renting a bangka from the little wharf in Badoc town.

Laoag

The congested streets of the Ilocos Norte provincial capital, **LAOAG**, can't compete with Vigan's historical core when it comes to aesthetic appeal, but there are a handful of things to do and see, and the city boasts one of the country's best museums. Laoag

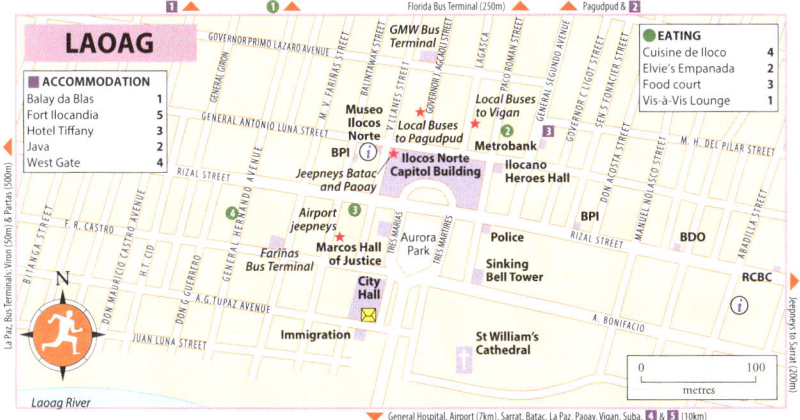

also makes an excellent base for exploring the beautiful coast at nearby **Suba** or touring sights associated with former dictator **Ferdinand Marcos**.

Museo Ilocos Norte

V. Llanes St at General Luna St • Charge • ⓦ museoilocosnorte.com

Laoag's most interesting attraction, the recently-renovated **Museo Ilocos Norte**, provides an overview of the province's history and culture. Close to the main plaza, it's housed in a restored Spanish-era tobacco warehouse. Exhibits include vintage costumes, farming equipment and tribal artefacts, with a replica of an ilustrado ancestral home complete with antiques. The souvenir shop has some appealing books and gifts.

Sinking Bell Tower and St William's Cathedral

Bonifacio St

It's worth taking a look at the **Sinking Bell Tower**, built by Augustinian friars in 1612, which has a door big enough for a man on horseback to pass through. Today, however, the tower has sunk so much that you can only get through by stooping – although sadly the tower is closed to visitors.

In principle the bell tower belongs to **St William's Cathedral**, the large church across the street, with its magnificent white and gold two-storey facade and simple, matching interior. The church, which became a cathedral in 1961, was originally constructed at the beginning of the seventeenth century to replace a simpler wooden structure. Most of what you see today dates from the 1870s however, when it was rebuilt after a fire. The inside was redecorated in the 1970s with money donated by the public, the chandeliers being the gift of one Mr and Mrs Ferdinand E. Marcos.

Marcos Hall of Justice

V. Llanes St • Free

The **Marcos Hall of Justice**, the square white building on the west side of Aurora Park, was where a young Ferdinand Marcos was detained in 1939 after being accused of the murder of one of his father's political opponents. Marcos wanted to graduate in law and used his time in detention wisely, swotting for the bar examination and successfully preparing his own defence.

ARRIVAL AND DEPARTURE | LAOAG

By plane The airport is 7km southwest of town (reachable by tricycle, or jeepney from Gabu terminal on Balintawak St). PAL and Cebu Pacific serve Manila (1–2 daily; 1hr 15min).

By bus Partas buses (ⓦ partas.online) from Manila (5 daily; 14hr) and Baguio (every 30–60min; 7–8hr) terminate at the Partas bus station on the western end of Rizal St. Viron (ⓦ virontransit.com; 6 daily to Manila) have a terminal on Rizal St slightly closer to town at Peralta St; Fariñas buses (ⓦ farinastrans.com) from Manila (11 daily) and Baguio (3 daily) drop passengers off at the corner of Fariñas and Castro streets. GMW buses from Tuguegarao (hourly; 6–7hr) arrive at the terminal at the corner of Gov. Agcaoli St and Primo Lazaro Ave. Local buses also connect Pagudpud (every 30min; 1hr 30min) and Vigan (every 30min; 3hr) to Laoag.

By jeepney Jeepneys to Paoay (every 30min; 40min) and Batac (every 30min; 30min) leave from the corner of Llanes St and Luna St, while those travelling to Sarrat leave east of town from F. Guerrero St (when full; 15min).

INFORMATION

Tourist information The helpful provincial tourist office kiosk is on Llanes St at General Luna St (daily 8am–5pm; ⓦ ilocosnorte.ph), while the Laoag City tourist office (Mon–Fri 8am–5pm; ☎ 077 772 0467) is on the second floor of the Pacific Building, Abadilla St.

ACCOMMODATION | SEE MAP PAGE 141

Balay da Blas 10 Giron St ⓦ balaydablashotel.com. A charming option, with superb-value warm and welcoming rooms decorated with antiques and colourful paintings. The larger family rooms also have a kitchenette, and there's a pleasant leafy seating area in the courtyard as well as an excellent restaurant attached. Breakfast included but wi-fi in the lobby only. $\overline{PP}$

Fort Ilocandia Brgy 37 Calayab (10km southwest of town) ⓦ fortilocandia.com.ph. Built in 1983 and hastily completed for the wedding reception of Ferdinand and Imelda Marcos's youngest daughter (see page 143), this expansive resort aims for classic elegance rather than modern chic. It's set in 77 hectares amid sand dunes and pine forests; amenities include a golf course, swimming pool, and a driving range. $\overline{PPP}$

Hotel Tiffany General Segundo Ave at M.H. del Pilar St ⓦ facebook.com/tiffanylaoag. This motel-style place has tried for a 1960s US theme, with mellow polka dot and stripy themed rooms and an attached American-style diner

serving cheeseburgers and milkshakes. The lobby wi-fi reaches some of the rooms. $\overline{PP}$

Java General Segundo Ave, 55-B Salet ⓦ javahotel.com.ph. A pleasant option in a stone building with thatched roof, with tastefully furnished rooms featuring modern amenities. There's a swimming pool, tennis court and gym, and an airy restaurant serving good Filipino dishes. Rates include breakfast. $\overline{PPP}$

West Gate 51B Jasmin St ⓦ facebook.com/westgate hotelofficial. A cheap and cheerful option, Westgate's rooms are plain but perfectly decent, and all have ensuite bathrooms. The main downside is its location, on the other side of the river from the centre. $\overline{P}$

EATING
SEE MAP PAGE 141

Cuisine de Iloco Hernando ⓦ cuisinedeiloco.com. Central restaurant serving up local Ilocano dishes, as well as a wider Filipino menu. The *bagnet sisig* (crispy chilli pork) is particularly good, but you could also try the *dinengdeng* (vegetable soup topped with grilled fish) or the grilled squid. There's a good selection of desserts too. $\overline{PP}$

Elvie's Empanada General Segundo Ave ☏ 0919 783 4185. The empanadas at this unassuming hole-in-the-wall place, a short walk north of the Sinking Bell Tower, are among the best in town. Choose your filling from chicken, pork or fish. Other simple quick eats are available too. $\overline{P}$

Food court Rizal St between Balintawak St and Llanes

St. This little market hosts a handful of stalls selling empanadas, *bulalo*, *miki* (noodle soup) and other tasty Filipino staples, with tables to eat them at. Not all the stalls are open round the clock, but there's always something good to eat, whether it's a meal you're after or just a snack. $\overline{P}$

Vis-à-Vis Lounge Corner of Giron St and A. Mabini St ⓦ facebook.com/Visavislounge. A smart and modern café which is a great place to relax with a coffee or milkshake, of which there are an astonishing number on the menu. Light meals such as sandwiches and burgers, as well as a few Filipino dishes, are also available. $\overline{PP}$

DIRECTORY

Banks and exchange There are plenty of banks along Rizal, including BDO and BPI.

Hospital Laoag General Hospital, Brgy 46 Nalbo, south of

town (☏ 077 772 8828).

Police Rizal St at Paco Roman St (☏ 077 771 1026).

Sarrat

Some 8km east of Laoag is the sleepy, pretty village of **SARRAT**, where the eighteenth-century **Santa Monica Church** hosted the wedding of Marcos's youngest daughter Irene in 1983. Preparations for the wedding – costing US$10.3 million – involved thousands of men remodelling the town and 3500 contracted employees renovating the two-hundred-year-old church. Large parts of Sarrat were reconstructed, with houses torn down and rebuilt in the old Spanish style.

Marcos Birthplace Museum

National Highway • Free • Jeepney from Laoag (leaving when full; 15min)

Ferdinand Marcos was born in Sarrat on September 11, 1917, and his former home has been turned into the **Marcos Birthplace Museum**. The ground floor displays traditional Ilocano weaving instruments, while the first floor showcases Marcos memorabilia, including a set of his clothes worn during infancy. This place is really for Marcos completists only.

Ferdinand Marcos Museum

Batac, 15km south of Laoag • Charge • ☏ 0917 772 6001 • Buses between Vigan and Laoag pass through Batac – ask the driver to let you off; Batac is also served by regular jeepneys from Laoag (every 30min; 40min)

Marcos spent his childhood in the pretty town of **Batac** before moving to Manila to take up law. The **Ferdinand Marcos Museum**, or "presidential centre", showcases Marcos memorabilia and traces his political career in glowing terms; there's also a section dedicated Imelda, who became his wife after only eleven days of courting. An adjacent building held his corpse until Imelda prevailed upon President Rodrigo Duterte to bury him in Manila's Libingan Ng Mga Bayani (Heroes' Cemetery) in 2016.

Paoay

A few kilometres west of Batac, **PAOAY** is the location of a UNESCO-listed **church** as well as the **Malacañang of the North**, the opulent mansion where **Ferdinand Marcos** stayed during presidential holidays.

St Augustine Church

Paoay Church Complex • Daily 6.30am–6pm • Buses between Vigan and Laoag pass through Paoay – ask the driver to let you off; there are also regular jeepneys (every 30min; 50min) from Laoag via Batac

St Augustine church is perhaps the best-known "earthquake Baroque" church in the Philippines. Begun in 1804, it took ninety years to build and has 26 immense side buttresses designed to keep it standing. Nearby is a bell tower dating from 1793, which you can climb for views of the area, although you may have to find the caretaker to open it up for you.

Malacañang of the North

Suba, 10km from Paoay • Charge • ☎ 0906 521 1139 • Tricycles from Paoay's St Augustine Church (25min) will then take you on to the Ilocos Norte Sand Dunes (see page 144)

The **Malacañang of the North** is named after the presidential palace in Manila. The mansion, set on a five-hectare estate of gentle lawns giving onto the beautiful Paoay Lake, was the Marcoses' holiday residence between 1977 and the revolution in 1986. The property also comprised a golf course – Marcos was an avid golfer – which is now part of the *Fort Ilocandia* resort (see page 143). In 2012 part of the building was transformed into a **pro-Marcos museum**, with seven galleries highlighting some of the major reforms – but, naturally, none of the corruption or human rights abuses – implemented during his presidency. The Agriculture Room focuses on the building of waterways and dams – aiming for self-sufficiency, Marcos implemented irrigation programmes in order to supply water to the entire archipelago – while the Nation Building Room highlights the president's achievement in uniting his country by connecting the islands via a number of ambitious highways and bridges.

Ilocos Norte sand dunes

Paoay Sand Dunes Adventures (Suba) (🏠 facebook.com/p/Suba-Sand-Dunes-4x4-ride-and-Sand-boarding-Ilocos-Norte-100076407068326/) arranges trips combining a 4WD ride and sandboarding

The coastline west of Laoag is a sight to behold. More like desert than beach, it measures almost 1km across at some points and reaches as far as the eye can see, fringed by huge **sand dunes**. The area has become a favourite among Manila film crews; the **Suba** dunes to the south – close to the *Fort Ilocandia* resort (see page 143) – are where Oliver Stone shot segments of *Born on the Fourth of July*.

Pagudpud and around

Seventy kilometres north of Laoag along the coastal road is **PAGUDPUD**, a typical provincial town providing access to several wonderfully picturesque **beaches**. The Pagudpud area is increasingly recognized as having all the beauty of Boracay, but just a fraction of the tourists and none of the nightlife.

Saud Beach

Tricycles from Pagudpud (15min)

Saud Beach ("Sa-ud"), a few kilometres down a narrow road to the north of town, is a beautiful long arch of white sand backed by palm trees. Resorts on the beach rent out snorkelling equipment, and can provide bangkas so that you can head to the best spots.

Kabigan Falls

Charge, including compulsory guide • Tricycle from either Saud Beach (35min) or Blue Lagoon (25min)

About halfway between Saud Beach and Blue Lagoon are the **Kabigan Falls**, a beautiful cascade of water flowing down a steep incline of 34m and nestled in a pretty stretch of thick vegetation. There's a refreshing pool at the bottom of the falls, perfect for a swim. At the main road, where tricycles drop off, you'll have to register and hire a compulsory guide who will lead you to the falls – a beautiful 1.5km (30min) walk through picturesque rice paddies and lush mountain scenery.

Blue Lagoon

Tricycles from Pagudpud (45min)

3

About 18km east of Saud is the glorious **Blue Lagoon** (also known as Maira-ira Beach). The setting is stunning, with dazzling water lapping a sugary crescent of sand; the breaks also attract surfers from July to January. One stretch of the beach has been overdeveloped with a large and incongruous resort, but it's possible to get away from that and still enjoy the sand and sea.

Kingfisher Beach

Tricycles from Pagudpud (30min)

Kingfisher Beach, a gem of a place just 6km north of Saud Beach, is one of the country's best kitesurfing spots, its strong northwest or side shore winds making it an ideal spot for advanced surfers, especially between October and March. The waters are so clear that you're likely to spot flying fish, sea turtles, jackfish and even tuna as you surf. The 250m-wide reef with a flat lagoon is perfect for snorkelling, stand-up paddling and kayaking. You can rent equipment from the well-stocked *Kingfisher Resort* just on the beach.

Cape Bojeador Lighthouse and around

Charge • To get here from Pagudpud take a jeepney or local bus towards Laoag and ask to be let off on the National Highway near the lighthouse; from here you can walk 900m up to the lighthouse (30min) or catch a tricycle (5min)

Some 36km west of Pagudpud is the **Cape Bojeador Lighthouse**, just outside the town of **Burgos**. Built in 1892, at 19.90m the lighthouse is the tallest in the country, and from the base there are unobstructed views of the coastline and across the South China Sea. It's still in use, but unfortunately you can't go inside the very top.

ARRIVAL AND INFORMATION

By bus Buses arrive on the main road in Pagudpud town. There are services from Manila (12hr), with local buses connecting the town to Laoag (every 15min; 2hr).

Tourist information In the town hall (Mon–Fri 8am–5pm).

PAGUDPUD AND AROUND

Services The Multi-Purpose Cooperative Bank has an ATM, and there is also one in the municipal hall, and another one in the nearby town of Bangui.

Tricycle tours Tricycles offer one-day tours taking in the area's major sights.

ACCOMMODATION AND EATING

Resorts around Pagudpud are a little pricier than similar establishments elsewhere, and many of them double their **prices** during high season (April & May, Holy Week & Christmas). It's always worth asking for a discount at other times. Budget travellers should consider a **homestay**. The tourist office has accredited more than a hundred, and there are also unofficial homestays in the area. Contact the tourist office for details, or just wander along the road behind the main resorts on Saud Beach.

SAUD BEACH AND AROUND

Apo Idon White Beach Cove ⓦ apoidon.com. This pleasant resort on Saud Beach offers a selection of comfortable rooms with dark wooden furniture. The more spacious suites have private balconies with sea views; there's also a small pool, and a restaurant giving onto a beautiful stretch of beach. The downside is the deafeningly loud hum of the generator around the reception area. $\overline{\text{PPP}}$

★ **BergBlick** Brgy Burayoc ⓦ bergblick-pagudpud.com. Halfway between Saud Beach and Blue Lagoon, this is an unusual find along the highway – a German-owned restaurant with waitresses in traditional Bavarian dress, offering excellent international and local dishes including home-made ravioli and *pinakbet* lasagne. Try the BergBlick Pan, a platter for 2-3 with pork chop, pork roast, pan-fried potatoes, cabbage roll and fresh mixed salad, followed by the home-made crème brûlée. $\overline{\text{PPP}}$

★ **Evangeline Beach Resort** Brgy Burayoc ⓦ evangelinebeachresort.net. An excellent option comprising comfortable rooms in a freshly painted thatched building with beautiful wooden interiors; there's also a spacious cottage with two double rooms, lounge area and fully equipped kitchenette. The beachside restaurant offers an extensive menu of Filipino and international dishes. $\overline{\text{P}}$

BLUE LAGOON

Casa Consuelo ⓦ facebook.com/CASACONSUELO. A laidback family-run place with comfy bedrooms set around a decent pool, beyond which are gorgeous views across the beach to the sea and Dos Hermanos island. There's good food, especially fish, available in the restaurant. $\overline{\text{PP}}$

Ikani Surf Resort ⓦ facebook.com/IkaniSurf. As the name suggests, this place is a good spot for those keen to indulge in watersports: there's not just surfing, but also paddleboarding, and if you'd prefer not to head into the sea, there's a decent pool too. The accommodation is good, but is beginning to show its age and could do with a bit of smartening up. $\overline{\text{PPP}}$

KINGFISHER BEACH

Kingfisher Resort ⓦ kingfisher.ph. Popular with kitesurfers, this is a particularly comfortable option, with tastefully decorated *casitas* with modern amenities, some with lofts. The cheapest rooms are little tiki huts with shared bath. The restaurant offers an extensive menu of Filipino and international dishes. $\overline{\text{PP}}$

The northeast

The **northeast** of Luzon, comprising the provinces of Nueva Vizcaya, Quirino, Aurora, Isabela and Cagayan, is one of the archipelago's least-explored regions, with kilometres of beautiful coastline and enormous tracts of tropical rainforest. Following the National Highway from Ilocos as it curves south brings you to the biggest city in the region, **Tuguegarao**, the starting point for trips to the **Peñablanca Protected Landscape and Seascape**. Turning off the highway and following the north coast road brings you to **Santa Ana**, departure point for boat trips to the rugged and isolated **Babuyan Islands**.

The coast south of Santa Ana and east of Tuguegarao is cut off from the rest of Luzon by the **Sierra Madre** mountains. One of the only significant settlements is **Palanan**, jumping-off point for the barely-explored **Northern Sierra Madre National Park**. The climbing and trekking possibilities here are exciting, but the area is so wild and remote that it's also potentially hazardous, with poor communications and areas of impenetrable forest. Further south on the coast – but unreachable by road from Palanan – is **Baler**, the best-known tourist destination in the northeast. This coastal town has become a popular surfing destination, but its location six hours from Manila means that it isn't swamped with weekenders.

Santa Ana and around

The northern coast of Luzon, part of Cagayan province, is skipped over by many visitors in their haste to head either west to Ilocos Norte or south to Tuguegarao. Yet the untouristy fishing town of **SANTA ANA** – on the northeastern point of Luzon – has much to offer, including some terrific white-sand beaches and a number of enticing offshore islands. **San Vicente,** 6km northeast of Santa Ana town centre, is the departure point for boats to the offshore islands and to Maconacon and the Northern Sierra Madre National Park (see page 149).

Anguib Beach

Charge • Bangkas from San Vicente (30min)

On the mainland, you can hire a bangka for the day to the lovely and secluded **Anguib Beach** on the eastern part of San Vicente. It's a beautiful 1.8km J-shaped stretch of beach with white sand and crystal-clear waters, and while you won't find any accommodation here, it's a great place to pitch a tent. Make sure to bring water and food, as there are no shops or restaurants.

Palaui Island

Various charges, including environmental fee local tax (payable at San Vicente), and compulsory guide • Bangkas from San Vicente to Punta Verde (15min) or Cape Engaño (45min)

The closest island to Santa Ana is **Palaui**, which has no roads, a few very basic homestays and only limited electricity. From the main settlement of **Punta Verde** on the east of the island, two trails head north to **Cape Engaño** on the island's northern coast, a beautiful crescent lagoon watched over by an old Spanish lighthouse – the walk will take about three hours. It's also worth taking a hike to the attractive Baratubot waterfall.

The Babuyan islands

Bangka from San Vicente (6hr) or negotiate passage on supply boat from Claveria

There's no longer a ferry, but fishing boats make the often rough crossing to the isolated and undeveloped **Babuyan islands**, a cluster of 24 volcanic and coralline islands 32km off the coast. Only five of the islands – Camiguin, Calayan, Fuga, Babuyan and Dalupiri – are inhabited and even **Calayan**, the most developed, has limited electricity. There are some beautiful beaches on several of the islands including Fuga and Dalupiri, and hot springs on the volcanic **Camiguin**.

ARRIVAL AND INFORMATION

By plane Cagayan North International Airport opened in 2014 at Lal-lo, 77km west of Santa Ana, but has no scheduled passenger flights.

By boat Irregular boat departures from San Vicente pier for Maconacon in the Northern Sierra Madre National Park (see page 149).

By bus GV Florida Trans (ⓦ gvfloridatrans.com) runs to Santa Ana from Manila (3 daily; 14hr), stopping opposite the main market, Centro Santa Ana, on the main highway.

SANTA ANA AND AROUND

They also have a less reliable service connecting Vigan to Santa Ana (1 daily; 12hr).

By van There are regular vans from in front of the main market to Tuguegarao (every 30–40min 3am–3pm; 3hr); change at Magapit (about halfway) for points west.

Tourist information In Santa Ana's municipal building (Mon–Fri 8am–5pm; ⓦ facebook.com/santaanatourismofc). They can offer advice on island-hopping and arrange homestays.

ACCOMMODATION AND EATING

In addition to the below, various homestay options are possible on the east coast of Palaui Island, and also the south coast of Babuyan Island, but none can be said to be reliable.

SANTA ANA AND AROUND

Cagayan Holiday & Leisure Resort San Vicente ☎ 032 844 0888. The best of a clutch of places to stay facing Palaui Island, with slick rooms, a skinny swimming pool facing the sea, and even a casino. **PPP**

Nassim Hotel & Beach Resort Aguinaldo St ☎ 0917 630 2335. The very smart exterior makes a great first impression; inside, rooms are a little less well maintained but still more than acceptable, and the common areas have a nice, homely feel. There's a decent-sized pool, containing dolphin fountains, and reasonable buffet meals in the evenings. **P̲**

BABUYAN ISLANDS

★ **Nouveau Resort** Camiguin Island ⓦ nouveauresort. com. A lovely top-end resort, Nouveau offers everything you could possibly want for a relaxing getaway. The pool is large and overlooks the sea, the restaurant is first rate, the rooms are large, the beds comfortable, and the bathrooms – especially those with free-standing baths – are gorgeous. If you can drag yourself away from the pool, there's a fantastic spa and a mini-golf course, and private island-hopping trips are available. **PPPP**

Tuguegarao

The capital of Cagayan province, **TUGUEGARAO** ("Too-GEG-er-rao") is a busy, tricycle-choked city with an airport that's convenient to fly to if you intend to explore the east coast around the Sierra Madre or the northernmost coast near Santa Ana, or head west into Kalinga province and its capital Tabuk. There are also small-aircraft flights from Tuguegarao to Batanes. The **city centre** is a kilometre south of **Tuguegerao Junction**, where the road from Santiago meets the National Highway that leads into town.

Tuguegarao is also the best starting point for a visit to a remarkable cave system at **Peñablanca**, and local travel agents offer **whitewater rafting** and **kayaking** trips on the Pinacanauan and Chico rivers, usually from August until February.

Tuguegarao Metropolitan Cathedral

Rizal Street at Luna St

The striking Baroque **Tuguegarao Metropolitan Cathedral**, dedicated to saints Peter and Paul, with its five-storey bell tower and striking red facade, is the region's biggest colonial church. Put up by the Dominicans in the 1760s, it survived quite serious damage in World War II. The facade is crowned with six little crests, and the windows and the columns are surrounded with moulded bricks adorned with crowns, stars and other symbols. Nor is this the town's only colonial church: the **San Jacinto Hermitage** at the western end of Legazpi Street is even older, dating from the seventeenth century.

Cagayan Provincial Museum

Provincial Capitol Compound, 3km north of Tuguegerao Junction • ☎ 078 255 7201 • Tricycle from city centre (15min)

The small **Cagayan Provincial Museum** traces the history of Cagayan province; displays include fossilized bones of extinct animals that roamed the area during the Ice Age. The highlight is the replica (the original is on display in Manila's National Museum) of the toe bone of Callao Man, discovered by a team of archeologists in 2007 in nearby Callao Cave and dating back 67,000 years. Other displays feature intricately designed Chinese bowls and porcelain vessels, and heirloom pieces from the Spanish and American eras.

ARRIVAL AND DEPARTURE — TUGUEGARAO

By plane Tuguegarao airport is 2km north of Tuguegerao Junction, easily reached from town by tricycle (15min). Cebu Pacific and PAL express fly to Manila (1–2 daily; 1hr); SkyPasada (🖥 skypasada.com) have flights to Basco in the Batanes Islands (3 weekly each; 1hr). For the Northern Sierra Madre National Park, SkyPasada fly to Palanan (3 weekly).

By bus Victory Liner buses (🖥 victoryliner.com) stop on the National Highway, 300m north of Tuguegerao Junction; Five Star (🖥 5starbus.com) stop just north of the junction; Dalin (🖥 facebook.com/dalinbuslineinc) arrive at Don Domingo Market, 100m southeast of the junction; GV Florida are on Diversion Rd, west of the junction.

Destinations Baguio (2 daily; 10–12hr); Laoag (8 daily; 7hr); Manila (1–3 hourly; 10–12hr); Vigan (6 daily; 9hr).

By van Vans for Santa Ana (every 30–40min; 3hr), Santiago (leaving when full; 3hr), and Tabuk (leaving when full; 1hr 30min) leave from a terminal on the National Highway, 300m south of Tuguegerao Junction. Vans for Santa Ana also leave from another terminal 200m further south. Vans for Santiago and Tabuk also leave from a terminal by Brickstone Mall, 100m north of the junction.

INFORMATION AND ACTIVITIES

Tourist information The regional tourist office (Mon–Fri 8am–5pm; ☎ 078 304 1499) is in the Regional Government Center at 2 Dalan na Pavvurulun, off the National Highway about 500m east of the airport. You can ask here about permits and guides for the Peñablanca caves, or book trips in other parts of northeast Luzon including the Northern Sierra Madre National Park (see page 149). The provincial tourist office (Mon–Fri 8am–5pm; ☎ 078 844 0203) is in the same building as the Cagayan Provincial Museum.

Activities For reliable first-hand information about caving, trekking, abseiling and climbing, contact the Sierra Madre Outdoor Club, aka SMOC (🖥 facebook.com/SierraMadreOC). Your accommodation may also be able to get you in touch with people who can organise kayaking and rafting trips locally and in Kalinga province.

ACCOMMODATION AND EATING

AdriNel's 29 Rizal St ☎ 078 844 1305. One of the city's few non-fast-food restaurants, offering a popular all-you-can-eat Filipino lunch. Other choices include the large family platter *familia sentenyal* (suitable for five people) that includes grilled and barbecued pork, vegetables, shrimp, crab and grilled fish. P̄P̄

Carmelita 9 Diversion Rd (150m west of Tuguegarao Junction) ⓦ facebook.com/Hotel-Carmelita-114886239939298. A handy budget hotel for lone travellers as it has cheap singles, and often promotional cheap rates on doubles too, although cheaper rooms tend to get taken up quite quickly, and the a/c can

be quite noisy. There's a pool and a decent restaurant, but breakfast isn't included. P̄

Hotel Roma Luna St at Bonifacio St ☎ 078 844 1057. The city's largest hotel offers comfortable private rooms, smoking and non-smoking (the former have balconies), but some give on to the interior patio and are consequently quite dark. It has a popular restaurant. P̄P̄

Mango Suites Rizal St at Balzain St ⓦ bit.ly/mango-suites. A good central option with modern, comfortable rooms and free airport transfers. A pleasant café-restaurant serves Filipino food and a smattering of Western dishes. P̄P̄

Peñablanca caves

The major tourist attraction around Tuguegarao is the marvellous **cave system** at Peñablanca, 24km to the east. Peñablanca, officially known as the **Peñablanca Protected Landscape and Seascape**, is riddled with more than three hundred caves, many of them deep and dangerous, and a good number still largely unexplored. Most of the caves are protected, but it's possible to visit three – **Callao**, **Musang** and **Lattu-Lattuc** – without permission; all three can be done in a single day. Several other caves in the area can be visited with permission from SMOC in Tuguegarao (see page 148), but note that some of them are suitable only for experienced cavers. Also be aware that typhoons between August and November can flood the caves and make them impossible to visit.

Callao Cave

Charge (plus guide) • Accessible by return boat trips to the bat cave (including waiting) for up to fifteen people; from the pier close to the cave entrance; or by kayak (in season), rentable by the hour

The easiest of the Peñablanca caves to visit is **Callao Cave**, which has seven immense chambers – previously nine but an earthquake in the 1980s cut off the last two. The 50,000-year-old remains of the archaic human species *Homo Luzonensis* were discovered here in 2007, eventually being confirmed as having belonged to a distinct species in 2019. The main chamber has a natural skylight and a chapel inside where Mass is celebrated on special occasions. You'll need a guide – there are plenty at the entrance. Note that there are 184 steps to climb before you reach the entrance of the cave, and inside the rocks can be slippery during the wet season. It's also possible to rent **kayaks** – ask at the cave entrance.

Another attraction here is a short **boat trip** that takes you to the **bat cave**, where at dusk you can see great flocks of the creatures leaving to hunt.

ARRIVAL AND INFORMATION PEÑABLANCA CAVES

By tricycle You can bargain hard to get a tricycle from Tuguegarao to Callao Cave, or, if you want to make a day of it and explore other caves nearby, it's worth hiring a van.

Guides Contact the SMOC (see page 148) for professional

guides in caving and other outdoor activities including mountaineering and trekking. You'll need one guide per five people, and possibly a porter as well.

Northern Sierra Madre National Park

At almost 3600 square kilometres, the **Northern Sierra Madre National Park** remains one of the country's last frontiers and well worth the trouble of getting there. Said by conservationists to be the Philippines' richest protected area in terms of habitat and species, the park is eighty percent land and twenty percent coastal area along a spectacular, cliff-studded seashore.

THE DUMAGATS

The people known as the **Dumagats** are among the original inhabitants of the Philippines. The word Dumagat translates roughly as "those who moved to the ocean", and the area around **Palanan** is the last stronghold of their vanishing culture and way of life. Some have now settled but others remain nomadic, living in small camps on the beaches around Palanan, where they build temporary sloping shelters from bamboo and dried grass. Life for the Dumagats is simple in the extreme: they survive by hunting and gathering, using little modern equipment. The main threats to their existence are through the commercialization and exploitation of their homelands, along with exposure to diseases previously unknown to them. Every March members of the nomadic Dumagat community join with the settled inhabitants of Palanan for the **Sabutan festival**.

One of the reasons for the health of the park's ecosystems is its inaccessibility. Though small aircraft connect the towns of **Palanan** and **Maconacon** to the outside world, to the east lies the Pacific, which is too rough for boats during much of the northeast monsoon (Dec–Feb) and typhoon (July–Oct) seasons. At present, no roads cross the park, but controversially – against opposition from environmentalists and the Church – a **road** is now being built from the provincial capital Ilagan across the park to Palanan on the coast; the project was initially scheduled for completion in 2020, but at time of writing, the road is still not open. Check online before you travel if you intend to use the road.

The park has few wardens and no fences, so you can visit any time you want without restriction; it is essential, however, to take a **guide** if you are to visit safely. A guide can take you down the Palanan River to the village of **Sabang**, from where you can walk through farmland and forest to **Disadsad Falls**, a high cascade that crashes through dense forest into a deep pool. For some of the trip there's no trail, so you'll have to wade upriver through the water. Another memorable trip from Palanan takes you northwards along the coast to the sheltered inlets around the towns of Dimalansan and Maconacon. On the isolated beaches here the **Dumagat** people establish their temporary homes (see box, above).

ARRIVAL AND DEPARTURE

NORTHERN SIERRA MADRE NATIONAL PARK

By plane The small town of Palanan is the main gateway to the park, and it is also possible to enter via Maconacon. From Cauayan, Cyclone Airways (W cycloneairways.com.ph) fly six-seater planes to Palanan and Maconacon depending on demand. From Tuguegarao, SkyPasada (W skypasada. com) fly to Palanan (2–3 weekly; 20min).

By boat and bus You can avoid flying by taking a long boat journey from San Vicente near Santa Ana (see page 147) to Maconacon (8–10hr), but it's basically a question of negotiating passage on a supply boat – check at the port for departure times. Alternatively, take a local bus from either Baler (see page 151) or from Santiago City in Isabela province (itself an 8hr trip from Manila) to Dilasag in Aurora province (1–2 daily,; 10–12hr), from where you

can take a boat to Palanan (no fixed schedules; 6–8hr). There are also boats from Palanan to Maconacon (no fixed schedules; 4hr) or to Divilacan, which is connected to Maconacon by road.

On foot For hardy visitors, the most interesting option is to trek into the park from San Mariano. It's a five- to seven-day trek that requires a guide; though no agencies were conducting this trip at the time of writing, if you're hell-bent on the walk you can arrive in San Mariano and ask around. San Mariano is served by direct buses from Manila (Five Star (W 5starbus.com): 6 daily; 8–10hr), and by local buses and vans from Ilagan and Cauayan (both served by vans on the Tuguegarao–Santiago route).

INFORMATION AND ACTIVITIES

Tourist information The park's tourism office (W facebook.com/nsmnpisabela) is based at the town hall in Palanan. Along with offering advice and information, they can help with arranging a homestay – there are no

guesthouses or hotels in Palanan – and can inform the Department of Environment and Natural Resources (DENR) that you are planning to hike in the area.

Baler

The laidback east-coast town of **BALER** is known for its excellent, if intermittent, **surfing**. Surfing scenes in Francis Ford Coppola's *Apocalypse Now* were filmed at a break known as **Charlie's Point** at the mouth of the Aguang River, which is a 45-minute walk north of the main surfing beach of **Sabang**. When the film crew departed they left the surfboards behind, kick-starting local interest in the sport.

Museo de Baler

Quezon Park • Charge

It's worth swinging by the central museum just to admire the fantastic bas-reliefs on its frontage, even if you don't go inside. Those who do enter will be rewarded with an exhibit on the Siege of Baler, a battle of the Philippine Revolution in 1898 when a Spanish garrison continued to defend their posts for a full six months. The upper floors contain artworks, ranging from paintings to a mechanical fish sculpture.

Dicasalarin Cove

Charge (halved if arriving by boat) • Walkable from Digisit (2–3hr) which is 5km beyond Cemento Reef; also accessible from Baler by motorbike or 4WD, or by chartering a boat (40min)

3

If you're not after surf, then you could try the white beach at **Dicasalarin Cove**. You can snorkel here too, and there is a spot for shallow diving at the site of a reef rehabilitation programme. There are no shops or restaurants – only picnic cottages, so bring drinks and snacks.

Casiguran Sound

Buses (every 2hr; 3–4hr) and vans (leave when full; 3–4hr) from Baler

The calm and picturesque inlet of **Casiguran Sound**, 120km northeast of Baler, is a lovely spot to while away a few hours. Protected from onshore winds and waves by a finger of hilly land, it makes perfect for **swimming** and is scarcely developed. You'll find little here in terms of restaurants and shops, apart from a few sari-sari stores around the fishing village.

ARRIVAL AND INFORMATION   BALER

By bus There are no road links north along the coast to the   Northern Sierra Madre National Park, but you can catch a

---

RIDING BALER'S WAVES

You can **surf** year-round at Baler, although the best waves usually come between September and March, especially early in the morning. The waves, averaging nearly 2m, are ideal for both amateur and experienced surfers. Lessons and kit rental are available at Sabang Beach.

Cemento Reef A strong world-class right-hand reef break, perfect for advanced surfers; competitions are held here.

Charlie's Point The most famous surf spot in Baler, gaining popularity in the late 1970s during the filming of *Apocalypse Now*.

Dalugan Bay, San Ildefonso This left-hand reef break peninsula offers good surf.

Dianed, Dipaculao North of Baler, this place has typhoon swells holding 1.2–1.8m waves.

Dicasalarin Point Right- and left-hand breaks, with reef breaks for the more experienced surfers and beach breaks for beginners.

Lobbot's Point, Dipaculao A left- and right-hand beach break holding 0.6–1.8m ground swells that break into the sandy gravel bottom.

Sabang Beach The sandy bottom beach break here is ideal for beginners; there are left and right breaks from September to March. You can rent surfboards and surfing lessons are available.

Secret Point, Castillo This surf spot breaks between two and four times a year and can offer a 140m ride.

bus to Dilasag (2 daily; 4hr 30min) where you can get a boat to Palanan (no fixed schedule; 6–8hr).

Destinations Baguio (2 daily; 9hr); Manila (4–8 daily, mostly by night; 5–6hr).

Tourist information The municipal tourist office is in the Municipal Building (Mon–Fri 8am–5pm; ⓦ baler. gov.ph). The provincial government also post some useful information on their website (ⓦ aurora.ph).

ACCOMMODATION AND EATING

All the best **accommodation** in Baler is on or around the beach at Sabang, which is a short tricycle ride from town. Apart from during the annual Aurora Cup in February, you won't have any problem finding somewhere to stay. The best eating options are in the hotels; all the options listed below have decent **restaurants**, some with lovely views.

Bay-Ler View Hotel ⓦ baylerviewhotels.com. Clean and comfortable accommodation right on the beachfront with lovely views over the ocean; the restaurant serves local and international dishes, staff are friendly and there's wi-fi in the communal areas. PP

Bay's Inn ⓦ facebook.com/baysinnresortofficial. One of the most popular resorts for budget tourists and out-of-town surfers, boasting panoramic views of Baler Bay, the Pacific Ocean and surrounding cliffs and beaches. It has clean fan or a/c doubles with private showers and a popular restaurant with views. Surfboard rental available. PPP

Costa Pacifica ⓦ costapacificabaler.com. The plushest hotel in town, and not a bad choice, with a pool and a variety of rooms available in the main hotel or its annexe across the way. Their restaurant, with chairs of a suitably ocean-blue in hue, also makes a good place to eat a mix of local and international cuisine. PPPP

The Cordillera

To Filipino lowlanders brought up on sunshine and beaches, the heartlands of the north and their spiny ridge of inhospitable mountains, the **Cordillera**, are seen almost as another country, inhabited by mysterious people who worship primitive gods. It's true that in some respects life for many Indigenous people has changed little in hundreds of years, with traditional ways and values still very much in evidence. If anything is likely to erode these traditions, it is the coming of tourists; already an increasing number of Indigenous people are making much more from the sale of handicrafts than they do from the production of rice.

The **weather** can have a major impact on a trip to the Cordillera, not least because landslides can cause travel delays during the rainy season (particularly May–Nov,

TREKKING IN THE CORDILLERA

Since the road network is poor in many parts of the Cordillera, and there are so many jungle-clad peaks and hidden valleys, **trekking** is the only way to see some of the region's secrets: burial caves, Indigenous villages and hidden waterfalls. Gentle **day-hikes** are possible, particularly in the main tourist areas of Banaue and Sagada, but there are also plenty of **two-or three-day treks** that take you deep into backwaters. Don't be tempted to wander off into the wilderness without a guide: good maps are almost nonexistent and it's easy to become disoriented and lost. Medical facilities and rescue services are few and far between; if you get into trouble and no one knows where you are then you'll have a long wait for help to arrive.

Most of the **best trails** are around Sagada, Banaue, Bontoc, Tabuk and Tinglayan. In each of these towns you'll find a tourist office or town hall where someone will be able to help arrange **guides**. In smaller settlements a good place to look for a guide is at the barangay hall. Many guides won't have official certification, but will know the area exceptionally well. Your guide may also agree to carry equipment and supplies, but don't expect him to have any equipment himself. Most guides happily wander through inhospitable landscapes with only flip-flops on their feet – don't follow suit, as the going underfoot is often extremely rugged. Rates vary so ask around, and check in advance if the guide is expecting you to provide food for them. Certainly, the guide will expect a tip, even in the form of a few beers and a meal, for getting you home safely.

but continuing until Jan or Feb). Since the rains come in from the northeast it's the places on the eastern side of the mountains – such as **Banaue** and **Batad** – that are usually worst hit, and fog can roll into those areas any time from October to February. Throughout the region it can get cold at night between December and February. Note that the rice terrace **planting seasons** vary significantly; the lower-lying areas typically have two plantings a year while the highlands have one. Terraces are at their greenest in the month or so before harvesting, although their barren appearance after a harvest can also be impressive.

Baguio and around

It's fair to say that **BAGUIO**'s heyday as a rural retreat from Manila now feels long past. The city centre is blighted by a polluted tangle of smoke-belching jeepneys and the large SM shopping mall hardly improves the scenery. Still, its position as a major hub for the Cordillera means that you're likely to pass through, and it does have some absorbing sights – plus, as a university city, a number of excellent restaurants and interesting nightlife. Baguio's municipal centre – the area around **Burnham Park** – was designed by renowned American architect Daniel Burnham in 1904, and based loosely on Washington DC. The main drag, **Session Road**, is lined with restaurants and shops, while the eye-catching **Baguio Cathedral** stands on a hill above.

Brief history

In the sixteenth century, intrepid **Spanish friars** had started to explore the region, finding a land of fertile valleys, pine-clad hills and mountains, lush vegetation and an abundance of minerals such as copper and gold. Soon more friars, soldiers and fortune-hunters were trekking north to convert the natives to Christianity and profit from the rich natural resources. In the nineteenth century, **colonizing Americans** took over and developed Baguio into a modern city, a showcase recreational and administrative centre from which they could preside over their precious tropical colony without working up too much of a sweat. In 1944, when American forces landed in Leyte, the head of the Japanese Imperial Army, **General Yamashita**, moved his headquarters to Baguio and helped establish a puppet Philippine government there under President José Laurel. In 1945 the city was destroyed and thousands lost their homes as liberating forces flushed out Yamashita and his army. The general quickly fled north into the interior.

The city is also etched on the Filipino consciousness as the site of one of the country's worst natural disasters, the earthquake of July 16, 1990, which measured 7.7 on the Richter Scale and killed hundreds, mostly in the city's vulnerable shanty towns, many of which cling precariously to the sides of steep valleys.

Burnham Park

Despite the efforts of the SM Mall, the city's centrepiece is still **Burnham Park**, a hilltop version of Rizal Park in Manila with a man-made boating lake at the centre. Even if it's a bit past its prime, the park is an interesting place to take a stroll and to watch the people of Baguio at play: there are boats for rent on the lake and tricycles for kids.

Baguio Cathedral

General Luna Rd • Free • ⓦ facebook.com/baguiocathedralofficial

Standing imperiously above Session Road, **Baguio Cathedral** is a striking example of "wedding cake Gothic" painted rose pink and with twin spires crowned by delicate minarets. Dating from 1936, it became an evacuation centre during World War II and withstood the US carpet-bombing of the city in 1945 – saving the lives of thousands who sheltered inside. There is a steep stairway to the cathedral from Session Road.

BAGUIO

BenCab Museum (6km), Lourdes Grotto & Dominican Hill (1.5km)

Jeepneys

St Louis University
Museum of Igorot
Cultures and Arts

St Louis
Hospital

CAMP H. ALLEN ROAD

Dangwa
Terminal

Baguio
Central
Mall

University
of Baguio

City Market

GENERAL LUNA STREET

Police
Station

KAYANG STREET

Fire Station

Jeepney to
Lourdes and
Bea Cab

Jeepney to
Tam-awan
Village

PCI

City
Hall

ABA NAO STREET

Vans to
San Fernando

PNB

ASSUMPTION ROAD

CHUNTUG STREET

SHAGEM STREET

MAGSAY SAY AVENUE

S E S S I O N R O A D

San Fernando
buses

Jeepneys to
Mines View Park

OTEK STREET

STREET

KMS
Bus Terminal

Ohayami
Bus Terminal

CHANUM

La Azotea
Building

HARRISON ROAD

Landbank

BDO

Burnham

LUNA DRIVE

LAKE DRIVE

Boating
Lagoon

Orchidarium

LAKE ROAD

ABAD SANTOS

Park

KISAD ROAD

Skating
Rink

DR. J. CARINO STREET

LEGARDA ROAD

DEL PILAR STREET

Baguio City
High School

Swimming
Pool

GOVERNOR PACK ROAD

● EATING	
Café by the Ruins	3
Chef's Home	1
Ebai's	7
Hill Station	6
Oh My Gulay	4
Rose Bowl	5
Solibao	2
Wood Nymph	8

■ DRINKING AND NIGHTLIFE	
108 Session Rd Café	2
Baguio Craft Brewery	4
Concoctions	3
Rumours	1

City Market

Magsaysay Ave, at the northern end of Session Rd • Daily 5am–8pm

The **City Market** is one of the liveliest and most colourful in the country, acting as a trading post for farmers and Indigenous people not only from Baguio but also from many of the mountain communities to the north. Bargains include strawberries, which thrive in the temperate north, and you can also buy peanut brittle, sweet wine, honey, textiles, handicrafts and jewellery.

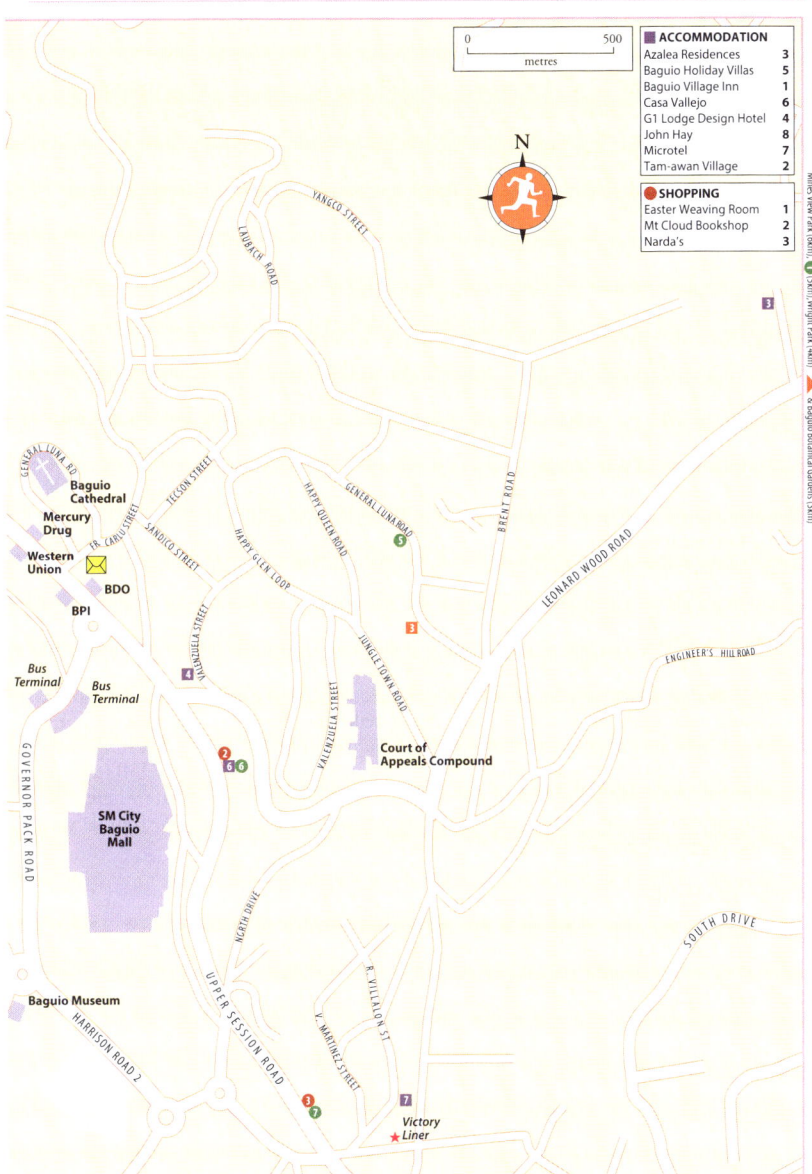

ACCOMMODATION	
Azalea Residences	3
Baguio Holiday Villas	5
Baguio Village Inn	1
Casa Vallejo	6
G1 Lodge Design Hotel	4
John Hay	8
Microtel	7
Tam-awan Village	2

● SHOPPING	
Easter Weaving Room	1
Mt Cloud Bookshop	2
Narda's	3

St Louis University Museum of Igorot Cultures and Arts

St Louis University Campus, Bonifacio St • Free, but bring ID • ☎ 074 442 2193

The **St Louis University Museum of Igorot Cultures and Arts** is a good place to get a general insight into the history of the north and explore the customs and traditions of the Igorot people. It displays hundreds of fascinating artefacts from the Cordillera including tribal costumes, weapons and fascinating black-and-white photographs of sacrifices and other rituals.

Baguio Museum

DOT Complex, Governor Pack Rd • Charge

The **Baguio Museum** showcases artefacts of the Indigenous people of the Cordilleras. There are separate displays about each of the major groups, including accessories, implements for rice farming, baskets, musical instruments, woodcarving and traditional dress. Upstairs is an exhibition on the history of Baguio. For an idea of how Baguio has changed, take a look at the set of three scale models of the city centre in 1909, 1928 and 2009.

Wright Park

Leonard Wood Rd, 4km east of the centre • Charge for pony rides • Take a taxi from city centre or the "Mines View" jeepney from Mabini St

Wright Park is a popular public space where you can hire a sturdy mountain nag – optionally with a dyed-pink mane – for a quick trot around the perimeter beyond. On the other side of Leonard Wood Road, still within the park, is **The Mansion** (not open to the public). Built in 1908 for American governor-generals to the Philippines and damaged in 1945, it was rebuilt in 1947 as a holiday home for Philippine presidents.

Baguio Botanical Gardens

Leonard Wood Rd, 4km east of the centre • Free • Take a taxi from city centre, or a Pacdal-bound jeepney from Magsaysay Ave

Travelling out of the city centre eastwards on Leonard Wood Road for 4km brings you to the **Botanical Gardens**, also known as the Centennial Park. You can wander through thick vegetation along winding concrete pathways, or join the locals relaxing and enjoying barbecued food at weekends.

Mines View Park

6km east of the centre • Taxi from city centre, or jeepney from Mabini St

Mines View Park has a viewing point overlooking an area that used to be the location of mining operations. To get there you have to make your way past countless souvenir stalls and hawkers – if you ever dreamed of having your photo taken with a sunglasses-wearing St Bernard dog then this is the place to do it. A short walk up the hill from the viewpoint is the **Good Shepherd Convent**, with a store inside the main gate where you can buy products made by the nuns, including strawberry, coconut or *ube* (purple yam) jam and cashew or peanut brittle.

Camp John Hay

Loakan Rd, 5km southeast of Baguio • **Historical Core** ☎ 074 444 8358 • Charge • Take a taxi from city centre

Named after US president Theodore Roosevelt's secretary of war, **Camp John Hay** used to be a rest and recreational facility for employees of the US military and Department of Defense. During World War II the property was used by the Japanese as a concentration camp for American and British soldiers. In 1991 the camp was turned over to the Philippine government for development into an upmarket country club, with hotels, a **golf course**, private mountain lodges and sundry restaurants and clubhouses.

The expansive, undulating grounds have some pleasant walks through the pine trees and are also ideal for jogging. Jeepneys can't enter the park itself, so it's best to get a taxi. If you don't have a particular destination in mind then ask to be dropped at the entrance to the **Historical Core**. Here you can buy a ticket to see the Bell House, the holiday residence of the Commanding General of the Philippines, the Bell Amphitheatre and the site where General Yamashita formally surrendered to US forces. At weekends, Filipino families congregate close to the entrance to the Historical Core to enjoy picnics. There have, in the past, been canopy rides, mini golf and a butterfly park on offer here; in recent years, visitors have had to content themselves with various walks, including the "eco trail", a "forest bathing trail", and the longer "red" and "yellow" trails heading south from the historical core. Note that it's also possible to stay here, at the fanciest hotel for many miles around.

Lourdes Grotto and Dominican Hill

Off Dominican Hill Rd • Take a taxi from city centre, or a Dominican-Mirador jeepney from Kayang St

High on a hill in the western part of the city is **Lourdes Grotto**, a Catholic shrine watched over by an image of Our Lady of Lourdes and reached by 252 steps. A kilometre further at the summit of the road is **Dominican Hill**, from where the views across the city are superlative. The crumbling Hotel Diplomat on the peak was built by a Dominican order, then later owned by a controversial entrepreneur and faith healer; it's now abandoned and rather eerie, making a popular spot for urban explorers, but you can no longer wander around inside.

BenCab Museum

6km west of the centre, Km 6 Asin Rd, Tadiangan, Tuba, Benguet • Charge • ⓦ bencabmuseum.org • From central Baguio, take an Asin-bound jeepney from Kayang St or a taxi

One of the best art galleries in the Philippines, the **BenCab Museum** is well worth the short trip out of the centre. Built to house the collection of local artist Ben Cabrera, who has a home and studio next door, it's an airy Modernist structure with lots of natural light and great views of the surrounding scenery. Two galleries house temporary exhibitions while the other seven contain permanent displays, including anything from Ifugao artefacts and old prints of the Philippines to paintings and sculptures by contemporary Filipino artists. Below the museum is an excellent **café** overlooking a duck pond and organic farm. The beautiful **garden** features cascading waterfalls and an eco-trail to a viewpoint on the hillside.

Tam-awan Village

366C Pinsao Proper • Charge • ⓦ tamawanvillage.com • Take a taxi from city centre or a jeepney from Kayang St

On the northwest outskirts of Baguio, 5km from the centre, **Tam-awan Village** is a replica Indigenous village established in 1996 by a group of Filipino artists, including Ben Cabrera and Jordan Mang-osan. There is a small gallery with changing exhibitions, a gift shop and café, and a cultural show with dancing every Saturday afternoon – you can even stay the night here in a tribal hut (see opposite). Tam-awan means "vantage point" – on a clear evening, you'll see magnificent China Sea sunsets and even the Hundred Islands in the distance.

ARRIVAL AND DEPARTURE BAGUIO AND AROUND

By plane Loakan airport is located 6km southeast of the city centre, though at the time of writing no scheduled flights were using it – the airport reopened in 2022 after years out of service, though due to slack demand all services had ceased by mid-2024. It has long been notorious among pilots (and, previously, passengers) for its extremely challenging approach, which when allied to a short runway and frequent low visibility, has caused numerous accidents.

By bus Though there are a number of terminals, most bus companies use Governor Pack Rd or the Slaughterhouse terminal on Magsaysay Ave. Victory Liner's Manila services (ⓦ victoryliner.com) use a terminal just off Upper Session Rd, KMS and Ohayami terminate on Chanum St, and local bus companies to La Union use a small terminal on Shagem St.

Destinations from Chanum St Banaue (3 daily; 8hr); Kiangan (1–2 daily; 7hr).

Destinations from Governor Pack Rd Bolinao (4 daily; 5hr); Dagupan (every 20min; 2hr 30min); Laoag (every 1–2hr; 7–8hr); Manila (1–3 hourly; 6–8hr); San Juan, stopping off at San Fernando (hourly; 2hr); Santa Cruz (5 daily; 6hr); Tuguegarao (3 daily; 12hr); Vigan (hourly; 5–6hr).

Destinations from Shagem St San Fernando (various: hourly; 2hr 30min).

Destinations from Slaughterhouse Bontoc (D'Rising Sun: hourly 6am–4pm; GL Trans: 5 daily; 6hr); Kabayan (Norton Trans: 9am, 11am & noon; 3hr 30min); Sagada (GL Trans: 5 daily; 5–6hr).

Destinations from Victory Liner terminal Manila Cubao (Victory Liner: hourly; 6–7hr), Manila Pasay (Victory Liner: hourly; 6–7hr).

By van A/c vans travel from the Slaughterhouse terminal to Banaue (6 daily; 6hr) and Kabayan (leaving when full; 3hr).

INFORMATION

Tourist information The department of tourism is in the Baguio Tourism Complex on Governor Pack Rd (Mon–Fri

8am—5pm; ☎074 442 7014), and there's a smaller city information centre on Lake Drive in Burnham Park (Mon—Fri 8am—5pm; ☎074 446 3434).

ACCOMMODATION

SEE MAP PAGE 154

Hotels in the centre can get quite noisy, so ask for a room away from the road; there are also a number of good choices **outside town** in peaceful pine forested areas – a much more pleasant way to experience Baguio than in its traffic-choked centre. You can also stay in traditional huts at the artist-run Tam-awan Village (see page 158).

Azalea Residences Leonard Wood Loop ⓦazalea baguio.com. In a quiet location on the northeastern outskirts of the city, these upmarket serviced apartments in a log-cabin-inspired hotel include living area, dining room and kitchen facilities. The only downside is that the lower-floor accommodation looks onto a wall – ask for a room on the fourth floor with views across the countryside. **PPP**

Baguio Holiday Villas 10 Legarda Rd ⓦbaguio holidayvillas.com. The apartments here have two bedrooms and a kitchenette, making them a good choice for families. There are also clean doubles that are good value, despite being on the smallish side. **PPP**

Baguio Village Inn 355 Magsaysay Ave ⓦbaguio villageinn.com. This spotless place, a 15min walk from the bottom of Session Road, is friendly and pretty homely, with wooden floors and wood panelling, although the single rooms in particular are rather small. Wi-fi in the restaurant area only. **PP**

★ **Casa Vallejo** Upper Session Rd ⓦcasavallejo.online. Built in 1909 to house government employees, this Baguio landmark became the city's first hotel in the 1920s. It was one of very few buildings to survive World War II, but by the 1990s it had fallen into disrepair. It reopened in 2010 after extensive renovation and now has bags of US colonial-era charm; rooms are tasteful, modern and a bargain even in peak season. The windows are not double-glazed, so ask for one away from the road. **PP**

G1 Lodge Design Hotel 2 Leonard Wood Rd, ⓦg1lodge.com. Architecturally distinctive, with small extensions jutting out at irregular angles, the G1 Lodge Design Hotel certainly makes a statement from the outside. The interior is perhaps a little less exciting, but the comfy international standard rooms certainly make a good place for a stay. It's in a good location near Burnham Park. **PPP**

John Hay Ordonio Dr ⓦcampjohnhayhotels.com. The various buildings making up this hotel look like buildings that have been magically transported from the Alps to more tropical climes. Your main choice will be between the Garden and Forest wings, which are separate entities in a sense, though largely the same, and share the same ample grounds and facilities. **PPPP**

Microtel Upper Session Rd ⓦwyndhamhotels.com. Right above the Victory Liner terminal, and now under the *Wyndham* umbrella, this hotel, with a blue wooden facade, is a good option; it has neat and tidy rooms set on four floors. **PPP**

Tam-awan Village 366C Pinsao Proper ⓦtamawan village.com. An unusual choice, featuring accommodation in traditional Ifugao and Kalinga huts that were acquired from the provinces and reassembled at this replica village (see opposite). The huts, all with shared bath, are simple but welcoming, and can sleep up to nine. Note that it can get surprisingly cold. **P**

EATING

SEE MAP PAGE 154

Baguio has some of the best **restaurants** in the country. There is also a good selection of street food, including a couple of places beside *Casa Vallejo* hotel serving *bulalo* (beef on the bone in a broth), and the usual fast-food outlets in the SM Mall.

★ **Café by the Ruins** 25 Chuntug St ⓦfacebook. com/cafebytheruinsph. Located in a breezy setting, with tables dotted around the World War II ruins of the residence of Baguio's first governor, this is one of the city's best restaurants, with excellent organic food prepared with home-grown herbs and served either indoors or in the shady yard. The duck *mami* is great, and there are home-made breads, pastries, muffins and scones too. **PP**

★ **Chef's Home** 13 Outlook Drive, Purok 3 ⓦfacebook. com/ChefsHomeBaguio. The Malaysian owner and chef rustles up exceptional Asian fusion dishes embracing Malay, Thai and Indian cuisine. Dishes are large enough to share, with most serving two to four; the crispy papaya salad is outstanding. **PPP**

Ebai's 151 Engineer's Hill, Upper Session Rd ⓦfacebook. com/EbaisCafeandPastry. The exquisite carrot cake at this little café was originally baked for the wife of former president Ramos; it's a great little spot to refuel with a slice of carrot cake, or a dish of Indigenous cuisine such as *bulalo* or pork adobo. **P**

Hill Station Upper Session Rd ⓦhillstationbaguio.com. This place is within the *Casa Vallejo* hotel, with a smart but unpretentious dining room and waiting staff in military-style uniforms to reflect Baguio's history as a US hill station. The international menu exclusively features home-made dishes and includes stews from other famous hill stations in countries such as India. There is also a pleasant café/bar with delectable cakes, as well as dishes such as Thai seafood curry and lamb tagine. **PPPP**

Oh My Gulay 5/F La Azotea Building, 108 Session Rd ⓦfacebook.com/OhMyGulayArtistCafeBaguio. On the top floor of a little shopping precinct, this quirky veggie restaurant and art space was designed by a renowned Baguio artist, and features stone walkways, mismatched furniture, a mock wooden boat and a little pond. **PP**

★ **Rose Bowl** 88 Upper General Luna Rd ⓦ facebook. com/rosebowlbaguio. This highly acclaimed Cantonese restaurant-cum-steakhouse follows family recipes brought over from China at the beginning of the twentieth century. Dishes use top-quality local vegetables, fish transported daily from the coast, and noodles from Manila's oldest noodle factory. Dishes serve three to four – try the roast bowl *pancit*, and if you need the roast bowl veg chop suey to be meat-free, let them know when you order. **PPP**

Solibao Puso ng Baguio Building, Session Rd ⓦ solibao.

com. This popular local restaurant may look like a fast-food franchise, but it's been dishing up solid Filipino food since 1972, no frills but reliably good, and it's an excellent place to check out the likes of *kare-kare* (stew of oxtail and banana flower in peanut sauce) or *lechon kawali* (crispy fried pork belly). **PP**

Wood Nymph 36 Military Cut-off Rd (100m from the junction with Session Rd) ☎ 074 446 0272. One of Baguio's many Korean restaurants, this airy place has been serving the city's Korean community for nearly two decades. Seafood is the speciality here – try the *haemultung* (seafood stew, enough for three people). The *galbichim* (braised short ribs) are great too. **PPP**

DRINKING AND NIGHTLIFE SEE MAP PAGE 154

108 Session Rd Café 2/F La Azotea Building, 108 Session Rd ⓦ facebook.com/108sessionrdcafe. Packed at weekends, this place is a good spot to enjoy a few beers and live music – anything from country to classical. The American menu features burgers, but the music and drinks are the main attraction.

Baguio Craft Brewery 4 Ben Palispis Hwy ⓦ baguio craftbrwery.net. The craft beer craze has reached Baguio, and has found a very welcoming audience. This place is admittedly about 3km out of town, but that hasn't stopped it becoming one of the city's most popular nightspots, with a huge variety of beers to try. The food on offer is good too, with innovative options such as strawberry-flavoured

chicken regularly hitting the menu.

Concoctions 86 Upper General Luna Rd ⓦ facebook. com/concoctionsbarandresto. The well-stocked bar at Concoctions makes it one of the best places in the city to seek out a cocktail, glass of wine or beer. There are regular musical performances, as well as the occasional stand-up comedy gig.

Rumours 55 Session Rd ☎ 074 246 1339. A straightforward place to enjoy a drink, without intrusive music or other distractions. There's a better than usual choice of beers and snacks to enjoy with them. The signature secret-recipe cocktail "Power of Rumours" mixes eight varieties of spirits.

SHOPPING SEE MAP PAGE 154

Easter Weaving Room 2 Easter Rd, Guisad ⓦ facebook. com/philippineeasterweaving. Handwoven articles such as rugs, tablemats, wall hangings, textiles, cushion covers and bed linen. You can watch the weavers at work on old handlooms and, if you've got a few weeks to wait, place a personal order. It's on the northwestern outskirts of town; take a Guisad jeepney from Kayang St, north of Burnham Park, or a taxi.

★ **Mt Cloud Bookshop** 1 Yangco Rd ⓦ facebook.com/

mtcloud. This small bookshop has an excellent selection of materials mainly on the Cordillera region, as well as works by local authors. There are monthly book launches and author talks, too.

Narda's 151 Upper Session Rd ⓦ nardas.com. The traditional Cordillera Ikat style of weaving has been adapted to contemporary tastes at this shop – choose from a variety of handwoven arts and crafts, including attractive clothes, bags, rugs, linen and tablemats.

DIRECTORY

Banks and exchange There are plenty of ATMs in the centre; you'll find moneychangers in the City Market at its

southern end.

Police 24hr police station on Abanao St (☎ 074 442 4119).

Kabayan and around

An isolated, one-road mountain village 85km northeast of Baguio, in Benguet province, **KABAYAN** makes a thrilling side trip – although because of the rough road you'll need to spend at least one night. There was no road here until 1960 and no electricity until 1978, and this extended isolation has left the place rural and unspoilt, a good place to experience the culture of the **Ibaloi**. The area around Kabayan is excellent **trekking** country, and climbers are also drawn here for the chance to ascend **Mount Pulag**, the highest peak in Luzon.

Kabayan came to the attention of the outside world in the early twentieth century when a group of **mummies**, possibly dating back as far as 2000 BC, was discovered in the surrounding caves. When the Americans arrived, mummification was discouraged as unhygienic and the practice is thought to have died out. Controversy still surrounds the Kabayan mummies, some of which have disappeared to overseas collectors, sold for a quick buck by unscrupulous middlemen. One was said to have been stolen by a Christian pastor in 1920 and wound up as a sideshow in a Manila circus. Some remain, however, and some have been recovered. Officials know of dozens of mummies in the area, but will not give their locations for fear of desecration. You can, however, see several of them in designated mountaintop **caves**.

Opdas Cave

At the southern end of Kabayan village; follow the signs from the main road • Free, but donation expected

Before heading on to the other burial sites, be sure to visit **Opdas Cave** at the southern end of Kabayan village. It contains around two hundred skulls and bones estimated to be up to a thousand years old, discovered in a pile but now arranged more neatly. Nobody knows why they were buried together, but one theory is that they died as a result of an epidemic. Call at the caretaker's house (the green corrugated iron building); a member of the family will open the gate and encourage you to pray to the spirits, asking them to allow you to enter and leave safely.

National Museum

At the western end of Kabayan beyond the bridge • Free

Kabayan's small branch of the **National Museum** displays the costumes and traditions of the people of Kabayan; exhibits include traditional dress, wild boar skulls, rice wine jars and woven rattan baskets. There is an informative display on centuries-old rituals and beliefs, including burial practices – take a look at the mummy in foetal position inside the coffin.

Tinongchol Burial Rock

3km north of Kabayan • Charge; extra for a guide • 4WDs can be arranged at the *Pinecone Lodge* (see page 161)

An hour's hike north of town is the **Tinongchol Burial Rock**, a large rock with deep niches that were carved to inter the mummified dead in coffins. Four of the seven man-made holes contain between five and ten coffins each – to this day it is unclear how the people of Kagayan hollowed these out.

Timbac Cave

1.2km above Kabayan • Charge; extra for Ibaloi accredited guide • Outside the wet seasons, 4WDs can be arranged at the *Pinecone Lodge* (see page 161)

MAKING A MUMMY

The history of the Kabayan **mummies** is still largely oral. It is even uncertain when the last mummy was created; according to staff at the town's museum, mummification was attempted most recently in 1907 but the wrong combination of herbs was used. It's possible that the last successful mummification was in 1901, of the great-grandmother of former village mayor Florentino Merino.

What is known is the general procedure, which could take up to a year to complete. The body would have been bathed and dressed, then tied upright to a chair with a low fire burning underneath to start the drying process. Unlike in other mummification rituals around the world, the internal organs were not removed. A jar was placed under the corpse to catch the body fluids, which are considered sacred, while elders began the process of peeling off the skin and rubbing juices from native leaves into the muscles to aid preservation. Tobacco smoke was blown through the mouth to dry the internal tissues and drive out worms.

When **Timbac Cave** is open, it's possible to hike up to see its mummies and return within the day. At last check the cave was closed for conservation work and no reopening date had been fixed. When visiting, it's essential to bring an Ibaloi guide not only to ensure that you don't get lost but also to respect local sensibilities: locals believe that unaccompanied outsiders will attract the wrath of the spirits. As one resident puts it, "If ever there is a curse, it will not be on you but on us." The tourist office (see page 161) can arrange an accredited guide.

It's a strenuous four- to five-hour climb to the cave. Take food and drink and aim to set off at around 6am. On the way ask your guide to point out the **Tinongchol Burial Rock**; you'll also see a number of **lakes** and **rice terraces** where farmers grow *kintoman*, an aromatic red rice. Your guide will retrieve the key to Timbac Cave from a caretaker who lives close by, and say the necessary prayers before you enter.

The walk back down to Kabayan takes three hours, or you can walk for an hour or so beyond the cave to the Halsema Highway and flag down a bus (the guide will charge extra for this) directly to Baguio, or head north to Bontoc and Sagada. Check the time of the last bus (usually late afternoon), and don't cut it too fine. It is not recommended that you do this in reverse and approach the cave from the highway, since you risk finding that the caretaker isn't there or offending locals by arriving without a guide.

3

Bangao Cave
Near Bangao village, 7km north of Kabayan • Charge; extra for guide • 4WDs can be arranged at *Pinecone Lodge* (see page 161)

If you don't have time to trek to Timbac Cave, or just want to see as much as possible while in the area, consider visiting the caves around Bangao village. The **Bangao Cave** has a handful of mummies in coffins, although they are in worse condition than those in Timbac. It's a two-hour walk from Kabayan, although you can reduce this to thirty minutes by hiring a 4WD to take you some of the way.

By bus Buses from Baguio's Slaughterhouse terminal (3 daily; 3–4hr) stop along Kabayan's main road.
By van Vans from Baguio's Slaughterhouse terminal serve

Kabayan (every 2hr; 3hr).

Tourist information The tourist information point is at the municipal hall (Mon–Fri 8am–5pm; ☎ 0917 521 5830).

ACCOMMODATION AND EATING

Brookside Café Main road, Kabayan. The friendly owner at this pleasant café with wooden benches rustles up simple dishes including soups, noodles and rice and meat, as well as sugary Benguet coffee that is just the thing on a cold Cordillera morning. ₱
Pinecone Lodge Main road, Kabayan ☎ 0927 586 0221.

As the name suggests, this lodge is decked out in pine; the clean tiled rooms are spacious and all have private bath, and the living area with fireplace gives the place a cosy touch. It also has a restaurant, which is by far the neatest and most reliable place to eat in town, and also serves great brewed coffee. ₱

Mount Pulag

Standing 2922m above sea level, **Mount Pulag**, located within Mount Pulag National Park, is the highest mountain in Luzon, and even experienced climbers are required to take a guide to climb it. The terrain is steep, there are gorges and ravines, and in the heat of the valleys below, it's easy to forget that it can be bitterly cold and foggy on top. Despite what villagers may flippantly say, don't underestimate the difficulty of this mountain. It's essential to treat the area with respect: a number of Indigenous communities including the Ibaloi, Kalanguya, Kankanay and Karaos live on Pulag's slopes and regard the mountain as a sacred place. They have a rich folklore about ancestral spirits inhabiting trees, lakes and mountains, and while they're friendly towards climbers you should stick to the trails.

The two best **trails** start from **Ambangeg** and **Kabayan**. Less used are the **Mountain Lakes Trail**, an hour's drive north of Kabayan, where you ascend Mount Tabayok and

3

THE IGOROTS

The Indigenous peoples of the Cordillera – often collectively known as the **Igorots** ("mountaineers") – resisted assimilation into the Spanish Empire for three centuries. Although the colonizers brought some material improvements, such as to the local diet, they also forced the poor to work to pay off debts, burned houses, cut down crops and introduced smallpox. The saddest long-term result of the attempts to subjugate the Igorots was subtler, however – the creation of a distinction between highland and lowland Filipinos. The peoples of the Cordillera became minorities in their own country, still struggling today for representation and recognition of a lifestyle that the Spanish tried to discredit as unchristian and depraved. The word Igorot was regarded as derogatory in some quarters, although in the twentieth century there were moves to "reclaim" the term and it is still commonly used.

Though some Igorots did convert to Christianity, many are still at least partly animists and pray to a hierarchy of **anitos**. These include deities that possess shamans and speak to them during seances, spirits that inhabit sacred groves or forests, personified forces of nature and generally any supernatural apparition. Offerings are made to benevolent *anitos* for fertility, good health, prosperity, fair weather and success in business (or, in the olden days, tribal war). Evil *anitos* are propitiated to avoid illness, crop failure, storms, accidents and death. Omens are also carefully observed: a particular bird seen upon leaving the house might herald sickness, for example, requiring that appropriate ceremonies are conducted to forestall its portent. If the bird returns, the house may be abandoned.

camp at the lakeside, and the **Enchanted Trail** starting in Tawangan, a two-hour drive north of Kabayan. Whichever way you choose to climb Pulag, the most exciting thing to do is to take a tent and expect to **spend the night** on top, but note that camping in the park is banned at weekends (Fri–Sun) and if weather conditions are bad. An alternative option to camping is accommodation in local homestays, which can be arranged by the Department of Environment and Natural Resources (DENR) Visitors' Center (see page 163). Two things to note before you set out are that visitor numbers may be restricted for conservation reasons, so it's wise to check ahead that you will indeed be able to visit on the date you have in mind; and that you'll need to pass a medical check-up before taking the hike (see page 163), or you won't be allowed to do it.

The Ambangeg trail

Ambangeg is a regular stop on the Baguio to Kabayan bus route; ask the driver to drop you at the visitor centre in the Bokod barangay of Ambangeg. It's a two- to three-hour walk from here to the **ranger station** where the hike officially begins, and where you can hire guides; you can also get a lift to the ranger station on a motorcycle (1hr). It's best to spend the night at the furthest campsite, about three hours from the ranger station, and ascend to the summit for dawn the next day. If you arrive in Ambangeg too late to ascend, staff at the visitors' centre can organize homestay accommodation.

The Kabayan trail

The trail from **Kabayan**, known as the **Akiki** or **Killer Trail**, starts 2km south of Kabayan on the Baguio–Kabayan road. As the name suggests this is a more difficult route than the Ambangeg trail, taking at least seven hours to reach the saddle camp near the summit. The next morning you will go to the peak, then descend.

INFORMATION   **MOUNT PULAG**

Trail information Before coming to Mount Pulag it's a good idea to contact Emerita Albas, the Protected Area's Superintendent, at the DENR Visitors' Center in the Bokod barangay of Ambangeg (☏ 0929 166 8864) for up-to-date information on which trails are most accessible at any given time of year. Be sure to check that you will be allowed to visit at the time you want to.

Medical certificate All climbers will have a health check performed prior to orientation.

Registration and fees You'll need to register and pay an entrance fee, camping fee and local government heritage fee, plus an extra fee for your health check. This

can be done at the DENR Visitors' Center in Ambangeg or at the municipal hall in Kabayan (see page 161).

Guides You can hire a guide for the Ambangeg trail at the DENR Visitors' Center. The tourist office in Kabayan can arrange guides for the Kabayan trail.

Bontoc and around

BONTOC lies on the Chico River, which divides Poblacion (the town centre) from the neighbourhood of Samoki. Primarily used by tourists as a transport hub, the town is also a good base for **trekking** and has easy access to the beautiful Maligcong

HIKES AROUND BONTOC

Around Bontoc a number of **mountain trails** snake their way through beautiful rice paddy scenery. Most places are far off the tourist radar, and you probably won't see any Westerners in any of the towns; accommodation is basic, but it's worth heading this way if you want to really get a taste of life in Mountain Province.

MALIGCONG

Nearly 7km north of Bontoc, the stone-walled rice terraces around **Maligcong village** are at their best in June and July immediately before the harvest. From the point where public transport stops, a path descends into a valley and follows the contour of the terraces to Maligcong. There's a friendly homestay (see page 165) and a sari-sari store here, but no café so it's best to bring your own food. Jeepneys to Maligcong from Bontoc (5 daily; 30min) leave from just above the market; the last return journey is at around 4pm.

MAINIT

From Maligcong it is a three-hour trek northwest through scenic rice paddies to **Mainit** ("Ma-i-nit"), a village known for its hot sulphurous springs, where you can also overnight (see page 165). Jeepneys to Mainit leave from just above the market in Bontoc (2 each afternoon; 1hr 15min); the return trips are the following morning, though sometimes you'll get lucky and be able to return the same day.

ALAB PETROGLYPH AND GANGA CAVE

A huge rock etched with drawings of humans with bows and arrows, the **Alab Petroglyph** is at the end of a two-hour hike uphill from the barangay of **Alab**, 9km south of Bontoc on the Halsema Highway. Although it was declared a national cultural treasure in 1975, little is known about who created these carvings or why. An hour further along is the **Ganga Cave**, a burial cave containing coffins and jars of bones. You'll need to find a guide in Alab for either destination. Regular jeepneys to Alab (hourly; 25min) leave from in front of Bontoc's market.

BARLIG AND KADACLAN

Two villages east of Bontoc are well off the normal tourist route, but their wonderful rice terraces are certainly worth the trip. The closest village to Bontoc is **Barlig**, 40km east, which is also the starting point for a trek up Mount Amuyao (2702m). The trek can be done in a day (guides will take up to five people), or you can continue to Batad (see page 174), 12km south, making it a two-day trip – ask about guides at the Barlig town hall. There are no-frills lodges in town (see page 165). Rarely visited by tourists, **Kadaclan**, 44km east of Bontoc, is in a scenic location and ideal for getting away from it all for a day or two; it has basic accommodation. Jeepneys to Barlig (2 daily; 2hr) and Kadaclan (2 daily; 5hr) leave from next to All Saints Cathedral in Bontoc.

3

rice terraces. The main road from Baguio to Bontoc (and through Poblacion) is the **Halsema Highway** or "Mountain Trail", a narrow, serpentine gash in the side of the Cordillera that's sometimes no more than a rocky track with vertical cliffs on one side and a sheer drop on the other. Although the road has been improved in recent years, it can still be an uncomfortable trip by public transport as some of the buses are crowded and not especially well maintained. The views, though, are marvellous, especially as you ascend out of Baguio beyond La Trinidad and pass through deep gorges lined with rice terraces.

Bontoc Museum

Uphill (west) from the market • Mon–Sat 8am–5pm • Charge • ☎ 0918 576 2170

Bontoc's one tourist sight is the **Bontoc Museum**, which includes wonderful artefacts and a collection of centuries-old Chinese porcelain and stoneware traded from different parts of the Cordillera region. Take a look at the disturbing photograph of a headhunting victim, whose corpse is being carried away for burial as his head is presented as a trophy around the village. There's a reconstruction of a traditional Bontoc village on the grounds. The shop sells items that include handmade jewellery, books and CDs of traditional music.

ARRIVAL AND INFORMATION
BONTOC AND AROUND

By bus GL Trans buses arrive at Circle Station in Bontoc (the main junction, by the market), while D'Rising Sun buses (ⓦ facebook.com/DRS.BUS) stop by the police station near the Municipal Hall on Halsema Highway. Coda Lines (ⓦ facebook.com/codalinescorporation) will pick up and drop off on the Poblacion side of the bridge across the river, but their actual terminal is at the *Cable Café* in Samoki (see below). Local buses to and from Tabuk and Tinglayan stop at Lower Caluttit opposite Bontoc's Polytechnic College.
Destinations Baguio (1–2 hourly; 5hr 30min); Manila (2

daily; 12hr); Tabuk (1 daily; 6hr); Tinglayan (1 daily; 3hr).
By jeepney Jeepneys for Sagada (hourly; 45min) leave from outside the *Walter Clapp Inn*, a block east of Bontoc's main drag.
By van Vans to Banaue (leaving when full; 2hr) leave from just off Halsema Highway beside Cooperative Bank.
Tourist information The municipal tourist office is by the Municipal Hall in Bontoc (Mon–Fri 8am–5pm; ☎ 0929 127 0892), while the provincial tourist office is on the second floor of the Provincial Capitol Building (Mon–Fri 7.30am–5pm).

ACCOMMODATION AND EATING

BONTOC

Bontoc Bed & Bistro By the market ⓦ facebook.com/pmabontocbAndBistro2019. Bontoc Bed & Bistro offers simple but clean rooms right in the centre of town, and the downstairs café is one of the nicest places in town for a coffee. Try and get a room at the back if you're a light sleeper. ̄P̄

Drop-By South of the museum. A no-frills place in the town centre to get a cheap and cheerful meal. There's both

Filipino and international choices on the menu, with the pizzas being perhaps the best choice. ̄P̄

Pines Kitchenette and Inn Above the market. This large family house was originally built to put up adopted World War II war orphans, as photographs in the lobby testify. Rooms are simple and the shared bathrooms (only one room has its own) just about pass muster, but the management is friendly and welcoming, and it's the most interesting place in town to stay. ̄P̄

KILLING ME SOFTLY

One Mountain Province delicacy, served in many restaurants, is **pinikpikan**, a chicken dish that translates as "killing me softly". The preparation involves beating the bird's wings and neck with a stick before it is killed in the belief that the beating brings blood to the surface, making the meat more tender and tasty. Once dead, the chicken is put on an open fire to burn off the feathers and is then mixed with cured pork; the burning of feathers and the blending of two types of meat adds to the flavour of the dish. When performing rituals, the local people traditionally eat the head and the innards for good fortune and good health the day after the chicken is butchered.

Samokey Coffee House Samoki ⓦfacebook.com/p/ Samokey-Coffee-House-100063796915442/. A pleasant place to enjoy a cup of coffee and a cake, as well as larger meals. There's decent wi-fi. P̄

MALIGCONG
Suzette's Maligcong Homestay ⓦmaligcong homestay.com. Small homestay that has three comfy little rooms with a couple of beds in each. The owner can also rustle up meals upon request, but let her know a few hours in advance. There are pretty views of the rice terraces from the breakfast table. P̄

MAINIT
Geston Minerals Spring Resort ☏0920 454 0963.

This green building has brightly painted rooms off a maze of narrow corridors. There are also two thatched cottages, built from stone and dried grass, giving on to four hot pools of varying temperatures – perfect for a soak after a long day's hike. P̄

BARLIG
Halfway Inn The seven tiny rooms at this simple place have wooden floorboards and spindly little desks; there's no hot water in the communal bathrooms (and no phone, either) but staff will happily boil a pot or two for you. There are pretty views from the terrace, and a restaurant serving very basic grub. P̄

Sagada

The small town of **SAGADA**, 160km north of Baguio, has long attracted curious visitors. Part of the appeal derives from its famous **hanging coffins** and a labyrinth of **caves** used by the ancients as burial sites. But Sagada also has a reputation as a remote and idyllic hideaway where people live a simple life well away from civilization. The landscape here is almost alpine and the inhabitants are mountain people, their faces shaped not by the sun and sea of the lowlands, but by the thin air and sharp glare of altitude. Sagada only began to open up as a destination when it got electricity in the early 1970s, and intellectuals – internal refugees from the Marcos dictatorship – flocked here to write and paint. They didn't produce much of note - it's said that this is perhaps because they spent much of their time drinking *tapuy* (the local rice wine). European hippies followed, as did the military, who thought the *turistas* were supplying funds for an insurgency.

While the town doesn't offer a lot to do, you'll find plenty of **activities** in the surrounding area. Other than that there's scope for just hanging out, settling down in the evenings by a log fire in one of the wooden cafés or restaurants. With so much fruit and vegetables grown nearby, the **food** in Sagada is among the best in the country, with lots of veggie choices – something of a rarity in the Philippines. A **curfew** means that you can't drink after 9pm, but almost everyone has gone to bed by then anyway.

Demang

If you have time then it's worth wandering 500m down to the village of **Demang**, reached from a turning on the right just beyond the *George Guest House*. The village is older than Sagada and

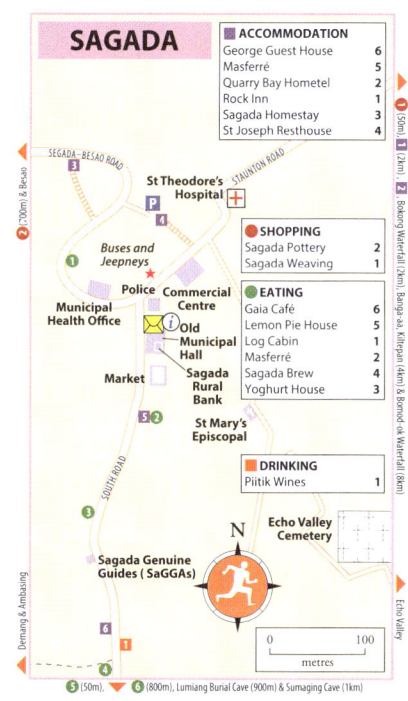

SAGADA

ACCOMMODATION
George Guest House	6
Masferré	5
Quarry Bay Hometel	2
Rock Inn	1
Sagada Homestay	3
St Joseph Resthouse	4

SHOPPING
Sagada Pottery	2
Sagada Weaving	1

EATING
Gaia Café	6
Lemon Pie House	5
Log Cabin	1
Masferré	2
Sagada Brew	4
Yoghurt House	3

DRINKING
Piitik Wines	1

remains practically untouched by tourism. It's a quiet residential area with several *dap-ay* (stone circles where community matters are resolved).

ARRIVAL AND INFORMATION SAGADA

By bus and jeepney Transport operates from the main junction, opposite the commercial centre. Coda Lines (ⓦfacebook.com/codalinescorporation) run a daily bus to Manila (13hr). GL Trans buses serve Baguio (5 daily; 5–6hr). Jeepneys run to and from Bontoc (1–2 hourly; 40min). For Banaue, take a jeepney to Bontoc and change there. Getting to Sagada or Bontoc from the coast involves taking vans in stages from Bitalag (just north of Tagudin on the San Fernando–Vigan road), via Cervantes and Abatan Bauko; set off early from Vigan or San Fernando if you aim to do this in a day.

Environmental fee All visitors to Sagada must register and pay an environmental fee, payable at the tourist information centre. Keep the receipt with you as you'll need to show it when visiting the main sights.

Tourist information There's a small tourist information centre in the old town hall (7am–5pm; ⓦfacebook.com/sagadatourism); they'll be able to give you a list of guided tours with fixed prices, and some information is also posted on their Facebook page.

ACCOMMODATION SEE MAP PAGE 165

The town gets packed out at Christmas and Easter, so if you're planning to visit at these times try to book ahead.

George Guest House ⓦfacebook.com/GGHSagada. A popular choice among travellers, with clean rooms with private showers and hot water; rooms in the annexe up the hill are more spacious but the same price; they also have another annexe down the hill with cottages sleeping six to twelve, all with kitchen, living area, TV and fireplace. $\overline{P}$

★ **Masferré** ⓦmasferre.blogspot.com. One of Sagada's best options right in the centre, offering spotless cosy rooms with pine-wood furniture and private bath. It's owned by the family of early twentieth-century photographer Eduardo Masferré, whose historical pictures of local Indigenous people decorate the (excellent) restaurant. $\overline{PP}$

Quarry Bay Hometel 1.5km east of town ⓦfacebook.com/RustyNailInnSagada. Ignore the slightly off-putting name and you'll find a large, welcoming place with comfortable beds, where the attractive rooms are set over six levels – a practical skyscraper. For those on a tighter budget, there are dorm rooms available. There's a basic but good bar and café, decorated with Indigenous

woodcarvings and artwork. $\overline{PP}$

★ **Rock Inn** Just over 2km east of town ⓦfacebook.com/RockInnSagada. Set on four verdant hectares with an orange grove, this place allows guests to pick their own fruit. The cosy rooms are in a large building with wooden furnishings, and there's a spacious attic dorm, too. Aptly enough, the airy restaurant serves dishes using fresh local produce. $\overline{PP}$

★ **Sagada Homestay** ⓦfacebook.com/Sagadahomestayinn.resto. This friendly, welcoming homestay offers neat and tidy rooms with or without private bath. It includes a couple of lounge areas that are perfect for meeting other travellers, as well as a guest kitchen. There's wi-fi in the main building, and a laundry service. $\overline{P}$

St Joseph Resthouse ⓦsaintjosephresthousesagada.blogspot.com. Converted from a convent and owned by the Anglican church, this guesthouse has cheap, basic rooms in a separate block, while those in the main building have more character and offer private bathrooms. There are also some cottages sprinkled along a grassy slope, the largest of which sleeps eight. $\overline{P}$

EATING SEE MAP PAGE 165

★ **Gaia Café** ☎0949 137 6777. Near the entrance to Lumiang Burial Cave, this wonderful eco-friendly restaurant offers inventive dishes, using largely organic ingredients and mostly vegan, including *miki mi na* – squash noodles sautéed with green beans, carrots and mushrooms, all served on a covered patio with terrific views over the rice terraces. $\overline{PP}$

Lemon Pie House ⓦsagadalemonpiehouse.blogspot.com. On the southern side of town, this place is renowned for its lemon meringue pie that customers enjoy at low wooden tables, all designed and assembled by the owner-cum-carpenter. Between March and May they also bake a great blueberry pie using local fresh fruits. $\overline{P}$

★ **Log Cabin** ⓦfacebook.com/logcabinsagada. Some of the best food in town. The welcoming wooden interior is warm and cosy, and the crackling fireplace further adds to the homely atmosphere. Sat evenings see a popular buffet with fresh ingredients bought from the market, while on other days there's an à la carte menu with a focus on French dishes. Reserve by mid-afternoon if you plan to dine in the evening, and preferably a day or two ahead for the buffet. $\overline{PPP}$

Masferré ⓦmasferre.blogspot.com. It's worth coming here to take a look at the wonderful set of black-and-white photographs of Sagada and various Indigenous mountain cultures taken by Eduardo Masferré in the late 1930s and early 1950s. The Western menu includes popular super-subs and sandwiches, as well as burgers and steaks. $\overline{PPP}$

Sagada Brew ⓦfacebook.com/sagadabrew. This Italian-influenced café offers scrumptious home-made brownies and Italian-style coffee, as well as such un-Italian confections as a Starbucks-style caramel "macchiato". The

ACTIVITIES IN SAGADA

TREKKING

One of the most popular hikes is to see the **hanging coffins** in **Echo Valley**. It's only a 25-minute walk from the centre of Sagada to the coffins, and it can be done alone with a map (souvenir shops sell sketch maps), but there are numerous paths and it isn't unknown for people to get lost. On the whole, it's better to take a guide who can also fill you in on local history and traditions. The coffins can also be visited as part of the popular three-hour Central Sagada Eco-Tour – ask at the Sagada tourist information centre (see page 166), who can arrange guides to take groups of up to ten. After the coffins, the path takes you along a short stretch of an underground river at Latang Cave and ends at the **Bokong Waterfall** on the eastern edge of Sagada, where you can swim. The waterfall can also be reached from town without a guide in about half an hour, although it's easy to miss the steps on the left about 500m beyond Sagada Weaving. Other guided hikes offered by the tourist office and Sagada Genuine Guides include a walk to the **Bomod-ok Waterfall**, rice terraces and villages north of Sagada (3hr); a trip to a scenic area of rice terraces known as **Kiltepan** (1hr 30min); and a trek on **Mount Ampacao** (3–4hr).

CAVING

Caving in Sagada's deep network of limestone channels and caverns is exhilarating but potentially dangerous. Many caves are slippery and have deep ravines. A small number of tourists have been killed in them, so it's essential to hire a reliable, accredited **guide**.

The most commonly visited cave is **Sumaging**, also known as Big Cave, a 45-minute walk south of Sagada. The chambers and rock formations inside are eerie and immense, named after things they resemble – the Cauliflower, the Rice Granary and such like. Guides with lanterns will take you on a descent through a series of tunnels you'll only be able to get through by crawling, ending in a pool of clear water where you can swim. Ideally you should wear trekking sandals, but otherwise shoes can be left at an appropriate point and the final sections negotiated barefoot.

Like many caves in the area, Sumaging was once a burial cave, although there are no coffins or human remains there now. However, a standard caving itinerary will also include a visit to the entrance of **Lumiang Burial Cave**, a short walk south of Sagada and then down a steep trail into the valley. Around a hundred old coffins are stacked in the entrance. Pointing at them is considered the worst kind of bad luck; lizards, on the other hand, are auspicious – you'll see their images carved onto some of the coffins.

Lumiang is also the starting point for the **Cave Connection** trip, which heads through passages linking it to Sumaging. It's a three- to four-hour excursion and not for the faint-hearted; it might be best to try Sumaging first. At points you'll need to descend a few metres without ropes, jamming your limbs against the rock walls and edging your way down.

RAFTING

Rafting is possible on the **Chico River** from June until December, although at the beginning of the season it may only be possible to raft the upper sections. October and November see the most pleasant weather, but the highest water is in December and early January, making it possible to go further downstream. You normally spend around 2hr in the water. Groups tend to be between three and seven; if there are just one or two of you, they may possibly be able to hook you up with a larger group.

MOUNTAIN BIKING

The mountainous landscape around Sagada offers rough terrain and remote trails that are ideal for **mountain biking**. Most tracts are steep and technical, and mainly suited to experienced individuals. Some back roads provide less technical riding, but there are still extended climbs. The cool mountain temperatures, fresh clean air and scenic beauty make this one of the country's best spots to explore on two wheels.

3

menu includes soups, sandwiches made with freshly baked focaccia and tasty pasta dishes. P̄

Yoghurt House ☎ 0908 112 8430. A popular place with travellers, this wood cabin offers hearty breakfasts and home-made yoghurt – try the fruit salad with yoghurt and honey. Main dishes are pretty good too; enjoy your meal on the narrow balcony as you watch life go by. P̄P̄P̄

DRINKING   SEE MAP PAGE 165

★ **Piitik Wines** ⓦ facebook.com/sagadaclayhaus. This place may sound boutiquey and modern, but it has been around since 2004; also known as the *Clay House*, it does indeed look like a giant school art experiment, but the fruit wines on sale are quite excellent. All ingredients are local – think guava, persimmon and guayabano – and visitors can sample by the tot, with payment via an honesty box.

SHOPPING   SEE MAP PAGE 165

Sagada Pottery A 15min walk west of the centre ⓦ facebook.com/SagadaPottery. High-quality stoneware, made on the premises. One of the potters will demonstrate their craft, and for a small charge you can have a go yourself.

Sagada Weaving Nangonogan ⓦ facebook.com/sagadaweaving1968. At this place a short walk east of the centre, you can buy fabrics and accessories produced using traditional tribal designs. More than half a dozen people work at sewing machines in the shop itself, while next door you can see the weaving being done on wooden looms. It's a good place to pick up a gift such as a *bahag* (loincloth), an exquisitely hand-loomed piece of long cloth traditionally wrapped around a man's middle, but increasingly bought by tourists as a throw or table runner.

DIRECTORY

Banks and exchange The best ATM is by the tourist office in the old town hall. There are others in the Sagada Rural Bank (Tues–Sat 8.30am–4.30pm), downstairs from the old town hall, and in the Treasure Link Cooperative Society on the top floor of the Commercial Centre (Mon–Sat 8.30am–3pm), but only accessible when those are open.

Hospital For minor ailments you can visit the Municipal Health Office (Mon–Fri 8am–5pm; ☎ 0945 481 7741); there's also a small hospital, St Theodore's (☎ 0917 570 4922), on the northeastern edge of the village.

Police Next to the Old Municipal Hall (24hr; ☎ 0998 967 4396).

Kalinga province

The mountains, rice fields and villages in **Kalinga province** rarely see visitors, never mind foreign tourists. This is real frontier travel, with massive potential for hiking and climbing. Outside the towns of **Tinglayan** and **Tabuk**, the only accommodation is in simple lodges or local homes, the only shops are roadside stores, and electricity is a rarity, so bring a flashlight.

The Kalinga, once fierce **headhunters**, are remembered for their indomitable spirit and their refusal to be colonized. Most Kalinga communities live on levelled parts of steep mountain slopes, where a small shrine called a *bodayan* guards the entrance to the village. You could also ask your guide (see box, page 168) about visiting a **tattoo artist**, many of whom still work using traditional materials and designs; it is possible to have a tattoo yourself, but if you do this, make sure that the thorn used to insert the ink is a fresh one.

HIKING IN KALINGA: GUIDES

Wherever you go hiking in Kalinga you'll need a **guide**: essential not only to avoid getting lost, but also to ensure that you respect local sensibilities. Occasionally there are disputes – over water rights, for instance – that result in violence, and a guide will stop you stumbling into any areas where tensions might be high. Law and order in the province still relies very much on pacts (*bodong*) brokered by elders. Your first point of contact should be your accommodation, who will either be able to put you on to a guide, or divert you to a place with more expertise in such matters.

RAFTING THROUGH THE RICE TERRACES

The area around Tabuk offers excellent **rafting** opportunities on the Chico River, which snakes its way through spectacular rice terrace scenery. The most reliable company is **Chico River Quest** (Ⓦfacebook.com/chicoriverquest), which runs trips for all levels – they don't go out as much as they used to, but get in touch and see what they can organise. The prime rafting season is July through to October; trips between October and December are dependent on rainfall.

The best run for **beginners** starts at the confluence of the Pasil and Chico rivers, and lasts about two hours. Groups must be a minimum of five people, and rates include transport and food. More experienced rafters should ask about a longer run which starts upriver in Tinglayan. This trip also allows you to stop off halfway down for a one-hour canyon hike.

Tinglayan

The town of **TINGLAYAN**, about 50km from Bontoc and 60km from Tabuk, is well placed if you want to explore Kalinga province. From here you can strike out on **mountain trails** carved by the Spanish when they tried, and failed, to bring the Kalinga people into the Catholic fold. Trails pass through villages and rice terraces at Lubo and Mangali, to the crater of the extinct volcano Mount Sukuok, and to a number of mountain lakes including Bonnong and Padcharao. Rice is planted twice a year around Tinglayan, and the fields are at their greenest from March to April and September to October.

Lubuagan

They don't see many tourists in **LUBUAGAN**, 18km north of Tinglayan on the road to Tabuk, but it makes for a worthwhile stop. The town itself has a makeshift air, lined with grey concrete buildings and with livestock wandering in the street, but it's beautifully located amid rice terraces. Remarkably, it was the capital of the free Philippines for 35 days in 1900, when the revolutionary President Aguinaldo established his headquarters in the town before being forced to flee the US army.

The barangay of Mabilong, east of the centre, is known for its **textiles** and you can arrange to visit one of the women who weave at home, sitting on the floor using rudimentary handlooms. Ask at the **town hall** to arrange a visit, or for advice about hiking routes and **guides**. You might also ask about the **cultural village**, around thirty minutes from the town, where traditional dance performances occasionally take place.

Tabuk

While it has little to see, the agricultural town and provincial capital of **TABUK**, 50km north of Tinglayan, offers a surprisingly decent choice of accommodation and the region's only internet access and banks. The town serves as a base and jumping-off point for trekking excursions, visits to Kalinga tattoo artists and **rafting** on the nearby Chico River.

Ryan's Farm

Mapaoay, Ipil, 6km north of Tabuk • Charge • ☎0916 755 7078 • Best visited by tricycle from Tabuk

While in Tabuk, take the time to visit **Ryan's Farm**, owned by Corazon and Jeremy Ryan. They have an orchard and fish ponds, and experiment with vermiculture (worm composting) and organic agriculture, but most of all it's just pleasant to enjoy their conversation – possibly over a glass of home-made *bugnay* (local berry) wine. They may also be able to prepare a meal and even let you camp overnight if you call in advance to arrange it.

3

ARRIVAL AND INFORMATION

In the **dry season** Tinglayan, Tabuk and Lubuagan can be reached by jeepneys from Bontoc, although services in this area are anything but regular and it's a bumpy road, so the trip can take many hours. In the **rainy season** (particularly July–Oct) it may be impossible to travel between Tinglayan and Tabuk due to the road conditions, in which case Tinglayan is best approached from Bontoc while Tabuk is reached via Tuguegarao.

TINGLAYAN

By bus There are two daily buses each way between Bontoc and Tabuk that stop in Tinglayan.

By jeepney A couple of jeepneys run from Bontoc to Tinglayan daily (2hr 30min), and a handful of between Tabuk and Tingalayan (3hr 30min).

LUBUAGAN

By bus There are two daily buses each way between Bontoc and Tabuk that stop in Lubuagan.

By jeepney A handful of jeepneys pass through Lubuagan on their way between Tabuk (2hr 30min) and Tingalayan (1hr 30min).

TABUK

By bus From Manila, Victory Liner (ⓦvictoryliner.com) and Dangwa buses run to Tabuk (2 daily; 12hr). There are more services from Baguio (7 daily; 10hr), and also two daily buses connecting Bontoc to Tabuk (4hr) via Lubuagan and Tinglayan.

By jeepney Jeepneys from Bontoc stop off in Tinglayan and Lubuagan on their way to Tabuk.

By van Vans from Tuguegarao (leaving when full; 1hr 30min) leave from the Santa Ana terminal on the National Highway and from Brickstone Mall terminal.

ACCOMMODATION AND EATING

TINGLAYAN

GL's Crib & Coffee ⓞ 0963 307 0218. Easily the best place to stay anywhere near Tinglayan, a remote homestay operation with cramped rooms (almost like a challenge to see how many mattresses can be squashed into one rectangular area), but better common areas, where you'll probably do most of your hanging out. The views are fantastic – gents will find that there's a great one from one of the urinals. PPP

TABUK

Davidson Provincial Rd, Bulanao ⓦfacebook.com/DavidsonHotel. One of Tabuk's better-equipped hotels, with a pool, gym and a good restaurant serving local and international dishes. Rooms vary considerably – some are spacious, clean and tidy while others are in disrepair – make

sure to take a look at a few before settling in. PP

Golden Berries San Juan ⓦgoldenberrieshotel.com. The owners here process, grind and package locally grown coffee beans on the premises – you can buy the finished product at the hotel's little shop. The rooms in the "old" building are a bit tired; those in the "new" block at the back are more comfortable with modern amenities. There's also a restaurant, although the food is less than average, and a swimming pool on site. PP

Grand Zion Resort National Highway, Purok 7, Bulanao ⓦgrandzionresort.com. Tabuk's most upmarket hotel features spacious, tastefully decorated rooms in an airy building resembling an alpine lodge. There are pleasant gardens at the back with an inviting swimming pool, and a restaurant serving an array of dishes. PPP

DIRECTORY

Banks You can withdraw cash at the PNB and DBP banks in the barangay of Dagupan, and Land Bank and Rural Bank in the barangay of Bulanao.

Ifugao province

Landlocked **Ifugao province** is characterized by spectacular rugged terrain, lush forests and verdant river valleys dotted with Indigenous villages. A number of Ifugao communities still wear traditional dress, although you'll have to trek to remote villages to experience authentic local life. The Ifugaos are a proud people who have preserved their ancestral past, largely because they managed to sustain resistance during the Spanish colonial regime, which, as in Kalinga, failed in subduing the highlanders. The highlights of the region are the spectacular **rice terraces**, handcarved in the mountainside more than two thousand years ago and now designated by UNESCO as a **World Heritage Site**.

Banaue

It may only be 300km north of Manila, but **BANAUE** might as well be a world away, 1300m above sea level and far removed in spirit and topography from the beaches and palm trees of the south. The town itself is small and not hugely impressive, centred on a marketplace, with a few guesthouses, some souvenir shops and a couple of good **museums**, but its location is superb. This is the heart of **rice terrace** country: the terraces in Banaue itself are some of the most impressive and well known, and there are hundreds of others in valleys and gorges throughout the area, most of which can be reached on foot. There is rustic accommodation at nearby **Batad** (see page 174), so you could stay overnight and hike back the next morning.

Museum of Cordillera Sculpture

Bissang Tam-an • Charge • ⓦ cordilleranmuseum.weebly.com/gallery-of-exhibits.html • Reached by tricycle from town, or on foot

The private collection of American expat George Schenk, the wonderful **Museum of Cordillera Sculpture** displays a fine array of Ifugao cultural objects. Highlights include *bulol* rice deities – guardian figures placed in the rice paddies in order to protect them from malevolent spirits and bring abundant harvests – and wooden statuettes of pregnant wives, carved by husbands who would devoutly pray to them believing that this would ease their spouse's pregnancy.

Banaue Museum

Poblacion • Charge • ☎ 0916 694 4511

The family-run **Banaue Museum** houses part of the collection of American anthropologist Henry Otley Beyer, and remains in the possession of his descendents. The objects were acquired from Ifugao province and the adjoining areas, and include ceremonial necklaces, black-and-white photographs of tattooed Ifugao ancestors, and wooden gods that were placed in rice granaries, serving as guardians of the harvest and the fields. Don't miss the Ifugao coffin – tradition dictates that the dead had to be sealed inside and kept under the house, with the top of the coffin serving as a bench.

Lookout points

Visit by tricycle

Two kilometres north of town is a series of five **lookout points** for the rice terraces, where Ifugao elders in traditional costume hang out and ask for a small fee if you want

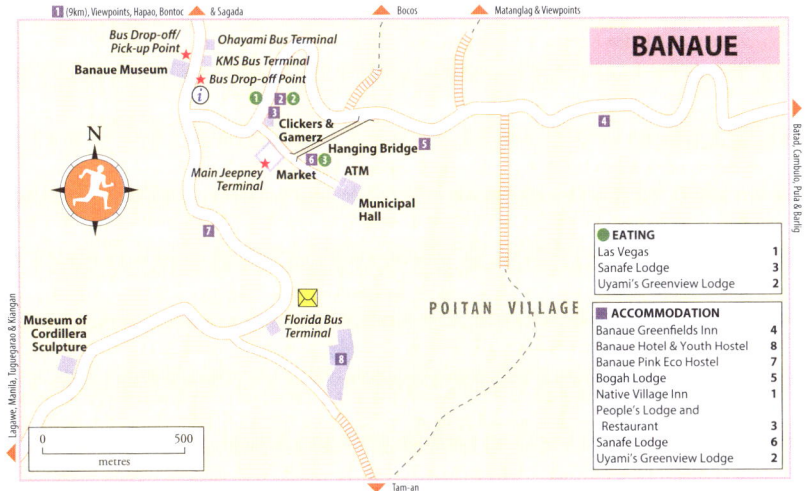

3

BANAUE'S STAIRWAYS TO HEAVEN

The **rice terraces** around Banaue are among the great icons of the Philippines, and were hewn from the land two thousand years ago by the Ifugao people using primitive tools, an achievement in engineering terms that ranks alongside the building of the pyramids. Called the "Stairway to Heaven" by the Ifugaos, the terraces would stretch 20,000km if laid out end to end. Not only are they an extraordinary sight, but they are also an object lesson in **sustainability**.

The terraces are on the UNESCO World Heritage list, and they will not last forever if they are not protected. They have always been subject to constant deterioration, due to erosion, imperfect irrigation systems and the actions of earthworms. Following a shortage of young people to help carry out repairs – rice farming held little allure for many of them, understandably tired of the subsistence livelihood their parents eked from the land – strict measures have been taken in recent years to protect and revive the paddies, and young farmers are slowly returning to work in the fields.

to take their photograph. The third lookout point has the view depicted on the P1000 banknote; you'll get the best vista from the fifth lookout.

ARRIVAL AND DEPARTURE   BANAUE

By bus Buses from Manila and Baguio drop passengers off outside the municipal tourist centre, but depart from their respective terminals. Coda Lines (ⓦfacebook.com/codalinescorporation), Ohayami (ⓦohayamitrans.com) and Dangwa all have evening services to Manila (8–9hr); Ohayami and KMS have early-evening departures for

Baguio (8hr).
By van Vans from Bontoc stop outside the municipal tourist centre (leaving when full, 11am–1pm; 1hr 30min). There are six daily departures for Baguio, best booked a day in advance at the office just below the municipal tourist centre (6hr).

INFORMATION

Environmental fee All visitors must register and pay the environmental fee at the municipal tourist centre.
Tourist information The municipal tourist centre is on the western end of the main drag, where the buses stop (daily 5.30am–5pm; ⓦfacebook.com/visitbanaue2016).

Tours You can hire an accredited guide to explore the surrounding area; rates vary depending on where you go – ask at the municipal tourist centre for a list of destinations with fixed rates. Guesthouses can enquire about motorbike rental.

ACCOMMODATION   SEE MAP PAGE 171

Banaue's **accommodation** is generally simple but clean and friendly, and many places have restaurants attached. Finding somewhere without a reservation is not a problem, except at Christmas and Easter.
Banaue Greenfields Inn East of town ⓦgreenfields. discoverbanaue.com. A walk out of town you'll find this deservedly popular place; it's hard not to be impressed by the rice-terrace views, whatever the weather, and the homely atmosphere makes guests look forward to returning when they're done with their day's activities (or evening's eating). Breakfast usually included and there's wi-fi in the lobby; just remember that countryside mornings can be quite loud. P̄P̄
Banaue Hotel & Youth Hostel Ilogui Tam-an ⓦbanaue hotelandyouthhostel.com. This vast, rambling hotel hasn't changed its decor much since opening in the 1970s. Rooms are comfortable and spacious nonetheless, and there are deluxe options and suites with nice views, plus a pleasant swimming pool and a bar with pool table. Wi-fi is available in

the lobby, and there's a youth hostel attached. P̄P̄
Banaue Pink Eco Hostel South of town ☏0927 854 9128. Relatively new budget spot, boasting a terrace with a view, tidy dorms, and decent advice when it comes to trekking or onward travel. P̄
Bogah Lodge Batunbinongle ⓦbogahlodge.weebly. com. An attractive and homely place a little way east of the centre of Banaue, with simple but comfortable rooms, some with lovely views across to the mountains. The food is good, and the owners can help with arranging local treks. P̄P̄
★ **Native Village Inn** Uhaj, 9km west of Banaue ☏0915 614 7778. On the road to Hapao, this wonderful place has stunning rice terrace views – there are two lookout points where guests are encouraged to take their breakfast, and where you can easily while away a few hours just soaking in the scenery. The food is another highlight, and includes fresh home-baked bread. Accommodation is in comfortable native huts dotted around the verdant

grounds. Call for a free pick-up from Banaue. $\overline{PP}$

People's Lodge and Restaurant Poblacion ⓦfacebook.com/conquer.banaue. This lodge offers simple rooms, some of which share cold showers and toilets, and more expensive, slightly more spacious rooms with private bath (otherwise, you pay extra for a hot shower, although cold ones are free). There's a terrace with excellent views and a lounge area with rustic wooden benches. $\overline{P}$

★ **Sanafe Lodge** Banaue Trade Centre, Poblacion ⓦfacebook.com/sanafelodge. A great option, with

clean rooms with wooden decor; some are more spacious than others so take a look at a few before choosing. The deluxe room is worth every peso – clean, spacious and with excellent views over the rice terraces. $\overline{PP}$

Uyami's Greenview Lodge Poblacion ⓦfacebook.com/banauegreenviewlodge. The homely doubles here have wooden floors and pine interiors, although the cheaper concrete rooms on the bottom floor aren't as snug, with common bathrooms and cold showers (hot water costs extra). $\overline{P}$

EATING

SEE MAP PAGE 171

Most of the best food is served in the town's various **lodges**.

Las Vegas Poblacion ☎0921 683 3431. This popular restaurant serving mainly Filipino food has a smattering of American and international memorabilia sitting alongside wooden Ifugao statuettes, and offers healthy salads as well as dishes such as beef *tapa*. $\overline{P}$

★ **Sanafe Lodge** Banaue Trade Centre, Poblacion

ⓦfacebook.com/sanafelodge. One of Banaue's better restaurants, where you can enjoy spectacular scenery from some tables. $\overline{PP}$

Uyami's Greenview Lodge Poblacion ⓦfacebook.com/banauegreenviewlodge. The restaurant at this lodge has wonderful rice-terrace views and wi-fi, and rustles up appetizing local dishes. $\overline{PP}$

DIRECTORY

Banks and exchange W&L moneychangers, 3/F Banaue Building in the main square (daily 8am–5.30pm) don't offer great rates. The ATM by the municipal hall accepts foreign

cards, but has been known to swallow them; most lodges, restaurants and shops don't take payment by card, so bring however much cash you're likely to need.

Around Banaue

The area around Banaue offers spectacular **rice terrace** scenery, with five areas designated UNESCO World Heritage Sites. **Trekking** through the stone-walled terraces and overnighting in typical Ifugao huts in rural villages is a major highlight. The most popular trek is to the remote little village of **Batad**, which has become something of a pilgrimage for visitors looking for rural isolation and unforgettable scenery. Other nearby villages include **Cambulo**, **Pula** and **Banga-an**. While less explored, the barangay of **Hapao** 16km southwest from Banaue, offers stunning terrace scenery that easily rivals that of Batad; 7km farther in the same direction is **Hungduan**, home to spectacular spider web terraces, mainly serving as a base for trekkers climbing Mount Napulawan (2600m).

Batad and around

BATAD nestles in a natural amphitheatre, close to the glorious **Tappia Waterfall**, which is 40m high and has a deep, bracing pool for swimming. There are signs that life here is beginning to change – the village has electricity and over a dozen simple **guesthouses** have sprung up – but it remains peaceful. There are several good hikes, including to **Banga-an**; ask around at the lodges for a guide, or try calling the numbers you'll find on a quick Google Maps search. One way to head back to Banaue from Batad is to backtrack south for about 16km to the tiny village of **Banga-an**, no more than a few dozen Ifugao homes perched between rice terraces close to the National Highway. You can **stay** here (see page 174), but it's a good idea to book ahead if you're relying on this after a hike – your guide will probably be able to do this for you.

ARRIVAL AND DEPARTURE

BATAD AND AROUND

On foot It is possible to walk the 16km to Batad from Banaue (3–4hr).

By jeepney Most people cut out the first 14km of the

walk from Banaue to Batad by taking a jeepney to just past Saddle (daily 8.30am; 1hr), from where it is a 30min walk downhill to Batad.

ACCOMMODATION AND EATING

BATAD

Batad Countryside Inn ☎ 0999 656 9136. The only vaguely flashy place to stay hereabouts, though you shouldn't expect too much more than more polished rooms and some modern decor here and there. The views are astonishing. $\overline{PPP}$

Batad Pension ⓦ facebook.com/batadpensionph. A pleasant *pension* decorated with wooden furniture made by the owner-cum-sculptor, whose little workshop is in the back yard. The simple rooms are brightened up with a thin layer of paint and colourful blankets – those upstairs have great views. Guests can also sleep in a native hut. $\overline{P}$

Rita's Mount View Inn ☎ 0905 144 2957. Homestay with a cheery atmosphere, awesome views (so good they're likely to make you linger over your morning cuppa), great information

and basic rooms. They're able to whip up meals, too. $\overline{P}$

Simon's Viewpoint Inn ⓦ facebook.com/simons viewinn. This popular guesthouse with walls covered in travellers' notes has a selection of clean simple rooms, some with excellent views over the terraces. There's a good restaurant serving a variety of international dishes, including freshly baked pita bread, Israeli-style *shakshuka*, and pizza. $\overline{P}$

BANGA-AN

Banga-an BnB & Coffee House ⓦ facebook.com/ bangaansagadabnb. A convenient place offering clean but basic dorms for the night, Bang-an BnB is a good choice with a decent restaurant serving (among other options) tasty banana pancakes, and a terrace with fantastic views. $\overline{PP}$

Pula and Cambulo

From the Banaue Awan-Igid viewpoint, 9km outside Banaue, you can trek east through fields and terraces to the villages of **PULA** and **CAMBULO**. There are some unforgettable sights along this route, including waterfalls, steep gorges and a hanging bridge near Pula that requires a bit of nerve to cross. The journey from Banaue viewpoint to Pula takes about four hours, and from Pula to Cambulo it's another two hours. You can camp or spend the night at one of the small **inns** or homestays in Cambulo. From here it's two hours to Batad, from where you can walk up to Batad Saddle and hop on a jeepney back to your hotel.

Pula is also the start of a hike up **Mount Amuyao** (2702m), a full day's walk and not something to be attempted without a guide and plenty of stamina. You'll need to sleep at the top and return next day, or you can continue to Barlig (see page 163) and eventually Bontoc.

Hapao and Hungduan

The rice terraces in the barangay of **HAPAO**, around 16km from Banaue, are spectacular. Hapao has a couple of homestays and is home to the **Hapao hot springs**, where you can take a dip in two natural pools. Further on, the small town of **HUNGDUAN**, less than 10km from Banaue as the crow flies but reached by a protracted looped road, is the location of the **Bacung spider web terraces**, at their best in April and May. The trip is well worth it, and you can overnight in the town itself. Hungduan is also the start of a hike up **Mount Napulawan** (2600m) for which you will need a guide.

ARRIVAL AND INFORMATION	HAPAO AND HUNGDUAN

By jeepney Jeepneys from Banaue run to Hapao (1hr) and Hungduan (1hr 30min).

By tricycle You can travel by tricycle from Banaue to Hapao (1hr) and Hungduan (1hr 30min).

Guides It is possible to organize guides to both Hapao and Hungduan at the tourist information point at Bokikwan on the way to Hapao; this is where all visitors must register and pay an environmental fee.

ACCOMMODATION

Native Village Inn Hapao ☎ 0915 614 7778. A fairly basic option that's perhaps a tad overpriced, with accommodation offered in traditional native huts with communal bathrooms. There are good views over the mountains and rice terraces, and meals are available; breakfast usually included. $\overline{PP}$

Pearl's Hungduan Homestay Hungduan ⓦ facebook.

com/umiyanan. Simple but not unpleasant rooms in a mint-green building, from which you can admire the marvellous views of the mountains. The restaurant serves great food, and will happily introduce you to the concept of a "boodle fight" – a Filipino term for eating with your bare hands from banana leaves. $\overline{PP}$

Mayoyao

There are buses to Mayoyao from Banaue (1 daily; 3hr) and Santiago (3 daily; 4–5hr)

Home to some arrestingly beautiful rice terraces listed as a UNESCO World Heritage Site, **MAYOYAO** is rarely visited due to the poor road condition, although it's well worth taking the time to travel here. The terraces are punctuated by distinctive pyramid-roofed local houses, and by stone burial mounds called Apfo'or. They are at their greenest from April to May and October to November.

ACCOMMODATION   MAYOYAO

Milcah Lodge ☎0905 199 3194. A cosy little place, conveniently located right in the middle of town, spotless and friendly, with great views. One room has its own bathroom; the others share. $\overline{P}$

Kiangan and around

On September 2, 1945, General Yamashita of the Japanese Imperial Army surrendered to US and Filipino troops in the town of **KIANGAN**, 10km from the provincial capital Lagawe (which is itself 24km south of Banaue). The event is commemorated with a large **shrine** although the actual site of the surrender (marked with a plaque) is now occupied by the library of the nearby Kiangan Elementary School. The hill on the right as you look out from the front of the shrine is where the Japanese holed up for their last stand; it's known as the **Million Dollar Hill** for the supposed cost of the artillery with which the US shelled it. Across from the shrine, the **Ifugao Museum** (Mon–Fri 9am–4pm; free) displays everyday local artefacts including men's hip bags used to store betel nut, and a mouth harp, considered to be a courtship instrument played to express intimate love.

The **rice terraces** around Kiangan are at their best in April and May. You can take a jeepney to the terraces at either **Nagacadan** (20min) or **Julungan** ("Hul-ungan"; 1hr). Tricycles also make it to Nagacadan (15min). Ask at Kiangan tourist office if you need a guide.

ARRIVAL AND INFORMATION   KIANGAN AND AROUND

By bus The nearest bus station to Kiangan is in Lagawe, 14km away, served by Ohayami buses from Manila (1 daily; 8hr) and Baguio (1 daily; 6hr).
By jeepney Jeepneys connect Kiangan and Lagawe (15min), from where there are regular jeepneys to Banaue

(1hr).
By tricycle There are tricycles from Lagawe to Kiangan (20min).
Tourist offices The tourist office is next to the municipal hall (Mon–Fri 8am–5pm; ☎0915 811 8500).

ACCOMMODATION

El Kikasa Tinoc-Kiangan-Asipulo-Lagawe Rd ⓦfacebook.com/elkikasa. Friendly and welcoming homestay just outside Kiangan, offering clean and comfortable rooms and a lovely terrace with fantastic views over the nearby hills. Breakfasts are tasty, and evening meals are available. $\overline{P}$
★**Ibulao B&B** Ibulao ⓦfacebook.com/ibulaoibulao bedandbreakfast. This highly acclaimed eco-lodge and

B&B, set in one hectare of land midway between Lagawe and Kiangan, has a selection of creatively presented rooms mostly decorated with Ifugao woodcarvings. The family room for six with stone floors is particularly impressive, built around exposed rocks. Bookings are essential (best via Facebook, and even then it can be an involved process); no walk-ins are accepted. $\overline{PP}$

Batanes province

Almost 150km off the northern coast of Luzon, **Batanes** is the smallest, most isolated province in the country – the islands are closer to Taiwan than to the northernmost tip of Luzon. This is a memorable place with otherworldly scenery, where doors are rarely locked and welcomes are warm even by Filipino standards. The people are different, the language is different, even the weather is different. The coolest months (Jan–March)

3

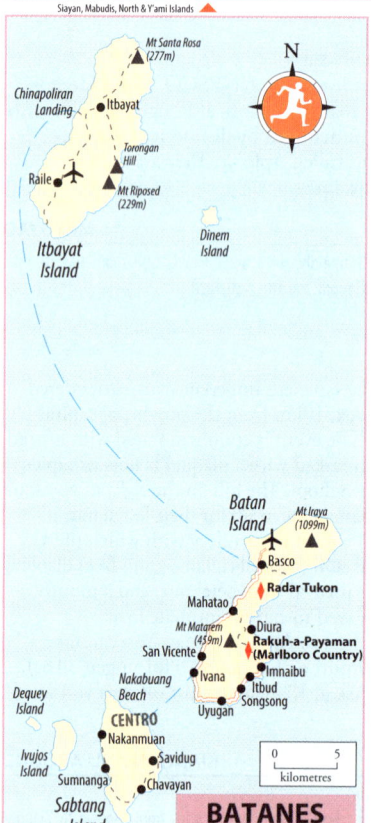

Siayan, Mabudis, North & Y'ami Islands

can get chilly, with temperatures as low as 10°C, while the hottest months (May and June) are searing. For visitors, the islands are at their best from February to June. Just three of the ten islands in the Batanes group are inhabited: **Batan** – the location of the capital **Basco** – **Sabtang** and **Itbayat**.

Batanes can be idyllic, but it would be wrong to portray it as a tropical utopia. Realities of life this far away from the rest of the world can sometimes be harsh. Petrol and provisions are brought in by ship, which means that they cost more, and when **typhoons** roar in from the east (July–Sept) it may be impossible for ships or aircraft to reach the islands. Boredom can set in and locals joke that during the typhoon season the cargo ship brings fifty thousand sacks of rice but sixty thousand crates of gin.

The native inhabitants of Batanes, the **Ivatan**, trace their roots to prehistoric Formosan immigrants. Most still make a living by cultivating yams and garlic or raising goats and cows; if you visit a village during the daytime, be prepared to find that almost everyone is out in the fields. Some women still wear rain capes called *vakul*, made from the stripped leaves of the *voyavoy* palm. The main **dialect**, Ivatan, includes some pidgin Spanish: "thank you" is *dios mamajes* and "goodbye" is *dios mavidin* (if you are the person leaving) or *dios machivan* (if you are staying behind).

Batan Island

Batan Island is the biggest in the group and site of the tiny capital, **BASCO**. The town boasts a spectacular location on the lower slopes of **Mount Iraya**, a volcano that hasn't erupted since the fifteenth century but is still officially active. You can walk around the town in half an hour, and there are no specific attractions, but it's a pleasant and friendly place, built around a rectangular plaza with the municipal buildings and church on the north side and the sea to the south.

Around the island

Most organized tours start by heading south from Basco along the coastal road for about 1.5km, before turning left up a narrow road to an abandoned weather station called **Radar Tukon**. This can also be done on foot as a day-hike: it's about an hour from Basco and from here the whole island is spread at your feet. Beyond the weather station is the swanky *Fundacion Pacita* hotel (see page 178), and some tunnels nearby created by the Japanese army during World War II.

After heading back to the coastal road you can return to Basco, or continue south through the pretty old Spanish village of **Mahatao** and on to **Ivana** ("Ih-va-na"), with its eye-catching yellow church, where ferries set off to Sabtang. Just opposite the church is the pier for ferries to Sabtang Island. In Ivana you will also find **Dakay's House**, the oldest stone house in Batanes, built in 1887. Although it is inhabited, you are usually welcome to poke your head in to take a look at the interior, which has wooden floors traditionally polished with banana leaves.

The coastal road round the southern end of the island brings you to the village of **Uyugan** before turning north to **Song Song**, where you can see the remains of stone houses that were washed away by a tidal wave. After Itbud there is a turning inland and uphill taking you through **Rakuh-a-Payaman** (known to tourists as "Marlboro Country"), elevated pastures inhabited by Ivatan bulls and horses, grazing against the backdrop of Mount Iraya and the Pacific Ocean.

After passing through the pastures you can either return to Mahatao (and from there to Basco) or continue to **Diura**, a small fishing village and the nearby Spring of Youth, a twenty-minute walk away. Here there's a wonderful stone pool perfect for a refreshing dip, with spectacular views over the ocean and Mount Iraya. There's no route for vehicles up the coast from Diura so unless you're hiking you'll need to head back to Basco via Mahatao.

3

Sabtang Island

Don't miss the opportunity to spend at least a day exploring **Sabtang Island**, a peaceful place dotted with Ivatan stone villages where life seems to have altered little in a hundred years. Ferries arrive in the port on the island's northeast coast, in the **Centro** area, where there's a Spanish church, a school and a few houses.

You can do a circuit of the island on foot, but with a vehicle it's necessary to double back and visit the eastern and western parts of the island separately. You could start by heading south from the port to **Chavayan**, about 10km away. On the way there are the remains of a fortress (*idjang*) that stands high on a hill; it served as a lookout point for the Ivatan to defend themselves from approaching invaders, as well as to monitor marine migration patterns. The path is steep in places, so take it slowly. Chavayan itself has some of the island's best-preserved traditional homes and a small chapel, as well as the Sabtang Weavers' Association, where you can purchase artefacts as well as enjoy fresh coconut and home-made biscuits prepared by members of the association.

From Centro you can also walk 9km to **Sumnanga**, passing through the tiny village of **Nakanmuan**, with a few traditional houses. About 3km further along is the fishing village of Sumnanga, home to the lovely Devuk Bay. From here you may be able to rent a boat to visit Ivujos Island, which is inhabited only by grazing cows. From Sumnanga you can hop on a scooter or tricycle to return to Centro.

Itbayat Island

Of the three inhabited islands in the Batanes group, **Itbayat Island** is the least accessible. There's no public transport, either, so you'll have to get around on foot or by asking one of the residents who owns a motorbike to give you a lift. It's crisscrossed by trails made by farmers and fishermen, making for superb trekking in good weather.

The ferry lands at the west coast harbour of Chinapoliran, from where you can walk or hitch a lift to the pretty little capital, **ITBAYAT**. There are great views of the island, and the others nearby, from the viewpoint of Mount Karaboboan, also known as **Mount Santa Rosa** (277m), on the northern side of the island. Alternatively, go looking for the stone boat-shaped burial markers at Torongan Hill, above a cave where the first inhabitants of the island are believed to have lived.

ARRIVAL AND DEPARTURE   **BATANES PROVINCE**

By plane The only way to get to the Batanes islands is   by air, with all flights landing in Basco. You can fly from

Tuguegarao with Sky Pasada (ⓦskypasada.com; 3 weekly; 1hr 30min), and from Manila with PAL (5 weekly; 1hr 45min). Basco is also connected to Itbayat (see below). A tricycle from the airport into Basco takes 5 minutes; many hotels offer free airport transfers.

GETTING AROUND

By plane North Sky has flights from Basco to Itbayat (no fixed schedule, but flying whenever they get eight bookings; 20min).

By ferry Ferries leave Ivana pier in Batan for Sabtang (1–2 daily; 30min). An early jeepney for Ivana leaves Basco to connect with the ferry, or you can take a tricycle.

The channel between Batan and Sabtang is known for its strong currents and big waves – avoid the crossing in rough weather. For Itbayat, ferries leave from Basco (1–2 daily; 3hr), but be warned that it can be a very rough and uncomfortable crossing, and may be cancelled for days in a row if sea conditions are particularly poor.

INFORMATION

Credit cards are almost never accepted in Batanes, so make sure that you have enough cash. You should be able to change dollars at PNB in Basco, but not at a favourable rate. PNB and Land Bank in Basco have ATMs, but it's probably best not to rely solely on them.

Tours Ivatan Travel & Tours (ⓦfacebook.com/ivatantravel) and Batanes Travel and Tours (ⓦfacebook.com/batanes tours) organize island tours, as well as biking and trekking. For scuba diving, contact Dive Batanes (ⓦdivebatanes.com).

BATAN ISLAND

Registration fee There is a "sustainable ecotourism fee" payable on arrival; keep your receipt on you as you may be asked to show it at places around the island. Leaving by air, you are charged a "terminal fee".

Tourist Information The heritage and tourism section of the governor's office is on National Rd (Mon–Fri 8am–5pm; ☎0929 230 5934, ⓦfacebook.com/batanes.province).

SABTANG ISLAND

Registration fee There is a registration fee payable at the tourist centre on arrival.

Tourist information The tourist centre (daily 8am–5pm; ☎0918 488 2424) is to the left as you leave the port. They have few maps or brochures but can provide advice on routes, and will collect your registration fee. If you want a tour of the island, call the tourist centre in advance or organize it in Basco.

GETTING AROUND

BATAN ISLAND

By jeepney If you are in a group, the easiest way to get a quick overall picture of the beauty of Batan is to hire a jeepney with driver for the day through your accommodation. It's also possible to travel in public jeepneys that connect settlements along the coastal road, but you'll have to be prepared to wait – and probably also to do some walking and hitching.

By tricycle To charter a tricycle with driver, contact BATODA (Batanes Tricycle Operators & Drivers Association; ☎0929 703 8404).

By bike Most lodges rent out regular and mountain bicycles, as do shops such as DLMV in Basco (☎0909 724 8476) and travel agencies such as Batanes Grand Holidays (ⓦbghtraveltours.wordpress.com). Batanes Scooters (ⓦbatanesscooters.com) rents out scooters. While the roads are very quiet, there are a number of blind bends, so take it easy and be sure to observe the speed limit of 20km/hr in towns.

SABTANG ISLAND

By tricycle You can charter a tricycle to tour the island.

ACCOMMODATION

BATAN ISLAND

The potential for trekking and camping on Batan is enticing. There are no campsites, but as long as you respect the landscape no one minds if you pitch a tent for the night near a beach. Whatever you do, take food and water, because there are few places to get provisions. All the accommodation listed below is in or around Basco; don't expect fast wi-fi or strong water pressure anywhere.

Amboy Hometel 3km south of Basco, Brgy Chanarian ☎0915 917 5808. This B&B has twelve a/c rooms with

private bath, all painted in different colours. There's a TV in each, while a restaurant by the little garden area serves seasonal dishes. ‾P‾P‾

Batanes Seaside Lodge National Rd, Brgy Kaychanarianan ⓦseasidebatanes.com. Right on the seafront, this lodge has fifteen decent-sized rooms and is very handy for the airport. There's a large restaurant serving Ivatan dishes, and a couple of lounge areas with armchairs. ‾P‾P‾

★ **Fundacion Pacita** Brgy Chanarian ⓦfundacion

pacita.com. The island's most upmarket accommodation option was the former home of artist Pacita Abad until her death in 2004; the common area exhibits Abad's art while the rooms, all with balconies and exceptional views, are tastefully decorated with works of Filipino artists. A portion of the proceeds goes to heritage conservation in Batanes, and provides art scholarships for Ivatan students and supplies for local schools. The restaurant serves wonderful Ivatan cuisine. ‾P‾P‾P‾P‾

Midtown Inn Abad St at Lizardo St, Brgy Kayhuvokan ⓦ midtowninnbatanes.com. The decor's a little bit lurid, but this is a good choice, reasonably spacious and centrally located, right in the middle of town, with breakfast included, and decent wi-fi, though only in the lobby area. ‾P‾P‾

Octagon Bed & Dine Brgy Kaychanarianan ⓦ batanes octagon.weebly.com. The three spacious rooms here are jam-packed with furniture and knick-knacks, including wooden trunks, vases, armchairs and chintzy bedspreads. Accommodation gives onto a balcony from where there are wonderful views of the ocean. ‾P‾P‾

Pension Ivatan Brgy Kayvalugan ⓦ facebook.com/ batanespensionivatan. Large place, now under the *RedDoorz* umbrella, whose exterior design would probably

make Wes Anderson go a little weak at the knees. Rooms have benefitted from a recent renovation, and there's an excellent restaurant on site (see below). ‾P‾P‾

Villa de Babat 305 Reyes St ⓦ villadebabatbatanes. com. Attractive B&B close to the airport, with simple but comfy bedrooms, a restaurant, a swimming pool, and even a tiny golf course in the garden. Staff can help arrange transport around the island. ‾P‾P‾

SABTANG ISLAND

Pananayan Pension Sabtang ☎ 0928 216 1829. Small homestay in the port of Sabtang, within sight of the attractive lighthouse. Rooms are basic but clean, and food is available. ‾P‾

ITBAYAT ISLAND

Abaya Hostel Itbayat ☎ 0999 390 9553. The most reliable accommodation on the island by far, with rooms set above a general merchandise store – this may not sound so salubrious, but it's more modern and comfortable than you might imagine for a place so far-flung (and, yes, sharing a building with a general merchandise store). Guests often end up draining a beer with a view on one of the intriguingly designed concrete tables. ‾P‾

3

EATING

BATAN ISLAND

Several of the lodges in Basco have restaurants or can make food to order, while elsewhere on the island you'll be reliant on the occasional small canteen so it's best to travel with at least a snack and some water.

Octagon Bed & Dine Brgy Kaychanarianan ⓦ batanes octagon.weebly.com. This octagonal restaurant, decorated with colourful paintings, wooden masks and other artefacts, offers what is probably the most extensive menu on the island, with most dishes large enough to serve two or three people. ‾P‾P‾

Pension Ivatan Brgy Kayvalugan ⓦ facebook.com/

batanespensionivatan. This friendly restaurant is decorated with beautiful glass buoys that were washed up ashore from nearby Taiwan. The menu focuses on traditional Ivatan cuisine – the large Ivatan platter will easily feed four to five; it includes coconut crab, lobster, cuttlefish, local salad and *uved*, a Batan delicacy of fish and pork sautéed with coconut. ‾P‾P‾

St Dominic College Canteen National Rd. This self-service canteen is used by students of the attached St Dominic College, but open to all. There are a variety of inexpensive dishes on offer, including *mami* (noodle soup), super-fresh local fish, and *halo-halo*. ‾P‾

Southern Luzon

CARAMOAN ISLANDS

Southern Luzon

Southeast of Manila, the provinces that make up Southern Luzon are home to some of the country's most popular attractions, particularly favoured by local tourists. The region is not yet on the backpacker trail, which can mean few budget accommodation options; however, it's blessed with some extraordinarily diverse natural phenomena. One of the area's top draws is the picturesque Mount Mayon volcano, whose cone is reputedly the most perfectly symmetrical in the world. Southern Luzon is also one of the few places on earth where you can swim with some of the world's largest fish, the gentle whale shark. It is also blessed with otherworldly underground rivers, glorious white-sand beaches, towering limestone cliffs, spectacular surfing waves, hot and cold springs, and well-preserved historic buildings dating all the way back to the Spanish colonial era.

The National Highway south from Manila takes you down to **Quezon province**, home to **Mount Banahaw**, a revered dormant volcano that presents one of the most rewarding climbs in the country. Quezon is linked by ferry to the beautiful island province of **Marinduque**, still largely untouched by mass tourism and best known for its Easter festival, the **Moriones**.

Beyond Quezon is the **Bicol** region, which encompasses the remainder of Southern Luzon and includes the mainland provinces of **Camarines Norte**, **Camarines Sur**, **Albay** and **Sorsogon** and the island provinces of **Catanduanes** and **Masbate**. Known throughout the Philippines as an area of great natural beauty – and for its delicious **cuisine**, characterized by the use of chillies and coconut milk – Bicol is studded with volcanoes, including **Mount Bulusan** and **Mount Mayon**, and offers superb coastline with some great beaches and island-hopping opportunities, particularly around **Legazpi** and **Sorsogon City**. Best of all is the **Caramoan Peninsula**, where tourism is developing apace but where it's still possible to find deserted hideaways. There are also attractions offshore, and although it can't rival the Visayas for scuba diving, Bicol does have an ace up its sleeve in the form of **Donsol**, home to huge whale sharks. Other water-based activities include surfing in **Daet** and wakeboarding at **CamSur Watersports Complex** near Naga. Two island provinces add further variety to Bicol's fabulous mix: **Masbate** is the Philippines' wild east, cattle country where the biggest tourist draw is the annual rodeo in April. **Catanduanes**, meanwhile, is infamous for its exposure to passing typhoons – ironically it's this extreme weather, however, that attracts surfers to its beaches.

ARRIVAL AND DEPARTURE
SOUTHERN LUZON

By plane There are commercial airports in Naga, Legazpi, Virac (Catanduanes) and Masbate City.

By train There is a train line between Manila and Legazpi via Naga, but at the time of writing, the only operational part of the route was between Sipocot (approximately 44km northeast of Naga) and Legazpi. The Philippine National Railway website (⊕ pnr.gov.ph) will have regular updates.

By bus There are plenty of buses running from Manila

down the National Highway via Naga and Legazpi, some going as far as Sorsogon City or beyond.

By boat In addition to ferries between the Luzon mainland and the islands of Catanduanes, Marinduque and Masbate, there are also regular services across the Bernardino Strait between Matnog in Sorsogon province and Allen and San Isidro ports on Samar in the Visayas. Masbate has ferry links to several provinces nearby including Romblon, Batangas and Cebu.

MAYON VOLCANO

Highlights

❶ Moriones festival Every Easter the beautiful little island of Marinduque lays on a boisterous religious pageant celebrating the life of Longinus, the Roman soldier who pierced Christ's side at the Crucifixion. See page 191

❷ Caramoan Peninsula Limestone cliffs, remote islands and beautiful secluded beaches much beloved by international TV companies – especially since the *Survivor* series was filmed here. See page 201

❸ Bicolano cuisine Savour spicy Bicolano cuisine, some of the country's best, prepared with chillies and plenty of coconut milk. See page 206

❹ Mount Mayon Even if you don't climb it, you can't miss its almost symmetrical cone standing imperiously above Legazpi. See page 207

❺ Swimming with whale sharks, Donsol Snorkel with the gentle giants of the sea, the world's largest fish. See page 212

❻ Ticao Island This small island in the Masbate province is well worth the extra boat ride, with deserted beaches, cascading waterfalls, native villages and excellent diving. See page 218

HIGHLIGHTS ARE MARKED ON THE MAP PAGE 184

SOUTHERN LUZON

Bagasbas Beach
Daet

Pandan
Caramoran
Panay Island
Panganiban

San Miguel Bay
Sipocot

Shrine of Our Lady The Most Holy Rosary †
Caramoan Peninsula

Bag'eing and Sabitang Laya Beach
Guinahoan Island
Lahuy Island
Maqueda Channel
Lahos Island
Matukad Island

Catanduanes
Gigmoto
Puraran Beach

CAMARINES SUR

Mt Isarog (1966m)
MOUNT ISAROG NATIONAL PARK

Sabang Port
Bikal Wharf
Paniman Beach
Caramoan
Gota Beach
Guijalo
Tugawe Cove
Codon Port

Naga
Nato Port

CamSur Watersports Complex
Pili
Pasacao

Mt Iriga (1196m)
Itbog Falls
Lake Buhi
Buhi
Iriga

CARAMOAN NATIONAL PARK
San Andres
Virac

CATANDUANES

Cabugao Bay

Rawis
San Miguel
San Antonio
Tabaco
Hacienda
Cagraray Island
Batan

Mt Mayon (2462m)
MAYON VOLCANO NATIONAL PARK
Calabidongan Cave
Cagsawa
ALBAY
Hoyop-Hoyopan Cave
Santo Domingo
Sula
Misibis Beach
Rapu-Rapu
Rapu-Rapu

San Pascual

Daraga
Legazpi
Albay Gulf
Libanon Beach
Pagurinan Beach
Prieto Diaz

Pio Duran
Bacon
Sorsogon City
Gubat
Rizal Beach
Barcelona

Burias Island
Burias Pass
Dancalan Beach
Pilar
Donsol
SORSOGON

Claveria
Mt Eganoso (428m)

Mt Bulusan (1559m)
Bulusan Lake
Bulusan
Irosin
Bulusan Volcano National Park

Bulan

Catandayagan Falls
Monreal
Manta Bowl Dive Site
Matnog

MASBATE
San Jacinto
Ticao Island
Ticao Pass
San Fernando
Allen
San Isidro

Aroroy
Kalanay Cave
Baleno
Batuan
Lagundi

Masbate City
Mobo
Bituon Beach
Matabao Island

Mandaon
Batongan Cave
Milagros
Bagacay
Uson
Dimasalang
SAMAR SEA

Masbate
Palanas

Palani Beach
Balud

Cataingan
Maripipi Island

Cawayan
Pio V. Corpuz

Placer
Esperanza

Jintotolo Island
VISAYAN SEA

Bogo (Cebu)
Bogo (Cebu)
Cebu City,

Ormoc (Leyte), Maasin (Leyte) & Surigao (Mindanao)

② ④ ③ ⑤ ⑥

Quezon province

Known as the "Coconut Province", as nearly half of the land is given over to cultivation of coconut palms, much of the northern part of **Quezon** is mountainous and hard to reach. The southern portion of the province serves mainly as a staging post on the road from Manila to the Bicol region, though it does have attractions such as a couple of excellent climbs, **Mount Banahaw** and **Mount Cristobal**. Further east you can explore **Quezon National Park**, which has some fairly easy marked trails. If you happen to be in Quezon in mid-May, check out what is by far the biggest festival in the province, the **Pahiyas**, held in and around **Lucban**, near the provincial capital, **Lucena**.

Lucena

The bustling town of **LUCENA** is worth considering for a stop on the route south, as a useful base during the **Pahiyas** festival in nearby Lucban or for those on their way to Marinduque via Dalahican port. The city itself doesn't offer much to visitors, but there are lots of sights in the surrounding area.

ARRIVAL AND INFORMATION
LUCENA

By bus The Grand Central Terminal is on the northern edge of the city, just off the highway. It's a 15min jeepney ride (every 15min; 10min) to Quezon Ave, the main thoroughfare. All departures given here are hourly at least in frequency; from Manila, you're best off departing from PITX. Destinations Daet (4–5hr); Legazpi (8hr); Manila (3–4hr);

Naga (5–6hr); Tabaco (9–10hr).
By jeepney Regular jeepneys travel from the Grand Central Terminal to Lucban (every 15min; 60min).
Tourist information The tourist office is on the second floor of the Provincial Capital Compound (Mon–Fri 8am–5pm; ☎042 373 7510).

ACCOMMODATION AND EATING

Isaiah's Kitchen 80 Allarey St ⓦ facebook.com/isaiahs kitchen.lc. Attractively minimalist in décor, Isaiah's Kitchen serves up delicious and authentic Japanese fare – there's some great sushi and maki on the menu, and excellent ramen too. The *aburi* salmon roll is particularly tasty. **PPP**
Luisa Quezon Avenue Extension, Brgy Gulang-Gulang ⓦ facebook.com/luisacaferesto. Long one of the best restaurants in the city. Sit in cosy booths, or in the courtyard outside, and choose from dishes such as Bangus sardines, filled crab and *ubod lumpia* (an egg roll filled with coconut heart, prawns and peanuts). Don't forget to try mango cheesecake for dessert. **PP**
Queen Margarette Hotel 1 People Square, M.L.

Tagarao St at Granja St ☎042 797 1881. Comfortable rooms with modern amenities, set on the fourth and fifth floors of an office block. Rates usually include breakfast at the Chinese restaurant within the same building. There's also a sister hotel just outside town, with a pool. **PP**
Saint Joseph Residential Suites 7 Trinidad St, Brgy 1 ⓦ thesaintjosephsuites.com. Located down a quiet street very close to the centre, this is easily one of the best-value accommodation options in Lucena. All suites come with mini-kitchens and living rooms, and if you don't mind the grandma-style decor and religious iconography everywhere, it's extremely homely and comfortable. **PP**

Lucban

Quezon province's major tourist draw is the **Pahiyas thanksgiving festival**, held every year on May 15 in **LUCBAN**, which sits at the foot of Mount Banahaw, 26km north of Lucena. It's a quaint little town and a pleasant spot to have a stroll, but there's not too much to see; it's worth taking a moment to visit the **St Louis Church**, which dates from the 1730s.

Kamay ni Hesus

Tricycle (10min), jeepney (every 15min; 10min)

The faithful climb **Kamay ni Hesus** – a hill on the edge of Lucban peppered with tableaux depicting the stations of the cross and topped with a large, open-armed statue of Christ – in the hope of being cured of various ailments. The route up is exposed,

PAHIYAS FESTIVAL

Each May during the **Pahiyas festival**, Lucban is transformed into something from a fairy tale, the houses decorated in the most imaginative fashion with fruit, vegetables and brightly coloured *kiping* (rice paper), which is formed into enormous chandeliers that cascade like flames from the eaves. The winner of the **best-decorated house** wins a cash prize and is blessed for twelve months by San Isidore (the patron saint of farmers). It's open house for visitors during Pahiyas, and people are especially honoured to have foreigners come in to admire their decorations.

The festival itself starts with a solemn Mass at dawn and goes on well into the night, with much drinking and dancing in the streets. There is a parade, a beauty contest, a marching band and a carabao parade in which enormous water buffalo, more used to rice fields and mud holes, are led through the streets in outrageous costumes.

and can be tiring on a hot day, but it's worth it for the wonderful views. Although a church stands at the base of the hill and masses are regularly held, the whole site has something of a theme-park feel, with a children's playground and replica Noah's ark.

ARRIVAL AND DEPARTURE | LUCBAN

By jeepney Regular jeepneys connect Lucban with Lucena (every 15min; 60min).

By van Regular vans run between Lucban and Lucena, and are slightly quicker than jeepneys. To get to Manila, you'll need to catch a van to Calamba (hourly; 2hr) and change there for an onward bus (every 15min; 40min).

ACCOMMODATION AND EATING

If you're coming to Lucban during the **Pahiyas festival** you should book **accommodation** well in advance – some places get their first reservations a year ahead. Expect the prices to be inflated. There are surprisingly very few good options in the centre, although staying in the colourful heart of town during festival time makes for a wonderful experience. Note that most accommodation options listed here do not have reliable **wi-fi**, and where available it's usually only in public areas such as the lobby. In terms of **eating**, be sure to try the famous garlicky **Lucban longganisa** (sausage) – particularly delicious when served with *achara* (pickled papaya) – and for dessert try **budin** (cassava cake). Cheap food stalls by the church sell **pancit habhab**, a local noodle dish served on a banana leaf and traditionally eaten with your hands.

Batis Aramin Resort ⊚ shouthotels.com. About 1km from the town proper, this large resort offers a range of spacious, plush rooms connected by a hanging bridge. There's a large pool with an artificial waterfall and slide, a basketball court, a lagoon, and an adventure camp with ziplines and rope courses. PPP

Buddy's Restaurant Rizal Park ⊚ buddys.com.ph. Located on the town's main square, this place may be a chain, but it's laidback and has colourful Pahiyas festival *kiping* (rice paper) decorations dangling from the ceiling. Seating is on small wooden benches, and the menu includes pancit Lucban (noodles with pork) and longganisa. PP

★ **Isabelito's** Deveza Farm, Arellano St at Placencia St ☎ 0915 847 9380. Located in a garden centre, surrounded by plants and ponds, this lovely, airy restaurant has chunky wooden tables and bamboo partitions. Bestsellers include crunchy Bicol Express, crispy *kare kare* (a Filipino curry made from stewed meats, vegetables and peanut sauce) and *papel de liempo* (bacon strips with smoky barbecue sauce). PPP

Patio Rizal 77 Quezon Ave ☎ 042 540 2107. This centrally located hotel is one of the most comfortable in town, offering decent rooms with carpet; the deluxe and premier suite are substantially larger and more welcoming. Each floor has a small seating area with wooden chairs and old paintings of the town centre, and there's a good restaurant on the ground floor serving a selection of Filipino dishes. Rates include breakfast. PP

Mount Banahaw and around

Northwest of Lucena, the town of **DOLORES** is the starting point for treks up **Mount Banahaw** and **Mount Cristobal**, which stand on either side of the town. Both mountains are protected areas and some of their hiking trails have been closed for several years to reduce human impact on the environment – at the time of writing, access to Banahaw was severely restricted, and it was difficult to climb thanks to the red tape involved, while Cristobal had been closed since 2014.

Considered sacred, 2188m Mount Banahaw has spawned a huge number of **legends** and superstitions: one says that every time a foreigner sets foot on the mountain it will rain. Members of various sects still live around the base of the mountain, claiming that it imbues them with supernatural and psychic powers. Its slopes thick with jungle, Banahaw is a challenging but rewarding **climb** (when it's allowed), with panoramic views of the surrounding country from the crater rim. Treat this mountain seriously, because although the trail looks wide and well-trodden, it soon peters out into inhospitable rainforest – even experienced climbers allow three days to reach the summit and get back down, while a crater descent should only be attempted by experts.

If you haven't time to reach the summit, you might prefer simply to trek to **Kristalino Falls** (Crystalline Falls) and back, which can be done in a day. One and a half hours further on is a second waterfall, whose surroundings make an ideal **campsite**.

Mount Cristobal

Mount Cristobal is seen as the negative counterpart to the positive spiritual energy of Mount Banahaw. It takes up to six hours of serious trekking along an awkward trail to reach Jones Peak, which is 50m lower than the inaccessible summit. The climb isn't recommended for beginners or unaccompanied trekkers; as things stood at the time of writing, you weren't allowed up anyway, but it was possible to make a partial ascent for a fine view.

ARRIVAL AND INFORMATION   MOUNT BANAHAW AND AROUND

By bus, jeepney and tricycle To reach the access town of Dolores, take one of the many buses that run hourly between Manila (PITX is best, but there are also services from Buendia or Cubao) and Lucena, and get off at San Pablo (a 2hr journey), from where there are jeepneys to Dolores (hourly; 25min) from the market. From Dolores, take a tricycle to the barangay of Kinabuyahan (20min).

Guides and permits The municipal tourist office, in the Municipal Hall, National Rd, Dolores (Mon–Fri 9am–5pm; ☏ 042 565 6515), can help organize guides and permits, though you may have better luck contacting specialist mountaineering agencies in Manila.

ACCOMMODATION AND EATING

Del's Garden and Resort Dolores ⓦ facebook.com/delsgardenandresort. Within the Protected Area, Del's Garden and Resort has a great location with views of the mountain from the garden and balconies. The rooms – many of them in individual villas – are fairly no-frills, but the grounds are well-maintained and there's a decent pool to cool off in. P̲P̲

Quezon Protected Landscape

Quezon Protected Landscape, about 25km east of Lucena near the town of **ATIMONAN**, is well off the beaten trail, far from the picture-postcard beaches of the Visayas and too distant from Manila to make it a viable weekend trip. Though relatively small at just ten square kilometres, the park is so dense with flora and fauna that you have a good chance of seeing anything and everything from giant monitor lizards to monkeys, deer and wild pigs. The park is also home to the *kalaw*, a species of hornbill.

It takes about an hour to walk along the paved trail to the highest point, 366m above sea level, which has a viewing deck from where you can see both sides of the Bicol peninsula. The summit is known as **Pinagbanderahan**, meaning "where the flag is hoisted", because both Japanese and American flags were flown there before the Philippine flag was raised in 1946. There are also numerous **caves** in the park that can be explored with guides, experience and the right equipment.

ARRIVAL AND INFORMATION   QUEZON NATIONAL PARK

By bus The turning for the park is on the Maharlika Highway, which runs from Lucena to Atimonan. The winding approach road to the park, known locally as *bituka* *ng manok* (chicken's intestine), is a challenge for buses: from Lucena's Grand Central station, you can get any bus heading east through Bicol (to Daet, for instance) or an

Atimonan-bound bus, as all these vehicles pass the park entrance (every 15min; 1hr).

Guides Enquire at the Atimonan Municipal Tourism Council, Aitmonan Old Municipal Hall Compound (☎ 042 316 6905).

ACCOMMODATION AND EATING

Borawan View Padre Burgos ⓦ borawan.com. Located along the coast, just a 25min drive from the park entrance, this is one of the best places to stay in the park's vicinity.

The rooms are nothing fancy, but they are clean and comfortable, and the titular view over the bay is lovely. P͞P

Marinduque

With its numerous caves and pretty beaches, tiny **MARINDUQUE** ("mar-in-DOO-kay") island, where most of the 240,000 residents lead a life of subsistence coconut farming and fishing, is a great place to get away from it all for a few days. The island is known as the "Heart of the Philippines" both due to its shape and location within the country. Work your way slowly around the coastal road south of **Boac**, then across the island to **Torrijos** and **Poctoy White Beach**, where you can live cheaply in the shadow of majestic **Mount Malinding**. There's some excellent island-hopping too, with spectacular beaches and coves to explore around the **Tres Reyes Islands** off the southwest coast and the **Santa Cruz Islands** off the northeast. Marinduque is known for its **Moriones festival**, an animated Easter tradition featuring masked men dressed like Roman soldiers (see box, page 191). If you plan to visit during Holy Week then you should book ahead.

Marinduque has had its share of problems. When copper mining was begun here in 1969, many thought it was the dawn of a new era. Sadly, the dream ended in disaster and recrimination as waste from disused pits flowed into the island's rivers on two separate occasions, destroying agricultural land, the livelihood of the locals and marine life – which is still trying to recover.

4

Boac

BOAC ("bow-ak") is an orderly, compact town with neat streets and low-rise buildings laid out around a central plaza. The area around the cathedral has numerous typical Filipino *bahay na buto* (wooden houses), the windows boasting carved wooden shutters instead of glass and the balconies exploding with bougainvillea and frangipani. Many of these houses were built in the nineteenth century and are now a photogenic, if faded, reminder of a style of architecture that is rapidly disappearing.

The cathedral

High Town

Construction of Boac's atmospheric Spanish Gothic **cathedral** started in 1580 in honour of the Blessed Virgin of Immediate Succour, and was used in its early years as a refuge from pirate attacks. Most of the original main structure, including the red-brick facade and the belfry, is well preserved and there's a pleasant garden outside. Look out above the main doors for a stone niche containing a statue of the Blessed Virgin, enshrined here in 1792. Devotees say it is the most miraculous statue in the country and tell of blind people who have regained their sight after praying fervently beneath it day and night.

Marinduque National Museum

Boac Plaza • Charge • ⓦ nationalmuseum.gov.ph

The small **Marinduque National Museum** is located in a lovely Spanish colonial building that previously served as a prison, a boys' school and a courthouse. The museum briefly charts the island's geological history, before introducing more recent history including evidence of pre-Spanish trade with China. Displays include sixteenth-century Chinese

4 | Mindoro

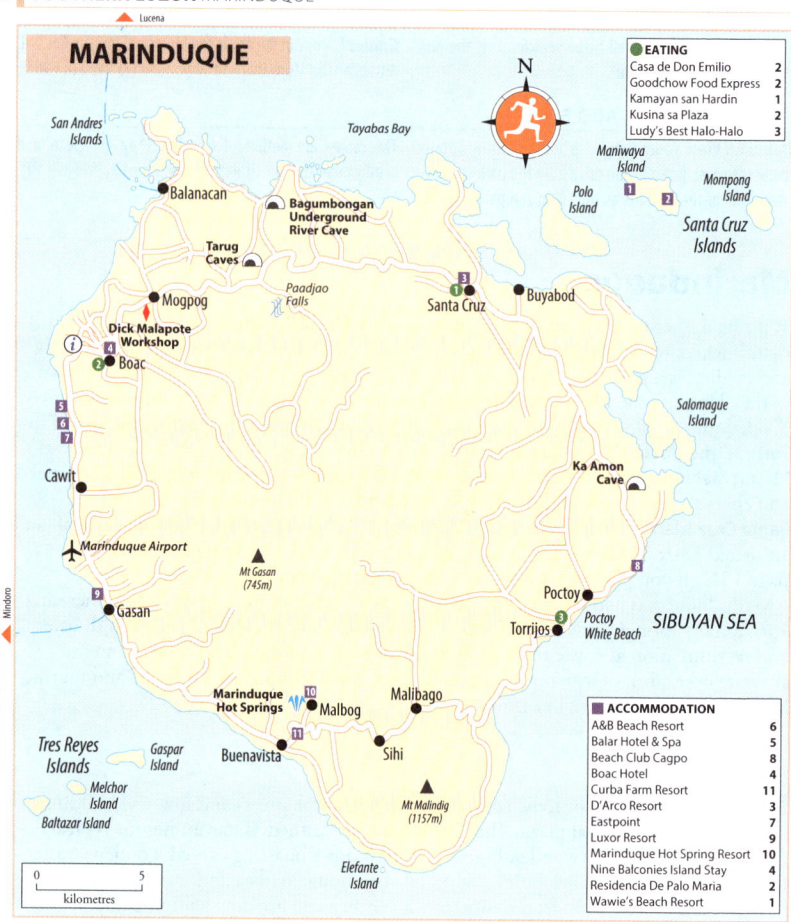

MARINDUQUE

Lucena

EATING

Casa de Don Emilio	2
Goodchow Food Express	2
Kamayan san Hardin	1
Kusina sa Plaza	2
Ludy's Best Halo-Halo	3

San Andres Islands

Tayabas Bay

N

Maniwaya Island

Polo Island

Mompong Island

Santa Cruz Islands

Balanacan

Bagumbongan Underground River Cave

Tarug Caves

Mogpog

Dick Malapote Workshop

Boac

Paadjao Falls

Santa Cruz

Buyabod

Salomague Island

Cawit

Ka Amon Cave

Marinduque Airport

Mt Gasan (745m)

Gasan

Poctoy

Torrijos

Poctoy White Beach

SIBUYAN SEA

Tres Reyes Islands

Gaspar Island

Marinduque Hot Springs

Malbog

Buenavista

Malibago

Sihi

Melchor Island

Baltazar Island

Mt Malindig (1157m)

Elefante Island

0   5
kilometres

ACCOMMODATION

A&B Beach Resort	6
Balar Hotel & Spa	5
Beach Club Cagpo	8
Boac Hotel	4
Curba Farm Resort	11
D'Arco Resort	3
Eastpoint	7
Luxor Resort	9
Marinduque Hot Spring Resort	10
Nine Balconies Island Stay	4
Residencia De Palo Maria	2
Wawie's Beach Resort	1

storage stoneware jars with dragon designs that were found on the seabed by Gaspar Island, as well as early musical instruments used during special events and celebrations. There is also a collection of Moriones masks, along with descriptive captions tracing the festival's roots.

Marinduque's west coast

The **west coast** from Boac south to **Gasan** and a little beyond boasts a number of **resorts**. The beaches are pebbly but they do offer fine views of the sunset and across the sea towards Mindoro in the distance. The resorts are often full for the Moriones festival (see box, page 191) and at Christmas, but at any other time you might find that you are the only guest. South of Gasan lies the sleepy town of **Buenavista**, where jeepneys usually terminate – so you'll have to wait here for onward transport.

Gasan

It's much better to stay in the nearby resorts than in **GASAN** itself, though the modern **St Joseph Catholic Church** is worth a look for its views, and the town has a few small souvenir shops selling Moriones-themed products and tasty arrowroot biscuits (which, along with *bibingka* rice cakes, are a Marinduque speciality).

St Joseph Catholic Church

Quezon Ave, Brgy 1, Gasan Poblacion

Perched on a hillside, **St Joseph Catholic Church** offers wonderful **bay views** from its leafy back terrace, especially at sunset. Built in the first decade of the new millennium, the church features a beautiful thick wooden door carved by a renowned Mogpog sculptor. The intricate ceiling was designed to resemble a palm leaf, while the inner side walls are lined with coconut shell dividers. At the back are the remnants of the old church, from 1609.

Tres Reyes Islands

Boat from Sitio Castillo, Gasan (15min), or arrange a private island-hopping trip with your resort

The beautiful **Tres Reyes Islands** – popularly known as **Baltazar**, **Melchor** and **Gaspar** after the biblical Three Kings – lie a few kilometres offshore of Gasan. There is some good **scuba diving** here, which can be arranged or at one of the resorts. On the far side of Gaspar Island there's a white-sand beach with good coral for **snorkelling**; a small fishing community is located on the eastern tip of the island, but there's no formal accommodation.

Marinduque hot springs

Sitio Mainit, Brgy Malbog, Km3 • Charge • ☎ 0917 382 9416 • Tricycle from Buenavista (10min)

Located in spacious grounds, the inviting **Marinduque hot spring** pools are a pleasant spot in which to while away a few hours. There are a couple of large pools, as well as three smaller pools that can be rented out privately (call in advance to arrange). There are picnic huts, too.

Mount Malindig

Enquire at the tourist office in Boac or at the barangay hall in Sihi, Buenavista to organize a compulsory guide

The highest peak of Marinduque is **Mount Malindig**, a 1157m volcano that's considered dormant. It's possible to climb to the summit; the hike can be done in a day starting from the barangay of Sihi in Buenavista, with the ascent taking about three and a half hours and the descent significantly less.

Marinduque's east coast

Marinduque's **east coast** offers a number of wonderful secluded beaches, the nicest of which is **Poctoy White Beach**. There are fewer resorts on this stretch of coast than on the west, and it's well worth spending a couple of days.

MORIONES FESTIVAL

The **Moriones festival** celebrates the life of Longinus, the Roman soldier who pierced Christ's side during the Crucifixion. Blood from the wound spattered Longinus's blind eye, which was immediately healed. Converted on the spot, he later attested to the Resurrection and, refusing to recant, was executed. The Marinduqueyo version of this tale is colourful and bizarre, involving fanciful masked figures dressed as centurions chasing Longinus around town and through nearby fields. Several Moriones pageants are staged in Marinduque during **Holy Week**, with extra events added in recent years for the benefit of tourists (see ⓦ marinduque. gov.ph for more information). Although the festival originated in Mogpog, and other towns including Santa Cruz have their own versions, these days the major Moriones celebrations are in **Boac**.

Poctoy White Beach

Environmental fee applies • Jeepneys between Santa Cruz and Torrijos stop off at Poctoy (hourly; 1hr 30min)

Just 2km from the barangay of Torrijos is **Poctoy White Beach**, where the sand is not as pale as the name suggests but still much better than the pebbles on the west coast. The views across the bay to Mount Malindig can also be spectacular. The stretch of beach is packed with huts which can be rented for the day, and it has a small market where you can buy the catch of the day by weight; pay a little more and you can have it cooked.

Ka Amon Cave

Brgy Bonliw • Compulsory guides can be organized at Bonliw Barangay Hall • ☎ 0926 648 7033 • Jeepneys from Torrijos to Brgy Bonliw (hourly; 20min)

Eleven kilometres north of Torrijos is the **Ka Amon Cave**, a series of seven chambers that were once pre-Hispanic funeral grottoes – you can still see skeletal remains and broken pottery as you enter the first chamber. Chambers six and seven are off limits to visitors in order to preserve the cave habitat and fauna, which includes bats and birds. You'll still be able to see about one hundred bats (more during the rainy season) in chamber five, where tours end.

Santa Cruz and around

If you're interested in exploring the caves and islands in the northeast of Marinduque, **SANTA CRUZ** is the best base for a day or two. That said, the town is unmemorable – the only sights a whitewashed Spanish-era church and the dilapidated wooden convent next to it – and the narrow streets in the centre are choked with tricycles and jeepneys from dawn to dusk. Be prepared for noise.

Santa Cruz Islands

Boats leave from Buyabod port, 5km east of Santa Cruz by tricycle (15min); your accommodation should be able to arrange a boat for island-hopping

The islands of Maniwaya, Mompong and Polo, collectively known as the **Santa Cruz Islands**, make for a wonderful day-trip. The closest to the mainland is **Polo**, which is rich in wetland forests and transient birds, local macaque monkeys and fruit bats. While the island is dotted with a few pleasant beaches, it's a good idea to head further on to **Maniwaya**, which boasts a long stretch of fine sand lined with a few accommodation options.

On the northeastern side of the island is the spectacular **Palad Sandbar**, a stretch of coral sands with crystal-clear waters that appears only during low tide. The furthest of the islands is **Mompong**, with its distinctive Ungab sedimentary rock formation that acts as a natural bridge – the waters here are emerald green, and it's a wonderful spot for a swim.

Bagumbongan Underground River Cave

Brgy San Isidro • Charge • Entry fee includes compulsory guides, who can be arranged at the tourist information centre on the way to the cave • Jeepneys from Santa Cruz (daily 11am & 4pm; 1hr); tricycles from Santa Cruz (45min)

About 24km west of Santa Cruz, the 2km-long **Bagumbongan Underground River Cave** is the longest underground river in the province. There are some fixed ropes and spots where water reaches chest height. Helmets, lights and gloves are provided. Guides will lead you inside the cave for about 1km, ending up at a cascading waterfall of about 10m before turning back; they can also take experienced cavers all the way to the other side. Note that you won't be able to explore the cave during heavy rains.

Mogpog

In the northwest corner of the island, the little town of **MOGPOG** doesn't offer much for visitors, although it is renowned across the island for being the birthplace of the **Moriones festival** (see box, page 191) and holds its own festivities – smaller in scale than those in Boac – during Holy Week. The word Mogpog comes from the tagalog word *mag-aapog*, which roughly translates as "abundance of lime" and the area around town is indeed rich in limestone, with a number of **caves** to explore.

Dick Malapote workshop

Brgy Janagdong, 1km west of Mogpog • ☎ 0939 468 2365 • Take a tricycle from Mogpog (10min), then ask around – locals know where Dick Malapote lives

One of the most famous Moriones **costume makers**, Dick Malapote has been creating centurion outfits since 1979, selling whole sets of armour for pretty princely sums, but getting more business for chiselled wooden masks. He welcomes visitors at his workshop but doesn't speak much English, so the best bet, if you are interested, is to enquire at the provincial tourist office near Boac (see page 193), who can arrange for someone to accompany you.

Tarug Caves

Brgy Tarug, Bocboc • By donation to local guides – ask around at the village you pass through on the way to the cave • Jeepney from Mogpog towards Santa Cruz (every 30min; 30min), followed by a 1.5km (45min) trek; ask the driver where to get off

The **Tarug Caves** are actually one enormous cave with three chambers set inside a 300m-tall limestone spire that's barely 3m wide at the top. You can climb to the top, where the reward is a panoramic view of the Bondoc peninsula to the east and the Tablas Strait to the west.

Paadjao Falls

Brgy Bocboc, 10km from Mogpog • Jeepney from Mogpog (daily); it's also worth visiting by tricycle (30min) and arranging waiting time

About ten minutes' uphill walk from the main road, nestled within coconut groves, are the gently cascading **Paadjao Falls**. There are a series of pools here, perfect for a little dip – the largest is at the foot of the uppermost fall. Join the locals sitting on the rocks, letting the strong jet stream of water massage your back and shoulders.

ARRIVAL AND DEPARTURE

MARINDUQUE

By plane The small Marinduque airport is sometimes served by flights to Manila (45min), but don't count on it.
By boat There are ferries from Lucena to Balanacan port (every 1–2hr; 3hr) with Montenegro Lines (🌐 montenegrolines.com.ph) and Starhorse (🌐 facebook.com/starhorseshippinglines). Jeepneys from Boac meet incoming ferries to Balanacan (1hr).

There are outrigger services between Gasan on Marinduque and Pinamalayan in Mindoro (1 daily; 3–4hr). Daily bangkas connect Buyabod port, which lies east of Santa Cruz, to Catanauan in Quezon province (1 daily; 3hr).
By bus Jac Liner travels between Boac and Manila using the roll-on-roll-off ferry (1 daily; 8–9hr; 🌐 jacliner.com).

GETTING AROUND AND INFORMATION

By jeepney No jeepneys loop the entire island; if you're planning on travelling to multiple destinations you'll have to change services from time to time. On the west and north coasts they run from Boac–Gasan–Buenavista, and Boac–Mogpog–Santa Cruz, while on the east coast there are services from Santa Cruz–Torrijos. To get to Buenavista from Torrijos you'll have to take a jeepney to Malibago and change there. It is possible to travel around the entire island by jeepney in two days, but four or five would be more comfortable, particularly since if you miss the last jeepney (most services stop at

4–5pm), you can easily find yourself stranded.
By van Easier than travelling by jeepney is renting a van. Most accommodation options can help organize this, or enquire at the provincial tourist office near Boac (see page 193).
Tourist information The helpful provincial tourist office (Mon–Fri 9am–5pm; ☎ 042 332 1177), in the Capitol Building complex on the road between Boac and the airport, has a handful of leaflets, but once on the road be prepared for a lack of reliable information.

ACCOMMODATION

SEE MAP PAGE 190

BOAC

Boac Hotel Deogracias St at Nepomuceno St 🌐 boachotel.com. This relatively big building is the oldest

hotel in town, and its antiques and wooden furniture lend it an appealing atmosphere. The single rooms with just one single bed allegedly sleep two, although they are

4

tiny, even just for one; you're better off going for a deluxe with a double bed. The cheapest rooms are fan only, while standard rooms and above have a/c. $\overline{P}$

Nine Balconies Island Stay Nepomuceno St ☎ 0928 517 2593. A more modern option than most of the town's scruffy offerings, with breakfast (included in most deals) taken in a kitchen-like room with chequered black-and-white tiling. Said snazziness continues up the ornate-ish stairs to spacious rooms, most of which have teeny weeny balconies. $\overline{PP}$

THE WEST COAST

A&B Beach Resort Brgy Balaring ☎ 042 754 5823. This lovely little place has warm and welcoming a/c rooms with private bath in a building overlooking the sea. The plant-festooned garden with a large pomelo tree is dotted with knick-knacks, including old carriage wheels, while the lounge area features fibre deck chairs and wicker sofas. There are also two outdoor jacuzzis. $\overline{PP}$

Balar Hotel & Spa Brgy Balaring ⓦ facebook.com/ balarhotelandspa. A smart international standard hotel, with spacious rooms containing lovely comfortable beds. There's a pool and a good restaurant on-site, and spa treatments and fitness classes available. $\overline{PPP}$

Eastpoint Brgy Balaring ⓦ eastpointhotel.com. This small, modern-looking hotel by the beachfront offers a range of clean and comfortable rooms, including family ones. It's worth upgrading to a twin or executive room, as standards are the only ones without a/c, hot showers and cable TV. $\overline{PP}$

★ **Luxor Resort** Brgy Pangi ⓦ luxormarinduque.com. Some 1.5km north of Gasan, with simple, bright-yellow concrete cottages set along a leafy pathway. All have a/c, flatscreen TV and private bathroom. The welcoming shaded area by the sea is the perfect spot to enjoy a sundowner, and there's a restaurant serving excellent artisan Italian pizzas. $\overline{PP}$

BUENAVISTA AND AROUND

Curba Farm Resort Brgy Uno ⓦ facebook.com/Curba FarmResort. There's a cowboy theme going on here, with framed guns and Wild West memorabilia decorating the premises, accompanied by a slightly incongruous model giraffe. The four rooms are on a grassy slope overlooking an inviting pool with an artificial waterfall; there's also a billiards table, and an attached restaurant/bar with outdoor seating serving local and international dishes, including mixed

seafood and T-bone steaks. Rates include breakfast. $\overline{PP}$

Marinduque Hot Spring Resort Sitio Mainit, Malbog, Km3 ☎ 0910 632 5924. Set in lovely verdant grounds, this resort offers a series of rooms connected by a pebbly pathway dotted with wooden statuettes; the spacious family rooms with two double beds are great value, though the cheaper a/c doubles and twins are not as appealing. You can also camp, though you'll need to pay the entrance fee to the springs. $\overline{PP}$

POCTOY AND AROUND

★ **Beach Club Cagpo** Brgy Cagpo ☎ 0921 993 2537. Located on a lovely stretch of sand, the blue and white rooms take their inspiration from Greece, with rough whitewashed walls and paintings of Greek islands. There's a welcoming a/c cottage, as well as one standard double with fan and a deluxe fan room. The restaurant serves international dishes prepared with fresh herbs from the garden, including great home-made burgers, vegetable curry and wood-fired pizzas. There's also an eight-bed dorm with lockers; blankets and pillows are not supplied. $\overline{PP}$

SANTA CRUZ

D'Arco Resort Brgy Maharlika ⓦ facebook.com/darco resorthotel. This resort offers simple no-frills rooms, set in well-maintained grounds with a decent-sized swimming pool. Meals are available on request, though it's only a short stroll into town. $\overline{PP}$

SANTA CRUZ ISLANDS

★ **Residencia De Palo Maria** Maniwaya Island ⓦ facebook.com/ResidenciaDePaloMaria. One of the best accommodation options on the island, offering comfortable a/c rooms with cable TV, as well as cheaper native cottages that are equally welcoming, and even feature their own little outdoor patio with TV. There's a breezy restaurant by the swimming pool serving local dishes, and the resort offers all manner of watersports, including banana boats, diving, waterskiing and kayaking. $\overline{PP}$

Wawie's Beach Resort Maniwaya Island ⓦ facebook. com/WawiesResort. Set on a lovely stretch of white-sand beach, backed by shady palms, *Wawie's* offers a range of native rooms with fans, as well as larger family rooms. Those on a budget can opt for 12-hr native-style *kubo* huts or tents on the beach. Can get very crowded. $\overline{P}$

EATING

SEE MAP PAGE 190

BOAC

★ **Casa de Don Emilio** Mercader St ⓦ facebook.com/ CasaDeDonEmilio. The best restaurant in town, set in a beautiful Spanish colonial building with polished hardwood floors. The owner, a keen musician, has a fascinating collection of old instruments, including an antique double bass, trombone, trumpet and sax – all displayed along the

restaurant's walls. The restaurant specializes in coconut dishes – try the native chicken cooked in coconut milk. $\overline{PP}$

Goodchow Food Express Mercader St ⓦ facebook. com/goodchowfoodexpress. Perennially popular with locals and tourists alike, Goodchow Food Express has been dishing up tasty fast food dishes for years. Options range from the international to the Filipino, with the fried chicken being a particular standout. $\overline{PP}$

Kusina sa Plaza Mercader St ⓦfacebook.com/ kusinasaplaza. Popular restaurant on Boac's main square offering a range of Filipino dishes. The attached coffee shop serves pizzas and pasta. $\overline{PP}$

POCTOY AND AROUND

★**Ludy's Best Halo-Halo** Brgy Torrijos ☎0967 433 7610. They're not kidding – this is the best *halo-halo* on the island (they've been doling them out since 1986), and

worth tracking down if you're anywhere on the east coast. Said desserts are quite beautifully served in coconut shells, and you can enjoy them in a garden-like covered area with fake grass and real plants. $\overline{P}$

SANTA CRUZ

Kamayan san Hardin Mabini St ☎0968 594 5680. A friendly restaurant serving up decent if unremarkable Filipino standards, accompanied by cold beer. It's pretty popular with expats. $\overline{P}$

DIRECTORY

Banks and exchange There are banks with ATMs in Boac, including Land Bank, RCBC and PNB, all along Reyes St.

RCBC and PNB also have branches in Santa Cruz.

Daet and around

The capital of Camarines Norte, **DAET**, 200km southeast of Manila, is overrun with tricycles, but the nearby coastline has more than its fair share of unspoilt beaches and islands; the fickle waves at **Bagasbas Beach** and **San Miguel Bay** are a particular attraction for surfers.

Daet's busy little central plaza is a popular meeting place in the evenings. One block north is the 1950s **Provincial Capitol**, in front of which Kalayaan (Freedom) Park features the tallest statue of **José Rizal** outside Manila. Erected in 1899, this was the first monument to Rizal in the country, and set the trend for thousands of others in plazas across the archipelago.

4

Bagasbas Beach

Reached by tricycle from Daet (20min)

The waves that crash in from the Pacific onto wild and windswept **Bagasbas Beach**, 4km northeast of Daet, are sometimes big enough for **surfing** (see box, page 196), particularly between November and March. In fact, the whole area of coast east of Daet has become something of a surfers' hangout, though the shore can be pretty much deserted by all but stray dogs on weekdays. Despite its reputation, the area is a little run-down and strong winds have ripped through most of the hotel and restaurant signs. Though not in surfing season, the beach gets more lively during the summer months of June and July, when the locals are on holiday.

ARRIVAL AND INFORMATION

DAET AND AROUND

By bus Buses arriving in Daet stop at the edge of the city on the National Highway, from where it's less than 2km into town; plenty of tricycles travel the route for P30. Various companies travel to Manila (roughly hourly; 7–8hr), stopping off in Altimoan (3hr 30min) and Lucena (5hr).

By van Regular vans connect Naga to Daet (every 30min;

2hr).

Information The municipal and provincial tourist offices are both in Daet on J. Pimentel St (both Mon–Fri 8am–5pm; provincial ☎054 721 3087; municipal ☎054 441 6163). There's also a tourist information centre on Magallanes Iraya St (Mon–Fri 8am–5pm, Sat 8am–noon; no phone).

ACCOMMODATION

DAET

Hotel Formosa Vinzons Ave, Brgy Lag-On ⓦhotel formosadaet.com. This is one of the city's best options, offering neat and tidy tiled rooms with flat-screen TV and

wooden furniture. Some rooms face the interior and as a result may be a bit dark, but the premises are kept spick-and-span and there's free welcome tea upon arrival. $\overline{PPP}$

One Platinum F. Pimentel Ave ⓦoneplatinumhotel.

SURFING AND KITESURFING ON BAGASBAS

Several places on **Bagasbas Beach** rent out surfboards and offer tuition. **Experienced surfers** who want to look beyond Bagasbas should ask about the breaks in nearby **San Miguel Bay**, which often has very good waves close to the town of Mercedes and around the seven islands known as the Siete Pecados.

Bagasbas Surfers Club ☎0915 202 8577. Surfing and kitesurfing lessons available, as well as equipment hire. Island hopping trips can also be arranged.

Hang Loose ☎0956 172 7459. Friendly outfit. The owners are a wealth of local info and offer surfboard rental and lessons.

---

com. About as far down the price scale as you'll probably want to go in Daet; there are cheaper options around, but here at least you get decent rooms, comfy beds, clean bathrooms and a modicum of service. Breakfast usually included. $\overline{PP}$

BAGASBAS BEACH

Bagasbas Lighthouse Hotel Resort ⓦfacebook.com/basagbasLH. On the seafront, this is by far the area's best option, with stylish accommodation in deluxe rooms or cheaper converted trailer rooms. There are also "backpacker rooms" with bunks. The poolside restaurant (see below) is worth a look too. $\overline{PP}$

EATING

DAET

K-Fisher 1101 V. Basit St ☎0946 768 4904. Though the decor screams cheap American diner, this places serves tasty local food. The speciality is seafood, ranging from *pusit* (squid) to sushi and sashimi. $\overline{PP}$

K-Sarap Vinzons Ave ⓦfacebook.com/KSarap. This very atmospheric bamboo-built restaurant, surrounded by leafy plants, fountains and colourful lanterns, is one of the best in Daet. Savoury dishes include empanadas, sizzling tofu with mushrooms or fish steaks; most people round things off with the ubiquitous *halo-halo*. $\overline{PP}$

BAGASBAS BEACH

Bagasbas Lighthouse Hotel Resort ⓦfacebook.com/basagbasLH. The poolside restaurant at this resort (see above) serves Filipino favourites and Bicol specialities (see box, page 206) including Bicol Express and *laing*. $\overline{PP}$

Kusina ni Angel Around for many a year, this no-frills restaurant has a nipa roof and tables clustered together both indoors and out. It's great for breakfasts, and also has a good range of typical Filipino meat, poultry and seafood dishes to share. $\overline{P}$

Leo's Cuisine ☎0917 315 5531. Good option right on the beachfront, with tables facing the ocean as well as an indoor area decorated with the owner's surfboards and surfing awards and a glass cabinet displaying all manner of knick-knacks. The fish- and seafood-based menu includes sizzling Thai squid and calamari. $\overline{PP}$

Camarines Sur province

Lying at the heart of Bicol, the laidback province of **Camarines Sur**, with a spectacular stretch of rugged coastline to the east, is rich in natural beauty, with secluded beaches and peaceful lakeside spots. The region is fast becoming a prime destination for young adventure sports enthusiasts, many of whom flock here from Manila to wakeboard at the **CamSur Watersports Complex**.

Naga

Centrally located in Camarines Sur, the lively university city of **NAGA** was established in 1578 by Spanish conquistador Pedro de Chavez. Although there are a couple of sights in the city itself, its place on the tourist map is due mainly to the success of the **CamSur Watersports Complex**, or CWC, in nearby Pili (see page 200). Naga offers an alternative base, with a fun nightlife scene thanks in part to its large student population. Things are particularly lively during the nine-day **Peñafrancia festival** in September, held in honour of Our Lady of Peñafrancia, when as many as a million devotees and tourists flood the streets. The city is also home to three impressive holy sites – the **Peñafrancia Basilica Minore**, **Our Lady of Peñafrancia Shrine** and the **Naga Metropolitan Cathedral**.

Naga centre is focused on two main squares, **Plaza Rizal** and **Plaza Quince Martires**, surrounded by fast-food restaurants, banks, convenience stores and pharmacies. The main drag, **Elias Angeles Street**, runs north to south; to the east, along Panganiban Drive, is the Naga River. Swish **Magsaysay Avenue**, to the northeast, running from Avenue Square mall to City Hall, has many of Naga's best bars and restaurants, as well as a handful of hotels.

University of Nueva Caceres Museum

J. Hernandez Ave • Free • ☎ 054 472 6100

The **University of Nueva Caceres Museum** gives an overview on the city's history from the ancient period to the present day. There is a very concise section on the Arab and Muslim influence in the southern Philippines, and details on Chinese trade. Highlights include Chinese porcelain and earthenware dishes that were bartered for local items, as well as local dresses showing how three hundred years of Spanish rule influenced the attire of Bicolanos.

Holy Rosary Minor Seminary

Elias Angeles St • **Archeological Museum** Charge • ☎ 054 473 8297

One of the country's oldest institutes for higher learning, the beautiful red-brick complex of the **Holy Rosary Minor Seminary** was built in 1785 as a vocation house. It was declared a National Historical Landmark in 1988, and still houses the dormitories of priests and active seminaries. It also holds the small, privately owned **Archeological Museum**, which was temporarily closed at time of writing. When it reopens, you'll be able to view its fascinating collection of trade wares from China, Vietnam and

4

Thailand, along with ancient relics – including the country's most extensive collection of primary burial jars from the Bicol region, dating back to 200 AD. By far the most unusual displays are dinosaur eggs from the Mongolian Gobi Desert, dating back 146–165 million years.

Metropolitan Cathedral
Elias Angeles St

The **Metropolitan Cathedral** is the largest church in Southern Luzon and the seat of the Archdiocese of Caceres. The original structure was built in 1595 near the Naga River; after being destroyed by fire in 1758, it was rebuilt on this site, only to be damaged by a typhoon in 1856, and subsequently an earthquake in 1887. The church was built in Romanesque Baroque style using Spanish Royal funds – note the Spanish royal seal above the door.

At daybreak on the opening day of the **Peñafrancia festival**, an image of the Virgin – known as "Ina" (Bicolano for mother) – is taken from its permanent home at the Peñafrancia Basilica Minore, east of town, and carried to the cathedral by barefoot devotees (*voyadores*); she then spends the nine days of the novena at the cathedral before being returned to her permanent home.

Our Lady of Peñafrancia Shrine
Peñafrancia Ave

Originally built by Spanish expat Miguel de Covarrubias from nipa and bamboo, **Our Lady of Peñafrancia Shrine** was reconstructed in stone around 1710, and reworked again by Bishop Isrido Arevalo around 1750. Today it boasts a charming Spanish-style red-brick and yellow-painted exterior with wide archways. The church used to be the home of the "Ina" Peñafrancia Virgin statue before the new Peñafrancia Basilica Minore (see below) was built.

Peñafrancia Basilica Minore
Balatas Rd

The **Peñafrancia Basilica Minore** is the newest of Naga's three religious sites: construction began in 1976 and wasn't completed until 1981. It was built as the new home for the "Ina" Peñafrancia statue of the Virgin Mary, which dates from 1710 and was commissioned by Miguel de Covarrubias, who also built the Our Lady of Peñafrancia Shrine (see opposite). A huge green- and yellow-painted structure, surrounded by sculpted gardens and palm trees, the basilica's facade is covered by a huge stained-glass window, said to be the largest in the Philippines. Created by stained-glass artist and mural painter Pancho Piano, it depicts the Peñafrancia Virgin surrounded by clouds, angels and religious figures. Inside, you'll find more stained-glass windows, as well as a stained-glass central dome and a beautiful altarpiece.

ARRIVAL AND DEPARTURE
NAGA

By plane Naga airport is 12km east of town, in the provincial capital Pili; taxis connect the city to the airport (15min). The only flights are to Manila, operated by Cebgo (2 daily; 1hr 20min).

By bus Buses to Naga arrive at the Central Bus Terminal in Central Business District 2 (CB2) on Ninoy and Cory Ave, which is across the river to the south of the town centre, close to the SM Mall; you'll have to take a tricycle from here (10min) to the centre. Many companies run the route to Manila (8–10hr), stopping off in Atimonan (for Quezon Protected Landscape; 6hr) and Lucena (6hr). Most buses to Manila depart between 6 and 10pm. There are also local buses to Legazpi (3hr) and Daraga (3hr), although for both these destinations it's quicker to catch a van.

By van Vans arrive and leave from opposite the Central Bus Terminal in Central Business District 2.

Departures Daraga (hourly; 2hr); Legazpi (every 30min; 2hr); San José (for Sabang port on the Caramoan Peninsula; hourly; 1hr 30min); Tabaco (every 30min; 2hr).

By train Naga is on the South Luzon train line, which will one day reopen all the way back to Manila. For now, your only options are eastbound to Legazpi (1 daily; 2hr 40min), or back west as far as Sipocot (1 daily; 1hr 10min), with the latter departing so early in the morning as to be useless from Naga.

INFORMATION

Tourist information The Naga City Arts, Culture and Tourism Office is in the DOLE Building, City Hall Complex, J. Miranda Ave (Mon–Fri 8am–5pm; ⓦnaga.gov.ph). Staff can provide city maps and organize traditional Bicolano cooking courses, as well as help organize guides for Mt Isarog (see page 201).

ACCOMMODATION

NAGA

SEE MAP PAGE 197

Many hotels, particularly the budget ones, are fully booked during the **Peñafrancia festival** so make sure to plan ahead if you're coming at this time. For the rest of the year, finding a room shouldn't be a problem. Unless otherwise stated, the **wi-fi** at most of the hotels listed here can be pretty unreliable, and may only be available in public areas.
Avenue Plaza Magsaysay Ave ⓦtheavenueplazahotel. com. In a class of its own in Naga, with rooms of an international standard, along with a swimming pool, gym and sauna, and an excellent restaurant, featuring fusion and international cuisine. The hotel is on Naga's entertainment strip, with plenty of restaurants and bars on its doorstep, and there's low-key piano music in the lobby in the evenings. P̄P̄P̄
Naga Land Elias Angeles St ⓦfacebook.com/Nagaland Hotel. With its refined lobby, fancy cake shop and grand staircase, this place initially seems like a very upmarket hotel, but the upper floors and rooms don't quite match up. Standard rooms are simple and comfortable, but have tired furniture, while the deluxe rooms have nicer decor. P̄P̄

New Crown P. Burgos St ☏054 473 8305. A decent option right in the centre of Naga, with a range of different rooms. Standards (with a double bed) are spacious and simple, while the deluxe rooms have better furniture. Suite A is a big jump up, featuring a comfortable living area and a king-size bed. There are a couple of 24hr restaurants offering a range of Chinese dishes. P̄P̄P̄
Robertson J. Miranda Ave ⓦrobertsonhotelnaga.com. More-than-acceptable option at the lower end of the price scale; go any cheaper and you might regret it. The family rooms are massive, standards are decent enough, and all are decked out in pleasing gold-and-brown tones. Breakfast available. P̄P̄
Villa Caceres Magsaysay Ave ⓦvillacacereshotel-naga. com. A classy hotel to the east of the town centre, Villa Caceres offers clean and attractively decorated rooms with comfortable beds. There's a pool and gym on-site, as well as a restaurant that serves up tasty food. Ask for a room at the back if you're a light sleeper, as those at the front overlook a busy street. P̄P̄P̄

EATING

SEE MAP PAGE 197

Naga's local specialities include **log-log, kinalas** (both noodle soup dishes) often served with toasted **siopao** (pork buns), and anything made with pili nuts. The town's restaurants are mostly along Magsaysay Ave, but there are also plenty of fast-food chain places in the centre.
★**Bob Marlin** Magsaysay Ave ⓦbobmarlin.ph. This popular restaurant has an atmospheric outdoor seating area with colourful low lighting and a roof of native reed and reclaimed wooden pallets; there's also an indoor area with wall-mounted plates signed by famous visitors, praising the restaurant's award-winning crispy *pata* (deep-fried pork leg; serves five people). As the name suggests, the music is laidback, with lots of reggae and ska. P̄P̄
Chef Doy's Cereza Compound, Magsaysay Ave ☏0928 554 6205. Doy rustles up imaginative Filipino fusion dishes that include sautéed baby squid with garlic, bay leaves and black pepper and boneless milkfish with vegetables in guava broth. Dishes are large enough to share, and you can either eat alfresco on the patio or in the dark interior,

where the walls are plastered with customers' notes and scribbles. P̄P̄P̄
★**Green Earth Café** Villa Sorabella Subdivision, Concepcion Grande ⓦfacebook.com/greenearthcafeph. An unusual but very welcome find in this country of meat-lovers, this excellent vegetarian health-food café serves creative dishes prepared with fresh local ingredients; the bread is home-made, as is the excellent dairy-free banana mango ice cream. The wide menu includes veggie burgers, rice-noodle pad Thai, *pako* salad (a type of fern mixed with salted eggs and tangy vinegar) and the bestselling club sandwich of home-made tofu and grilled vegetables. It's 4km east of Naga; to get here catch a jeepney heading for "Centro Concepcion" (every 30min; 20min), and it's the third turning on the right off Soriano Ave. P̄P̄P̄
Mang-koks Kinalas 2 Solid St ⓦfacebook.com/profile. php?id=100063902539771. A solid choice on Solid St, this is a great little local spot serving up the best kinalas in Naga City. P̄P̄

DRINKING AND NIGHTLIFE

SEE MAP PAGE 197

Magsaysay Ave is the centre of the city's nightlife, with many of the more expensive restaurants and a few bars. The *Bob Marlin* restaurant (see above) is also a great drinking spot.
Back Draft Resto Bar Magsaysay Ave ☏0917 501 6215. A popular bar in the town centre, Back Draft is a great place for a beer or cocktail. Drink anything containing Jack Daniels and you'll be contributing towards the enormous wall of empty Jack Daniels bottles. P̄

4

SHOPPING

SEE MAP PAGE 197

House of Pili Magsaysay Ave ☎ 0970 480 4046. More conveniently located than the factory, this small shop is located right in the centre of town and is the best place to pick up all manner of pili nut products, from tarts and sweets to cookies.

House of Pili Factory 178 Jacana St, RJ Village, Haring,

Canaman ☎ 054 871 3935. Some 3km north of town, this is a family-run pili production factory where, during working hours, it's possible to watch staff coating, glazing and packaging all manner of pili products – which you can then buy at the attached shop. If you can't make it out to the factory, note that there's also a shop in town.

DIRECTORY

Banks There are plenty of banks, including Metro Bank, BPI and PNB on Plaza Rizal.

Police City Hall Complex, Miranda Ave (24hr hotline ☎ 054 472 3000).

CamSur Watersports Complex (CWC)

Provincial Capitol Complex, Brgy Cadlan, Pili • Charges vary by activity, plus equipment rental • ⓦ cwcwake.com

Located just under 10km southeast of Naga, **CamSur Watersports Complex (CWC)** is an international-standard wakeboarding course. There is a beginners' winch park, where you can practise standing up on a straight run, and it's also possible to use a kneeboard on the main course, which involves six turns and an assortment of ramps and rails for those who know what they're doing. The complex also has a swimming lagoon and a pool, while you can also go speeding around the "adventure trail" on a buggy or ATV.

ARRIVAL AND DEPARTURE

CAMSUR WATERSPORTS COMPLEX (CWC)

By shuttle The easiest way to get to CWC is to take a free shuttle, departing from Naga's SM Mall and along Magsaysay Ave – contact CWC for the current timetable. There is also a free shuttle service that meets incoming flights at Naga airport.

By bus and jeepney From the bus terminal in Naga you

can take a bus towards Legazpi (20min) or a jeepney to Bula or Partido (every 30min; 25min); ask the driver to let you off by the CWC entrance by the highway. At the entrance, you can take a tricycle (10min) or habal-habal (5min) to get into the complex itself.

ACCOMMODATION AND EATING

Villa del Rey Hotel ⓦ cwcwake.com. A huge range of accommodation options, from simple tiki huts to cute cabanas, converted containers and cosy wood cabins. There are also private villas with small gardens and breezy

outdoor bathtubs surrounded by greenery and bamboo shoots. The wi-fi reaches some of the rooms, and there are a couple of restaurants and bars. It has, however, seen better days, and is rather expensive for what you get. $\overline{PP}$

Lake Buhi

Regular vans connect Naga to Buhi (hourly; 1hr 30min)

Mostly enclosed by hills – some of which rise as high as 300m – **Lake Buhi** lies 52km southeast of Naga. From the lakeside market in the surprisingly busy town of **BUHI**, on the south shore, you can charter a **bangka** to take you across the water (20min); once you're across, it's a fifteen-minute walk to the wonderful twin **Itbog Falls** in the barangay of Santa Cruz, 5km from Buhi. The falls crash through thick rainforest into deep pools that are perfect for swimming. You can also trek to the falls from Buhi, a terrific hour-long hike through rice paddies and along rocky trails. You'll have to organize a guide with Mary Grace Oafallas, the Executive Director for Culture and the Arts (☎ 0947 187 0457), or via Lake Buhi Resort (see below).

ACCOMMODATION

LAKE BUHI

★ **Lake Buhi Resort** Brgy Cabatuan ⓦ facebook. com/thelakebuhiresort. Owned and run by affable Cyrus Obsuna, this wonderful resort, 4km northwest of Buhi, has tastefully furnished accommodation in well-manicured

grounds; a spiral staircase leads up to a series of spacious rooms in the main building – the cosy attic room is probably the most inviting, with a living area and terrace. There's also a swimming pool. Rates include breakfast. $\overline{PP}$

Mount Isarog National Park

One of the Philippines' most spectacular and least trampled areas, **Mount Isarog National Park** covers forty square kilometres in the heart of Camarines Sur, about 40km east of Naga. At its centre stands **Mount Isarog** (1966m), the second-highest peak in Southern Luzon and part of the Bicol volcanic chain that also includes Mayon. Isarog is considered potentially active, although it is not known when it last erupted.

The jungle is thick and steamy, and the **flora and fauna** are among the most varied in the archipelago. Long-tailed macaques and monitor lizards are a pretty common sight, while with a little luck you may also spot the indigenous shrew rats, reticulated pythons and rare birds such as the bleeding-heart pigeon, red-breasted pitta and blue-nape fantail. Reaching the summit (see box opposite) takes two days of strenuous climbing. At the top is a large crater with a couple of sulphuric rivers that meet here and stream down the southeastern part of the mountain.

A number of paths on Isarog's lower slopes lead to **waterfalls** – including Mina-Ati, Nabuntulan and Tumaguiti – all of which are surrounded by thick rainforest and have deep, cool pools for swimming. The easiest to reach is beautiful **Malabsay**, a powerful ribbon of water that plunges into a deep pool surrounded by forest greenery. It's a delightful place for a dip. There are also hot springs in the barangay of **Panicuason** (charge), the most popular starting point for climbing the mountain.

ARRIVAL AND DEPARTURE   MOUNT ISAROG NATIONAL PARK

By jeepney To get to the barangay of Panicuason, starting point for the Panicuason trail (see box above), take a jeepney (hourly; 40min) from close to the market in Naga.

There are no jeepneys from Panicuason back to Naga after 3pm (4pm in summer), so keep an eye on the time. If you get stuck you can catch a habal-habal (15min).

ACCOMMODATION

Panicuason Hotspring Resort ⓦfacebook.com/Isaroganic. The closest accommodation to the national park, offering simple rooms in the "old" building along with much more appealing doubles with modern bathrooms in a newer block. There is no hot water, but the four hot spring pools are just at your feet. Facilities include two ziplines, a waterball, a heart-shaped pool of which the management are very proud, and a restaurant. PP

Caramoan Peninsula

The wild and sometimes windswept **Caramoan Peninsula**, 50km east of Naga, is blessed with limestone cliffs and blue-water coves to rival the Visayas or Palawan. Until recently its relative isolation and lack of infrastructure meant that it attracted only a handful of tourists. Then in 2008 the French version of the *Survivor* TV show was filmed here, and other international productions swiftly followed suit. While the area hardly rivals somewhere like Boracay in terms of development, it is attracting increasing numbers to its rugged, scenic landscape. The **dry season** runs from February to September, while October to December sees the most rain.

CLIMBING MOUNT ISAROG

The easiest and most commonly used route to the summit of **Mount Isarog** is the **Panicuason trail**, which starts at the barangay of Panicuason and takes two days. There are two other recognized routes on the mountain – the PLDT trail and the more challenging Patag-Patag trail – both of which also take two days.

You will need a climbing **permit** and a local **guide** to climb Mount Isarog – contact the Naga City Arts, Culture and Tourism Office in the DOLE Building, City Hall Complex, J. Miranda Ave (Mon–Fri 8am–5pm; ⓦnaga.gov.ph).

The **best time** to trek is between March and May, but it is possible at other times, weather allowing; September to December is particularly wet.

> ## ISLAND-HOPPING FROM THE CARAMOAN PENINSULA
>
> **Island-hopping tours** are a good way to visit Guinahoan, Lahos, Matukad and Lahuy islands as well as Bag'eing and Sabitang Laya beaches. Trips can be arranged through most accommodation or tour operators in Caramoan town; Caramoan Islandhopping at Caramoan Rd (☏0919 982 4730), are recommended. Alternatively you can hire a bangka direct from Bikal Wharf or from Paniman Beach, both around 5km north of Caramoan town, though be prepared to haggle quite a bit to get a decent price.

Caramoan

There isn't much to delay you in the town of **CARAMOAN** other than a few souvenir shops, a couple of simple restaurants and some decent enough accommodation options. If you have a bit of time to kill, it's worth taking a stroll to the **Michael the Archangel Parish Church** on National Road, a pretty red-brick building constructed in the 1600s. The church was originally built with light materials such as bamboo, wood and nipa, but in the 1800s it was renovated using clay, stone and adobe. Opposite is the covered produce **market**.

Gota Beach

6km northeast of Caramoan town • Charge • Tricycle from Caramoan town (20min)

Part of the **Caramoan National Park**, the government-owned **Gota Beach** became a tourist attraction when accommodation for the filming crew of the *Survivor* series was built here. Reachable from Caramoan town along a surfaced but damaged road, the beach itself is a bit of a let-down, although it continues to attract tourists who head to the resort intrigued to see what put this place on the map.

Guinahoan Island

With its grassy terrain and grazing cows, the inhabited **Guinahoan Island** is an unusual sight among the Caramoan Peninsula's jagged limestone cliffs. The island has some lovely **beaches** with white and pink sand; it's a 45-minute trek from the shore to the **Guinahoan Lighthouse**, which still functions as a beacon for fishermen at night and offers wonderful views of the nearby islands.

Lahos Island

Also known as Bichara, the small **Lahos Island** consists of two stunning limestone formations connected by a short stretch of sand. Except during high tide, you can spend some time on the beach that cuts through from one side of the island to the other, which has deep, clear water.

Matukad Island

One of the smallest islands in Caramoan, **Matukad Island** is a pretty spot with some of the whitest sand in the area. Within the island there's a hidden lagoon; you'll have to scramble to the top of rugged limestone cliffs to find it, and you shouldn't attempt to do so without a guide – contact the Caramoan tourist office (see page 203). The lagoon is allegedly inhabited by one milkfish; legend says that the little creature protects the island, and brings ill fortune to those who harm it.

Lahuy Island

At 10km long and 3.5km wide, **Lahuy** is the largest island in the northern part of the Caramoan Peninsula; it is also known as "Treasure Island" because of its history of gold mining. There is still small-scale gold panning in the barangay of **Gata**, and visitors can try their hand for a minimal fee. The island is wonderful at low tide when you can see the beautiful white sandbar of **Manlawe** covered in a thin layer of crystal-clear water.

Bag'eing and Sabitang Laya beaches

Located on a triangular-shaped island of the Lucsuhin group of islands, the lovely **Bag'eing and Sabitang Laya beaches** are among the filming locations of the *Survivor* series. Both have coral-yellow sand dotted with rock formations and shallow emerald-green waters that are perfect for swimming and snorkelling.

Paniman Beach

Paniman Beach is one of the jumping-off points for island-hopping tours. The black sand is nothing to write home about, but there are a few accommodation options, so if you don't want to head inland to Caramoan town, you may want to consider overnighting here.

The Shrine of Our Lady The Most Holy Rosary

From the main road in the barangay of Tabgon, 9.5km northwest of Caramoan town, you can climb 524 steps to the top of Caglago Mountain to reach the **Shrine of Our Lady The Most Holy Rosary**, a white concrete statue of the Virgin Mary spreading her arms in benediction; from the 213m summit, you will be rewarded with wonderful views over the peninsula and the surrounding islands. It's a great spot to watch the sun rise over the bay.

ARRIVAL AND DEPARTURE   CARAMOAN PENINSULA

By plane The closest airport is in Virac, on Catanduanes (see page 219), from where you can catch a tricycle to Codon port (1hr), and then hire a private bangka to Guijalo ("Gee-ahlo") port (45min).

By bus Visitors coming direct from Manila can take a Raymond Transport bus to Sabang Port (5 daily; 12hr; ⓦraymondbus.com) or all the way to Caramoan town (2 daily; 15hr). These buses all pick up and drop off passengers in Naga, which is a good place to break the long journey;

from here there are more regular services to Caramoan (6 daily; 4hr). The road to Caramoan, despite the upgrade, remains very slow.

By boat The easiest way to reach the peninsula was, for decades, by taking a sea trip to Guijalo from the port of Sabang, or from Nato Port. However, since the upgrading of the road, these services have essentially dwindled away to nothing, and it's not even easy to organise a private boat.

4

INFORMATION

Tourist information The tourist office is in the Municipal Compound in Caramoan town (Mon–Fri 8am–5pm; ☎0928 407 9960).

ACCOMMODATION

The two jumping-off points for island-hopping tours, **Paniman Beach** and **Bikal Wharf**, make good bases if you have limited time in the area. It's possible to **camp** on some of the islands, including Matukad, Lahuy and Bag'eing Beach; the inhabited Lahuy Island is probably the most recommendable as there is a fresh water source. Unless otherwise stated, all accommodation options listed here have **limited wi-fi**.

BIKAL WHARF

Rex Tourist Inn Tawog ☎0919 882 1879. Nearly 1km from Bikal Wharf, this pleasant resort has twenty clean and comfortable rooms in well-tended grounds, all with cable TV and a/c. There's a good-sized pool, climbing wall and a rustic bamboo bar looking over the Lubok River, which is a tranquil spot for a few hours' kayaking. In busier months, bands play at the lovely on-site restaurant in the evenings. They also offer tour packages which include accomodation, food and island-hopping adventures. P̄P̄

CARAMOAN TOWN

La Casa Roa Teoxon St ☎0917 596 5881. The most atmospheric hotel in town, this welcoming place offers comfortable, private colour-coded rooms with mock-period furniture. The spacious rooms on the first floor have beautiful parquet floors; no.1 is the nicest. There's also a communal lounge with wicker furniture and a large sunny terrace. The annexe is not as inspiring, with small bare rooms. P̄

West Peninsula Villas San Andres St ⓦfacebook. com/westpen. Conveniently located near the bus station, West Peninsula Villas offers simple standalone villas with a swimming pool. The food at the restaurant is good, and the owners can arrange island-hopping tours in the vicinity. P̄

GOTA BEACH

Gota Village Resort ⓦfacebook.com/gotavillage. This resort, built to house the crew of the *Survivor* TV series, has more than 130 cabañas cluttered together on a grassy slope, which come in small, medium and large, and are much more appealing inside than out, with rustic cosy interiors more suited to an alpine lodge than a beach resort. There is also pricier VIP accommodation on nearby Hunongan Cove. Between Feb and June it's often block-booked for filming, but there's a bit of an eerie feel when the place is empty. **PPP**

PANIMAN BEACH

Magindara ☎ 0945 392 9631. Named after a Siren-like being of Bikolano mythology, Magindara is a great no-frills resort in which you'll stay in a traditional seaside hut. It's a very authentic experience, but there's no restaurant, and the beach in the immediate vicinity isn't that great; luckily, prices are low for most of the year. **P**
Paniman Bay Lodge ⓦ facebook.com/islandview lodge. Once the *Island View Lodge* (which presumably will lead to a change of Facebook address at some point), this is a reliable place to bed down. Some rooms are in

thatched shacks, and others in the sturdier-looking main building; they all feel a bit cheap, and it's hard to escape the conclusion that it's a bit pricey for what you get, but breakfast is included with most bookings. **PP**

LATUGAWE COVE

Tugawe Cove Resort ⓦ tugawecoveresort.com. One of the nicest places to stay on the Caramoan Peninsula – and offering the only way to get to see the private Tugawe Cove – this lovely resort is located on a wonderful stretch of private beach with crystal-clear waters. Accommodation is in comfortable cabañas with modern amenities, set around a lake and dotted along the hillside. On the hilltop are the restaurant and an inviting infinity pool with incredible views over the coast and surrounding islands. In the evenings, it's worth heading out on a trip to see bioluminescent plankton within the cove. **PPPP**

DIRECTORY

Banks and exchange There is a UCPB bank with ATM on Real St in Caramoan town, although it's unwise to rely upon

it – be sure to bring enough pesos.

Albay province

Thanks to its central location, **Albay province** is considered to be the gateway to the Bicol region. At the heart of Albay is **Mount Mayon**, with its almost perfect cone-shaped bulk rising from paddy fields to the north and majestically looming over the city of **Legazpi**. Legazpi is the jumping-off point for the rest of the region, where highlights in the lovely countryside include quiet beaches around the town of **Santo Domingo**, the eerie remains of a church at **Cagsawa**, and the **Hyop-Hoyopan** and **Calabidongan caves**. Northwest of Legazpi is the little port of **Tabaco**, from where there are regular ferries across to Catanduanes.

Legazpi

About 100km south of Naga, the busy port city of **LEGAZPI** (sometimes spelt Legaspi) is the jumping-off point for climbing **Mount Mayon** and makes a convenient base to explore the surrounding area. The city centre is divided into two parts at either end of the National Highway. The **old town**, where you'll find the City Hall and most of the top-end hotels, is centred on Peñaranda Park and known as the **Albay district**. A couple of kilometres to the northeast is the new town, or **City Proper**, a muddle of small businesses, banks, cinemas and market stalls where the rest of the hotels are located, along with the waterfront **Embarcadero de Legazpi**, a large mall that also offers go-karting, arcade games, watersports and live music. It's a 25-minute walk between Albay and City Proper, along a busy, polluted road lacking a decent pavement – a tricycle or jeepney is a better option.

Lignon Hill

Charge • ☎ 0922 883 6722 • Jeepney Loop 1 or 2 (every 20min; 10min), then 2km uphill walk (30min)
Northwest of the city centre, **Lignon Hill** is popular with local families and is not only a great viewpoint for Mayon but also a destination in its own right. Attractions include a zipline, hanging bridge, Japanese war tunnels and quad bikes that can be rented at the base of the hill for tours to see volcanic rock formations. The hill is also the location of the **Philippine Institute of Volcanology and Seismology** (PHIVOLCS) research station.

ARRIVAL AND DEPARTURE

LEGAZPI

By plane Bicol airport, which superseded Legazpi's own in 2021, is 12km southwest of the city centre near Daraga; taxis are on hand at the airport (up to 30min into town). PAL, Cebgo and Cebu Pacific operate flights from here, and the airport's increased capacity has seen it become a very minor hub of sorts.

Destinations Cebu (1–2 daily; 1hr 20min); Iloilo (2 weekly; 1hr 10min); Manila (6 daily; 1hr 15min).

By bus All buses arrive at the Grand Central Terminal on the western edge of City Proper. Dozens of a/c buses ply the route to Manila, and there are plenty of local buses.

Destinations Manila (dozens daily; 11–12hr); Naga (every 15min; 2hr); Sorsogon City (every 15min; 1hr 30min); Tabaco (every 20min; 1hr).

By jeepney Regular jeepneys make the trip to Santo Domingo (hourly; 30min).

By van Vans arrive at and leave from the Grand Central Terminal.

Destinations Bulan (hourly; 2hr 30min); Donsol (hourly; 1hr 30min); Naga (every 30min; 2hr); Pio Duran (hourly; 2hr); Sorsogon City (every 30min; 1hr 20min); Tabaco (every 30min; 45min).

By train The station, just north of the city centre, sends trains out west as far as Naga (2 daily; 2hr 45min), from where you could catch another service west to Sipocot, but probably won't thanks to the awkward timings.

By boat The wharf is at the eastern end of Quezon Ave in City Proper. Outrigger boats travel to Rapu-Rapu, Albay (2 daily; 3hr).

INFORMATION AND TOURS

Tourist information The city tourist office is in the City Hall Building on Rizal St in Albay district (Mon–Fri 8am–5pm; ⊛ legazpi.gov.ph), while the provincial tourist office is on F. Aquende Drive, also in Albay district (Mon–Fri 8am–5pm; ⊛ albay.gov.ph); there is also an info kiosk at the airport that opens when flights arrive.

Tours For private tours, car rental, trekking (including Mount Mayon), ATV rides and other adventure tourism, try Your Brother Travel & Tours (⊛ mayonatvtour.com) or Bicol Adventures and Tours (⊛ bicoladventureatv.com). You can also ask at the tourist offices about arranging a guide for Mount Mayon (see page 207).

4

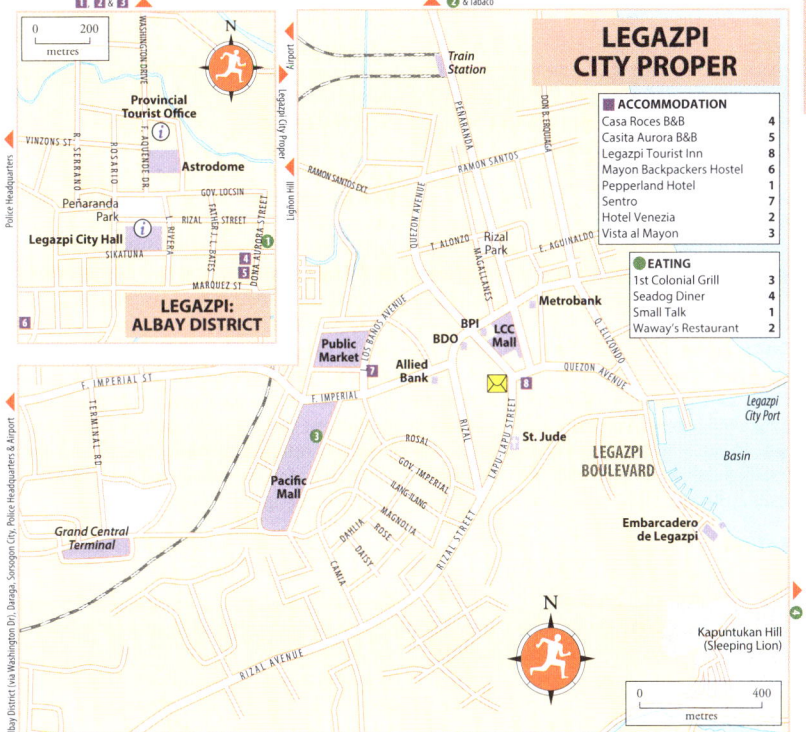

SPICING IT UP IN BICOL

Bicolano **cuisine** is unusual in the Philippines, and is noted for its use of coconut and chillies. Most Bicolano dishes are prepared by sautéeing or simmering ingredients in coconut cream – traditionally minced, diced or ground pork, smoked fish (*tinapa*) or small shrimps. Among the most common dishes are **Bicol Express**, named after a famous train service, made with coconut cream, diced pork, small shrimps, chilli and garlic, and sometimes pineapple; **laing**, a spicy dish of delicious taro leaves, coconut cream, ground pork and minced small shrimps; and **pinangat**, which uses the same ingredients as *laing*, although the taro leaves here are tied together and wrapped around the ground pork and small shrimps, before being submerged in coconut cream. To sample some of the best Bicolano cuisine, head for *Seadog Diner* or *Waway's Restaurant* in Legazpi (see opposite).

ACCOMMODATION

SEE MAP PAGE 205

Poor **wi-fi** is less of an issue than it once was, though brownouts still happen from time to time.

CITY PROPER

Legazpi Tourist Inn 3rd Floor, V&O Building, Lapu-Lapu St at Quezon Ave ⓦfacebook.com/legazpitouristinn03. On the second floor of an office block, this simple place offers plain rooms, some with fan. The more expensive standard rooms have a/c and cable TV, but the deluxe rooms are worth the extra – they're much larger and in better condition than the standards. $\overline{P}$

Sentro F. Imperial St at Los Baños Ave ⓦhotelsentro legazpi.com. The nicest place in the centre, for what it's worth, though overpriced for sure; rooms at the lower end of the price scale can feel cramped, but there's a friendly feel to things, and a good breakfast usually comes included. $\overline{PPP}$

ALBAY DISTRICT

Casa Roces B&B Sikatuna ⓦfacebook.com/casa rocesbb. The rooms at this B&B are large and comfortable, and the common areas are decorated with pleasant, homely touches. Breakfast is very tasty, and the location is central and convenient. $\overline{PP}$

Casita Aurora B&B Doña Aurora St, Old Albay ⓦfacebook.com/casitaaurorabedandbreakfast. Owners Martin and Elizabeth offer just four rooms in their cosy home, which is decorated with stained glass, small trinkets, and with vintage wooden and wicker furniture. The tasty breakfasts (included in rates) are served in the country-kitchen-style dining room. There's also a large leafy garden

and rooftop patio offering spectacular Mayon views. $\overline{PP}$

Mayon Backpackers Hostel Brgy Maoyod ⓦmayon backpackers.com. Legazpi's best hostel has a series of tiled four- and six-bed dorms, each with its own bathroom and wooden bunks and lockers. There's one double room with a/c and private bath, a communal guest kitchen and all-day tea and coffee; rates include a light breakfast of toast and fruit. $\overline{P}$

Pepperland Hotel Airport Rd, Washington Drive ⓦthepepperlandhotel.com. Not far from the old airport, this stylish Spanish colonial-style hotel is named after that Bicol favourite, the chilli pepper – evident from the giant chilli sculpture which adorns the front of the building. Rooms are plush and colourful, and there's also an excellent restaurant and trendy café. $\overline{PPP}$

Hotel Venezia Renaissance Gardens, Washington Drive ⓦhotelvenezia.com.ph. Close to the airport, this upmarket hotel oozes minimalist chic, with rooms set on three floors. Standard rooms are tiny, while the much larger junior suites with king-size beds, sacrifice a little style for a lot more space. There's a café in the lobby serving delectable cakes. $\overline{PP}$

★ **Vista al Mayon** Washington Drive ⓦfacebook.com. In a good location close to the area's prime restaurants, this is a good choice among the city's inexpensive options, with knick-knacks dotted about the entrance hall and comfortable rooms with little wicker details; there's also a piano, billiards table and a small swimming pool in the courtyard (the pool is used for children's lessons at the weekend, when it can get a bit noisy and crowded). Rooms upstairs in the annex offer those sought-after Mayon views, as well as kitchenettes. $\overline{PP}$

EATING

SEE MAP PAGE 205

CITY PROPER AND AROUND

1st Colonial Grill Pacific Mall ⓦfacebook. com/1stcolonial. This popular restaurant within Pacific Mall is renowned for its unique pink chilli ice cream that gives quite a kick; other flavours include roasted rice (*tinutong*) and pili nut. The menu features fish and seafood

dishes such as grilled mussels and barbecue pork that are large enough to share. There are a couple of other branches elsewhere in town. $\overline{PP}$

★ **Seadog Diner** Legazpi Boulevard, Barangay Puro ☎0918 952 2996. Cosy little restaurant right on the waterfront, offering brick-oven-baked pizza and Bicolano classics. Try the lunchtime set menu of Bicol Express with *pinangat* and a drink. $\overline{P}$

Waway's Restaurant Albay 647 ⓦfacebook.com/waways1967. Join the local working crowd for an all-you-can-eat buffet lunch of native Bicolano specialities in a large and airy restaurant. The evening menu is not so good. $\overline{PP}$

ALBAY DISTRICT

Small Talk 51 Doña Aurora St, Albay district ☎ 0917 624 9279. The most atmospheric dining experience in the city, located in an ancestral home complete with family pictures and old photographs of Mayon. The menu covers all the Filipino standards, with some twists on Bicolano cuisine (see box, page 206) including pasta with Bicol Express and the fiery Mayon stuffed pizza, with *laing*, *longganisa* sausage and Bicol Express. $\overline{PP}$

DIRECTORY

Banks There are numerous banks on Rizal Ave as well as ATMs in the shopping malls. In the Albay district, you'll find a Land Bank ATM in the Provincial Capitol Annex.

Police The Albay police provincial office is at Camp Gen. Simeon A. Ola (☎ 052 820 6440), west of the Albay district.

Mount Mayon

The elegantly smooth cone of **MOUNT MAYON** (2460m) may look benign from a distance, but don't be deceived. The most active volcano in the country, Mayon has **erupted** more than forty times since 1616, the date of its first recorded eruption. The most deadly single eruption was in 1814 when around 1200 people were killed and the church at Cagsawa (see page 208) was destroyed; 77 people, including American volcanologists, were killed in a 1993 eruption. In August 2006, an "extended danger zone" was enforced but the expected eruption did not occur. Three months later, however, Typhoon Durian caused mudslides of volcanic ash and boulders on Mayon that killed hundreds. Further eruptions and ash ejections have occurred since, with tens of thousands of locals evacuated during periods of particularly increased activity in 2018 and 2023.

The presence of Mayon results in strange **weather conditions** in and around Legazpi, with the volcano and the surrounding area often soaked in rain when the rest of the country is basking in unbroken sunshine.

4

CLIMBING MOUNT MAYON

The traditional window of opportunity for an ascent of Mount Mayon is **February to April**, and even then you'll have to be well prepared for cold nights at altitude and the possibility of showers. At any other time of year you could be hanging around for days waiting for a break in the weather. Though the slopes look smooth, it takes at least two days to reach the highest point of the trail, working your way slowly through forest, grassland and deserts of boulders. Above 1800m there's the possibility of being affected by poisonous gases, and climbers are not allowed past 2000m even if there's no imminent threat of eruption.

There are various approaches to Mayon, although the accredited and authorized jump-off point is at **Lidong**, Santo Domingo, where the **Mayon Volcano National Park** is located. You'll have to bring all your food with you from Legazpi; there are sources of water on the volcano, but you'll need purifying tablets.

INFORMATION AND GUIDES

Whatever you do, don't attempt the climb without a **guide**. Guides are mandatory and setting out without one would be foolhardy in the extreme. Local guides at Lidong, Santo Domingo, can assist tourists, although it's probably wise to arrange one in advance at the tourist offices in Legazpi (see page 205), where you can also check to see whether conditions are suitable for an ascent. Another good source of information is the Institute Of Volcanology And Seismology (ⓦphivolcs.dost.gov.ph), in Legazpi on Lignon Hill (see page 204).

Daraga

Jeepney from Legazpi (every 5min; 30min)

Five kilometres west of Legazpi, the busy market town of **DARAGA** is much more visited than it was previously, after becoming host to Legazpi's new aiport. It's also home to **Daraga Church**, an imposing eighteenth-century Baroque structure built by Franciscan missionaries from blocks of volcanic lava. The exterior was decorated by skilled stonemasons with statuary, carvings, alcoves and niches, but until the early 2000s had been falling into disrepair. It was declared a national cultural treasure in 2008 and has now been restored to its former glory.

ACCOMMODATION AND EATING   **DARAGA**

Daraga offers a couple of surprisingly good **dining** options in pleasant surroundings, while **staying** here provides a good alternative to the hustle and bustle of central Legazpi. **Balay sa Bicol** Pagasa St ☎ 052 483 2083. Located in a beautifully restored ancestral home with wooden furniture and nick-nacks all over the place, this restaurant serves a decent range of local food, including seafood (try the prawns, which come in garlic, sweet chilli and sometimes coconut guises), Bikol Express, various types of *pancit*, and more. ‾P‾P‾P‾

Casa Bicolandia Suites Malvar St 🌐 facebook.com/casa bicolandiasuites. Just outside the centre of Daraga, and offering fantastic views of Mount Mayon, Casa Bicolandia is a friendly place with several bedrooms and a shared lounge area. Kitchen facilities are also available, though it's only a short walk to the restaurants in the centre. ‾P‾P‾

Cagsawa ruins

Ruins Charge • **Swimming Pool** Charge • Take a jeepney from Legazpi in the direction of Malabog or Polangui; make sure to tell the driver where you want to get off

Eight kilometres northwest of Legazpi, beyond Daraga, the **Cagsawa ruins** are the remains of a Spanish church, dating back to 1773. Much speculation surrounds the church as some claim that it was destroyed by the 1814 eruption of Mayon, while others say it was by earthquakes and typhoons. The ruins are small and there's not much to explore, but they are picturesque, standing in gardens close to paddy fields with marvellous views across the plain to Mount Mayon. This is a popular spot, so if you want peace and quiet – or if you want to take photographs before the cumulus roll in to obscure the volcano's tip – take an early jeepney. You can buy drinks and snacks from the souvenir stalls and sari-sari stores outside the ruins.

There's a **swimming pool** just by the ruins, while the area has also become popular for (short) ATV excursions, and even as a place to stay the night.

Hoyop-Hoyopan Cave

17km west of Legazpi • Daily 7am–7pm • Charge for 1hr guided tour; guides only receive 20 percent of the entrance fee so tips are appreciated • Jeepney from Legazpi to Camalig (every 20min; 45min), then change to another jeepney towards Cotmon or catch a habal-habal (15min)

Hoyop-Hoyopan – meaning "Blowing Wind" due to the breeze inside – is the most easily accessible of fourteen limestone **caves** near Legazpi. It's a well-established attraction, privately owned, and guides are available at the entrance, although you could try local guide Bam Nuylan (☎ 0927 969 9855) if nobody is there. Guides will point out fragments of burial jars dating back two thousand years; incongruously, there is also a concrete dancefloor built in 1972, when parties were held in secret to avoid the curfew of the martial law era.

Calabidongan Cave

24km west of Legazpi, 7km from Hoyop-Hoyopan • Charge for 3hr tour (compulsory) with guide

Calabidongan (Cave of the Bats) is a more difficult cave to explore than Hoyop-Hoyopan as it is always partly flooded and at one point requires a very short swim.

It is best visited in April and May, as at other times the water level can be too high. Make sure to bring a torch and wear rubber shoes or sandals; don't take a camera unless you have a waterproof bag. Hoyop-Hoyopan is the jumping-off point for Calabidongan; guides there can arrange a habal-habal (15min) for those who don't want to walk (7km; 1hr).

Santo Domingo and around

About 13km northeast of Legazpi along the coastal road, the small town of **SANTO DOMINGO** is a tidy, friendly little settlement with an atmospheric old Spanish church on the north side of the narrow main street. In the barangay of **Buyuan** is a signposted turning for a nine-hole golf course and stables offering horseriding (there's a good choice of rides, some take you to the lowest camp on Mount Mayon).

Calayucay Beach

East of Santo Domingo, a concrete road winds its way up and down through some delightful, pristine countryside, with the main destination being **Calayucay Beach**, 2.5km east of the town. It's pretty but not spectacular, though the views across Albay Gulf are attractive and its resorts are good places to relax.

Sogod Beach

About 10km north of Santo Domingo, near Bacacay, is **Sogod Beach** – a pleasantly rustic stretch of black volcanic sand sometimes known as the Mayon Riviera. As well as day-cottages for picnickers, there are a couple of resorts with accommodation.

Cagraray

You can reach Cagraray by boat from Tabaco (the island's resort organizes boats for their guests), or by taking the bridge from the peninsula east of Santo Domingo – more reliable than a boat during typhoon season, but not used by public transport, so you'll have to rely on taxis

The island of **Cagraray**, 26km east of Santo Domingo, connected to the mainland by bridge, has some wonderful white-sand beaches in **Sula** and **Misibis** on the southeast coast. The sand here is naturally black thanks to Mount Mayon's volcanic activity: the white sand that covers the beaches now was brought over from nearby Masbate. There is only one resort here, on Misibis beach (see below), although you can camp out. Hiring a bangka for a full day is a doable option.

ARRIVAL AND DEPARTURE · SANTO DOMINGO

By jeepney Jeepneys connect Legazpi to Santo Domingo (hourly; 30min) from where there are services to Calayucay Beach (hourly; 30min). Jeepneys also connect Sogod Beach to Tabaco (every 30min; 30min).

By van From Legazpi there are vans to Bacacay (for Sogod Beach; hourly; 45min).

By tricycle You can get a tricycle from Santo Domingo to Calayucay Beach (10min) or Sogod Beach (30min). A tricycle from Bacacay to Sogod Beach takes 10min.

ACCOMMODATION

Poor **wi-fi** can still be an issue here, as can power cuts.

Coastal View Beach Resort Calayucay Beach ☏ 052 437 8170. The first resort you come to on Calayucay Beach is also one of the best on this strip, albeit on slightly overbuilt grounds with a concrete promenade by the sea. The standard rooms are spacious, with poolside or Mount Mayon views, while the executive rooms have more attractive decor. **PP**

Costa Palmera Resort Calayucay Beach ⓦ facebook. com/costapalmeraresort. This is a decent option with a range of a/c economy rooms as well as suites. Best of all are probably the two poolside rooms, and the views from the wall wrapping around said pool. **PP**

Misibis Bay Misibis Bay, Cagaray ⓦ misibisbay.com. This large high-end resort, set in generous grounds, offers luxurious rooms and villas with prices to match. Facilities include seven swimming pools, a spa, restaurant, an excellent bar, and a range of watersports. **PPPP**

Tabaco

TABACO, 26km northeast of Legazpi, is a busy little port that functions as the gateway to **Catanduanes** (see page 219). The town itself doesn't offer much to visitors, although it's worth knowing that it has a couple of surprisingly decent hotels, should you happen to get stuck here for the night to catch the early ferry to Catanduanes.

ARRIVAL AND DEPARTURE   TABACO

By bus Buses arrive at the bus terminal 1.5km outside the centre; a pedicab to the centre of Tabaco takes 10min, while a tricycle is 5min. A/c buses travel to Manila (2–4 daily; 10–12hr); plenty of local buses also make the journey, with most leaving around 5pm (15 daily; 10–12hr).

By jeepney The jeepney terminal is on the main street just by the Tabaco City mall and market.
Destinations Bacacay (for Sogod Beach; every 30min; 30min); Legazpi (every 15min; 40min); Santo Domingo (every 30min; 30min).

By boat The port is a 10min walk from the jeepney terminal down the road running next to the market. There are ferries to Virac (1 daily; 4hr) and San Andres (2–5 daily; 1hr 30min–3hr) on the southwest coast of Catanduanes, which can be a rough crossing, particularly from October to December.

By van Vans to and from Legazpi (every 30min; 40min) and Naga (every 1–2hr; 2hr 30min) use the bus terminal.

ACCOMMODATION AND EATING

Amore Coffee Arellano St ☎0998 978 7986. This little café with wooden stools, a couple of armchairs and a sofa offers eight varieties of coffee beans including the prized civet coffee; desserts include Belgian waffles and coffee brownies, and there are savoury snacks too, such as sandwiches and nachos. P̅

HCG Ziga Ave ⓦhcg-residence-mansion-hotel-and-resto.business.site. Located in the centre of town, opposite the jeepney terminal, this is a good, safe option with clean, tiled a/c rooms. Those on a tight budget may want to opt for the 12hr option (6pm–10am). There's also an in-house restaurant serving Japanese dishes. P̅P̅

Ishiaya's Garden Bistro Villaruel St ⓦfacebook.com/

IshiAyasGardenBistro. Owned and run by Filipina celebrity Aya Medel, former actress and sex symbol, this lovely restaurant serves up Japanese and Bicolano fusion dishes in a leafy garden filled with fountains and fish ponds. Plates include pili-crusted fish fillet, yakisoba noodles and various types of sushi. P̅P̅

JJ Midcity Inn Herrera St ⓦjjmidcityinn.com. Above a small shopping complex, this place is a pleasant surprise – rooms are clean and modern, although the standard single with bunk bed is a bit of a squeeze. There's a karaoke bar within the hotel, so it can be quite noisy until it closes at midnight. Rates are cheaper for stays of up to 12hr. P̅P̅

Sorsogon province

A toe of land with a striking volcanic topography and some little-known beaches, lakes, hot springs and waterfalls, **Sorsogon province,** south of Albay, is the easternmost part of mainland Bicol. The province is best known to tourists for the chance to snorkel with whale sharks off the coast near **Donsol**, but it's also a great area for activities such as hiking and caving. **Sorsogon City** makes a good base for exploring the area's many lovely beaches – the nicest stretch of sand being **Rizal Beach**, in the barangay of Gubat to the east of Sorsogon City. There are many pristine coves to explore along the coast around **Bacon**, while south of Sorsogon City **Mount Bulusan** is a climbable, active volcano.

Driving through Sorsogon province you will pass many stalls selling items made from **abacá**, the fibre of a species of banana tree and one of the major products of the province. Sometimes known as Manila hemp, although it also grows in Malaysia and Indonesia, it is processed to make everything from banknotes to teabags.

Donsol

The area around the sleepy town of **DONSOL** is best known for one of the greatest concentrations of **whale sharks** in the world. The number of sightings varies: during the **peak months** of January to April there's a very good chance of encountering these

SORSOGON OUTDOOR ACTIVITIES

Although Donsol is famous for its whale shark watching, there are plenty of other activities elsewhere in Sorsogon for nature lovers and outdoor enthusiasts.

SCUBA DIVING

There's scuba diving at the infamous **Manta Bowl** (see page 218); though it's actually closer to Ticao Island (see page 218), it is best reached from the dive shops attached to several of the resorts in Donsol. The site is far from shore, and requires divers to descend rapidly and cling onto rocks – try to get a reef hook or gloves. You then use the strong drift to move towards the Manta Bowl, and if you're lucky you will be rewarded with close-up views of mantas or even whale sharks. This is not a dive for beginners, whatever the dive shops may tell you when trying to get your business. Also, be on the lookout for shoddy equipment. Bicol Dive Center (🅦bicoldivecenter.com) are a reputable choice for Manta Bowl dives.

OTHER ACTIVITIES

The Sorgoson area is home to a large number of fireflies, and in certain conditions they create a huge spectacle along the riversides. **Firefly-watching** has become a popular attraction; one of the best companies to do this with is **Buhatan River Eco Adventure** (🅦facebook. com/BuhatanRiverEcoAdventure). As well as the fireflies, they offer **birdwatching**, sunset **cruises** with dinner, kayaking and **mangrove tours**. A cruise down the river in a floating cabana, combining firefly-watching, birding, local snacks and live music is an excellent evening experience.

A day of **island-hopping** near the island of Ticao in Masbate province can be arranged through the visitor centre in Donsol (see page 211), who can also sort out **kayaking** trips on the Ugod River.

4

gentle creatures, but on some days (particularly early or late in the season, which stretches from December to early June) you might see none. **Swimming** with these colossal sharks as they sedately glide through the clear waters, their enormous mouths opening more than 1m wide to gulp down huge quantities of plankton, is a truly unforgettable experience, but remember that you need to be a good swimmer and a decent snorkeller to get into the water with them. Outside of whale shark season, there's not much here for travellers, and most of the accommodation options and even some restaurants are **closed**.

ARRIVAL AND DEPARTURE
DONSOL

By bus Philtranco has a daily bus from Manila (12hr). Buses travelling between Sorsogon City and Donsol (every 15min; 1hr) arrive at Junction Putiao (see below).

By jeepney Jeepneys and a/c minivans arrive at a terminal on the southern edge of town. For Sorsogon City, catch a jeepney towards Daraga and ask the driver to let you get off at Junction Putiao (every 30min; 1hr), from where the buses leave.

By van There are regular vans to Legazpi (hourly; 1hr 30min).

By boat Ferries from Masbate City arrive at Pilar port, 15km south of Donsol by jeepney (every 30min) or tricycle (30min). There is one daily roll-on-roll-off ferry (3hr) and three fast crafts (2hr).

INFORMATION

Tourist information The Visitor Centre (daily 7am–6pm; ☎ 0950 236 4663) is northwest of Donsol among the resorts in the barangay of Dancalan, reachable by tricycle from the centre of town. You'll need to check in here if you want to swim with the whale sharks (see box, page 212).

ACCOMMODATION

The **resorts** are about 2km northwest of the town centre, on **Dancalan Beach**, and most are closed outside of the whale-shark-watching **season** (Dec–June). Donsol itself is becoming more tourist-oriented as locals aim to capitalize

WHALE SHARKS IN DONSOL

Known locally as the *butanding*, the **whale shark** is a timid titan resembling a whale more than the shark that it is. It can grow up to 20m in length, making it the largest fish in existence. These gentle giants gather around Donsol every year, around the time of the northeastern monsoon, to feed on the rich shrimp and plankton streams that flow from the Donsol River into the sea, sucking their food through their gills via an enormous vacuum of a mouth.

Whale sharks were rarely hunted in the Philippines until the 1990s, when demand for their meat from countries such as Taiwan and Japan escalated. Cooks have dubbed it the "tofu shark" because of the meat's resemblance to soybean curd. Its fins are also coveted as a soup extender. Tragically, this has led to its near extinction in the Visayas and further south in Mindanao. In Donsol, however, where the creatures are protected, attitudes seem to be changing, with locals realizing that whale sharks can be worth more alive than dead, attracting tourists and thus investment and jobs.

WHALE-SHARK-WATCHING

At the Donsol Visitor Centre (see page 211) you can complete all the formalities for **renting a boat** for a whale-shark-watching trip. In peak season, especially at weekends, queues can start to form before the centre opens, so arrive early.

Before boarding you will need to watch a video briefing in which a **Butanding Interaction Officer** (BIO) explains how to behave in the water near a whale shark. The number of snorkellers around any one shark is limited to six; flash photography is not allowed, nor is scuba gear; and the animal's tail should be avoided as it can do serious damage. Some boatmen flout these rules in order to keep their passengers happy, but this risks distressing the whale sharks and should not be encouraged. Check, too, that your boat has one of the mandatory propeller guards.

Snorkelling equipment can be rented from outside the visitor centre. Each boat has a crew of three, the captain, the BIO and the spotter, each of whom would welcome a token of your appreciation. All this makes it an expensive day out by Philippine standards, but your money is helping the conservation effort. Take plenty of protection against the sun and a good book. Once a whale shark has been sighted you'll need to get your mask, snorkel and flippers on and get in the water before it dives too deep to be seen.

on growing visitor numbers; although there are few hotels, there are numerous **homestays**. Contact the Visitor Centre (see page 211) for an up-to-date list.

DONSOL TOWN
Aguluz San Jose St ⓦ facebook.com/aguluzbutanding. This welcoming homestay has beautiful *narra* wood floors and spacious, clean and comfortable rooms. Guests can also use the lounge and kitchen, as well as request home-cooked meals. P̲P̲

Giddy's Place 54 Clemente St ⓦ giddysplace.com. This place offers standard rooms at the back by the pool, and deluxe rooms at the front. All have kettle, fridge and TV, and there's a dive shop and restaurant. Limited wi-fi. P̲P̲

DANCALAN BEACH
AGM Beachfront Resort ☎ 0919 688 2264. This is the first resort on the strip if you're coming from Donsol town, and it has rows of thatched bamboo-fronted cottages and clean and tidy a/c concrete rooms with hot and cold

showers. There's also a pool overlooking the sea, and a casino. P̲P̲

Amor Farm Beach Resort ⓦ facebook.com/p/Amor-Farm-Beach-Resort-100064129171824/. Well-maintained resort in which guests can stay in rooms in the main building or in individual villas. Some villas have lovely sea views, and there's bonus points for having large models of whale sharks dotted around the grounds. P̲P̲

Elysia Beach Resort ☎ 0917 547 4466. This resort is the most upmarket choice along the strip, with minimalist decor, bamboo beds and wooden loungers by the pool. There are a few hammocks slung along the beach and a restaurant serving Filipino and Italian dishes. The resort accepts credit cards. P̲P̲P̲

Vitton Beach Resort ⓦ facebook.com/vittonand woodlandresorts. One of the area's best resorts, with clean and spacious rooms, most with private veranda. The restaurant serves good international food. The *Woodland Beach Resort* next door, owned by the same people, offers "backpacker rooms" which sleep three. Limited wi-fi. P̲P̲

EATING AND DRINKING

DONSOL TOWN

Justea Café 55 Clemente St 🌐facebook.com/ jusTeaCafe. Modern café in Donsol town which offers cheap and cheerful meals, though it's probably more recommended for a tea or coffee stop. P̲

DANCALAN BEACH

★ **Baracuda** Dancalan Beach ☎0961 588 7474. You'll find potent margaritas, daiquiris and piña coladas at this lovely bamboo restaurant with cushioned seating. The food is delicious, too, including mouthwatering sashimi, squid salad and prawns with garlic and olive oil. Lunch is available upon request. P̲P̲

Sorsogon City

There are few attractions in **SORSOGON CITY**, although it serves as a base to explore the area's natural sights and has a range of good accommodation. Along the pier, vendors crack open large clams and display them in buckets. The **boardwalk** on the pier is a good place to watch the sun set, with views of Mount Pulag and Mount Bulusan. Every year, the **Kasanggayahan festival** (roughly Oct 17–23) celebrates the town's history with street parades, traditional dances and beauty pageants. Dancing is clearly in the blood of this city: in 2019, it was the location of the Guinness World Records certified largest ever Filipino folk dance, which involved more than 7000 participants.

Museo Sorsogon

Capitol Compound • Free

The small **Museum and Heritage Center** displays a number of ancient artefacts, including burial jar covers dating back as far as 1000 BC that were found in caves in Bacon. Among the other exhibits are beautiful Chinese porcelain bowls from the Ming dynasty, chairs with Chinese-inspired designs and anchors believed to have been used during the Spanish colonial era. Highlights include the skull of a sperm whale, the skeletal system of a dolphin and a 10m-long vertebra of a whale shark that was washed ashore at nearby Donsol in 2010.

4

ARRIVAL AND INFORMATION

SORSOGON CITY

By bus Buses use the Grand Terminal 2km south of the city centre, a short tricycle ride away. Local buses make the trip to Legazpi (every 15min; 1hr 30min). Philtranco, among other companies, runs a daily service to and from Manila (13 daily; 10–12hr), as do a number of local companies.
By jeepney Jeepneys travel to Gubat (every 10min; 30min),

Bacon (every 10min; 30min) and Bulan (every 30min; 2hr).
By van Regular vans connect the city to Legazpi (every 15min; 1hr 15min).
Tourist information The provincial tourist office is in the Capitol Compound (Mon–Fri 8am–noon & 1–5pm; ☎056 421 5632).

ACCOMMODATION AND EATING

★ **Antonio's Bed & Breakfast** Calle Nueva 🌐facebook.com/antoniosbnbhotelsor. A genuinely lovely and characterful B&B in the heart of Sorsogon City, Antonio's offers comfy rooms decorated in traditional style, and the ambience is reinforced by the gorgeous wooden bench on the hallway's attractively tiled floor. The breakfast is excellent, and the owner is extremely friendly. A top choice for experiencing real Filipino hospitality. P̲P̲
The Chancery Magsaysay St 🌐facebook.com/ thechancery2021. Pretty café and religious store that's about as good a place as you'll find in which to sate any caffeine cravings. P̲
Fernando's N. Pareja St ☎0928 412 4520. As well as simple budget rooms, this hotel has cosy coconut-and-

bamboo-clad rooms, and newer deluxe ones with private balconies. There's also a large pool, which is a great for a cooling swim. P̲P̲
Rosario's J. Alegre St ☎0929 880 5199. Probably the best restaurant in town, this welcoming place whips up all sorts, from pasta dishes to seafood via salad options, and the regular roster of Philippine staples, all prepared well and served beautifully. P̲P̲
★ **Siama Hotel** Sitio San Lorenzo, Bibincahan 🌐siama hotel.com. This chic designer hotel offers stylish rooms with creative furniture made from wood. The welcoming rooms are set around an inviting 25m pool with a giant over-water hammock – a pleasant spot to sip a cocktail at sunset. The hotel organizes pick-up from Legazpi airport. P̲P̲P̲P̲

Rizal Beach

A short tricycle ride beyond the barangay of **Gubat**, which lies about 12km east of Sorsogon City on the eastern tip of the province, **Rizal Beach** stretches for 2km in a perfect crescent. It's a pleasant spot that can be suitable for **surfing** between October and January; for further information contact Lola Sayong (see below), who rent boards and organize lessons.

ARRIVAL AND DEPARTURE   RIZAL BEACH

By bus Several companies connect Manila to Gubat (5 daily; 12hr).

By jeepney Jeepneys from Gubat travel to Bulusan (every

15min; 45min) and Sorsogon City (every 10min; 30min).

By tricycle A tricycle from Gubat to Rizal Beach takes 10min.

ACCOMMODATION

Lola Sayong Eco-Surfcamp Rizal Beach, ⓦ lolasayong. org. An excellent budget choice, offering beachfront bamboo cottages and tents, both with shared bathrooms. There are plenty of shady palm trees and hammocks for

relaxing, as well as a communal kitchen and restaurant serving local dishes. Surfboard rental and surf lessons are also available. An extra environmental fee is added to your bill. P̄

Bacon and around

The small town of **BACON** (pronounced "backon"), 9km north of Sorsogon City by jeepney, has a grey-sand beach with a handful of resorts. Just a ten-minute tricycle ride west is the black-sand **Libanon Beach**, where surf hammers dramatically against immense, black rocks that were spewed out centuries ago by Mayon. The volcano is visible in the distance.

Paguriran

Bacon is a good base for exploring some of the **islands** in the eastern half of Albay Gulf. The best of these is **Paguriran**, a circle of jagged rock, much like the rim of a volcano, inside which is a seawater lagoon that's wonderful for swimming. The access point from the mainland is **Paguriran Beach**, 20km east of Bacon, from where you can walk across to the island at low tide; make sure to check your timings. Otherwise, you'll have to hire a boatman to paddle you across. Paguriran Beach is a wonderful spot to while away a few hours – the water is crystal clear, and there are lovely views over the neighbouring islands.

ARRIVAL AND DEPARTURE   BACON AND AROUND

By jeepney Regular jeepneys connect Sorsogon City to Bacon (every 10min; 30min) and Paguriran Beach (every 20min; 1hr 30min).

By tricycle A tricycle from Bacon to Paguriran Beach takes 45min.

ACCOMMODATION

Fisherman's Hut Brgy Caricaran ⓦ facebook.com/ fishermanshutofficial. Small, welcoming resort 1km east of Bacon, offering a series of comfortable rooms in cute A-frame nipa huts with private bath; four are duplexes that can sleep up to four, while one has a kitchenette with microwave. P̄P̄

Jefstar Resort Brgy Sugod ☎ 0912 381 8380. Very modest resort where life revolves around the swimming pool and jacuzzi tub, perhaps because there's not all that much else to do, distant as the place is from the beaches and town. Not a bad choice, though. P̄P̄

Bulusan Volcano National Park

Mount Bulusan, in the heart of **Bulusan Volcano National Park**, is one of three active volcanoes in the Bicol region. Trekking has resumed following a series of periods of increased seismic activity and a small eruption in June 2022, but it remains essential to check the situation before considering an ascent. From **Lake Bulusan** a 6.3km trail (3hr) leads to Aguingay Lake at 940m above sea level. This is where trekkers camp before setting off early to ascend the volcano in time for sunset. At the peak is the Blackbird Crater Lake (1565m), from where there are wonderful 360° views over Mount Mayon to the north, the Philippine Sea and Masbate to the west, the Pacific to the east, and as far afield as the Visayas to the south. Although it is possible to climb the volcano year-round, the **best months** are April and May. Pre-pandemic, Bulusan was the setting for the annual **Sky Run**, a race to the volcano's peak that starts in **Bulusan town**, 8km from Lake Bulusan – the record holder is a Kenyan who raced to the peak and back in 3hr 47min in June 2013 – but this rather energetic activity is yet to resume; some local bicycle teams, however, have got into trying an approximation of the route on two wheels.

ARRIVAL AND INFORMATION

By jeepney You can take a jeepney to the town of Irosin from Sorsogon City (every 15min; 45min) or Bulan (15min; 30min) and then another towards Bulusan town (hourly; 30min) – you'll need to jump off at the junction to the volcano, so ask the driver where to get off.

Guides and information Hikers will be refused access by rangers if an eruption warning is up; for guides and up-to-date details about the state of the volcano, contact the environmental organization AGAP, who can also provide accredited guides who will take groups of up to five (☎ 0919 223 1536). You should also consult the Philippine Institute of Volcanology and Seismology website (🌐 phivolcs.dost. gov.ph).

BULUSAN VOLCANO NATIONAL PARK

ACCOMMODATION

Balay Buhay Bee Farm ☎ 028 986 4355. A lovely bee farm, 5km south of Lake Bulusan, offering accommodation in pleasant grounds with one thousand bee colonies, a tilapia pond and a freshwater shrimp hatchery. There's also a pretty stone swimming pool with fresh water flowing directly from a spring. As well as simple cottages, there are twin rooms and rooms with two sets of bunks. PP

Masbate province

The province of **Masbate** ("maz-bah-tee") lies in the centre of the Philippine archipelago. It comprises the **island of Masbate**, site of the small capital of **Masbate City**, plus two secondary islands – **Burias** and **Ticao** – and numerous smaller islands. There are a number of attractions here – exceptional beaches on Masbate island, such as **Bituon**, for example, along with immense caves in thick jungle such as **Kalanay** and **Batongan** – but it's the infrastructure that's lacking. This is slowly changing, however, with an increased emphasis on tourism and a new ferry route to Manila via Caticlan (and Boracay).

The position of Masbate at the heart of the Philippines leads to some complicated **cultural blending**, with a mix of **languages** including Cebuano, Bicolano, Waray, Ilonggo, Tagalog and Masbateño. The province has long had something of a reputation for violence, with an image throughout the Philippines as a lawless "Wild East" frontier. Like many isolated areas of the archipelago, Masbate does seem a law unto itself and political killings are certainly not unheard of, but its reputation for unfettered goonish violence is mostly unfair. It is highly unlikely that tourists will feel any less **safe** here than in most other parts of the country.

The Wild East moniker is, however, apt for reasons other than lawlessness: Masbate ranks second only to the landlocked province of Bukidnon, Mindanao, in raising **cattle**. There's even an annual **rodeo** in Masbate City in the first or second week in April, where cowboys do battle for big prize money. If you're on the island on a Thursday, take the time to visit the **Uson Livestock Auction Market**, 42km southwest of Masbate City. It is one of the country's largest, with traders from various islands selling carabao, pigs, horses, chickens and goats.

Masbate City

The provincial capital of **MASBATE CITY** is attractively situated, nestling between the sea and the hills, but spoilt slightly by unstructured development. The best time to come is during the **Rodeo Masbateño**, a four-day orgy of bull-riding and steer-dogging held every April (usually the first half of the month).

A number of activities and sights around Masbate City together make a good day-trip by **bangka**. The tourist office (see page 216) should be able to help with arrangements for bangka rental, or you could bargain directly with a fisherman at the pier close to the main transport terminal.

Pawa boardwalk

4km southwest of Masbate City centre • Accessible by jeepney or tricycle (15min)

The **Pawa boardwalk** was built primarily to shorten the distance to school for students in the barangay of Pawa. The 1.3km path extends into protected **mangroves** at each side, where migratory birds can be seen, particularly at low tide.

Buntod Sandbar

Conservation fee • From Masbate City, take a tricycle (10min) to the barangay of Nursery, where there are bangkas for private hire

Out in the pass between Masbate and Ticao islands, in a marine protected area, the **Buntod Sandbar** is a popular spot at the weekend but empty during the week. After paying your conservation fee at the large open-fronted hut, you can relax at a picnic table – be sure to bring some supplies – or on one of the four floating platforms. There's decent snorkelling, too – and equipment for rent at the hut.

ARRIVAL AND DEPARTURE   MASBATE CITY

By plane The airport is on the southern edge of town; a tricycle to the centre takes 5min. Oddly, at the time of writing there were no flights to Manila, only nearby Clark/Angeles. Destinations Cebu (3 weekly; 1hr 10min); Clark (4–7 weekly; 1hr 30min).

By boat Masbate City's ferry pier is west of the centre. Services have been curtailed in recent years, though note that as well as the services listed below, there are also boats to Cawayan, on the southern side of Masbate island, from Bogo on Cebu (1 daily; 5hr) and to Mandaon, on the west side, from Roxas (2 weekly; 4hr 30min) and Cajidiocan on

Sibuyan (1 weekly; 4hr). Bangkas connect Masbate with Lagundi on Ticao Island (every 30min; 45min).
Destinations (ferries) Cebu (1 weekly; 12hr; ⓦtransasiashipping.com); Pilar, 15km south of Donsol, Sorsogon province (7 daily; 2–4hr; ⓦmontenegrolines.com.ph); Pio Duran, Albay (2 daily; 3hr; ⓦfacebook.com/santaclarashippingcorporation).

By bus and jeepney Buses, jeepneys and vans use a terminal on Diversion Rd on the southern edge of town, a little beyond the fishing port.

INFORMATION

Tourist information The provincial tourist office (Mon–Fri 8am–5pm; ☏056 333 2220) is in the Capitol Building, while the city tourist office is in the City Hall (Mon–Fri

8am–noon & 1–5pm; ☏056 588 2402). Both can advise on itineraries, although they have little in terms of printed materials.

ACCOMMODATION AND EATING

GV Hotel Danao St ⓦgvhotels.com.ph. Cheap, cheerful and convenient – don't expect great things from this central place, but if you just want a budget bed for the night, this is your spot. Try to get a room at the back as front-facing rooms can be noisy. P̲

★ **Patio Dada's** South of town, off Central Nautical Hwy ☏0998 432 8866. Zanily decorated restaurant with crockery on some walls, crockery here and there on the ceiling, crockery in wooden cupboards, and then of course more crockery when you're served your food. "Fusion" is probably the simplest description; it's a bit far out, but

there's bound to be something you like on the menu. P̲P̲

★ **Ranchelle Hotel & Resort** Masbate Circumferential Rd ⓦfacebook.com/RanchelleBeachResortKainanSaTabingDagat. A pleasant resort right on the seafront, with attractive villas and rooms set around a swimming pool in the courtyard. There's a gym on-site, as well as a café that serves good food and coffee. P̲P̲

Sutukil South of town, off Central Nautical Hwy ☏0921 629 1468. A little out of the centre, it's worth making the journey out to Sutukil for the excellent seafood. The menu also includes a fine selection of Filipino meaty dishes, with the lechon particularly good. PP

Tio Jose Quezon St ☎056 582 0193. This popular restaurant is a stab at a US-style bar, with sizzlers, steaks and grills on the menu, as well as Spanish-style tapas.

Dishes include *calamares fritos*, onion rings and buttered chicken, plus plenty of Filipino dishes. It gets pretty lively in the evenings, when locals belt out karaoke. PP

Bituon Beach

The sand at **Bituon Beach** (aka Bagacay Beach), 14km south of Masbate City and 2km down a dirt road from the barangay of **Bagacay**, is not as blindingly white as some, but that's a minor quibble. Some 2km long, the beach, with palm trees at the edge and beautifully clear shallow water, is nonetheless a pretty crescent bay.

ARRIVAL AND DEPARTURE

BITUON BEACH

By jeepney From Masbate City it's a short jeepney ride to Bagacay (hourly; 20min); they stop on the main road from where you can either walk to Bituon Beach (20min) or take a tricycle down the track (5min).

By tricycle A tricycle all the way from Masbate City will take 1hr 30min.

ACCOMMODATION AND EATING

Bituon Beach Resort ⓦfacebook.com/bituonbeach resortmasbate. Offering simple rooms in an idyllic location, this is a good place to relax on the beach or indulge in watersports if you're feeling active. The restaurant is good if not outstanding. PP

Batongan Cave

20km inland from Mandaon • Charge for local guide; ask around where the jeepney drops you off, or organize in advance at the Masbate City tourist office (see page 216) • Jeepneys (hourly; 45min) and buses (hourly; 1hr) run from Masbate City towards Mandaon; ask the driver to let you off at the caves; there are also boats to Mandaon from Cajidiocan on Sibuyan (2 weekly; 3hr)

The town of **MANDAON** is 64km west of Masbate City on the opposite coast. The trip by jeepney takes you along a scenic road that passes through pastureland, paddy fields and a number of isolated settlements inhabited by subsistence farmers. There's not much in Mandaon itself, but it's a good base for exploring two of the island's most noted natural wonders: **Kalanay Cave** on the northwest coast 40km from Mandaon, and, 20km nearer town, **Batongan Cave**. Both make excellent day-trips, but Batongan is the better of the two, with immense caverns and a large population of bats whose guano is collected and used as fertilizer. About 100m away is an **underground river**, which you can swim in. It's easy to get lost in these parts, and if you fall and get injured you might not be found for days, so don't explore the caves or the river without a **local guide**.

Palani Beach

About 5km north of **BALUD** on Masbate's western coast is **Palani Beach**, a wonderful, 5km-long virgin stretch of sand fringed with palm trees and lapped by crystal-clear waters. There are only a handful of simple resorts here, but if you're happy to stay in basic accommodation then it's a wonderful place to unwind for a few days. During the week you'll have the entire beach to yourself, while on weekends it gets busy with *masbateños* from all over the island. You can also camp here.

ARRIVAL AND DEPARTURE

PALANI BEACH

By jeepney Regular jeepneys make the journey from Masbate City to Balud (hourly; 3hr), from where you can take a tricycle to Palani Beach (15min).

ACCOMMODATION

Paraiso de Palani Palani Beach ⓦfacebook.com/ paraisodepalani. One of an increasing number of small resorts along this beautiful stretch of coast, this place is a beaut – modern, pleasingly decorated rooms surrounded by

> ### SNORKELLING AND DIVING FROM TICAO ISLAND
>
> Ticao Island is surrounded by spectacular **dive sites**, one of the best known being the huge Manta Bowl, the cleaning and feeding station for local manta rays. There are five different dive sites within the bowl, with depths ranging from 14 to 29 metres. Most of these are for advanced divers, so if you're after something less intense, head north of Ticao to the island of **San Miguel**, which has another twelve dive sites, better suited to less experienced divers. Night dive options are available at the **Pasil Ree**, found in front of *Ticao Island Resort* (see page 219). The waters in the **Ticao Pass**, to the east of Ticao island, are rich in plankton and attract many types of sharks including black-tip reef sharks, tiger sharks, hammerheads and even the mighty whale shark; many of these sharks can be spotted while diving and snorkelling here.
>
> The best way to organize **dive or snorkel trips** to these sites is to contact the excellent dive shop at *Ticao Island Resort* (⌨ ticao-island-resort.com), which also offers PADI and SSI dive courses. Manta Bowl (see page 211) also lies within easy reach of Donsol and trips can be arranged from here too.

palm fronds, with an inviting little pool and an even more   inviting stretch of beach. PP

Placer

On Masbate island's southwest coast, the small town of **PLACER** doesn't offer much to visitors, but it does have a pleasant stretch of beach with a few newish resorts. The waters around here are rich in giant squid, scallops and, in particular, **crabs** – the provincial tourist office in Masbate City (see page 216) can help organize a visit to a crab production plant.

ARRIVAL AND DEPARTURE   PLACER

By jeepney Regular jeepneys make the journey from Masbate City to Placer (hourly; 2hr). There are also boats from Bogo on Cebu (daily noon; 5hr) to Cawayan, which is 60km north of Placer.

ACCOMMODATION

Virginia Resort Pasiagon ☎ 0939 627 3269. One of the best places to stay on the whole of Masbate island, this pretty resort is a 5min tricycle ride from Placer. As well as one *kubo* beach hut, there are tastefully furnished rooms facing a leafy pool area with wooden four-poster beds, kitchenette with fridge and kettle, and patios with cushioned rattan seating. The resort organizes bangka hire to nearby islands. PP

Ticao Island

Beautiful and laidback **Ticao Island**, across the Masbate Passage from Masbate City, is well worth the one-hour bangka trip. The infrastructure is mostly basic and the roads can be very difficult in the rainy season, but Ticao is home to beautiful scenery and lovely **beaches** with crystal-clear waters, and it's deliciously unvisited. A convenient way to get around is to hire a bangka and explore the coast. Ask the boatman to take you to **Talisay**, the island's finest beach, and then on to **Catandayagan Falls**, the only waterfall in the country – and one of the very few in the world – where fresh water cascades directly into the sea. It's an impressive sight, plunging 60m into the emerald-green waters below. It's a perfect spot to have a swim, too.

ARRIVAL AND DEPARTURE   TICAO ISLAND

By boat Bangkas connect Masbate pier to Lagundi, on Ticao's southwest coast (every 30min 8am–4pm; 45min); there are also bangkas from Bulan in Sorsogon province to San Jacinto on the northeast of Ticao Island (5 daily; 1hr) and from Pilar to Monreal in the north (2 daily; 1hr 30min).

ACCOMMODATION

Ticao Altamar Boutique Resort ⓦ ticaoaltamar.com. Set in large, lush grounds, this lovely resort consists of a hilltop villa, Yellow House, with a welcoming lounge and four cosy private rooms decorated with vases, rugs, books and wicker and wood furniture. There are also attractive cottages set around the grounds, with neat and tidy rooms, although they are smaller than in the main building, and not quite as homely. Activities include kayaking, horse riding along the beach and island-hopping trips. Full board only. <u>PPP</u>

★ **Ticao Island Resort** ⓦ ticao-island-resort.com. This friendly place has four welcoming budget rooms and, on a pretty stretch of beach, nine comfortable a/c cabañas with parquet flooring and spacious bathrooms. The resort grows its own vegetables, and the restaurant menu includes delicious home-made bread, pizza and pasta. Staff can organize fishing trips, kayaking, firefly river tours, horse riding and cooking lessons. There's limited wi-fi available in the restaurant only. <u>PP</u>

Catanduanes Island

Once known as the "Land of the Howling Winds" thanks to its reputation for typhoons, the eastern island province of **Catanduanes** has rebranded itself as "The Happy Island" in honour of the affability and resilience of its people. Ripe for exploration, it's a large, rugged, rural island with endless stretches of majestic coastline. While **surfers** have known about Catanduanes for some time, attracted to the big waves off **Puraran Beach** on the wild east coast, the island has barely felt the impact of tourism, although with four flights a week from Manila and improvements to the main road around the island, this is slowly changing. There are several good beaches within easy reach of the capital **Virac**, along with the immense caves in **Lictin**, while the undeveloped west coast offers the opportunity to blaze a trail into areas few travellers see. Above all Catanduanes is a friendly, down-to-earth place to hang out for a few days, adjusting to a slower pace of life and travel.

When Filipinos think about Catanduanes they think mostly of **bad weather** – the island lies on the exposed eastern edge of the archipelago, smack in the middle of the "typhoon highway". Unless you are a surfer (surf season is roughly July–Oct), the best time to visit is from March to June, when the chances of rainfall are slight and the wind is less wicked. During the wet season (July–Nov), the island can be hit half a dozen times by **typhoons**, causing extensive damage to crops and homes and sometimes loss of life.

Virac

VIRAC is an anonymous provincial town, busy with mercantile activity and the noise of jeepneys. There is a small central plaza with a cathedral and a lively market, and an interesting local **museum**, but for most visitors Virac will simply be a base for exploring the rest of the island.

Museo de Catanduanes

Old Capitol Building, Santa Elena St • Mon–Fri 8am–4pm • Charge

The **Museo de Catanduanes**, within the same building as Virac's tourist office, is worth a look. Artefacts include fishing implements and trumpet shells used to send out signals to local communities. Objects from the Spanish colonial era include the intricately decorated walking cane of a Spanish congressman, which he allegedly used to accessorize his sharkskin coat and felt hat.

Around Virac

You will find some good **beaches** west of Virac in the villages of **Magnesia** and **Palawig**, particularly good for sunbathing and swimming, and east at **Buenavista**, although Puraran (see page 220) is the best for surfing. Inland from Palawig there are enormous limestone **caves** near the village of **Lictin**. To get there you'll have to find a guide in Lictin (there are no established rates, so ask around); contact the tourist office in Virac (see below) before setting out, or ask at the barangay hall in Lictin or in any of the village stores. The best known is **Luyang Cave**, whose waters are said to have healing properties. Another good short trip from Virac is to the **Maribina Falls**, between the barangays of Marinawa and Binanwahan – thus the name – fifteen minutes inland by jeepney. The waterfall plunges more than 10m into a crystal-clear pool that's good for swimming.

Puraran Beach

30km northeast of Virac • Surfboard rental and lessons available for a charge • One morning jeepney from Virac passes Puraran (1hr) on its way to Gigmoto; there are also jeepneys from Virac to Baras (hourly; 40min), from where it's a 20min tricycle trip to the beach; beach resorts can arrange a tricycle back to Baras

The break at beautiful **Puraran Beach** is referred to as **Majestic** by surfers. Majestic is fickle but it's generally thought that the best bet is to come here between **July and October**, when low-pressure areas lurking out in the Pacific help kick up a swell (though if these areas turn into tropical storms or typhoons, surfing is not advisable).

Luckily, you don't have to be a surfer to enjoy a few days on a beach as lovely as this. Extensive **coral gardens** just offshore make for wonderful snorkelling, and swimming is safe inside the line of the reef and away from the rocks – ask for advice at your resort before heading out, though, as it is not unknown for swimmers to get into trouble. Puraran is still mercifully undeveloped, with just a couple of basic resorts.

ARRIVAL AND DEPARTURE

By plane Virac's airport is 4km west of the town. Tricycles are available to take you into Virac: these cost less if you walk away from the airport waiting area. Cebu Pacific has flights from Manila (1 daily; 1hr 15min).

By boat From Tabaco, there are ferries to Virac (1 daily; 4hr) and to San Andres (2–5 daily; 1hr 30min–3hr); note that this can be a rough crossing, even with no typhoons around. In addition to the ferry ticket

CATANDUANES ISLAND

price, you'll need to pay a terminal fee. From Guijalo port in the Caramoan Peninsula you can hire a private bangka to Codon port on the western coast of Catanduanes island (45min), from where you can catch a tricycle to Virac (1hr).

GETTING AROUND

By rental car Hiring a car with a driver is a good if expensive way to see the island; try the drivers at the airport, visit the provincial tourist office in Virac (see page 220) or simply ask your accommodation to arrange it.

By motorbike Motorbikes are a cheaper way of exploring independently; the provincial tourist office in Virac (see page 220) can help arrange rental.

By bus, van and jeepney Buses, vans and jeepneys to destinations on the west side of Catanduanes leave from the barangay of Gogon in Virac. From Gogon, buses and vans to Pandan (3–4hr) pass through Caramoran (2hr 30min–3hr 30min); there are also regular jeepneys to San Andres (20min). From Virac pier, vans run to Bagamanoc (every 1–2hr; 1hr 30min) and Viga (hourly; 1hr 15min); there are also local buses to Bagamanoc (2 daily; 2hr).

INFORMATION AND ACTIVITIES

Tourist information The provincial tourist office (Mon–Fri 8am–5pm; ⓦ gocatanduanes.com) is on

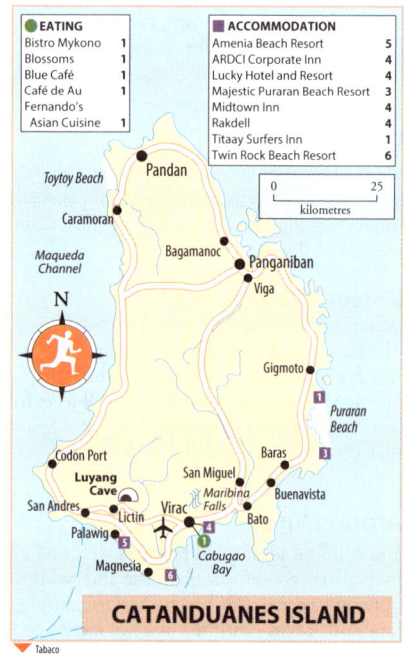

● EATING		■ ACCOMMODATION	
Bistro Mykono	1	Amenia Beach Resort	5
Blossoms	1	ARDCI Corporate Inn	4
Blue Café	1	Lucky Hotel and Resort	4
Café de Au	1	Majestic Puraran Beach Resort	3
Fernando's		Midtown Inn	4
Asian Cuisine	1	Rakdell	4
		Titaay Surfers Inn	1
		Twin Rock Beach Resort	6

CATANDUANES ISLAND

the second floor of the Old Capitol Building on Santa Elena St in Virac.

Surf lessons The resorts at Puraran Beach (see page 221) offer surf lessons, with costs including board rental.

Services All the services are in Virac. There are a few banks on the main plaza, and on the ground floor of the Old Capitol Building, just below the tourist office. The post office is at the back of the municipal building.

ACCOMMODATION
SEE MAP PAGE 220

If you're keen to stay out of town, but within reach of Virac's amenities, try the *Twin Rock* or *Amenia Beach* resorts. The resorts at **Puraran Beach** are very laidback and it is not unusual to end up staying for longer than you had planned. Note that electricity is often limited, and that **wi-fi** can be unreliable.

VIRAC
ARDCI Corporate Inn 4th Floor, ARDCI Corporate Building, San Roque ☏ 0998 988 2476. On two floors of an office block with floor-to-ceiling windows, this is a good option; rooms are comfortable and the bathrooms have rain showers. There's a café with views over the rice paddies and Virac. Breakfast included. $\overline{\underline{PP}}$

Lucky Hotel and Resort Rizal Ave ☏ facebook.com/ LuckyHotelandResort. This concrete monolith in the town centre is perhaps pushing it a little to refer to itself as a resort, but that aside, it's a decent place with comfortable and clean, if not especially exciting, rooms. There's a very small indoor swimming pool, which is perhaps suited more for exhibitionists than swimmers. $\overline{\underline{PP}}$

Midtown Inn San José St ☏ catmidinn.com. One of the best options in town, just off the main roundabout, with a little communal lounge on the first floor. Most rooms have a/c, cable TV and private bathrooms with hot showers. $\overline{\underline{PP}}$

Rakdell San Pedro St ☏ facebook.com/rakdellinnvirac. Budget option with acceptable a/c rooms with private bath and hot shower – but its location opposite a popular nightspot means that it can be noisy. On the plus side, there's a roof-deck restaurant where guests can enjoy their meals. Limited wi-fi. $\overline{\underline{P}}$

AROUND VIRAC
Amenia Beach Resort Palawig Beach, San Andres ☏ 0932 958 6074. Some 12km west of Virac, the real draw here is the lovely beach outside, which is popular with day-trippers but is also a pleasant spot to stay. The nine rooms here, named after local trees, are appealing enough, with decent-sized beds, and there are a couple of swimming pools. $\overline{\underline{PP}}$

Twin Rock Beach Resort Brgy Igang ☏ facebook.com/ twinrockbeachresort. About 10km south of Virac, this is one of the island's most developed resorts, with leafy grounds on a lovely stretch of beach in front of two jagged rock formations. It offers a range of room options, from claustrophobic rock cottages without pool access to larger deluxe a/c rooms with pool access included. There's a zipline over the sea, a climbing wall, kayaks and a pool with two slides. The noisy karaoke is something of a drawback. $\overline{\underline{PP}}$

PURARAN BEACH
Majestic Puraran Beach Resort ☏ facebook.com/ majesticpuraranresort. Rustic, fan-cooled, thatched cottages set around a wide garden at the far end of the beach, with wooden balconies with swinging hammocks. There are also a couple of a/c rooms in a concrete block, which are not nearly as nice. $\overline{\underline{P}}$

Titaay Surfers Inn ☏ facebook.com/p/Titaays-Surfers-Inn-100083031623999/. Welcoming surfer hangout with simple bamboo and palm-leaf cottages with wooden beds that look like a good kick would turn them into matchsticks, plus sturdier metal bunk beds in some rooms. There's also a "restaurant". $\overline{\underline{P}}$

4

EATING
SEE MAP PAGE 220

Unless you're staying in one of the upmarket resorts, the best **restaurants** can be found in the city of Virac. The only places to eat at Puraran Beach are within the three simple resorts.

VIRAC
Bistro Mykono Imelda Blvd ☏ facebook.com/bistro mykono. This ostensibly Greek restaurant does offer a couple of Mediterranean dishes such as souvlaki, but the majority of the menu is made up of Filipino classics and international dishes. No matter, though – it's all very tasty. $\overline{\underline{PPP}}$

Blossoms Salvacion St ☏ facebook.com/blossoms restoph. The most atmospheric restaurant in town, with wooden chairs set around a breezy dining area. They serve pasta and pizza, as well as seafood, noodles and cakes. $\overline{\underline{PPP}}$

Blue Café Gogon ☏ 0915 420 8434. This cosy café, located on the second floor of Virac Town Centre shopping mall, offers a good selection of savoury dishes such as pastas and panini, as well as waffles and cakes. $\overline{\underline{P}}$

Café de Au Imelda Blvd ☏ 0918 682 9817. Small café with quirky decoration – a sort of baffling cross between surfer hangout and industrial chic, via garden centre. The coffee's good, though, as are the sarnies. $\overline{\underline{P}}$

Fernando's Asian Cuisine Gogon ☏ 0908 977 1162. On the third floor of Virac Town Centre mall, this large and friendly restaurant filled with cosy booths and long tables serves all kinds of Asian cuisine, from Japanese and Thai to Korean and Chinese, as well as Filipino. Dishes include aubergine and beef hot pot, Korean *bibimbap* and California maki sushi. It also offers fabulous city views. $\overline{\underline{PPP}}$

Mindoro

SNORKELING NEAR APO ISLAND

5 Mindoro

Within a few hours of Manila, yet worlds away, Mindoro remains undeveloped even by Philippine provincial standards. Much of the island is wild and rugged, with some near-impenetrable hinterlands and an often-desolate coastline of wide bays and isolated fishing villages. The island, seventh largest in the archipelago, is divided lengthways into two provinces, Mindoro Occidental and Mindoro Oriental; the latter is the more developed and visited, if mainly on its northern, Luzon-facing fringe. Most travellers head this way only for the beaches, scuba diving and nightlife around picturesque Poblacion (Puerto Galera town) on Mindoro Oriental's northern coast, a short ferry trip across the Isla Verde Passage from Batangas, but there is much more to Mindoro than this. Few people, Filipinos included, realize that the island is home to several areas of outstanding natural beauty, all protected to some degree by local or international decree.

ARRIVAL AND DEPARTURE | MINDORO

BY PLANE
San José airport In the south of Mindoro Occidental, the airport is served from Manila with Cebu Pacific (1 daily; 1hr). There is no airport serving Puerto Galera.

BY BOAT
Manila to Puerto Galera A good way to reach Puerto Galera and Sabang from Manila is to buy a combined bus-boat ticket with Si-Kat (w sikatferrybus.com; 1 daily; 5hr total to Puerto Galera, via Batangas); the bus departs from their office at City State Tower, 1315 Mabini St, Ermita.
Batangas City to Puerto Galera and northern Mindoro The main ferry port for departures to Muelle pier in Poblacion (Puerto Galera town) is Batangas City (see page 114). There are frequent departures (daily 6.30am–5pm; 1–2hr) from Batangas to Muelle pier, Sabang and White Beach on large outriggers, easy to find on arrival at Batangas Port Terminal 3; companies running them include Montenegro Shipping Lines (w montenegrolines.com.ph). Galerian Water Transport vessels are the fastest, with

speedboats to Balatero, 3km west of Poblacion (45min); Montenegro Lines also operate a car ferry on this route (1 daily; 2hr). In addition to fares, you may have to pay a terminal fee, and an environmental fee upon arrival.
Batangas City to Calapan and Abra de Ilog Port Various companies run ferries to Calapan, 44km southeast of Galera (regular; 1hr 30min–2hr), including Montenegro Lines, who also sail to Abra de Ilog Port (9 daily), 30km west.
Roxas to Caticlan (for Boracay) Roxas (163km southeast of Puerto Galera) is a key link on the route to Boracay, and there are regular ferries departing for Caticlan (4hr) with Starlite Ferries (w starliteferries.com)
Bulalacao to Caticlan (for Boracay) FastCat (w fastcat.com.ph) sail from Bulalacao, 44km south of Roxas, to Caticlan (2 daily; 3hr 30min).

BY BUS
Manila to San José Partas Bus (w partas.online) and Penafrancia (w penafranciabus.com) run direct bus routes to Mindoro from Manila (3 daily, 9–10hr).

Mindoro Oriental

Most visitors head to **Mindoro Oriental**, which is more accessible and developed than its poorer neighbour across the mountains, to dive in the marine reserve at **Puerto Galera**, in the north of the province. Nearby **Mount Malasimbo** is also protected because of the biodiversity of its thickly jungled slopes. To the east of Puerto Galera, near the port of **Calapan**, is **Mount Halcon** – at 2587m, Mindoro's tallest peak and a difficult climb even for experienced mountaineers. The south of the island is less populated than the north, with few tourists making it as far as

Highlights

❶ Puerto Galera The area around this picturesque coastal resort has fine beaches, challenging treks and scuba diving for every level. See page 226

❷ Mount Halcon Mindoro's highest peak is a serious hiking challenge through mist-shrouded jungle, with jaw-dropping vistas of the whole island. See page 235

❸ Indigenous people Get an intriguing insight into a marginalized culture by meeting the island's original inhabitants, the Mangyan. See page 236

❹ Mounts Iglit-Baco National Park See the rare tamaraw, a type of water buffalo, as you trek through some of the most enchanting countryside on Mindoro. See page 240

❺ North Pandan Island Idyllic island hideaway just off the west coast, a tranquil resort offering scuba diving, snorkelling or the chance to just laze on the bone-white sands. See page 241

❻ Apo Reef Superlative diving in one of the most pristine marine environments in the world, where sharks, rays and other pelagics are common sightings; you can spend the night on a remote islet, too. See page 241

HIGHLIGHTS ARE MARKED ON THE MAP ON PAGE 226

5

Roxas on the southeast coast unless they're taking a ferry to Caticlan (for Boracay) from **Bulalacao**, around 44km south of Roxas.

Puerto Galera

One of the country's most popular resorts, **PUERTO GALERA** (meaning "Port of the Galleons") boasts some of the most diverse coral reef diving in Asia and gorgeous, sugar-sand beaches, as a result of which the whole area is often mobbed during national holidays. Arriving by ferry is a memorable experience, the boat slipping gently through

MINDORO

HIGHLIGHTS

1. Puerto Galera
2. Mount Halcon
3. Indigenous people
4. Mounts Iglit-Baco National Park
5. North Pandan Island
6. Apo Reef

Dense & largely impenetrable

0   50
kilometres

N

aquamarine waters past a series of headlands fringed with haloes of sand and coconut trees. Brilliant white yachts lie at anchor in the innermost bay, and in the background looms the brooding hulk of Mount Malasimbo, invariably crowned with a ring of cumulus cloud.

Founded by the Spanish in 1574, the town was once an important port and served as Mindoro's capital until 1837, when Calapan assumed the role. Today it's a natural choice for escaping Manileños, so book ahead if you're planning to visit during Easter and summer weekends. There's also plenty on offer in addition to diving, including excellent snorkelling, trekking into the mountains and beach- and island-hopping by bangka.

Poblacion (Puerto Galera town)

Poblacion, basically Puerto Galera town itself, occupies a marvellous location, overlooking Muelle Bay on one side, with green hills behind it. Despite its picturesque location, the town is a little chaotic – filled with tricycle traffic, and offering few good restaurants and places to stay. Other than watching the bangkas phut-phut back and forth from one of the waterfront cafés and bars near Muelle pier, there's not much to see or do. Most tourists move straight on to the beaches and dive resorts, but with some time to kill you might visit the small **Excavation Museum** or take a glance at the canon-flanked marble **Cross at Muelle**, near the pier; it was erected by the Spanish to commemorate the sinking of the battleship *Canonero Mariveles* in 1879 during a storm.

Sabang and around

Set in a pretty cove, **Sabang** is jam-packed with hotels, restaurants and dive schools, and appeals to primarily foreign tourists. Despite its popularity, there's not much of a beach here, so it's not great for swimming; and there's a very visible go-go bar scene that comes as a shock to many visitors. At night the small rabbit warren of streets behind the beach can feel a little seedy. If you arrive here by bangka from Batangas City, you'll be dropped right on the beachfront.

Small La Laguna

Just a few minutes' walk northwest along the coast from Sabang beach, **Small La Laguna** is the ideal choice if you're looking for a range of friendly accommodation in a quiet location – most of it right on the water – with good dive operators and a handful of informal bars and restaurants. The beach here is still not great, however, so if you're looking for something more tropical, head around the headland to Big La Laguna (see page 228).

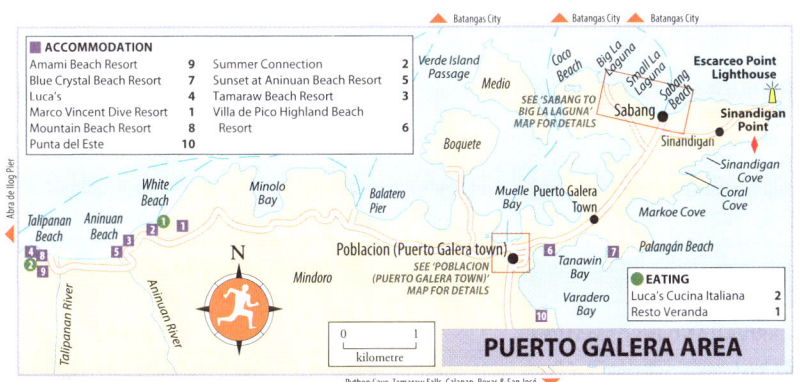

ACCOMMODATION

Amami Beach Resort	9	Summer Connection	2
Blue Crystal Beach Resort	7	Sunset at Aninuan Beach Resort	5
Luca's	4	Tamaraw Beach Resort	3
Marco Vincent Dive Resort	1	Villa de Pico Highland Beach	
Mountain Beach Resort	8	Resort	6
Punta del Este	10		

EATING

Luca's Cucina Italiana	2
Resto Veranda	1

PUERTO GALERA AREA

5

PUERTO GALERA ORIENTATION

Though Puerto Galera does have a commercial centre (aka **Poblacion** or **Puerto Galera town**), the name is generally used to refer to the whole area between **Sabang**, 5km to the east, and **White Beach**, 8km to the west. Most visitors head straight for Sabang and the nearby beaches of **Small La Laguna** and **Big La Laguna**, home to a diverse range of accommodation, diving, restaurants and nightlife. There are a couple of resorts near the village of **Palangán**, about halfway along the road from Puerto Galera to Sabang. Northeast of Palangán there's a small isolated cove at **Sinandigan** with a handful of very peaceful options. In the other direction, picturesque White Beach has plenty of accommodation and is popular with partying Manileños at the weekends. For the best beaches and more of a remote experience, walk – or take a tricycle – further west to beautiful **Aninuan Beach** with its range of plush resorts; or **Talipanan Beach**, which has a couple of comfortable and affordable places to stay.

Big La Laguna

The sheltered cove of **Big La Laguna** has dive shops and a few good accommodation options, some with convivial beach-style bars and restaurants attached. With largely clean sands, this is the best spot in the Sabang area for swimming, and there's safe snorkelling over the offshore coral reef (boats are prohibited).

Palangán and Sinandigan Cove

To the southeast of Sabang lies quiet **Sinandigan Cove**, also known as Coral Cove, dominated by the Escarceo Point lighthouse. Other than a few abandoned resorts, there's not much here, but it makes for a lovely walk from Sabang and offers spectacular coastal views. Six kilometres to the southwest you'll find the barangay of **Palangán**, home to a few quiet and comfortable places to stay. Some are on the ridge above the road, with marvellous views across Puerto's bays and islets, and are just a short walk from the beach. Not all of these resorts have dive centres, but they can all help arrange diving through operators in Sabang.

White Beach

A once quiet crescent of sand, spectacular **White Beach** has in recent years been populated by small resort hotels and cottage rooms popular with Filipino families. Unlike Sabang, there are not many go-go bars and fewer scuba divers too, but it does have a number of lively discos and bars that can get a bit noisy. White Beach gets especially busy at peak times, notably New Year and Easter, when backpackers and students from Manila hold all-night rave parties on the sand. There are still some quieter spots on the beach, but those looking for an isolated and quiet beach experience should head on to Aninuan and Talipanan (see page 228).

Aninuan and Talipanan

By far the two best beaches in the Puerto Galera area, **Aninuan** and **Talipanan** both have vast swathes of empty golden sand and good range of accommodation options, from upmarket resorts to laidback guesthouses. While slightly more difficult to reach via public transport, they can both be accessed by walking along the shoreline (20–30mins from White Beach) and, when the tide is in, via a pathway that leads up over the headland. Aninuan is more popular, while Talipanan is for those seeking real solitude. There's little nightlife and no karaoke – probably just you, the fishermen and the fireflies.

ARRIVAL AND INFORMATION   PUERTO GALERA

By boat Most travellers arrive at Puerto Galera via boat   from Batangas (see page 114) at Muelle pier in Poblacion, or direct to Sabang (see page 227) and White Beach (see page 228). For Abra de Ilog Port, further west in Mindoro Occidental (the road to Abra is impassable except on foot or trail bike; it's an hour's walk), there are bangkas from Balatero (30min), providing the seas aren't too rough (check with your hotel), although if headed that way you may as well go directly from Batangas.

By jeepney Jeepneys to Calapan (1hr 30min) leave when full from the Petron petrol station on the southern edge of Poblacion from early morning until mid-afternoon; a/c minivans also make the trip from a depot 2km further out of town; they're slightly more expensive, but will get you there quicker.

GETTING AROUND

By tricycle Tricycles are always available and the most convenient way to zip between the various beaches in Galera, though drivers are notorious for ripping off tourists. Ask at your accommodation what the going rate ought to be; once you've got an idea of local prices, you'll need to bargain hard. Note, however, that the road to Talipanan is pretty bad and becomes almost impassable when it rains, so walking via the beach is the best option.

By bangka Bangkas regularly ply between Sabang and White Beach (40min); for an extra charge the boat will wait for you. You can arrange bangkas between just about any beach; rates will depend on how long you need the boat for

and your haggling skills. Small pumpboats travel between Sabang and Big/Small La Laguna beaches.

By jeepney Jeepneys shuttle back and forth between Sabang and Poblacion (they depart up the hill from Muelle pier, on P. Concepcion St; 6am–6pm; 15min), although these won't leave until they are overflowing. Jeepneys also run along the west coast to White Beach and Aninuan. Most routes stop running after 5pm, when you'll be at the mercy of the tricycle drivers.

By scooter/motorbike You can rent scooters and motorbikes in Poblacion and Sabang; try asking at *Badladz Dive Resort*.

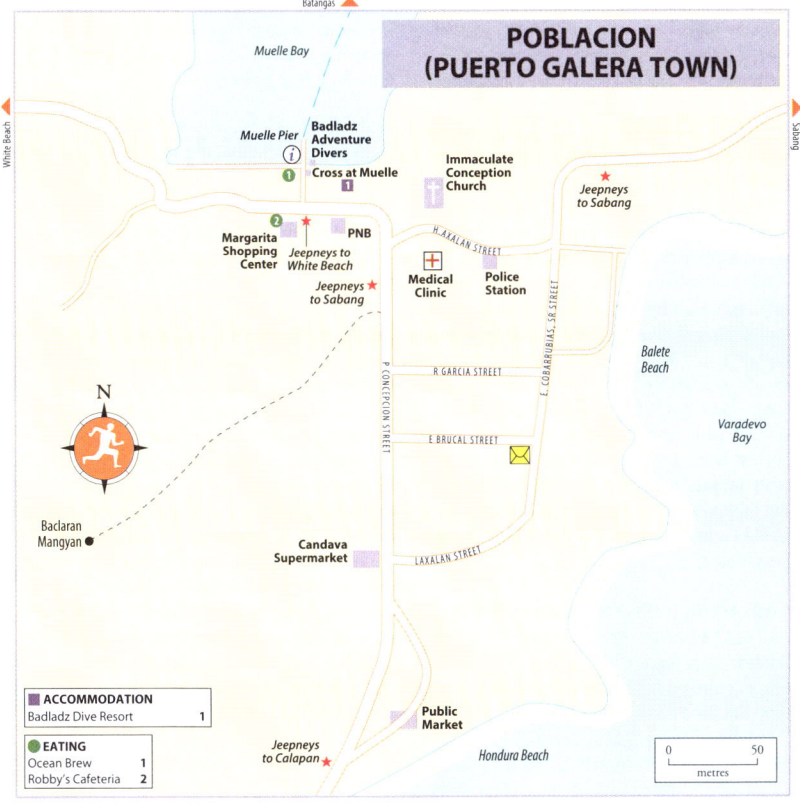

POBLACION (PUERTO GALERA TOWN)

Batangas

Muelle Bay

White Beach

Sabang

Muelle Pier

Badladz Adventure Divers

Cross at Muelle **1**

Immaculate Conception Church

Jeepneys to Sabang

Margarita Shopping Center **2**

PNB

Jeepneys to White Beach

Jeepneys to Sabang

H. AXALAN STREET

Medical Clinic

Police Station

E. COBARRUBIAS, SR STREET

P. CONCEPCION STREET

R GARCIA STREET

Balete Beach

Varadevo Bay

E BRUCAL STREET

Baclaran Mangyan

Candava Supermarket

LAXALAN STREET

ACCOMMODATION
Badladz Dive Resort   1

EATING
Ocean Brew   1
Robby's Cafeteria   2

Public Market

Jeepneys to Calapan

Hondura Beach

0   50
metres

5

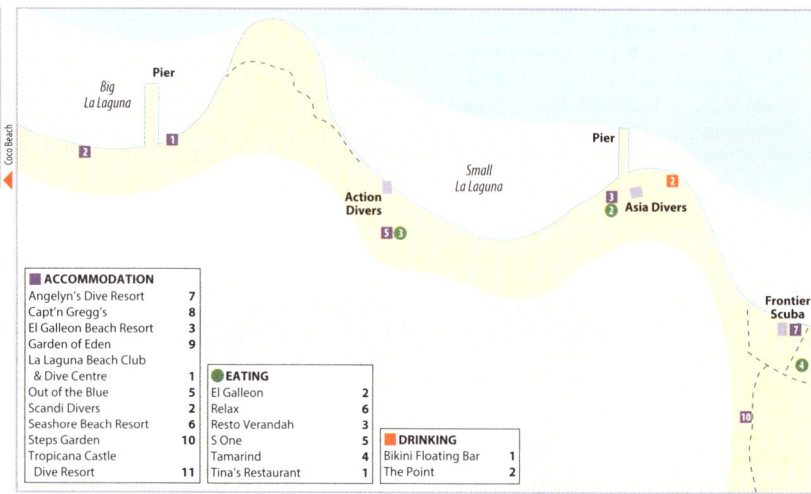

ACCOMMODATION

Angelyn's Dive Resort	7
Capt'n Gregg's	8
El Galleon Beach Resort	3
Garden of Eden	9
La Laguna Beach Club & Dive Centre	1
Out of the Blue	5
Scandi Divers	2
Seashore Beach Resort	6
Steps Garden	10
Tropicana Castle Dive Resort	11

EATING

El Galleon	2
Relax	6
Resto Verandah	3
S One	5
Tamarind	4
Tina's Restaurant	1

DRINKING

Bikini Floating Bar	1
The Point	2

INFORMATION AND TOURS

Tourist information There's a small tourist office (daily 7.30am–5pm; 043 287 3051) at Muelle pier.

Jeepney tours There are a couple of tour operators in town, but their offices are hardly ever open and they're pretty unreliable. Your best bet is to hire a local jeepney to take you round the sights; most drivers have photos and descriptions of local attractions plastered up inside their jeepneys to give you an idea of where to go. Prices for a day's private hire are for the whole jeepney, so it's cost-effective to join up with other travellers.

ACCOMMODATION

With direct boats from Batangas to Sabang and White Beach, there's really little need to stay in **Poblacion (Puerto Galera town)**; that said, if you want to escape the beach scene, there are a couple of decent hotels here. Accommodation choices in **Sabang** range from small resorts to more expensive dive resort options. Generally speaking, the accommodation to the west of the main road, which is closer to the nightlife, is pricier than that to the quieter east. **White Beach** is now very popular, and room prices have rocketed. It can be hard to find a decent budget room, particularly at weekends and holidays; it's definitely worth booking in advance. **Aninuan Beach** has the best range of both upmarket and mid-range resorts, while **Talipanan** has some good budget options. Note that though **wi-fi** is available in most resorts listed here, it's often unreliable and limited to public areas such as the lobby or poolside.

POBLACION (PUERTO GALERA TOWN), SEE MAPS PAGES 227 AND 229

Badladz Dive Resort Muelle pier ⓦbadladz.com. Geared to divers rather than beach-lovers, with great bay views and spacious rooms with hot water, a/c and cable TV. There's also a dive shop (see box, page 232). $\overline{PP}$

Punta del Este Off Calapan N Rd ⓦpuertogaleravilla. com. A complex whose villas occupy the tip of a promontory, providing wonderful views out east – great news for those who are able to haul themselves out of bed in time for sunrise. The villas themselves are a little basic in feel for the price, but they have four or five bedrooms each – great for groups, and there's a good swimming pool. Meals included with some deals. $\overline{PPPP}$

SABANG, SEE MAP PAGE 230

Angelyn's Dive Resort ⓦangelynsdiveresort.com. Good location right on the beach, at the far western end, and only a short walk from dive operators, bars and restaurants. All rooms have a/c, cable TV and mini-fridges and some have private balconies. There's also a small open-air restaurant. $\overline{PP}$

Capt'n Gregg's ⓦcaptngreggs.com. Turn left at the end of the road in Sabang, and it's a 2min walk along the beach to get to this popular, well-established resort catering mainly to divers, with acceptable rooms (the cheapest come with fans only, but all have TVs), decent food and useful advice from the resident divers in the dive shop, many of whom have lived in Sabang for years. $\overline{PP}$

⭐ **Garden of Eden** ⓦgoeresort.com. Just east of Sabang Pier, this is one of the area's most attractive and relaxed resorts, with thatched fan-cooled bungalows (ones with a/c are more expensive) set in a tropical garden with a lagoon-shaped pool. There's also a good beachfront

Bangkas to Batangas City

SABANG TO BIG LA LAGUNA

5

0   50
metres

Sabang
Beach

Ferry Terminal

General
stores

N

Maxbank & Poblacion (Puerto Galera Town)

restaurant. PPP

Seashore Beach Resort ☎ 043 287 3021. A good choice if you're on a bit of a budget, Seashore Beach Resort offers decent if unremarkable rooms close to the beach. There's a pool in the courtyard, and the food at the restaurant isn't at all bad. It can suffer a little from internal noise so earplugs are recommended. PP

★ **Steps Garden** ⓦ stepsgarden.com. Discreetly tucked into the western end of the cove, some 60m inland, *Steps* has a wide variety of comfortable a/c huts spread through the lovely hillside gardens (inspired by the Greek island of Santorini). There's also an attractive pool, a good restaurant and friendly staff. PP

Tropicana Castle Dive Resort Sabang Rd ⓦ cocotel. com. Set on the main road coming into Sabang from Poblacion, this extraordinary faux-German *schloss* has medieval-themed rooms with four-poster beds and all mod cons, although it's seen better days. There's a swimming pool, a small spa and a restaurant, which are also rather tired-looking. Many guests are on all-in packages from Europe that include diving. PP

SMALL LA LAGUNA, SEE MAP PAGE 230

El Galleon Beach Resort ⓦ asiadivers.com. Professionally run, tropical-style hotel with airy bamboo a/c rooms, many with balconies, ranging from no-frills budget to spacious sea-view cottages; there's also a pleasant seaside restaurant (see page 234). PPP

★ **Out of the Blue** ⓦ outoftheblue.com.ph. Sophisticated villas and apartments on the hillside above the beach, 30m back from the sand, most of which feature huge sea-view windows and balconies. There are also two pools, and a great restaurant, *Verandah* (see page 234). PPP

BIG LA LAGUNA, SEE MAP PAGE 230

La Laguna Beach Club & Dive Centre ⓦ llbc.com.ph. Substantial resort with palm-roofed rooms and cottages surrounding a beautiful swimming pool. All rooms have a/c, hot water, cable TV and DVD player. On site are a reputable diving school, a first-class restaurant and *Gecko Bar* with a large balcony for sunset-watching. PP

Scandi Divers ⓦ scandidivers.com. Attractive place in the centre of the beach offering rooms and cottages, some with sea views and others facing the pool area. There's a good diving school here, offering an extensive programme of trips in the area. There are two restaurants on site too, offering a varied and tasty menu. PPP

PALANGÁN, SEE MAP PAGE 227

Blue Crystal Beach Resort ⓦ bluecrystalbeachresort. com. For those seeking a remote escape without foregoing everyday luxuries, this imposing colonnaded building right on the seashore may be the answer. Rooms have a/c and cable TV, and are grandly decorated with heavy furnishings; some have kitchenettes. There's also a decent pool and beautiful coastal vistas. In fact the only downside is that the beach here isn't that great. PP

Villa de Pico Highland Beach Resort ⓦ villadepico highlandbeachresort.com. A lovely peaceful spot, Villa de Pico offers rooms and cottages set in gorgeous grounds with fantastic views over the sea and mountains. The friendly owners can arrange outings to Tamaraw Falls and Mount Malasimbo, as well as diving and snorkelling trips. The food at the restaurant is excellent. PP

WHITE BEACH, SEE MAP PAGE 227

Marco Vincent Dive Resort ⓦ marcovincent.com. Set a few hundred metres back from the beach, with plush

5

DIVING IN PUERTO GALERA

The beauty of scuba diving around Puerto Galera is the number and variety of **dive sites** that can be reached by boat in a matter of minutes. These offer something for everyone, from exhilarating dives in raging currents to gentle drifts along sheltered coral reefs.

A good option for novices is West Escarceo, a drift dive sloping down gently from 5m to 30m. Look out for electric clams in the small caves here and big schools of snapper, trevally and sweetlips. Just west of here, **Hole in the Wall** is another popular spot to see large schools, particularly of drummer fish and batfish. The **Sabang Wrecks**, two wooden wrecks and a steel yacht, are home to surgeonfish, moray eels, lionfish, and even quirky frogfish and stargazers. In the shallow areas around the sea grass you can also see green sea turtles. Finally, don't miss the **Alma Jane Wreck**, where advanced divers can safely swim below deck to explore the cargo holds. The ship is now a refuge for lionfish and rabbitfish, among others.

A more challenging dive is the **Canyons**, a healthy reef split into three slab-like sections with deep troughs (hence the name) and some fierce currents. It's the best place in the area to encounter large pelagics such as sharks and barracuda. **Verde Island Dropoff** is another for advanced divers only: a rocky pinnacle 400m off Verde Island, where sloping reefs and coral-carpeted walls are home to banded sea snakes, scorpionfish, nudibranchs and a variety of colourful reef fish.

DIVE OPERATORS

There are dozens of dive operators in Sabang, Small La Laguna and Big La Laguna, and a smattering in White Beach and the beaches nearby. Rates are dependent on whether you hire all equipment or if you bring your own wetsuit and buoyancy control device; in addition, the more dives you do, the cheaper it gets. Established firms include:

Action Divers Next to Out of the Blue villas, Small La Laguna ⓦ actiondivers.com.

Asia Divers Next door to El Galleon resort, Small La Laguna ⓦ asiadivers.com.

Badladz Adventure Divers Badladz Dive Resort, Muelle pier, Poblacion (Puerto Galera town) ⓦ badladz.com.

Capt'n Gregg's Sabang ⓦ captngreggs.com.

Garden of Eden Sabang ⓦ goeresort.com.

---

a/c rooms set around a central courtyard with pool, this hacienda-style development is as grand as it gets in White Beach. There's a dive centre on site. $\overline{PPP}$

Summer Connection ⓦ facebook.com/Summer Connection. At the attractive western end of the beach, *Summer Connection* has managed to retain much of its original charm despite having added a modern concrete block. The simple nipa huts at the back are the least expensive option, but there are also clean and functional standard rooms with a/c, cable TV, fridge and shower; deluxe rooms have hot water. Spotty wi-fi in public areas. $\overline{PP}$

ANINUAN, SEE MAP PAGE 227

Sunset at Aninuan Beach Resort ⓦ aninuanbeach.com. Right on the sand halfway along the beach, this marble-floor complex has tastefully styled a/c rooms which look out over the sea. The reef right in front of the resort is perfect for snorkelling, and there's a relaxing pool, open-air bar and a good restaurant. $\overline{PPP}$

Tamaraw Beach Resort ⓦ facebook.com/tamaraw beachresort. *Tamaraw* has an unbeatable location on the sand at the White Beach end of Aninuan, and pleasant rooms with balconies overlooking the sea, perfect for watching the sunset. The main building is an ugly motel-style box with simple, sparsely furnished rooms; the separate cottages are more appealing. They also do good, reasonably priced food, mostly salads and grills with rice. $\overline{PP}$

TALIPANAN, SEE MAP PAGE 227

Amami Beach Resort ⓦ amamibeachresort.com. Found in the centre of the beach, Amami Beach Resort offers accommodation in traditional-style rooms, cottages and even a tree house. The very helpful staff can arrange diving trips or outings to local sights. Food at the restaurant is good but a tad expensive. $\overline{P}$

Luca's ☎ 0916 417 5125. At the far end of the beach, *Luca's* has well-designed rooms with a/c, cable TV, fridge and hot water, plus genuine Italian food at the beautifully situated restaurant (see page 234). $\overline{PP}$

Mountain Beach Resort ☎ 0920 725 1058. In the middle of the beach, offering a good choice of rooms, from basic doubles to nipa huts with kitchens and cable TV, and a/c bungalows on the sand. $\overline{P}$

EATING

Restaurants are quite overpriced in the whole of the Puerto Galera area, so be prepared to pay more than you might be used to in other parts of the Philippines. Most of the area's resorts have their own simple restaurants, and in-hotel places are the only option at **Aninuan** and **Talipanan**. Outside of these, there are good restaurant scenes at **Sabang**, though the places here are generally more expensive, and at **White Beach**, which has some small-scale cafés and restaurants serving simple, relatively inexpensive food.

POBLACION (PUERTO GALERA TOWN), SEE MAP PAGE 229

Ocean Brew Muelle pier ☎ 0927 927 2361. Popular spot for a drink or light meal as you watch the boats come and go in the beautiful natural harbour. The menu includes tasty pizzas, burritos and toasted sandwiches. P̄

Robby's Cafeteria Calapan North Rd ☎ 0916 609 2502. Popular with tourists and locals, *Robby's* is one of Poblacion's many Italian restaurants. The menu features delicious pizzas and classic steaks. P̄P̄P̄

SABANG BEACH, SEE MAP PAGE 230

Relax ⓦ facebook.com/RelaxBarAndRestaurant. Tasty local dishes in a humble-looking venue festooned with flags – like an old-school go-go bar, but without the seediness. The *sisig*, curry and squid dishes are particularly recommended. P̄P̄

S One no phone. If you're in the mood for something a little different, give this Korean restaurant a try – not terribly authentic, and the dishes are hit and miss, but if you've made it as far as Mindoro you may be keen to tingle your tastebuds with some Korean spice. Give the BBQ a go, or the *jjigae* (broths). P̄P̄P̄

DAY-TRIPS AROUND PUERTO GALERA

MANGYAN VILLAGES AND MUSEUM

Two Mangyan villages (see box, page 236) are easily accessible from Puerto Galera, while others require a bit more effort in the form of some stiff uphill hiking, but are rewarded with a more genuine experience. To get the most out of your visit it's worth calling the **Oriental Mindoro Heritage Museum** in Calapan (see page 235), who can provide an interpreter and cultural etiquette tips. The **Baclaran Mangyan** village is just a thirty-minute walk from Poblacion, while the barangay of **Dulangan** is a short jeepney ride from Baco, 34km southeast of Puerto Galera.

TAMARAW FALLS

Off the main road to Calapan lie a number of caves and thundering waterfalls, and thirty minutes from Puerto Galera, in the barangay of Villaflor, the **Tamaraw Falls** (charge) is the mother of all cascades. Here cool mountain water plummets over a 132-metre precipice and into a natural pool and man-made swimming pool. The falls have become a popular sight (hence the entrance fee), so avoid going at the weekend, when they are overrun. Lots of travellers hire scooters or motorbikes in town to save the cost of a guided tour (and to spend more time at the falls). The cheapest option is to take the Calapan-bound jeepney at Poblacion and ask to get off at the falls, which are right beside the road (30min).

MOUNT MALASIMBO

One of the best day-treks is from White Beach into the foothills of **Mount Malasimbo** (1168m), where there are a number of Indigenous communities, as well as waterfalls with cold, clear pools big enough for swimming. To tackle the summit itself, pick up the trail at Talipanan Beach (take a tricycle) and through the Iraya Mangyan village just inland. Total trek time is around 5hrs for a reasonably experienced hiker (no permits necessary); watch out for leeches.

PYTHON CAVE AND HOT SPRINGS

This popular day-trek takes you 3km out of town along the Calapan road, from where a narrow, unsigned 2km trail leads up to the immense **Python Cave** through thick vegetation and piping-hot springs deep enough for a swim.

5

Tamarind ☎ 0956 693 4888. On the front at the western end of the beach, *Tamarind* is one of Sabang's most popular restaurants, offering tropical charm, wonderful ocean vistas and tasty international and Filipino dishes. The menu includes burgers and steaks. PP

★ **Tina's Restaurant** ☎ 043 287 3046. At the far eastern end of the beach, this is a pleasant little restaurant with chequered tablecloths, bamboo chairs and nice sea views, serving a range of Filipino, German and Asian dishes at reasonable prices, as well as breakfasts. The mango pancakes are exceptionally good. PPP

SMALL LA LAGUNA, SEE MAP PAGE 230

El Galleon El Galleon Beach Resort ⓦ asiadivers. com. Great views and good European and Filipino cuisine continue to make this a popular Small La Laguna choice; the French chef whips up dishes such as *coq au vin*, *quenelles*, *quiche lorraine* and *pot au feu*. They sometimes also offer themed buffet nights, such as Mongolian and Indian. PPP

★ **Verandah** Out of the Blue ⓦ outoftheblue.com.ph. Perched high above the beach, this is the best restaurant in Small La Laguna and serves salads, excellent Australian Wagyu beef steaks and pizzas, either in the tasteful wood-furnished interior or out on a breezy terrace overlooking the ocean. There's also a decent wine list. PPPP

WHITE BEACH, SEE MAP PAGE 227

Resto Veranda ⓦ restoveranda.com. This restaurant on the seafront is extremely popular, and not without reason: there's something for everyone on the extensive menu, which ranges from seafood and curries to burgers and pizzas, all cooked perfectly. PPP

TALIPANAN BEACH, SEE MAP PAGE 227

★ **Luca's Cucina Italiana** Luca's ☎ 0916 417 5125. Italian seems to be the order of the day in Puerto Galera, and few places are as good and as relaxed as *Luca's*. At the far western end of the beach at the resort of the same name, it's a tranquil spot with beachside views and authentic Italian food such as thin-crust pizzas and hearty pasta dishes with tangy tomato sauce. PPP

DRINKING

Most of the dive resorts in **Sabang** have their own bars where visitors tend to congregate at the end of the day for a beer, but outside of these, Sabang's night scene is dominated by go-go bars, and gets seedier as the night progresses. **White Beach** is lined with small-scale cafés and restaurants which serve Puerto Galera's trademark cocktail, the "**Mindoro Sling**" (basically a combo of rum, Sprite and various fruit juices). For something a bit more romantic and low-key, head to the resorts in **Aninuan**, most of which have good beach bars.

SMALL LA LAGUNA, SEE MAP PAGE 230

Bikini Floating Bar Off the beach ⓦ facebook.com/ bikinifloatingbar.sabangpuertogaleraphilippines/. The location on our map isn't wrong – as you may have deduced from its name, this bar is located a little way off shore, and accessible on small tenders from the pier. Given this location, the prices aren't actually that steep, and many choose to come here for a sunset meal and a drink afterwards.

The Point El Galleon Beach Resort ⓦ asiadivers.com. Though it's located on the headland between Sabang and Small La Laguna, this popular sunset drinks spot with amazing views is part of the *El Galleon* resort, with a huge cocktail list and food available from the hotel menu.

DIRECTORY

Banks and exchange Few of the ATMs in Puerto Galera accept foreign bank cards, and even when they do they're often out of cash; in addition, few local places take card, so it's best to bring enough pesos, or dollars, for your time here. The well-stocked Candava Supermarket at 62 P. Concepcion St changes dollars. The most reliable ATM in the area is the PBM one in Poblacion.

Clinics and pharmacies As well as a hospital in Poblacion, there are a number of other rudimentary clinics in town; if in doubt you can always ask the dive operators, who know where the best doctors are. There are also a few small pharmacies in town.

Police station The police station (☎ 043 281 4043) is inside the municipal compound.

Calapan

About 45km east of Puerto Galera, the busy port city of **CALAPAN** is the capital of Mindoro Oriental. It's not a tourist destination, depending for most of its livelihood on trade, but it has good transport connections and is the base for a trek up **Mount Halcon** (see box, page 235), supposedly the toughest mountain in the Philippines to climb. Calapan's main road is **J.P. Rizal Street**, which is only 500m long and runs past Calapan Cathedral south to Juan Luna Street.

CLIMBING MOUNT HALCON

Rugged **Mount Halcon** rears up dramatically from the coastal plain of Mindoro Oriental, 28km southwest of Calapan. At an altitude of 2586m, it's Mindoro's highest peak, and surrounded by some of the most extensive tracts of rainforest on the island. Conquering the summit is a major target of mountaineers from all over the globe, though in 2006 the trails found themselves officially closed. In 2013 hikes unofficially resumed, with the blessing of the local Mangyan community, though the situation remains confusing; it's currently only possible from Feb–May, with the mountain given a breather for the rest of the year. Don't even think about climbing Mount Halcon on your own – hire a Mangyan guide at **Bayanan**, just south of Calapan city.

Unusually for the Philippines, Halcon is not of volcanic origin, created instead by a massive geological uplifting millions of years ago. The total climb – the barangay of Dulangan and Halcon combined – is longer than that to the summit of Mount Everest from Base Camp; allow four to five days for the ascent and descent (the latter is possible in a day, if you're fast and in luck with the weather). There are many obstacles, not the least of which is the sheer volume of **rain** that falls on the mountain. There is no distinct dry season here and heavy rain is virtually a daily occurrence, resulting in an enormous fecundity of life – massive trees, dense layers of dripping moss, orchids, ferns and pitcher plants – but also making the environment treacherous and potentially miserable for climbers. Another irritation is the *limatik*, a kind of small leech that quietly clings to your boots and skin. You'll be sleeping on the mountain for at least three nights, so you will need to bring a tent and other equipment. Make sure you have good waterproof clothing and a waterproof cover for your backpack.

PRACTICALITIES

The lower slopes of Mount Halcon are about an hour from Calapan; to **get there**, take a jeepney to Baco, where you should register at the town hall. From Baco take a tricycle up an unsealed track to the barangay of Bayanan, where you pay a small charge to the barangay head and can organize guides. You can also approach the mountain from Puerto Galera, taking a jeepney for Calapan and getting off at the Baco turn-off. Alternatively, you can charter a van at Baco market to Bayanan. Fees for the climb should include **permit** and **guide fees** but exclude food and water, and there's an additional fee for entry to the trail. Check ⓦpinoymountaineer.com for up-to-date **information** on the ascent.

Oriental Mindoro Heritage Museum

Next to the cathedral, off Quezon Dr • Free

The **Oriental Mindoro Heritage Museum** took over from its predecessor, the Mangyan Heritage Center, as the place to go for an in-depth introduction to the culture of Mindoro's oft-misunderstood Mangyan peoples (see box, page 236). There's plenty to see in this attractive, well-laid-out facility, including local pottery and traditional clothing, plus weapons and handicrafts. If you're in luck, you can learn how to write your name in Mangyan script.

ARRIVAL AND INFORMATION   CALAPAN

By boat Arriving in Calapan by ferry from Batangas City (see page 114), the city centre is a 15min ride away by tricycle.

By bus and jeepney If you're heading for Puerto Galera, many resorts will send transport to meet you if you book and pay in advance. Otherwise you can take a jeepney (every 45min 6am–5pm; 1hr 30min) from the petrol station out beyond the Provincial Capitol building on J.P. Rizal St. Many of these jeepneys don't go as far as Sabang

or White Beach, so you'll need to change to tricycle or taxi at Poblacion (Puerto Galera town). For Roxas (3–4hr), jeepneys head out from the market, small buses leave from a terminal on the corner of Roxas and Magsaysay streets, and there are also minivans from the Angel Star terminal on Mabini St (every 15min daily 5am–5pm; ☎02 783 0886).

Tourist information The main tourist office for Mindoro Oriental is in the Provincial Capitol building on J.P. Rizal St (daily 9am–4pm; ☎043 288 5622).

5

THE MANGYAN

It's estimated that there are around one hundred thousand of Mindoro's original inhabitants, the **Mangyan**, left on the island, who have a way of life not much changed since they fought against the invading Spanish in the sixteenth century. With little role in the mainstream Philippine economy, the Mangyan, who divide into eight groups, subsist through slash-and-burn farming of taro and yams, a practice the elders insist on retaining as part of their culture despite the destruction it causes to forests.

You may well see Mangyan as you travel around the island, often wearing only a loincloth and machete and carrying produce for market, but if you want to actually visit them in their villages, it's best to go with a guide who can act as an interpreter. You can break the ice with gifts such as cigarettes, sweets and matches, but if you want to take photographs make sure you have permission. Treks to Mangyan villages are possible in several parts of the island (see box, page 233). Visit the Mangyan Heritage Center in Calapan (see page 235) for a more in-depth introduction to the culture.

ACCOMMODATION AND EATING

Accommodation options in Calapan don't set the pulse racing and most are located outside the centre. Note that **wi-fi** at the places listed below is sometimes only available in public areas, such as the lobby or the restaurant, and can be pretty unreliable. In terms of **eating**, a walk along the traffic-clogged length of J.P. Rizal St in town will take you past the usual fast-food outlets, including *Jollibee*, *Chowking* and *Mister Donut*.

Anahaw Island View Resort Brgy Balite ⓦ facebook. com/AnahawIslandViewResort. Located just west of the city, this resort offers simple native cottages with fan (or a/c for an extra charge), as well as cottages with or without hot tubs and deluxe rooms in the main building. There's a covered pool area and waterside restaurant, but there's not much of a beach and the water is quite dirty. P̄

Calapan Bay Hotel Nautical Hwy (Quezon Drive), Salong. Bright and clean a/c rooms with cable TV and hot water. There's also an atmospheric restaurant with a patio overlooking the ocean. P̄P̄

Parang Beach Resort Brgy Parang ⓦ parangbeach resort.com. Some 15min southeast of town, with a number of plain but comfortable and well-kept rooms in tin-roofed cottages right on the shore, plus a beachside restaurant. P̄P̄

DIRECTORY

Banks There are numerous banks with ATMs along J.P.Rizal St, including Metrobank (Mon–Fri 9am–5pm; ☎043 288 1985).

Immigration The immigration office (Mon–Fri 8–5pm; ☎043 288 2245), where you can extend visas, is on J. Luna St.

Roxas

Unless you just have a penchant for rough-road driving and are planning to head across the mountains to San José and beyond, the main reason for heading down the east coast to **ROXAS** is to take the ferry to Caticlan (for Boracay) or Romblon. Roxas is a busy town, with a lively **market** (Wed & Sun) and a few hotels and beach resorts with long, hot stretches of grey sand at **Dalahican Beach**, 5km along the coast from Dangay pier.

As ferries leave around the clock, there's really little reason to stay in Roxas unless you're too late to get onward transport to San José or Calapan. If you find yourself with a few hours to kill while waiting for a ferry, the best thing to do is to head for the Dalahican Beach resorts, which have day rates for non-guests (although most get very busy on weekends).

ARRIVAL AND DEPARTURE   ROXAS

By bus Buses and jeepneys run north and south from Roxas, leaving from near the market on Administration St, and from Dangay pier on the eastern edge of town. Heading north to Calapan is simple enough, and there are a series of minivan depots on Magsaysay St which operate cramped but speedy trips (3–4hr). A couple of jeepneys journey west over the mountains to San José (2hr) every morning.

By ferry Roxas is a key link on the Strong Nautical Highway route to Boracay, and there are regular ferries departing for Caticlan (4hr) from Dangay pier (best reached by tricycle from the market) with Starlite Ferries (ⓦstarliteferries. com).

INFORMATION

Tourist information There's a tourist office (Mon–Fri 8am–5pm; ☎ 043 289 2824) at the entrance to Dangay pier.

ACCOMMODATION AND EATING

Casa Gracia Catalina Beach ⓦ casagraciashotel.com. Both a good place to stay and a "garden" restaurant – all you really need if hunkering down in Roxas. Rooms are in A-frame huts that are pretty basic, though they do have a/c and private bathrooms. The restaurant is perhaps more appealing, serving a range of hot local dishes, plus *halo-* *halo* for dessert. PP

L.D. Ignacio's Island Resort Off Nautical Hwy ⓦ facebook.com/LDIGNACIORESORT. Clean, comfortable and smart, with rooms set around an attractive pool, this resort makes a good stab at being the best choice in town. The downside is that karaoke parties are not unknown. PP

DIRECTORY

Banks and exchange There are plenty of banks with ATMs here. There's a Mercury Drug pharmacy next to *Roxas* *Villa Hotel*, and a doctor's surgery at the *RL Ganan Hotel*.

South of Roxas

The coastal road south from Roxas trundles through **Mansalay** and on to the small town of **Bulalacao**, the jumping-off point for a bangka ride to some beautiful and remote islets, including Target, Aslom, Buyayao and **Tambaron Island**.

ARRIVAL AND DEPARTURE   SOUTH OF ROXAS

By bus The road between Bulalacao and San José is surfaced all the way, making the journey to the airport just 45min. Vans and jeepneys ply the coast north to Roxas (1hr) and Calapan (4–5hr), and across to San José.

By bangka From Bulalacao you can hire bangkas to the islands.

Mindoro Occidental

Aside from a few intrepid wildlife enthusiasts and divers around Sablayan, **Mindoro Occidental** remains wonderfully undiscovered, and travellers with flexible travel plans and a penchant for bumpy jeepney rides will have their efforts rewarded with wild jungle-covered mountains, remote beaches, and maybe meetings with a few local Mangyan people along the way.

San José on the southwest coast has the only functioning airport on Mindoro and makes a logical gateway for trips north to the fishing town of **Sablayan**, itself the jumping-off point for a sight no scuba diver should miss, the **Apo Reef Marine Natural Park**, a vast reef complex offering some of the best diving in the world. As well as organizing a trip from Sablayan, you can do so in advance at a dive shop in Manila (see page 84) or Busuanga (see box, page 378). Sablayan is also a base for a visit to the **Mounts Iglit-Baco National Park**, home to the tamaraw – a dwarf buffalo endemic to Mindoro and in acute danger of extinction – and to **Sablayan Watershed Forest Reserve**, a lowland forest with beautiful **Lake Libuao** at its centre. The northwest of the island is little-visited, though there are some unspoilt beaches around the town of **Mamburao**, the low-key capital of Mindoro Occidental.

San José

On Mindoro's southwest coast, the intensely sun-bleached and noisy port town of **SAN JOSÉ** is a quintessential Philippine provincial metropolis, with traffic-dense streets lined with pharmacies, cheap canteens and fast-food outlets. Travellers usually only see

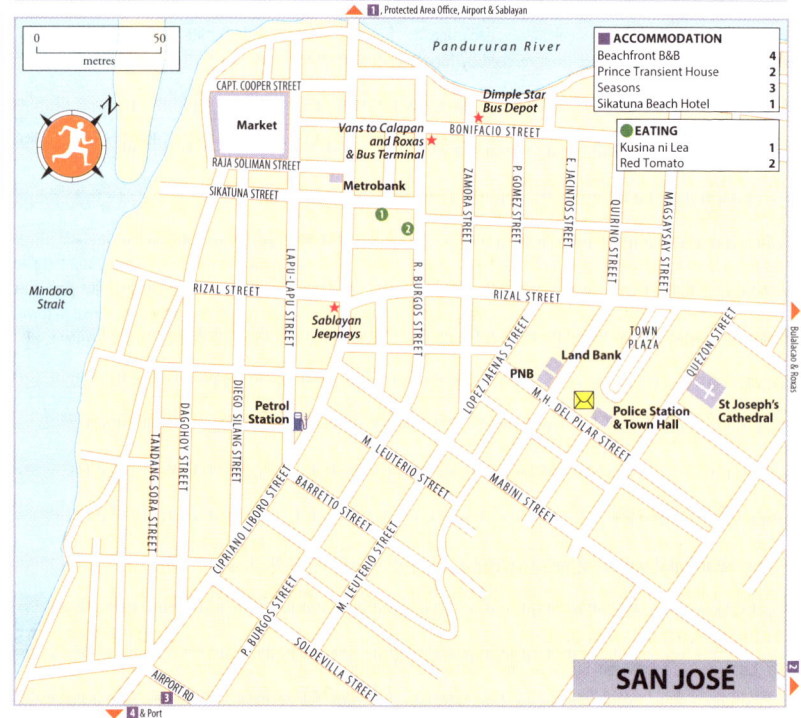

San José as they pass through on their way from the airport to Sablayan or the Mounts Iglit-Baco National Park (see page 240), for which permits can be obtained here. Though Apo Reef is close by, there are no major dive operators in town and it's best to organize a trip through the *Pandan Island Resort* (see page 241) or in Sablayan (see page 239).

San José is bounded on its northern edge by the **Pandururan River**, beyond which are the pier and the airport. Arriving by jeepney from Roxas, or bus from Sablayan, you'll find yourself on **Cipriano Liboro Street** in the west of town. From here it's a short walk (or tricycle ride) to the main thoroughfare, **Rizal Street**, which runs across town and turns into the National Highway in the east, where it runs inland to Magsaysay.

ARRIVAL AND DEPARTURE

SAN JOSÉ

By plane Northwest of town, San José Airport is a 20min tricycle ride from the centre; you could also take one of the private cars that act as airport taxis (fix the price before you get in). The airport is served by one daily flight from Manila (1hr) with Cebu Pacific, whose office is at the airport.

By boat Cheap flights have superseded boats to San José, and there's little benefit from taking a long-distance ferry here – in fact, in recent years it hasn't even been possible. One route worth checking out is the informal "Bunso boat" bangka service to Coron (see page 375; buy tickets from any agent in town), which leave 2–3 times per week; the trip is supposed to take 6hr but can take much longer. You must embark via a smaller boat from the beach in front of

central San José (for which there's another small charge).

By bus Buses leave from the depot on Bonifacio St for Sablayan (7 daily; 3hr), Mamburao (5–7hr) and Abra de Ilog (7hr), while vans for Calapan via Roxas leave from just outside the bus terminal on Bonifacio St (usually 2 daily; check the latest times in advance). All of these services continue on to Batangas by ferry, and then Manila by bus, but if you're not planning to stop anywhere along the way, it's almost as cheap (and obviously much quicker) to fly. If you want to reach Puerto Galera, you'll need to take a bus to Abra de Ilog, then a jeepney to the Abra de Ilog pier at Wawa on the north coast, and finally take (or charter) a bangka the rest of the way.

By jeepney Two or three jeepneys depart every morning (check in advance) from just south of Rizal St on C. Liboro for Sablayan (3–4hr) and Roxas (2hr).

INFORMATION

Permits and guides You can apply for a permit (free) and organize a local guide for Mounts Iglit-Baco National Park (you'll meet the guide at the park entry station) at the Protected Area Office (Mon–Fri 8am–4pm; ☎ 043 491 4200) in the LIUCP Building on Airport Rd.

ACCOMMODATION SEE MAP PAGE 238

Unless you arrive too late to move on, there's little reason to **stay** in San José, but if you find yourself with a night here, the choices are between out-of-the budget options in town, or spending a little more out at the beach on the edge of town in the barangay of San Roque.

Beachfront B&B Off Felix Y Manalo Ave ☎0960 381 3263. A stylish and modern place on the seafront, with friendly staff and a tasty breakfast, this is one of the best places to stay in town. The downside is that it's perhaps a little overpriced. P̄P̄P̄

Prince Transient House Mabini Extension ⓦfacebook. com/princetransienthouse. If you're just wanting a cheap and cheerful place to lay your head while waiting for a ferry, Prince Transient House is a good option. It's simple but clean, and offers a reasonable breakfast, though it is a bit of a walk from the centre. And yes, there's a typo in the Facebook address, which they may or may not correct in due course. P̄P̄

Seasons Airport Rd ⓦseasonshotelmindoro.com. Aiming for smart but landing on rather bland, this is nonetheless a decent enough choice for an overnight in San Jose. Noise carries quite easily, so ask for a quiet room away from the reception area. The restaurant isn't marvellous – it's probably better to eat elsewhere. P̄P̄

Sikatuna Beach Hotel Airport Rd, Brgy San Roque ⓦfacebook.com/sikatuna.beachotel. Pleasant beachside spot with friendly staff and simple, ageing rooms with cable TV (some with a/c look out to the ocean). It could do with renovation, and it's worth haggling for a lower rate and checking your room before paying. There's also a decent open-sided restaurant. P̄P̄

EATING SEE MAP PAGE 238

Sit-down **dining options** in San José principally revolve around the hotels, and of these the best options are the restaurants at *Sikatuna Beach Hotel*, *El Mora Hotel* and the canteen at the *Mindoro Plaza*.

Kusina ni Lea Sikatuna St ⓦfacebook.com/KNLSJOM. Inexpensive soups, sandwiches and local dishes in a traditional Filipino-style wooden dining hall, cooled by a/c. P̄P̄

Red Tomato Burgos St. The most notable eatery in town, serving "modern Italian" food, by which they mean rather substandard facsimiles of pizza, lasagne and the like. Not bad, though, and fairly priced. P̄P̄

DIRECTORY

Banks and exchange There are a number of banks, with ATMs, on Sikatuna St (at Liboro St).

Sablayan

A very bumpy 40km north of San José, the unhurried fishing town of **SABLAYAN** is the perfect jumping-off point for several nearby attractions, including Mounts Iglit-Baco National Park, the Sablayan Watershed Forest Reserve and Apo Reef. The town, small enough to cover on foot, has a central plaza (with free wi-fi) with a town hall, and a stretch of scrappy black-sand beach lined by bangkas.

ARRIVAL AND INFORMATION SABLAYAN

By bus There are buses and jeepneys north to Mamburao (3hr) and Abra de Ilog (4hr), and south to San José (3–4hr) from the bus station, which is at the southern edge of town on the National Highway. The pier is a 5min walk south of the bus station.

Tours, permits and guides To arrange permits for Mount Iglit-Baco National Park (free), guides and boats to North Pandan Island and the Apo Reef Marine Natural Park, head to the friendly Sablayan Eco-Tourism Office (Mon–Sat 8am–noon & 1–5pm; ⓦsablayan.net) in the town plaza.

ACCOMMODATION AND EATING

Camalig Restaurant National Hwy ☎0926 990 4573. A wide range of dishes from local seafood and sweet-

5

and-sour pork to noodles, burgers and pastas, as well as vegetable options such as steamed okra with fish sauce and mixed veg in oyster sauce. The restaurant is a 5min tricycle ride from the main plaza. PP

Gustav's Place Santo Niño ⓦgustavs-place.com. This simple Austrian-owned resort, a little out of town, has a number of cosy thatched bungalows in a palm-shaded garden by the seafront. There are two nipa huts with fan, as well as one standard fan bungalow and one deluxe air-con bungalow. There is also a simple restaurant. PP

Sablayan Adventure Camp Punta, Poblacion

ⓦsablayanadventurecamp.com. Out by the pier, this cheery establishment has spacious a/c rooms set in cottages looking out to the beach, although the walls dividing the rooms don't stretch to the ceiling, meaning you'll hear everything that your neighbours do. They also have a fairly basic restaurant and can arrange boats to Pandan. PP

Wency Amor C. Salvo St ⓦfacebook.com/WencyAmor Hotel. Housed in an attractive colonial-esque building, the Wency Amor is a smart and reasonably priced hotel with simple, clean rooms. The friendly staff can help arrange diving trips to Apo Reef. PP

Mounts Iglit-Baco National Park

The isolated and wonderfully raw jungles of **Mounts Iglit-Baco National Park** are dominated by the twin peaks of **Mount Baco** (2488m) and **Mount Iglit** (2364m). It can take up to two days of tough hiking to reach the peak of Mount Iglit, while the vegetation is so dense that there have been no officially recorded ascents of Mount Baco.

There are also a number of more leisurely treks through the foothills to areas in which you are most likely to see the endangered **tamaraw** (*Bubalus mindorensis*), a dwarf buffalo endemic to the island; numbers are small but steady, with annual headcounts usually finding around 500 individual animals in the wild. The tamaraw, whose horns grow straight upwards in a distinctive "V" formation, has fallen victim to hunting, disease and deforestation in the past, and to create more awareness of its plight there is talk of designating it the country's national animal. The Sablayan Eco-Tourism Office (see page 239) can advise on visits to the **Tamaraw Conservation Program**, known as the "Gene Pool Farm", a small laboratory where scientists are trying to breed the tamaraw in captivity.

Apart from tamaraw, the park is also prime habitat for the Philippine deer, wild pigs and other endemic species such as the Mindoro scops owl and the Mindoro imperial pigeon. It's also home to two **Mangyan** groups – the Tau-Buid and Buhid – some of whom you are likely to meet on guided hikes.

ARRIVAL AND INFORMATION   MOUNTS IGLIT-BACO NATIONAL PARK

By bus/jeepney Reaching the park by public transport from Sablayan means taking one of the regular buses or jeepneys south along the coastal road to the barangay of Popoy, then a jeepney up the bumpy and rutted track to the park itself.

Guided hikes To visit the park, you'll first have to secure a permit (free) and arrange a guide (charge), either in San José at the Protected Area Office (see page 239) or

the Sablayan Eco-Tourism Office (see page 239). Both of these offices can help put together all of the logistics for your trip, including camping options. Guided hikes usually include a 3hr stroll to the park bunkhouse (aka station 2) where you can stay the night, before the steep hike up to Mt Magawang (just above station 3; 2hr) where you should see the famed tamaraw (and can also spend the night).

Sablayan Watershed Forest Reserve

Entry permits (charge) must be secured from the Sablayan Eco-tourism Office in advance • Hire a vehicle and driver in Sablayan, or take a bus along the coastal road and ask to be dropped at the turn-off for the penal colony, near the town of Pianag; buses and jeepneys run from Pianag for the return trip

The **Sablayan Watershed Forest Reserve** is unusual among protected wilderness areas because it surrounds the **Sablayan Prison and Penal Farm**, a huge open "prison without bars" established in the 1950s and surrounded by agricultural lands worked by the prisoners. The inmates also produce handicrafts, and are distinguishable from the guards by their orange T-shirts, saying "minimum" or "medium", depending on their crime (maximum-security inmates are kept away from visitors).

Nearby are a number of villages where staff and prisoners' families live; beyond the last of these villages is a motorable track that ends at the edge of the dense **Siburan Rain Forest**, close to Lake Libuao and the largest lowland forest on Mindoro.

Both the forest and the whole reserve are superb **birdwatching** spots; you might see species such as the endangered bleeding-heat pigeon, serpent eagle and black-hood coucal; prisoners can act as guides, taking you to the best birding areas and pointing out individual species.

Lake Libuao

The entry permit for the Sablayan Watershed Forest Reserve (see page 240) includes access to the lake

Within the grounds of Sablayan Prison Farm, shallow and roughly circular **Lake Libuao** is covered in lotuses and alive with birds, including kingfishers, bitterns, egrets and purple herons. An undulating footpath around the shore makes for some wonderful walking, taking you through the edge of the forest and through glades from where there are views across the water; you'll see locals balanced precariously on small wooden bangkas fishing for tilapia. If you're reasonably fit you can walk round the lake in three hours, starting and finishing at the penal colony, though allow an hour to get between the colony and the main road.

North Pandan Island

Idyllic **North Pandan Island**, ringed by a halo of fine white sand, coral reefs and coconut palms, lies 2km off the west coast of Mindoro. In 1994 a sanctuary was established around the eastern half of the island so the **marine life** is exceptional; with a mask and snorkel you can see big grouper, all sorts of coral fishes and even the occasional turtle. Sharks are very rare, however.

The island is the site of the well-run *Pandan Island Resort* (see page 241), but is open to day guests from 8am to 6pm. On most days the resort's scuba-diving centre organizes day-trips to **Apo Reef** (see page 241), and longer overnight safaris both to Apo and to Busuanga, off northern Palawan (see page 378), if there are enough passengers. Even if you don't dive, there's plenty to keep you occupied on and around the island itself, including kayaking, jungle treks, windsurfing and sailing.

ARRIVAL AND DEPARTURE   **NORTH PANDAN ISLAND**

By boat If you want to visit the island for the day, contact the Sablayan Eco-Tourism Office (see page 239) who can arrange transport on the *Pandan Island Resort* bangka (charge); to get to the departure point, you need to take a tricycle to "Punta". Once there, the *Pandan Island Resort's* dive shop will kit you out for snorkelling or a "fun dive" (both chargeable). There's an additional "environmental fee"; guests at the resort also pay these fees.

ACCOMMODATION AND EATING

★ **Pandan Island Resort** ⓦ pandan.com. This well-run, back-to-nature private hideaway was developed by the French adventurer who "discovered" the island in 1986. As well as the budget rooms, there are standard double bungalows, larger bungalows for four and family houses for up to six. During the diving season (Nov–May) the island is so popular that all rooms are often taken, so it's important to book in advance. Guests are required to take at least one buffet meal at the resort restaurant every day, and this is no bad thing: the chef dishes up excellent European and Filipino cuisine (try the tangy fish salad in vinegar) and the beach bar serves some unforgettable tropical cocktails. Limited wi-fi available. PP

Apo Reef Marine Natural Park

Lying about 30km off the west coast of Mindoro, magnificent **Apo Reef Marine Natural Park** stretches 26km from north to south and 20km east to west, making it a significant marine environment and one of the world's great dive destinations. There are two main atolls, separated by deep channels, and a number of shallow

5

lagoons with beautiful white sandy bottoms. Only in three places does the coral rise above the sea's surface, creating the islands of Cayos de Bajo, Binangaan and **Apo**, the largest.

Apo Island is home to a ranger station and a lighthouse, and you can spend a magical night here in tents (turtles often lay eggs on the beach), though the experience comes at a price. The diving is really something special, with sightings of manta rays, sharks (even hammerheads), barracuda, tuna and turtles fairly common. Most of the Philippines' 450 species of coral are here, from tiny bubble corals to huge gorgonian sea fans and brain corals, along with hundreds of species of smaller reef fishes such as angelfish, batfish, surgeonfish and jacks.

ARRIVAL AND INFORMATION APO REEF MARINE NATURAL PARK

Fees Experiencing Apo Reef isn't cheap. For starters, everyone who visits needs to pay an "environmental fee": the fee for divers is larger than that for everyone else (including snorkellers). Transport by boat (1hr 30min from *Pandan Resort*) is extra, and you'll pay additional fees if you want to dive (as opposed to just snorkel).

Tours from Pandan Island Resort *Pandan Resort* rates for scuba-diving trips to Apo Reef depend on the boat and the number of people on it, which can range between two and eight: naturally, per-person prices are lower if there are more people on the boat, so it may be worth teaming up with other divers. Trips can include three dives plus equipment, or can involve an overnight expedition (costing

considerably more) for six dives plus equipment. If you just want to snorkel, prices for a day-trip to the reef (including environmental fees and food) also reduce if you have more people.

Tours from Sablayan You can visit the reef on one of the liveaboard trips offered by many dive operators in Coron Town in Busuanga (see box, page 378) or Manila, or organize a trip with the Sablayan Eco-Tourism Office in Sablayan (see page 239); these trips involve a ten-person boat out to the reef for a day-trip or overnight (snorkelling only). There is also a guide fee and an environmental fee, and you must bring your own food and drink.

The northwest

It's hard to believe that the quiet, relatively isolated west-coast town of **MAMBURAO**, 80km north along the coastal road from Sablayan, is the capital of Mindoro Occidental. With a population of around forty thousand, Mamburao is significant only as a trading and fishing town, although the coastal road is undeniably scenic, with blue ocean on one side and jungled mountains on the other. North of town there are some alluring stretches of white-sand **beach**, which is slowly being developed for tourism. The best of these is **Tayamaan Bay**, 4km north of Mamburao, where day-trippers can use the beach at the Tayamaan Beach Resort for a small charge.

North of Mamburao the road forks. From here, jeepneys and some buses head northwest along the coast to Palauan or northeast to **ABRA DE ILOG**, near the north coast; the journey to Abra de Ilog takes you past dazzling green paddy fields and farmland planted with corn. The easily motorable road ends at the Abra de Ilog pier at **Wawa**, 1km past Abra de Ilog, although the coastal track to Puerto Galera is a popular route with bike riders, and hikers have also made the trip.

ARRIVAL AND DEPARTURE THE NORTHWEST

By bus The most comfortable way to traverse the west coast is via the 4–5 daily bus services, which shuttle between Mamburao and San José (5–7hr), Sablayan (2–3hr) and Abra de Ilog (2hr), with connections to Batangas and Manila.

By boat From the Abra de Ilog pier at Wawa, the easiest way to get to Puerto Galera is to take a bangka. There are sometimes morning passenger bangka services, but don't be surprised if you end up having to charter your own (about 2hr).

ACCOMMODATION

There are a few accommodation options in the vicinity of Abra de Ilog, though none are truly reliable, and some

require a bangka ride (or long walk) from Abra pier.

5

MAMBURAO

La Gensol Plaza Hotel National Hwy ☎ 043 711 1072. No-frills hotel where the cheapest rooms are fan singles with tiny cold showers, though they also have larger, more comfortable doubles with a/c and cable TV. It enjoyed a renovation in 2022, which gave it a new lease of life. The attached restaurant offers decent burgers, pizza and pasta. P̄

The Western Visayas

A PARTICIPANT OF DINAGYANG FESTIVAL

The Western Visayas

The Visayas, a collection of large and small islands in the central Philippines, are considered to be the cradle of the country. The western half of this sprawling group contains an absorbing array of islands of all sizes, which offer everything from powdery beaches and dazzling coral reefs to thickly forested mountains. This spectrum of natural assets provides superb opportunities for diving, snorkelling and other watersports, as well as great hiking. There are also a few surprisingly pleasant towns where you can enjoy small-scale urban life.

The jewel in the crown of **the Western Visayas** is undoubtedly **Boracay**, which though diminutive in size utterly dwarfs the larger islands surrounding it in terms of its touristic profile. By contrast, the **Romblon** group to the north and sizeable **Panay** to the south are far less visited, although the latter is home to the country's liveliest festival, **Ati-Atihan**. Yet further south, the largest island of **Negros**, famed for sugar-cane production, has a varied assortment of attractions and is conveniently located between the smallish but enticing islands of **Guimaras** and **Siquijor**, both favourites of the discerning traveller. Wherever you go in this region, the locals are invariably welcoming and more than happy to assist you in having a great time.

As with the whole of the Visayas, those who live in the western half are quite a diverse bunch. Visayan is the umbrella **language** group in the Visayas, the most widely spoken form of which is Cebuano (see box, page 301), the native language of Cebu. Cebuano has an audible presence in eastern Negros and Siquijor, due to their proximity to Cebu. The language with most speakers in the westernmost regions is Ilongo, although Panay has tongues as diverse as Aklan, Karayan and Kuyan; all contain elements of Malayo-Polynesian. Even the modest-sized islands of Romblon are home to several linguistic varieties. This diversity of languages is a symptom of the region's fractured topography; many of these islands are culturally and economically isolated from those around them.

Boracay

Some 350km south of Manila, and just off the northeastern tip of Panay, the island of **BORACAY** is famed for the picture-perfect **White Beach**, a quality dining and wild nightlife scene, plus activities from scuba diving to kitesurfing. It may be only 7km long and 1km wide at its narrowest point, but Boracay has over thirty beaches and coves, and enough accommodation options to suit all budgets. Watching the graceful *paraws* (sailing boats) setting sail at sunset is worth the journey on its own.

Though Boracay is popular with domestic tourists, they are heavily outnumbered by foreigners, both on package and independent holidays; this gives the island a strong international feel. For all its beauty, Boracay is far and away the most developed island resort in the Philippines, a situation which has its downsides – it can be hard to relax with the constant blare of music on the beach and the hum of tricycles on the island's main road. Many resort owners are aware of how fragile the island is and organize beach clean-ups and recycling seminars. The authorities have finally woken up to some of the island's problems, and threats to demolish resorts that have been built without permission have actually come into effect, plus a beach **smoking ban** has been in force for several years. In 2018, the island was entirely closed to tourists for six months to facilitate renovations and clean-up: the loss of business for resorts was not helped by the enforced closure during the Covid-19 pandemic two years later. Even so, most

Highlights

❶ Boracay Though overdeveloped, Boracay's White Beach is still one of the best anywhere, with great dining and nightlife; and there's so much to do, you'll never be bored. See page 246

❷ Romblon This little-visited island group includes relaxed Romblon Town and challenging Mount Guiting Guiting on neighbouring Sibuyan. See page 256

❸ Ati-Atihan Festival, Kalibo The biggest bash in the Philippines: wild costumes and copious food and drink. See page 271

❹ Silay Stay in the converted mansions of sugar barons and visit a sugar-cane factory in Silay. See page 279

❺ Mount Kanlaon National Park Active volcano at the centre of dense forest offering some extreme trekking and climbing. See page 281

❻ Sugar Beach Negros' most delightful strip of sand is a superb place to unwind and a good jumping-off point for magnificent Danjugan Island. See page 282

❼ Apo Island Robinson Crusoe-esque hideaway off Negros, with excellent diving. See page 289

❽ Siquijor Very laidback island with a reputation for sorcery and a fine balance between gentle commercialization and unspoilt natural beauty. See page 291

HIGHLIGHTS ARE MARKED ON THE MAP ON PAGE 248

resorts have weathered the storm, and Boracay is once again welcoming tourists.

Note that, for all the hordes of visitors hell-bent on partying, locals are keen to keep the island a family destination; overt public displays of affection are discouraged, and **topless sunbathing** is only tolerated in quiet parts of the less frequented beaches.

White Beach

To many visitors, the 4km talcum-powdery sand strip of **White Beach** *is* Boracay, and while the carnival of activities, touts and tourists is hardly an accurate representation of Philippines beach life, it is certainly fun. A short walk along the beach takes you past restaurants serving a veritable United Nations of cuisines, including Greek, Indian, Caribbean, French, Thai and more. The beach is also dotted with interesting little bars and bistros, some of them no more than a few chairs and tables on the beach, others where you can sit in air-conditioned luxury eating Chateaubriand and smoking Cuban cigars.

Not so long ago, bangkas from Caticlan would pull up directly to White Beach, at one of three **boat stations**. Though the stations themselves have disappeared, their names continue to be used to describe the three respective segments of the beach. The smartest places to stay are mostly towards the quieter far north section of the beach, beyond Boat Station 1. To the south in Boat Station 2 the lively heart of the beach focuses on **D'Mall**, a warren of outdoor lanes and one main street, which is packed with cafés and shops. Things gradually quieten down as you move south towards Boat Station 3, where there's a clutch of budget accommodation set back from the beach.

Around the island

Most visitors fall in love with White Beach, but you shouldn't leave out **Puka Beach** on the north coast, so named for its famous shiny white seashells (*puka*). A pleasant way to get there is to hire a bangka on White Beach, and then take a tricycle back.

BORACAY

● EATING	
Barlo	2
Congas	4
Indigo	3
Red Apol	1

■ ACCOMMODATION	
Cocoloco	8
Crimson Resort & Spa	3
Discovery	6
The Lazy Dog B&B	7
The Lind	5
Microtel	4
Oasis Resort & Spa	2
Shangri-La	1
Shore Time Dormitel	10
Signature Boracay	9

6

Immediately north of White Beach sits the little village of **Diniwid** with its 200m beach, accessible from White Beach on a path carved out of the cliffs. At the end of a steep path over the next hill is the tiny **Balinghai Beach**, enclosed by walls of rock. On the other side of the island, **Bulabog Beach** has developed from a small fishing village into a popular kitesurfing destination.

Around 500m north of Bulabog Beach, Mount Luho is an easy ascent. The tallest point on the island (though only about 100m high), it affords terrific 360-degree views of the island and neighbouring Romblon. On the northeast side of Boracay, **Ilig-Iligan Beach** has coves and caves, as well as thick jungle, which is full of flying fox fruit bats.

ARRIVAL AND DEPARTURE   BORACAY

Travelling to and from Boracay has never been easier, and long-distance **ferries** here have largely been superseded by countless **flights**. Unless you're coming from Carabao Island in the Romblon group, all visitors must pass through the hectic little town of **Caticlan**, from where frequent bangkas shuttle visitors across to **Cagban pier** in the south of Boracay (15min). Boats run day and night, with night trips costing slightly more; whatever time you travel, you'll also need to pay an environmental fee and a boat terminal fee as well as the boat fare. From Cagban it's just a short tricycle journey to White Beach or you can jump in a shared van. If you're flying in and have booked to stay at one of the pricier resorts, you might be met at the airport by a hotel representative.

By plane Caticlan airport – also known as Boracay airport, and often written that way on departure boards – connects the island with Manila, Cebu and a few other domestic destinations, as well as some charter flights from abroad.

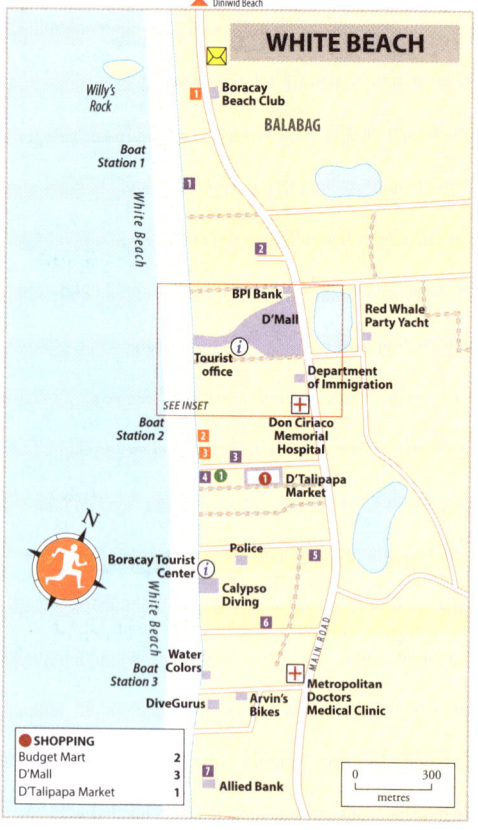

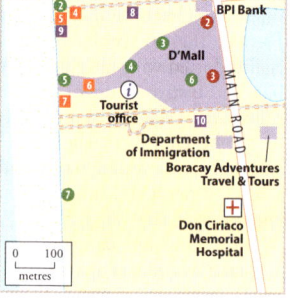

■ ACCOMMODATION

Bamboo Bungalows	9
Fat Jimmy's	10
Frendz Resort & Hostel	2
Hue Resort	5
Monallan Boracay Hotel	7
The Muse	1
Nigi Nigi Nu Noos 'e' Nu Nu Noos	4
Ocean Breeze Inn	6
Seabird Resort	8
The Tides	3

● EATING

Aria	5
Cyma	6
Hobbit Tavern	3
I ♥ Backyard BBQ	1
Lemoni Café	4
Munimuni	2
Real Coffee and Tea Café	7

■ DRINKING & NIGHTLIFE

Coco Bar	5
Epic	7
Exit Bar	4
Paraw Beach Club	1
The Poodle Bar	6
Summer Place	3
Wave Bar & Lounge	2

● SHOPPING

Budget Mart	2
D'Mall	3
D'Talipapa Market	1

WET SEASON ON BORACAY

The two distinct **climatic seasons** in the Philippines have a marked effect on Boracay. Because of the island's north–south orientation, White Beach takes the brunt of onshore winds during the wet season (June–Oct), so don't expect it to look at its well-barbered best at that time. The waves can be big, washing up old coconuts, seaweed and dead branches. Many beachfront resorts and restaurants are forced to erect unsightly tarpaulins to keep out the wind and sand, and some even close during July and August, the wettest months. The onshore wind makes for some thrilling windsurfing and kitesurfing, but other ocean activities move to calmer waters on the island's east side.

6

The airport is a 3min tricycle ride from the ferry terminal, or you can walk it in less than 10min. Note that there's another airport 75km to the east – Kalibo (see page 269), which also has a handful of flights to other Asian countries (see page 269).

Destinations Cebu (3–7 daily; 1hr); Clark (1 daily; 1hr); Davao (2 weekly; 1hr 35min); El Nido (1 daily; 1hr 10min); Manila (1–3 hourly; 1hr 10min).

By boat From Mindoro there are regular Starlite (w starliteferries.com) ferries from Roxas to Caticlan, and less-regular ones from Batangas; 2GO also run the latter route. For Romblon there are slow bangkas from Caticlan to Looc on Tablas, plus a car ferry to Odiongan. Alternatively, you can negotiate with a boat captain on White Beach to take you to Carabao, and then travel onwards to the main island group.

Destinations Batangas (2 daily; 10hr); Looc (on Tablas; 2 daily; 4hr); Odiongan (5 weekly; 3hr); Roxas (on Mindoro; 6 daily; 4hr).

By bus and van Buses drop you on the main road through Caticlan, about 1km from the pier and airport, from where there are tricycles to take you the rest of the way. Many vans from Kalibo (particularly from the airport) will take you all the way to the ferry pier.

Destinations Iloilo (hourly until 4pm; 6hr); Kalibo (every 10–15min; 1 hr 30min); San José (6 daily; 3hr 30min).

GETTING AROUND

By tricycle Tricycles (including an ever-increasing number of electronic ones) are easy to pick up for a trip along the length of the island's main road – make sure you agree a fare before you climb on board as some drivers have a habit of adding "extras" at the end of the journey.

By bangka You can hire four- to six-person bangkas or *paraw* by the hour.

By scooter Many resorts and a number of outlets on the main road rent scooters.

INFORMATION

Tourist information The Department of Tourism has a small, ineffectual tourist office (☎ 036 288 3689) in D'Mall, on the right-hand side as you enter from the beach. A few minutes' walk to the south, the Boracay Tourist Center (daily 9am–10pm) is far more useful.

Listings The *Boracay Sun* (w boracaysunnews.com), , plus *Boracay Info Guide* (w boracayinfoguide.com) and *Boracay Beach Guide* (w boracaybeach.guide), have the latest details of what's new and happening in Boracay.

ACCOMMODATION   SEE MAPS PAGES 249 AND 250

There are hundreds of **places to stay** on little Boracay, which means that except at peak times (Christmas, Easter and Chinese New Year, when prices can rise by as much as fifty percent) you should be able to find a room simply by taking a stroll down White Beach. Rates can be extravagant, with the best rooms in high-end places going for sky-high sums, but there are still cheapies out there, especially away from the beach. Broadly speaking, the beach is divided into three sections: **Boat Station 1 and north** is high end, **Boat Station 2 and around** is generally mid-range, while the lanes behind the beach **south of Boat Station 3** hold a selection of budget backpacker options, plus a smattering of mid-range and high-end places. At the mid-to-upper end, there are usually great advance online deals, and budget places will often give decent discounts for longer stays or at slack times.

WHITE BEACH

BOAT STATION 1 AND POINTS NORTH
★ **Discovery** At the northern end of White Beach, beyond Boat Station 1 w discoveryboracay.com. At the upper end of Boracay's price spectrum, *Discovery Shores* features bright, spacious and ultramodern rooms and suites stretching back up the hill behind the beach. All rooms are luxurious and contain an impressive array of amenities,

6

BORACAY'S ACTIVITY BONANZA

Boracay has the biggest range of **activities** to be found anywhere in the Philippines. In addition to the sports below, there are numerous dive sites and operators (see box, page 254).

KITESURFING AND WINDSURFING

Windsurfing has been popular in Boracay since the 1990s, and more recently the **kitesurfing** boom has seen the island emerge as one of the world's premier locations for this sport. Boarders gather on Bulabog Beach to take advantage of the constant wind during the peak season, while in the off-season the focus shifts to White Beach. There are a number of schools offering both windsurfing and kitesurfing equipment rental and lessons (see below) covering everything from basic introductory classes to full-blown courses.

OTHER WATERSPORTS

Other watersports on offer include **jet-skiing**, **waterskiing**, **banana boat rides**, **boat hire** (on both sailing boats and speedboats), **glass-bottom boat rides**, **fly-fishing**, **ocean kayaking** (including a completely translucent "Crystal" kayak), **parasailing** and even **mermaid swimming** (yes, you read that correctly – stick on a mermaid tail and take to the ocean).

For a true adrenaline experience, you can try **flyboarding**, which involves a jet propulsion tube sending riders several metres above the water. More natural highs can be achieved by **cliff diving** at Ariel's Point, a thirty-minute boat ride away from White Beach; trips can include transport, lunch, and unlimited beers (though not before the diving).

LAND SPORTS

On land, the choices are equally extensive. Take your pick from: **quad biking**; **golf** at Fairways & Bluewater, Newcoast (ⓦfairwaysandbluewater.com); **horseriding** in Balabag; **ziplining** at Mount Luho; **zorbing**; and **mountain biking**. One of the nicest rides is to cycle from Punta Bunga to Tambisaan Beach, where the shoreline is dotted with installation art, including the famous Boracay Sandcastle. Up in the air you can get great views from even a ten-minute **helicopter ride**.

TIBIAO ACTIVITIES

Several hours away at **Tibiao** (see page 267), on the Panay mainland, are a host of adrenaline-inducing options including **whitewater kayaking**, **canyoning**, **trekking** and more **ziplining**: excursions here from Boracay can be arranged through Tribal Adventures (see below).

OPERATORS

You'll find **touts** offering almost all of the activities above along the beach, but for specialist activities it's best to head direct to the operators.

Boracay Adventures Travel & Tours 2/F Sunflower Resort ⓦboracayadventures.com. Offers the usual activities, plus tours in other parts of the Philippines. They'll get you on an ATV tour, on a "UFO" in the sea, and more besides.

Hangin Kite Center Bulabog Beach ⓦhangin kitecenter.com. One of the best-established kitesurfing schools offering rental, storage, lessons and more. There are beginner lessons and various courses up to the full one with IKO Certification. The scene shifts to White Beach from May–Oct.

Isla Kitesurfing & Wingfoiling School Bulabog Beach ⓦislakitesurfing.com. Kitesurfing and wingfoiling specialists who offer lessons from beginner to pro.

Red Whale Party Yacht Balabag Lake ⓦredwhale. ph. One of the most popular activities on Boracay in recent years – no real balance or command of the waves required, until perhaps you've had one too many.

Tribal Adventures Boracay Sandcastles ⓦtribaladventures.com/adventure-packages. Another popular option for kayaking and rafting.

which include espresso machines, smart TVs and desks suitable for work. The premier rooms have an expansive outdoor living area with a large jacuzzi and views down to the sea. There's also a pool, bar, two superb restaurants (see page 255) and a spa. **PPPP**

Frendz Resort & Hostel 100m towards the beach from Main Rd ⓦfrendzresorthostels.com. Tucked halfway between the beach and main road, the simple cottages at *Frendz* present no-frills laidback living. The native huts have double beds, hot and cold showers and nice verandas. There are also separate male and female dorms (a/c and fan) and a café with wi-fi. Bring a padlock for your locker. **PP**

★ **The Lind** At the northern end of White Beach, beyond Boat Station 1 ⓦthelindhotels.com. A relative newbie on what is still often called "Friday beach", despite the demise of the resort bearing that name; this is a highly swanky replacement, with smart rooms – most with sizeable balconies – gazing inwards towards a quirkily-shaped swimming pool, which itself gazes outwards to a pristine stretch of beach, and the sea beyond. The restaurant and other facilities are also top-notch. **PPPP**

The Muse On the beachfront, Boat Station 1 ⓦthemuse boracay.com. Dazzling white marble luxury hotel, with a snazzy lobby and spacious, comfortable rooms arranged around the rectangular pool. The rooms themselves feature toothpaste-white linens and light pine furniture, plus mini-bars and cable TVs. There is also a café, roofdeck and spa. **PPP**

BOAT STATION 2 AND AROUND

★ **Bamboo Bungalows** Just north of D'Mall ⓦbamboo bungalowboracay.com. Great choice in the heart of the action, a stone's throw from D'Mall. There's a range of cottages and apartments set around the lush garden, and some rooms at the front of the main building with beach views. Discounts off the rack rate are always available. **PPP**

Fat Jimmy's 200m inland, south of D'Mall ⓦfat jimmysresort.com. One of a number of budget resorts along a path next to D'Mall. Relaxed, quiet and friendly, *Fat Jimmy's* has sixteen simple but charming fan or a/c rooms, five of which have their own small patio garden. Family rooms sleep four with a bunk bed for the kids and rates include a choice of Filipino or American breakfast. **PP**

Hue Resort Down the footpath beside the Tourist Center ⓦboracay.thehuehotel.com. Leafy, good-value, comfortable hotel that's close to the beach but away from the noise of the bars and clubs. Three levels of rooms curl around a pool that usually has at least some shade, and atop facilities including a restaurant and bar. **PPP**

Nigi Nigi Nu Noos 'e' Nu Nu Noos 5min walk north of the Boracay Tourist Center ⓦniginigi.com. Long-standing and enduringly popular White Beach guesthouse featuring Indonesian-style cottages set in tranquil tropical gardens. All of the spacious cottages have thatched pagoda

roofs and shady verandas. Also has a decent, very popular bar-restaurant. Breakfast and mineral water included. **PPP**

Seabird Resort Set back from the beach a short walk north of D'Mall ⓦfacebook.com/seabirdresort. An oldie but a goodie, *Seabird* continues to renovate to keep up with the new crowd and offers a range of rooms set in pleasant and quiet gardens just a minute's walk back from the beach. Good coffee, pancakes, breakfasts and fish in the restaurant. **PP**

The Tides Just south of D'Mall ⓦtidesboracay.com. The centrally located Tides impresses with its lovely friendly staff and spacious comfortable rooms. There's a pool and a bar on the roof, making it a great place to watch the sunset. **PPP**

BOAT STATION 3 AND POINTS SOUTH

Cocoloco At the southern end of the beach ⓦcocoloco boracay.com. A long-established hotel, Cocoloco has years of experience, with the result that the team here really know what tourists are looking for. Many of the comfortable rooms offer sea views, there's a great bar and restaurants, and watersports activities can be arranged. **PPP**

Monallan Boracay Hotel Inland from the southern end of the beach ⓦmonallan.com. A homey spot a couple of minutes' walk from White Beach, Monallan is a decent hotel with friendly staff, comfy rooms and a relaxing shared lounge, but it's hard to escape the conclusion it's a little expensive compared to similar hotels at Boracay. **PPP**

Ocean Breeze Inn Just inland, a few mins' walk south of Boracay Tourist Center ⓦoceanbreezeinn.info. You can choose between a/c rooms in the pleasant sky-blue painted house or the more humble but airy nipa huts (fan) in the adjacent plot. Wi-fi in the house only. **PP**

Shore Time Dormitel Main Road ⓦshoretime hotelboracay.com/home. Among the cheapest places you'll find on Boracay, Shore Time Dormitel offers comfy beds in clean dormitories with shared bathrooms. Breakfast costs extra, and it's a short walk to the beach, but if you just want a bed for the night, it's absolutely perfect. **P**

Signature Boracay At the southern end of the beach, next to Cocoloco ⓦfacebook.com/signature boracaysouthbeach. One of the best options in this price range, an attractive small hotel on the seafront, offering comfortable and clean if not enormously exciting bedrooms, with curiously space-age toilets in the en-suites. The better rooms have beach-facing balconies affording gorgeous sunset views. **PP**

ELSEWHERE ON BORACAY

Crimson Resort & Spa Punta Bunga Rd ⓦcrimsonhotel. com/boracay. A great choice for a splurge, Crimson sits in a prime location above Punta Bunga Beach, and comes with top-notch amenities and service. The pool is enormous, there's a selection of excellent restaurants, the spa is marvellous, and if you can tear yourself away from all that, it's easy to arrange watersports and boat rides. The only

6

6

DIVING AROUND BORACAY

Boracay's diving isn't as varied or extreme as diving in Palawan or Puerto Galera, but there's still enough to keep everyone happy. The dive sites around the island, all easily accessible by bangka, include gentle drift dives, coral gardens and some deeper dives with a good chance of encounters with sharks. At **Crocodile Island**, fifteen minutes southeast of Boracay, there's a shallow reef that drops off to 25m and a number of small canyons where sea snakes gather. **Big and Small Laurel** are neighbouring islets with some of the best soft coral in the Visayas and shoals of snappers, sweetlips, eels, sea snakes, morays, puffers and boxfish. Probably the star attraction for divers here is **Yapak**, where you freefall into the big blue, eventually finding at 30m the top of a marine wall where there are batfish, wahoo, tuna, barracuda and cruising grey reef sharks. **Lapu Wall** is a day-trip from Boracay to the northern coast of Panay, but the diving is some of the most challenging in the area, with overhangs and caverns. Another good day-trip is north to Carabao Island (see page 259), in the province of Romblon, where there are splendid reefs, some peaceful, powdery beaches and a resort if you want to stay overnight.

DIVE OPERATORS

There are dozens of licensed dive operators along White Beach, offering introductory sessions with a dive master and a full PADI **Open Water Course** (3–4 days). Of the countless dive operators on the island, the following are well established and PADI five-star rated:

Calypso Diving Boat Station 2 ⓦ calypso-boracay.com.

DiveGurus Boat Station 3 ⓦ divegurus.com.

Fisheye Divers Boat Station 1 ⓦ fisheyediversboracay.com.

Water Colors Boat Station 3 ⓦ watercolors.ph.

---

downside is that you're a little way from the centre of the action at White Beach. **PPPP**

The Lazy Dog B&B Bulabog Beach ⓦ lazydogboracay.com. With an emphasis on sustainability, the Lazy Dog is one of the best places in Boracay to experience some genuine Filipino hospitality – and meet some outstandingly friendly dogs. Make sure you have at least one meal here – the food is excellent and extremely generous. **PP**

Microtel Brgy Vapak ⓦ wyndhamhotels.com. A small and attractive hotel in a quieter part of town, this *Wyndham* hotel offers simple rooms, some of which come with basic kitchen facilities. There's a little pool, and a decent restaurant on-site. It's just a short walk down to Diniwid Beach. **PP**

Oasis Resort & Spa On the road to Ilig-Iligan Beach

ⓦ facebook.com/oasisresortandspa. If you're truly looking to get away from the hustle and bustle of White Beach, *Oasis* – on the northeast corner of the island – is a good choice. With easy access to the comparatively little-visited Ilig-Iligan Beach, it's a quiet, peaceful and good-value place to stay. The downside is that the facilities aren't as good as most places on Boracay, and you'll probably want to head into town to eat. **PP**

Shangri-La Brgy Vapak ⓦ shangri-la.com. Perched above its own private beach, the *Shangri-La* presents a range of attractively styled rooms and villas which blend comfortably into the lush hills. Service is top-notch, and all of the facilities typical of the chain are on offer, along with nature trails and a dive centre. The palatial Presidential Villa is staggering, both in terms of décor and cost. **PPPP**

EATING

SEE MAPS PAGES 249 AND 250

Boracay has a more diverse dining scene than most cities in the Philippines, and even in a two-week stay you can only sample a fraction of the options. Many restaurants are listed in the local info booklet *My Boracay*, which has meal discount vouchers. As well as the listings below there are also plenty of **local vendors** who set up barbecues on the beach at sundown to cook everything from fresh lapu-lapu and squid to tasty local bananas sprinkled with muscovado sugar. Conversely, the big international chains also have a noticeable presence. A **cautionary note**: be wary of the big seafood buffet places on the seafront, as sometimes the fish isn't quite as fresh as it appears and can cause stomach problems.

CAFÉS

★ **Lemoni Café** D'Mall ⓦ facebook.com/Lemonicafe. Boracay. Terrific bright and airy little café. Breakfast items include eggs Benedict and delicious coconut pancakes. For lunch or dinner there's outstanding pan-fried mahi-mahi with warm potato salad and lemon butter garlic sauce, lemon and thyme roast chicken with sautéed potatoes and a range of lemon desserts. Drinks range from refreshing calamansi juice to "lemonijito" and other cocktails. **PP**

Munimuni Boat Station 2 ⓦ facebook.com/munimunibora. A great spot on the beachfront, offering decent coffee and a small menu of Mexican-inspired dishes.

The interior is pretty funkily decorated, but you're more likely to want to sit outside and take in the views. $\overline{\text{PP}}$

Real Coffee and Tea Café Boat Station 2 ⓦfacebook. com/originalrealcoffeeandteacafe. The upstairs location overlooking the beach is pleasantly removed from the hubbub. The bamboo interior harks back to a simpler time when this was the first "real" coffee on the beach. Good breakfasts, as well as a great selection of teas (try the punchy ginger tea) and cookies. Make sure to try the delicious calamansi muffins. $\overline{\text{PP}}$

RESTAURANTS

Aria Beach entrance to D'Mall ⓦaria.com.ph. This popular Italian place offers attractive alfresco dining under the palms. Pizzas and pastas are reliably good, and coffee and desserts are available from neighbouring *Café del Sol*. $\overline{\text{PP}}$

Barlo At the Two Seasons Resort, north of Station 1 ⓦtwoseasonsresorts.com/boracay/dining. The *Barlo Lounge* has acquired a reputation for serving up the best four-cheese pizza to be found in Boracay – go along to see if you believe the hype. The menu also includes a similarly famous sizzling oyster *sisig*, delicious curries, and excellent *lechon* (crispy pork). $\overline{\text{PPP}}$

Congas Road 1-A, east of Balabag Lake ⓦfacebook. com/Congasrestaurantboracay. Excellent and authentic Thai dishes are served up at this small place a little way from the centre. There's a lot to choose from on the menu, but it's hard to go wrong with the classic Thai green curry, and the

pad thai comes highly recommended too. $\overline{\text{PP}}$

Cyma D'Mall ⓦcymarestaurants.com. The owners may not be Greek, but *Cyma* serves the best tzatziki in Boracay in a tiny but boldly decorated restaurant. Delicious *horiatiki* (Greek salad), chicken souvlaki and baklava are also on the menu, and it's worth checking the specials board. $\overline{\text{PP}}$

Hobbit Tavern D'Mall ⓦfacebook.com/HobbitTavern Boracay. Western-themed restaurant serving large portions of roulade and burgers, as well as juicy steaks. Live country and folk music at lunchtime and in the evening. Free wi-fi. $\overline{\text{PP}}$

I ♥ Backyard BBQ D'Mall ☎036 288 6980. Brightly lit, reliable local joint serving whole roast chicken to a carnivorous crowd, as well as other good barbecue options such as ribs and grilled squid. $\overline{\text{PP}}$

Indigo Discovery Shores, north of Boat Station 1 ⓦdiscoveryshoresboracay.com. The place to come for a splurge, with tables on the sand and in the suave interior. Classy dishes such as blackened grouper or mussel Madras curry are great choices, or you could splash out on a US Angus steak. Creative set menus are also available. The hotel's *Sands* and *Forno Osteria* restaurants are also good, but less costly. $\overline{\text{PPP}}$

Red Apol On the main road, just off Puka Beach, ☎036 288 6705. This humble restaurant is nothing fancy, but people go back for its delicious fresh seafood, which includes garlic prawns with buttered honey, and tangy *sinigang* soup with the catch of the day. Head here for a lazy lunch if you're in the Puka Beach area. $\overline{\text{PP}}$

DRINKING AND NIGHTLIFE

SEE MAP PAGE 250

Nightlife in Boracay starts with drinks at sunset and continues all night. Hard-core partiers don't warm up until around midnight, with many dancing and drinking until sunrise. As well as the listings below, there are countless other options which range from upscale resort bars to beach shacks.

BARS

Coco Bar Red Coconut Resort, Boat Station 2 ⓦfacebook. com/CocoBarInBoracay. This loud and lively bar serves cocktails and bills itself as a "husband daycare centre".

Exit Bar Next to Coco Bar ⓦfacebook.com/EXIT.Bar. Boracay. Popular and friendly, with well-priced drinks and occasional DJ sets, the *Exit Bar* is a lively spot that keeps going until the early hours.

The Poodle Bar D'Mall ☎036 288 5553. An unexpectedly cute little cocktail bar in the mall; don't expect anything too fancy, but the cocktails are fine, and every now and then a guitar comes out.

Summer Place 200m south of D'Mall ☎036 288 3144.

U-shaped bar facing the beach, with a dancefloor and music until the sun comes up, or until the last customer leaves. Don't confuse it with the *Boracay Summer Palace* resort nearby.

CLUBS

Epic On the edge of D'Mall ⓦepicboracay.com. In the daytime, *Epic's* kitchen turns out tasty dishes from its international menu, and in the evening it transforms into one of the most popular clubs on the strip. Resident DJs serve up dance music, and guest DJs rock up for party nights.

Paraw Beach Club Boat Station 1 ☎036 288 6151. Spilling out onto the sand, this popular club plays everything from EDM to R'n'B. There's a cover charge in peak season, but it includes a drink.

Wave Bar & Lounge Hennan Regency, near Boat Station 2 ⓦfacebook.com/WaveBarAndLounge. Part of an upmarket resort, this trendy, modern beach lounge bar-club hosts DJs whose tunes are piped out to the dancefloor via state-of-the-art Swiss "plane wave" speakers.

SHOPPING

SEE MAP PAGE 250

Budget Mart Where D'Mall meets the main road ☎036 288 5983. Boracay's most accessible decent-sized

supermarket.

D'Mall Behind the beachfront restaurants. D'Mall has

a warren of alleys packed with stalls and boutiques where you can pick up everything from clothes to dive gear and imported foods.

D'Talipapa Market Sprawling market with the best and cheapest selection of beachwear in Boracay, plus a fruit, veg and wet market, with simple restaurants that will cook your freshly bought produce.

DIRECTORY

Banks and exchange There are numerous banks with ATMs on Boracay, but during peak season they sometimes run out of cash by the afternoon or at weekends, so it's best to go on weekday mornings. All banks offer exchange. Any number of banks, private exchange agents and resorts will change cash.

Hospitals and clinics The main hospital is the 24hr Don Ciriaco S. Tirol Hospital (☎ 036 288 3041) on the main road a little south of D'Mall. There are numerous 24hr clinics able to provide first aid or deal with emergencies, including MedExpress (☎ 0969 479 1691).

Immigration Visa extensions (see page 50) are available at the small Department of Immigration office, just off Main Rd south of D'Mall (Mon–Fri 7.30am–5.30pm; ☎ 036 288 5267).

Laundry The place you're staying will probably arrange laundry for you, but for a cheaper service there are several launderettes on the island; ask at your accommodation for the closest to you.

Pharmacies There are pharmacies selling most necessities in D'Mall, Boracay Tourist Center and D'Talipapa.

Police The police station (☎ 036 288 3066) is a short walk inland between Boat Stations 2 and 3, immediately behind the Boracay Tourist Center. If you have lost something, you can ask the friendly staff at the local radio station, YES FM 91.1 (☎ 036 288 6107, ♥ facebook.com/yesboracay), to broadcast an appeal for help. They claim to have a good record of finding lost property, from wallets and passports to Labrador puppies. The station office is on Main Rd close to Boat Station 1.

Romblon

Off the northern coast of Panay, between Mindoro and Bicol, the province of **ROMBLON** consists of three main islands – **Tablas**, **Romblon** and **Sibuyan**, plus a dozen or so more smaller islands. The province is largely overlooked by visitors because of limited transport connections, and once you're here, to put it simply, there's not that much to do. However, as Boracay becomes increasingly crowded, Romblon makes an ever-more appealing option, and little by little it is making its way onto travellers' radars, aided by the opening of new resorts and activities, particularly on the southernmost island of **Carabao**. For now, though, most of Romblon remains wild and untouched and is home to some beautiful and rarely visited **beaches** and coral reefs, making it an excellent off-the-beaten-track destination for **scuba diving**. **Mount Guiting Guiting**, on Sibuyan, also offers one of the country's most challenging hikes.

ARRIVAL AND DEPARTURE

BY PLANE

Tugdan Airport There's a small airport at Tugdan on Tablas Island, which has in the past been served by flights from Manila; these were not operating at the time of writing. Jeepneys meet flights when they *do* exist, and run to Looc (40min) and San Agustin (1hr). If you don't have too much luggage, you can take a habal-habal to Looc or to destinations further afield. Many resorts across the island group can arrange airport pick-up, although it will cost far less to make your own way.

BY BOAT

From Batangas 2GO (♥ 2go.com.ph) operate ferry services from Batangas to Odiongan, on Tablas Island (2

weekly; 6hr) and Romblon Town (1 weekly; 7hr), which carries on to Roxas on Panay (see page 262). Montenegro Shipping Lines (♥ montenegrolines.com.ph) has a slower service for Odiongan (3 weekly; 10hr). Finally, Navios Shipping Lines (☎ 0908 146 2243) has sailings to San Agustin (2 weekly; 9hr) then on to Cajidiocan on Sibuyan's east coast (12hr).

From Mindoro There are three weekly bangkas from Roxas on Mindoro to Odiongan (3–4hr).

From Panay and Boracay 2GO run services from Caticlan to Odiongan (2 weekly; 2hr) and Roxas (2 weekly; 5hr). Alternatively, there are also bangkas (2 daily; 3–4hr) from Caticlan to Looc, or you can charter bangkas in Boracay itself for Carabao Island. From Tabon Baybay port there are

Batangas

Banton

Simara

Kobrador

Calatrava • Carmen   Alad
                Lugbung   Romblon
Tablas   Lonos   Romblon
San   San   San Pedro   Town
Andres   Agustin

Magdiwang

Sibuyan

Odiongan
            Concepcion   Mount Guiting
                           Guiting (2050m)
                                        Cajidiocan
         Tugdan
Looc   San Fernando
Looc Bay
Marine Refuge
& Sanctuary
         Alcantara
      Santa Fe
San
José
Carabao
Lanas   Port Said
Boracay
         Caticlan
Panay

Roxas (Mindoro)

Mandaon

Roxas (Panay)

ROMBLON

0 ——————— 50
kilometres

N

6

---

also small boats to Carabao (2 daily; 45min). If the sea is calm and the weather okay, there are also bangkas every morning from Roxas to Sibuyan Island (4–5hr).

From Masbate Cajidiocan is linked by occasional bangkas with Mandaon on Masbate.

GETTING AROUND

BY BOAT
From Tablas Island There are bangkas from San Agustin on Tablas to Romblon Town (2 daily; 1hr), and San Fernando on Sibuyan (1 daily; 2hr). There are also bangkas from Santa Fe to Carabao (2–3 daily; 40min). Direct Odiongan–Romblon ferries run three times per week.
From Romblon Island There are bangkas from Romblon Town to San Agustin (2 daily; 1hr) on Tablas, and Magdiwang (1 daily; 2hr) and San Fernando on Sibuyan (1 daily; 2hr 30min). Twice a week, Navios ferries (☎ 0908 146 2243) go from Romblon to Cajidiocan (2hr) on Sibuyan.
From Sibuyan Island Daily bangkas run from San Fernando to San Agustin on Tablas and Romblon Town (both 2hr 30min). There are also daily bangkas from Magdawing to Romblon Town (2hr), and twice weekly ferries from

Cajidiocan to Romblon (2hr).

BY ROAD
Once you've made it to the islands, the main modes of transport are jeepneys, tricycles and motorbikes, with the odd bus.
By jeepney Jeepneys run set routes and tend to be most frequent in the mornings.
By tricycle and motorbike taxi Motorbike taxis are one of the speediest if not always most comfortable ways to get around. Short journeys are pretty cheap and a full day-trip is eminently affordable.
By van and motorbike Resorts can also help to arrange transport, including van and motorbike hire.

Tablas Island

Tablas, the largest and best connected of the Romblon group, is a narrow island with a sealed coastal road. Chartering a jeepney for a tour around the island is worth considering. The road that cuts across the island from Concepcion to Odiongan is a real thrill, winding along a ridge with views as far as Sibuyan in the east and Boracay in the south on clear days.

Odiongan and San Andres

If you arrive by air, it's typical to head first to **ODIONGAN**, the island's main town, which has a few simple places to stay. From Odiongan it's easy to explore the beautiful northwest coast up to **SAN ANDRES**, a neat and tidy little place with paved roads and low-rise wooden houses. The town has a beautiful sweeping bay of fine sand on one side, and on the other dazzling paddy fields that stretch to the foothills of **Mount Kang-Ayong** (Table Mountain), which can be climbed with a guide – ask at the town hall in the plaza.

Calatrava and San Agustin

The next town north of San Andres is **Calatrava**, from where you can charter a bangka for the short hop to the **Enchanted Hidden Sea**, an incredibly beautiful 40m-wide pool of water barely 10m from the sea through a gap in the rocks. To most local folks the pool is an enchanted place, home to supernatural beings, though you're more likely to see white-breasted eagles, monkeys, butterflies, sharks and turtles.

For bangkas to Romblon or Sibuyan, go by bus or jeepney to dull **San Agustin** on the northeast coast; the only reason to stay over here is if you miss the last one.

Looc and Santa Fe

The sleepy town of **LOOC**, a scenic place huddled among palm trees against a curtain of jungled hills and facing a wide natural harbour, is not really worth going out of your way for but is a useful entry point from Caticlan. Further south, the district of **Santa Fe** is home to some good beaches, although the town itself is little more than the jumping-off point for boats to Carabao.

Looc Bay Marine Refuge and Sanctuary

Arrange snorkelling through the KOICA office beside the pier (daily 8am–4pm; snorkel & mask rental extra; ☎ 0935 590 2204)

Looc's main attraction is the **Looc Bay Marine Refuge and Sanctuary**, an area of the bay guarded 24 hours a day to allow corals damaged by dynamite fishing to regenerate. The guards, all volunteers, are stationed on a bamboo platform; you can organize a visit to snorkel from it through the KOICA office.

INFORMATION
TABLAS ISLAND

Tourist information The tourist office is in the Capitol Building on Looc's town plaza (daily 8am–noon & 1–5pm; ☎ 0995 393 0805) but is often left unmanned and isn't much help anyway.

Services In Odiongan, there's a bank with ATM on the plaza, plus another on Formilleza St.

ACCOMMODATION AND EATING

ODIONGAN

Lyn's Snack Bar Rizal St ☎ 042 567 5812. Directly below the *Odiongan Plaza Lodge*, this place has outdoor seating where you can fill up on cheap local dishes. P̄

Sato Hotel and Resort Just off MA Roxas St, 200m north of the Plaza ☎ 042 567 6070. Painted bright yellow, this modern business/accommodation complex has fan and a/c doubles, a large suite and a dorm. P̄

Skyluxe Festin St ⓦ facebook.com/61572895175919/about/?_rdr. Convenient for a short stay due to its acceptably central location, and one of the only places in town bookable on online accommodation engines, this newbie (opened 2025) has surprisingly nice rooms, and a decent-enough swimming pool. P̄P̄

Star Palace Restaurant & Pizzeria Bonifacio St
ⓦpizzadito.com. Tasty stone-baked pizzas are the top
choice at Star Palace, but there are plenty of other options,
ranging from pastas to curries, by way of some pretty decent
fried chicken. There's also a bewildering array of flavoured
milk teas. **PP**

SAN AGUSTIN

Seashore Inn Seafront ⓦfacebook.com/p/Seashore-
Inn-61558691084903/. The only reliable accommodation
in the town centre, right by the pier and with cute little
rooms. Free coffee available through the day. **P̄**

LOOC

Angelique Inn Gonzales St, southeast cnr of Plaza de la
Paz ☏0916 344 6946. *Angelique* offers basic rooms, a bit
dusty but with clean linen, all with shared bathrooms. The
simple restaurant is one of the few places to eat in town. **P̄**

SANTA FE

Beachaus Resort About 4km west of Santa Fe
ⓦfacebook.com/BeachausResortCanyayo. The cheapest

acceptable accommodation around, but actually quite nice
– the house contains rooms that are simple but bright (a/c
in some of them, balconies on most), and the beach is right
there. All you need to know, really. **P̄**

Dreamshore Kiwi Beach Resort About 5km south of
Santa Fe ☏0981 731 6714. Right by the beach, and also
a jetty that's ideal for snorkelling, this simple spot has clean
accommodation and a winningly relaxed vibe. **PP**

Morel's Private Island Resort Guinbiyaran Bay
ⓦmorelisland.com. Sitting on its own tiny island, this
charming resort has a budget beach cottage with kitchen
sleeping six, and small, attractive rooms, mostly with shared
bathrooms. The resort can arrange pick-up from Santa Fe, a
20–30min drive from the pier at Guinbiyaran and then a
short bangka ride. Alternatively, they can arrange a boat
direct from Boracay. **PP**

Pili Beach Resort About 8km south of Santa Fe
ⓦpilibeach.com. Found in an isolated location towards
the south of the island, *Pili Beach Resort* offers simply
decorated rooms, a relaxing pool, and an excellent bar. They
can arrange scuba-diving courses and trips. **PPP**

Carabao Island

Only 6km wide from the capital of **San José** on the east coast to **Lanas** on the west,
beautiful little **Carabao Island** is an idyllic place where fishing is the main industry
and tourism has only just begun to have an impact. **Divers** arrive on day-trips to
explore the dozen well-known dive sites in the reefs around the island, although,
if you want to stay longer, there are a few decent resorts at **Inobahan Beach**, the
island's best – a 1km stretch of powdery white sand a couple of minutes' walk
from **Port Said**, where bangkas arrive. It's easy to hire a motorbike in San José to
get around; an enjoyable ride takes you to **Tagaytay Point**, the highest point on the
island from where there are magnificent views across to Boracay and beyond. Note
that Carabao's electricity supply is only switched on for part of the day.

ACCOMMODATION AND EATING   **CARABAO ISLAND**

LANAS BEACH

The Beach House ⓦthebeachhouse-carabao.com.
With a decent restaurant and bar set out along a gorgeous
expanse of sand, the Beach House makes a great first
impression. Some rooms, however, are beginning to look a
little shabby, though others are well-kept, so ask to see a
few. Scuba diving trips can be arranged. **PP**

Lanas Beach Resort ⓦlanasbeachresort.com. British-
run resort on a beautiful and quiet stretch of beach. The
seven a/c apartments and suites are well designed and
set in lush, landscaped grounds. The restaurant is highly
recommended too, serving a range of dishes, including
burgers and Thai green curry. **PP**

Romblon Island

Romblon Island has been extensively quarried for decades to get at the beautiful
Romblon marble, a favourite with the rich and famous in Manila. It's a picturesque
island, with a pretty harbourside capital, an interior buzzing with wildlife and a coastal
road, partly cemented, that you can whip around in half a day past some enticing
beaches. **Romblon Town** itself is a pretty place, with Spanish forts, a venerable cathedral
and breathtaking views across the Romblon Strait.

6

Romblon Town

One of the most attractive towns in the Philippines, low-rise **ROMBLON TOWN**, the provincial capital, sits at the back of a deep, twisting bay, with red-roofed houses lining the water's edge and thickly jungled hills behind. Happily dozing in the balm of a more sedentary age, the town feels decades behind the rest of the Philippines. In the mornings, the only sound is that of crowing cockerels, and most activity stops for a siesta in the afternoons. The town has developed a small but discerning and somewhat quirky expat community. The only time the place gets busy is around the second Saturday of January for the **Fiesta of Santo Niño**, celebrating the failure of the Spanish to steal the holy image of baby Jesus from the local cathedral.

The town has a few sights, all reachable on foot. Slap in the middle, overlooking the quaint little Spanish plaza, is **St Joseph's Cathedral**, a richly atmospheric church built in 1726. Overlooking the seafront are the remains of renovated **Fort San Andres** and less well-preserved **Fort San Pedro**, reminders of the risk Romblon Town once faced from pirates. Accommodation choices in Romblon Town, however, are extremely limited.

Beaches and resorts

Romblon island has some good beaches with very simple hut accommodation on the coast near **Lonos**, 3km south of Romblon. Around 500m long, **Bonbon Beach** is accessed from the road between Romblon and Lonos, and has a gently sloping ocean floor that makes it safe for swimming. A little south of here, **Tiamban Beach** (charge) is a short stretch of white sand backed by palm trees and wooden refreshment shacks. Further still, a number of resorts have sprung up along the stretch of coast from Tiamban south to **Ginablan** and the nearby barangay of **San Pedro**.

ACCOMMODATION — ROMBLON ISLAND

ROMBLON TOWN

★ **Stone Creek House** Gov. Fetalvero Ave w stonecreek houseromblon.com. Just beyond the covered market, this three-storey boutique hotel boasts three splendid units, crowned by the spacious self-catering penthouse suite, complete with classy decorations and top-notch appliances. PPP

ELSEWHERE ON THE ISLAND

Horizon 3km west of Romblon Town w horizonhotel romblon.com. Within walking distance of Romblon Town you'll find this large-for-Romblon hotel, whose infinity pool does indeed allow guests to gaze longingly at the horizon. It's not a bad horizon from here, either, and the rooms are no slouch in the looks department either. PPP

Lamao Beach Resort Brgy Lamao, 14km east of Romblon Town w facebook.com/LamaoBeachR. Four spacious and neatly tiled nipa huts, smaller huts with shared bathrooms and two a/c rooms, all set in a peaceful beachfront compound with a large pool and simple restaurant. P

The Three P Beach Resort & Dive Center 7km west of Romblon Town w the-three-p.com. A gorgeous resort on the west coast that's particularly tailored to divers, but it's equally enjoyable if you're not going beneath the water. Rooms are comfortable and unfussy, the restaurant serves good food, and the staff can arrange island hopping and trekking. PP

EATING

ROMBLON TOWN

JD & G Just inland from the harbourfront. The Italian owner makes sure that the pizzas and pasta dishes here pass muster. There's also tasty fresh fish and some fine desserts. PP

Joe-Ra Cafe t 0998 990 125. Not just a café, but a place for proper meals too – bright, cheery and facing the sea, just a short walk west of the town centre. Decent desserts round out the picture. P

ACTIVITIES

Ducks Diving Amihan Resort, San Pedro w ducks-romblon.com. Professional diving centre, which specializes in macro diving for avid underwater photographers but also offers fun dives when not booked up.

The Three P Beach Resort & Dive Center 7km west of Romblon Town w the-three-p.com. The diving centre at this excellent resort (see page 260) is first-rate, offering tuition in underwater photography in various conditions, including the remarkable blackwater diving. There's some serious expertise here; this is a great opportunity to take perfect pictures of the fascinating underwater life around the island.

Sibuyan Island

The easternmost of the Romblon group, verdant **Sibuyan Island** has everything the adventurous traveller could dream of: a sparkling coastline; a thickly forested interior; and a couple of daunting mountain peaks, most notably the ragged, saw-like bulk of **Mount Guiting Guiting**. Dubbed "The Galapagos of Asia", the island boasts an extraordinarily rich range of **wildlife**, including 700 plant species and 131 species of bird. Five mammal species (one fruit bat and four rodents) are unique to the island.

Much of Sibuyan was declared a nature reserve in 1996. However, this has not prevented the island from being targeted as a potential mineral-mining site. In 2017, the environment secretary banned mining on Sibuyan; this order was reversed in 2021, and in 2023 tensions arose regarding a nickel-mining concession. Sibuyan's 60,000-odd residents, mostly subsistence farmers and fishermen who rely on the forest and the ocean to supplement their meagre incomes, see relatively few tourists, but some who know every cove, trail and cave on the island are happy to act as guides. Most Sibuyan residents live in three towns, **San Fernando**, **Cajidiocan** and **Magdiwang**; most boats dock at the latter.

Mount Guiting Guiting

Permits, guides and porters can be organized at Mount Guiting Guiting Natural Park headquarters (☎ 0928 490 1038) • The park is accessed by an 8km tricycle ride from Magdiwang

Rising directly from the coastal plain to a height of 2050m, the extinct volcano **Mount Guiting Guiting** is an unforgettable sight. This is not a climb to be undertaken lightly, though, and if you plan on doing any serious trekking or climbing, you'll have to bring all your equipment with you. The trail to the top of the mountain (affectionately known as G2 by climbers) starts from the **Mount Guiting Guiting Natural Park** headquarters. It begins gently enough, winding through pleasant lowlands, but soon becomes very steep and culminates in a precarious traverse across "the knife edge" to the summit. Even experienced mountaineers regularly fail to summit, and you'll need to allow three days for the round trip (guide compulsory) including ten hours for the ascent.

Next to Guiting Guiting is **Mayo's Peak** (1530m), a secondary summit that, like its neighbour, is cloaked in mossy forests, ferns and rare orchids. The trek to the top is more straightforward, requiring only 24 hours. Check at the park headquarters for more information and advice.

ACCOMMODATION   SIBUYAN ISLAND

Cantingas River Resort The island's southwest, on the Cantingas River. The accommodation here is pretty rough and ready, but it's worth stopping by to enjoy a swim in the gorgeous river, which comes down fresh and clear from the mountain. Rooms are basic, and there's no food available. P̄

Sanctuary Garden Resort By the start of the trail up Mt Guiting Guiting ⓦ sanctuarygardenresort.net. This well-located place provides a great alternative to a beach stay, and offers everything from camping and dorm beds to a/c rooms with fridges, TVs and private bathrooms. They also rent out bicycles. P̄

Panay

The substantial, vaguely triangular-shaped island of **PANAY** has been largely bypassed by tourism, perhaps because everyone seems to get sucked towards **Boracay** off its northern tip instead. There's room enough on Panay, though, for plenty of discovery

6

and adventure: the island has a huge coastline and a mountainous, jungle-filled interior that has yet to be fully mapped.

Panay comprises four provinces: **Antique** ("ant-ee-kay") on the west coast; **Aklan** in the north; **Capiz** in the northeast; and **Iloilo** ("ee-lo-ee-lo") running along the east coast to the capital of the province, **Iloilo City**, in the south. The province that most interests tourists is Aklan, whose capital, **Kalibo**, is the site of the big and brash **Ati-Atihan festival**, held in the second week of January (see box, page 271). This doesn't mean that you should give the rest of Panay the brush-off. The northeast coast was badly affected by Typhoon Odette in 2021, but it still offers bangka access to a number of unspoilt islands, while on the west side, Antique is a raw, bucolic province of picturesque beaches and scrubby mountains.

ARRIVAL AND DEPARTURE   PANAY

By plane There are four major airports on Panay, all served by daily flights from Manila: Panay's principal airport is in Iloilo, while on the north coast there are airports at Roxas, Kalibo and Caticlan. Roxas only has a few flights per day, while busier Kalibo and particularly Caticlan are mainly used by visitors on their way to Boracay. Kalibo is also served by international flights from South Korea, and Iloilo from Thailand, Hong Kong and Singapore, making them alternative ports of entry into the Philippines. See the individual town accounts for flight schedules.

By boat Frequent passenger ferries link Iloilo with Bacolod on nearby Negros; a few also sail to Manila and Cebu. Large bangkas ply the route to Guimaras. In the north, Caticlan is served by boats from Batangas, Roxas on Mindoro Oriental (see page 236), and a couple of destinations on Tablas Island in the Romblon group (see page 258). Roxas receives ferries from Batangas (see page 114) via Romblon Town and bangkas from Sibuyan, as well as ferries from Mandaon on Masbate.

Iloilo City and around

ILOILO CITY is a useful transit point for Guimaras (see page 271) and has good ferry connections to many other Visayan islands, but there's nothing to keep you here for more than a day or two. The **city centre** occupies a thin strip of land on the southern bank of the Iloilo River, with views across to Guimaras. **General Luna Street** runs for nearly 3km along the northern boundary of the centre, and is one of the city's major arteries, lined with banks, hotels and restaurants. It's worth heading across the river to the **Riverside Boardwalk** for dining and nightlife, made all the more attractive by the proximity to the splendidly landscaped riverside **Esplanade**. For more of a sense of history, the old areas of **Molo**, 3km west of town, and **Jaro**, 3km north, both make pleasant distractions. There are also more adventurous pursuits to be enjoyed around Iloilo, including trekking and caving in **Bulabog Puti-An National Park**, and trips to local Ati villages.

Over the fourth weekend of January, the **Dinagyang** festival (❂facebook.com/iloilodinagyangofficial), loosely based on Kalibo's Ati-Atihan, adds some extra frenzy to the city. The **Paraw Regatta** falls in the third week of February and includes a race across to Guimaras.

Plaza Libertad and J.M. Basa Street

In the southeastern quadrant of the city is **Plaza Libertad**, where the first flag of the Philippine Republic was raised in triumph after Spain surrendered the city on December 25, 1898. There's little to remind you of the history, though – the square today is a concrete affair with fast-food restaurants and busy roads on all sides. The few old residential and commercial buildings that survive date back to Spanish and American colonial periods, and are mostly in **J.M. Basa Street**, which runs past the square linking Ledesma Street to the port area.

Museo Iloilo

Bonifacio Drive, just south of the river • Charge • A short walk north of General Luna St, or hop on a Jaro-bound jeepney

An engaging and clearly presented repository of Iloilo's cultural heritage, the **Museo Iloilo** has a diverse range of exhibits including fossils, shells and rocks indicating the age

6

ILOILO CITY

● EATING	
Afrique's Gourmet	3
Bavaria	2
Bluejay Coffee	4
Buto't Balat	6
Kogi & Vegi	5
Ted's Oldtimer	
Lapaz Batchoy	1/7

■ ACCOMMODATION	
Century 21	6
Go Hotel	7
Highway 21 Pension House	4
Hotel del Rio	2
La Fiesta	5
Smallville 21	1
Vermillion	3

SM City Mall, ① Tagbac Bus Terminal (9km) & Airport (15km)

② Jaro & Bulabog Puti-An National Park

Asilo De Molo (1km) & Molo (1km)

Smallville Commercial Complex

Medicos Medical Center

BENIGNO AQUINO AVE

Esplanade

San Pedro Terminal

M. H. DEL PILAR STREET

Molo Church

All Seasons Travel & Tours

YBIERNA S AVENUE

WEST AVENUE

University of the Philippines

TIMAWA AVENUE

TANZA STREET

SAN AGUSTIN STREET

DELGADO STREET

LEDESMA STREET

DE LEON STREET

MABINI STREET

QUEZON STREET

GENERAL LUNA STREET

City Police

St Paul's Hospital

Mercury Drug

BPI

Gaisano City Mall

Iloilo River

BONIFACIO DRIVE

Forbes Bridge

Museo Iloilo

PNB

Provincial Capitol Building

MUELLE LONEY STREET

Atrium Mall

SOLIS STREET

YULO STREET

VALERIA STREET

VALERIA STREET

RIZAL STREET

SM Mall

Marymart Mall

IZNART STREET

Metrobank

Mercury Drug Store

Jeepney Terminal

Robinsons Place Shopping Mall

Central Market

University

J. M. BASA STREET

Bureau of Immigration

City Hall

Plaza Libertad

ORTIZ STREET

Ortiz Wharf

RIZAL STREET

MUELLE LONEY STREET

ZAMORA STREET

DELA RAMA STREET

Bacolod Fast Ferry Terminals

San José Church

Land Bank

FORT SAN PEDRO DRIVE

Slow Ferry Port

Iloilo Strait

N

0   500   metres

of Panay Island. There are also ornamental teeth, jewellery excavated from pre-Spanish burial sites, pottery from China and Siam, coffins, war relics and some modern art, including large wooden sculptures.

Molo

Molo can be reached by taxi, or on foot from the city centre in 30min by heading west down M. H. Del Pilar St, or by tricycle or jeepney (10min)

On the western edge of the city, the district of **Molo** makes for an interesting wander. In the sixteenth and seventeenth centuries, Molo was a Chinese quarter, much like Parian in Manila. The main sight is **Molo Church** (St Anne's), a splendid nineteenth-century Gothic Renaissance edifice made of coral, with rows of female saints lining both sides of the aisle.

Asilo de Molo

Donation expected • Ⓦ facebook.com/asilodemoloinc

About 1km west along the road from Molo Church is the **Asilo de Molo**, formerly an orphanage where vestments were hand-embroidered by orphan girls under the tutelage of nuns. The orphans have since been transferred to Manila, and the Asilo, still run by the Sisters of the Daughters of Charity, is now home to Iloilo's elderly poor, who also turn out local handicrafts.

Jaro

Taxi, or jeepneys marked Jaro or Tiko (10min), or about a 45min walk

Three kilometres north of the centre across the Forbes Bridge, the historical enclave of **Jaro** is worth exploring. You can also wander among the old colonial homes of sugar barons and mooch through a number of dusty old antique shops, where prices are lower than in Manila. Jaro's **plaza** is an inspiring little piece of old Asia, dominated by Jaro Cathedral, and lined with *bibingka* stalls and colourful flower shops.

Jaro Metropolitan Cathedral

Jaro Plaza • ☎ 033 329 1625

The Spanish-era **Jaro Metropolitan Cathedral**, with its ivory-white stone facade and dignified but crumbling old belfry that was partially destroyed by an earthquake in 1984, is the seat of the Catholic diocese in the Western Visayas. Steps either side of the main doors lead up to a platform and the Shrine to the Divine Infant and Nuestra Señora de la Candelaria (Our Lady of Candles).

Nelly Garden mansion

Set back from Luna St, south of Jaro Plaza • Charge; tours available in groups (min five) • ☎ 033 320 3075

The grandiose **Nelly Garden mansion** stands down a picturesque driveway lined with eucalyptus. The mansion, which has murals on the walls and a U-shaped dining room with a fountain in the middle, no longer has to be visited by arrangement, but they do need a minimum of five visitors, which can be tough to rustle up – otherwise you'll have to cover all five tickets yourself.

Bulabog Puti-An National Park

Charge, plus additional cost for guide • To reach the park independently from Iloilo City, charter a taxi (cost dependent on vehicle size and how long you stay) or take a jeepney to Dingle (1hr), then tricycle to the park entrance; or book a trip through the tourist office (see page 265)

Some 40km north of Iloilo, **Bulabog Puti-An National Park**, established in 1961, sits along a ridgeline of intact primary forest. The region's caverns were used as a hideout by revolutionary forces during the Spanish period, and inscriptions penned on the cave walls still bear testament to this time. Today the park offers a healthy choice of adventurous outdoor pursuits such as trekking and cave exploration, plus the chance to spot monkeys, pythons and a host of creepy-crawlies.

You can easily visit as a day-trip from Iloilo, but for those who want a closer look, an **overnight stay** can be arranged at the simple cabins in the ranger's office, or at a homestay in Dingle. You can get to Bulabog Puti-An independently – in which case hiring a **guide** on arrival is recommended – but for fuller exploration it's worth arranging a trip in advance through the tourist office.

ARRIVAL AND DEPARTURE
ILOILO CITY

By plane Iloilo's airport is at Cabutuan, 15km from the city. A taxi to the city centre is easy to pick up, or you can take a share-van.

Destinations Cebu (4–6 daily; 45min); Davao (1–2 daily; 1hr 10min); Manila (9–13 daily; 1hr 10min); Puerto Princesa (3 weekly; 1hr).

By boat Slow ferries from Cebu and Manila arrive at the wharf on the eastern edge of the city, a 15min walk or short jeepney/tricycle ride from General Luna St. Fast ferries for Bacolod arrive a few hundred metres beyond the post office on Muelle Loney St. Ortiz wharf, used by bangkas from Hoskyn on Guimaras, is at the southern end of Ortiz St near the market.

Destinations Bacolod (frequent; 1hr); Cagayan de Oro (1 weekly; 14hr); Cebu City (8 weekly; 12–13hr); Hoskyn (on Guimaras; every 30min; 15min); Manila (2 weekly; 24hr).

Puerto Princesa (3 weekly; 25–27hr).

By bus and minivan Most buses now arrive at the Tagbac bus terminal, 9km northeast on the outskirts of town, from where it's a 20min ride into town by taxi or jeepney. The most comfortable and reliable bus company is Ceres Liner (ⓦceresliner.com), which has frequent a/c and ordinary services. Non-stop minivans from here are slightly quicker, but more expensive. Both services are most frequent until 1pm. For San José, capital of Antique in the west, and Libertad to the north, you'll need to head to the old San Pedro terminal on M.H. Del Pilar St in the west of town.

Destinations Caticlan (every 45min–1hr; 6hr); Estancia (every 20min; 3hr 30min); Kalibo (every 30min; 4–5hr); Roxas (every 30min; 3hr); San José (every 30min–1hr; 2hr 30min).

GETTING AROUND, INFORMATION AND TOURS

By taxi and jeepney There are plenty of taxis in Iloilo, but the city centre is compact enough to cover on foot. There's a jeepney terminal on Ledesma St.

Tourist information The helpful tourist office (Mon–Fri 8am–5pm; ☎033 337 5411) is in the grounds of the Capitol Building on Bonifacio Drive, one block north of J.M. Basa St and next to the Museo Iloilo.

Tours The tourist office has a list of accredited travel agencies, guides and drivers and can help you arrange trips

in the surrounding region including to Guimaras, Bulabog Puti-An National Park and the churches of the south coast.

Health St Paul's Hospital is at the eastern end of General Luna St (☎033 337 2742, ⓦsphiloilo.com), towards the junction with Bonifacio. The Medicus Medical Center is just off the Esplanade (☎033 328 7777, ⓦmedicusmedicalcenter.com). There are pharmacies in every mall.

Immigration The Bureau of Immigration (☎033 509 9651) is at the Old Customs House on Aduana St.

ACCOMMODATION
SEE MAP PAGE 263

Century 21 Quezon St ☎033 335 8821. Mid-sized, glass-fronted building offering basic, affordable rooms with a/c and cable TV. Singles are among the cheapest in town for this sort of quality, and family rooms for four are good value. P̲P̲

Go Hotel Robinsons Mall, Ledesma St at Mabini St ⓦgohotels.ph. Increasingly popular franchise, always attached to a Robinsons Mall. Rooms are bright, modern and comfortable. The earlier you book online, the better the price. P̲

Highway 21 Pension House General Luna St ☎033 335 1220. Excellent budget choice with modern rooms and staff who are on the ball. All rooms have a/c, cable TV and hot water, but some are windowless. Good location not far from the Esplanade and Smallville. P̲

★ **Hotel del Rio** M.H. Del Pilar St, Molo ⓦhoteldelrio.xyz. Stylish and very professional hotel in a pleasant location on the river. Standard rooms have a/c, fridge, cable TV, king-size bed and river views. Superior and deluxe rooms

are newer and more tastefully styled, but don't overlook the river. There's also a popular coffee shop and a good pool. P̲P̲

La Fiesta MH del Pilar St ⓦfacebook.com/lafiestahotelioilo. Well-located and reasonably-priced hotel with a very smart lobby and restaurant. Rooms, however, vary considerably – some are smart while others are rather dingy, so ask to see a few before settling. P̲P̲

Smallville 21 Smallville Complex, Diversion Rd ⓦfacebook.com/smallville21iloilo. This addition to the home-grown *21* chain is perfect for those who want to have some of the city's best nightlife and restaurants on their doorstep. Rooms are well kept, modern and fitted with dark wood furnishings. Breakfast included. P̲P̲

Vermillion General Luna St ⓦthevermillionhotels.com/. Formerly the Sarabia Manor, then The Mansion, Iloilo's biggest hotel has been given yet another new lease of life by yet another change of name and ownership – the lobby now looks quite stylish, and the pool out back fine but maybe a little cheesy. The cheapest rooms are small, but

6

their pricier counterparts are fancier and include breakfast. All room types come with a/c and have cable TV. Promo rates usually available. PPP

EATING
SEE MAP PAGE 263

Across the river from the city centre, you'll find everything from coffee shops and restaurants to bars featuring live bands, and full-blown clubs. Also worth a mention is **Coffeebreak**, a citywide chain that does good coffee and cakes.

Afrique's Gourmet Red Square Building, Smallville ⓦ facebook.com/AfriquesPizza. Atmospheric restaurant in a lovely old colonial house right behind Jaro cathedral. The menu is largely Italian and includes a huge range of pizzas along with specialities such as *osso bucco* pasta. They also have a more modern branch at Smallville. PPP

Bavaria 113 Seminario St ⓦ facebook.com/Bavaria restaurant. A true taste of Germany in the Philippines – walk in here and you could be forgiven for thinking you've been transported to a bierkeller in Munich. There's authentic German food and, perhaps more importantly, real German beer. It's a favoured hangout of expats. PPP

Bluejay Coffee Smallville Commercial Complex, Diversion Rd ⓦ facebook.com/bluejaycoffeeiloilo. Relaxed blend of comfy chairs and tasty food, serving all-day American, Filipino, German or Spanish breakfasts. The chunky apple and tuna salad sandwich is also excellent, as is the coffee. PP

★ **Buto't Balat** Solis St ⓦ facebook.com/official butotbalatrestaurant. A haven of tropical tranquillity and greenery in the midst of the downtown mayhem, this popular restaurant offers candlelit dining under thatched cabanas surrounding a small pond. Dishes to try include chilli shrimps, pork Bicol Express, beef *kare kare*, and there's fish by weight. PP

Kogi & Vegi Boardwalk, right off Esplanade ⓦ facebook.com/p/Kogi-Vegi-100057220069002/. Pleasantly decorated modern Korean restaurant, where you can enjoy well-prepared, authentic dishes such as beef *bulgogi*, *ddeokbokki* (stir-fried rice cake in a spicy sauce), soups and the like. PPP

Ted's Oldtimer Lapaz Batchoy Valeria St & SM City Mall ⓦ facebook.com/TedsLapazBatchoy. Though the precise origins of *batchoy*, the famed Illonggo dish (see box below), are something of a mystery, *Ted's*, open since 1945, is without question *the* place to get an authentic helping of it. P

The south coast

Heading southwest from Iloilo City along the coastal road takes you through the atmospheric Spanish-era towns of **Oton**, **Tigbauan**, **Guimbal**, **Miag-ao** and **San Joaquin**. Each has a historic **church**, notably Tigbauan's Baroque church (22km from Iloilo City) and Guimbal's Catholic (35km from Iloilo) church, which stands close to a number of ruined seventeenth-century watchtowers.

Miag-ao Church
Miag-ao, 40km west of Iloilo

Pride of place along the southwest coast goes to **Miag-ao Church** (also known as the Church of Santo Tomas de Villanueva), built by the Augustinians between 1786 and 1797 as a fortress against Moro invasions. Declared a national landmark and a UNESCO World Heritage Site, the church is built of a local yellow-orange sandstone in Baroque-Romanesque style, a unique example of Filipino Rococo.

ARRIVAL AND DEPARTURE
THE SOUTH COAST

By car The easiest way to visit the church towns of the southwest is to hire a vehicle and driver in Iloilo for a day-trip.

By bus and jeepney If you have time, it's simple enough

ILOILO SPECIALITIES

Iloilo City is one of the best places in the country to try **seafood**, and it's also known for a number of unique regional Illonggo delicacies, including **pancit Molo soup**, a garlicky noodle soup containing pork dumplings, which is named after the Molo area of the city and is sold at numerous street stalls. **Batchoy**, an artery-hardening combination of liver, pork and beef with thin noodles, is also widely available.

to travel between the towns by public transport. All buses from Iloilo City bound for San Joaquin (1hr) pass through Oton (10min), Tigbauan (15min), Guimbal (25min) and Miag-ao (50min), and plenty of jeepneys also ply the west-coast route.

ACCOMMODATION

Bantayan Beach Resort Guimbal ☎ 033 315 5009. Named after the squat, Spanish-era watchtower on the property, this place has a/c cottages, all fully renovated. There's a pool table and wi-fi in the restaurant. PP

Sol y Mar Resort Oton ⓦ solymariloilo.com. Smart rooms and cottages set in impeccably manicured grounds, this welcoming place has a pool and pizza restaurant, and also boasts an eco-farm of which you can take tours. PP

The west coast

Most of the west coast of Panay, made up largely of the province of **Antique**, is untouched by tourism. This is one of the poorest areas of the Philippines, with a solitary coastal road connecting a series of isolated villages and towns. It's an attractive coastline with a savage backdrop of jungled mountains that are only just beginning to be explored and climbed. The journey along the province's coast, from **San José** in the south to **Libertad** in the north, provides an excellent opportunity to experience a simple provincial life, shielded from the rest of the Philippines by mountains on one side and sea on the other.

San José

SAN JOSÉ is a busy little port town whose major claim to fame – apart from being capital of Antique – seems to be that its cathedral has the tallest bell tower in Panay. There are no tourist sights here, just a chaotic wharf, a cracked plaza and a main street, the National Highway, lined with pawnshops, canteens and rice dealers. The town's annual **Binirayan festival**, held from April 30 to May 2, commemorates the thirteenth-century landing of ten Malay chieftains who established the first Malayan settlement in the Philippines.

Tibiao

About halfway along Panay's west coast, **TIBIAO** is best used as a base for **whitewater kayaking**, **rafting** and **trekking** on the Tibiao River, at the head of which the town stands. Tibiao also stands in the shadow of Panay's highest peak, **Mount Madja-as** (2090m) – it's possible to climb this daunting peak, but a permit and guide are essential. The town itself is a relaxed spot, with a lively central plaza – complete with basketball court – less than 200m inland from the long stony beach full of fishing boats.

Tibiao Eco Adventure Park

Daily 8am–5pm • Charge, additional for zipline and guided kayaking tours • From Tibiao take a shared tricycle 3km north to the junction at Importante, then a habal-habal ride, or a 40min walk; you can also visit as part of a tour with Katahum Tours (see page 267) • ⓦ facebook.com/tibiaotourismofficeteapark

A few kilometres inland is the **Tibiao Eco Adventure Park** (aka TEA Park), which offers a host of outdoors activities from gentle introductory kayaking lessons through to whitewater rides, canyoning (through the Bugtong Bato falls) and rappelling. There are also a few places hereabouts in which you can take a hot spring bath.

ARRIVAL AND DEPARTURE   THE WEST COAST

By bus San José's bus station is in Isabel St, 1km west of the centre, and the pier is on the western edge of the town.

Buses running between San José and Caticlan pass through Tibiao.

ACTIVITIES

Katahum Tours Tibiao ⓦ facebook.com/calawag

mountain. Tour operator (as well as a fish spa and hotel;

see below) where you can arrange everything from gentle day-tours to rafting and trekking.

ACCOMMODATION AND EATING

SAN JOSÉ
Esprutingkle Hotel Brgy Bantayan ⓦfacebook.com/ esprutingklebusinesshotel. Set above a small shopping mall, this place has clean, well-maintained rooms with a/c and cable TV, and also serves the best meals in town. PP

TIBIAO
Calawag Mountain Resort Beyond TEA Park, in the foothills outside Tibiao ⓦfacebook.com/calawag mountain. Simple lodge up the river from TEA Park, with basic bamboo nipa huts; you can soak yourself in a *kawa*, a large wok-like bath heated by fire (originally used for cooking muscovado sugar), or even have a massage down by the riverside. Their restaurant also serves good-value "boodles" of local food. PP

Godo's Hotel & Restaurant Culasi ⓦfacebook.com/ godoshotel. There are a handful of hotels and homestays in Culasi, about 15km north of Tibiao, of which Godo's is one of the most reliable. Rooms aren't exciting, but they are clean and decent value. The restaurant's not bad either, and there are sometimes live music performances while you eat. PP

Kasa Raya Travelers Inn Near the crossroads at Importante ⓦfacebook.com/KasaRayaInn. Comfortable modern rooms, some fan, some a/c, all including breakfast. The knowledgeable owner runs eco-trips to inland and islet destinations. PP

Mammamia 8km along the road heading north from Tibiao ⓦfacebook.com/p/Mammamia-Pizzeria-and-American-Diner-61557431612917/. An unexpected find along a relatively quiet stretch of coast, this small beachside restaurant serves up delicious and authentic Italian pizza. It's a good spot for sunset-watching. PP

The east coast

Panay's **east coast** – from Iloilo City north to **Estancia** – is an undeveloped area of wilderness and sun-drenched barangays rarely seen by tourists. There are some wonderfully pristine islands off the coast, many of them unfamiliar even to locals, but to explore them you'll need time on your hands, patience and a willingness to spend nights camped on beaches. This region was badly hit by Typhoons Yolanda and Odette, with heavy loss of life. It has largely got back on its feet, but developing tourism is still not a priority.

Roxas

ROXAS, the capital of Capiz province, is renowned for its seafood, and also has a reputation among Filipinos as being a hotbed of witches and shamans. The city is well connected by air, sea and land. However, aside from taking a trip out to the pleasant if unremarkable stretch of golden sand and row of seafood restaurants at **Baybay Beach**, 3km north of town en route to the port, and the finds at the **Ang Panublion Museum**, there is little to keep visitors in Roxas for long.

Tibiao Eco Adventure Park
Hughes St • Free

If you're in town for more than an hour, you may want to have a quick look at the local historical artefacts in the **Ang Panublion Museum** on the elongated, rather traffic-choked plaza in the town centre. The circular, whitewashed building it's set in looks quite fancy from outside, like something teleported here from Europe; inside the exhibits are a little more modest (bar the classic car), but you may learn something about local musical instruments.

ARRIVAL AND INFORMATION   ROXAS

By plane The airport, 10min north of the city by jeepney or tricycle in Arnaldo Blvd, is served daily from Manila (2–3 daily; 1hr 10min).

By boat Ferries dock at the Calusi pier, 3km west of Baybay Beach. Tricycles run out to the pier, plus there are jeepneys. Providing the weather is agreeable, bangkas leave every morning for Sibuyan Island in the Romblon group (4–5hr). There are also ferries to Batangas (2 weekly; 13hr) via

Romblon Town (5hr) and to Mandaon on Masbate (4 weekly; 5hr), and also sailings to Manila (2 weekly; 18hr) with Morta Shipping Lines (⒲ moretashipping.com).
By bus Services for Iloilo, Kalibo and Estancia use the bus terminus 4km south of the Panay River, reachable by

tricycle. Direct services stop early, so another alternative is to catch one of the frequent buses to Sigma (till 6.45pm), and then change there for Kalibo or Caticlan.
Destinations Caticlan (every 30min–1hr; 3hr); Iloilo (every 20–30min; 3–4hr); Kalibo (every 30min; 2hr).

ACCOMMODATION

ROXAS
Asia Novo Boutique Arnaldo Blvd ⒲ meacohotel.com. This outlet of the national chain is a reliable place to get a cheap bed for the night. It's fairly central, and the staff are friendly, but it can suffer from noise both internal and external. Try to get a quiet room at the back. P̄
Roxas President's Inn Rizal Ave at Lopez Jaena St ⒲ roxaspresidentsinn.com. This hotel is strewn with antiques. Rooms are cosy and clean, with a/c, cable TV and hot showers attached. There's a convivial café. P̄P̄

BAYBAY BEACH
Casita Juan ⒲ facebook.com/casitajuan.baybay. A small and friendly hotel close to the beach, with stylishly minimalist rooms; the "loft", which sleeps up to six (in theory, at least) is quite something. There's a pleasant terrace on which to enjoy drinks. P̄P̄
San Antonio Resort ⒲ thesanantonioresort.com. A range of rooms from tiny budget rooms to luxurious suites overlooking an attractive lagoon just back from the beach. There's also a pleasant pool, and kayaking on the lagoon. P̄P̄

EATING

ROXAS
Eleckuisine Lopez Jaena St, ☎ 0906 368 6944. There are a surprising number of Mexican places in Roxas City; Eleckuisine is probably the best, with decent tacos and burritos served up in an atmospheric streetside spot decorated with excellent Mexican-themed murals. P̄P̄

BAYBAY BEACH
Almax Grill ☎ 0929 834 8628. In a long hall of a building

on the seashore, *Almax* serves standout *gambas*, grilled fish and smaller snacks like squid or catfish on a skewer. P̄
Coco Veranda ⒲ facebook.com/cocoverandacapiz. Pretty beachside restaurant with friendly service and a huge seafood menu. As well as excellent crab, scallops, oysters, mussels and prawns, there's also pink salmon sashimi, plus meat dishes, cocktails and desserts. Free wi-fi. P̄P̄

Kalibo

KALIBO, the capital of Aklan province, is the biggest – in fact the only – attraction of Panay's **north coast**, which from Roxas in the east to Caticlan in the west (see page 268) is mostly industrial and has no notable beaches. Served by flights from around Asia, Kalibo lies on the well-trodden path to Boracay; for most visitors, this is simply the place to transfer from plane to bus.

The town's major thoroughfare is **Roxas Avenue**, which runs into town from the airport in the southeast, with most streets leading off it on a southwest–northeast axis. It's really just another small town, full of tricycles and fast-food outlets, but it does have an interesting **museum**, and every second week of January it hosts what is probably the biggest street party in the country, the **Ati-Atihan**, an exuberant festival that celebrates the original inhabitants of the area and the later arrival of Catholicism (see box, page 271).

Museo It Akean
San Martelino St at Archbishop Reyes St • Charge • ⒲ facebook.com/MuseoItAkean

Kalibo is home to one of Panay's best museums, the **Museo It Akean**. Though modest, it's the only museum to document the cultural heritage of the Aklañons (Aklan people), and contains exhibits of the area's old *piña* textiles, pottery, religious relics, literature and Spanish-era artefacts, many on loan from affluent local families. Among the most interesting exhibits are rare costumes that were worn by the Aklan people during festivals. Despite serious earthquake damage in the 1980s, the museum building

6

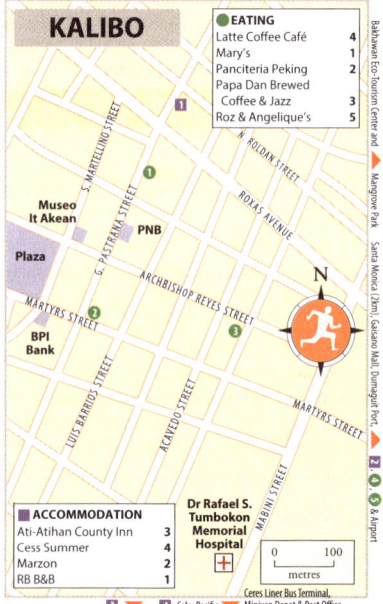

retains some of the original features; since its construction by the Spanish in 1882, it has also been used as a school, a courtroom and a garrison.

Bakhawan Eco-tourism Centre and Mangrove Park

Bakhawan, around 3km east of town • Charge

A short tricycle ride from town, the **Bakhawan Eco-tourism Centre and Mangrove Park** is the site of a mangrove-replanting project. The project was principally initiated to prevent flood and storm surges, but also benefits local wildlife and affords visitors the chance to experience this little-seen habitat up close. Once here, you can walk along a pretty 1km-long boardwalk through the tangled mangrove thickets to the beach.

ARRIVAL AND DEPARTURE　　　　KALIBO

By plane The tricycle ride into town from the airport, a distance of about 6km, takes 10min. As well as flights to Manila (4 daily; hr 10min), there are flights to Kalibo from South Korea, and charter services from a few Chinese cities; other international destinations have also been served in the past.

By boat Ferries arrive in Dumaguit Port, a 15min jeepney ride (around 12km) outside Kalibo. Shuttle buses take passengers from Kalibo's Ceres Liner terminal to Caticlan port, from where ferries run to several other destinations (see page 262); from Kalibo you can get combined bus-ferry tickets all the way to Manila (17hr approx).

By bus and van Regular buses and vans serving Caticlan (the jumping-off point for Boracay) arrive and depart directly from the airport (1hr 30min). Cheaper buses and vans to Caticlan leave from the Ceres Liner terminal on Osmeña Ave, from where there are also regular buses and vans to all other destinations listed.

Destinations Caticlan (every 20min; 1hr); Iloilo (every 20–30min; 4–5hr); Roxas (every 30min; 2hr); San José (hourly; 4–5hr).

ACCOMMODATION　　　　　　　　　　　　SEE MAP PAGE 270

Good accommodation can be hard to find during the Ati-Atihan, when rates double or triple, so if you're visiting during the festival, make sure you've booked a room (and, if you want to fly in, your plane ticket) in advance.

Ati-Atihan County Inn D. Maagma St ⓦfacebook.com/AntiAtihanCountyInn. Government-owned place offering good-value rooms with fans or a/c, cable TV and hot showers, set around a communal living area that has wi-fi. P̲

Cess Summer Jaime Cardinal Sin Ave ⓦfacebook.com/p/Cess-Summer-Hotel-100057351262602/. A little way south of the town centre, this friendly hotel offers spotless comfortable rooms with enough stylish touches to keep them from feeling bland. P̲P̲

★**Marzon** Jaime Cardinal Sin Ave, Santa Monica, 2km southeast of town ⓦmarzonhotelkalibo.com. Surprisingly upscale hotel for this part of the world – perhaps a sign of things to come. Owned by the same company as *Marzon* in Boracay, this modern hotel on the road out to the airport has comfortable, stylish rooms and a huge swimming pool. *Latte Coffee Café* (see page 271) is almost next door, and *Roz & Angelique's* (see page 271) just down the road. P̲P̲

★**RB B&B** G. Pastrana St ⓦfacebook.com/RBBedandBreakfast. Good-value hotel. The cheapest fan rooms are small and dark, but the better a/c rooms are quiet and tastefully furnished, though the phrase "you get what you pay for" comes to mind. There's also a coffee shop on site, which is where the second "B" from "B&B" comes in. P̲

EATING　　　　　　　　　　　　　　　　SEE MAP PAGE 270

Kalibo's dining options have improved in recent years, particularly out in Santa Monica on the way to the airport. In town there are a few independent places, but otherwise it's a choice of hole-in-the wall carinderias or fast-food chains

6

ATI-ATIHAN: KEEP ON GOING, NO TIRING

Ati-Atihan is a quasi-religious mardi gras held every January in Kalibo. The culmination of the two-week event is a procession through the streets on the third Sunday of the month, a sustained three-day, three-night frenzy of carousing and dancing. Transvestites bring out their best frocks, and schoolgirls with hats made of coconuts join aborigines, celebrities and priests in fancy dress. Throw in the unending beat of massed drums and the average Filipino's predisposition for a good party, and the result is a flamboyant alfresco rave that claims to be the biggest and most prolonged in the country. The Ati-Atihan mantra *Hala Bira, Puera Pasma* translates as "Keep on going, no tiring."

The festival's **origins** can be traced to 1210, when refugees from Borneo fled north to Panay. Panay's Negrito natives, known as Atis, sold them land; both parties celebrated the deal with a feast, which was then repeated year on year. The fancy-dress element derives from the lighter-skinned Borneans blacking up their faces in affectionate imitation of the Atis. Later, Spanish friars co-opted the festival in honour of the **Santo Niño**, spreading the word among islanders that the baby Jesus had appeared to help drive off a pirate attack. It was a move calculated to hasten the propagation of Catholicism throughout the Philippines, and it worked. Ati-Atihan has since become so popular that similar festivals have cropped up all over the Visayas. Historians generally agree, however, that the Kalibo Ati-Atihan is the real thing.

which include *Chowking, Jollibee* and *Andok's*.

★ **Latte Coffee Café** Jaime Cardinal Sin Ave, Santa Monica ☎ 036 268 9026. Pleasant coffee shop that, as you'd expect of a place with not one but three terms used to order coffee in the English language, offers great coffee, as well as sandwiches and light meals, alongside Havaiana flip-flops. P̄

Mary's G. Pastrana St ⓦfacebook.com/Marys Refreshment. Clean, bustling, canteen-style place serving huge bowls of noodles, sandwiches, desserts and coffee. P̄

Panciteria Peking Martyrs St ⓦfacebook.com/panciteriapeking. Kalibo's most popular Chinese restaurant is often full of folk enjoying delicious but inexpensive food such as seafood fried rice and noodle dishes. PP

Papa Dan Brewed Coffee & Jazz United Veterans Ave ⓦfacebook.com/papadanfoodandjazz. This place does pretty much what it says on the tin – it does indeed offer coffee and there are regular jazz performances in the evenings. There's also a short but good menu of pizzas, sandwiches and burgers. PPP

Roz & Angelique's Jaime Cardinal Sin Ave, Santa Monica ⓦfacebook.com/RozAndAngeliquesCafe. A popular dining spot for Kalibo's well-to-do, this formal restaurant has an extensive menu featuring everything from crispy *pata* (good for three) to crêpes, burgers, sandwiches, crème brûlée and shakes. No MSG is used in the cooking. PPP

Guimaras

Separated from the Panay mainland by the narrowest slither of ocean, the small island of **GUIMARAS** is best known for producing the tastiest mangoes in the Philippines. The bounteous fruit is celebrated on the third weekend of April at the **Manggahan Guimaras festival** in San Miguel, the island's capital, which includes an eating contest that sees competitors consuming as many of the super-sweet mangoes as they can in thirty minutes.

The island has some good, affordable **resorts**, exceptional **beaches** – especially around **Nueva Valencia** on the southwest coast – and a few enticing **islands** offshore. Its undulating **interior** makes it a beautiful place to explore by mountain bike – main roads are reasonably signed, though there are a bewildering array of secondary roads, trails and tracks. There's also a smattering of history, with defiant old Spanish churches and the country's only **Trappist monastery**. During the Filipino–American War, General Douglas MacArthur, then a first lieutenant, built the wharf near Buenavista, which is still being used by ferries today.

Guimaras has been affected by a couple of oil spills during the last couple of decades, and although the beaches look to the casual observer as if they are back to their pristine best, it will take decades longer for the island's mangrove ecosystems – and fish stocks –

6

to fully recover. One thing that might help the island, at least in an economic sense, is the envisioned **Panay–Guimaras–Negros Island Bridge**, for which ground is set to break around the time you read this; it's hoped to be in operation and cutting hours off travel in 2030, though knowing the Philippines, don't hold your breath.

Jordan and San Miguel

Tourists only visit **JORDAN**, in the north of the island, because most bangkas from Iloilo arrive at Hoskyn port 2km to the west. Nearby **SAN MIGUEL**, the capital, is on the island's major crossroads and, although few people choose to stay here, it has most of the facilities, including a couple of ATMs, as well as several simple local restaurants.

GUIMARAS

■ ACCOMMODATION	
JM Hometel	2
The Lazy Tiki	1
The Pitstop	4
Raymen Resort	5
Zemkamps Chalet	3

Kokomojo Farms

Around 4km from San Miguel • Free • ⓦ facebook.com/kokomojomango

You could hardly leave Guimaras without a visit to one of the **mango plantations**. All have just the right soil, elevation and exposure to the elements to produce succulent fruit ready for the main harvest season in April and May. The most visitor-friendly plantation on the island is **Kokomojo Farms**, near Millan, roughly in the centre of Guimaras, where the owners will show you around personally if you call ahead.

Our Lady of the Philippines Trappist Monastery

2km south of San Miguel

Founded in 1972 by Americans, **Our Lady of the Philippines Trappist Monastery** lies on the main road southwest from San Miguel. Orchards grow assorted tropical fruit, and there's an interesting souvenir shop where monks sell banana fries, cashews, guava jelly, mango jam and even holy water under the Trappist Monastic Products brand name. Unfortunately, you cannot enter the monastery itself, although you can attend one of the seven daily church services.

Sad-Sad Falls

1.5km west of the San Miguel to Nueva Valencia road, down an unmarked track about 500m south of Guimaras Memorial Gardens Park; about a 10min walk from the car park

Guimaras has some pretty waterfalls in its hinterland, the best of which is **Sad-Sad Falls**, south of San Miguel. You can swim in the chilly mountain pool formed by the gushing water, or just have a picnic.

Nueva Valencia and the south

NUEVA VALENCIA in the southwest is nothing more than a ramshackle crossroads town. However, it's close to a couple of the island's better resorts and the **JBLFMU Ecopark** (dawn to dusk; charge), a convoluted promontory featuring a marine sanctuary, a sea cave with coral, sea grass monitoring station and a butterfly garden.

Taklong and Sereray islands

Bangkas can be hired through resorts or direct from boat owners

Exploring the beautiful islands and islets in the south of Guimaras by bangka makes a good day-trip. Off the southwest coast is **Taklong Island**, a marine reserve whose mangroves and beds of sea grass are breeding grounds for hundreds of marine species. Off the southeast coast there's **Sereray Island** and **Nao-wai Island**, both with tiny sandy coves where you can picnic and swim.

Navalas and the north

6

The seventeenth-century **Navalas Church**, an atmospherically decrepit relic of the Spanish regime, is a good starting point for exploring the barangay of **NAVALAS** on Guimaras' northern coast. A short walk away on a promontory overlooking Iloilo Strait stands a villa known as **Roca Encantada** (Enchanted Rock) or, more sneeringly, Lopezville, vacation house of the wealthy Lopez clan who hail from Iloilo.

Siete Pecados

30min by bangka from Navalas • Small boats (fitting four to six people) charge by the hour • Bring your own snorkel; many accommodations rent them out

Opposite the Roca Encantada's promontory is a picturesque group of coral islets called **Siete Pecados** (Isles of the Seven Sins). The largest of these has an impressive house perched on top, but the others are bare. There are no beaches, but it's worth the trip for the snorkelling.

ARRIVAL AND INFORMATION

GUIMARAS

To/from Panay Frequent bangkas (20min) leave Ortiz wharf in Iloilo City for Hoskyn port on the west coast of Guimaras. Some resorts can send a bangka to collect you at Iloilo.

To/from Negros There are ferries from Sebaste on the southeast coast to Pulupandan (2–3 daily; 1hr), which also receives two daily bangkas from Suclaran further up the east coast. There is also a daily bangka from Cabalagnan on Guimaras' south coast to Valladolid, south of Bacolod.

Tourist Information On arrival at Hoskyn port, look for the Guimaras Tourism Assistance kiosk (daily 7.30am–4.30pm; ☎ 0999 332 1727).

Banks San Miguel has the island's only ATMs; you'd best bring some cash along for the ride, in any case.

Hospitals Medical care is better than you might expect, with a provincial hospital in San Miguel and others at Buenavista and Nueva Valencia.

GETTING AROUND

By jeepney Open-sided minivans and jeepneys make regular circuits of the island's major towns and ports and can be useful for touring the island if you're not laden down with luggage. Jeepneys charge by the section (for example Jordan to San Miguel, or San Miguel to Nueva Valencia); the journey from Jordan to Nueva Valencia takes 45min–1hr.

By tricycle and habal-habal Since many of the resorts

lie off the main jeepney and minivan routes, hiring a tricycle or habal-habal is the most convenient option for getting to your accommodation.

By motorbike and bicycle To get the most out of exploring the island on two wheels, it's worth enquiring about a guide at the tourism assistance kiosk in Hoskyn. Many resorts rent out mountain bikes and motorbikes.

ACCOMMODATION AND EATING

SEE MAP PAGE 272

Guimaras is small enough that it doesn't matter too much where you **stay**. Even if you choose the solitude of a resort on one of the smaller islands nearby, it's easy to hop on a bangka back to Guimaras itself. **Eating** is almost exclusively in the resorts, apart from some humble local joints, mainly in San Miguel, serving *lechon* and the like.

JM Hometel San Miguel ⌾ bit.ly/JMBackpackers Homotel. One of the very few choices if you want a central location in the capital, this fine modern hostel has compact

rooms, some with a/c and all featuring cable TV and separate shower and toilet cubicles. $\overline{PP}$

The Lazy Tiki Buenavista ⌾ the-lazy-tiki. tagaytaycountryhotel.com.ph. The island's most relaxed accommodation is hiding up near its northern tip. Its rooms are quite charming, decorated as they are with images of yesteryear; the beach is right there, there's a swimming pool if you don't fancy sea water, and rocking chairs on which to idle away the time. $\overline{PP}$

6

The Pitstop Jordan ⓦfacebook.com/pitstop mangopizza. Everyone's looking for their individual niche these days, and the Pitstop, found in the centre of Jordan, seems to have found theirs: mango pizzas. It's certainly something to try, but perhaps only once. Ask them to go easy on the cheese if you don't want your pizza overloaded. Other, safer, options on the menu do exist. $\overline{PP}$

Raymen Resort Alubihod, 1.5km west of Nueva Valencia ⓦraymenresort.com. Located on the island's southwest coast, *Raymen Resort* has clean a/c rooms with TV and hot showers in a building set back from the beach, as well as cheaper fan rooms. There's a simple restaurant, which you should avoid at weekends if you don't like karaoke. $\overline{PPP}$

Zemkamps Chalet Jordan ⓦfacebook.com/zemkamps chalet. Attractive and well-maintained hotel in Jordan, with comfortable – if a little bland – rooms. The breakfast is good, and the restaurant is open for tasty evening meals too. $\overline{PP}$

Negros

The island of **NEGROS**, fourth largest in the country and home to 3.5 million people, lies at the heart of the Visayas, between Panay to the west and Cebu to the east. Shaped like a boot, it's split diagonally into the northwestern province of Negros Occidental and the southeastern province of Negros Oriental. The demarcation came when early missionaries decided that the thickly jungled central mountain range was too formidable to cross, and this is still felt today with each side of the island speaking different main languages – Cebuano to the east and Ilonggo to the west.

Today, Negros is known as "Sugarlandia"; its rich lowlands grow two-thirds of the nation's sugar cane, and you'll see evidence of this in the vast silver-green expanse of sugar-cane plantations stretching from the Gulf of Panay across to the gentle foothills off the volcanic mountains of the interior and beyond. The mountains rise to a giddy 2465m at the peak of **Mount Kanlaon**, the highest mountain in the Visayas. For the intrepid, this means there's some extreme trekking and climbing on Negros, from Mount Kanlaon itself to **Mount Silay** in the north.

From **Bacolod**, the capital of Negros Occidental, you can follow the coastal road clockwise to **Silay**, a beautifully preserved sugar town with grand antique homes and old sugar locomotives. Much of the north coast is given over to the port towns through which sugar is shipped to Manila, but at the southern end of the island around **Dumaguete** there are good beaches and scuba diving, with a range of excellent budget accommodation. The **southwest coast** – the heel of the boot – is home to the island's best beaches, and remains charmingly rural and undeveloped, with carabao in the fields and chocolate-coloured roads winding lazily into the farming barangays of the foothills.

Brief history

Among Negros's earliest inhabitants were dark-skinned natives belonging to the **Negrito** ethnic group – hence the name Negros, imposed by the Spanish when they set foot here in April 1565. After appointing bureaucrats to run the island, Miguel López de Legazpi placed it under the jurisdiction of its first Spanish governor. Religious orders wasted no time in moving in to evangelize the natives, who were deemed ripe for conversion to the true faith. The latter half of the eighteenth century was a period of rapid economic expansion for Negros, with its **sugar industry** flourishing and Visayan ports such as Cebu and Iloilo open for the first time to foreign ships. In the last century, the rapacious growth of the sugar industry and its increasing politicization were to have disastrous consequences that are still being felt today (see box opposite).

ARRIVAL AND DEPARTURE   NEGROS

By plane The main airports on Negros are Bacolod and Dumaguete, both with flights from Manila and Cebu City.
By boat The biggest and busiest ports on the island are Bacolod and Dumaguete, which are connected by regular ferries with Manila and Mindanao. Bacolod also has ferry connections with Iloilo on Panay, while Dumaguete and

THE BITTER HISTORY OF SUGAR IN NEGROS

Land reform – or the lack of it – has been at the root of simmering discontent on Negros that began in the 1970s under Ferdinand Marcos and continues to this day. All of Negros's sugar-producing land is held by two percent of the people, and half the arable land by five percent. Negros's gentry see the land as a way of life, while the Church, the New People's Army (NPA; see page 419) and various peasant organizations see it as a source of food. The NPA has been screaming about land reform for years, intimidating *haciendoros* and seizing land. The *haciendoros* have responded with private armies and acts of repression, turning Negros into a battleground for the struggle between rich and poor, in which the rich have all the guns.

In the 1970s and 1980s this struggle was played out against the background of Ferdinand Marcos's thieving dictatorship. Marcos monopolized sugar trading, placing it in the hands of crony **Roberto Benedicto**, who ended up controlling 106 sugar farms, 85 corporations, 17 radio stations, 16 television stations, a Manila casino, a *Holiday Inn* and a major piece of the national oil company. Known as the Sugar Czar, he effectively controlled the supply chain, allowing him to steal tens of millions of dollars from his neighbours on Negros by paying them a quarter of the price he received when he resold their sugar. For good measure Marcos gave him control of the bank that was the planters' principal lending agency.

In 1974, as prices of sugar on the world market rose steadily, Benedicto began hoarding, speculating that the price would continue to rise. When sugar prices plummeted in 1984, Benedicto responded by paying planters less for their sugar than it cost to grow. The planters took their land out of cultivation and, as a result, production in 1985 was half that of ten years earlier. Thousands were thrown out of work and hunger and malnutrition set in on a massive scale. Benedicto got out of the sugar business and was promptly appointed Philippine ambassador to Japan.

In 1981, the **Pope** visited Negros and thrust the island into the international limelight with his words of condemnation ("injustice reigns"), in stark contrast to Imelda Marcos's message that "Negros is not an island of fear, but an island of love". Five years later Marcos was overthrown, and **Cory Aquino** gave the impression during her election campaign that she was willing to give up her family's hacienda north of Manila in the name of nationwide land reform. But once elected she produced a watered-down land bill which she dumped in the lap of a newly elected Congress dominated by landed oligarchs. "She might as well have appointed a crack addict to run her drug treatment programme," said an opposition senator.

As for Benedicto, he was allowed to keep US$15 million of the fortune he amassed, and he lived quietly in Negros until his death in 2000. Although no longer ruled by a single overlord, since the millennium the Negros sugar-cane industry has been in gradual decline, trying to compete with globalized market forces. Meanwhile, even when they do have work, the 300,000 labourers who toil in the fields continue to survive on barely subsistence wages.

its satellite ports have various services to Cebu, Tagbilaran (Bohol) and Siquijor. Many other coastal towns have smaller ferries and bangkas going to neighbouring islands as well as to other destinations on Negros itself. Boats from San Carlos, on the east coast, head to Toledo (7 daily; 2hr) on Cebu, while Cadiz has reliable connections to the local Bantayan Island.

Bacolod

On the northern coast of Negros, **BACOLOD** is a half-million-strong provincial metropolis, known as the "City of Smiles" and famed for its flamboyant **Masskara Festival** (third week of Oct). Its tourist attractions aren't significant enough to make you linger for more than a day or two, but it's a major transit point and a good base from which to visit nearby historic towns such as Silay and Victorias, or to arrange more adventurous excursions to Mount Kanlaon.

The old **city centre**, chaotic and choked with traffic, is best defined as the area around the **City Plaza** at the northern end of Araneta Street. North of here, Bacolod's main thoroughfare, and the city's social hub, is **Lacson Street**, which runs past the Provincial Capitol Building and has good restaurants, shops and bars. There are more places to stay, eat and party 3km south of the town centre at the **Goldenfields Commercial Complex**.

Negros Museum
Gatuslao St • Charge • ⓦ ncfiph.org

Housed in an elegant Neoclassical building dating from the 1930s (though badly damaged by a storm in 2012), the **Negros Museum** details five thousand years of island history and has artefacts from other parts of Asia. Its star exhibit is the "iron dinosaur" steam engine on the upper floor, once used to haul sugar cane. The 1930s Provincial Capitol Building next door is another of the city's few architectural highlights.

Negros Forest and Ecological Foundation
South Capitol Rd, opposite the Provincial Capitol • Charge • ☏ 034 433 9234

The rescue centre at the **Negros Forest and Ecological Foundation** is an unexpected reprieve from the streets. It's not a huge site, but conservationists do what they can to care for endangered animals endemic to Negros, including leopard cats, the Visayan spotted deer, the writhed hornbill and the Negros bleeding-heart pigeon.

The Ruins
Talisay • Charge • ⓦ theruins.com.ph • Best visited on a round trip by taxi, or take a tricycle ride from the crossroads immediately south of the North bus terminal

Seven kilometres north of the Provincial Capitol Building, on the edge of town, **The Ruins** make a great short excursion from the city. Officially the Don Mariano Ledesma Lacson Mansion, it is billed as the "Taj Mahal of Negros", more for its sad story of love lost than its architectural splendour, although it does have a haunting beauty. The Lacsons were one of the island's pre-eminent sugar families in the nineteenth century. When Maria Lacson died during pregnancy with the couple's eleventh child, Don Mariano was inconsolable and set about building a memorial mansion. During the outbreak of World War II, the building was razed to prevent it being used as a headquarters by the Japanese. The fire left behind the building's complete superstructure, including the double-M motif used throughout. Mariano died in 1948, and the building was largely forgotten until his great-grandson decided to open it to the public. On site you'll also find the interesting *Tractor Café*.

ARRIVAL AND DEPARTURE   BACOLOD

By plane Bacolod-Silay Airport is located 15km northeast of town and is linked to Bacolod by taxi, shuttle buses from SM City Mall or, cheapest but least convenient, by jeepney from the North bus terminal to Silay, from where it's a short tricycle ride.
Destinations Cebu City (5–7 daily; 45min); Davao (3 weekly; 1hr 10min); Manila (10–14 daily; 1hr 15min).
By boat Most ferries come from Iloilo and dock at Bredco port, a short walk or tricycle ride west of City Plaza. Oceanjet (ⓦ oceanjet.net), 2GO (ⓦ travel.2go.com.ph) and Weesam Express (ⓦ weesam.ph) have ticket offices here. Long-distance ferries to Manila and Mindanao leave less often and use the old Banago wharf, 8km north of Bacolod. You can pick up a jeepney from Banago into town. Smaller vessels for Guimaras leave from either Pulupandan or

Valladolid, 20km and 25km southwest respectively.
Destinations Cagayan de Oro (1 weekly; 21–22hr); Iligan (1 weekly; 14hr); Iloilo (every 20–40min; 1hr); Manila (4 weekly; 20–24hr); Ozamiz (1 weekly; 18–19hr).
By bus Ceres Liner buses (ⓦ ceresliner.com) drop passengers at one of two main terminals. The South terminal, for destinations south, is on Lopez Jaena St, just east of the old city, while the North terminal is around 4km north of town on the National Highway (continuation of Lacson St). Buses from the North terminal head along the coastal road to Cadiz, from where there are boats to Bantayan Island; some continue on to San Carlos and round the long way (313km) to Dumaguete, while others board ferries at San Carlos for Toledo on the western coast of Cebu and continue on to Cebu City. The quickest way to

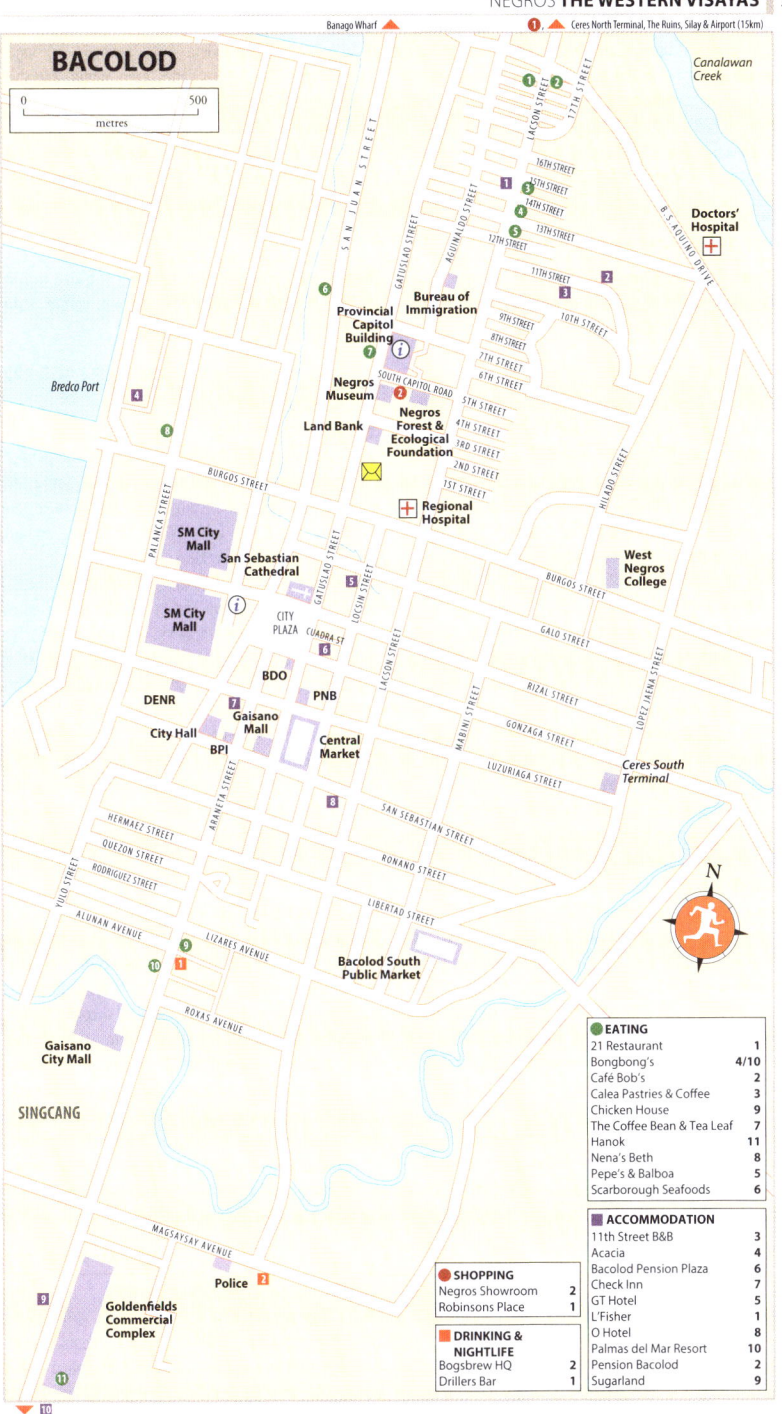

BACOLOD

Banago Wharf

Ceres North Terminal, The Ruins, Silay & Airport (15km)

Canalawan Creek

0 — 500 metres

Doctors' Hospital

Bredco Port

Bureau of Immigration

Provincial Capitol Building

Negros Museum

Land Bank

Negros Forest & Ecological Foundation

Regional Hospital

West Negros College

SM City Mall

San Sebastian Cathedral

SM City Mall

CITY PLAZA

BDO

DENR

PNB

Gaisano Mall

City Hall

BPI

Central Market

Ceres South Terminal

Bacolod South Public Market

Gaisano City Mall

SINGCANG

Police

Goldenfields Commercial Complex

STREETS

LACSON STREET · 12TH STREET · SAN JUAN STREET · GATUSLAO STREET · AGUINALDO STREET · B.S. AQUINO DRIVE · 16TH STREET · 15TH STREET · 14TH STREET · 13TH STREET · 12TH STREET · 11TH STREET · 10TH STREET · 9TH STREET · 8TH STREET · 7TH STREET · 6TH STREET · 5TH STREET · 4TH STREET · 3RD STREET · 2ND STREET · 1ST STREET · SOUTH CAPITOL ROAD · MILADO STREET · BURGOS STREET · BURGOS STREET · GATUSLAO STREET · LOCSIN STREET · LACSON STREET · GALO STREET · RIZAL STREET · MABINI STREET · GONZAGA STREET · LOPEZ JAENA STREET · LUZURIAGA STREET · PALANCA STREET · ARANETA STREET · CUADRA ST · SAN SEBASTIAN STREET · HERMAEZ STREET · RONANO STREET · QUEZON STREET · RODRIGUEZ STREET · LIBERTAD STREET · YULO STREET · ALUNAN AVENUE · LIZARES AVENUE · ROXAS AVENUE · MAGSAYSAY AVENUE

N

6

● EATING	
21 Restaurant	1
Bongbong's	4/10
Café Bob's	2
Calea Pastries & Coffee	3
Chicken House	9
The Coffee Bean & Tea Leaf	7
Hanok	11
Nena's Beth	8
Pepe's & Balboa	5
Scarborough Seafoods	6

■ ACCOMMODATION	
11th Street B&B	3
Acacia	4
Bacolod Pension Plaza	6
Check Inn	7
GT Hotel	5
L'Fisher	1
O Hotel	8
Palmas del Mar Resort	10
Pension Bacolod	2
Sugarland	9

● SHOPPING	
Negros Showroom	2
Robinsons Place	1

■ DRINKING & NIGHTLIFE	
Bogsbrew HQ	2
Drillers Bar	1

Dumaguete is from the South terminal down the west coast and then via the inland road that runs from Kabankalan across the mountains. A few services cover this route directly, but most of the time you'll need to change in Kabankalan. Buses heading south along the coast road for Sipalay also leave from the South terminal.

Destinations Cadiz (every 15–30min; 1hr 30min); Cebu City (7 daily; 8–10hr); Dumaguete (every 30min; 6–7hr); Sagay (every 30min–1hr; 2hr); San Carlos (every 30min–1hr; 3hr); Silay (every 10–15min; 20min); Sipalay (hourly; 4–5hr).

By jeepney Jeepneys, vans and tricycles ply short journeys within the city. For Silay you'll need to change at the North bus terminal. Jeepneys to Pulupandan (40min) and Valladolid (50min) leave from outside the South terminal.

INFORMATION AND ACTIVITIES

Tourist information The Negros Occidental Tourism Center (Mon–Fri 8am–5pm; ☎ 034 433 2515) is in the Provincial Capitol Building.

Hiking and cycling To arrange hiking or biking trips in the foothills of Mt Kanlaon, contact the tourist office, or the DENR on Luzuriaga St (ⓦ denr.gov.ph).

ACCOMMODATION
SEE MAP PAGE 277

Hotels are spread throughout the city but there are three main areas to choose from: foodies will relish the uptown choices around the northern section of **Lacson St**; bargain-hunters are best off in the shabbier **town centre**; and nightlife fiends will find surprisingly quiet accommodation around **Goldenfields**, a modern complex 3km south of town and also the city's red-light district.

CITY CENTRE

Acacia P Hernaez St Ext ⓦ acaciahotelsbacolod.com. Conveniently located by the ferry, the international-standard rooms at the *Acacia* are large with comfortable beds, and some come with sea views. There's a pool for guest use, which is ideal on warmer days. Breakfast is a bit limited but tasty enough, and the meals at the restaurant aren't bad either. P̄P̄

Bacolod Pension Plaza Cuadra St, opposite City Plaza ☎ 0915 363 7138. Not to be confused with *Pension Bacolod*, this place is bigger and more central, with dozens of old but well-maintained a/c rooms. P̄

Check Inn Luzuriaga St ⓦ reddoorz.com. Decent-value option – now under the *RedDoorz* umbrella – near the old town centre with modern, clean and comfortable rooms, the best of which are on the business floor, set around the roof garden. P̄

GT Hotel Locsin St at Galo St ⓦ facebook.com/ GTHotelBacolod. One of the city's newer hotels, with friendly staff and attractive, modern rooms styled in muted tones. Mod cons include central a/c, low lighting, flatscreen TV and fridge. P̄P̄

O Hotel 52 San Sebastian St ⓦ ohotel.com.ph. Large, modern motel-style hotel with brightly coloured lobby and rooms, all with cable TV, fridge and mini-bar, although those facing the front are noisy. There's also an ATM in the lobby. P̄P̄

LACSON STREET

★ **11th Street B&B** 14 11th St ⓦ facebook. com/11thstreetbedandbreakfast. A great-value pension set around a leafy courtyard with a fountain, just a few minutes' walk from the Lacson St restaurants. Rooms are clean and simple with cable TV and bathrooms, and a/c rooms have hot water. Breakfast included. P̄P̄

★ **L'Fisher** Lacson St ⓦ lfisherhotelbacolod.com. One of Bacolod's best top-end hotels, this glass-fronted establishment is in a great location right on Lacson St. The deluxe rooms are extremely comfortable, with a/c, cable TV, fridge and safe. There's also a 24hr poolside café that offers buffet lunches and dinners. Within the same complex are two more modest sister hotels. P̄P̄P̄

Pension Bacolod 11th St ☎ 0943 561 9173. Not as welcoming as the *11th Street B&B* along the road, this popular cheapie is still great value, though both the walls and mattresses are thin. The cheapest rooms have shared bathrooms. P̄

ELSEWHERE IN THE CITY

Palmas del Mar Resort J.R. Torres Ave, 2km southwest of Goldenfields ⓦ facebook.com/palmasdel marresortbacolod. Family resort in a residential area close to the sea, with a good range of accommodation, including regular a/c rooms, family rooms and cottages. There's a decent-sized pool and the restaurant serves local specialities and European dishes. You might have the pool to yourself on weekdays, but weekends can get busy. P̄P̄P̄

Sugarland Araneta St ⓦ sugarlandhotel.com. Good-value modern hotel with stylish and well-kept a/c rooms. There's also a small pool and a couple of good restaurants in the hotel, plus a massage service. P̄P̄

EATING
SEE MAP PAGE 277

Bacolod's dining scene has moved uptown and upscale in recent years, with a cosmopolitan range of trendy cafés and restaurants along northern **Lacson St**, while time-tested favourites still hold their own in the **old city**. As well as the listings below, it's worth checking out the row of identikit chicken restaurants at **Manokan Country**.

★ **21 Restaurant** 21st St at Lacson St ⓦ facebook. com/21-Restaurant-174681132582731. Popular with Bacolod's elite and middle classes, this institution dishes out amazing *batchoy* (noodle soup with crispy pork) and

excellent seafood, from blue marlin with herb butter to good old-fashioned fish and chips. White tablecloths and attentive service complete the picture. $\overline{PPPP}$
Bongbong's Araneta St ⓦfacebook.com/bastapasalubong. For a real taste of Sugarlandia, *Bongbong's* sells everything from banana-honey chips to *piyaya* (a hardened pancake with sugar melted inside) and delicious *bay ibayi* (sugar and coconut bar). They also have outlets at the ferry terminal, on the plaza and at the corner of 13th St at Lacson St. $\overline{P}$
Café Bobs 21st St at Lacson St ⓦfacebook.com/cafebobs. Super-popular diner that efficiently turns out pizzas, sandwiches and burgers, plus coffees. It also a huge range of imported goods for sale in the deli. $\overline{PP}$
Calea Pastries & Coffee 15th St at Lacson St. Hugely popular spot, not so much for the comestibles hidden within its name, but for their tempting array of cakes, most of which are available by the slice. $\overline{PP}$
★**Chicken House** Araneta St ⓦfacebook.com/chickenhousebacolod. An oldie but a goodie, *Chicken House* has been serving up sumptuous roast chicken and other grilled meat for three decades and continues to draw in the local crowds with its distinctive flavours and low prices. Other branches around town. $\overline{PP}$
The Coffee Bean & Tea Leaf Gatuslao St ⓦcoffeebean.

com. If you've never been to a *Coffee Bean & Tea Leaf* before (there are over one thousand of them, in two dozen countries), here's your chance. It's as good a place as any in town to get a brew and chill out while enjoying one of the excellent cakes or pastries – the carrot cake is particularly good. $\overline{PP}$
Hanok Araneta Ave, Goldenfields ☎034 704 6137. Billing itself as an "authentic Korean restaurant", this place gets off to a bad start by spelling its name (*hanok* being traditional wooden houses in Korea) incorrectly in Korean on the sign outside. Nevertheless, the dishes served inside are actually pretty good; they focus on broths and BBQ. $\overline{PPP}$
Nena's Beth Palanca St. Popular, canteen-style place that's great for delicious Inasal chicken, pork, liver and *bangus* (milkfish), all at great prices. $\overline{PP}$
Pepe's & Balboa 13th St at Lacson St ⓦfacebook.com/pepesxbalboa. *Balboa* is a clean, bright diner with a Negrense twist. Along with diner staples including pizza and spareribs, local offerings include *kare kare* and *lechon kawali*. $\overline{PPP}$
Scarborough Seafoods San Juan St, opposite the fish market ⓦfacebook.com/scarboroughseadoodPala2x. Massive fish restaurant with indoor and outdoor seating, where you can get the catch of the day at near-market rates, plus delights like crab-meat soup or shrimp tempura. $\overline{PPP}$

DRINKING AND NIGHTLIFE
SEE MAP PAGE 277

The city's nightlife district is cited as **Goldenfields Commercial Complex** in Singcang, but while there are a few regular bars and clubs, in truth many of the places here are go-go bars catering to an exclusively male crowd, so the atmosphere is rather seedy.
Bogsbrew HQ Magsaysay Ave ⓦinstagram.com/bogsbrew. You can tell that Bacolod is on the up – it not only has a craft beer bar, but one selling beer brewed right

here in the city. Oddly, rather than opting for the generic stylings of such venues, they've made the place look more like a café.
Drillers Bar Alunan St ⓦfacebook.com/drillersbar168. The city's most enjoyable bar (unless, of course, you're into the go-go variety), with a youthful clientele filling the two spacious levels. Cold beer and cheap cocktails – a winning mix.

SHOPPING
SEE MAP PAGE 277

Negros Showroom S Capitol Rd ☎034 468 8857. This extensive showroom has top-quality handicrafts from all over the island.
Robinsons Place Lacson St, 1km north of B.S. Aquino

Drive ⓦrobinsonsmalls.com. Located on the northern section of Lacson St, this popular countrywide mall has dozens of shops to supply your everyday needs, as well as clothes stores and fast-food outlets.

DIRECTORY

Cinema There's a cinema in the SM City Mall, off Rizal St (ⓦsmcinema.com).
Hospitals Bacolod Doctors' Hospital (☎034 468 2100, ⓦthedoctorshospital.com) is on B.S. Aquino Drive, northeast of the centre.

Immigration The Bureau of Immigration is at the back of the National Bureau of Investigation office on Aguinaldo St (☎034 433 8581).
Police Police headquarters is at Magsaysay Ave, south of the centre, in Singcang (☎034 434 1152).

Silay

The elegant town of **SILAY**, about 15km north of Bacolod, is an atmospheric relic of a grander age, when Negros was rich from its cultivation of sugar cane. In the late eighteenth century it was talked about as the "Paris of Negros", with music performers

6

from Europe arriving by steamship to take part in operettas and *zarzuelas*. This passion for music and the arts gave Silay – and the Philippines – its first international star, **Conchita Gaston**, a mezzo-soprano who performed in major opera houses in Europe in the postwar years. Japanese forces occupied the city in World War II, after which the sugar industry declined and Silay lost its lustre – many of its European residents departed for home. Today, Silay's major tourist draw is its **ancestral homes**, most of them built between 1880 and 1940. Some of the best are open to the public or have been converted into hotels, offering a glimpse of what life was like for the sugar barons.

The main road runs through Silay as **Rizal Street**, passing the central public plaza halfway along its kilometre strip of shops, hotels and restaurants. The major annual festival in town, the **Kansilay**, lasts one week and ends every November 13 with a re-enactment of a folk tale showing the bravery of a beautiful princess who offered her life for justice and freedom.

The Balay Negrense Museum

Cinco de Noviembre St, a 5min walk west of the central plaza • Charge • ☎ 034 445 4282

The **Balay Negrense Museum** was once the home of Don Victor Gaston, eldest son of Yves Leopold Germaine Gaston, a Frenchman who settled in Silay in the mid-nineteenth century. After World War II, the house was left deserted; by 1980, it was a sad ruin, known only by locals for the ghosts that were said to roam its corridors. Now restored by the Negros Foundation, the house is a glorious monument to Silay's golden age, with rooms of polished mahogany furnished with antiques donated by locals.

Don Bernardino-Ysabel Jalandoni House Museum

Rizal St • Charge • ☎ 034 495 5093

Hard to miss at the northernmost end of Rizal Street is the pink **Don Bernardino-Ysabel Jalandoni House Museum**, known throughout town as the Pink House. Built in 1908, it gives some idea of the luxury of the time and features displays of antique law books and Japanese occupation currency. The price includes a guided tour – ask them to show you the huge metal vat in the garden, which was used to make muscovado sugar.

Manuel and Hilda Hofileña ancestral house

Cinco de Noviembre St • Charge • ☎ 034 495 4561

The first ancestral home in Silay to open its doors to the public, the **Manuel and Hilda Hofileña ancestral house** is one of the last vestiges of the city's artistic history. The house holds a gallery of works collected by Manuel and Hilda's son, Ramon, which includes contemporary Filipino painters and masters such as Juan Luna and Amorsolo, as well as two nude sketches of Ramon in a state of arousal. Also on display are countless fascinating antiques and curiosities which include part of a meteorite fragment, one of Negros's oldest pieces of pottery and (allegedly) the world's smallest dolls, visible through a magnifying glass. An incongruously modern DVD collection caps it off.

Church of San Diego

Zamora St, on the north side of the public plaza

Built in 1925, the **Church of San Diego** is a dramatic sight, with a great illuminated crucifix on top of the dome that is so bright at night that it was once used by ships as a navigational aid. Behind the church are the ruins of the original sixteenth-century Spanish church, now converted into a grotto and prayer garden.

Guinhalaran

About 2.5km from town; 10min by tricycle or jeepney

Silay is known for **pottery** made from the red clay endemic to the area. In the barangay of **Guinhalaran** on the National Highway, you can visit the potters and watch them making high-quality jars and vases, which are for sale at bargain prices.

Hawaiian Philippines Sugar Company

About 7km from town; 15min by tricycle • Hours vary • ☎ 034 495 2085 • Visits can be arranged through the tourist office (see page 281)

Just a short drive from Silay, this historic **Hawaiian Philippines Sugar Company** mill offers the chance to take a ride on one of the famed "iron dinosaurs" and see the workings of a genuine sugar mill. North from here along the rugged coast is Victorias Milling Company (🖰victoriasmilling.com), the largest integrated mill and sugar refinery in Asia.

ARRIVAL AND INFORMATION   SILAY

By bus and jeepney Buses and jeepneys from Bacolod either terminate at the southern end of Rizal St, from where it's a short walk to the centre, or pass right through the plaza.

Tourist information The Silay tourist office (Mon–Fri 8am–noon & 1–5pm; ☎ 034 495 5553) is in the central plaza. The helpful staff can arrange informal guided tours of some ancestral houses that aren't usually open to the public, and will open the small historical museum (same hours) opposite the office for you.

ACCOMMODATION AND EATING

1898 Casa and Restaurante Zamora St 🖰facebook. com/1898CasaAndRestaurante. Housed in an attractive period building, this restaurant dishes up a menu of international standards, including pizzas, sandwiches and the like. You can't miss the place – there's a trio of statues outside which depict the Negros rebellion against the Spanish. Rooms are also available. P̄P̄P̄

Balay 8 Suites Senator Jose Locsin St 🖰facebook.com/balay8. Smart, spacious and reasonably priced rooms await at Balay 8 Suites, found a little way south from the town centre. P̄P̄

Café 1925 4 J. Ledesma St ☎ 034 714 7414. This pretty little place dishes up Italian classics, sandwiches, pasta, squid balls and excellent coffee. P̄

El Ideal 118 Rizal St. Established in 1920, this bright and airy café-deli does a range of sweet and savoury items, including noodles, sandwiches and rice meals, cassava cake, and *halo-halo*. P̄

★ **German Unson Heritage House** Zamora St, 150m east of the plaza 🖰facebook.com/german unsonheritagehouse. This superbly renovated property, full of original furniture and artwork, exudes period charm while offering modern comforts. The biggest of the four ample-sized rooms has a huge shower and oval stone bath. There are balconies, gardens and complimentary breakfast. P̄P̄

Mount Kanlaon

Thirty kilometres southeast of Bacolod, **Mount Kanlaon** (2435m) is the tallest peak in the central Philippines and one of the thirteen most active volcanoes in the country. Climbing it offers a potentially dangerous challenge, with the real possibility of violent eruptions – climbers have died scaling it – and the crater's rim is a forbidding knife-edge overhanging an apparently bottomless chasm. The dense surrounding **forest** contains all manner of wonderful fauna, including pythons and tube-nosed bats, and locals believe the mountain is home to many spirits. It also features in Philippine history – it's where President Manuel Quezon hid from invading Japanese forces during World War II. Unfortunately, a series of large **eruptions** in late 2024 and early 2025 meant that the mountain was off limits at the time of writing; the effect was also felt by the local sugar industry, with many hectares of crop being lost, while farmers lost thousands of head of livestock.

There are, when the thing isn't blowing its top, three main routes up the volcano itself. The **Guintubdan trail** is the easiest and most common ascent, but even this should not be underestimated. From here, although it's only 8km to the top, the trail is best broken with an overnight stop (see page 282). The 14km-long **Mananawin trail** works best over three days and offers the chance to really get to know the region, while the short, steep **Wesey trail** is very exposed and only for experienced tropical mountaineers. It goes without saying that for whichever route you choose, you'll need a guide.

ARRIVAL AND INFORMATION   MOUNT KANLAON

By jeepney Guintubdan is 2hr by jeepney from Bacolod, with a change at La Carlota.

Guides Whichever way you choose to ascend, a permit and guide are mandatory, and a porter might come in handy. The easiest way to make all of these arrangements is through the Department of Environment and Natural

Resources (⚉ denr.gov.ph), or directly with Angelo Bibar (📞 0917 301 1410). Contact Angelo as far in advance as possible (ideally a month) and he can arrange everything from permits, guides and porters to tents and meals. Various other agents and hotels throughout Negros also run trips.

6

ACCOMMODATION AND EATING

The recent eruptions saw a couple of the mountain's already-tiny number of accommodation options close, so do check ahead to see what's available.

Guintubdan Mountain Resort Guintubdan 📞 034 460 0286. Clean and simple accommodation, with cold showers, in an attractive lodge nestled in the forest. Rooms are more attractive than you might think for such a far-flung location, and there's even a swimming pool with views out over the surrounding jungle (though, somewhat ironically, it can be hard to see said jungle for the compound's trees). P̄

Sagay and around

SAGAY is a hectic industrial and fishing city 15km east along the coast from the sugar port of **Cadiz**, at the mouth of the Bulanon River. Head for the city plaza and take a look at the **Legendary Siete**, or Train Number Seven, an "iron dinosaur" that once hauled lumber for the Insular Lumber Company and now stands in the middle of the plaza, restored and sparkling in all her 75-tonne liveried glory.

Sagay Marine Reserve

Free • Bangkas leave from Sagay wharf (30min)

Sagay is the jumping-off point for one of the Philippines' least-visited natural wonders, the beautiful **Sagay Marine Reserve**. The sanctuary boasts some marvellous beaches, and with its maximum of seventy visitors per day, its reef remains a picture of health; with a mask and snorkel you can see giant clams, puffer fish, immense brain corals and the occasional inquisitive batfish.

ARRIVAL AND DEPARTURE SAGAY AND AROUND

By bus Regular buses from Bacolod stop in Cadiz (1hr 30min) and Sagay (2hr) on their way along the coastal road.
By boat There are three services each week from Cadiz (usually early morning) for Bantayan Island, off the north coast of Cebu (3–4hr).

Sipalay and around

Nearly 200km south of Bacolod, on the heel of Negros, **SIPALAY** is the access point for the lovely resorts of **Sugar Beach** and **Punto Ballo**, a few kilometres north and south of town respectively. There are a couple of hotels in town, but given the proximity of the beaches there's no need to stay unless you arrive late. Sipalay's historical focal point is the plaza and the church, but these days most activity centres around its pier and the main drag, **Alvarez Street**, where there are numerous canteens, bakeries and convenience stores.

Punta Ballo and Campomanes Bay

Punto Ballo can be reached by tricycle from Sipalay; it's a 25–30min walk from Punta Ballo to Campomanes Bay

Just 6km south of Sipalay, **Punto Ballo** has a pretty stretch of beach and offers great snorkelling and diving from the shoreline. A couple of kilometres south, **Campomanes Bay**, also known as Maricalum Bay, is a natural harbour that's said to be deep enough to hide a submarine. Shaped like a horseshoe, 2km wide and backed by steep cliffs, it's a fantastic day-trip with some good snorkelling and scuba diving, though there's little accommodation here.

Sugar Beach

Resorts can arrange boat transfer, picking you up from Poblacion Beach in Sipalay; a cheaper, less direct alternative is to take a tricycle to Nauhang, then a small paddle boat across the creek, and walk around the headland – better still, ask to be let off the bus in Montilla, 5km northeast of Sipalay, only a short tricycle ride from Nauhang

Although it's just 5km as the crow flies from Sipalay, the absence of road access to beautiful **Sugar Beach**, cut off by knobbly green hills, makes it feel more like an island. While it may not have the white sand and azure waters of Boracay, it offers a relaxed vibe, plus a good selection of small resorts ranging from ultra-budget to mid-range.

ARRIVAL AND INFORMATION

SIPALAY AND AROUND

By bus If you're coming from Dumaguete, the quickest bus route follows the coast south around the toe of the island and then north through Hinoba-an, but an equally scenic option is to head north and then across the mountains to Kabanklan before travelling south for Sipalay. Buses from Bacolod or Dumaguete stop at Poblacion Beach in Sipalay Town. For moving on, there are hourly buses from Sipalay for Bacolod (5–6hr), but only one direct service for Dumaguete (5am; 5hr), so you're best hopping on the first southbound bus and then changing in Hinoba-an. You may even require a further change at Bayawan.

Tourist information There's a small tourist office at the beach end of Alvarez St in Sipalay (Mon–Fri 8am–noon & 1–5pm; ☎034 473 2101).

ACCOMMODATION AND EATING

SIPALAY

Jamont Mercedes Blvd ⓦjamonthotelsipalay.com. The most comfortable place to stay in town has clean but characterless rooms right behind the beach. They also have a nice pool, and their beach restaurant is fairly decent. P̄P̄

PUNTA BALLO

★Arteva Beach Resort ⓦartisticdiving.com. Beachfront accommodation in simple fan or a/c rooms, fan or a/c bungalows, and larger villas with cable TV. There's also a decent bar and restaurant, plus a pool and dive centre. P̄P̄

Easy Diving & Beach Resort ⓦsipalay.com. Pleasant fan bungalows and even smarter a/c stone cottages, with spacious verandas and attractive rattan and wooden furnishings, set in hillside gardens looking down to the white-sand beach. P̄P̄

SUGAR BEACH

Bermuda Beach Resort Next to Takutuka Lodge ⓦbermuda-beach-resort.com. *Bermuda* offers spacious and tastefully decorated fan-cooled beachfront bungalows and smaller a/c rooms at the rear of the property. The restaurant serves Italian and Thai cuisine, but the Filipino dishes are recommended. P̄P̄

Big Bamboo Beach Resort Just north of the centre of the beach ⓦbigbamboobeachresort.com. Accommodations range from tiny overpriced nipa huts just bigger than the mattress, to larger bamboo cottages and through to concrete a/c rooms; there's also a dorm and simple restaurant. P̄P̄

★Driftwood Village Halfway along the beach ☎0920 900 3663. A backpacker favourite with a superb vibe, Swiss-built *Driftwood* has a wide range of budget huts, some with private bathrooms, set in palms behind the beach. There's also a basic dorm, an excellent restaurant that does great Thai food, Italian dishes and fish, and a lively bar. P̄

Sugar Lounge Northern end of the beach ⓦsugar lounge.ph. A series of simple huts (no a/c) with pretty interiors, and of course mosquito nets. Slightly questionable value for what you get, so perhaps more notable for its restaurant and bar – it's perhaps the most popular place for a drink on the whole strip. P̄P̄

Sulu Sunset Beach Resort Towards the northern end of the beach ⓦsulusunset.com. German-owned *Sulu* has simple but attractive fan cottages – which look straight out onto the beach – and a larger bungalow. The restaurant serves Filipino food, a few European dishes including schnitzel, and cold beer. Free transfer from Sipalay if you stay three nights or more. P̄

★Takatuka Lodge The furthest south of the resorts ⓦsipalay.net. Wonderfully wacky *Takatuka* displays the unhinged creativity of the Swiss-German owners who started the place. Each room features one-of-a-kind furnishings, from the pink Cadillac bed in the Superstar room, to the microphone light fittings in Rockadelic. All rooms have verandas and cost a little more for a/c and hot showers. The restaurant serves Filipino and international dishes – some of the best food on the beach, with menu items such as *tuktoro-ok* (crispy fried chicken with creamy, green coconut-pandan rice and a Malay peanut sauce). There is also a reputable dive centre here, and a nice swimming pool. P̄P̄P̄

Danjugan Island and Bulata

Lying 3km off the southwest coast of Negros and accessible through the small town of **Bulata**, about 10km north of Sipalay, **Danjugan** (pronounced "Danhoogan") **Island** is a little gem. Managed as a nature reserve by the Philippine Reef and Rainforest Foundation (PRRCFI; ⓦprrcf.org) NGO, it's entirely fringed by vibrant coral reefs.

Danjugan is so well forested that it's home to rarities such as the white-bellied sea eagle and barebacked fruit bat. Around five thousand **bats** of various species reside in a **cave** on the island; resident pythons feed on them from the rocky ledges by the entrance.

There are also a number of small **islets**, including Manta Island and Manta Rock, and three protected offshore **reefs**, home to about 570 species of fish. An overnight stay (see below) is a truly magical experience, as you're lulled to sleep by the sound of lapping waves on the beach.

ARRIVAL AND DEPARTURE

By bus and tricycle Buses driving the coastal road pass through Bulata. For Danjugan, ask to be let off at Crossing Remollos, a short walk from the pick-up point for the island's bangka service, which should be arranged in advance.

DANJUGAN ISLAND AND BULATA

Tours Day-trips to Danjugan from the *Punta Bulata Resort & Spa* (see below) and some of the Sugar Beach resorts should include transfers, lunch, snacks, a trekking guide and kayaking. Shorter ecotours are available.

ACCOMMODATION

★ **Danjugan Sanctuary** ⓦ danjuganisland.ph. The atmosphere at *Danjugan Sanctuary* is extremely sociable and blissfully relaxed. Accommodation is in beautifully designed rooms at Typhoon Beach or more basic huts at Moray Lagoon. Rates include return transfers, all meals, a boat tour, trekking guide, plus snorkel and kayak use. Wi-fi at certain spots. PPP
Punta Bulata Resort & Spa Accessed along a 2km dirt

road from Cartagena ⓦ puntabulata.com. The resort has a good range of comfortable huts, rooms and family cabins (for six), all a/c. There's also a spa, a pleasant bar and a hillside native-style restaurant with ocean views. Wi-fi in common areas. To get here, take the coastal road bus and ask to be let off at Cartagena, from where you can take a tricycle or arrange with the resort to send one. PPP

Dumaguete

DUMAGUETE ("dum-a-get-eh"), known in the Philippines as the City of Gentle People, is capital of Negros Oriental and lies on the southeast coast of Negros, within sight of the southernmost tip of Cebu Island and Siquijor. With its attractive architecture, laidback university town ambience and lovely **seafront promenade**, shaded by acacia trees and coconut palms and lined with lively bars and restaurants, it's easy to see why the town is increasingly becoming a mainstream tourist destination – having an airport has certainly helped things along, too.

While Dumaguete doesn't possess major sights, it is a great base from which to explore the region. **Day-trips** include the Twin Lakes of Balinsasayao and Danao (see page 291) and dolphin- and whale-watching at Bais (see box, page 290), while scuba diving can be arranged from the affordable resort accommodation around Dauin (see page 288).

St Catherine of Alexandria Cathedral

Governor Perdices St, Quezon Park • ⓦ facebook.com/DumagueteCathedralParish

Dumaguete is centred on the grand **St Catherine of Alexandria Cathedral**, which dominates Quezon Park. The cathedral was originally built in 1754, although the current version dates from 1957. Standing next to the cathedral is the **belfry**, which was completed in 1867, and its statue of the Lady of Lourdes is a popular site of worship in its own right.

National Museum

Burgos St, Quezon Park • ⓦ nationalmuseum.gov.ph

Dumaguete's newest sight is located in one of its oldest buildings – the **National Museum** (which is one of several nationwide... Dumaguete isn't *that* special), set in a beautiful building of 1937 vintage. Designed by Juan Arellano, a Filipino architect who designed basically all major structures that went up in Manila in the 1930s, it incorporated elements of Spanish, American and local design motifs, and served as the seat of power for local officials. Their successors threw a bunch of money at this museum prior to its revamping; it finally opened in 2022, and while the result is very

DUMAGUETE

ACCOMMODATION

Bethel Guest House	6
Coco Grande	2
Essencia	3
Harolds Mansion	1
Nicanor	4
Hotel Palwa	5

EATING

Casablanca	4
Dayo Seafood	3
Jo's Chicken Inatô	2
Lantaw	1
Sans Rival	5/6

DRINKING & NIGHTLIFE

| Game On Sports Bar | 1 |
| Why Not? Music Box | 2 |

SHOPPING

| Robinsons Place | 2 |
| Terracotta Haus | 1 |

MINDANAO SEA

6

pretty and the exhibits well presented, it has to be said that the latter are perhaps a little dull.

Silliman University

Anthropological Museum: SE corner of main campus, near the church • Charge • Ⓦ su.edu.ph/academics/museums/anthropology-museum

The oldest Protestant university in the Philippines, **Silliman University**'s strong reputation has largely been built on the work of its marine laboratory, which has

6

spearheaded efforts to protect the island's mangroves and stop illegal fishing. The university also has an interesting **Anthropological Museum** housing some Song and Ming dynasty porcelain, as well as relics from Indigenous people in the Philippines.

ARRIVAL AND DEPARTURE — DUMAGUETE

By plane Dumaguete's small airport is in Sibulan, 4km north of the centre; you may see either name – Dumaguete or Sibulan – on departure boards and booking engines. Tricycles make the trip to the city; there are also jeepneys from outside the airport perimeter fence, or you can haggle with one of the private car and van drivers who greet incoming flights. Grab cabs are also bookable here.
Destinations Cebu (1–2 daily; 40min); Iloilo (3 weekly; 50min); Manila (4–6 daily; 1hr 25min).
By boat The ferry pier is near the northern end of Rizal Blvd, within easy walking distance or short tricycle ride from the centre. 2GO (travel.2go.com.ph) have a weekly ferry to Manila, while Cokaliong (cokaliongshipping.com) has ferries direct to Cebu. Oceanjet (oceanjet.net) run daily services to Tagbilaran on Bohol. For Dapitan on Mindanao, FastCat (fastcat.com.ph) run a fast daily service (3hr), while Cokaliong, Aleson Shipping (alesonshipping.com) and Montenegro Shipping Lines (montenegrolines.com.

ph) all have slower boats. For Siquijor, GL Shipping Lines (035 480 5534), Aleson, Montenegro and Oceanjet all operate services, mostly to Siquijor Town or, less frequently, Larena. For southern Cebu, it's quicker to cross from one of the ports near Dumaguete (see box, page 286).
Destinations Cebu City (3 weekly; 6–7hr); Dapitan (6–7 daily; 3–4hr); Manila (1 weekly; 19hr); Siquijor (9–11 daily; 45min); Tagbilaran (1–2 daily; 2hr).
By bus and jeepney The Ceres Liner terminal (035 225 9030) is on Governor Perdices St, 1km south of Quezon Park. Tricycle rides are pretty cheap, but if you haven't got much luggage you can walk it almost as fast. For departures to the north of the island, it's worth making sure that you get on an express bus, which will shave hours from journey times. There are hourly buses to Sipalay (4–5hr), with changes in Kabankalan or Hinoba-an, and Bacolod (6–7hr). For the short hop to Dauin, there are plenty of jeepneys and buses going back and forth most hours of the day and night.

INFORMATION AND TOURS

Tourist information In town, there's a tourist office kiosk in Quezon Park (Mon–Fri 8am–5pm; 035 225 0549).
Tours There are a number of decent travel agencies and tour operators in town who can arrange trips to nearby attractions.

Harold's Mansion (see page 287) runs good budget trips to Casororo Falls, Bais and dive trips to Apo Island. Orientwind at 201 Flores Ave (orientwind.com.ph) offers an extensive line-up of tours in the region and beyond.

ACCOMMODATION — SEE MAP PAGE 285

Dumaguete has plenty of inexpensive accommodation in the city centre or within walking distance of it, but rooms can get booked up fast in high season. Another option is to base yourself in Dauin (see page 288) and see Dumaguete on a day-trip.
Bethel Guest House Rizal Blvd 035 422 8000. In an excellent location on the seafront, this modern four-storey building has clean studio rooms and doubles, some with a sea view (for which you'll pay extra). Rooms at the front are big and bright, with picture windows. Staff are efficient and friendly, and there's a

reasonable restaurant. Strictly no alcohol or smoking. PP
Coco Grande Hibbard Ave, just north of Silliman University cocograndehotel.com. Under the same ownership as *Coco Grove* on Siquijor and *Apo Island Resort* on Apo, this remains one of the best places in town. The lobby and lounge are quaintly old-fashioned, while the spacious rooms and suites are attractively styled and come with a/c, cable TV and fridge. Breakfast included. PP
Essencia 39 Real St hotel-essencia.com. This nine-storey hotel has become rightfully popular for its clean, comfortable and stylish rooms in a central location. Staff are

FROM DUMAGUETE TO CEBU

To get to **Cebu island** from Dumaguete, take a van, jeepney or tricycle north to Sibulan, from where there are boats to Lilo-An (every 30min; 30min); from Lilo-An, buses run up the east coast to Cebu City. Alternatively, continue beyond Sibulan to Tampi, from which boats go to Bato on Cebu (every 1hr 30min; 30min). From Bato, buses go north to Moalboal, and then on to Cebu City. You can get a chit (a numbered scrap of paper which guarantees you a place; you'll pay on the bus) for the connecting Cebu bus at the Sibulan pier ticket office. For all that, sometimes it works out almost as cheap to fly – it has, occasionally, been possible to find return tickets between Cebu and Dumaguete for less than some people pay for a cocktail.

friendly, and there's a good restaurant, as well as a spa. $\overline{P}$
★ **Harolds Mansion** 205 Hibbard Ave, just north of Silliman University ⓦharoldsmansion.com. This hostel offers great-value rooms, plus a sociable roof-deck restaurant where you can get on the wi-fi. A/c rooms have cable TV and hot-water showers; fan rooms are actually preferable, as the a/c units can be noisy. Harold is a great source of travel information and can arrange all sorts of tours. They also have a basic ecolodge up in Valencia. Simple

breakfast included. $\overline{P}$
Nicanor San José St ⓦthehotelnicanor.com. Modern, comfortable rooms with a/c, cable TV, hot showers and free wi-fi. Standard rooms are windowless, making it worth the extra cost to upgrade to a larger superior room. $\overline{PP}$
Hotel Palwa Locsin St ⓦpalwahotel.com. One of the town's cheaper options, offering small but nicely styled a/c rooms with flatscreen TV, and there's also a pleasant café. $\overline{P}$

EATING

SEE MAP PAGE 285

Dumaguete has an expanding food scene which features everything from fresh seafood stalls to quality international cuisine.

★ **Casablanca** Rizal Blvd ☎0917 300 9708. Movie-themed, Austrian-owned restaurant which offers fine European cuisine to a mainly expat clientele. Most dishes such as pasta and Indian chicken curry are good, though it's worth splashing out for the undeniably excellent signature Brazilian beef tenderloin. *Casablanca* also has its own bakery and deli, a decent wine list and a changing daily menu. $\overline{PPPP}$

Dayo Seafood San Juan St ⓦfacebook.com/nine degreesdgte. Once the extremely popular *Nine Degrees* seafood restaurant, this restaurant had recently morphed, at the time of writing, into a Chinese restaurant that also serves seafood – hopefully it will maintain its popularity, though most patrons now seem to be tucking into *mapo* tofu, fried rice and the like. $\overline{PPP}$

Jo's Chicken Inatô Silliman Ave ☎035 225 4412. This outlet of the popular chain serves up uncomplicated Filipino-style grilled chicken, as well as other barbecue options. It's generally not service-with-a-smile, but the food makes it worth a visit. $\overline{PP}$

★ **Lantaw** 201 Flores Ave, around 1km north of the ferry port ⓦfacebook.com/lantawdumaguete. Deservedly Dumaguete's most popular seafood restaurant, with a spacious interior, large courtyard and sea-facing wooden deck. Excellent-value dishes include *sinigang* shrimp soup, served in more of a vat than a bowl, and sizzling marlin. $\overline{PPP}$

Sans Rival Bakery: San Jose St; restaurant: Rizal Blvd ⓦbit.ly/SansRival. The original little cake shop on San Jose St still turns out delicious cakes and coffee, while its larger sister round the corner on Rizal serves a host of tasty but inexpensive meals including tapas and sizzling shrimp *sisig*. $\overline{P}$

DRINKING AND NIGHTLIFE

SEE MAP PAGE 285

Nightlife is mostly focused on **Rizal Blvd**, although, like many Philippine port towns, the scene gets a little sleazy here as the night wears on.

Game On Sports Bar North end of Rizal Blvd ☎0906 865 9485. Small, popular bar-restaurant playing fairly eclectic and varied music, and putting major sports games on the TV. Nowhere near as interesting as it was under its previous guise of *Bogarts*, but hey.

Why Not? Music Box 70 Rizal Blvd ⓦwhynot dumaguete.com. The most popular nightlife venue in town, *Why Not?* has a selection of bars plus a very popular disco. There's also a games room, and even a deli.

SHOPPING

SEE MAP PAGE 285

Robinsons Place On the southern edge of town ⓦrobinsonsmalls.com. Decent-sized mall with supermarket, National Book Store, plenty of clothes and electronics stores, cafés and restaurants, plus a bouncy castle for kids.

Terracotta Haus Silliman University Co-operative. For Negros souvenirs including basketware and bags, seek out the tiny souvenir kiosk in the Silliman University Co-operative.

DIRECTORY

Hospitals Dumaguete's best hospital is the Silliman Medical Center (☎035 420 2000) on Venencio Aldecoa Rd.
Immigration Dumaguete's bustling immigration office is at Lu Pega Building, 38 Dr V. Locsin St, at the end of a

narrow shopping arcade signed off Dr V. Locsin St (Mon–Fri 8am–5pm; ☎035 225 4401).
Police The main police station is at the west end of Dr V. Locsin St, near the Central Bank.

Valencia and around

An 8km drive inland and uphill from the coast, the town of **VALENCIA** offers fresh air, thundering waterfalls and adventurous trekking nearby, and a quirky museum. While there are a few places to stay here, Valencia can easily be visited as a day-trip (or half-day-trip) from Dumaguete or Dauin. The town itself has an attractive main square and a few cafés, but the reason to come out here is to experience the beauty of the mountain scenery.

Casororo Falls

Apolong • Charge • Habal-habal from Valencia to drop-off point of Casaroro Falls, or you can take one of the day-trips from Harold's Mansion in Dumaguete (see page 287)

It's a steep 5km drive up from Valencia to the starting point of the steps down to **Casororo Falls**. Once you've descended the steps, it's then a 400m scramble up the valley, with a couple of quite tricky river crossings before you round a bend to view the towering 30m falls, surrounded by lush tropical greenery. Locals (or your habal-habal driver) might offer to show you the way, in which case it's a good idea to tip them a small amount.

Mount Talinis

You can either hire local guides and porters or take an organized trip from Harold's Mansion in Dumaguete (see page 287) – they can arrange day-hikes, overnight treks, and full mountain assaults

The challenging trail up **Mount Talinis** (1903m) begins at Apolong near the entrance to Casororo Falls and *Harold's Eco Lodge*. There are several different routes up the mountain, all of which require two to three days of steep jungle-trekking through dense foliage, but are rewarded by steaming fumeroles, tranquil lakes and spectacular views. You're definitely best with a guide for this trek, and you will need to bring tents, sleeping bags and food with you.

Cata-al WWII Museum

Jose Romero Rd at Legarda St • Free, but donations welcome

The slopes of Mount Talinis were a hotbed of activity during World War II and were bombarded by US ships trying to force out the entrenched Japanese forces. Local resident Felix Constantina V. Cata-al (aka "Tantin") has been hunting out war memorabilia from the surrounding forests since he was a boy, and his huge and captivating collection is now on display at the **Cata-al WWII Museum**. Samurai swords, dog tags, old uniforms and radios are just a few of the bewildering array of items on show. Indeed, Cata-al's collection now has so many missile shells that he's ingeniously constructed a stair balustrade from them.

ARRIVAL AND DEPARTURE

VALENCIA AND AROUND

By bus, van and jeepney Regular jeepneys leave Dumaguete for Valencia (1hr); you can also take a tricycle. Vans, jeepneys and tricycles can also be chartered.

Alternatively, you could hire a tricycle at Bacong, halfway between Dumaguete and Dauin, for the steep ride up to Valencia.

ACCOMMODATION

The Forest Camp On the road up to Casororo Ⓦ facebook.com/forestcampresort. This family-run camp has grown over the years and now has attractive cabins where you can overnight, as well as day-use cottages. There's also a network of trails, some lovely pools and a simple restaurant. There's an entrance fee if you're not staying. **PPP**

Tejero Highland Resort and Adventure Park On the road up to Casororo Ⓦ tejerohighlandresort.com. There's surprisingly good value to be found at this family resort, with decent little rooms surrounding a swimming pool – the "adventure" part of the resort's name refers mainly to the water slides plopping people down into said pool, though you can always walk up to the Casororo Falls from here, which counts as a kind of adventure too. **PP**

Dauin and around

South of Dumaguete is beach-and-dive-resort country, with a decent range of accommodation. However, beaches are brown sand and the sea can be choppy from November to May, which makes the nearby island of Siquijor (see page 291) a more appealing prospect for pure beach enthusiasts. This said, divers will find the quality of nearby dive sites more than adequate compensation.

DAUIN is a popular port of call 15km south of Dumaguete. The beach has a dramatic backdrop of palm trees and ruined watchtowers, which were built in the nineteenth century as protection against raiding Moro pirates.

Malatapay market

Malatapay, Zamboanguita, 20km southwest of Dumaguete and 10km southwest of Dauin • Wed dawn–noon • Most of the resorts in Dauin arrange trips to the market (20min drive); alternatively, flag down a jeepney or charter a tricycle

One of the most unusual markets in the Philippines is held every Wednesday in the seaside barangay of **Malatapay**. Buyers and sellers at **Malatapay market**, also known as **Zamboanguita market**, still use the traditional barter system, with farmers from the surrounding villages and Bukidnon Indigenous people from the interior meeting with fishermen and housewives to swap everything for anything – livestock, fish, exotic fruit, strange vegetables and household items. You'll have to be up bright and early to

---

APO ISLAND AND OTHER DIVE SITES

Tiny, volcanic **Apo Island**, 7km off the south coast of Negros, has become a prime destination for divers, most of whom head out for the day from Dumaguete, Dauin or Siquijor. Site of one of the Philippines' first and most successful marine reserves, Apo has a series of reefs teeming with marine life, from the smallest nudibranch to the largest deepwater fish. The sanctuary area is on the island's southeast coast, while much of the flat land to the north is occupied by the only village, home to four hundred fisherfolk and farmers. Non-divers needn't be bored; Apo has some fantastic snorkelling and it's a great little island to explore on foot.

Organized trips from Dumaguete or Dauin are priced depending on the level of comfort and number of people in your group, or you can travel independently on one of the regular bangkas from Malatapay. Alternatively you can arrange a place on one of the four daily *Liberty Lodge* shuttles (see below). There's a charge for **admission** to the marine sanctuary, where you can snorkel with turtles in guided groups of four, though it can get rather like a watery zoo.

Among other dive sites, **Calong-Calong Point** off the southern tip of Negros is known for its dazzling number of smaller reef fish. Nearby is **Tacot**, a tricky deep dive where sharks are common. From the coastal towns to the south of Dumaguete, you can take a bangka to Siquijor (see page 291), where sites such as **Sandugan Point** and **San Juan** go as deep as 65m, and where you can expect to see tuna, barracuda and sharks – plus, from March to August, manta rays.

Sightseeing trips to Apo can be arranged through most hotels in Dumaguete, but for dive trips you're best to book through dive resorts in Dauin or Siquijor – *Atmosphere* (see page 290), *Liquid* (see page 290) and *Coco Grove Beach Resort* (see page 295) are all recommended. In Dumaguete, *Harold's Mansion* (see page 287) runs day-trips on which you'll get between 1–3 dives, or you can just snorkel.

APO ISLAND ACCOMMODATION

Apo Island Beach Resort ⓦ apoislandresort.com. A few minutes' walk over a path from the village, under the same ownership as *Coco Grove* in Siquijor and *Coco Grande* in Dumaguete, this lovely little place sits at the back of a tiny isolated sandy cove, hemmed in by rocks. It's expensive, and the beach and restaurant can get overrun with day visitors, but once they've left, the true magic of this location reveals itself. Breakfast included. P̄P̄

Liberty's Community Lodge ⓦ facebook.com/apoislandlibertys. Set above the main beach, *Liberty's*

offers good views and reasonable rates for the sweet little rooms, which are inclusive of all meals. Wi-fi is available for a small charge (if there is electricity) in the restaurant. Shuttle boats run to Malatapay four times a day. P̄P̄

Mario Scuba Diving & Homestay ⓦ mariosscubadivinghomestay.com. In the thick of the village, this humble place offers the cheapest non-homestay rates on the island, either in the eight-bed dorm or simple private en-suite rooms. P̄

6

visit the market: the bartering begins at first light and is usually more or less finished by noon. Malatapay is also the departure point for boats to Apo Island (see box, page 289), so a visit to the market and island can easily be combined.

Tambobo Bay

Most resorts can arrange trips, or you can hop on any bus or jeepney from Dumaguete or Dauin heading south along the coast – get off at Siaton and then take a tricycle for the last few kilometres to the beach; if you have your own vehicle it's far simpler to leave the main road at Mayabong Crossing (Km39) from which it's a beautiful but very bumpy 10km to Tambobo

Forty kilometres south of Dumaguete, at the very southern tip of Negros near the small town of Siaton, **Tambobo Bay** is a beautiful, serpentine bay, popular with foreign yachties for the protection it affords from storms, but also for its laidback lifestyle and pretty mangrove- and palm-fringed beaches. It's a great place to spend a lazy afternoon swimming and snorkelling, and there are also a few decent places to stay.

ARRIVAL AND DEPARTURE

By bus and jeepney Buses and jeepneys leave Dumaguete for Dauin (20–30min), Malatapay (40min), Zamboanguita (45min) and Siaton (1hr) from either the Ceres Liner terminal or the area around the market. An alternate route to Valencia leaves the main highway at Bacong, halfway between Dumaguete and Dauin; tricycles can be chartered from here for the steep ride up to Valencia.

DAUIN AND AROUND

ACCOMMODATION

DAUIN

Atlantis Brgy Lipaya, 800m north of Dauin ⓦ atlantishotel.com. A/c cottages with TV, mini-bar and private bathrooms, set amid lovely gardens, and for a little more, you can get sea views. *Atlantis* is primarily a dive resort, though it offers non-divers a large pool, loungers on the sand and day-trips to Dumaguete, Bais (for dolphin- and whale-watching) and Apo Island. $\overline{\text{PPPP}}$

★ **Atmosphere** Maayong Tubig, 5km south of Dauin ⓦ atmosphereresorts.com. British-owned *Atmosphere* is easily the most upmarket place in this part of the world. Beautiful suites, apartments and penthouses, with state-of-the-art facilities and wonderful outdoor bathrooms, are spread through well-manicured gardens. There's also a quality dive shop, the excellent Sanctuary spa, a top-class restaurant and a lovely infinity pool. The Kids Cove day-care centre also makes *Atmosphere* a good choice for families. $\overline{\text{PPPP}}$

★ **Liquid** Brgy Bulak, 2km north of Dauin ⓦ liquiddumaguete.com. This low-key dive resort has eight attractively decked-out beach huts, all with sea views, and six a/c cottages. There are also some cheaper concrete rooms at the back, discounted if you are diving. There's a sociable pool bar and an upstairs restaurant, which serves tasty meals and has a small bakery. $\overline{\text{PPP}}$

Mike's Dauin Beach Resort Poblacion, Dauin ⓦ mikesbeachresort.com. Attractive, small-scale and homely resort on a pretty stretch of beach. Rooms are spread over two floors in one large block, and there's a lovely pool down by the beach. Also has a popular dive centre. $\overline{\text{PP}}$

Pura Vida Brgy Lipayon, Dauin ⓦ pura-vida.ph. Stylish option with a range of tastefully designed native fan and a/c huts, and a lovely beachside pool. $\overline{\text{PPP}}$

ZAMBOANGUITA

Kav's Beach Resort ⓦ kavsbeachresort.com. Hidden away in super-chilled Zamboanguita, just south of Dauin, this is a fine place to unwind. Well-soundproofed rooms run alongside a cute little pool, across from which is a bar that'll happily cut open a coconut for you to splosh some rum into. The beach isn't far away, and the villagers nearby are often surprised to see a foreign face – you're pleasingly far from mainstream tourism out here. $\overline{\text{PP}}$

WHALE-WATCHING AROUND BAIS

The city government operates the cruise vessels *Dolphin I & II*, *Vania I & II* and *Horizon* out to view the **whales and dolphins** in Bais Bay, each of which accommodates 15–20 people. Tours operate all the way through to October, and bookings are recommended at least a month in advance, especially during the peak whale-watching season (March–Sept) – to arrange, call the tourist office (see page 291) or ☎ 035 402 8174. It is also possible to just turn up at Bais pier and negotiate with local boatmen or, more easily, to take a day-trip from Dumaguete.

TAMBOBO BAY

Kookoo's Nest ⓦkookoosnest.com.ph. Wonderfully remote little British-run place with simple cottages on stilts overlooking a pretty cove at the entrance to Tambobo Bay. There are kayaks for rent and the restaurant turns out tasty meals and snacks. $\overline{PP}$

EATING

DAUIN

Dauin Dive Café Bonafacio St ☎0969 555 6863. Simple spot close to the seafront that serves an eclectic mix of dishes, including pasta, panini, schnitzel and even a full English breakfast. It's a good place for a cold beer too. $\overline{P}$

MALATAPAY

Dream Beach Café Just along from the Apo Island bangka station ⓦfacebook.com/p/Dream-Beach-Cafe-100094487277027/. Opened in 2013 by a British-Filipino couple, this lovely little café right on the seashore makes a great stop after a visit to to Malatapay market or Apo Island. They serve decent omelettes, pancakes, coffee and juices, plus home-made mango ice cream. $\overline{PP}$

Bais and around

The town of **BAIS**, about 40km north of Dumaguete, is a good place to see **dolphins and whales** in Bais Bay as they migrate through the Tanon Strait separating Negros from Cebu. Tours run between March and October (see box, page 290).

Twin Lakes

Daily 8am–5pm • Charge, extra for kayak rental • From Bais either take a jeepney to Amlan and then a motorcycle taxi up to the lakes or hire a van from Bais or Dumaguete; day-trips and hikes from Dumaguete can be booked through *Harold's Mansion* in Dumaguete (see page 287)

Nestled in a jungled crater 15km west from the main coastal road, the **Twin Lakes** of Balinsasayao and Danao make for an excellent day out. Getting there is part of the adventure and is best done by motorbike, as the last part of the track is often inaccessible to larger vehicles. Alternatively, you can make the strenuous 15km **hike** in from the little town of **San José**, nearly midway between Dumaguete and Bais. The hike takes you past a couple of waterfalls, where you can swim, and through settlements of the Indigenous Bukidnon people who inhabit the area. Once at the lakes, it's possible to rent a kayak and head out onto the water, and to hire a pair of binoculars to check out the wildlife, which includes tarictic hornbills, monkeys and eagles; there's also a café.

ARRIVAL AND INFORMATION

BAIS AND AROUND

By bus and jeepney Bais lies on the main coastal road and is well served by buses and jeepneys from Dumaguete (1hr).

Tourist information The tourist office (Mon–Fri 8am–5pm; ☎035 402 8338) is in the public plaza in the centre of town.

ACCOMMODATION AND EATING

Campuyo Aroma Beach Resort Manjuyod ⓦfacebook.com/OfficialCampuyoAromaBeachResort. A few kilometres north of Bais and right on the beach, *Aroma* has clean, a/c rooms with cable TV. They also have a restaurant with free wi-fi and can arrange dolphin-watching trips. $\overline{PP}$

Casa Sandoval Western Nautical Hwy ⓦfacebook.com/CasaSandovalPR. Clean and comfortable rooms and dorms in a convenient location by the main road. Ask for a room at the back if you're a light sleeper. $\overline{PP}$

Siquijor

Small, laidback **SIQUIJOR** lies between the islands of Cebu, Negros and Bohol and makes a worthwhile stop on a southern itinerary. Very little is known about the island and its inhabitants before the arrival of the Spanish in the sixteenth century, who named it the Isla del Fuego ("Island of Fire") because of the eerie luminescence

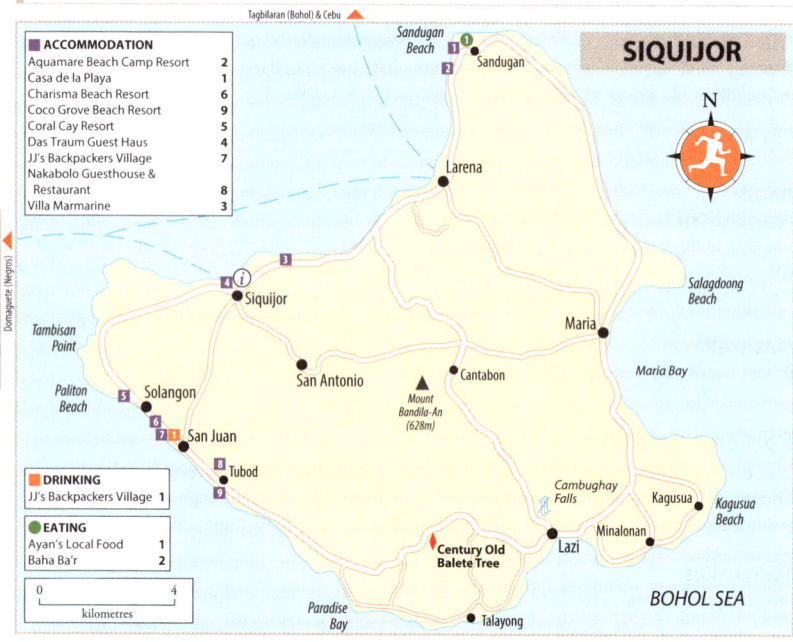

ACCOMMODATION

Aquamare Beach Camp Resort	2
Casa de la Playa	1
Charisma Beach Resort	6
Coco Grove Beach Resort	9
Coral Cay Resort	5
Das Traum Guest Haus	4
JJ's Backpackers Village	7
Nakabolo Guesthouse & Restaurant	8
Villa Marmarine	3

DRINKING

JJ's Backpackers Village	1

EATING

Ayan's Local Food	1
Baha Ba'r	2

generated by swarms of fireflies. This sense of mystery still persists today, with many Filipinos believing Siquijor to be a centre of **witchcraft** (see box, page 292). Shamans aside, the island is peaceful, picturesque and a pleasure to tour, whether by bike, tricycle, motorbike or jeepney – the entire 72km coastal road is paved (a rare delight in the Philippines) and traffic is light. The **beaches** alone make it worth a visit, but there are also **mountain trails**, waterfalls and old churches to explore as well as decent scuba diving. The island is gradually becoming more popular, but for now it remains relatively unexplored by tourists.

Most places to stay are within half an hour of the port towns of **Siquijor** and **Larena**, notably around **San Juan**, south of Siquijor, and at **Sandugan**, north of Larena. A number of resorts have certified **dive operators** who will take you on trips to places such as Sandugan Point and Tambisan Point, both known for their coral and abundant

---

SORCERORS ON SIQUIJOR

Every Good Friday, herbalists from around Siquijor and from the rest of the Visayas and Mindanao gather in **San Antonio**, in Siquijor's pea-green hinterlands, to prepare potions made from tree bark, roots, herbs and insects. The culmination of this annual Conference of Sorcerers and Healers – now rebranded the **Folk Healing Festival** because it sounds less menacing – is the mixing of a mother-of-all potions in a large cauldron. As the mixture is stirred, participants gather in a circle and mumble incantations said to imbue it with extraordinary healing powers. The ceremony takes place on Good Friday in the belief that on Christ's day of death, supernatural forces are free to wander the earth. The brew is evidently strong, with wide-ranging powers that include provoking a good harvest, securing a spouse or getting rid of that troublesome zit. The festival attracts spiritualists and tourists from across the Philippines and beyond – be sure to book your accommodation well in advance if you plan to visit at that time.

marine life. At Paliton Beach there are three submarine caves where you can see sleeping reef sharks, and at Salag-Doong Beach, on the eastern side of the island, divers have occasionally reported seeing manta rays and shoals of barracuda. Further afield but still within easy reach, Apo Island (see box, page 289) is another dive favourite, and is worth a visit even if you stay above water.

Siquijor Town

SIQUIJOR TOWN is a likeable enough place though without anything to keep you there for long. There is an atmospheric eighteenth-century church on the seafront, the **Church of St Francis of Assisi**, which was built in 1783 partly from coral. You can climb its bell tower for views across the town and out to sea.

The north coast

Some slow ferries arrive at the port of **LARENA**, from where the beaches of Sandugan are only a brief jeepney or tricycle ride to the north. From the pier it's just a short walk to Larena's centre, which has a town hall, plaza and church, but not much else. There are a couple of basic lodges, but with plentiful jeepneys and tricycles to nearby Sandugan, there's really no need to stay.

Six kilometres northeast of Larena is the village of **SANDUGAN**, where there's a beach and a number of resorts, one with professional **scuba-diving** facilities. To reach the beach, take a tricycle or jeepney from Larena to Sandugan and then negotiate the rutted path that leads to the shore. All the tricycle drivers know it, so you won't get lost.

The west coast

Twenty minutes west of Siquijor you come to beautiful and undeveloped **Paliton Beach**, 1km down a bumpy track from the main road (take the turn-off at the church in Paliton Town), but well worth the journey. A west-facing cove of sugary-white sand, Paliton is sheltered from big waves by the promontory of **Tambisan Point**, and has views of tropical sunsets you'll never forget.

A few kilometres further south, the small town of **SAN JUAN** has an unusual focal point: the sulphurous **San Juan de Capilay Lake**, where locals gather (especially at weekends) to wallow in the eggy water, said to have miraculous healing qualities. For more energetic activity, try the scenic but strenuous trek from San Juan along a jungled trail to San Antonio.

The east coast

Siquijor's picturesque east coast is a rural littoral of sun-bleached barangays and hidden coves, some of the most secluded around **Kagusua Beach**, reached through **Minalonan** and then the sleepy little fishing village of **Kagusua**. There's a sealed road from the village to the edge of a low cliff, where steps take you down to the sand and a series of immaculate little sandy inlets. To proceed north from Kagusua you'll have to backtrack to the coastal road at Minalonan, where you can catch a jeepney through sleepy **Maria** and on to **Salagdoong**, which has a resort popular with locals at weekends. For Salagdoong Beach, look out for the signposted turning about 6km north of Maria. You can walk it in about twenty minutes from the main road.

Southern Siquijor

The main east-coast road meets the island's north–south dissecting road at **Lazi**, with its delightful nineteenth-century church built of coral and stone. Right opposite it is the

6

oldest convent in the Philippines, a low-rise wooden building now sagging with age, but still beautiful. A couple of kilometres inland from Lazi, **Cambughay Falls** are the island's most accessible and popular waterfalls. Steep steps lead down to the pretty falls, which are a pleasant spot for a picnic or a swim.

Continuing clockwise, the main road cuts a fair distance inland, passing the **Century Old Balete Tree**; sheltered under its massive branches are a few stalls and a popular pond with a fish spa (charge). If you have a motorbike, you can explore the partly paved tracks that lead down to the coves around **Talayong** and **Paradise Bay**. You may also pass the island's main **dairy farm** – Siquijor is famed for its fresh milk, which is quite a rarity in the Philippines.

Mount Bandila-an

You can enquire about guides at the tourism assistance centre in Siquijor Town, although many resorts can also offer advice and arrange for a local to show you the way • Access is via either the village of Cantabon (book a tricycle or jeepney from Larena), or from Cangmonag in the south

At 628m and right at the island's heart, **Mount Bandila-an** is Siquijor's highest point and accessible to anyone who's reasonably fit. It lies at the centre of the island in an area that suffered serious damage during World War II, when acres of forest were razed by retreating Japanese troops. Now the entire area is part of the Siquijor Reforestation Project; while rehabilitation is not yet complete, wildlife such as the leopard cat and long-tailed macaque survive.

Mount Bandila-an can be climbed in a day, and you'll need a guide. On the way to the peak you'll pass the **Stations of the Cross**, where a solemn religious procession re-enacting the Passion of Christ is held every Easter, and there are a number of springs and caves. Ask your guide to point out another huge old balete tree at the side of the trail, said to be home to spirits, imps and guardians of the forest. To ask their permission to pass, the polite thing to say is "*tabi tabi lang-po*" ("excuse me, please step aside").

ARRIVAL AND DEPARTURE   SIQUIJOR

By plane Siquijor's airport opened for commercial flights in summer 2021, and is served by infrequent Air Juan (why couldn't it have been "Air Force Juan"?; ⊕airjuan.com) flights to Cebu.

By boat GL Shipping Lines (☎035 480 5534), Aleson (⊕aleson-shipping.com), Montenegro (⊕montenegro lines.com.ph) and Oceanjet (⊕oceanjet.net) operate eleven daily services from Dunaguete, mostly to Siquijor Town but some to Larena (45min–1hr 30min). Oceanjet also has a combined service from Cebu to Tagbilaran, then Dumaguete and finally on to Larena (3 weekly; 4hr 50min). Onward boat tickets can be arranged through most resorts or directly at Siquijor Town and Larena piers.

INFORMATION

SIQUIJOR TOWN
Tourist information There's a tourism assistance centre (Mon–Fri 8am–noon & 1–5pm; ☎035 344 2088) at the pier in Siquijor Town, which has a few maps and brochures and can also help arrange transport and guides in the local area.

Services There are a few banks with ATMs in town.

THE NORTH COAST
Tourist information There's a friendly private tourist office (daily 8am–9pm) in a building by the pier in Larena, which also has a pleasant café and a well-stocked souvenir shop.

Services Larena has a good post office and a bank with an ATM.

GETTING AROUND

If you've booked accommodation in advance, you may get a free pick-up from your port of arrival; otherwise there are tricycles from the main port of Siquijor, and jeepneys from Larena. You could also arrange a tour through your resort.

By bike and motorbike Renting a bicycle or motorbike is the cheapest and best way to get around the island. Bicycles can be rented from certain resorts and dive centres. Motorbikes can be rented from many resorts, or at Scandinavian Rent-A-Motorbike on the National Highway in Siquijor Town.

By bangka To travel the coast by sea, charter a bangka in Larena, Siquijor Town or Lazi.

ACCOMMODATION SEE MAP PAGE 292

SIQUIJOR TOWN
Das Traum Guest Haus East of the hospital ☎0917 429 0299. Fairly basic rooms in an impressive colonial-era house, in a convenient location for the ferry. Nothing fancy, but very affordable, and great for the faded grandeur. $\overline{\text{PP}}$

★ **Villa Marmarine** Candanay, 2.5km east of Siquijor Town ⓦ marmarine.jp. Wonderful place on a peaceful stretch of beach, with spacious, well-constructed huts and rooms, as well as a fine restaurant serving authentic Japanese and Filipino food. Occasional tennis lessons are conducted on the resort's court. $\overline{\text{PP}}$

THE NORTH COAST
Aquamare Beach Camp Resort Sandugan ⓦ facebook. com/aquamarebeachcampresort. A beach resort with a difference – here, you sleep in comfortable beds in pod tents pitched on the beach, with some transparent panels so you can get a great sea view. There's a pool too, and a lovely relaxing wooden decking area for great meals and drinks. $\overline{\text{PP}}$

Casa de la Playa Sandugan ⓦ siquijorcasa.com. A New Age tropical spa that offers yoga sessions, food made with organic vegetables from the resort's own garden and even massages from a local shaman. Accommodation is in a range of lovingly built fan and a/c huts, and houses with kitchenettes, either in a pretty garden bursting with frangipani and white *sampaguita* blossom or right on the beach. $\overline{\text{PP}}$

THE WEST COAST
Charisma Beach Resort Solangon, 2km northwest of San Juan ☎035 481 5033. British-owned place with dorm beds, simple bamboo cottages right on the beach and spick-and-span, white, motel-style rooms arranged around a swimming pool. Wi-fi in the restaurant. $\overline{\text{P}}$

★ **Coco Grove Beach Resort** Tubod, 2km southeast of San Juan ⓦ cocogroveresort.com. By far the island's most luxurious resort, *Coco Grove* occupies a prime stretch of palm-fringed beach. Rooms range from modest but tasteful standards to newer executive suites and luxury villas, all of which have a/c. There are three restaurants, two pools, a swim-up bar, a reputable dive centre, kayaks, spa, and wi-fi in the common areas. $\overline{\text{PPPP}}$

Coral Cay Resort Solangon Beach, 3km west of San Juan ⓦ coralcayresortsiquijor.com. Accommodation ranges from clean, simple rooms with fan and cold shower to spacious a/c cottages with a small living area and separate bedroom. $\overline{\text{PP}}$

JJ's Backpackers Village 1.5km northwest of San Juan ⓦ instagram.com/jjsbackpackers. Good budget choice, where the simple rooms have fans and shared bathrooms. There are also tents for rent and a dorm, but many visitors aren't here to stay – it's a renowned party spot. $\overline{\text{P}}$

Nakabolo Guesthouse & Restaurant 2km north of Coco Grove ⓦ facebook.com/nakabologuesthouse. Very smart rooms in a pleasant resort a little way inland. There are marvellous views from the infinity pool, and excellent meals are served at the restaurant. $\overline{\text{PP}}$

EATING SEE MAP PAGE 292

SIQUIJOR TOWN

THE NORTH COAST
Ayan's Local Food Larena. Marvellous Filipino specialties are served up at this small place that has a lovely welcoming vibe. The seafood is particularly good, but the banana blossom balls also come highly recommended. $\overline{\text{PP}}$

THE WEST COAST
Baha Ba'r 500m south of San Juan ⓦ baha-bar.com. Hip place with a shady courtyard and smart upstairs wooden deck, where you can enjoy breaded calamari, chicken tacos and fresh fish while listening to live acoustic music. $\overline{\text{PP}}$

DRINKING SEE MAP PAGE 292

JJ's Backpackers Village 1.5km northwest of San Juan ⓦ instagram.com/jjsbackpackers. Even if you're not staying, come to party at the island's most prominent nightlife spot – the offerings of the live bands and DJs are kind of hit and miss, but things can get nice and rowdy.

The Eastern Visayas

TAOIST TEMPLE, CEBU

The Eastern Visayas

The Eastern Visayas, a collection of jigsaw-shaped islands in the heart of the Philippines, are considered the cradle of the country. It was here that Ferdinand Magellan laid a sovereign hand on the archipelago for Spain and began the process of colonization and Catholicization that has since shaped so much of the nation's history. The islands were also the scene of some of the bloodiest battles fought against the Japanese during World War II, and where General Douglas MacArthur waded ashore to liberate the country after his famous promise, "I shall return".

7

Comprising thousands of islands and atolls, this relaxing region is a bounty of tropical sands and coral reefs; everywhere you turn, there seems to be another beach or dive site. There are four major island groups – **Cebu**, **Bohol**, **Samar** and **Leyte** – but it's the hundreds of tropical enigmas in between that make this part of the Philippines so irresistible.

Of the smaller islands, some are world-famous for their scuba diving, such as **Malapascua**, off the northern tip of Cebu; some for their extraordinary better-than-Boracay beach life, such as **Panglao**; and some for the ability to take you back in time to the Philippines as it once was, such as **Biliran** and **the Camotes**. Travelling here is a slow, easy-going, and ultimately rewarding experience.

The Eastern Visayas suffered a great deal of damage back in 2013, with a substantial quake in Bohol in October, and then in November **Typhoon Yolanda** tore through the region, leaving a band of destruction along its path. Numerous destinations were affected, including southeastern Samar, Tacloban, Ormoc, the Camotes, Bantayan and Malapascua. The area was mostly back on its feet by 2021, when it was ravaged by **Typhoon Odette**. While most areas have returned to normal, some parts, in particular eastern Leyte and southeast Samar, remain a shadow of what they once were, and the legacy of all these disasters continues to be felt.

Cebu

Right in the heart of the Visayas, nearly 600km south of Manila, the island of **CEBU** is the most densely populated in the Philippines and home of the second-largest metropolis, **Cebu City**, an important transport hub with ferry and air connections to the rest of the country. Cebu is a long, narrow island – 300km from top to bottom and only 40km wide at its thickest point – with a mountainous and rugged spine. Most tourists spend little time in the towns, heading off on island-hopping adventures to the north or venturing west for world-renowned scuba diving. The closest beaches to Cebu City are the resort-fringed sands on **Mactan Island** to the southeast, although they are by no means the best. Head north instead to the marvellous island of **Malapascua**, where the toothpaste-white beach is as fine as Boracay's; to tranquil **Bantayan** off the northwest coast; or to really get away from it all, to the isolated **Camotes Islands**. Alternatively, to the south of Cebu City, you can cross to the west coast diving haven of **Moalboal** to explore its offshore caves and canyons. Finally, down in the south, **Oslob** has become famous for nose-to-nose encounters with whale sharks.

ARRIVAL AND DEPARTURE CEBU

By plane Getting to Cebu is simple. There are dozens of flights daily from Manila to Cebu City, and less frequent flights from a number of other key destinations within the Visayas (Dumaguete, Kalibo and Tacloban), the rest of the Philippines

ALONA BEACH

Highlights

❶ Cebu City It's not Manila, but the Philippines' second-biggest metropolis is still a hectic introduction to modern Filipino life. Beyond the packed malls and thronging markets, there's plenty to savour in its museums, churches and happening restaurant and bar scene. See page 301

❷ Malapascua A little nugget of paradise north of Cebu, boasting the dazzling Bounty Beach, plenty of islets to explore and scuba diving with thresher sharks. See page 318

❸ Pescador Island Marine Reserve Off the coast of Moalboal, tiny Pescador is only 100m long, but has a glorious reef attracting whale

sharks and divers from around the world. See page 322

❹ Bohol Everything good about the Philippines in one compact island package: superb diving, fine beaches, Gothic churches, the postcard-perfect Chocolate Hills and, uniquely, tarsiers – the world's smallest primates. See page 324

❺ Beaches Beaches, beaches and more beaches. From Alona Beach's restaurant- and bar-lined strip to the pinch-yourself-you're-dreaming blue of Bantayan and White Beach, the Eastern Visayas has them by the bucket-load. See pages 328, 316 and 323

HIGHLIGHTS ARE MARKED ON THE MAP ON PAGE 300

THE EASTERN VISAYAS

N

Luzon

Donsol

Burias

Luzon

Bulan

Ticao

Masbate

Mandaon

Masbate Town

Matnog

Biri-Las Rosas Islands

Balicuatro Islands

Capul

San Antonio

Dalupiri

Allen

Victoria

San Isidro

San José

San Catarman

Laoang

NORTHERN SAMAR

Tarangban Falls

Samar

WESTERN SAMAR

Calbayog

Taft

Maripipi

Jiabong Cave

Catbalogan

BILIRAN

Kawayan

Almería

Biliran

Culaba

Higatangan

Naval

Biliran

San Isidro

Langun Gobingob Cave

Borongan

EASTERN SAMAR

Divinubo Island

Gigantes

Sicogan

Pan de Azucar Islands

Bantayan Islands

5 Bantayan

2 Malapascua

Tacloban

Marabut Islands

Basey

Hernani

Palompon

Leyte

Lake Danao

SOHOTON NATURAL BRIDGE NATIONAL PARK

Marabut

Guiuan

Calicoan Island

Cadiz

Sagay

Escalante

Mt Silay (1535m)

Mt Mandalagan (1879m)

San Carlos

Ormoc

Burauen

LEYTE

Camotes Islands

Ponson

Homonhon

CEBU

Balamban

Danao

Poro

Poro

Ponson

Baybay

Toledo

1 Cebu

Hilongos

Bato

SOUTHERN LEYTE

Tangil

Carcar

Mactan

Olango

Talibon

Maasin

Dinagat

Guihulngan

3 Moalboal

Jetafe

Danao

Ubay

Padre Burgos

Sogod Bay

Panaon

5

Badian

Argao

Tubigon

Sagbayan

Carmen

BOHOL

Anda

Limasawa

Bato

Oslob

Lilo-An

Tagbilaran

Panglao

5

Jagna

Pamilacan

Surigao

Bucas Grande

Camiguin

Mindanao

Benoni

0	100
kilometres	

HIGHLIGHTS

1 Cebu City

2 Malapascua

3 Pescador Island Marine Reserve

4 Bohol

5 Beaches

(Camiguin, Siargao, Coron, Davao and Puerto Princesa) and the rest of Asia (Hong Kong, Seoul, Singapore and Taipei).
By ferry Cebu's position in the middle of the country makes it an excellent place to journey onwards by ferry, with frequent sailings to Luzon, Mindanao and elsewhere in the Visayas.

Cebu City

Gateway to the Visayas, **CEBU CITY** is the Philippines' second-largest city, home to nearly a million people. Nicknamed the "Queen City of the South", it's peppered with historic attractions and is worthy of a day or two's exploration before moving on to the beaches and islands beyond. While a far easier introduction to urban life in the Philippines than Manila, Cebu is not without its problems: streets are often clogged with smoke-belching jeepneys, and "rugby boys" (see box, page 44) are common. The October 2013 Bohol earthquake also shook Cebu, not that the happy-go-lucky Cebuanos would let you know it. Buildings have been restored and it's very much a modern, happening metropolis: all over you'll find colossal shopping malls (around which the whole city seems to rotate), praiseworthy restaurants and buzzing coffee shops.

Many of Cebu's attractions are associated with Magellan's arrival in 1521, and are to be found near the **port** in the old part of the city. West of here, a seething cobweb of sunless streets spreads out between **Carbon Market** and **Colon Street**, the latter anchoring the oldest mercantile quarter in the country. You can explore the area on foot, picking your way carefully past barrow boys selling pungent fruits, hawkers peddling fake mobile-phone accessories and, at night, pimps whispering proposals from dark doorways. A vibrant, humming, occasionally malodorous area of poorly maintained pavements and thick diesel fumes, it's by no means a mainstream tourist sight, but it's worth some of your time in order to experience the daily realities and pulsating energy of downtown Cebu.

7

A QUICK GUIDE TO CEBUANO

Filipino (Tagalog) might be the official language and English the medium of instruction, but **Cebuano**, the native language of Cebu, is the most widely spoken vernacular in the archipelago, not used only in Cebu but also throughout most of the central and southern Philippines. Cebuano and Tagalog have elements in common, but also have significant differences of construction and phraseology – it's quite possible for a native Manileño to bump into a native Cebuano and not be able to understand much of what he or she says.

Cebuano is evolving as it assimilates slang and colloquialisms from other Visayan dialects, as well as from Tagalog and English. Confused? You will be. Most Cebuano conversations veer apparently at random between all three languages, leaving even Filipino visitors unable to grasp the meaning.

Bold vowels below indicate where to lay emphasis.

SOME CEBUANO BASICS

Good morning Maayong buntag
Good afternoon Maayong hapon
Good evening Maayong gabi
How are you? Kumusta?
I'm fine Maayo man
Very well Maayo ka'ayo
What's your name? Umsay pangalan ni mu?
Where are you from? Taga din ka?
Thank you Salamat
You're welcome Walay sapayan
Goodbye Ari na ko
Yes O-o

No Dili
OK Sigi
How much is this? Tag-pila ni?
Expensive Mahal
Cheap Barat
Idiot! Amaw!
Go away! Layas!
Who? Kinsa?
What? Unsa?
Why? Ngano?
Near/Far Duol/Layo

> ## CEBU CITY ORIENTATION
>
> Cebu City's main north–south artery is **President Osmeña Boulevard**, running from the Provincial Capitol Building (northwest of the centre) down to **Plaza Independencia**, the old centre, which is sort of to the west or southwest of what *probably* constitutes the new one. However, in true Philippine urban tradition, the jumble of streets that constitutes Cebu City itself appears to have no particular centre. Return visitors may cite the earthy, careworn charms of Colon Street and the **port** as the beating heart of Cebu, while others focus on the hotel and bar hub of **Fuente Osmeña**, 1km north, but these days the best dining and shopping are to be found in the malls at the **Ayala Center** and the trendy residential northern suburbs of **Lahug** and **Banilad**. Thirty minutes' drive north of the city proper, **Mandaue** is an industrial suburb that functions as one of the city's economic and transport hubs. However, for many a Cebuano, city life revolves around the malls, and its these that you'll most commonly find used as landmarks when giving directions – or perhaps even when trying yourself to make some sense of this happy mess of a city.

7

Further inland, the excellent **Casa Gorordo Museum** and **Museo Sugbo** are rich with colonial splendour and offer more historical insights, while for a break from the serious stuff, **Tops Lookout** is true to its name; it offers a sigh-triggering view across the city, along with a much-needed breath of fresh air.

Cebu City's main tourist event is the Mardi Gras-style **Sinulog festival** in January (see box, page 303).

Magellan's Cross

Magallanes St • Free

Cebu City's spiritual heart is an unassuming stone rotunda in the middle of busy Plaza Sugbo that houses the **Magellan's Cross**. The first of the conquering Spaniards to set foot in the Philippines, Magellan began a colonial and religious rule that would last four hundred turbulent years. The rotunda's ceiling is exquisitely painted with a scene depicting his landing in Cebu in 1521 and the planting of the original cross on the shore. It was with this crucifix that Magellan is said to have baptised the Cebuana Queen Juana and her followers. The cross that stands here today, however, is only a modern reproduction, apparently containing fragments of the conquistador's original.

Basilica del Santo Niño

President Osmeña Blvd, next to the Cross of Magellan • Free • No shorts, sleeveless tops, flip-flops or other clothing deemed improper • ⓦ santoninodecebubasilica.org

Heralded by vendors selling religious icons and amulets offering cures for everything from poverty to infertility, the **Basilica del Santo Niño** was first founded in 1565 – making it the oldest church in the country – and is home to probably the most famous religious icon in the Philippines: the statue of the **Santo Niño**. The figure, which looks like an extravagantly dressed children's doll, is said to have been presented to Queen Juana of Cebu by Magellan after her baptism, considered the first in Asia, in 1521. Another tale has it that 44 years later, after laying siege to a pagan village, one of conquistador Miguel López de Legazpi's foot soldiers found a wooden chest that had survived the bombardment inside a burning hut. Inside this box was the Santo Niño. If you want to see the statue, let alone touch it, you'll have to join the queue of devotees that often squirms through the doors and outside.

Carbon Market

MC Briones St • Free

No longer the coal unloading depot from which its name is derived, **Carbon Market** is now an area of covered stalls where the range of goods on offer, edible and otherwise, will leave you reeling – shining fat tuna, crabs, lobsters, coconuts, guavas, avocados, mangoes and more. The market is alive from well before dawn and doesn't slow down until after dark.

National Museum

Off Plaza Independencia • Free • Ⓦ nationalmuseum.gov.ph

Set in an old yellow creamcake of a building, **National Museum** possesses quite a colourful history. It was designed by American architect William Parsons and built in 1910; after serving as a customs house for many decades, it suffered heavy damage during the earthquake of 2013, and finally assumed its current guise when inaugurated as a national museum in 2023. The place has already become one of the most popular sights in the city; three permanent galleries on the first floor feature model ships, paintings and some short takes on the city's history, while in the halls upstairs the exhibitions rotate, and usually focus on local art in some form.

Fort San Pedro

Near the port area at the end of Sergio Osmeña Blvd • Charge • ☎ 032 256 2284

When he arrived in 1565, conquistador Miguel López de Legazpi set about building **Fort San Pedro** to guard against marauding Moros from the south. It was here, on December 24, 1898, that three centuries of Spanish rule in Cebu came to an end when their flag was lowered and they withdrew in a convoy of boats bound for Zamboanga, on Mindanao – their way station for the voyage to Spain. The fort has been used down the centuries as a garrison, prison and zoo, but today is little more than a series of walls and ramparts. On Sundays, the park opposite, **Plaza Independencia**, gets packed out with locals playing ball games and enjoying picnics.

Cebu Metropolitan Cathedral

Legazpi St • Free • Ⓦ facebook.com/katedralsasugbo

An imposing sixteenth-century Baroque structure, **Cebu Metropolitan Cathedral** has felt the force of nature and conflict several times in its four hundred-year history. An early version was completely destroyed by a typhoon before construction was finished, and the cathedral was almost razed to the ground during World War II. It was quickly rebuilt, and then renovated in 2009, but damaged (only superficially, thankfully) once again by the 2013 earthquake.

Yap-Sandiego Heritage House

Mabini St • Charge • ☎ 032 266 2833

Distilling the essence of Cebu before the mall and mobile era is the **Yap-Sandiego Heritage House**, which was built between 1675 and 1700 and is one of the oldest

---

SINULOG

Almost as popular as Kalibo's Ati-Atihan (see box, page 271), the big, boisterous **Sinulog festival**, which culminates on the third Sunday of January with a wild street parade and an outdoor concert at Fuente Osmeña, is held in honour of Cebu's patron saint, the Santo Niño. The Santo Niño statue itself (see page 302) is brought on a boat from Mandaue to the city proper, festooned with candles and garlands, and then paraded through the streets. Sinulog is actually the name given to a swaying **dance** said to resemble the current (*sulog*) of a river and supposedly evolved from tribal elders' rhythmic movements. Today, it's a memorable, deafening spectacle, with hundreds of intricately dressed Cebuanos dancing through the streets to the beat of noisy drums. Most of the action happens on President Osmeña Boulevard, but to escape the crowds, grab a spot on one of the nearby roads where security is less zealous and you can slip underneath the velvet ropes and join the dancers. If you plan to visit Cebu City during Sinulog, make sure you book accommodation well ahead of time.

Airport (9km)

Mandaue

Beverly Hills (2km), Busay (5km), Tops; Cebu,

7

CEBU CITY

Ayala Malls Central Bloc

Crossroads Mall

Cebu IT Park

LAHUG

J. ABAD SANT.

GEN. ECHAVERRIA

NRT. A RACI

GOV. CUENCO AVENUE

GEN. ECHAVERRIA

PRES. MAGSAYSAY

PRES. ROXAS

PRES. M QUEZON

F. CABAHUG

PRES. AGUINALDO

E. GOCHAN

P. ALMENDRAS

TRES BORCES PADRES

B. COLINA

P. ALMENDRAS EXT.

EDROS ROAD

J. SENG

J. LUNA AVENUE

J. LUNA AVENUE

SALINAS DRIVE

ARCH. REYES AVENUE

MINDANAO AVENUE

CARDINAL ROSALES AVENUE

Cebu Business Park

CAMOTES ROAD

SAMAR LOOP

LEYTE LOOP

Ayala Center

Jeepney Terminal

LUZON AVENUE

BANTAYA N.

J. SOLON DRIVE

APITONG

MOLAVE

C. ROSAL

N. ESCARIO

Cebu Holidays Tours & Travel

TOJONG

ACACIA

MYS Tower

Cebu City Police Office

GENERAL MAXILOM AVE.

Perpetual Succour Hospital

Land and Sky Travel

Iglesia ni Cristo

Mango Plaza

Horizons 101 Condo

N. ESCARIO

ELIZABETH POND

JUANA OSMEÑA

MA. CRISTINA

JANSALEM

E. BENEDICTO

R. BAHANAN

GENERAL MAXILOM AVE. | MANGO AVENUE

F. RAMOS

Provincial Capitol

Cebu Doctors' University Hospital

PRES. OSMEÑA BLVD

Bo's Coffee

Chong Hua Hospital

FUENTE OSMEÑA

JUANA OSMEÑA

M. ZOSA

J. AVILA

J. AVILA

G. GARCIA

M. CUI

M. BRIONES

J. LLORENTE

F. RODRIGUEZ

P. RODRIGUEZ

J. ALCANTARA

D. JAKOSALEM

B. RODRIGUEZ

VISITACION

B. OSMEÑA

E. OSMEÑA

M. VELEZ

M. VELOSO

D. JAKOSALEM

V. RAMA AVENUE

B. BACALSO

D. R. ROAD

● SHOPPING	
Ayala Center	1
The Buzz Cafe	4
Casa Gorordo	6
Fully Booked	1
Island Souvenirs	7
National Book Store	1/2/3
Robinsons Galleria	5
SM City	3

N

CEBU

■ ACCOMMODATION	
Castle Peak	11
Cebu Hotel Plus	10
Cebu Parklane International	7
Cebuview Tourist Inn	21
Crowne Garden	1
Fuente	15
Harolds	4
Hop Inn	16
Hostel 7	14
Hotel Asia	6
Kiwi Lodge	17
Murals Hostel & Café	5
One Central	19
The Pad Co-Living	3
Palm Grass	2
Pensionne La Florentina	9
Pillows	13
Radisson Blu	18
Seda Ayala Center	12
Sugbutel	20
Vacation	8
Waterfront Cebu City	3

● EATING	
Abaca Baking Company	7
Anzani	1
Banana Pancake Trail	8
Bo's Coffee	15
Chika-An Sa Cebu	4
House of Lechon	10
La Vie Parisienne	3
Lemon Grass	11
Maco Manok	2
The Original AA BBQ	16
Persian Palate	13
The Pig and Palm	14
Pungko-pungko sa Fuente	12
Sparrow Café Culture	6
STK ta Bay!	9
Yukga	5

■ DRINKING AND NIGHTLIFE	
Ambiance	2
Cebu Icon	7
The Distillery	4
Draft Punk	9
G-Spot Bar	1
Maya	3
Sunset Soirees	5
Turning Wheels Craft Brewery	8
Verified Lounge	6

homes in the Philippines, evidenced by the dusty antiques and warp and weft of the floorboards. It's owned by a descendant of the original residents; current landlord Val Sandiego, a choreographer and antique collector, still sometimes stays over at weekends with his extended brood. The house is located across the road from the overtly patriotic, flag-waving **Heritage of Cebu Monument**.

Casa Gorordo Museum

35 Lopez Jaena St, off Mabini, off the eastern end of Colon St • Charge • ⓦ casagorordomuseum.org

Built in the 1850s by wealthy merchant Alejandro Reynes, the marvellous **Casa Gorordo Museum** building is one of the few structures of its time in Cebu that survived World War II. Owned by a succession of luminaries, including the first Filipino Bishop of Cebu, Juan Isidro de Gorordo, it was acquired in 1980 from the bishop's heirs and opened as a museum three years later. The museum enjoyed extensive structural renovations, including the addition of a new shop and café (the best-located branch of Cebu's own *Bo's Coffee* chain; see page 311), in the mid-2010s.

The house is a striking marriage of late Spanish-era architecture and native building techniques, with lower walls of Mactan coral cemented using tree sap, and upper-storey living quarters built entirely from Philippine hardwood held together with wooden pegs. The interior offers an intriguing glimpse into the way Cebu's aristocracy once lived, and is elegantly furnished with original pieces like a Viennese dining set, a German piano and Catholic icons from Spain.

Museo Sugbo

MJ Cuenco Ave • Charge (including guided tour) • ⓦ facebook.com/museosugbo

Housed in the former Carcer del Cebu (provincial jail), the excellent **Museo Sugbo** traces the island's history from early Chinese and Siamese trading to the arrival of the Spanish and the modern era. The highlights are the first-floor World War II exhibits, including banned "guerrilla money" that was issued after the Japanese had instituted their own currency, and possession of which was punishable by death. There are also wartime notices detailing the types of foods Filipinos weren't allowed to eat: one of the few staples not on the list was sweet potato, meaning that during the occupation, many people survived on these alone. Towards the complex's rear, a separate room houses finds excavated from Plaza Independencia, including a spooky fifteenth-century death mask made of gold leaf.

Tops Cebu

Busay • Charge • Busay jeepneys from SM City and Ayala Center stop 1km from Tops, from where there are habal-habals, or you can brave the steep walk up • ⓦ topscebu.ph

The road that winds northwards out of Cebu City eventually finds its way to **Busay**, the high mountain ridge that rises immediately behind the city. At the top, there's a wide, recently prettified lookout area known as **Tops Cebu**, where visitors pay an entrance fee, buy some barbecued chicken from a vendor and watch the plum-coloured sunset. It's popular at dusk, so don't expect romantic solitude, but the view is great and the air cooler and cleaner than in the concrete jungle 600m below.

Jumalon Museum and Butterfly Sanctuary

Jumalon St, Basak • Charge • ☎ 032 261 6884 • Best reached by taxi (20min); alternatively, take any jeepney heading along Cebu South Rd to Friendship Village or Basak, get off at the Holy Cross Parish Church and look out for Jumalon St near Basak Elementary School

Four kilometres west of the centre in the largely residential suburb of Basak, the **Jumalon Museum and Butterfly Sanctuary** is lepidopteran heaven, with rooms full of glass display cases and a large garden at the back with butterflies fluttering around. As well as everyday species, such as monarchs and viceroys, there are also rare examples such as albinos, melanics, dwarfs and conjoined twins. It's home to a fascinating art gallery, too.

BY PLANE

MACTAN CEBU INTERNATIONAL AIRPORT
Cebu flights land at Mactan Cebu International Airport (ⓦmactancebuairport.com), the second busiest in the land, over the way on Mactan Island. There is a tourist information counter in the arrivals hall, which also has car rental booths; all the rental agencies are reputable and offer cars at competitive rates. You'll need to pay a departure tax from Cebu, but this is now included in almost all airfares.

Getting into town White taxis are generally cheaper than yellow taxis, and Grab cabs cheaper still, but there isn't much difference between them. The journey into town is 8km across the suspension bridge, and fares will depend on your destination and the time of day. MyBus, a welcome airport transfer running to and from Mactan from SM City Cebu, is also in service (every 20–30mins, 6am–10pm; ⓦfacebook.com/MyBusPH).

Domestic destinations Bacolod (8 daily; 45min); Busuanga (3 daily; 1hr 30min); Butuan (4 daily; 50min); Cagayan de

---

CEBU FERRY SCHEDULES

7

Note that **ferry schedules constantly change**, especially those for slower boats; what follows should be viewed as a guide only. Also note that for many destinations, there are major differences between slower and faster sailings – although the slow ones can sometimes end up saving you a night's accommodation.

DESTINATION	FREQUENCY	DURATION
BILIRAN		
Naval	1–2 daily	3hr 40min–9hr 30min
BOHOL		
Tagbilaran	1–2 hourly	2–5hr
Tubigon	1–2 hourly	1hr 20min–3hr
CAMOTES		
Poro	3–4 daily	1hr 30min 4hr 30min
LEYTE		
Hilongos	3 daily	4hr 30min
Maasin	2–3 daily	3–6hr
Ormoc	13 daily	2hr 30min–6hr
LUZON		
Manila	1–2 daily	23hr
MASBATE		
Masbate City	2–3 weekly	12–14hr
MINDANAO		
Cagayan de Oro	1–3 daily	8–10hr
Dapitan	1–2 daily	9–15hr
Iligan	1–2 daily	13hr
Nasipit	1–2 daily	10hr 30min
Ozamiz	1–2 daily	8hr – 9hr 30min
Surigao	6 weekly	8hr 30min
NEGROS		
Dumaguete	1–2 daily	4–6hr
PANAY		
Iloilo City	1–2 daily	12hr
SAMAR		
Calbayog	3 weekly	11hr
Catbalogan	2 weekly	12hr
SIQUIJOR		
Siquijor Town	1 daily	4hr–6hr (via Tagbilaran and Dumaguete)

7

Oro (6–7 daily; 45min); Camiguin (1–2 daily; 45min); Caticlan (3 daily; 1hr); Clark (6 weekly; 1hr 25min); Davao (6–9 daily; 1hr); El Nido (1 daily; 1hr 40min); Iloilo City (4–6 daily; 50min); Kalibo (3–7 daily; 50min); Manila (1–3 hourly; 1hr 10min); Puerto Princesa (2–3 daily; 1hr 15min); San Vicente (3 weekly; 1hr 45min); Siargao (8 daily; 1hr); Surigao (2 daily; 45min); Tacloban (3–4 daily; 45min); Zamboanga (2 daily; 1hr 5min).

BY BOAT

ESSENTIALS

Piers The arrival points for ferries are eight large piers stretching along the harbour area beyond Fort San Pedro. Pier 1 is closest to Fort San Pedro, just a few minutes on foot, while Pier 8 lies several kilometres to the northeast. Jeepneys and buses line up along nearby Sergio Osmeña Blvd for the short journey into the city. Taxis wait to meet arriving ferries.

Tickets and information As well as ticket offices at the piers, travel agents and hotels throughout the city can book ferry tickets (see page 309). Generally speaking, tickets for fast ferries on the main inter-island routes are very reasonably priced, while slower services are, as you'd expect, even cheaper. The shipping pages of local newspapers are a good place to get up-to-date ferry information. There's also a shipping schedules channel on the local Sky Cable TV network, available in some hotels. To get a better idea of which companies go where, try using an agglomerate site – ⓦ 12go.asia has been the most useful of late in such regards, and offers online ticket purchase for the routes it displays.

SHIPPING LINES AND FERRIES

The three main fast boat companies are Oceanjet (ⓦ oceanjet.net), Weesam (ⓦ weesam.ph) and 2GO (ⓦ travel.2go.com.ph). 2GO is a conglomerate of companies which operates both fast and slow ferries, and generally – alongside rival operator OceanJet – offers the most comfortable and professional service. For a fuller list of ferry companies and their contact details, see Basics (see page 27).

DESTINATIONS

Cebu is connected by boat to almost every major port in the Philippines, and a number of minor ones (see box, page 307). Fast boat and catamaran services link Cebu with Bohol and Leyte all within 3hr, but these services are more expensive than regular ferries. As well as ferries to Dumaguete, another way to Negros is to ride the bus to Bato, Lilo-An or Toledo, and take a ferry or big bangka (see page 274).

BY BUS

Bus terminals Ceres Liner (ⓦ ceresliner.com) is the main bus company in Cebu, and operates out of two terminals. The Northern bus terminal, served by jeepneys marked "Mandaue", is just south of SM City Mall (and thus actually not that far north at all), and used by buses and jeepneys for destinations north of the city (all every 20–30min), plus services to the airport. The Southern bus terminal, for buses south, is on Bacalso Ave, west of President Osmeña Blvd and is accessible by jeepneys marked "Basak".

Destinations from Northern terminal Danao (for Camotes; frequent; 1hr); Hagnaya (for Bantayan; every 30min; 3hr 30min); Maya (for Malapascua; every 30min; 4hr).

Destinations from Southern terminal Badian (4hr); Bato (4hr); Lilo-An (3hr); Moalboal (3hr); Oslob (4hr); Toledo (for San Carlos; 2hr 30min).

GETTING AROUND

By bus Cebu City's Bus Rapid Transit System, though it's been in development since 2012, only started construction in 2023 (a mere seven years after it was supposed to be completed), meaning that for now jeepneys and vans remain the principal public transport.

By taxi Taxis are plentiful and it's not hard to find a driver who's willing to use the meter. The Grab app works well here, and will almost always be cheaper than regular cabs.

By jeepney and van Jeepneys and open-sided vans painted in outrageous colours ply dozens of cross-city routes. From Colon St, they run almost everywhere; ask local advice if you want to get around in this manner.

By car You may prefer to charter a car with driver to get around the island; many tourists simply negotiate a flat rate with a tax driver, or else see how much point-to-point services cost on Grab (they can be quite affordable). Many of the bigger hotels have their own cars with drivers, but charge significantly more. Plenty of rental firms have kiosks at the airport, or in town.

INFORMATION

Tourist information The main tourist office is the Department of Tourism's Cebu regional office (Mon–Fri 8am–5pm; ☎032 254 2811) in the LDM Building on Legazpi St, near the junction with Lapu-Lapu (close to Fort San Pedro). There's also a branch at the airport (opening hours vary).

Maps There are plenty of free maps to pick up from hotel receptions, tourist kiosks and at Mactan airport, while apps such as Google Maps and Maps.me work very well in the city.

Newspapers There are a number of English-language local newspapers, including the *Cebu Daily News*

AIRBNB IN CEBU CITY

While accommodation is generally very affordable in Cebu City, even relative to Manila, you may get better value on Airbnb and similar sites, especially if you're staying for a few days or more. Some buildings have plenty of rooms to let on such platforms, like the lofty towers of the *Horizons 101 Condo* (which is cheating somewhat, since it doesn't have 101 levels; this is the sum of the levels of its two towers, though they're both pretty tall anyway). As in Manila, for the same price as you'd pay for a hotel or guesthouse room, you can get a small apartment with cooking facilities, and a pool with a view.

(ⓦcebudailynews.inquirer.net), and the *Sun Star Cebu* (ⓦsunstar.com.ph), both of which have ferry timetables (sadly in the printed version alone), events listings and restaurant reviews.

TOURS

Travel agents These can be found in most malls and hotels, and can arrange tours of the city, ferry tickets, flights and vehicle hire (with driver). A few to try include: Cebu Trip Tours (F.E. Zuellig Ave ⓦcebutriptours.com); Grand Hope Travel and Tours (Lower Ground Level, SM City Mall, Juan Luna Ave ⓦfacebook.com/grandhopetravelinc); and Cebu Tours (Ibabao-Gisi Rd ⓦcebutours.ph).

ACCOMMODATION SEE MAP PAGE 304

Some of the cheapest accommodation in Cebu City is in the old **Colon Street** area, though the streets in this neighbourhood can be a little daunting at night, with roaming pimps and a number of shabby massage parlours and go-go bars. Hotels around **Fuente Osmeña** are better, and, further out, glitzier options near the **Ayala Center** and in **Lahug** and **Banilad** are close to the city's hyper-real malls and many of the more fashionable restaurants.

COLON STREET AND AROUND

Cebuview Tourist Inn 200 Sanciangko St ⓦcebuview touristinn.com. Reasonably comfortable and secure, offering a/c rooms with cable TV and Filipino breakfasts. Long-term deals are available and it's right in the mix of the shopping and fast-food outlets outside. P̄P̄

One Central Sanciangko St at Leon Kilat St ⓦone centralhotel.com. Rooms here offer good value, and they're pleasant and comfortable. The hotel boasts a decent gym and a good rooftop swimming pool – not exactly luxurious, but far fancier in feel than the price-tag may suggest. P̄P̄

Palm Grass 68 Junquera St ⓦpalmgrasshotel.com. ph. Pitched as Cebu's first heritage hotel, *Palm Grass* is decorated in faux-vintage maps, teak furniture and gold curtains. Deluxe rooms are well lit and modern, while staff are super-helpful. Breakfast is included, and there is a mini rooftop bar – great for sunset beers. P̄P̄

FUENTE OSMEÑA AND AROUND

Cebu Hotel Plus 332 Don Mariano Cui St ⓦcebuhotel plus.com. The not particularly exciting bedrooms at this international standard hotel are spiced up by some fairly funky bed linen, some of which make you feel as though you're in an Escher cartoon. There's a restaurant on site, though the food is a little underwhelming. P̄P̄

Fuente 0175 Don Julio Llorente St ⓦfuentehoteldecebu. com. The spotlessly clean lobby makes the *Fuente* seem like a boutique hotel at first glance, but the rooms are simple and good value. All have hot water and cable TV, and the rooftop restaurant has free wi-fi. They offer 24hr rates, regardless of when you check in, and reliable airport and pier pick-up and drop-offs. P̄P̄

Hostel 7 101 E. Ramon Aboitiz St ⓦfacebook.com/ HostelSevenCebu. Just next to Casa Rosario, Hostel Seven remains the best backpacker option in this part of town. With clean, comfy and rather stylish dorms, friendly staff, and a great bar with regular live music , it's a great place to bed in for a couple of days and meet fellow travellers. P̄

Hotel Asia 11 Don Jose Avila St ⓦhotelasiacebu.com. In a good location north of Fuente Osmeña, this neat, well-run, Japanese-themed hotel has an airy white-tiled lobby, plenty of Mt Fuji motifs and well-appointed, box-sized rooms, each with a high-tech toilet; the place comes across as very 1980s, which is actually true of lots of urban Japan too. Larger, deluxe rooms (some laid-out tatami-mat-style) have stone bathtubs. There's also an acceptable Japanese restaurant on lobby level. P̄P̄

Pillows 208 Gov. M. Roa St ⓦpillowshotel.ph. Pillows Hotel offers classy international standard rooms, some with balconies and city views, in a good central location. There's a decent café, and a few pieces of artwork about the place to keep it from feeling too bland. P̄P̄

Vacation 35 Juana Osmeña St ☏032 253 2766. It may look a bit like a prison from outside, but things *do* get better. The best a/c rooms at this charming mid-range choice, north of Fuente Osmeña, are on the second floor, with balconies

7

overlooking the small pool. Downstairs, some rooms at the front have little verandas centred around a garden, but others are darker and less enticing – ask to see a few. P̄P̄

AYALA CENTER AND AROUND

Cebu Parklane International N Escario St ⦿ parklane hotels.com.ph. A swish but affordable option, the Parklane is a bit corporate but the great service and comfy rooms certainly makes up for that. There's a gym, a pool and several different good restaurants to choose from – *Kananan* is a great place to sample Cebuano cuisine, even if you're not staying here. P̄P̄P̄

Harolds 146 Gorordo Ave ⦿ haroldshotel.com. With a bustling all-day café and 360-degree rooftop live music bar, this business hotel is an exciting proposition. Daily rates are on the high side, but over-the-counter promos are great value. Rooms come fitted with mini-bars, rainfall showers and comfy memory foam beds. P̄P̄

★ **Hop Inn** Samar Loop ⦿ hopinnhotel.com. Sharing a modern tower block with the *Holiday Inn*, this has an admirable bang-to-buck ratio – rooms are small but contain everything you might need, while the swimming pool is also tiny but boasts a gorgeous cityscape view (which you may well have from your room, at higher levels). P̄

Kiwi Lodge 1060 G. Tudtud St, Mabolo ⦿ kiwilodge. centralcebu.com. Small hotel in a residential area south of Ayala Center, with a range of comfortable a/c rooms at reasonable prices. Superior rooms in the new wing have TVs and safes, while elsewhere on the premises you'll come across a pool table, fitness centre and restaurant – all quite modest, but very welcome in this slightly out-of-the-way location. P̄

Pensionne La Florentina 18 Acacia St ⦿ pensionne laflorentina.business.site. Family-friendly cheapie in a rambling old building set back from Gorordo Ave. The best rooms on the upper floors have a/c and cable TV, while the pokey street-level veranda is the ideal place to plan your next move. There's a cute little café on reception level, and plenty of street eats immediately outside. P̄

★ **Seda Ayala Center** Cardinal Rosales Ave ⦿ seda hotels.com. Formerly the *Marriott*, this classy but affordable hotel is housed in a twelve-storey building near the Ayala Center. There are over three hundred rooms, all remodelled in sleek, modern style, plus three restaurants, a poolside café and a health club. P̄P̄P̄

LAHUG AND BANILAD

Crowne Garden Salinas Drive ⦿ crownegarden.ph. In a price war with *Cebu Northwinds* across the road, this hotel just edges it for service. Its entrance is hidden around the back of a car park, but don't let that put you off: rooms are bright, clean and comfortable and have a/c, hot water, cable TV and fridge. P̄

Murals Hostel & Café Pres Roxas Rd ⦿ facebook.com/ muralshostels. The most popular of the city's new breed of modern hostels, and one of those places that some guests choose to hunker down in for weeks on end; the rooms aren't all that great, in all honesty, and neither are the shared bathrooms, but the café down below and bar on top are enduringly popular, with the latter often hosting live music or other fun events. P̄

★ **The Pad Co-Living** 101 Gov. Cuenco Ave ⦿ thepad coliving.com. A really interesting cheapie, billed as a co-living spot but actually just a bunch of cheap, bare (but perfectly adequate) rooms facing off across a car park. However, it's an interesting complex with cafés and snack restaurants down below, and a swimming pool and bar on top of the main block; breakfast is included if you book directly, and usually not otherwise. P̄

Waterfront Cebu City Salinas Drive ⦿ waterfront hotels.com.ph. A mid-city landmark, the *Waterfront* is a brash slice of Las Vegas, Cebu-style. Despite the name, it's nowhere near the coast. A world unto itself, with a 24hr casino, several upscale restaurants and bars, and a gym and large pool, this is as showy as the city gets; popping in can be quite fun even if you're not staying, and the café, bakery and snack shop are very affordable. P̄P̄P̄

ELSEWHERE IN THE CITY

Castle Peak F. Cabahug St at President Quezon St, Mabolo ⦿ hotelcastlepeak.com. Affordable hotel in a quiet area east of Ayala. Although showing signs of age, the rooms are spacious and the bathrooms well maintained. There are two decent on-site restaurants, *The Pizza Pub* and *The Dining Room* – the latter does a recommended *lechon*. Popular with Chinese salarymen. P̄P̄

★ **Radisson Blu** S. Osmeña Blvd ⦿ radissonblu.com. Cebu's City's premier international hotel is a gigantic palace with a monstrous lobby, hundreds of spacious, tastefully decorated rooms and the most overwhelming breakfast spread (included) in the city at *Feria* – cooking stations offer everything from Korean BBQ to French crêpes. Better still, the service is so good that you'll rarely have to lift a finger. P̄P̄P̄P̄

Sugbutel S. Osmeña Blvd ⦿ sugbutel.com. The economy version of Japan's capsule hotels, this bizarre green-and-white budget stopover has the cheapest comfy beds in the city. Large rooms have been subdivided into train-like compartments which house two to six bunk beds, each of which has an overhead light, small safety box and plug socket. The lobby feels like a train station waiting room, but it's functional and – most importantly – dirt cheap. P̄P̄

EATING

SEE MAP PAGE 304

Cebu's cosmopolitan dining scene is seriously on the up, offering everything from excellent snack joints to top-end restaurants. Though there are places to eat all over downtown, many of the best options are to be found in the city's malls, notably **The Terraces** at the Ayala Center, a tastefully designed food court overlooking atmospheric gardens. North of the centre, the **Crossroads** and Ayala Central Bloc malls are also home to the city's best international restaurants. Fast-food chains and coffee shops – including Cebu's own *Bo's Coffee*, which is actually very good – are so commonplace that it can feel as if there's one on every corner. It's also hard to talk about Cebu without mentioning lechon (spit-roasted pig), since it's the most famed place in the land for the Philippines' signature style, which Anthony Bourdain famously referred to as the "best pig ever".

COLON STREET AND AROUND

★**Bo's Coffee** Eduardo Aboitiz ⓦboscoffee.com. If you're at all into coffee, you absolutely have to visit a *Bo's* during your time here – the Philippines' best and most successful café chain, serving several types of quality beans from across the nation, it started life right here in Cebu. This is the best-located branch, snuggled as it is within the Casa Gorordo complex (see page 306) – with fine architecture right outside and greenery even closer, it makes for a delightful place to drain a mug of local coffee. $\overline{PP}$

FUENTE OSMEÑA AND AROUND

Persian Palate Mango Plaza, General Maxilom Ave ⓦpersianpalate.ph. Well-spiced Indian and Middle Eastern dishes, including biryanis, samosas and baba ghanoush. There are four other outlets, including one at Ayala. $\overline{PP}$

Pungko-pungko sa Fuente 52 J. Llorente St ⓦfacebook.com/pungkopungkosafuente. The best and most entertaining food court in a city full of them – so long as you don't mind deep-fried stuff, with *chicharron* and the like making up the artery-clogging majority of what's eaten here. The place is popular and tables are large, so you may have to share – a great way to get into the local vibe. $\overline{P}$

STK ta Bay! 6 A.Climaco St ⓦfacebook.com/PaolitosSTK. *STK* stands for Cebu's three most famous cooking methods – *sugba* (grill), *tuwa* (soup) and *kinilaw* (ceviche) – while the wall of fame showing a who's who of Filipino diners underlines the restaurant's credentials. Set up in an old home, diners are seated among family heirlooms and instruments, including locally-made guitars and an enormous goatskin drum. Despite the distractions, the seafood remains the star: try the adobo eel or black pepper crabs, or one of the many non-seafood options. $\overline{PP}$

AYALA CENTER AND AROUND

★**Banana Pancake Trail** N. Escario St ⓦfacebook.com/bptcebu. As it says on the sign outside this industrial-chic spot, what we have here is "Southeast Asian Street Food" – bringing such fare together from what simply have to be the world's best street-food nations is a really good idea, and it's largely been well executed. Take your pick from Burmese

tofu salad, Vietnamese spring rolls or *com tam* ("broken" rice with grilled meat and egg), Singa-Malay *kaya* toast (coconut-pandan jam and lots of butter), Thai *pad krapao* (stir-fried minced meat and basil), and much more. $\overline{PPP}$

★**House of Lechon** Acacia St ⓦfacebook.com/HouseOfLechonCebu. To go the full hog in the company of smiling, grease-chinned locals, there really is nowhere better in Cebu. With cherry-red, succulent barbecued pig that's been voted the best in the city (no small feat with so much competition), the restaurant prices its secret-recipe *lechon* by weight, serving it in little piggy-shaped crockery that may make you question your carnivorous choices. It's an attractive place, and you may have to queue to get in at mealtimes, though those willing to forgo a/c and eat in the outdoor section often get a table more quickly. $\overline{PPP}$

Lemon Grass Garden Level, The Terraces, Ayala Center ⓦlagunagroup.ph. Staff at this bright, garden-view restaurant really know how to lure customers through the door. Thai and Vietnamese dishes are as close to authentic as you can expect round here, with lots of well-seasoned and spicy coconut curries. The *banh xeo* (sizzling Vietnamese crêpes) are also delicious. $\overline{PPP}$

The Pig and Palm MYS Tower, Pescadores Rd ⓦthepigandpalm.ph. Located on the ground floor of the MYS Tower, this Spanish tapas restaurant is run by a Michelin-starred British chef. The creative sharing plates are highly recommended, with dishes like beef-and-foie-gras burgers and tipples made with bacon butter bourbon. Needless to say, the place is hugely popular with expats and moneyed locals. $\overline{PPPP}$

LAHUG AND BANILAD

Abaca Baking Company Crossroads Mall, Banilad ⓦtheabacagroup.com. Tucked away at the back of the Crossroads Mall, this small but sophisticated café has a wide-ranging menu offering everything from gourmet sandwiches to cupcakes and Danishes, all served up by staff clad in sleek black. They have branches around the city, but this one strikes the best balance between demand (you won't have to queue) and style. $\overline{PP}$

Anzani Panorama Heights, Nivel Hills ⓦanzani.com.ph. Run by an Italian chef and his Filipino wife, this classy hilltop restaurant is an award-winner for Mediterranean fusion cuisine. Dishes are pricey, but for something totally different, try the ostrich carpaccio or pan-seared crocodile tail. $\overline{PPPP}$

Chika-An Sa Cebu Salinas Drive ☎032 233 0350. A Cebu institution that serves popular rustic food such as chicken or pork BBQ sticks, *lechon kawali* (crispy pork), sizzling *bangus* (milkfish) and various soups, as well as really, really good *halo-halo* for afters. $\overline{PP}$

★**La Vie Parisienne** 371 Gororodo Ave ⓦlavielifestyle.ph. Affectionately known as "the Pink Restaurant", this converted villa looks like the French embassy from the

7

street, but is in fact a smart restaurant, outdoor patio and a patisserie and fine-food emporium. In the restaurant, dishes such as duck confit and escargots make it a culinary utopia for Francophiles, but with fresh-baked pastries and macarons, the patisserie is worth a pit stop too. **PPPP**

Maco Manok 2916 Holy Family Rd ☎ 0917 153 3788. Delicious Filipino dishes, particularly chicken, served at a classy restaurant with fabulous views over town. It's a little way out, on the road to Tops Lookout, but worth the trip. There's another branch on AS Fortuna St, so be sure you know which you're headed to. **PPP**

Sparrow Café Culture V. Padriga St ☎ 0999 229 2433. The most appealing café in this fancy area, with excellent coffee, a chic design, and a tempting array of cakes and desserts on display – one of those places you could quite easily stay in for an hour or two, or more if you've work to do. **PP**

★**Yukga** Garden Row, Ayala Malls Central Bloc ⓦ facebook.com/Yukgakoreanbbq. The best of many Korean restaurants in this newly-developed area, with plenty of meat cuts to choose from, mostly lined up in cool-looking refrigerators. These are meant for sharing; solo diners can have a pop at *naengmyeon* (buckwheat noodles either in a spicy paste or a spicy, ice-cold soup) or *jjigae* (broth), and everything's served with an admirable armada of *banchan* (free side dishes). **PPP**

ELSEWHERE IN THE CITY

The Original AA BBQ Ouano Ave, Mandaue. This branch of the low-key, self-service, Cebu-wide chain offers a butcher's shop's worth of authentic Filipino skewered meats and fish. Dishes like sweet and sour pork and baked scallops bring in locals by the busload. **P**

DRINKING AND NIGHTLIFE SEE MAP PAGE 304

Cebu, like its big sister Manila, is a city that never – or rarely – sleeps. You don't have to walk far in the centre to pass a pub, karaoke lounge or a music bar, although you'll want to choose your venue carefully. Many of the biggest clubs are to be found in **Mango Square** on General Maxilom Ave, though some are distinctively seedy; others change their name so often it can be hard to keep up with what's going on. While many of the most appealing places are at the **malls**, a more cosmopolitan drinking scene is emerging, with the epicentre around the trendy **Cebu IT Park** and **Crossroads Mall** in Banilad.

BARS

Ambiance Garden Row, Ayala Malls Central Bloc ⓦ ambiance.com.ph. This popular spot offers a decent range of snacky meals, but it's with its cocktails that it really excels – all the old favourites are here, plus some of the bar's own invention. You'll sometimes find live bands playing.

The Distillery Crossroads Mall, Banilad ☎ 032 266 9064. One for real night owls, this connoisseur's drinking hole is set up like a liquor store, yet turns into a lively party spot with DJs and fresh-faced youngsters supping on single malts.

Draft Punk Juana Osmeña St ⓦ draftpunk.ph. Worth including just for its name, Draft Punk happily is more than a pun: it's got a great range of draft beers on offer, occasional live music nights, and surprisingly good food. Very popular, and with good reason.

Maya Crossroads Mall, Banilad ⓦ theabacagroup.com. The place to whet your sombrero with an exhaustive tequila

list, as well as blue agave tasting tours. There are also authentic Mexican dishes (including burritos and fajitas), and energetic salsa classes.

Sunset Soirées The Pad Co-Living, 101 Gov. Cuenco Ave ⓦ thepadcoliving.com. Set atop a cheap "co-living" hotel, this bar-with-a-view has decent drinks (and not-so-great food), and fun themed nights on weekends.

Turning Wheels Craft Brewery P. Almendras St, ⓦ turningwheelsbeer.com. Excellent spot with an industrial vibe, Turning Wheels offers a good selection of IPA and pale ales, as well as serving up tasty burgers and tacos, making it a great place to settle in for the evening.

Verified Lounge Rooftop, Avenir Building, Archbishop Reyes Ave ⓦ facebook.com/verifiedlounge. This elegant bar is found on the 22nd floor of the Avenir Building – come by for the fabulous city views and stay for the expertly mixed cocktails.

CLUBS

Cebu Icon 6 F. Cabahug St ⓦ cebuicon.com. Probably Cebu's glitziest club, with mirror balls and lasers aplenty, Icon is a great spot to dance the night away to EDM and hip-hop played by a daily-changing cast of DJs. Drinks are decent but not cheap, and it's best to avoid the food.

G-Spot Bar 3rd Floor, JCA Pizza Building, 935L Salinas Drive ⓦ facebook.com/gspotbargaming. Hugely popular rooftop bar-club with an ever-changing rotation of local and national DJs, as well as fun events including dance-offs and beer pong. It doesn't get going till it's late, and it doesn't close until it's early.

SHOPPING SEE MAP PAGE 304

BOOKSHOPS

Fully Booked Level 2, The Terraces, Ayala Center ⓦ fullybookedonline.com. This branch of the country's

best bookstore has a broad range of titles and also sells magazines and stationery.

National Book Store SM City Mall ☎ 032 231

5496; Ayala Center ☏ 032 231 4006; Mango Plaza ⓦ nationalbookstore.com. A great YA and kids' selection as well as plenty of bestsellers, staff picks and classics, plus stationery and writing supplies galore.

MALLS

Ayala Center Cebu Business Park ⓦ ayalamalls.com/main/malls/ayala-center-cebu. Opened in 1994, the Ayala Center still welcomes around 135,000 shoppers every weekend. It plays host to a huge selection of local and international stores, along with coffee shops, cinemas, dentists and internet cafés – and the excellent The Terraces dining complex.

Robinson's Galleria Gen. Maxilom Ave at Sergio Osmena Blvd ⓦ robinsonsmalls.com. More than two hundred shops, a 3D cinema, open-air American-style food court and the largest flower-power guitar you're ever likely to see.

SM City Juan Luna Ave ⓦ smsupermalls.com. Another megamall, this retail labyrinth has all the usual shops, movie theatres and services – plus a bowling alley – spread between the old Southern Wing and the newer Northern Wing. Another location at SM Seaside City, southwest of the city.

SOUVENIRS

Besides the malls, there are also a half-dozen souvenir stalls inside the airport departure lounge. As well as Alegre on Mactan (see page 315), for handmade guitars and ukuleles, you could also try Borremeo St, a 10min walk south of Colon St.

The Buzzz Cafe Robinson's Galleria ⓦ boholbeefarm.com. A first for Cebu, this fine food shop and café (from the wildly popular Bohol farm-to-fork outfit) showcases a variety of gourmet honeys, tropical fruit-flavoured jams, organic teas and honey wine.

Casa Gorordo Eduardo Aboitiz, ⓦ boscoffee.com. If you're visiting Casa Gorordo (see page 306), you'll come out through this souvenir shop, which is worth at least a little pause – all manner of cool souvenirs, and fairly priced to boot.

Island Souvenirs P. Burgos St ⓦ theislandsgroup.com. A peso's throw from The Cross of Magellan, this downtown emporium sells Cebu-branded T-shirts, hats, bags and all sorts of fun-in-the-sun, Visayan-inspired goodies. Look for the bright-green "I Heart Cebu" monogram outside. There's also a small branch inside *Waterfront Cebu City* (see page 310).

7

DIRECTORY

Banks and exchange There is no shortage of places to change currency, particularly along the main drag of President Osmeña Blvd, on Fuente Osmeña and in all shopping malls. The main banks are BDO, PNB and Allied. Beware the 24hr exchanges in the bar districts unless you really have to – rates are often substantially lower than elsewhere. Also try to use guarded indoor ATMs if you need to withdraw cash late at night – ATM muggings are not unheard of.

Cinemas Ayala Malls (see page 313) has the most comfortable movie theatre in Cebu, and shows the latest movies in English daily.

Consulates A number of countries have consular offices in Cebu, among them the UK, at Villa Terrace, Greenhills Rd, Mandaue City (☏ 032 238 9055) and the US, *Waterfront Cebu City*, Salinas Drive, Lahug (☏ 032 231 1261), though these are open only part-time and don't offer a full consular service.

Emergencies ☏ 161.

Hospitals Among the best equipped are Cebu Doctors' University Hospital, President Osmeña Blvd (☏ 032 255 5555); Chong Hua Hospital, Don Mariano Cui St, just north of Fuente Osmeña (☏ 032 255 8000, ⓦ chonghua.com.ph);

and Perpetual Succour Hospital on Gorordo Ave (☏ 032 233 8620, ⓦ perpetualsuccorhospital.com).

Immigration The Cebu Immigration District Office is on the Level 2 of J. Centre Mall on A.S. Fortuna St, Mandaue (usually daily 8am–6.30pm; ☏ 032 345 6441). You can extend your 30-day visa to 59 days here in a few hours. There's also a sub-office on the ground floor of the Gaisano Mactan Island Mall Annex Building on Quezon Ave in Lapu-Lapu, Mactan Island (usually daily 8am–6.30pm; ☏ 032 495 2852).

Pharmacies There are large pharmacies in all malls, and you'll also find 24hr pharmacies that are often little more than holes in the wall, but carry a good stock of essentials. There's a big branch of Mercury drugstore at Fuente Osmeña, and a Watson's just round the corner on President Osmeña Blvd.

Police The main Cebu City Police Office is on Gorordo Ave (☏ 032 231 5802), while there is another handy branch south of Fuente Osmeña close to Cebu State College (☏ 032 253 5636). There's a branch of the tourist police unit opposite Cebu City Hall near Fort San Pedro (☏ 032 412 1838).

Mactan Island

The closest beaches to Cebu City are on **MACTAN ISLAND**, which is linked to the main island of Cebu by the Mandaue–Mactan Bridge and the Marcelo Fernan Bridge. Off the southern coast of Mactan and linked by two short bridges is **Cordova Island**, a relatively undeveloped slab of land with a couple of secluded, upmarket resorts on the beach. While the sands and scuba diving on these islands

7

THE BATTLE OF MACTAN AND THE DEATH OF MAGELLAN

Everything seemed to be going well for Portuguese explorer **Ferdinand Magellan** when he made landfall in Samar early in 1521 and claimed the pagan Philippines for his adopted country, Spain, and the true religion, Catholicism. He stocked up on spices and sailed on, landing in Cebu. It was here that he befriended a native king, Raja Humabon and, flush with his conquest of the isles, promised to help him subdue an unruly vassal named **Lapu-Lapu**. Early on the morning of April 27, 1521, Magellan landed at Mactan and tried to coerce Lapu-Lapu into accepting Christianity. Lapu-Lapu declined and when Magellan continued to hector he angrily ordered an attack. As his men fled quickly to their ships, Magellan, resplendent in polished body armour, backed away towards safety, but was felled by a spear aimed at his unprotected foot. Lapu-Lapu's men quickly moved in for the kill. In the north of Mactan, at the Mactan Shrine, are two memorials to the battle: **Magellan's Marker** and **Lapu-Lapu's Monument** (an odd cross between King Neptune and Rambo, sculpted in bronze). Seventeen months later, on September 8, 1522, the last remaining ship in Magellan's original fleet sailed into Seville with eighteen survivors on board. After three years, and the loss of four ships and 219 lives, the first circumnavigation of the globe was complete.

don't compare with Malapascua, for instance, they are easier to reach, and the many package-style resorts here (see page 319) offer plenty of watersports and day-trips to nearby islands.

Lapu-Lapu

On the island's northern shore, close to the Mandaue–Mactan Bridge, the small capital of **LAPU-LAPU** has a heaving central market, a mall, a post office and some small hotels, but not much for tourists. For many, an obligatory souvenir purchase is a handmade **guitar** from one of Mactan's world-famous Cebuano guitar factories (see page 315).

The east coast

The beach on Mactan's **east coast** is not especially attractive and in some cases has been expensively dredged, groomed and landscaped to try to make it look like a tropical beach should, with the predictable result that it looks fake.

ARRIVAL AND DEPARTURE   MACTAN ISLAND

By jeepney Mactan is a short ride from the terminal by Cebu City's SM City Mall on J. Luna Ave Extension, close to the *Radisson Blu Cebu*. In Lapu-Lapu, jeepneys stop near the small market square, where you can catch another onwards towards the beaches dotted along Mactan's east coast.

By taxi From the airport to anywhere on Mactan is a short journey, so taxi fares will not be high. Getting to Cordova takes a little longer.

INFORMATION AND ACTIVITIES

Scuba diving The experienced SiDive agency (🌐 sidive. com) offer competitive rates for dives and PADI packages, and can also help organize trips to swim with the whale sharks in Oslob (see box, page 325). Scotty's Dive Center, inside the plush *Shangri-La's Mactan Resort & Spa* on Punta Engaño Rd (🌐 divescotty.com) is also highly recommended for dive courses and trips from Mactan.

Tours Island-hopping day-trips are bookable through most resorts.

ACCOMMODATION AND EATING

Lapu-Lapu has a handful of functional, affordable hotels with a/c and restaurants. On Mactan's **eastern shore** there are about twenty beachfront resorts, mostly overpriced mid-range resorts or top-of-the-line international affairs set up for the package crowd, but there are a couple of cheaper options in **Maribago**. While there's some good dining here, it's also expensive.

LAPU-LAPU
Goldberry Suites Quezon Hwy, Lapu-Lapu City 🌐 the

bellavista-hotel.com. This bright golden box has sleek, modern rooms, with good amenities – three-star comfort at two-star prices. There's a café on site, and room rates usually include breakfast and round-trip airport transfers. PP

Little Norway Guest House 3359 Greenfield Village, off Pusok Rd, Lapu-Lapu City w littlenorwayguesthouse. com. Friendly, affordable, quiet and stylish – the *Little Norway Guest House* is a great find. Rooms are comfortable and decked out with lovely, homely touches, while the pleasant terrace is a super place to relax. P

Manna Sutukil Mactan Shrine, Lapu-Lapu w manna stk.webs.com. One of three waterfront point-and-cook seafood grills hidden behind the souvenir market at the Mactan Shrine, this stands out for its vast selection of shellfish and friendly service. Get the likes of meaty prawns or grouper grilled, sautéed in garlic, or fried. PPP

EAST COAST

Dusit Thani Punta Engaño Rd w dusit.com. Right on the northeast tip of Mactan, the Dusit Thani resort is a fantastic place to get away from it all. Boasting a spa, a gym and a gorgeous infinity pool, along with a choice of five restaurants and bars, it's easy to see why most guests rarely leave the compound. PPPP

Plantation Bay Resort & Spa Marigondon w plantationbay.com. Home to one of the world's largest man-made saltwater lagoons, this colossal resort offers all manner of water's edge activities, including a comprehensive scuba programme. Rooms range from poolside villas to riverboat suites. It's usually packed with Chinese and Korean families. PPPP

★ **Shangri-La Mactan** Punta Engaño Rd w shangri-la. com. The ultimate in Cebuano luxury, the Mactan *Shangri-La* is super-comfortable and has every amenity imaginable. There are five hundred rooms, eight restaurants and bars, and it has a speedboat, yacht, luxury sedan or helicopter to meet you at the airport. There are plenty of activities on offer, including scuba diving, windsurfing, banana-boat rides and, for relaxation, the renowned Chi Spa. PPPP

WEST COAST

Lantaw Floating Native Restaurant Cordova w facebook.com/LantawSeafoodandGrill. Fresh fish and fantastic sunsets are the order of the day at this native Cebuano over-water restaurant anchored off the western coast. The breezy terrace attracts large parties and families, while its beer promos and piled seafood plates make it a messy affair. PPP

SHOPPING

Alegre Guitar Factory Pajac–Maribago Rd, Lapu-Lapu ☎ 032 238 6263. A visit to this famous guitar factory offers the chance to see instruments being made, as well as doing a little souvenir shopping. The cheapest steel-stringed acoustics are not that well constructed, but for serious enthusiasts there are top-quality models made with Indian rosewood or mango wood. The factory is a 30min taxi ride from central Cebu.

DIRECTORY

Banks There are multiple ATM branches across the island.
Hospital The best hospital is the Mactan Doctor's Hospital (☎ 032 236 0000), near the airport in Basak.

Police In Lapu-Lapu, the police station (☎ 032 341 1311) is on Basak Maringondon Rd at the intersection with the Quezon National Highway.

Olango Island

Five kilometres east of Mactan Island, **Olango Island** supports the largest concentration of **migratory birds** in the country. Of the 97 species found here, about 48 – including egrets, sandpipers, terns and black-bellied plovers – use the island as a layover on their annual migration from breeding grounds in Siberia, northern China and Japan to Australia and New Zealand. The island is also home to about sixteen thousand resident native birds, which live mostly in the northern half; the southern half is made up of expanses of mudflats and mangroves, including the **Olango Island Wildlife Sanctuary**.

Olango Island Wildlife Sanctuary

Magallanes St • Charge • w olangowildlifesanctuary.org

Set in the southern part of the island is the rudimentary **Olango Island Wildlife Sanctuary**. The reserve is at its best during peak migration months: September to November for the southbound migration, and February to April northbound.

ARRIVAL AND TOURS   OLANGO ISLAND

Day-trips Most resorts on Mactan can organize an island-hopping day-trip to Olango (including snorkelling equipment), though you could visit independently.

By boat There are regular bangkas (every 40min) to Santa Rosa on Olango Island from the wharf near the *Mövenpick* at the far north of Mactan Island, or you can hire your own

bangka from Maribago Wharf to the island and back. From the small Santa Rosa wharf, it's a short 15min tricycle ride to the wildlife sanctuary.

ACCOMMODATION AND EATING

There has been a recent increase in homestays and low-end resorts on Olango; though nothing truly stood out at the time of writing, it's worth a quick online hunt if you're aiming for the lower end of the budget scale.

Nalusuan Island Resort & Marine Sanctuary Nalusuan Island ⓦ nalusuanislandresort.com. *Nalusuan* is set on an islet rising out of Olango's western coastal reef, and has a choice of rooms or stilted cottages on the water. The open-air restaurant specializes in seafood caught on the

doorstep, and there are nightly campfire cookouts. There are kayaks and paddleboards available to explore the area, but better yet, the house reef is fabulous for snorkelling. PPP

Sagastrand Beach Resort West coast of Olango Island ☎ 0956 245 6508. The best place to stay on the island, though you'll pay for the privilege, and the value for money is quite questionable. Rooms are sharp, the pool is fine (though smallish), and the restaurant excellent; the grounds are manicured, and you're right by the sea. PPPP

Toledo and Balamban

On the west coast of Cebu, less than two hours from Cebu City by road, **TOLEDO** has several daily ferries to **San Carlos** in Negros (see below) – be sure to there before mid-afternoon, as Toledo isn't a place you'd choose to stay. You're better off heading twenty minutes north to the town of **BALAMBAN**, which has slightly more to offer with its clutch of deserted black-sand **beaches**.

ARRIVAL AND DEPARTURE   TOLEDO AND BALAMBAN

By bus Buses leave Cebu City's Southern bus terminal for Toledo from 5am daily (2hr 30min). If you're heading from Cebu City to Negros, catch an early bus to Toledo to make sure you don't miss the last ferry.

By ferry Several ferries and ROROs, including fast E. B. Aznar Shipping (1hr; ⓦ aznarshipping.ph) and slow Lite Shipping (2hr; ⓦ liteferries.com.ph) run daily to San Carlos in Negros.

ACCOMMODATION AND EATING

The Ranch Resort Laguna Rd, Toledo ⓦ facebook.com/TheRanchResortOfficial. Given the very few options in town, this powder-blue saloon-style Texan farmhouse is by far the best choice, even if it is about 8km south on the main westcoast highway. The highlights are its five pools and horse-riding opportunities. PP

Treehouse de Valentine 7.5km east of Balamban town ⓦ treehousedevalentine.com. A real escape, the Treehouse de Valentine is a resort with a difference. Found out in the jungle by a tiny waterfall, the treehouse itself is gorgeously rustic: it's constructed of beautiful, treated wood

and bamboo, with balconies looking out into the forest, and the bathtub is made from a hollowed-out tree trunk. There's also a small pool and, for those who don't want to stay in the treehouse, a self-contained geodesic dome. The only downside is the hefty price tag. PPP

Villa Adela J Gonzales St, Balamban ⓦ villaadelabalamban.com. Villa Adela offers reliable if unexciting rooms inside an attractive colonial-style building. It's good value if you're looking for a place to stay in Balamban, but it does suffer from noise from the road outside. PP

Bantayan Island

Just off the northwest coast of Cebu, quiet, bucolic and pancake-flat **BANTAYAN ISLAND** is the place to go for pleasant, low-key resorts, a smattering of sparkling sandy beaches and friendly open–armed welcomes. While Malapascua takes the lion's share of visitors this far north, that makes Bantayan all the quieter: visitors here are occupied by little more than sand, sunshine and seafood. The island was badly hit by Typhoon Yolanda in November 2013, but the island has made a strong recovery, and fortunately escaped the brunt of Typhoon Odette in 2021. Most of the resorts and beaches are around the little town of **SANTA FE** on the southeast coast, which is where ferries from mainland Cebu arrive at the boat terminal.

Bantayan Town

Along the west coast, the port town of **BANTAYAN** has no decent accommodation, but it's worth a quick visit. There's an elegant Spanish-style plaza on the south side of which stands the **Saints Peter and Paul Church**. The original structure was torched by marauding Moros in 1640, with eight hundred local folk taken captive and sold as slaves to Muslim chieftains in Mindanao. Every Easter during Holy Week, Bantayan holds solemn processions of decorated religious *carozzas* (carriages), each containing a life-sized statue representing the Passion and death of Jesus Christ. Thousands turn out to join in the processions, many setting up camp on the beaches because the resorts are full.

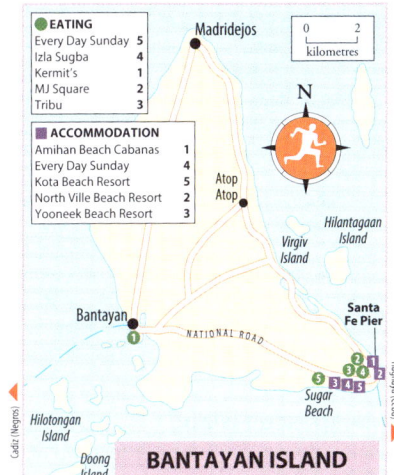

ARRIVAL AND DEPARTURE
BANTAYAN

By bus To reach Bantayan from Cebu City you can take a bus (7 daily; 3hr 30min) from the Northern bus terminal to the port town of Hagnaya, where you can pick up the ferry crossing to Santa Fe (6–7 daily; 1hr).

By taxi Taxis from Cebu to Hagnaya tend to be more expensive on the outward journey than the return.

By bangka There are big bangkas to Bantayan from Cadiz on Negros. Coming from Malapascua, you can charter a bangka, but you should only do so in good weather. If you intend to stay in Santa Fe, you can get a tricycle from the pier to your accommodation, though some resorts can send a representative to collect you at the pier.

GETTING AROUND AND INFORMATION

By habal-habal The only local transport is a habal-habal, known on Bantayan as a *tricikad*.

By motorbike It's fun to hire a motorbike or moped and tour the island yourself by the coastal road, though inspect the rental thoroughly beforehand.

Money There are a couple of ATMs on Rizal Ave in Bantayan Town, but it's best to bring enough cash to last your stay. Currency can be changed at many resorts, and at the MoneyGram exchange office across from the Santo Niño Parish Church in Santa Fe.

ACCOMMODATION   SEE MAP PAGE 317

Amihan Beach Cabanas East side of Santa Fe ⓦ amihanbeachcabanas.com. Six lovely bamboo-and-nipa cabins spread around a sandy courtyard, a coconut shell's throw from hammock-hung palms and the clear sea. Rooms come with mosquito nets, cable TV, hot and cold showers, and there is a breezy restaurant. PPP

Every Day Sunday C. Batiancila Street, Santa Fe ⓦ everydaysundayhotelcafe.com. A super-friendly and affordable place just to the west of Santa Fe, this is a laid-back spot offering spacious accommodation in the main building. Food is good (see below), and there are hammocks to lounge in on the terrace. P

Kota Beach Resort On the main Santa Fe beachfront ⓦ kotabeachresort.com. *Kota* has a range of tightly packed

cottages set in regimented lines on a lovely stretch of beach. The superior cottages are right on the sand, while the cheaper economy rooms at the back offer decent value. PPP

North Ville Beach Resort East side of Santa Fe ⓦ cocotel.com.ph. This stylish and colourful place, part of the national *Cocotel* chain, offers characterful rooms with a small pool and easy access to the beach. Note that breakfast is not included, and there's no restaurant. PP

Yooneek Beach Resort A short ride west of Santa Fe ⓦ yooneekbeachresort.com. Plonked on a quiet part of Sugar Beach, this laidback, nine-room complex has a variety of a/c and fan rooms, some with balconies, fridges and TVs. It's also home to one of the best backpacker bars on the beach. PP

EATING AND DRINKING   SEE MAP PAGE 317

Bantayan has a way to go before it becomes a culinary destination, but there are a few places to try after a hard day

at the beach. A great cheap breakfast option is to buy banana bread from the bakery by the main junction in Santa Fe and some fresh mangoes from the market across the road.

Every Day Sunday C. Batiancila Street, Santa Fe ⓦeverydaysundayhotelcafe.com. Not only a good place to stay on the cheap, but an excellent place to eat even if you're not staying here, with breakfast/brunch fare served all day – Filipino *silog* meals, smoothie bowls, waffles and the like. P̄P̄

Izla Sugba G. Borraska St, Santa Fe ⓦfacebook.com/ izlasugbantayanisland. A no-frills restaurant serving up excellent Filipino dishes, with a particular emphasis on fish and seafood. The scallops and crab are especially good. P̄P̄

Kermit's B. Rodrigues St ⓦfacebook.com/kermits bantayan. The best of the places to have opened up in the newly-popular area around Bantayan Park, in the west

of the island; not an amazing café by any means, but the coffee is okay, the pastries good, and the *halo-halo* worth trying. P̄

★ **MJ Square** Off the main strip in Santa Fe ☎032 438 9013. This community collective of lively, pop-up style restaurants has a dozen or so choices with everything from Tex-Mex burritos and burgers to cupcakes, coffee and cheap Filipino eats. P̄

Tribu Santa Fe ☎0916 534 0667. Authentic Italian restaurant (complete with authentic Italian chef) in the backstreets of Santa Fe, with pizzas, pasta dishes, panini and desserts such as tiramisu doled out to customers who inevitably walk out satisfied. A simple-looking place, but it does the job well. P̄

Malapascua Island

Eight kilometres off the northern tip of Cebu, the tiny island of **MALAPASCUA** is often erroneously touted as the next Boracay, largely due to **Bounty Beach**, a blindingly white stretch of sand on the island's south coast. Yet Malapascua is a world apart from its Western Visayan counterpart, and the islanders have no interest in seeing their paradise lost.

The island's trump card is its world-class **diving**, and it is also renowned for the chance to see thresher sharks congregate in shallow waters (see box, page 319). The sting in the tail is that Malapascua was just emerging onto the main tourist stage when **Typhoon Yolanda** struck. Almost every roof on the island was destroyed, and most of the local population was left without shelter. Substantial private reparations and contributions have helped the island get its groove back and the inhabitants of Malapascua remain some of the warmest people you'll meet. They're also renowned for their love of a party, especially during the annual fiesta from May 11–12 when the whole island gets into carnival mode.

Around the island

It's worth taking a stroll in the cool of the late afternoon to explore the island's glorious main beachfront. You'll also find, radiating from the jetty, a web of traffic-free sandy lanes home to beach bars, low-key seafood grills, and divers relaxing after the drama of the sea. For more of an adventure, you can **walk** the entire circumference of the island in a few hours, a journey which will take you through sleepy fishing villages lined with mangroves to remote white-sand beaches.

Kalanggaman and Carnasa islands

Accessible by bangka or group tour

Whether you're diving or not, don't miss the opportunity for a day-trip to unwind on **Kalanggaman**, a beautiful, tiny islet that consists of no more than a spectacular narrow, arcing sandbar, a handful of windswept trees and some shaded picnic benches. Another full-frontal stunner in the area – two hours northeast of Malapascua by bangka – is **Carnasa Island**, a tropical paradise where you land at a picturesque bay fringed by palm trees.

ARRIVAL AND DEPARTURE   **MALAPASCUA ISLAND**

From Cebu Most visitors head from Cebu City's Northern bus terminal to Maya by Ceres Liner bus (3–4hr) or private taxi, and then take a bangka (hourly) across to the island. The last boat to Maya is usually at 4pm, although boatmen

may try to tell you it's earlier to get you to charter a bangka (the price depends on the boatman and your bargaining skills). When its low tide, you'll likely need to transfer to a smaller boat to get you to the shoreline (which may involve

DIVING AT MALAPASCUA

Although some shallower dive sites around Malapascua were damaged by Yolanda, the major attraction – the distinctively tailed **thresher sharks** – remain in residence, and anyone staying more than a few days is almost guaranteed a sighting. The vortex of this activity was long **Monad Shoal**, the only place in the world where the trident-tailed swimmers could be seen like clockwork before sunrise and just before sunset; in 2022, they migrated to the nearby **Monad Shoal** instead. At shallow depths of around 20m, they congregate on the sea plateau in huge numbers, using the seamount as a symbiotic cleaning station where fish remove (and eat) parasites from the sharks' skin; also plentiful here are hammerheads and devil rays. There are also plenty of wrecks in the vicinity, including the passenger ferry **Doña Marilyn**, which went down in a 1988 typhoon and is now home to scorpionfish, flamefish and stingrays. Dive companies collect a daily marine conservation tax, and there is an additional charge to visit the shoals.

DIVE OPERATORS

Divelink Ⓦ divelinkcebu.com.
Evolution Diving Resort (see page 319).
Malapascua Exotic Island Dive and Beach Resort

(see page 319).
Sea Explorers Ⓦ sea-explorers.com.
Thresher Shark Divers Ⓦ malapascua-diving.com.

an additional charge).
From Bantayan You'll need to charter a bangka from Malapascua (2–3hr); only undertake this trip if the weather is fair and set to stay that way.

From Leyte There is a daily boat from San Isidro to Maya (2hr), returning the same morning. From the city of Bogo, one hour south, operator Super Shuttle Ferry runs a daily service to Palompon.

INFORMATION AND ACTIVITIES

Money There are a couple of ATMs on Malapascua, but it's best to bring enough pesos with you.
Sunset cruises Sunset cruises involving swimming,

snorkelling, and cliff jumping can be great fun; to arrange one, ask at your resort.

ACCOMMODATION

There are about a dozen **dive resorts** on Bounty Beach and a number of others dotted around the island. Budget rooms at the most popular book up fast in peak season. Bear in mind that **swimming pools** are illegal on the island, and even though many have been built, they are a major drain on the island's water resources; the best accommodation providers don't have them.

BOUNTY BEACH

★ **Evolution Diving Resort** Far eastern end of the beach Ⓦ evolution.com.ph. If only all dive resorts were like this welcoming hideaway, tucked out on the loveliest stretch of real estate on the island. Rooms are split between fabulous bungalows and deluxe rooms further back from the beach, while the personable staff make sure that your A–Z of diving needs is taken care of. **PP**
Malapascua Exotic Island Dive and Beach Resort Far eastern end of the beach Ⓦ malapascua.net. One of the best-established resorts on the island (they opened its first dive shop, way back in 1998), there's a huge range of rooms to choose from here, from standard a/c to pricey beachfront deluxe rooms. Full board is available, and the restaurant

pumps out good European and pan-Asian food. **PPP**
Mike & Diose's Far eastern extreme end of the beach Ⓦ malapuasca.de. A collection of simple fan beach huts, plus kitted-out deluxe cottages with a/c, cable TV and fridge. It's tucked away in a garden, by some fishing boats and next door to *Evolution*. Management are as friendly as can be. Wi-fi doesn't reach the back rooms. **PP**
Ocean Vida Beach and Dive Resort Middle of Bounty Beach Ⓦ ocean-vida.com. Plush rooms right on the beach make *Ocean Vida* a popular choice for both divers and sun-seekers. Prices are high, but then so is the quality of service and rooms, and the restaurant-bar is one of the liveliest on the strip. **PPP**

AROUND THE ISLAND

Angelina Logon Beach Ⓦ angelinabeachresort.com. An excellent resort in Malapascua's southwestern corner, Angelina offers stylish rooms outfitted with classy dark wood furnishings and exposed stone walls. The hotel's grounds are a lovely place to relax, and the on-site restaurant (see page 320) is one of the island's best places to eat. **PP**

Buena Vida Resort & Spa On the lane behind Bounty Beach ⓦ buenavida-malapascua.com. For those seeking a respite from early-morning dives and late-night beach bars, this perfumed oasis, hidden in the riddle of lanes off the beach, is a rare blissed-out sanctuary. There are twelve fabulous en-suite garden rooms, all with private wooden terraces, hammocks and chill-out beanbags. For a tranquil treat, checkout the on-site Vida Spa, the only one on the island. Run by the same team behind *Ocean Vida*. PPP

Tepanee Beach Resort Logon Beach ⓦ tepanee.com. On a lovely headland just west of Bounty Beach, *Tepanee's*

owners have glamorized Logon Beach, causing locals to nickname the area the "Italian Quarter". A/c ocean-view cottages and rooms are decorated with bamboo furniture and have queen-size beds. This is the place to come for a zoned-out beach holiday. PPP

White Sand Bungalows Logon Beach ⓦ whitesand. dk. Overlooking the boat landing, this low-key collection of six fan nipa huts is as simple as Malapascua gets. The balconies come draped with hammocks and out front, on a raised wooden platform, is a Thai restaurant. PP

EATING

Amihan Logon Beach ⓦ tepanee.com. Next door to island favourite *Angelina's*, this Italian-run joint is part of *Tepanee Beach Resort* (see page 320) and comes with a fabulous crow's-nest view above the beach line of foaming surf. Lunch is a steal (there's usually a meal deal comprising pizza or pasta with a beer or soft drink) while dinner is a more refined affair. PPP

★ **Angelina** Logon Beach ⓦ angelinabeachresort. com. Easily the best (and most expensive) place to eat on the island, *Angelina's* serves top-quality Italian dishes on

gingham tablecloths looking out over pretty Logon Beach. Top dishes include beef or fish carpaccio and *tartar di tonno*, but the wood-fire pizza and pasta dishes are also excellent. PPP

Ocean Vida Bounty Beach ⓦ ocean-vida.com. The restaurant at the Ocean Vida resort serves up a great menu of Filipino and international choices, all dished up on the terrace with gorgeous views of the sea. It's a good spot for lunch, with an extensive range of paninis, omelettes and soups. PPP

DRINKING

Kokoy's Maldito Logon Beach ⓦ kokaysmaldito diveresort.com. The island's prime sunset beach bar, barn-like *Maldito's* has pool tables, table football, happy hours, an

outdoor screen for live sports, and plenty of other reasons to keep you socializing later than planned.

The Camotes Islands

About 30km northeast of Cebu City, the friendly, peaceful **CAMOTES ISLANDS** are named after camotes, the sweet potatoes which thrive on the islands' rocky topsoil cover. Known as the "lost horizon of the south", the island group once sheltered Magellan's fleet; it now serves as a refuge for travellers, thanks to a reliable ferry route from Cebu and Danao. The two principal islands, **Pacijan** and **Poro**, are linked by a mangrove-shaded causeway. While those two islands are seeing increasing visitors, the third, **Ponson**, is as off-the-track as this part of the country gets. Villages have little in the way of modern services, and residents experience daily power outages.

Pacijan

The main town on Pacijan is **SAN FRANCISCO**, on the eastern edge of the island, where the causeway runs across to Poro. "San Fran" has a pretty 18th-century church, but little else to detain you; most of the resorts are scattered around the powdery sands of the northwest and along Santiago Bay to the south.

Beaches

A ten-minute habal-habal ride from **Consuelo**, on Pacijan's west coast (where boats arrive), **Himensulan Beach** is a short, attractive stretch of oceanfront with a handful of resorts. Pacijan's widest stretch of sand is **Santiago Beach**, another ten minutes around the toe of the island, which also has a selection of hotels to choose from. In the northwest of the island, low-key **Bakhaw Beach** (also referred to as Borromeo Beach) is the closest the Camotes gets to the sugar-white-sand of Boracay.

Lake Danao and around

Charge for Greenlake Park; additional for boat rides and kayak rental

To get the lay of the land, make for the **Arquis Viewing Deck** in the heart of the island. From here you can see guitar-shaped **Lake Danao**, an extensive body of murky water, and the site of the privately owned **Greenlake Park** where you can take *sakanaw* (local boat) trips or a kayak out to the mangroves, then have lunch in one of the simple shorefront restaurants.

Tulang

Accessible by bangka or private boat

North of Lake Danao lies **Tulang**, a picturesque islet lapped by turquoise waters, which has good snorkelling and diving and is accessible by a short bangka ride from Tulang Daka Beach.

Poro

Across the causeway on the more rugged Poro, **Buho Rock Resort** (charge) is stretching the use of the word resort (there are no rooms or places to eat), but it does have a lovely swimming spot, slides and six-metre-high rock platforms where you can dive into the sea. At the eastern edge of the island near MacArthur, you can swim in a series of subterranean sea caves at **Bukilat** (charge), while easier swimming awaits at **Busay Falls** just a short walk from Tudela on the south coast.

Ponson

Take a ferry from Tudela on Poro's south coast (2hr), or a bangka from Puerto Bello on Poro's northeast coast to Kawit (20min)

To really get away from it all, make for the easternmost and smallest of the Camotes, **Ponson**, where there are several quiet, attractive white-sand beaches. Bangkas arrive at the main settlement of Kawit. You're likely to attract attention on Ponson, as few travellers make it this far; the interest is genuine – the locals will simply want to find out where you're from.

ARRIVAL AND GETTING AROUND THE CAMOTES ISLANDS

By boat The Camotes are accessible by fast ferry from Cebu City with OceanJet (2 daily; 1hr 30min; ⓦoceanjet. net). The reliable Jomalia Shipping (ⓦjomaliashipping. com) connects Danao to Consuelo on Pacijan (6–7 daily; 2hr), while Super Shuttle Ferry has a service from Poro to Danao (1 daily; 3hr; ⓦsupershuttleroro.com). Danao is 1hr from Cebu City's northern terminal by bus, and you could also come by taxi. There's a terminal fee to leave Danao.

Jomalia Shipping also connects Tudela (on Poro) and Pilar (on Ponson) with Ormoc on Leyte (2 daily; 1–2hr 30min). This route is subject to change, so check ahead of any planned travel.

By motorbike Hiring a motorbike is the easiest way to get around; you can rent one from most resorts.

By habal-habal Short trips are cheap, and it's also possible to arrange a full-day island tour.

ACCOMMODATION

The Camotes' resorts are rustic and low-key affairs, so there is sometimes little in the way of **wi-fi**; those that do have it – or, at least, say they do – are prone to power blackouts and patchy connections.

DANAO

El Salvador Beach Resort 3km south of the port ⓦelsalvadorresort.com. Danao isn't the most inspiring place to spend a night, so if you get stuck in town, it's worth making the trip south to this decent resort. Rooms are clean and stylish, and there's a small pool and access to the beach. **PPP**

PACIJAN

Camotes Hidden Huts Bakhaw Beach ⓦcamotes hiddenhuts.com. Ideal for those seeking real isolation, nipa huts near one of the island's most alluring beaches. There's a swimming pool here, and you're bound to spend some time on the chill-out platform just above it. **PP**

Mangodlong Rock Resort Heminsulan Beach ⓦfacebook.com/MangodlongRockResort. The most upmarket choice on the Camotes, *Mangodlong Rock* has a range of clean, comfortable beachfront units with cable TV set around a large oceanfront garden and pool. **PP**

Santiago Bay Garden and Beach Resort Santiago Beach ⓦfacebook.com/SantiagoBayGardenAndResort.

7

Owned by the same team behind the *Mangodlong Rock Resort*, this hotel has a huge choice of room types, all set on a prime slice of hillside overlooking pretty Santiago Beach. The villas and bungalows are the best value, but the fan rooms offer a budget alternative and full use of the resort's facilities, which include two pools. P̅

Villa Marquez Tulang Beach. A no-frills resort on Pacijan's north coast, Villa Marquez offers clean if basic rooms, hosted by hugely friendly owners. It's easy to arrange a trip to Tulang Island from here. P̅

PORO

Flying Fish Resort 5km east of Esperanza ☏ 0915 593 8636. Snorkelling – and the off-beach coral shelf – is the chief draw at this very isolated resort on the north of the island. The reef was badly damaged by Odette, but it's still a great place to hang out for a few days. Seafront a/c cottages include breakfast, but power can be hit and miss. P̅P̅

My Little Island Esperanza ⓦ mylittleislandhotel.com. If you don't mind being away from the beach, you'll find some of the best-value rooms on the island at this quiet, clean, business hotel. There's a restaurant and swimming pool, and the reception staff are as helpful as they come. If you're feeling particularly exravagant, splurge on the penthouse suite with custom bed, kitchen, living room, and rose-petal-filled jacuzzi. P̅P̅

EATING

Pito's Sutokil Santiago Beach, Pacijan. Laidback and popular little beach café serving breakfasts, simple meals and seafood right on the sand. P̅

DIRECTORY

Money There's an ATM here, but it's not to be relied upon, so bring enough cash to last.

Moalboal and around

Three hours by road and 89km from Cebu City, on the southwestern frontier of Cebu Island, lies the sleepy inland town of **MOALBOAL**, jumping-off point for the nearby resorts of **Panagsama Beach**, the boozy hangout for travellers and scuba divers chasing the **sardine run** (see box opposite). Sun-worshippers looking for a Boracay-style sandy beach will be disappointed: there isn't one – the shoreline is rocky in places and not generally suitable for recreational swimming. Nonetheless, Panagsama's village makes up for this in other ways, with a great range of accommodation, marvellous sunset views over distant Negros and good discounts on diving and rooms. Sunbathing by resort pools, diving and drinking take centre stage, and there's little else to do in town. If baking on the sand

---

DIVING AT MOALBOAL

Pescador Island, thirty minutes by bangka from Panagsama, is one of the best dive sites in the country; it's surrounded by a terrific reef that teems with marine life, and is renowned for its swirling **sardine shoals**. Barely 100m long, the island is the pinnacle of a submarine mountain reaching just 6m above sea level and ending in a flat surface, making it look from a distance like a floating disc. The most impressive of the underwater formations is the **Cathedral**, a funnel of rock that is open at the top end and can be penetrated by divers. Pelagic fish are sometimes seen in the area, including reef sharks and hammerheads, while at lesser depths on the reef there are Moorish idols, sweetlips, fire gobies and batfish. There are at least ten other dive sites around Panagsama, including the gentle Balay Reef, Ronda Bay Marine Park, Airplane Wreck (which was sunk by Savedra Dive Center) and Sunken Island (an advanced site).

Arranging diving trips is easy, with a **dozen operators** at Panagsama Beach:

DIVE OPERATORS

Blue Abyss Dive Shop South end of Panagsama Beach ⓦ blueabyssdiving.com.

Freediving Planet North end of Panagsama Beach ⓦ freediving-planet.com. For something a little different, try a free-diving course at this outfit. The aim is to train guests how to hold their breath longer and dive deeper unassisted.

Quo Vadis Dive Resort (see page 324).

Savedra Dive Center North end of Panagsama Beach ⓦ savedra.com.

is top of your list, head 8km north to **White Beach**, an attractive strip with several far quieter mid-range resorts. Note that – confusingly – the whole area around Panagsama is often referred to as Moalboal.

Away from the coast, the jagged limestone peaks and lush river valleys of Cebu's central mountains offer white-knuckle canyoning, hiking, kayaking, mountain biking and horseriding all within easy reach of Panagsama.

Kawasan Falls

Badian • Charge • Visit by southbound bus or tricycle; it's a 20min walk from the main road to the falls

With such a spellbinding oceanfront in Panagsama Beach, it may come as a surprise to learn that **Kawasan Falls** is the most popular place to swim in Moalboal, even if it is 17km to the south. Made up of a series of cascades – some as high as 20m – this jungle-fringed waterfall is a great place for a taster of Cebu's interior.

ARRIVAL AND DEPARTURE

By bus A number of bus companies, including Ceres Liner (🖥 ceresliner.com), run regular services to Moalboal town from Cebu City's Southern bus terminal (3hr), but make sure that the driver knows where you want to get off, as most buses continue beyond Moalboal. Moalboal proper is on the road that follows the coast; however, Panagsama Beach and White Beach are a short tricycle ride from the main road where buses drop passengers. Heading south for Lilo-An and Bato, for onward ferries to Negros and Dumaguete, there are regular Ceres Liner buses (1hr 30min), or you can arrange a van through one of the resorts.

By taxi A quicker option from Cebu City than the public bus is to negotiate a rate with a taxi driver.

INFORMATION AND ACTIVITIES

Cooking classes Ven'z Kitchen in Panagsama (🖥 facebook.com/VenzKitchen) is a dinky cooking school offering a great hands-on introduction to the hybrid Spanish-Asian cuisine of the Philippines. Tutors will guide you around the local market to select ingredients before returning to the kitchen to show you how to make dishes such as pork adobo and *biko*, a gooey desert made with sticky rice, brown sugar and coconut milk. Great fun.

Outdoor activities To get away from the dive scene and explore the wild hinterlands of western Cebu, head for Planet Action Adventure (🖥 action-philippines.com) at the *Tipolo Beach Resort* (see page 324), who can organize caving, trekking, canyoning and mountain-biking tours.

ACCOMMODATION

PANAGSAMA BEACH, SEE MAP PAGE 323

Chief Mau 50m inland from the beach path's north end 🖥 facebook.com/ChiefMauMoalboal. This place knows how to keep budget backpackers happy. Set around a sociable bar terrace with a driftwood shack vibe, you'll find both fan and a/c six- and eight-bed dorms, a handful of privates, plus board games and beer pong. You can't beat the banana pancakes, either. P̄P̄

Love's Beach & Dive Resort A 5min walk from Quo Vadis 🖥 loves-beach-resort.com. Attractive and well-

7

White Beach (8km)

ATM

Freediving Philippines

Cyan Adventures

Savedra Dive Center

ACCOMMODATION	
Chief Mau	1
Love's Beach & Dive Resort	5
Maya's Native Garden	2
Quo Vadis Beach Resort	4
Tipolo Beach Resort	3

DRINKING AND NIGHTLIFE	
Chili Bar	1

EATING	
The Last Filling Station	5
Le Café Français	1
Nomad Music and Art Bar	2
The Pleasure Principal	3
Tan-aw	4

Planet Action Adventure

Blue Abyss Dive Shop

N

0   100
metres

PANAGSAMA BEACH

& Moalboal

Moalboal

Moalboal (2.1km)

cared-for resort on a quiet section of coast. There's a wide variety of fan and a/c rooms to choose from, a decent pool, and a lovely restaurant looking out to Pescador Island. Breakfast included. PP

Maya's Native Garden Opposite Tipolo Beach Resort ⓦmayasnativegarden.com. You won't find a more exotic setting in Moalboal. With five thatched, stilted native huts, centred around a rough-and-ready garden (look out for hummingbirds), *Maya's* excels, with clean, affordable rooms and friendly service. For local craft beers and Mexican food, prop up on a stool at the restaurant-bar out the front. PP

Quo Vadis Dive Resort At the beach path's southern end ⓦquovadisresort.com. Attractive place, set in coastal gardens, with a relaxed poolside atmosphere. Economy rooms are in a block at the back, while stylishly decorated a/c nipa huts and cottages are closer to the front. There's also a bar-restaurant looking straight out to sea, and a great dive shop on-site. PPP

Tipolo Beach Resort South of the centre ⓦtipoloresort.com. Lovely little seaside resort whose a/c rooms look out onto an attractive garden, with the sea beyond, and are tastefully furnished in bamboo, with tiled floors, hot showers and mini-bars. PP

WHITE BEACH

Blue Orchid At the beach's northern end ⓦblue orchidresort.com. Beautifully isolated property at the end of the road with a landscaped garden, pool, dive school, well-designed rooms, massage pavilions and nose-to-nose views of Negros across the Tañon Strait. The resort is showing signs of age, but remains a good choice for peace and quiet. PPP

Dolphin House Southern end of the beach ⓦdolphin-house.com. Long considered the most sophisticated place to stay on White Beach, this dive and spa resort is pricey, but has a lovely pool and a very professional on-site diving school, plus comfy and wonderfully decorated rooms. Note that the shoreline is a bit rocky here. PPP

★ **Hale Manna** Next to Blue Orchid ⓦhalemanna. com. If there's a more relaxing place in Cebu, we've yet to find it. Overlooking a landscaped tropical garden with yucca huts, pool and an unbeatable strip of white beach out front, this former family home has been turned into a beautifully decorated Cebuano-meets-Hawaiian lodge that celebrates the best of both heritages. The restaurant serves fantastic thin-crust pizzas. PPP

EATING

SEE MAP PAGE 323

The Last Filling Station Tipolo Beach Resort ⓦtipoloresort.com. Right at the heart of the Moalboal scene, this laidback place rustles up tasty international dishes and top-notch wood-fired pizzas, as well as freshly baked bread and heaped breakfasts. Free wi-fi. PPP

Le Café Français North end of the beach path ⓦfacebook.com/frenchcoffeeshop2021. This friendly place offers freshly brewed coffee, croissants and crêpes and great breakfasts (try the Parisienne), as well as daily specials. PP

Nomad Music and Art Bar C. Schmitz Rd ⓦfacebook. com/thenomadmusicandartbar. This laid-back place serves up some of the best Mexican food you'll find in the

Philippines, with delicious burritos, tacos and quesadillas on offer. If there's a live band in, relax and enjoy the music – otherwise, entertain yourself with the board games. PPP

★ **The Pleasure Principle** North end of the beach path ☎032 474 3988. Basque-style fish, Arabic-spiced pizzas, Indian curries and Godzilla-sized shellfish are the speciality at this deservedly popular jack-of-all-trades fusion restaurant on the main strip. PPP

Tan-aw Opposite Chili Bar ⓦneptunediving.com. Hidden from the beach path, above the Neptune Diving Shop, this bamboo hut kitchen has mastered the tricky art of Indian, Indonesian and Thai cuisines. Come for deliciously zingy curries, stay for the epic sea views. PPP

DRINKING AND NIGHTLIFE

SEE MAP PAGE 323

Chili Bar Midway along the beach path ⓦfacebook. com/chilibar2003. This waterfront bar remains resolutely popular with divers ("get out of that wet suit and into a dry

martini"). Great sea views, two pool tables and cut-price beers to the last man or woman standing.

DIRECTORY

Money Moalboal has a number of ATMs which accept foreign cards.

Bohol

BOHOL, a two-hour boat ride south of Cebu, is an attractive little island where life today is pastoral and quiet. The only sign of heavy tourist activity is on the beautiful beaches of **Panglao**, a magnet for scuba divers and sun-worshippers, which is close to the utilitarian port capital of **Tagbilaran**. Most visitors only leave the beach for a day-

SWIMMING WITH WHALE SHARKS AT OSLOB

Once a sleepy little town, **Oslob**, at the southern tip of Cebu, has become famous for the near-guaranteed chance to swim with **whale sharks** off the coast of Tan-awan, a barangay of Oslob. Marine biologists raise **ethical questions** about the adverse effects of human–whale shark interaction and doubt whether the Oslob population can even be considered wild anymore, but while the opportunity to swim with the animals remains, tourists flock here on a daily basis. Visitors are given a mandatory orientation, and those who plan to swim with the gentle giants are required not to wear sunscreen, not to use flash photography, and not to get closer than 5m to the whale sharks. Unfortunately, these rules are often flaunted the moment a shark is sighted from the boat.

The most painless way to arrange a visit is to book through **Oslob Whale Sharks** (ⓦoslobwhalesharks.com), or a dive shop in Cebu, Moalboal, Panglao (in Bohol) or Dauin (on Negros). Tours from Cebu leave early morning and head first for the whale sharks, then stop for lunch before heading back to the city. It's far cheaper to arrive independently by Ceres Liner bus from Cebu (3–4hr) and then organize the trip in Tan-awan. Given the large number of visitors, a morning visit is recommended.

If you've got time while you're in the vicinity, and fancy something different, consider stopping off at Cuertal Ruins in Oslob: this picturesque construction was built in the late 1800s to house Spanish soldiers, but was never completed owing to the arrival of the Americans in 1899.

ACCOMMODATION

GT Seaside Inn San Jose Rd ⓦfacebook.com/gtseasideinnoslob. A good all-rounder with simply but attractively decorated rooms, it's a little way up the coast from Tan-awan Pier but is just a 5 minute walk from Oslob town centre. P̄P̄

Sharky Hostel Oslob Tan-awan ☏0927 936 5090. With a choice of dirt-cheap eight- or ten-bed mixed dorms, this spartan guesthouse has little more than an outdoor terrace and travel desk to recommend it. But what it lacks in character, it makes up for with a stellar location. Stay here and you'll be one of the first out on the boat in the morning – the dock is 50m away. P̄

tour taking in Bohol's most famous attractions: the postcard-perfect **Chocolate Hills**, a glimpse of the world's smallest primate (the endangered **tarsier**), lunch on the **Loboc River**, and a visit to the **Blood Compact** site, memorial to Bohol's violent past. Those with more time can be rewarded by trips to other parts of the province, including the adventure centre at **Danao**, the attractive island of **Pamilacan** and the forgotten-by-time beaches of **Anda**.

Bohol is also renowned for its wonderfully creaky Spanish churches – many of them built with coral, which can be found all over the island – though several were damaged during the October 2013 quake, which, with a magnitude of 7.2, did damage as far away as Cebu City. On Bohol, more than two hundred people died, and thousands of homes and buildings were destroyed, though a reconstruction programme has done a good job of restoring the town. May is **fiesta** month on Bohol, with island-wide celebrations including barangay festivals, beauty pageants, street dancing and solemn religious processions. Another highlight is the annual Bohol Day on July 22.

ARRIVAL AND DEPARTURE BOHOL

By plane Bohol Panglao International Airport on Panglao Island, which opened in 2018, is the main gateway to Bohol. It's served by flights to Manila and Davao, as well as as a few other domestic destinations and international flights to Korea, Taiwan and China.

By boat Tagbilaran is Bohol's principal port, though there are also services from Jagna (see page 335), Tubigon and Ubay (see page 334). Starcraft (ⓦfacebook.com/

MVstarcrafts) also operates fast ferries to Cebu from Jetafe (3 daily; 1hr), in the northwest, and Lapu-Lapu Shipping Lines (ⓦlapulines.wixsite.com) operates a slow ferry from Talibon (4 weekly; 4hr), in the north.

By road Discussions about a bridge between Cebu and Bohol have been taking place on and off since 2016, though the project is yet to be fully green-lighted.

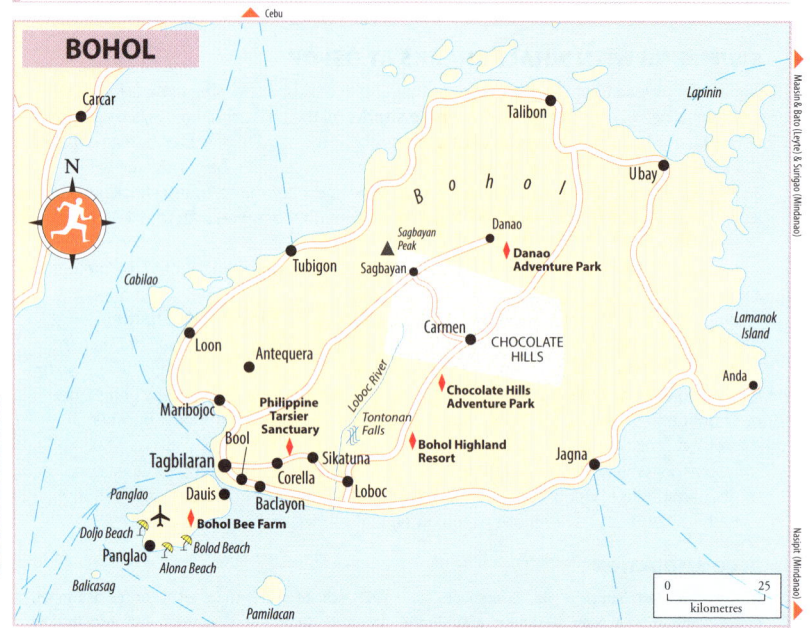

Tagbilaran

There are plenty of hotels and lodges in **TAGBILARAN**, the hectic port capital of Bohol, but with so many beaches and sights nearby, there's no real reason to stay here. From Tagbilaran, you can be on Panglao Island in less than twenty minutes; even the Chocolate Hills, hidden in the hinterlands, are less than an hour away by road.

Aside from the **museum**, the only sight in Tagbilaran itself is the **Cathedral**, opposite the plaza in Sarmiento Street, a nineteenth-century hulk standing on the site of an original that was destroyed by fire in 1789. Located on the edge of town is **Island City Mall**, which is packed full of shops, cafés and restaurants. The **Tagbilaran City Fiesta** takes place on May 1.

National Museum

Plaza Rizal • Free

Set in the former home of Carlos Garcia (the fourth President of the Philippine Republic), the **National Museum** isn't worth a special trip, but if you have some time to kill before catching a ferry or bus, the presidential memorabilia and anthropological collection of shells will help pass half an hour.

ARRIVAL AND DEPARTURE   TAGBILARAN

By boat The ferry pier in Tagbilaran is off Gallares St, a 1km tricycle ride from the city centre. Taxis and vans for hire wait like hawks to meet passengers arriving on ferries. The Cebu–Tagbilaran route is operated by several fast ferry companies (2hr), including Oceanjet (w oceanjet.net) and SuperCat (w supercatschedule.com). Other operators such as Cokaliong (w cokaliongshipping.com), Lite Shipping (w liteferries.com.ph) and Trans-Asia Shipping Lines (w transasiashipping.com) also have cheaper slower services (4–5hr) on this route. Bear in mind that the Cebu

Passenger Terminal has airport-style security and charges a terminal fee, so plan to arrive at least 30min in advance. Destinations Argao (2 daily; 2hr), Cagayan de Oro (3 weekly; 10hr), Cebu City (1–3 hourly; 2–5hr); Larena, Siquijor (2 daily; 3hr 30min), via Dumaguete (2 daily; 2hr). **By bus** All bus journeys around the island start at Dao Integrated Terminal, near Island City Mall and the Central Market, 10min outside Tagbilaran by jeepney or tricycle. Buses leave here (every 30min–1hr) for all destinations both clockwise and anticlockwise around the main coastal road, as well as along the cross-island road via Carmen and the Chocolate Hills. For Alona Beach, the most convenient buses leave from a scrap of waste-ground at the corner of Hontanosas and F. Rocha streets.

Destinations Anda (2hr 30min); Baclayon (20min); Bool (10min); Carmen (1hr 30min); Jagna (1hr 30min); Tubigon (1hr 30min); Ubay (4hr).

By taxi, van and tricycle Travel agents and most hotels in Tagbilaran and Panglao can arrange car or van hire, but the cheapest way is to negotiate directly with a taxi. If you're heading for Panglao, it's not hard to find a taxi, van or tricycle at the pier to whisk you across the bridge and out to the beaches.

By jeepney Jeepneys leave from Dao, making trips clockwise and anticlockwise around the coast, but they stop often and become uncomfortably overloaded, so are best used only for short trips.

By motorbike The whole island is accessible by motorbike – a cheap, fun and flexible way to see Bohol. Rentals are easily available in Tagbilaran and Panglao.

INFORMATION AND ACTIVITIES

Tourist information You can find small information kiosks at the airport and ferry pier. The Bohol department of tourism is one of the country's most proactive provincial tourist boards and can provide plenty of up-to-date information, maps, ideas and itineraries. Visit the friendly staff at Governor's Mansion on CPG Ave (w aroundbohol. com).

Tours and activities For a highly recommended backwater paddle through island mangroves at night, book a trip with Kayakasia, an outfitter based out of Maribojoc

TAGBILARAN

ACCOMMODATION
Nisa Traveller's Hotel	3
Sweet Home Boutique Hotel	2
Travelbee Seaside Inn	1

EATING
The Garden Café	2
Gerarda's	1
Jose	4
Payag	3

(w kayakasiaphilippines.com). Under cover of darkness, informative guides lead small group tours on a 2hr paddle along the palm-lined Abatan River, finishing up beside hundreds of fireflies that glow in the moonlight. It just may well be the highlight of your trip to Bohol.

ACCOMMODATION   SEE MAP PAGE 327

Nisa Traveller's Hotel 14 CPG Ave ☎ 038 411 3731. The best budget option in town, featuring good a/c doubles, hot water and clean bathrooms, as well as more expensive rooms with king-size beds. Note that rooms at the front contend with constant traffic noise. P̅

Sweet Home Boutique Hotel Remolador St w facebook.com/sweethomeboutiquehotel. A very pleasant choice in the town centre, Sweet Home offers stylish and attractive bedrooms – to really splash out, treat

yourself to the presidential suite, which has a hot tub on the (fortunately not overlooked) balcony. The breakfasts are made to order and delicious. P̅P̅P̅

Travelbee Seaside Inn Celestino Gallares St w travelbee.ph. In an extremely handy location near the pier, this is a fairly uninspiring option that suffers from internal and external noise. Still, rooms are clean, the staff are friendly, and it's good for those on a budget. P̅P̅

EATING   SEE MAP PAGE 327

★ **The Garden Café** Plaza Rizal w facebook.com/ GardenCafeTabiglaran. Established by the Bohol Deaf Academy and providing training for up to forty deaf students, *The Garden Café* has a menu mixing Mexican and Filipino dishes. You can communicate with the staff in writing or with sign language (a few basic signs are listed in the menu). P̅P̅

Gerarda's J.S. Torralba St w facebook.com/gerardas resto. A short walk from Plaza Rizal, *Gerarda's* is easily

Tagbilaran's most sophisticated restaurant. Popular with local Filipino celebrities, it's a riot of wooden furniture and parquet floors with diners tucking into heaped seafood plates of *gambas* and succulent pork. A sign of its enduring popularity, two other branches have opened in town, as well as others on Cebu. P̅P̅P̅

Jose Tamblot Circumferential Road at CPG Ave w facebook.com/Kambingderia. Offering generous portions of good Filipino food, Jose is a popular venue for locals. The sisig is a particularly good choice, but you won't go wrong with anything on the menu here. $\overline{PP}$

Payag S. Matig-a St ⓦfacebook.com/payag restaurantofficialpage. Hidden on the second floor of an antiquated Spanish-era home, this terrace-style restaurant's sizzling pork *sisig* and BBQ *lechon* is as authentic as any you'll find anywhere in Bohol. $\overline{P}$

DIRECTORY

Banks There are plenty of banks with ATMs on CPG Ave. You can also change money in Tagbilaran City Square Mall.

Hospitals The Governor Celestino Gallares Memorial Hospital (☎038 411 4868 ⓦgcgmh.doh.gov.ph) is on M. Parras St.

Immigration The Bureau of Immigration (☎038 235 6084) is on CPG Ave, a 10min walk north of the downtown core.

Police The police station is near City Hall, behind St Joseph's Cathedral.

Panglao Island

Across one of two bridges from Tagbilaran, **PANGLAO** boasts beautiful beaches, first-rate diving and historic Spanish churches. The whole island is enjoying increasing popularity, nowhere more so than **Alona Beach**, and while there is a great choice of hotels and restaurants, this also means high room and food prices. With the new international airport now open and a colossal *Hennan* luxury hotel found on the beachfront, things are changing at pace. Despite rapid development, quieter stretches of white sand can still be found, particularly at **Bolod Beach**, **San Isidro Beach** and **Bikini Beach**, all on the south coast, and **Doljo Beach**, near the westernmost tip of the island.

Away from the reefs and beaches, Panglao has two main towns, **Dauis** and **Panglao**, on the east and west sides of the island respectively, both of which centre around pretty Spanish churches. The rest of the interior feels like a giant replica of a batik, filled with nipa huts and flowering palms – perfect for short walks, cycle rides, or motorbike tours.

Bohol Bee Farm

Dao, Dauis • Free • ⓦ boholbeefarm.com

ALONA BEACH

EATING
Barwoo	3
MoCoo	2
The Monkey Bar	5
Saffron	4
Wonderland	1

ACCOMMODATION
Alona Grove Tourist Inn	6
Alona Vida Beach Resort	7
Amorita Resort	5
Eyy Hostel	1
Island World	2
Oasis Resort	4
Tamarind	3

DRINKING AND NIGHTLIFE
The Monkey Bar	2
Panglao Birdwatchers	1

Panglao Bay

0   200
metres

DIVING AT PANGLAO

The **reef** at the western end of Panglao, a few minutes by bangka from Alona Beach, has healthy soft corals, a multitude of reef fish and perpendicular underwater cliffs that drop to a depth of 50m. This is where most of the island's dive sites are, though you can go further afield to **Doljo Point** and **Cervira Shoal**, or use Alona Beach as a base for diving at Cabilao (see page 333). Day-trips also run to **Balicasag**, a beautiful halo of coral with steep drop-offs to the southwest.

DIVE OPERATORS

Alona Divers Alona Beach ⓦalonadivers.com. A professional outlet who've been running trips since 1996, Alona Divers are still going strong despite increasing competition from new kids on the block.

Sea Quest Dive Center Alona Beach ⓦseaquest divecenter.com. Offering dive safaris and island-hopping, Sea Explorers are one of the best outfits in Alona.

Near Dao on the island's southern coast, **Bohol Bee Farm** is one of the island's star attractions and offers the chance to tour an organic bee and vegetable farm. Afterwards, you can sample the delicious produce at the restaurant or buy some of the goodies to take home. They have accommodation on the farm too (see page 330), and you can try their produce elsewhere at the *Buzzz Café* chain (see page 313).

7

Pamilacan Island

Visit by boat tour; every Wed there are large and cheap group boat tours– alternatively, take a bus to Bacalayon and arrange a trip with Pamilacan Island Dolphin & Whale Watching Tours (ⓦ whales.bohol.ph)

Off the south coast of Panglao Island is whale territory, and the tiny **Pamilacan Island** is a prime jumping-off point for **whale-watching and dolphin-spotting**. Once home to generations of whalers, the island now excels at community-focused tourism; boat crews make the daily ocean run in converted whaling ships, armed with eco credentials rather than harpoons and nets. The best time of year to visit is from February to June.

ARRIVAL AND DEPARTURE
PANGLAO ISLAND

By plane Bohol Panglao International Airport is just north of Alona Beach, the main area of tourist interest; you can even walk to or from your plane in under 30min, though of course there will be wheels waiting to make that journey a bit faster. Destinations Davao (1–2 daily; 1hr); El Nido (3 weekly; 1hr 45min); Iloilo (3 weekly; 50min); Manila (7–10 daily; 1hr 25min).

From Tagbilaran Almost everyone arrives overland at Alona by van or tricycle from Tagbilaran port, in which case you'll be dropped as close to your accommodation as possible (you'll need to walk to get to some of the beach cottages).

From elsewhere in Bohol You might arrive via Dao Integrated Terminal (see page 326), from where there are jeepneys and buses to Panglao. These services will drop you on the main road, from where it's a 5min walk down to the beach.

INFORMATION AND TOURS

Tourist information There is no official tourist information centre in Alona, just a number of glorified confectionary shops that dispense tours. In case of any trouble, there is a tourist police assistance centre at Rona's Corner (☎038 502 8365).

Tours Southwest Tours (ⓦsouthwesttours.com.ph), not too far from the beach, can book all ferry tickets, as well as arrange day-trips around Bohol, van hire and boat trips. Alternatively, try Bohol Nature Tours (ⓦboholnaturetours.com), whose office is some distance to the northwest.

ACCOMMODATION

Hotel prices have gone skywards in **Alona**, and there are hardly any budget options on the beach, but if you don't mind a short walk or tricycle ride to the sea, there are still a few cheap (and fairly good quality) place to be found in the area.

ALONA BEACH, SEE MAP PAGE 328

Alona Grove Tourist Inn Set back from the western end of the beach ⓦfacebook.com/AlonaGroveTouristInn. One of a number of off-beach budget resorts with a row of simple thatched huts, some with a/c, fridge and cable TV. Popular with money-conscious backpackers. P̲P̲

Alona Vida Beach Resort Halfway between the main access road and the east end of the beach ⓦalonavida. com. Excellent rooms decorated in earthy tones just a few metres back from the beach. Deluxe and superior rooms come with fridges, mini-bars, kettles, safety deposit boxes and room service, plus there's one budget room, though it's a little too close for comfort to the lively *Coco Vida* bar. Sea Explorers dive centre (see box, page 329) is also on-site. P̅P̅

★ **Amorita Resort** Along the clifftop at the beach's eastern end ⓦamoritaresort.com. The infinity pool overlooking the sea at this fabulous clifftop retreat is one of the many highlights at this luxury resort, which includes polished service, stunning food, free bikes, day-beds and a very good cocktail bar. Rooms are huge, with balconies, flatscreen TVs and rainfall showers. Superb, if pricey. P̅P̅P̅P̅

Eyy Hostel Hontanosas Rd, towards Panglao ☏0991 313 2887. Right by the main road, this is a good budget choice, despite the obvious lack of beachfront – partly made up for by the pleasant swimming pool. Clean four-bed dorms, fan and a/c rooms, and a common area with hammocks, dartboard and board games. P̅

Island World Purok 7, Tawala ⓦisland.world. A very smart resort boasting stylish bungalows set around a long swimming pool, Island World offers top-end service at mid-range prices. There's a spa and restaurant, and a free shuttle bus will ferry you down to the beach if you want to leave the site. P̅P̅

Oasis Resort Eastern end of the beach ⓦoasis resortbohol.com. In the thick of things in the middle of Alona Beach, this sprawling dive resort has a lovely pool, bucolic garden and great people-watching opportunities; there's a garden lounge, as well as a beachfront cocktail bar and restaurant. Standard rooms have bamboo-frame beds, whirring fans and a veranda, while the deluxe options come with pool or garden views and enough room to loll around like a whale. P̅P̅P̅

Tamarind Purok 7, Tawala ⓦfacebook.com/Tamarind-521122198274286. A friendly place with simple and comfortable rooms, Tamarind is a bit of a walk from the beach, but there's a good pool, and the distance does mean the resort doesn't suffer from traffic and tricycle noise. P̅P̅

BOLOD BEACH

Amarela Resort Brgy Libaong, western part of Bolod Beach ⓦamarelaresort.com. Perched on top of a hill looking out to the sea, *Amarela* is an intimate, sophisticated hideaway with stylish rooms, good amenities and its own art gallery. Heavy wood furnishings define the rooms, all of which have a/c, balconies, hot showers and cable TV. The popular restaurant enjoys wonderful views. From the main house, steps lead down to a pretty stretch of white beach, plus there's a cracking pool. P̅P̅P̅

Bohol Beach Club Bolod Beach ⓦboholbeachclub. com.ph. Large VIP resort split into two wings named after the Philippines' two monsoons: "Habagat", with recently renovated native-style cottage blocks, and the plusher "Amihan", which boasts more elegant rooms surrounding two swimming pools. Watersports are on offer, along with a range of other highlights including a gym, pizzeria and herb garden for the restaurant. Day visitors can use the beach and pool for a charge, which includes an advance towards food and drinks. P̅P̅P̅P̅

Bohol Bee Farm Dao, Dauis ⓦboholbeefarm.com. As the name suggests, this ranch-style place offers the unique opportunity to get busy with the bees. As well as getting to enjoy the farm's organic produce from the vegetable and herb garden in the excellent restaurant, overnight guests are given a complimentary tour. Comfortable cottages with a/c, cable TV and hot water are dotted throughout the property, and there's a pool and ocean swimming platform. The store, selling organic goodies, is the pride of Bohol. P̅P̅

ELSEWHERE ON THE ISLAND

The Bellevue Resort Doljo Beach ⓦthebellevuebohol. com. A top-end resort on Panglao's northwest tip, the Bellevue offers all the luxuries you'd expect in this price bracket: a marvellous infinity pool, an excellent restaurant, and a private beach. Watersports activities can be arranged, as island hopping tours and hot air balloon trips. P̅P̅P̅P̅

Panglao Sea Resort Tabuan Beach ⓦpanglao searesort.com. If you're looking for peace and quiet away from the busy strip along Alona Beach, but still want the luxury of a beach resort, this place could be for you. With a pool and easy access into the sea (though no beach), Panglao Sea Resort also offers comfy rooms with balconies and gorgeous sea views. P̅P̅

EATING

ALONA BEACH, SEE MAP PAGE 328

★ **Barwoo** Circumferential Rd ⓦinstagram.com/barwoo_bohol. Industrial-chic spot that's proof of how the Alona Beach scene is changing – two attractive levels (prettier by night) on which Korean fusion food is served – try some sea urchin bibimbap (actually a thing in Korea, or at least it was for a while), *jjamppong* rice (spicy seafood rice; not a thing in Korea, even though it should be), or classics from South East Asia such as Thai *pad krapao* (minced meat with basil), or something more Western like chilli cheese fries (which may count as Wild Western, rather than regular Western). P̅P̅P̅

★ **MoCoo** Circumferential Rd ⓦfacebook.com/mocoobohol. Attractive bamboo restaurant offering up a range of tasty international dishes, including black-ink risotto, beef *tagine*, *shakshuka*, and some excellent burgers. It's popular after dark for cocktails. PP

The Monkey Bar Towards the beach's western end ☎ 038 412 9000. Relatively new beachfront spot, started by a renowned local chef, and a beautiful place to enjoy dishes from a menu full of comfort food – "easy eats" such as pulled pork fries, soups, salads, sandwiches, and heartier meaty mains and steaks. PPP

Saffron Amarito Resort, at the east end of the beach ⓦ amaritaresort.com. One of a new breed of trendy places to eat in Alona, *Saffron*'s team of chefs present Filipino salads, chicken and inventive seafood. Among its mouthwatering signatures are sea-bass ceviche, tuna *kinilaw* and line-caught white marlin. Perfect for a date night. PPPP

Wonderland Circumferential Rd. There's tasty Thai food available at this attractively decorated restaurant: the pad thai and the spring rolls are particularly recommended, as is the crab curry. PP

BOLOD BEACH

Buzzz Café Centre of the beach ⓦ boholbeefarm. com. On *Bohol Bee Farm* (see page 330), this dependable breakfast and lunch spot serves excellent waffles with bacon and eggs, ice cream, and regular lunch dishes. PPP

DRINKING AND NIGHTLIFE

Nightlife mainly revolves around resort and dive-shop bars, but there are a few independent party places by the beach turn-off.

ALONA BEACH, SEE MAP PAGE 328

The Monkey Bar Towards the beach's western end ☎ 038 412 9000. This restaurant (see above) also has a mean drinks list, including plenty of spirits, cocktails, and no fewer than three kinds of IPA. Try to nab one of the outdoor tables, so long as you don't mind kicking off your footwear and sitting on the floor.

Panglao Birdwatchers Towards the beach's western end ⓦ panglaobirdwatchers.com. Beachfront bar (with super-cold beers) that's big on sunset happy hours, booming tunes and good times. If the quirky staff, cocktails, live sports, occasional live music and zingy tacos don't convince you, little else will.

DIRECTORY

Banks There are several ATMs on the Alona Beach access road. There are also plenty of places to change money in Alona, but it's best to hunt around to find the most competitive rates.

The interior

In addition to the ubiquitous Chocolate Hills, which appear on every tourist brochure and postcard from Manila to Mindanao, Bohol's **interior** hosts a range of sights worth exploring. Take your pick from historic churches, markets, river cruises, waterfalls, a tarsiers sanctuary, and a jungle adventure camp.

Antequera Market

Bus or jeepney from Tagbilaran, or visit as part of a day-trip

A number of resorts offer half-day trips to the town of **ANTEQUERA**, 20km north of Tagbilaran, to see the lively Sunday **market**. Craftsmen and traders from around the island congregate to sell handicrafts such as baskets, hats and various home decor items like linen tablecloths, mirrors and attractive bowls made from stone or coconut shells.

Philippine Tarsier Sanctuary

Charge • Hiking guides extra charge • ⓦ tarsierfoundation.com • No flash photography • Bus or jeepney from Tagbilaran to Corella and then a tricycle for the last 4km; or stay on the bus towards Sikatuna and ask to be dropped at the entrance, from where it's a 500m walk to the sanctuary

Ten kilometres northeast of Tagbilaran outside the village of Corella, the **Philippine Tarsier Sanctuary** is dedicated to protecting what is left of the native population of tarsiers, saucer-eyed creatures you will see on posters throughout the country. Often mistakenly referred to as the world's smallest monkey, the cuddly **tarsier** – all 10–15cm of it – is more closely related to the lemur, loris and bushbaby and has been around for a staggering 45 million years.

After a brief induction at the base camp, knowledgeable **guides** lead visitors into the jungle, but spotting the sanctuary's hundred-or-so free-to-roam residents among the foliage can be challenging, especially as the creatures are nocturnal and rarely move. Upon being found, the tarsier study visitors with wide-eyed curiosity, sometimes swivelling their heads a disconcerting 180 degrees to get a better look.

Loboc River
Visit on a private boat trip or on the all-you-can-eat floating barge buffet

Eleven kilometres east of Corella, the town of **Loboc** is the starting point for enormously popular **jungle boat trips** along the **Loboc River** to **Tontonan Falls**. Whichever way you choose to cruise, it's a lovely, if very touristy, journey past idyllic villages, green paddies, twisted roots and towering palms. The majority of visitors are whisked away on a floating restaurant barge, stopping off at riverside shacks to see local women sing and dance, before arriving at the somewhat underwhelming waterfall.

Bohol Highland Resort
Bilar • Charge (including guided tour) • ⓦ facebook.com/HabitatBoholWildlifeAdventure

Halfway between Loboc and Carmen, the **Bohol Highland Resort** contains a bird and butterfly park – a popular tour-group stopover – with over 150 different types of lepidopterans and plenty of bats, insects and fireflies. Night safaris can be organized, in order to see nocturnal wildlife, including – of course – tarsiers. Proceeds from the tours go towards better habitat protection. Recent years have also seen the resort flourish into a wellness centre – forest bathing, qigong sessions, massages and south baths are just some of the activities on offer, though most taking part are actually staying here too.

The Chocolate Hills
Viewpoint Daily dawn to dusk • Charge • ⓦ chocolatehills.net • **Adventure Park** Daily 8.30am–5.30pm • Charge; extra for buggy tours
• **Sagbayan Peak** Daily dawn to dusk • Charge • To get to the Adventure Park or Viewpoint independently, take a bus to Carmen (hourly; 2hr) from the Dao terminal in Tagbilaran, and then hop on a habal-habal; for Sagbayan Peak, take a bus from Tagbilaran to Sagbayan town, then rent a habal-habal

Renowned throughout the Philippines, the surreal **Chocolate Hills** are one of the country's biggest tourist attractions. Some geologists believe that these unique 40m mounds – there are said to be 1776 of them, if you care to count – were formed from deposits of coral and limestone sculpted by centuries of erosion. Most locals, however, will tell you that the hills are the calcified tears of a broken-hearted giant; others prefer the idea that they were left by a giant carabao with distressed bowels.

What you think of the hills will depend largely on the time you visit. During the glare of the day, the light casts harsh shadows and the hills lose their definition. But at **dawn or dusk** they look splendid, especially during the dry season (Feb–June) when the scrub vegetation covering the hills is roasted brown. At such times, they really do live up to their billing.

Most visitors head for the 360-degree viewpoint at the **Chocolate Hills Viewpoint**. Built atop one of the unearthly formations, it's reached by a winding road and a steep climb up two hundred or so rough-hewn steps.

Different views are on offer at the privately run **Chocolate Hills Adventure Park**, where the main draw is a host of thrilling activities (see box, page 333). The centre also offers ATV and buggy tours around the bases of the hills.

Prior to the 2013 earthquake, visitors wanting solitude to escape the crowds would continue further north to **Sagbayan Peak**, northwest of Carmen. The area, however, was the epicentre of the Bohol quake and has since been reborn as a Disneyfied funfair.

ACCOMMODATION AND EATING   THE INTERIOR

★ **Fox and the Firefly Cottages** By the Petron Gas cottages.com. Five hundred metres off the main Loboc Station, Barangay Valladolid ⓦ foxandthefirefly Rd, this chilled-out collection of riverside cabanas is a great

THRILL-SEEKING IN BOHOL

Bohol's interior is packed with **activities** that'll encourage you to step out of your comfort zone. From stand-up paddleboarding down a jade river to ziplining on a bicycle or surfboard (yes, really) above the forest canopy, the Eden-like combination of the island's jungle, rivers and mountains provides the perfect backdrop to let loose and get wild. Here are some places to embrace your inner Tarzan or Jane.

Chocolate Hills Adventure Park ⓦchocolatehills adventurepark.com. Based at the Chocolate Hills, activities include an eco-trail canopy walkway, Tarzan high-rope challenges and a bike or surf zipline.

Danao Adventure Park ⓦfacebook.com/danao adventureparkbohol. A few kilometres from the small town of Danao, north of the Chocolate Hills, Danao Adventure Park occupies an area of rugged jungle-covered massif cut by deep valleys. Established in 2006, the park has become the centre for outdoors pursuits in Bohol, offering everything from river trekking, white-knuckle-inducing "plunge" canyon swinging, climbing, extreme caving and kayaking. The easiest and quickest way to get here is to arrange a car and driver through your resort; alternatively, take a bus from Tagbilaran

to Danao via Sagbayan (3hr), where you can charter a tricycle.

SUP Tours Philippines ⓦsuptoursphilippines. com. Running fantastic stand-up paddleboarding and biking trips along the Loboc and Abatan Rivers (as well as further afield in Negros, Palawan and Siargao), this paddle centre is based on a bend of the river a few kilometres from the south coast. The real star is the outfit's full-day journey into the island interior along a jade-like river, but for those who want something less strenuous, shorter three-hour waterfall and estuary excursions are available. Various paddleboarding trips, including waterfall and river tours are good options, and they also do guided mountain biking.

7

place to soak-up the sights and sounds of the Bohol jungle for a day or two. With great home-made food, lovely staff and a choice of six-bed dorms or comfy privates, the only decision is whether to read a book by the riverside or hop on a paddleboard. P̄P̄

Nuts & Huts 2km north of Loboc ⓦnutshuts.org. Simple

dorms with mosquito nets and far bigger rooms with private bathroom and balcony, and the perched-up outdoor restaurant has attractive views across the dense green canopy of rainforest. Activities on offer include rafting, trekking or mountain biking. P̄

The west and north coasts

Bohol's pretty northwest coast is lined with mangroves and dotted with Spanish-era ruins, and is also the access point for the dive sites of **Cabilao Island**. Further north, **Tubigon** has fast craft to Cebu, while on the opposite side of Bohol to Tagbilaran, the agricultural town of **Ubay** has handy transport connections to Leyte.

Maribojoc

Take a bus or jeepney from Tagbilaran (30min)

The pretty coastal town of **MARIBOJOC** lies just 14km from Tagbilaran and is worth a quick stop. The town is the site of the old Spanish **Punta Cruz watchtower**, one of a number of old watchtowers of note on Bohol. Once a lookout for marauding pirates, Punta Cruz is now a viewing deck from where you can gaze across to Cebu and Siquijor.

Cabilao Island

Bus to Loon from Tagbilaran (1hr) and then change to a jeepney or habal-habal for Mocpoc pier on Sandingan Island; bangkas from Mocpoc to Cabilao take 20min

Off the radar for most divers, the pretty little island of **Cabilao** has a handful of modest, but very comfortable resorts, making it an appealing option. With limited beachfront, these chilled-out resorts can also arrange trips to local dive sites such as the **Wall at Cambaquiz**, where there are turtles and baby sharks, and **Shark View Point**, where one of the attractions – apart from sharks, as you'd expect – is the easy-to-miss pygmy sea horse.

7

Lapinig

Just offshore from Ubay, the undeveloped island of **Lapinig** offers good diving, some of it for experts only in extreme subterranean caves. To explore, you can rent a bangka for the day at the small pier in Ubay, but the easiest way to dive is to arrange a trip through one of the operators in Panglao (see box, page 329).

ARRIVAL AND DEPARTURE THE WEST AND NORTH COASTS

By boat Fastcat (Ⓦfastcat.ph) operates fast ferries between Cebu City and Tubigon (11 daily; 1hr 20min), while Lite Shipping (Ⓦliteferries.com.ph) runs a slower ferry (9 daily; 2hr). Super Shuttle Ferries depart from Ubay to Bato on Leyte (daily; 3hr 30min).

ACCOMMODATION

CABILAO ISLAND

Polaris Dive Centre On the main beach on the northwest coast Ⓦpolaris-dive.com. Family-style resort with a choice of cottages ranging from simple wooden treehouses to more substantial a/c doubles and bungalows. At low tide, the nearby sandbar is ideal for snorkelling; kayaks are also available. <u>PP</u>

Pura Vida Cabilao On the northeast coast Ⓦcabilao. com. From the same team as *Pura Vida* in Dauin, Dumaguete (see page 290), this sibling offers the same standard lodgings at a range of budgets all the way up to a honeymoon suite. There are five economy rooms on the beachfront, while deluxe a/c rooms sit atop a small cliff looking out over the ocean. There's also a popular beach bar and the Sea Explorers dive centre. <u>PPP</u>

The south coast

Most travellers only make it this far in order to catch the boat from the busy little port town of **Jagna** to Camiguin Island and Mindanao. But those that have the time to stop for a few days are spoilt with beautiful beaches and diving at **Anda**, as well as a few Spanish-era ruins along the way.

Bool

Some 5km east of Tagbilaran, the coastal fishing town of **BOOL** is said to be the oldest settlement on the island. It's also the location of the **Blood Compact Site**, marked by a bronze sculpture on the seafront, as well as dozens of tour buses stopping off for photo opportunities. This is the spot where local chieftain Rajah Sikatuna and Miguel López de Legazpi concluded an early round of Philippine–Spanish hostilities in 1565 by signing a compact in blood. Every year for one week in July, Boholanos gather in Bool for the **Sandugo Festival**, which, apart from the usual beauty pageants and lashings of roast pig, includes an eyebrow-raising re-enactment of the blood ceremony.

Baclayon Church
Museum daily 8am–5pm • Charge

About 2km east of Bool, **BACLAYON** is the site of **Baclayon Church**, the oldest stone church in the Philippines, which was badly damaged by the 2013 quake. Much of the newer Augustinian facade collapsed, along with the upper half of the bell tower; renovations were completed in 2017. The rest dates back to 1595 and was declared a national historical landmark in 1995. The church's convent functions as an intriguing **ecclesiastical museum** housing a number of priceless religious icons and oddities.

Anda and around
Buses run from Tagbilaran (3hr)

Around 100km east of Tagbilaran, the countless white-sand coves of beautiful Guindulman Bay have made the once forgotten town of **ANDA** an emerging choice for those looking to escape Panglao's commercialized beach scene. Most of the resorts which have popped up in recent years are high-end, although there are also a few budget options. Offshore, **Lamanok Island**'s haematite cave paintings add credence to Anda's claim as the "cradle of Boholano culture", while on land there are several caves offering clear-water swimming – **Kabagno Cave** has a 6m-deep pool.

ARRIVAL AND DEPARTURE · THE SOUTH COAST

By boat Super Shuttle Ferry (ⓦsupershuttleroro.com) runs from Jagna to Balbagon on Camiguin Island (3 weekly; 2hr). Cokaliong Shipping Lines (ⓦcokaliongshipping.com) also operates a daily service from Jagna to Nasipit on Mindanao (5hr 30min).

ACCOMMODATION

ANDA

Amun Ini Beach Resort and Spa Western end of the beach ⓦamunini.com. Meaning "this is ours" in the local Ilonggo dialect, this remote hideaway, reached after a long drive, has a private beach, infinity pool and the kind of exemplary service that means you'll be handed a cold-pressed towel as soon as you start sweating. **PPPP**

Anda White Beach Resort Eastern end of the beach ⓦandabeachresort.com. For pure beach-lovers, this place can't be beaten, with attractive rooms, the best of which front onto a bright white strip of sand. There's also a palm-fringed pool, kayaks, an on-site dive shop and a buzzy bar. Wi-fi in public areas. **PPP**

Blue Star Dive and Resort Western end of the beach ⓦbluestardive.com. One of the first to venture this far east, *Blue Star* still stands out for scuba-lovers and has a good dive centre, pool, a tiny beach at low tide, and good snorkelling on the house reef. There is a choice of ten standard bungalows, or ocean- and pool-view a/c rooms, all of which are spacious and tastefully designed. Wi-fi reaches some rooms. **PPP**

Three Little Birds Resort Next to Anda White Beach Resort ⓦthreelittlebirdsresort.com. Gorgeous resort offering accommodation in traditional thatched cottages with all mod cons, set around a lovely swimming pool. It's just a few steps from the beach, and there's a great bar and restaurant waiting for you when you return. **PP**

Samar

The island of **SAMAR**, between Bicol and Leyte and 320km from top to toe, has yet to take off as a major tourist destination, which is both a shame and a blessing. Administratively divided into three parts, **Northern, Western and Eastern Samar**, large parts of each remain unspoilt, wild and beautiful. Homonhon Island in Eastern Samar is where **Ferdinand Magellan** is reputed to have set foot for the first time on Philippine soil in 1521, but these days the island is better known as the arrival point for many of the Philippines' worst storms. As well as suffering under **Typhoon Yolanda** in 2013, Samar was rocked by **Typhoon Odette** in December 2021, devastating numerous cities, towns and villages in its path. As well as the terrible human costs, the typhoon's aftermath continues to have serious economic implications.

The ongoing impact of these typhoons is evident in the east-coast surfing mecca of Guiuan, which has so far failed to live up to its pre-storm promise, and **Sohoton Natural Bridge National Park**, a prehistoric wilderness in Western Samar, which continues to be overlooked. Further north, however, the towns of **Calbayog** and **Catbalogan** offer plenty of adrenaline-rush activities in their hinterlands, including the chance to explore some of Southeast Asia's biggest cave systems.

ARRIVAL AND DEPARTURE · SAMAR

By plane There are airports at Calbayog and Catarman, both served by PAL to Manila. Cebu Pacific also flies to Calbayog.

By boat Coming from Cebu there are numerous slow ferry connections to various ports along Samar's west coast, including Calbayog and Catbalogan. Ferries from Matnog on Bicol in Luzon arrive in Allen, in the northwest of the island.

By bus and minivan Tacloban on neighbouring Leyte is linked to Samar by regular buses and minivans, crossing the 2km San Juanico Bridge. From Manila, several operators including Philtranco (ⓦphiltranco.net) cross on the Matnog–Allen ferry and run down the coastal road to Catbalogan (17–23hrs).

Northern Samar

Served by flights from Manila and boat from Luzon, **Northern Samar** is primarily used as an entry and departure point to and from the island, but there are also some beautiful islands offshore. The **Balicuatro** and **Biri Island** groups are slowly being developed for tourism, but most remain wonderfully pristine and untouched.

Allen

Arriving from Luzon by bus or ferry, your first taste of Samar is the small port town of **ALLEN**, in northwestern Samar, which has basic services and amenities but little else of interest to travellers. Most people head straight from the boat onto a bus or van, or out to the nearby Balicuatro or Biri Islands.

ARRIVAL AND DEPARTURE   ALLEN

By boat Roll-on, roll-off ferries from Matnog on the southernmost tip of Bicol (Luzon) make the return trip to the Balwharteco terminal in Allen, several times each morning (1–1hr 30min). As in other ports, there is a terminal fee to pay.

By bus and jeepney Dozens of buses and jeepneys run east every day from Allen to Catarman (1hr) and beyond, as well as south to Calbayog (2hr) and Catbalogan (4hr), where you can catch an onward bus to the southern half of the island. Buses heading south and east from Allen also pick up passengers at the port itself.

ACCOMMODATION

Birmingham Allen Resort Rizal St, Allen ☎ 0929 293 9152. There's no real beach here, but this four-room resort is a great option for a stopover, with tasty food, clean rooms, and helpful staff. As a welcome bonus, it's in a great location in which to see the to-die-for sunsets as the sun dips behind Dalupiri Island. P̲P̲P̲

The Balicuatro Islands

The remote, marine-protected **Balicuatro Islands**, off Samar's northwest coast, afford the chance to find your own slice of paradise for the day, although only a couple of them have anywhere to stay. The capital of **Dalupiri Island**, where most bangkas arrive, is **San Antonio**, a sleepy barangay with dozens of little bangkas that can take you on day-trips to tranquil islands nearby.

The rest of the islands, also largely unexplored by tourists, are mostly home to farmers and fishermen. **Capul**, for example, is a picturesque little atoll about one hour from the San Isidro Sea Port on Samar, with the empty shell of a seventeenth-century fortified stone church built by the Spanish, and an almost derelict coastal road that takes you past some incredible coves and beaches.

ARRIVAL AND DEPARTURE   THE BALICUATRO ISLANDS

By boat Scheduled morning bangkas leave from Victoria, 8km south of Allen, to San Antonio on Dalupiri (30min). Private bangka trips can also be arranged direct to resorts on Dalupiri from San Isidro, 7km south of Victoria. There is one morning bangka from Looc ferry terminal in Allen to Capul (1hr), or you can arrange a private trip.

ACCOMMODATION

Haven of Fun Beach Resort Just south of San Antinio ☎ 0917 790 6594. Concrete-and-thatch cottages in a pretty shoreside spot just south of town. They're able to whip up simple meals, but you're better off heading into town. P̲P̲

DIRECTORY

Money and services There are no ATMs on the islands. San Antonio in Dalupiri has a pharmacy and a small medical clinic.

Catarman

The ramshackle north coast port city of **CATARMAN** is served by flights from Manila and – though it has never been a major tourist destination – makes a good point of entry to Northern Samar if you want to save yourself a long bus or ferry journey. It's also only a short hop from the Biri group of islands.

By plane The airport received an upgrade in 2021, though flights are still pretty infrequent – they run to Cebu (3 weekly; 1hr) and Manila (4 weekly; 1hr 20min).

By bus and van Buses run from the terminal behind the market. A quicker way for destinations south, rather than a public bus, is to take a van, which leaves 1–2 times hourly.

Destinations Allen (hourly; 1hr); Calbayog (hourly; 2hr); Catbalogan (hourly; 3hr); Tacloban (hourly; 7hr)

ACCOMMODATION

Café Eusebio Bed and Breakfast 1071 Anunciation St ☎ 055 500 9245. This is the closest thing that Catarman has to a boutique hotel. Located next to shops, banks and restaurants, *Café Eusebio* has modern rooms, designer fixtures and fittings, and great Filipino breakfasts. It also does great coffee and cakes in the café. **PP**

Pink City Pension House Roxas St ⓦ facebook.com/pinkcitypension. True to its name, this place has bright-

pink rooms set around a central water feature. Standard rooms have a/c and cable TV, but for hot water you'll need to fork out for an executive or family room. **PP**

Sasa Pension House Jacinto St ⓦ facebook.com/sasapensionhouse. The clean, comfortable fan and a/c rooms at this four-storey, family-run pension offer great value, and it's often fully booked as a result. The cheapest rooms have shared bathrooms. **P̄**

EATING

Beehive Resto-Bar 211 Bonifacio St ⓦ facebook.com/BeehiveGelera. A great family-run place, the *Beehive* offers hearty mains such as steak and rice or salmon and veg, as well as a great selection of freshly baked cakes. Before paying up, the only decision is whether to take a slice of blueberry cheesecake, mango cake, or chocolate brownie to go. **PP**

Collin's Coffee Shop Bonifacio St ⓦ facebook.com/

collinscoffeeshop. Pretty café that's not a bad spot for a coffee or other drink to relax with; they also serve simple meals such as sandwiches, pasta and fried chicken. **PP**

Michz Café Western end of Jacinta St ⓦ facebook.com/Michzcafeofficial. Popular café serving pastas, salads and the best pizza in town, including a devilishly spicy tuna and pepperoni half-and-half. Cool down afterwards with a Willy Wonka-esque *halo-halo*. **PP**

DIRECTORY

Money There are a few banks with ATMs in Catarman, including on Anunciation St and Del Pilar St.

Biri-Las Rosas Islands

Charge for marine protection fee

Somewhere among the tantalizingly undeveloped cluster of idyllic outcrops known as the **Biri-Las Rosas Islands**, you'll be able to find one to call your own for the day. Most of the islands are only inhabited by fisherfolk, and the infrastructure is non-existent, but there are a few places to stay. Beyond the white sand, there are a number of more beguiling attractions, including weird rock formations, majestic cliffs, tidal pools and – at the right time of year, after the annual monsoons – sea waterfalls.

By boat Bangkas from Lavezares, 8km east of Allen, go to Biri (1hr) until an hour before sunset. Alternatively, you can charter a boat from San José (where all buses stop) for a

day-trip; bear in mind that restaurant options on the islands are slim, so it's likely that you'll have to provide food for you and the boatman.

Western Samar

Western Samar is dominated by its limestone topography, and has **caves**, gorges and waterfalls galore. Aside from the famous **Sohoton Natural Bridge National Park**, most natural attractions are still relatively undiscovered, and there is little tourist footfall and infrastructure. The provincial towns of **Calbayog** and **Catbalogan** are the best bases for exploring the region.

Calbayog and around

Sitting pretty, wedged between the Calbayog River on one side and the Samar Sea on the other, **CALBAYOG** makes a pleasant enough place for a stop on the west coast on

7

SAMAR UNDERGROUND

Catbalogan is not known as the capital of **caving** in the Philippines for nothing. Below the surface, a whole new world exists; it's a must-see on any visit. Of the many caves in Samar, **Jiabong**, just 12km from Catbalogan, is the easiest to explore, and has plenty of weird and wonderful features, including a ceiling carpeted with miniature stalactites. Further away, some 50km south of the city, **Langun-Gobingob** in Calbiga stretches 7km through twelve different chambers, and is one of the largest cave systems in Southeast Asia. This utterly dark environment is home to blind crabs, fish and thousands of fluttering bats. Both caves offer extreme caving – plenty of wading, swimming and squeezing through narrow spaces, with only your guide's lantern (or your torch) to guide you. **Permits** are required.

CAVING TRIPS

Trexplore Allen Ave, Catbalogan ⓦ trexplore.ph. The best way to get underground is to arrange a guided trip through these local cave gurus. If there's anything they don't know about the subterranean passages below the Catbalogan jungle, then it's not worth knowing about. They can arrange day- or overnight trips to the caves including meals, permits, equipment and transport.

your way through Samar. **Bangon and Tarangban Falls** are within easy reach of the city on the way to Catbalogan. To get to the falls, take a jeepney to Tinaplacan, and then walk (45min), or take a habal-habal direct (20min). Once there, you can swim in the plunge pool at Bangon Falls, or hike up to Tarangban Falls.

Guinogo-an Cave

Free • Take a jeepney from Calbayog to Lungsod, from where you can hire a boat, then walk the last 15min to the cave – bring a torch

After entering **Guinogo-an Cave**, you'll quickly find yourself wading through chest-deep water, before you emerge into a series of vaulted caverns, home to *kabyaw* (fruit bats), snakes, spiders and crabs. It's far safer to take a guide with you, which can be organized through the tourist office (see page 338). The vast Calbiga cave system is also accessible from Calbayog, but it's best to organize trips here through Trexplore (see box, page 338).

ARRIVAL AND DEPARTURE

CALBAYOG AND AROUND

By plane The airport is 8km out of town; tricycles are readily available to take you into the centre.
Destinations Cebu (1 daily; 1hr); Manila (1 daily; 1hr 25min).

By boat Calbayog has ferries for Cebu (3 weekly; 11hr), operated by Cokaliong (ⓦ cokaliongshipping.com). The ticket office is at the port, which lies on reclaimed land 2km from town. Tricycles into town are easy to find.

By bus and jeepney Buses and jeepneys arrive at the Capoocan transport terminal north of the river, 10min by tricycle from the town centre.

Destinations Allen (jeepneys; 2hr); Catarman (4 daily; 2hr 30min); Catbalogan (every 30min; 2hr); Tacloban (every 30min; 4hr).

By van A quicker alternative to the bus is to take a Grand Tours or Van-Vans shuttle van, which leave from their private terminals. Grand Tours is on the corner of Burgos St and the National Highway, while Van-Vans can be found at the bus station and on Bugallon St.

Destinations Allen (hourly; 1hr 45min); Catarman (hourly; 2hr); Catbalogan (every 30min; 1hr 30min); Tacloban (via Catbalogan; 3hr–3hr 30min).

INFORMATION

Tourist information Next to City Hall, Calbayog's friendly tourist office (Mon–Fri 8am–5pm; ⓦ facebook. com/TurismoCalbayog) has a few brochures about local attractions and can offer transport advice as well as helping

to arrange guides.

Services There's a daily produce market in Orquin St, on the northern edge of town near the river. There are several banks with ATMs.

ACCOMMODATION AND EATING

Café Buenaventura Northwest of town up Cajurao St ⓦ facebook.com/CafeB2020. With one eye firmly on the

Instagram market, Café Buenaventura offers the chance to be photographed in front of a variety of entertaining backgrounds while you enjoy your coffee, which is incidentally very good. The only downside is that it's a bit of a way from the centre. P̄

Carlos n' Carmelos Nijaga St ⓦfacebook.com/CarlosandCarmelosBistro. Simply the best ribs in the Eastern Visayas. This fast-food favourite wows locals and newcomers alike with sizzling grilled-rib platters as well as burgers, pastas, tacos, cheese sticks and fancy fries. PP

Ciriaco South of town on the National Hwy ⓦfacebook.com/ciriacohotel. By far Calbayog's best hotel, with excellent rooms, the more expensive of which look straight out to sea. There's a lobby café and a pool. Staff bend over backwards to help. PPP

S&R B&B Northwest of town on the National Hwy ⓦsrbedbreakfast.blogspot.com. This hotel is comfy, clean and cosy. The single-storey, red-and-yellow block overlooks a clean garden, while the five rooms have mini balconies, cool tiled floors, queen beds and TVs. Deluxe rooms, with deep-soaking tubs, cost extra. P̄

Catbalogan and around

Seventy kilometres south of Calbayog, the bustling port town of **CATBALOGAN** is the capital of Western Samar. For travellers, the city is mostly of interest as a base from which to head out climbing, canyoning and caving in the labyrinthine **cave systems** found within a couple of hours drive of the city (see box opposite); it's also a popular birdwatching area.

Ulot Torpedo Boat Extreme Ride

Charge per boat (for up to five people) • ⓦfacebook.com/TorpedoBoat • Take a bus or shuttle van bound for Borongan from Tacloban or Catbalogan and jump off at Samar Island National Park in Brgy Tenani; book in advance

Ulot Torpedo Boat Extreme Ride is a community-run initiative located on the cross-island Taft-Paranas Road that heads to Borongan on the east coast, 16km from the Catbalogan junction. The organization is successfully bringing visitors to a once-remote part of Samar. The idea is simple: a torpedo-shaped pumpboat whisks you up through the rapids into the island's last virgin forest, where you embark on a jungle adventure involving trekking, swimming and wildlife-watching. The longest river in Samar, the 90km Ulot was named for the local term for monkey, but it's unlikely you'll see any. Instead, keep your eyes peeled for soaring hawks and eagles.

ARRIVAL AND INFORMATION

CATBALOGAN AND AROUND

By ferry Roble Shipping (ⓦ robleshipping.com) has a ferry service to Cebu (2 weekly; 12hr), which leaves from the Catbalogan pier at the end of Allen Ave.

By bus and van Buses leave from the Catbalogan Bus Terminal, between Pier 1 and Pier 2, departing every 30min 1hr.

Destinations Borongan (5hr); Calbayog (2hr); Catarman (4hr); Tacloban (3hr).

By van A quicker alternative to the buses is to take a Duptours, Grand Tours or Van-Vans vehicle. All three companies have regular services for Calbayog and Tacloban, which leave from their private terminals – Grand Tours and Van-Vans on San Bartolome St, and Duptours just around the corner on Allen Ave. For Catarman, you need to transfer in Calbayog.

Destinations Calbayog (every 30min; 1hr 30min). Tacloban (every 30min; 2hr).

ACCOMMODATION AND EATING

Alegro 7th St ☎0919 073 9663. One of the best of Catbalogan's pretty limited accommodation options, this somewhat overpriced hotel offers simple and clean rooms, and not a whole lot more, though it's not a bad place at all. Get a room at the back, as those at the front can be noisy. PP

Fortune Del Rosario St ☎055 512 1147. It might be the poster child for "nothing special", but this hotel is conveniently located by the pier and the rooms are clean, reasonably comfortable, and pretty cheap, so it's by no means a bad choice for Catbalogan. P̄

King Bean Café Allen Ave ⓦfacebook.com/Kingbeancafecatb. Shiny and modern coffee shop that offers a decent menu of international dishes such as pasta, sandwiches and waffles, in addition to a Starbucks-esque range of lattes, Americanos, cappuccinos and frappes. PP

Rolet Hotel Mabini Ave ⓦfacebook.com/rolethotel. Starting to show signs of age, this was once the best option in town, with a/c rooms, slightly worn furniture, cable TV and good bathrooms. PP

Secret Café 170 Del Rosario St ⓦfacebook.com/thesecretcafeofficial. With sparse yet stylish décor, the Secret Café is one of Catbalogan's best places to grab a bite to eat. The menu ranges from Filipino to international, with particularly good burgers, and it's a fun place to while away the evening with a beer too. PPP

7

Money and services Catbalogan has most things a traveller should need, and ATMs aren't hard to come by.

Sohoton Natural Bridge National Park

Best known for a rock that has formed a natural bridge across a gorge, the **Sohoton Natural Bridge National Park** includes some remarkable limestone caves and chasms, and lowland rainforest where you can see, even around the park's picnic areas, monitor lizards, macaques and wild boar. Heavy rains cause flash floods, and the park is often closed during the monsoon from late November to early March.

Much of the area can be toured by boat and kayak, although to reach the **natural bridge** itself you'll have to get out and walk; and as there are few marked trails, you'll need to hire a **guide** to find your way around. The boat trip into the park is spectacular, heading up the **Cadacan River**'s estuary, which is lined by mangroves and nipa palms. As you approach, the river begins to twist and is then funnelled into a gorge of limestone cliffs and caves.

The most accessible of the park's many impressive caves is **Panhuughan I**, which has extensive stalactite and stalagmite formations in every passage and chamber. If you're lucky you might come across a number of specialized spiders and millipedes that eke out lives here in total darkness, and there have been many significant archeological finds in the caves, including burial jars, decorated human teeth and Chinese ceramics. During World War II, Filipino guerrillas used the caves as hideouts in their campaign against the occupying Japanese forces.

ARRIVAL AND INFORMATION   SOHOTON NATURAL BRIDGE NATIONAL PARK

Access The park is in the southern part of Samar, with the only approach being through Basey, on Samar's southwest coast, where you can arrange a bangka for the 10km-long, 2hr river trip to Sohoton. The quickest way to get to Basey is via Tacloban on Leyte, from where you can catch an early minivan or jeepney from the New Bus Terminal (40min); a tricycle will then take you to the Basey Municipal Tourist Office, near Basey's plaza.

Fees, guides and information It's both complicated and expensive to get into the heart of the park. At the regional tourist office (☎ 055 276 1471) you pay the entrance fee, and can arrange a guide, head torch and a bangka to take you to and from the park; prices fluctuate wildly, so be prepared to haggle.

Marabut Islands

A hundred kilometres southeast of Catbalogan lies the small settlement of Marabut. This is the jumping-off point for exploring the **Marabut Islands**, a striking collection of toothy limestone karsts rising out of the sea only a few hundred metres offshore, and reminiscent of Krabi's outcrops on Thailand's Andaman Coast and the rock formations in Halong Bay, Vietnam. There's no **accommodation** on any of the islands, but there are some options on the mainland.

ACCOMMODATION   MARABUT ISLANDS

Caluwayan Palm Island Resort Brgy Caluwayan, 17km northwest along the coast from Marabut ⓦ caluwayanresort.com. *Caluwayan* offers luxurious accommodation with a/c and TV, in lovely native-style cottages on a stretch of beach. There is a choice of rooms, villas and cottages, and plenty of distractions, including kayak hire, rock climbing and a stellar infinity pool. **PPP**

Eastern Samar

Eastern Samar is surf country, particularly around **Borongan**, and further south on beautiful Calicoan Island, which is accessed from the small and sleepy town of **Guiuan**. **Calicoan** island has plenty of beaches, caves and lagoons and was only just starting to see tourism development when Yolanda devastated the island, and almost entirely demolished Guiuan. The area was further impacted by Odette in 2021, but tourism is beginning to recover.

The bus trip from Catbalogan across to the east coast is one of the great little road journeys in the Philippines, taking you up through the rugged, jungle-clad interior past isolated barangays and along terrifying cliff roads. After four hours, the bus emerges from the wilderness onto the typhoon-battered east coast at Taft and turns south towards Borongan.

Borongan and around

BORONGAN has good surf at most times of year, and the entire coastline remains largely untouched by developers and hotels. Confident surfers can slip off the country's main surfing circuit to discover reef and beach breaks all to themselves here. If the surf's not up, you could always hire a bangka and take a trip along the coast, or out to the pretty island of **Divinubo**, dubbed the hidden paradise of Eastern Samar. It's an idyllic day-trip destination for exploring and snorkelling, but as there are no facilities on the island, make sure that you take something to eat and drink.

ARRIVAL AND INFORMATION

By bus and jeepney There are a few buses that ply the mountain route between Borongan and Catbalogan (5hr), as well as jeepneys and vans for Guiuan. The Duptours terminal is on Real St, and Van-Vans is on E. Cinco St.

BORONGAN AND AROUND

Tourist information The small tourist office (Mon–Sat 8am–4pm; ☎ 0917 426 9167) is in the Provincial Capitol Building facing Borongan plaza.

ACCOMMODATION AND EATING

Boro Bay North of town on Baybay Blvd ⓦ facebook. com/BoroBayHotel. Situated away from the bustle of downtown, this quiet property has an impressive pavilion-style lobby and entrance, and welcoming and friendly staff. The clean rooms have all the mod cons, including a/c, cable TV and en-suite showers with hot water. Basic breakfast included of beef or milkfish, with egg over rice. **PP**

Dona Vicenta Real St ⓦ facebook.com/Donavicenta hotel. The most luxurious accommodation in the town is to be found at this grand-looking business hotel on the main highway. Comfortable, box-like rooms and junior suites have cable TV, although many suffer from being too close to the noisy bar, which often stays open until the wee hours. The higher you go – towards the presidential suite,

no less – the better the mountain and ocean views. There's a refreshing pool, too. **PP**

Primea Abogado St ⓦ primeahotel.com.ph. A solid, no-nonsense, international-standard hotel in the centre of town, offering comfortable but rather bland rooms. Staff are friendly, and there's a small pool. Make sure to get a room at the back, as those at the front can be very loud. **PP**

Rawis Resort & Restaurant Real St ⓦ facebook.com/ rawisresorthotel. Aside from at the hotels, Borongan's dining options are limited, which makes this international all-rounder overlooking the estuary and Baybay beach a solid option. It has live music almost every night, cold beers, and meals such as chop suey and fried chicken. **PP**

DIRECTORY

Money There's are several ATMs in town.

Guiuan and around

At the far end of the road in southeast Samar, protruding out into the Leyte Gulf like a skeletal finger, is **GUIUAN** and the forgotten-by-time surf outpost of **CALICOAN ISLAND**. Such exposed topography meant that when Typhoon Yolanda hit in 2013, with vicious 400km/h winds, the area stood no chance. The casualties were lower than they could have been – fewer than two hundred people were killed – but the storm caused untold damage to the area's hotels and restaurants, and the emerging surf scene was literally wiped off the map. The resilient community was just beginning to recapture its pre-Yolanda spirit when the area was forced to shut down during the Covid-19 pandemic, and further - if less severe - damage was wrought by Typhoon Odette in 2021. Recovery is now underway, with the re-emergence of remote surf camps along Calicoan's **ABCD Beach**, and fishermen eager to show you **Kantican** and **Tubabao** – Eastern Samar's best white-sand islands – by bangka.

Calicoan Island

Catch a jeepney to Sulangan via ABCD Beach from Guiuan Terminal, or charter a habal-habal for a round trip

Accessible across the Guiuan bridge, **Calicoan Island** ticks a lot of boxes – quiet towns, empty beaches, frothing surf and grand sunsets. Prior to Yolanda, it was rapidly developing, but most surf camps were completely destroyed in the almighty storm. The island was thrown back to far simpler times, and there are still few resorts to choose from.

Most surfers base themselves in Guiuan, content with day-trips to ABCD Beach, for the Pacific reef breaks. The best surfing season is from June to October.

ARRIVAL AND INFORMATION

GUIUAN AND AROUND

By bus and jeepney The quickest way to get to Guiuan is with a Van-Vans or Duptours shuttle bus from Tacloban, which leave when full (3hr 30min). Regular buses may take nearly double that time. If coming from Borongan, a jeepney is by far your best bet (3hr).

Tourist information The Guiuan Tourism Council, based at the Town Plaza (Mon–Sat 9am–6pm; ☎0917 426 9167), can help with information on the region.

ACCOMMODATION AND EATING

La Luna Beach Resort North of Sulangan Bridge, Calicoan ⓦfacebook.com/lalunabeachresortofficial. Owned by long-time Italian ex-pat Giovanni, this little four-room resort – two look out to sea, two are out the back – is a great place to detox for a few days, with its saltwater pool and well-stocked bar. Remote, but worth the effort of getting here. P̄P̄

La Tazza Café-Bar Conception St, Guiuan town ⓦfacebook.com/latazzacafebar. A small and stylish café in the centre of Guiuan, La Tazza is a popular spot to enjoy a coffee and a pancake or waffle. It also offers a menu of more substantial fare, including burgers and curries. P̄

Sea Quest Lodge 2km north of Guiuan town, Brgy Luboc ☎0919 446 8231. Formerly called Tanghay View, this very clean, three-storey oceanfront property overlooks Tubabao Island and the Leyte Gulf. The lodge is home to the best restaurant in town, with a Filipino menu that changes daily. P̄P̄

DIRECTORY

Money There's an ATM near the Guiuan Integrated Transport Terminal, and more in town.

Leyte

The east Visayan island of **LEYTE** ("LAY-tay"), separated from Samar to the north by a mere slither of ocean, the San Juanico Strait, is another sizeable chunk of the Philippines that has a great deal to offer visitors but is regularly overlooked. You could spend months here and still only scratch the surface: the coastline is immense, the interior rugged and there are lakes and mountains that are well off the tourist map, known only to farmers who have tilled their shores and foothills for generations.

In the sixteenth century, Magellan passed through Leyte on his way to Cebu, making a blood compact with the local chieftain as he did so. But to manyFilipinos and war historians, the island will always be associated with **World War II**, when its jungled hinterlands became the base for a formidable force of guerrillas who fought a number of bloody encounters with the Japanese. It was because of this loyalty among the inhabitants that General Douglas MacArthur landed at Leyte on October 20, 1944, fulfilling the famous promise he had made to Filipinos, "I shall return".

Around the provincial capital of **Tacloban**, the usual arrival point, there are a number of sights associated with the war, notably the **Leyte Landing Memorial**, marking the spot where MacArthur waded ashore to liberate the archipelago. Tacloban is also now remembered as the site of the worst of Typhoon Yolanda's devastation – as well as the powerful winds and rain, a huge storm surge decimated large chunks of the city. To the north of Tacloban is the beautiful island of **Biliran** and, a short bangka ride away from Biliran, the islands of **Maripipi** and **Higatangan**, which both have terrific beaches, rock formations and caves. To the south of the bayside town of **Ormoc**, the coastal road takes you through the ferry ports of **Baybay** and **Maasin** before reaching **Padre Burgos**, which is gaining a reputation for its scuba diving and whale shark encounters.

ARRIVAL AND DEPARTURE   LEYTE

By plane Leyte's only major airport is at Tacloban (see page 343).

By boat Fast ferry connections link the port of Ormoc with Cebu, and there are also boats from Cebu and Bohol to Bato, Baybay, Hilongos, and Maasin on Leyte's west coast.

By bus Buses to Leyte operate from Manila (using ferries to cover the watery bits, obviously), and there are also regular daily services from Biliran to Tacloban and Ormoc, and from Samar via the San Juanico Bridge.

Tacloban and around

On the northeast coast, **TACLOBAN** is associated by most Filipinos with that tireless collector of shoes, Imelda Marcos, who was born a little south of here in the small coastal town of Tolosa to the prominent Romualdez family. In her youth, Imelda was a local beauty queen, and referred to herself in later life as "the rose of Tacloban". The famed **San Juanico Bridge**, presented by Ferdinand to Imelda as testimony to his love, is another legacy of the Marcos connection. You'll probably see it when flying in or out of the airport, which still bears the Romualdez name.

Typhoon Yolanda will live long in the memory for the survivors in Tacloban, which became the epicentre of recovery efforts, but it's now business as usual in the city, which remains a typically frenetic Filipino city, with most activity centred around the port and the market. There are few tourist attractions, though if you are here for a day or two you'll find that the city has everything you need: good accommodation, numerous travel agencies, and banks and restaurants crammed into the grid-like centre between **Avenida Veteranos** and **J. Romualdez Street**.

The city's major fiestas are the Mardi Gras spectacles of **Pintados-Kasadyaan**, a celebration of the body-painting traditions of the island's ancient tattooed warriors, and **Sangyaw**, a carnival with parades and floats. Both are held in the last week of June.

Santo Niño Shrine and Heritage Museum

Real St, 2km south of town • Charge, including guide

The first stop on any tour of Tacloban should be to gawp at the **Santo Niño Shrine and Heritage Museum**. A grand folly of a house that Imelda Marcos ordered built but, in fact, never slept in, it was sequestered by the government after the Marcos regime was overthrown. Inside, there is evidence aplenty that nothing was too opulent or tasteless for the Iron Butterfly. Her personal chapel has sparkling diamond chandeliers, gold-framed mirrors and an expensive replica of the miraculous Santo Niño de Leyte (the original resides in the **Santo Niño Church** opposite Rizal Park in Real Street).

San Juanico Bridge

Free • Take a bus from the New Bus Terminal to anywhere on Samar (Marabut, Basey, Borongan, Guiuan) and jump off beforehand (20min)

Completed in 1973, the monumental, humpbacked landmark of **San Juanico Bridge** stretches from Leyte to Samar, and at 2.16km is the longest bridge in the Philippines. Though such a statistic may not be all that impressive, its arch-shaped truss design is still an engineering marvel. On a good day, the bridge offers fabulous views across the San Juanico Strait to Tacloban and beyond; by night, the bridge has been illuminated since receiving an LED-driven makeover in 2022.

Calvary Hill

Ave Veteranos, on the western edge of the city, 1km from the centre

It's worth the sweat of a walk up to the top of **Calvary Hill**, which is a place of pilgrimage during Holy Week before Easter: the ascent is marked by the fourteen **Stations of the Cross**, with a five-metre statue of the Sacred Heart of Jesus at the

TACLOBAN

● EATING	
Chew Love	6
Dream Café	3
Espazio Arts + Food + History	7
Giuseppe's	4
Ocho	1
Sal's Restaurant	2
Stephanie's Smokehaus	5

■ ACCOMMODATION	
Alejandro	2
Ambassador	3
Asia Stars	1
HIS Capsule Hostel	6
Ironwood	4
Rosvenil	5

6. Santo Niño Shrine & Heritage Museum, Palo & Airport

summit. A good time to start the climb is late afternoon, so you reach the top in time to watch the sunset.

Palo and around

Reach by taxi, tricycle and jeepney

About 5km south of Tacloban is the small town of **PALO**, known for its associations with MacArthur and the liberation. It was at Palo's **Red Beach**, about 1km from the town centre, that MacArthur waded ashore on October 20, 1944, fulfilling his famous vow to return. The spot is marked by the dramatic **Leyte Landing Memorial**, an oversized sculpture of the general and his associates, among them Sergio Osmeña walking purposefully through the shallows to the beach.

ARRIVAL AND DEPARTURE

TACLOBAN AND AROUND

By plane Daniel Z. Romualdez Airport is located on a spit of land southeast of Tacloban, 10km by road from downtown. Jeepneys and tricycles can be picked up to take you into town. Destinations Cebu (3 daily; 50min); Davao (3 weekly; 1hr 10min); Iloilo (3 weekly; 1hr); Manila (1–2 hourly; 1hr 10min).
By bus and jeepney Buses and jeepneys from all points

arrive at the New Bus Terminal in Abucay, 2km west of the city. Services to destinations within Leyte and Samar run regularly, but are most frequent in the mornings.
Destinations Borongan (4hr 30min); Calbayog (hourly; 4hr); Catbalogan (hourly; 3hr); Catarman (hourly; 6hr); Maasin (hourly; 5hr); Manila (3 daily; 24hr); Naval (every

30min; 3hr); Ormoc (hourly; 3hr).

By van Many of the bus routes are also covered by the far quicker Duptours Shuttle Services, Grand Tours and Van-Vans minivans, each of which leaves from their designated terminal: Duptours on Santo Niño St; Grand Tours from Trece Martires St, near the post office; and Van-Vans terminal on P. Burgos St.

Destinations Catbalogan (every 30min; 2hr); Maasin (every 30min; 4hr); Naval (every 30min; 2hr 45min); Ormoc (every 30min; 2hr 30min).

INFORMATION

Tourist information The regional tourist office on Magsaysay Boulevard on Kanhuraw Hill can provide information, maps and travel tips (☎ 053 832 0901).

ACCOMMODATION   SEE MAP PAGE 344

Accommodation ranges from quirky budget rooms to affordable mid-range places.

Alejandro P. Paterno St ☎ 053 321 7033. From the outset more museum than hotel, this bragging old-timer in an attractive 1930s colonial villa was used as a refuge for evacuees in World War II. Rooms are tastefully styled and have a/c, cable TV, and fridges, although not all have external windows. There's a fascinating display of historic photographs, and downstairs the restaurant and coffee shop have wi-fi. Worth a look round, even if you're not staying. PP

Ambassador Real St ⊕ facebook.com/TheAmbassador Hotel. Housed in a grandiose building, but in need of a bit of a spruce-up inside, the Ambassador is a decent central option. Some rooms are considerably better than others so ask to see a few. PP

Asia Stars Zamora St ⊕ facebook.com/asiastars hotelcorporation. Unattractive from the outside, but the rooms are fine, the staff friendly and the central location unbeatable. Quiet doubles with fan or a/c, all with private shower, plus some rooms which have cable TV and a fridge. Deluxe rooms have bigger beds. PP

HIS Capsule Hostel 13 Real St ⊕ facebook.com/his capsulehostel.ph. Very basic and very cheap, this capsule hostel – bearing a very slight resemblance to such places in Japan, the birthplace of the concept – is an excellent choice for those wishing to stay in Tacloban on a budget. The dorm berths are comfortable, with more privacy than you get in the average bunk bed, and there are also a couple of private rooms available. It's a bit of a trek from the centre, though. P̄

Ironwood P. Burgos St at Juan Luna St ⊕ ironwoodhotel. com. Sleek, modern, and a world apart from the competition, the *Ironwood* is a business hotel with a fine selection of premium doubles, kings and deluxe executive suites. Rooms come with all mod cons and fragrant bathroom amenities, but you'd expect as much for the price. PPP

Rosvenil 302 P. Paterno St ⊕ facebook.com/Rosvenil hoteltac. Part Spanish farmhouse ranch, part Swiss mountain lodge, this homely mid-range option has clean if bare-boned rooms with comfy beds and a choice of a/c or fan. Out front is a sociable garden, and the hotel is in walking distance to all the downtown restaurants. PPP

EATING   SEE MAP PAGE 344

These days Tacloban has a pretty sophisticated **restaurant** scene, including weekend pop-ups and American-style smokehouses. In between meals, there are plenty of local specialities to **snack** on – *binagul*, a hot sticky concoction made of coconut and nuts, and chocolate *meron* can be bought freshly made every morning from hawkers along Rizal Ave.

Chew Love P. Gomez St ⊕ facebook.com/chewlove tacloban. If any restaurant can create a social media buzz in Tacloban, it's *Chew Love*. Don't be put off by the twee, candy-cane look of this emoji-influenced café-restaurant. Past the eye-popping wall-art mural and toy-town design, it's a fun place to eat. There are plenty of fish, steak, pork and chicken soul-food dishes to choose from, served with heart-shaped rice. Understandably, it's popular with families and teenagers. PPP

Dream Café 222 M.H. Del Pilar St ⊕ facebook.com/ dreamcafetacloban. This jack-of-all-trades diner serves all-day breakfasts, burgers, paninis, Aussie rib-eye steaks, freshly baked breads, packed lunches and imported wines. The terrace is one of the few places in the city to grab a cold beer, while on weekens, it often hosts live acoustic shows. PPP

★ **Espazio Arts + Food + History** 130 Juan Luna St ⊕ facebook.com/espazio.tacloban. Is this the coolest place in town? There's a lot to look at here, in any case – old photos, old cameras and old typewriters vie for your attention with art of a more modern nature (and furnishings that are somewhere in the middle), while there's also a garden area out back. After all this, the food and drink seem almost by-the-way; simple meals and good coffee mean that the whole place works just fine. PP

★ **Giuseppe's** 173 Ave Veteranos ⊕ facebook.com/ giuseppesresto. It seems like every town in the Philippines has an Italian place like this, but *Giuseppe's* is a genuine cut above the rest. The stone-baked pizzas are as good as you'll find in this part of the world, and there's also ravioli ragu, baked lasagne, spaghetti marinara and top-notch coffee. It's as sophisticated as the Tacloban dining scene gets. PPP

Ocho Senator Enage St ⊕ ochoseafood.com. Stylish restaurant where you choose from super-fresh salads, fish, fruit and desserts laid out at the back of the restaurant, or

7

opt for market-fresh fish or shellfish cooked to your taste. For something different, try one of the *amapalaya* specials (bitter tropical melon with fish). $\overline{PPP}$

Sal's Restaurant 163 Salazar St ⓦfacebook.com/salstacloban. Housed in a lovely older building, and decorated simply but attractively, Sal's Restaurant is a lovely welcoming choice for a top-notch evening meal. The menu is almost exclusively Filipino, with marvellous lechon, delicious ribs and great seafood. $\overline{PP}$

Stephanie's Smokehaus Ave Veteranos ⓦfacebook.com/StephaniesEatAllYouCan. Ludicrously popular buffet restaurant, where a pleasingly low price buys a great-value, all-you-can-eat spread. It's hugely popular with locals, and queues out the door aren't unheard of at weekends. $\overline{PP}$

DIRECTORY

Hospital There are a number of private hospitals and medical clinics in the city, including Divine Word Hospital on M. H. Del Pilar St, and R.T. Romualdez Hospital and Mother of Mercy Hospital south of the city centre.

Police Local police headquarters are located on the P. Paterno Extension near the RTR Plaza Park.

Biliran

The beautiful and largely undiscovered Eden of **Biliran** lies off the north coast of Leyte, connected by a bridge. An autonomous island province governed from **NAVAL**, the sleepy capital on the west coast, Biliran is the Philippines in microcosm: there's a lengthy coastline of deep coves and palm-fringed white beaches; a mountainous interior; and the **Sampao rice terraces**, the island's own small version of Banaue's agricultural steps at Iyusan.

Among the many natural wonders are nearly a dozen thundering **waterfalls**, most with deep, clear pools that are perfect for swimming: Kasabangan Falls is in the barangay of Balaquid on the south coast; Casiawan Falls, a little further along the coast near Casiawan village; and Tinago Falls, near Gabibihan, is in the island's east. For something different, and to see where the future of tourism in Biliran may lie, stop at the **Canaan Hills Farm & Honey Garden** outside Caibiran. A tropical fruit farm, landscaped garden and organic café, it paints a romanticized picture of rural Leyte life.

Two of the best **beaches** on Biliran are on opposite sides of the island, but even on a day-trip you'll have time to see them both. On the east coast, near Culaba, is the deserted Looc White Beach, while the Shifting Sand Bar, 45 minutes by bangka towards **Higatangan** from Naval, is a 200m-long curving spit of sand surrounded by shallow water.

Maripipi and Higatangan islands

There are boats each morning from Naval for Maripipi (2 daily; 1hr) and Higatangan (2 daily; 40min), though all return the following day – unless you charter a bangka, overnighting is necessary on both islands

If you get to Biliran, make sure that you allow enough time to take a bangka to some of the surrounding islands. **Maripipi** is a picturesque place for a backwoods adventure, dominated by a stunning 924m volcano, while Higatangan Rocks on **Higatangan Island** is well worth a visit. The beach here is beautiful, and the rocks have been carved into extraordinary formations by time and tide. Both islands have simple, often power-free (or power-limited) places to stay.

ARRIVAL AND GETTING AROUND   BILIRAN

By bus and minivan There are buses and minivans to Naval from Tacloban and Ormoc (both every 30min; 2–3hr).

By boat Roble Shipping (ⓦrobleshipping.com) have ferries from Cebu City to Naval (3 weekly; 9hr), but if you want to save time, it's far quicker to take a fast ferry to Ormoc and then take a minivan from there.

By bus and jeepney From Naval there are sporadic buses and jeepneys north to Almeria (20min), Kawayan (40min) and east to Caibiran and Culaba (1hr), but no further in either direction.

By habal-habal To explore the island at leisure, it's most convenient to hire a habal-habal to take you around for the day.

By car Alternatively, try Biliran Island Rent-A-Car (ⓦtourism.biliranisland.com).

INFORMATION

Tourist information The small tourist office (Mon–Fri 8am–5pm; ☎053 500 9571) and museum is on the second floor of the Provincial Capitol Building in Naval. To explore the more remote areas of the islands and to find the waterfalls, it's best to employ the services of a local guide – staff at the tourist office can help arrange one. It's also worth checking out ⊛ biliranisland.com, which is a volunteer-driven website that comes across as quite official. **Services** There are banks, with ATMs, on P. Inocentes St near the WAD Mall in Naval.

ACCOMMODATION AND EATING

As tourism has yet to really take off on Biliran, hotels and guesthouses are accustomed to **power blackouts**, and **electricity** often only runs at certain times of the day. In conditions such as this **wi-fi**, particularly on the remoter islands, is still not all that reliable.

NAVAL

Chamorita 5km south of town ⊛ chamoritaresort.com. Located just off the island ring road, this homely waterfront resort has a mixture of a/c rooms, including budget options for backpackers, standard doubles and deluxe rooms with French-louvre windows and power-showers. There's a restaurant and bar on site, and a whole host of activities on offer. P̄P̄

D'Mei Residence Inn 213 P. Inocentes St ⊛ facebook. com/DMeiResidenceInn. Hands down the best overnight option in Naval, with attractive, clean and brightly painted a/c rooms with flatscreen TVs. Considering the noise outside, the rooms are surprisingly quiet. There's a handy mini-mart on the ground floor. P̄

Marvin's Seaside Inn 2km north of town, Brgy Atipolo ⊛ marvinsseasideinn.com. A far better bet than staying in town, *Marvin's* is a quiet, safe and clean choice with seaside rooms (without views or any kind of beach) in the main banana-yellow block, and larger, nicer rooms set around the pool in a building across the road. All rooms come with cable TV and hot showers, and the restaurant has a decent range of Western and Filipino dishes. P̄P̄

TJ Pensione Magallanes St ⊛ facebook.com/tjpensione naval. If you get stuck in town and need a bed for the night, you could do worse – though the rooms are looking pretty worn, it's clean, cheap and central. Rooms at the back are distinctly quieter. P̄

ELSEWHERE ON BILIRAN

Agta Beach Resort Almeria, 12km north of Naval ⊛ agtabeachresort.com. Something of a scuba pioneer, *Agta* was the first dive resort on Biliran, and continues to prioritize what's under the sea rather than what's on land. This means that its rooms could do with an update, but staff make up for it by being amiable and eager to help. P̄P̄

MARIPIPI AND HIGANTANGAN ISLANDS

Napo Beach Resort 20min habal-habal from pier, Maripipi ☎ 0921 212 5164. For those who won't mind if the power generator cuts out at night or not, Maripipi's only reliable place to stay is an attractive shoestringers' resort with budget rooms and brightly painted fan and a/c huts set at the base of mountains. Breakfast included. P̄

Ormoc and around

For such a small, quiet town, **ORMOC**, on Leyte's west coast, has endured a surprising amount of turmoil in its recent history. Scene of some of the bloodiest battles during World War II, Ormoc Bay, at the mouth of the Isla Verde River, hides dozens of shipwrecks. In 1992, floods caused untold damage and resulted in the loss of eight thousand lives. Then, in 2013, Yolanda tore through the city, demolishing countless homes and damaging almost every roof. The city has recovered well, though, and its bay-side park is a lovely place to watch the sunset.

Lake Danao National Park

Charge for raft rental • Jeepney from Ormoc or hire a van for the day

Lake Danao National Park, 19km away from Ormoc and at a far cooler 650m above sea level, makes for a pleasant half-day trip. Once there, you can hike to a number of different waterfalls, including Inawasan Falls (30min), Tigbawan Falls (2hr) and Mag-aso Falls (3–4hr). For something more relaxing, you can explore the park's lake by renting a raft.

ARRIVAL AND INFORMATION · ORMOC AND AROUND

By ferry Oceanjet (⊛ oceanjet.net), SuperCat (⊛ supercat. ph) and Weesam (⊛ weesam.ph) all have fast ferry sailings between Cebu and Ormoc (11 daily; 2hr 30min). 2GO (⊛ travel.2go.com.ph), Lite Shipping (⊛ liteferries.com.

ph) and Roble Shipping (⊛ robleshipping.com) run slower services for Cebu (5–6hr).

By bus, jeepney and van The main bus terminal and jeepney terminal are next to each other on Ebony St, near the pier. Jeepneys also operate some of the routes below but are far slower. The quickest way to move on is with a Duptours Shuttle Services van, which costs slightly more than the buses, and leaves from the terminal on Bonifacio St.

Destinations Baybay (hourly; 1hr); Maasin (hourly; 3hr); Naval (every 30min; 3hr); Tacloban (hourly; 3hr).

ACCOMMODATION

★ **IA Lodge** Bonifacio St ⓦ ialodge.ph. Situated right by the central park, the IA Lodge is an excellent budget choice, with clean and comfortable, though fairly unexciting, rooms. There's also a 15-bed dormitory for super-cheap digs. P̄P̄

Niko's Ark Voyager's Inn Real St ⓦ nikosarkhotel. wixsite.com. Niko's is a unique concept. Decked out to look like the inside of Captain Nemo's submarine, this boutique hotel has ship's cabins for rooms, with nautical memorabilia, lifebuoys, and frigate ropes hung from the walls. Bunk-bed dorms for shipmates are a bargain, and there are capsule-like single rooms and doubles with power-showers and flatscreen TVs. Lovely, if a little odd. P̄

Pongos Bonifacio St ☎ 053 255 2211. During Yolanda, Pongos flung open its doors to help as many people as possible in the aftermath – and people in Ormoc continue to have a soft spot for it. It has a vast array of rooms, ranging from tatty doubles in the main building to better a/c rooms in the new building. P̄

Rosetta Guest House Rizal St ⓦ rosettagh.com. Smart, shiny and modern, the Rosetta Guest House offers several rooms of differing size, as well as a self-catering suite. It's in a good location just a short walk from the centre. It's perhaps a little on the pricey side, though. P̄P̄P̄

EATING

Lorenzo's Café Larrazabal St ⓦ facebook.com/Lorenzos CafeOrmoc. Pleasant Starbucks clone with indoor seating and people-watching tables outside, which look across to the sea. The menu includes sandwiches, salads and pastas. P̄

Milagrina's 134 Real St ☎ 053 561 1697. A fast-food style place with a good menu of Filipino dishes, though the most popular order by some distance is the chicken, which is fried with a lipsmacking combination of herbs and spices. P̄P̄

Sutuwaki Larrazabal St ⓦ facebook.com/sutuwaki restaurant. Popular open-sided restaurant by the harbour, where you choose from the meat and fish at the counter and get it cooked to order. P̄P̄P̄

DIRECTORY

Hospital The city's most convenient hospital is Ormoc Doctors' Hospital (☎ 053 560 8222), on the corner of Aviles St and San Pablo St.

Police Ormoc's police station is on J. Navarro St at Aviles St.

The southwest coast

If you're heading south along the coast, you'll find several towns which offer transport connections with Cebu and thus an alternative gateway to the diving to be found further south at Padre Burgos (see page 349). Fifty kilometres south of Ormoc, the frenetic port of **BAYBAY** is a functional town with a very busy wharf area and a main street lined with *carinderias*, convenience stores, pawnshops and a few banks. About halfway between Baybay and Maasin, clean, easy-going **HILONGOS** has a number of canteens huddled around a simple pier, but nowhere to stay. A little south of Hilongos, the port town of **BATO** is a useful jumping-off point for Padre Burgos. At the mouth of the Maasin River, the otherwise dull, industrial port of **MAASIN** makes a good starting point if you're heading for the far south of Leyte, an area that's opening up for scuba diving and whale-shark-watching, particularly around Sogod Bay.

ARRIVAL AND INFORMATION   THE SOUTHWEST COAST

By boat Both Baybay (2–3 daily; 6hr) and Hilongos (1 daily; 3hr 30min) are connected by regular ferries to Cebu, and have onwards transport connections by bus, jeepney and van further south; Cokaliong (ⓦ cokaliongshipping. com) and Roble Shipping (ⓦ robleshipping.com: daily; 6hr) run to Baybay, and Gabisan Shipping (ⓦ facebook.com/ gabisanshipping) to Hilongos. From Maasin, Cokaliong runs slow ferries to Cebu City (4 weekly; 6hr), while Weesam Express (ⓦ weesam.ph) runs two fast services (daily; 3hr; check ahead of travel). From Ubay on Bohol, Super Shuttle Ferry (ⓦ supershuttleroro.com) runs trips to Bato (daily; 3hr 30min).

By bus If you're arriving by air in Tacloban you can catch an a/c minivan direct to Maasin (4hr). Otherwise, buses from Tacloban take up to 6hr. A trip from Ormoc should take around 3hr.

Tourist information You can get up-to-date information on diving and whale-shark-watching from any of the resorts, particularly *Peter's Dive Resort* and *Sogod Bay Scuba Resort* (see page 349).

ACCOMMODATION

Caimito Beach R. Kangleon St, 7km south of Maasin ⓦcaimitobeachhotel.com. This pool resort is a short drive along the coast, but worth it for the waterfront location, pools and patios. Tiled floor rooms are no-frills, but come with extra perks including mini-bar, tea-and-coffee-making facilities and bathroom amenities. Single rooms are available. P̄P̄

Villa Romana R. Kangleon St, Maasin ⓦfacebook.com/villaromanamaasin. A mix of Spanish bodega-style and downtown Filipino, this central hotel is a reliable option to break up a journey. It's on the waterfront, overlooking the Port of Maasin, and within walking distance of the city's best shops, bars and restaurants. P̄P̄

Padre Burgos and around

The area around **PADRE BURGOS** on Leyte's southern tip has developed as an under-the-radar **scuba-diving** destination, with dozens of sites, including the impressive **Napantao Marine Sanctuary**. The region has a frontier atmosphere, and remains firmly off the main tourist path. Those who come this far are rewarded with eerily quiet deep-wall and cave dives in **Sogod Bay** and unpredictable **whale shark** sightings that – on a good day – can beat anywhere in the country.

7

Limasawa Island

Bangkas leave Padre Burgos 3–4 times early in the morning for Magallanes Brgy on Limasawa (45min)

It was atop a prominent hill on tiny **Limasawa Island** that Magellan is said to have conducted the first Catholic Mass in the Philippines on March 31, 1521. After an often choppy boat ride from Padre Burgos, visitors can walk up 450 concrete steps to a monument at the top of the hill, from where there are commanding views over the whole island.

Coral Cay Conservation

In the village of Napantao on Panaon Island • ⓦcoralcay.org

Established in 1986 way out in Belize, **Coral Cay Conservation** is an international group with an ongoing project in Southern Leyte, focused on protecting the coral reefs in and around Padre Burgos and **Panaon Island**, further east across Sogod Bay. Volunteers are welcomed to the headquarters in the village of **Napantao**, where a variety of programmes are available, including everything from two-week stints to more immersive four-month marine conservation surveys.

ARRIVAL AND ACCOMMODATION

By ferry The closest major port to Padre Burgos is Maasin, which is served by ferries from Cebu City (see page 308).

By jeepney Jeepneys head up the coast to Maasin (1hr) from where there are transport connections to the rest of Leyte.

v ★ **Peter's Dive Resort** Padre Burgos ⓦpetersdiveresortph.com. For those who want excellent service and plenty of time in the water beyond the pebble beach, this is a superb option. There's affordable accommodation in dorms, better standard rooms or duplex cottages. The views of Sogod Bay are breathtaking. The main building's lower terrace has a games room, and there's a pool and an excellent little restaurant serving home-cooked food. Cheaper rates for divers. P̄P̄

PADRE BURGOS AND AROUND

Sogod Bay Scuba Resort Lungsodaan, 1km north of town ⓦsogodbayscubaresort.com. Don't be put off by the concrete rooms: the real draw is the professional diving outfit and the location, a flipper's throw from the best scuba sites. Even if you're not here to dive, the owners can help arrange everything from trekking to motorbike hire and caving trips. P̄P̄

Southern Leyte Divers San Roque, Macrohon ⓦleyte-divers.com. This small lodge is some 15min northwest of Padre Burgos by jeepney, with charming native-style cottages and hammocks in a lazy beachside location. The terrace restaurant serves Bavarian sausages, fish dishes and curry; the owners can, of course, arrange all sorts of diving trips. P̄P̄

Palawan

EL NIDO, PALAWAN

Palawan

Tourism is on the up in Palawan, and for good reason. Surrounded by the 1,780-odd islets that make up Palawan province, the main island is the fifth largest in the Philippines, with a lush jungle-swathed interior surrounded by floury white beaches lapped by gin-clear waters and overlooked by towering limestone outcrops. Its location southwest of Luzon on the very edge of the archipelago, as close to Borneo as it is to Manila, has seen Palawan influenced by many external cultures and religions, and it instantly has a different feel to the rest of the Philippines. While the centres of Coron, El Nido, Sabang and Puerto Princesa have become popular tourist hubs, the southern part of the 450km-long, sword-shaped main island remains largely unexplored. But whichever parts of the province you choose to visit, you'll be treated to a Jurassic landscape of coves, beaches, lagoons and forests. Offshore, meanwhile, despite some damage from dynamite fishing and coral bleaching, there's always an untouched reef to discover.

8

The capital of Palawan, **Puerto Princesa**, is the main entry point, and located close to the mangrove islands of **Honda Bay** and the immense flooded cave systems that make up the mind-boggling **Underground River**. Further north you'll find the pretty beach resort town of **Port Barton**, the old fortress town of **Taytay** and the incredibly beautiful islands and lagoons of **El Nido** and the **Bacuit archipelago**. Some areas are still relatively unaffected by tourism, such as the friendly little fishing village of **San Vicente** and nearby **Long Beach**, one of the finest stretches of sand anywhere. Undeveloped **southern Palawan** contains some of the least-visited areas in the whole country, from the remains of a Neolithic community in the **Tabon Caves** and the turtle and cockatoo sanctuaries at **Narra** to **Brooke's Point**, the access point for **Mount Mantalingajan**; off Palawan's southern tip, the island of **Balabac** has, however, seen a recent spike in popularity, though it requires some effort to get to and certainly won't be roping in package groups for some time to come.

The **Calamian group** of islands, scattered off the northern tip of the main island of Palawan, has a deserved reputation for some of the best **scuba diving** in Asia, mostly on sunken World War II wrecks. Even if you're not a diver, there's plenty to do here. The little town of **Coron** on Busuanga is the jumping-off point for trips to mesmerizing **Coron Island**, with its hidden lagoons and volcanic lake and, to the south, the former leper colony of **Culion**.

Note that while most tourist hubs now have ATMs, smaller places such as Sabang and Port Barton do not; even in these tiny towns, card use is quite widespread, but it's still wise to bring some cash for your stay.

ARRIVAL AND DEPARTURE
PALAWAN

By plane There are four airports that you can use to get to Palawan: the one in the island capital of Puerto Princesa is the main hub, though further north there's a tiny one near San Vicente (see page 367), a slightly larger one in El Nido, and one on Busuanga Island (see page 374) in the Calamian chain.

By boat 2GO (⊚ travel.2go.com.ph) operate a ferry between Puerto Princesa, Coron and Manila (1 weekly; 14hr to Coron, 30hr to Manila). There's also a RoRo ferry with Montenegro (☎ 043 740 3201) to Puerto Princesa from Iloilo (4 weekly; 36hr), via Cuyo.

GETTING AROUND

By bus, jeepney and van Services run throughout the main Palawan island. From Puerto Princesa you can travel

THE PUERTO PRINCESA SUBTERRANEAN RIVER NATIONAL PARK

Highlights

❶ Dining out in Puerto Princesa With its top-notch seafood restaurants, this is the best place in Palawan to indulge in the local cuisine. See page 358

❷ Underground River Pass under limestone cliffs and through sepulchral chambers on a boat trip along the world's longest navigable subterranean river – a true wonder of nature. See page 364

❸ Port Barton A laidback and convivial beach town with simple accommodation, rustic nightlife and a pristine bay of reefs and untouched islands. See page 365

❹ Long Beach Enjoy one of the nation's most alluring stretches of bone-white sand – and get there before the developers arrive. See page 367

❺ Bacuit archipelago Explore the majestic limestone islands, beaches and lagoons that stud the bays around El Nido. See page 370

❻ Lake Kayangan Hop on a bangka to a hidden blue lagoon off Coron Island, from where you scramble uphill to this dazzling volcanic lake. See page 377

❼ Scuba diving around Coron Some of the wildest diving in Asia, around sunken Japanese World War II wrecks. See page 378

HIGHLIGHTS ARE MARKED ON THE MAP ON PAGE 354

south to Brooke's Point and Quezon, or north to Sabang, Roxas, San Vincente, Taytay and El Nido. While jeepneys are the cheapest way to travel, they're slow and you have to change often; vans run between all the main tourist hubs and are the most convenient transport for travellers. Lexxus Shuttle (facebook.com/lexusshuttle1025) are reliable van services, though most people simply book through their accommodation.

Puerto Princesa

PUERTO PRINCESA is the only major urban sprawl in Palawan, and its population of just over 250,000 makes up a third of the island's total. Even so, it manages to live up to its name as the "City in the Forest" – a few minutes' wander up any side street will soon find you amid greenery. As Southeast Asia's first carbon-neutral city, it's an eco-friendly capital where the mall is entirely run on solar power and littering can earn you a prison sentence. There are a few sights around Puerto Princesa, as well as a couple of worthwhile ones in the city itself, although most visitors treat it as a one-night stop

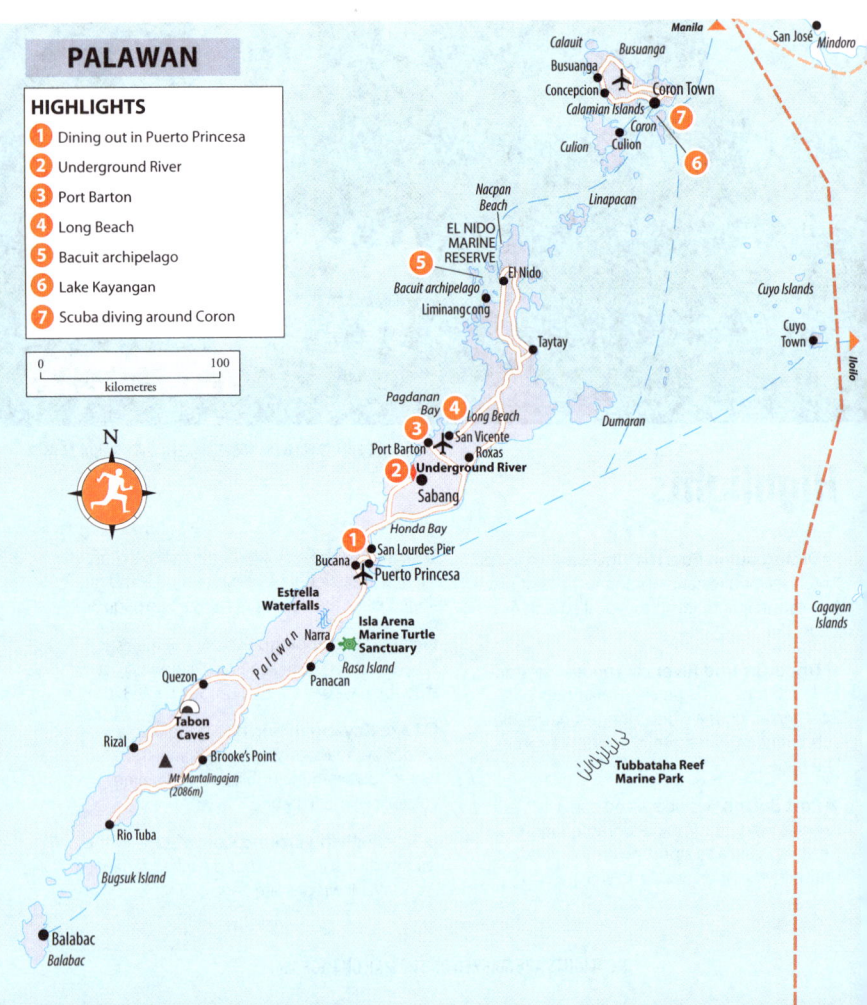

PALAWAN

HIGHLIGHTS

1. Dining out in Puerto Princesa
2. Underground River
3. Port Barton
4. Long Beach
5. Bacuit archipelago
6. Lake Kayangan
7. Scuba diving around Coron

0   100
kilometres

on the way to or from Palawan's beaches and islands. **Rizal Avenue**, the main drag, runs west from the airport 3km through the centre of the city to the ferry port. Just east of the port along the seafront, the lively **Bay Walk** promenade is a popular spot for an evening stroll, with a string of alfresco seafood shacks along the water's edge.

Immaculate Conception Cathedral

Plaza Cuartel, Rizal Ave • Free

At the west end of Rizal Avenue, on **Plaza Cuartel** is the **Immaculate Conception Cathedral**, a pretty white- and blue-painted Neo-Romanesque structure with twin towers. The plaza has a memorial dedicated to the 143 American soldiers who were burnt alive near the city by the retreating Japanese Army during the "Palawan Massacre" of 1944.

Palawan Museum

Mendoza Park, Rizal Ave • Charge

The small **Palawan Museum** offers an overview of the history, art and culture of the region. Most of the exhibits are fossils and old tools but there are, at least, informative English captions. Look out for shells in the biology section and, in the archeological displays, the Neolithic-era Manunggul burial jar.

Palawan Heritage Centre

8

Fernandez St • Charge

A small but reasonably engaging museum that focuses on the Indigenous heritage of Palawan. Exhibits consist largely of pottery and jewellery, punctuated by waxwork models of Indigenous people coupled with informative text. It won't take up much of your time, but if you're at a loose end, it's worth a stop.

ARRIVAL AND DEPARTURE
PUERTO PRINCESA

By plane Puerto Princesa airport is located at the eastern edge of the city on Rizal Ave. A small tourist office (☎048 434 4211) opens to meet flights. Some local hotels will arrange to pick you up for free, or tricycles to the centre are easy to pick up; you can even walk to the centre of town in 20min. Though designated an international airport, at the time of writing no flights from abroad were landing here.

Destinations Angeles (2–3 weekly; 1hr 30min); Cebu (2–3 daily; 1hr 15min); Davao (3 weekly; 1hr 40min); Iloilo City (3 weekly; 1hr 5min); Manila (1–2 hourly; 1hr 20min).

By boat Services to and from Puerto Princesa (see page 352) arrive and depart from the port at the western end of Malvar St, a short walk north of Rizal Ave.

By bus, jeepney and van Most services depart from the San José terminal (also known as "New Market" after the market next door), 7km north of the centre. Tricycles will take you between the city centre and San José; you

can also catch multicabs (a minivan version of a jeepney) and jeepneys from the corner of Rizal Ave and the National Highway (junction 1). Departures to all points north are most frequent in the early mornings; the times quoted here are guidelines only. Vans are typically 25 percent faster than buses and slightly more comfortable, but are also correspondingly more expensive. Booking is a cinch, since most travellers simply reserve a seat through their accommodation, and get picked up there; fees can vary (sometimes your accommodation can ask for less than the bus company would if you went directly), so if you're on a budget, ask around.

Destinations Brooke's Point (4 daily; 5hr); El Nido (10 daily; 6–8hr); Port Barton (6 daily; 3hr); Quezon (hourly; 4hr); Roxas (10 daily; 3hr); Sabang (8 daily; 2hr 30min); San Vicente (2 daily; 5hr); Taytay (10 daily, mornings; 5hr).

GETTING AROUND

Tricycles Tricycles are an easy way of taking short hops within the city, and to the airport and port.

Motorbike rental There are numerous motorbike rental shops near the airport on Rizal Ave, offering scooters

and bigger motorbikes. Kim Rentals (🌐facebook.com/ Palawanrentalseldrive) near the airport is a reputable operator, and will also deliver to your hotel.

PUERTO PRINCESA

● EATING

Badjao Seafront Restaurant	10
Bona's Chao Long Haus	9
Guni Guni Hostel	8
Haim Chicken	7
Itoy's Coffee Haus	5
Ka Joel's	1
Kinabuchs Grill & Bar	4
Namaskar Vegetarian House	6
Painted Table	2
Smoke Shack	3

■ ACCOMMODATION

Balai Princesa	1
Blue Lagoon	7
Canvas Boutique	5
Cleon Villas Pension	2
Dolce Vita	4
Guni Guni Hostel	9
Hibiscus Garden Inn	10
Lokal Hut B&B	8
Palacio	3
Puerto Pension	6

□ DRINKING

Kinabuchs Grill & Bar	2
Palaweño Brewery	3
Tiki Restobar	1

● SHOPPING

SM City	1

TOURS FROM PUERTO PRINCESA

There are several attractions around Puerto Princesa that you can easily visit in a day or less, including **Honda Bay** (see page 362) and the **Underground River** (see page 364), though note that for the latter you need to sort out a permit at least a day in advance (see page 365). Many hotels and agents in the area sell essentially the same tours, taking in the nearest sights by tricycle or in a minivan, or simply packaging tour-agency fare as their own and getting you in the same bus for a mark-up.

Most "city" tours take in the **Palawan Butterfly Eco-Garden and Tribal Village** (daily 8am–5pm; charge), where you can see butterflies, tandikan (small native peacocks), bearcats (a member of the civet family) and leopard geckos, as well as meet some of Palawan's native people; and **Baker's Hill** (daily 7am–8pm; free), a beautiful sculpture-filled garden with an excellent bakery selling *hopia ube*, mooncake-like pastries filled with bright purple *ube* (purple yam). Some tours also visit the **Iwahig Prison and Penal Farm** (daily 8am–7pm; free), an interesting "Prison Without Bars" established in 1904, and the **Crocodile Farm and Nature Park** (daily 8am-5pm; charge), though the welfare of the animals at the latter is a bit suspect for a "conservation centre", and it's probably best avoided. Lastly, night-tours take in the **fireflies** near Bucana, out across the bay.

RECOMMENDED TOUR OPERATORS
Corazon Travel and Tours Junction 1, Rizal Ave, Ⓦtoursbycorazon.com.
Travel Palawan Manalo St, Ⓦtravel-palawan.com.

INFORMATION

8

Tourist office Provincial Capitol Building, Rizal Ave, 1km west of the airport at the junction with the National Highway (Mon–Sat 9am–5pm; ☏048 433 2968).
Underground River permits If you're planning to visit the Underground River independently (see page 365), you can arrange a permit on the spot if you take your passport along to the park office in the City Coliseum, north of the centre via the National Highway at San Pedro (daily 8am–5pm; ☏048 433 4297).

ACCOMMODATION

SEE MAP PAGE 356

Puerto Princesa's many places to **stay** are concentrated on and around Rizal Ave; the most pleasant are towards the eastern end of the strip. Those in the leafy northern suburbs are a tricycle ride from the centre.

CITY CENTRE

Blue Lagoon Purok Malaya Ⓦbluelagoon.com.ph. Close to Rizal Ave, offering clean, comfortable cottages with cable TV and fridge. Staff are friendly and welcoming, and there's a decent restaurant. $\overline{P}$

★ **Canvas Boutique** National Hwy Ⓦcanvas boutiquehotel.com. One of the best and most innovative accommodation options in the city, this modern industrial-style boutique hotel is covered in murals by local artists and offers chic rooms with polished concrete floors and creative touches such as bamboo speakers and colourful lamps. There's also a pool area with plants and sunken seating, and an excellent restaurant (see page 358). $\overline{PPP}$

Dolce Vita 4 Victoria Romasanta St, San Pedro ☏0917 503 2855. This hotel, northeast of the centre, has romantic canopy beds and fancy bathrooms set in two-storey pavilions (cable TV, breakfast and a/c included). There's a decent pool and bar, as well as family rooms and suites. $\overline{PP}$

Guni Guni Hostel Manalo St Ⓦfacebook.com/GuniGuni Hostel. By far the best hostel option in town, a modern-looking place with cosy pine berths, a TV/games room, and an excellent bistro-bar out front. $\overline{P}$

Hibiscus Garden Inn Manalo Extension Ⓦfacebook. com/hibiscusgardeninn. Just south of the airport, with great staff and friendly service, and huge rooms with spotless tiled floors, a/c, cable TV and hot showers. There's also a peaceful garden with hammocks and outdoor tables where breakfast is served. The attached restaurant serves some of the best pizzas in town. Free airport pick-up. $\overline{PPP}$

★ **Lokal Hut B&B** Trinidad Rd, off Rizal Ave. Just set back from the thick of things, there's a lovely out-of-the-way feel at this simple, amiable B&B. Simple a/c rooms surround what's effectively a manicured piece of jungle, which is great for hanging out – and also where you'll enjoy a yummy breakfast. $\overline{PP}$

Puerto Pension 35 Malvar St Ⓦpuertopension.com. Located at the back of the lively Bay Walk promenade, this three-floored nipa-hut-style building is set in a lush tropical garden. The cosy a/c rooms all have mini-fridges and cable TV, and are decorated with local Palaweño artwork. There's also a lovely rooftop restaurant with spectacular bay views, and free use of an outdoor hot tub in the evenings. $\overline{PP}$

NORTH OF THE CENTRE

Balai Princesa Socrates Rd ⓦ balaiprincesa.com. A little north of the centre, Balai Princesa is a quiet and relaxing spot, boasting a spa and a decent café as well as tastefully decorated and comfortable rooms. The outdoor jacuzzi, set beneath an attractive pagoda, is a lovely touch. $\overline{PPP}$

Cleon Villas Pension Pineda Rd ⓦ cleonvillaspension. hotelia.top. Some 2.5km north of town (a 10min tricycle ride), this friendly hotel is housed across a number of villas arranged around a garden area. Its distance from the centre

means it's quiet and peaceful (despite the rather ominous claim on the website that "there's never a dull moment at this hotel"), and its excellent value. $\overline{P}$

★ **Palacio** Puerto Princesa South Rd ⓦ hotelpalacio palawan.com. Often the best bargain in Palawan, this sizeable hotel – set on its lonesome up by the bay – exudes an air of faded grandeur; it's in need of a little polish, but rooms here can be incredibly cheap. Rolling along from the large lobby, head past the pool table to the bay-viewing deck, where you can have a cocktail or so-so meal; steps lead down to the lovely little swimming pool. $\overline{PP}$

EATING SEE MAP PAGE 356

CITY CENTRE

★ **Badjao Seafront Restaurant** Abueg St, Bagong Sikat ⓦ badjaoseafoodrestaurant.shop. Open-air, native-style restaurant with terrific views of the sea. It's reached on foot from Abueg Rd, at the end of Bonifacio St across a dainty bamboo bridge. Highlights include the fresh, tasty grilled seafood such as sizzling squid, and there are also a couple of veggie dishes including stuffed aubergine and breaded okra. If you're here in the evening, getting transport back to the centre can be tricky, so you might want to pay a tricycle driver to wait for the return trip. $\overline{PPPP}$

★ **Bona's Chao Long Haus** Manalo St ☎ 048 434 8420. Extremely popular place specialising in *chao long* soup, a cousin of (and certainly influenced by) Vietnamese *pho*: of the small number of variations on the menu, the spicier beef noodle option is perhaps the best. It makes for a cheap and satisfying lunch, especially if you add a little spice, vinegar and pepper from the table. $\overline{P}$

Guni Guni Hostel Manalo St ⓦ facebook.com/GuniGuni Hostel. The restaurant fronting this hostel (see page 357) is open to all, and about as good a place as you'll find in town for Western fare, including good breakfasts and brunch specials. $\overline{PPP}$

Haim Chicken 294 Manalo Extension ⓦ haimchicken. com. Despite sounding like a fast-food chicken chain, this

family-run restaurant serves quality Filipino dishes. You can dine on mains such as grilled tuna belly, *ginataang ubod ng rattan* (young rattan vine with coconut milk and small fish) and vegetable curry while seated in bamboo huts decorated with vibrant artwork. $\overline{PP}$

Itoy's Coffee Haus Rizal Ave ☎ 048 433 5182. Convivial local café with a huge range of coffee-based drinks. They also have decent desserts, including cassava pudding. $\overline{PP}$

★ **Kinabuchs Grill & Bar** Rizal Ave ⓦ facebook.com/ kinabuchs. The huge and enticing bar and garden at this Filipino restaurant is usually packed. The main attraction is the *tamilok* or "mangrove worms", believed to be an aphrodisiac rich in protein (actually a mollusc that tastes a bit like squid). Equally adventurous and more palatable dishes include Croc à la Bicol Express, with crocodile meat, while the classic Filipino food is also excellent; try the sizzling seafood *sisig* or *sinigang na baboy*, or the delicious *laing* (creamed spinach-like taro leaves with pork, lemongrass, coconut milk, spices and more). $\overline{PP}$

Namaskar Vegetarian House Burgos St ☎ 0918 705 0124. Long-established and popular vegetarian restaurant, offering a wide range of choices for veggies and vegans. Their take on a vegetarian barbecue is excellent. Most dishes involve tofu or meat substitutes. $\overline{PP}$

Painted Table Canvas Boutique Hotel, National Hwy

TUBBATAHA REEF NATURAL PARK

Located in the middle of the Sulu Sea, 181km southeast of Puerto Princesa, **Tubbataha Reef Natural Park** has been inscribed on the UNESCO World Heritage List thanks to its huge number of marine species. Unsurprisingly, it has become a magnet for scuba divers, who reach it on liveaboard boats – most departing from Puerto Princesa between March and June. The reef is one of the finest in the world, with sightings of sharks, manta rays and turtles a daily occurrence. Dive operators in Manila, Puerto Princesa and Coron Town can arrange one-week **liveaboard** trips, which include onboard accommodation and meals, the conservation fee, and up to four dives a day. For details, visit the park office on Manalo Extension in Puerto Princesa (ⓦ tubbatahareefs.org), or take a look at international liveaboard websites (such as ⓦ liveaboard.com).

ⓦ canvasboutiquehotel.com/the-painted-table. This hotel café and restaurant is a stylish, modern place to eat, serving Filipino cuisine alongside popular Western dishes – all quite affordable for an attractive hotel restaurant. Try the soy-fried chicken with Palawan honey glaze or local mussels in a ginger and lemongrass broth. If you're here with a large group, ask to sit at the eponymous brightly coloured painted table. PPP

Smoke Shack Rizal Ave ⓦ facebook.com/smoke shackBBQhouse. Unprepossessing little place that serves up excellent smoked meat barbecue dishes – the pulled pork quesadillas are a particularly good choice. PP

NORTH OF THE CENTRE

★ **Ka Joel's** Abanico Rd ⓦ instagram.com/kajoelsresto. If you're staying anywhere north of central Puerto Princesa, you shouldn't need cajoling to swing by this large, attractive, hugely popular restaurant. The food they serve is a real mix of Philippine and island classics; they're famed for their "cocotopus" (a mix of octopus and coconut milk), though their *kilawin* (ceviche) is a tasty bargain. They've plenty of other meaty and veggie mains, as well as plenty of juices. However, a note to the stinky-footed – footwear has to be set aside on entry, to keep the wooden floorboards nice and clean. PP

DRINKING
SEE MAP PAGE 356

Kinabuchs Grill & Bar Rizal Ave ⓦ facebook.com/ kinabuchs. Probably the best of the restaurants to drink at, especially since cocktails here are as cheap as fruit shakes.
Palaweño Brewery 28 Manalo St ⓦ palawenobrewery. com. The first craft brewery in Palawan, this small bar was set up by two Filipina women, and also offers microbrewery tours. Beers use indigenous flavours from Palawan

(including a couple made with honey from tribal lands in the island's south), and there's a small discount for a tray of four to sample.
Tiki Restobar Jct 1, Rizal Ave ☎ 048 434 1797. This big, busy open-sided bar on the city's main junction is its major venue for live bands. They also serve set meals and seafood dishes.

SHOPPING
SEE MAP PAGE 356

SM City Malvar Rd ⓦ smsupermalls.com. This large mall is a good place to head to for all sorts of potential reasons: if you need some new travel togs, if your mobile phone cable

has broken, if you want some snack food – or if you simply want to walk around in a/c for a little while.

DIRECTORY

Banks and exchange There are stacks of banks with ATMs on Rizal Ave, and elsewhere too.
Hospitals and clinics There are two good hospitals, the Palawan Adventist Medical Center (☎ 048 433 1247) on the National Highway, 4km north of the city centre; and the Provincial Hospital (☎ 048 434 4088), 1km north of the city centre on Malvar St.

Immigration The office on Rizal Ave(Mon–Fri 8am–4.30pm; ☎ 048 433 2248) can easily extend visas on the spot.
Pharmacies Mercury Drug (daily 6am–midnight; ☎ 048 433 3875) on Rizal Ave, opposite Mendoza Park. The branch at the Alicon Building, Malvar St (☎ 048 434 8618) is open 24hr.

Southern Palawan

A journey through southern Palawan represents one of the last great travel challenges in the Philippines. Much of the area is sparsely populated, with limited accommodation and nothing in the way of dependable transport, communications or electricity. The major attractions, south of **Quezon** village, are **Tabon Caves** – among the country's most significant archeological sites. On the east coast, around **Brooke's Point**, there are hardly any buses and few jeepneys, but if you do make it here you'll find unspoilt countryside, quiet barangays and deserted, palm-fringed beaches backed by craggy mountains. Beyond the whole lot lies **Balabac**, an island that has been gaining favour of late with independent travellers.

Narra and around

The small town of **NARRA**, about two hours by bus and 92km south of Puerto Princesa, makes a good introduction to southern Palawan: there are several empty beaches in the area as well as **Rasa Island**, 3km offshore, one of the only places in the wild where you can see the endangered **Philippine cockatoo**. Around 250 of the estimated wild population of only one thousand reside here, although their habitat was threatened in 2013 by plans for a 15MW coal-fired power plant less than 1km from the island; fierce opposition stalled the project, but the plans are by no means dead. The island is a thirty-minute boat trip from the village of Panacan, a short tricycle ride from Narra. Further offshore, the **Isla Arena Marine Turtle Sanctuary** is a major nesting site for green turtles, where the tiny hatchlings are protected before being released into the wild. The main hatching season is between February and April.

Inland, the most rewarding excursion is to the **Estrella Waterfalls**, around 15km from Narra on the road back to Puerto Princesa. The water is wonderfully fresh and pure (you can swim here), and the falls are surrounded by lush jungle inhabited by monkeys.

Tabon Caves and around

It was inside the **Tabon Caves** in 1962 that archeologists discovered a fragment of the skull dubbed "**Tabon Man**", dating back 22,000 years, which made it the oldest-known human relic from the archipelago at the time. Crude tools and evidence of cooking fires going back some fifty thousand years have now been unearthed in the caves, along with fossils and a large quantity of Chinese pottery dating back to the fifth century BC. Most of these artefacts have been transferred to the National Museum in Manila for preservation, though some are on display in the caves. It's still intriguing to wander through the damp caverns and tunnels, which may have been a kind of Neolithic workshop for making stone tools; researchers are still working here and are happy to show visitors the latest finds.

Quezon

The Tabon Caves are accessible from **QUEZON**, a fishing village consisting mainly of wooden houses on stilts, around 150km southwest of Puerto Princesa. Before visiting the caves, stop first at the **National Museum** (Mon–Fri 9am–4pm; free) inland from Quezon wharf for orientation and information. There are actually more than two hundred **caves** in the area, but only 38 have been established to be of archeological and anthropological significance. Of these, only seven are **open** to the public; Tabon is the most interesting. You can visit Tabon independently but it's much better to set up a tour via one of the operators in Puerto Princesa (see box, page 357).

ARRIVAL AND DEPARTURE	TABON CAVES AND AROUND
Tours Hotels and travel agents in Puerto Princesa (see page 357) organize day-trips to the Tabon Caves.	Princesa to Quezon (3–4hr). At Quezon wharf, bangkas can be chartered for the 30min ride to the caves and back.
By bus and bangka You can catch a bus from Puerto	

ACCOMMODATION

Fontera Garden Suites Punta Baja Rd ⓦ fonteragardensuite.wixsite.com/mysite. Out of fairly slim pickings, Fontera Garden Suites is the best accommodation choice in Tabon. Rooms are clean and comfortable, and there's decent food available. P̱

Brooke's Point and Mount Mantalingajan

Deep in the southern half of Palawan, a four- to five-hour drive south of Puerto Princesa, the town of **BROOKE'S POINT** is flanked by the sea on one side and formidable mountains on the other. It was named after eccentric nineteenth-century British adventurer James Brooke, who became the Rajah of Sarawak (now Malaysia) after helping a local chieftain suppress a revolt. From Borneo he travelled north to Palawan, landing at what is now Brooke's Point and building an imposing **watchtower**, the remains of which stand next to a newer **lighthouse**. Today, the main attraction here is the ascent of nearby **Mount Mantalingajan** (2086m), Palawan's highest peak. It's a seriously tough climb, which can take up to a week, so make sure you come well prepared; there's no equipment for rent locally. The usual route actually starts on the west coast from the barangay of Ransang near **RIZAL** (6hr from Princesa by Charing Bus Lines). Enquire at Rizal town hall, staff at which can help to arrange a guide and porter, or give the Puerto Princesa tour agencies a go.

ACCOMMODATION   BROOKE'S POINT AND MOUNT MANTALINGAJAN

Maruyog's Ridge Brooke's Point ☎0905 390 0944. The rooms here are nothing fancy, but if you find yourself in need of accommodation in Brooke's Point you could do much worse. There's a good restaurant and bar on-site, which is handy as it's a bit of a walk to the town centre. P̄

Balabac and around

Beyond the main island's sourthern tip lies a small archipelago, of which beautiful Balabac is the largest island. Almost unexplored by foreign travellers until a recent social media-driven mini-surge, it is now making a modest name for itself among independent travellers; plans are in place to make this a kind of southern El Nido, and though this still seems a little fanciful, for now Balabac still feels like one of those well-kept secrets.

Such development would rob this island of what currently constitutes its main draw – a sense of remoteness and an ability to disconnect, the latter somewhat simplified by the fact that Balabac is, itself, totally disconnected from the national electricity grid. Some places do have solar panels (so you may be able to charge your phone from time to time), though mobile coverage is patchy at best (so you may not be able to do much with that phone other than take photos). Toilets tend to be of the bucket-flush variety, and most "beds" are in tents; needless to say, you should probably bring as much cash here as you think you'll need.

ARRIVAL AND DEPARTURE   BALABAC AND AROUND

By van and bangka The long, arduous journey to Balabac, for most, starts with an insanely early departure from Puerto Princesa, from which it's a 6hr minivan ride down to Rio Tuba (including a break or two). From here, it's a boat ride to Balabac, and usually this means a little island-hopping on the way. Some travellers opt to break up a long day by taking a regular bus down to Rio Tuba, staying the night, and then taking the boat the next day – not such a bad idea, if you value your sleep.

Tours Hotels and travel agents in Puerto Princesa (see page 357) can get you to Balabac, as can all of the accommodation options listed here.

ACCOMMODATION

Balabac Eco Resort Balabac ⌨balabacecoresort.com. Simple A-frame huts, and a few dome-tents. Toilet and shower facilities are all shared, but they're some of the better ones you'll find in the archipelago; the huts and tents, however, are not in such great condition, and you'll have to make your own entertainment of an evening. Including transfers, it's one of the more expensive options, but they use speedboats instead of slower vessels, which for some is worth the extra expense. P̄P̄

Tatak Balabac Beach Came Bancalan Island ⌨instagram.com/tatak_balabac. Without doubt the best-looking camp on the archipelago, with creature comforts like nice sinks (gasp!) and cushions (double gasp!). The food's good, too, but the experience doesn't feel as seamless as with other places – you'll have to work harder to get here, but many find it worth such endeavour. P̄P̄

★ **Wanderwalkers** Bugsuk Island ⌨balabac.ph. Officially known as "Sibaring Island Camp", most visitors know this places as Wanderwalkers, since it's where the agency of that name sets down its groups. Accommodation is in A-frame huts, which are kept in good nick, and there are hammocks to lie in while you're not busy island-hopping. P̄P̄

Northern Palawan

Most visitors to Palawan focus their time in **northern Palawan**, a wild, mountainous land that crumbles into the mesmerizing islands of the Calamian chain (see page

373). Two hours north of Puerto Princesa, the UNESCO World Heritage-listed **Underground River** meanders past a bewildering array of stalactites, stalagmites, caverns, chambers and pools. From here, **Port Barton** makes for a soothing stopover on the journey north to **El Nido**, with a wide range of accommodation options and enticing snorkelling spots in the bay. El Nido town itself is a little chaotic, but occupies a very scenic spot and is the gateway to the clear waters and jungle-smothered limestone islands of the **Bacuit archipelago**.

Honda Bay

Picturesque **Honda Bay**, 10km north of Puerto Princesa, is a shallow, lagoon-like expanse of water, backed by the spectacular range of mountains on the main island. The bay contains seven low-lying **islands**, most of them little more than sandbars fringed by mangrove swamp and small beds of coral – perfect for a day of island-hopping, lounging and snorkelling. Note that Snake Island, formerly one of the most popular visitor destinations, has been sold to a private owner and is now off limits.

To snorkel at the lush **Pambato Reef**, the best place in Honda Bay for coral and giant clams, you can join a tour from Puerto Princesa (see box page 357); boats moor up at a floating pier with a giant turtle-shaped roof. Some trips take in the swanky **Dos Palmas resort on Arreceffi Island**, where the day-guest rate will usually be included in the price of your tour.

Luli Island

A laidback stop in Honda Bay, **Luli Island** sinks and rises with the tide and is sometimes almost completely covered by water. At low tide it has a beautiful beach, where locals create imaginative sand sculptures. There is also a large area where operators often encourage the rather dubious practice of fish feeding. Although you may see visitors taking part, it's not advisable, and is in fact banned on the reef itself.

Cowrie Island

As the main lunch stop for tours of Honda Bay, **Cowrie Island** has a number of thatched cabanas, as well as a fine sandy beach – great for swimming and sunbathing, but not so much for snorkelling, as it's not close to the reef. This island provides a welcome rest during a tiring day of swimming.

Starfish Island

Starfish Island is a sandbar backed by mangroves named after the abundant **horned sea star** (starfish) that carpet much of the inner shallows here. The island has some fine snorkelling towards the northern end, but it's not advisable as the water is so shallow that it's difficult to avoid touching the coral, causing damage to it and yourself. As a result, lots of tour operators no longer stop here.

Isla Pandan

Isla Pandan offers expensive beach huts, umbrellas, table and chair sets and massages – along with everything from paddleboards to buckets and spades. Simple seafood meals are also available from local vendors.

ARRIVAL AND INFORMATION   HONDA BAY

Organized tours Corazon Travel and Tour in Puerto Princesa (see page 357) offer Honda Bay tours for a set fee, including pick-up and drop-off at local hotels, transport to the San Lourdes pier, stops at three islands (usually Luli, Cowrie and Pandan) and a buffet lunch. While this is convenient, you can save money if you're in a large group by arranging tours independently (see below); on the other hand, most accommodation options in and around Puerto Princesa will get you on a Honda Bay tour, either of their own or with an affiliated agency.

By boat Outrigger bangkas tour Honda Bay from the San Lourdes pier, 11km north of Princesa. Boats are rented by the day (there's also a terminal fee to pay), and it's usual to make just three stops, plus Pambato Reef, but you can specify which islands you want to visit. You can rent masks, fins and booties (reef shoes), and it's good to tip your boatmen if they've looked after you well. To get to the pier, the departure point for which is signposted around 1km off the National Highway, hotels can arrange minivans or tricycles, which comes with the convenience of return transport guaranteed. It's cheaper to grab a tricycle on the street, though you might have to wait a while to get one heading back.

Island fees There are fees payable to visit Luli Island, Cowrie Island, Pambato Reef, *Dos Palmas* resort (if and when it reopens), Starfish Island and Isla Pandan.

ACCOMMODATION AND EATING

Astoria Palawan Km62, North National Hwy ⌨ astoria palawan. The swankiest accommodation in the area, a family-friendly spot with large rooms and plenty of pools, water-slides and the like, as well as good places to eat and drink. The only drawback is that it feels a little out on its own, though the adventurous may enjoy the village-style life on offer immediately outside the compound walls. $\overline{\text{PPP}}$

★ **A Touch of Pink** Salvacion ⌨ facebook.com/puerto princesapalawanph. A really, really cute little place, though a "touch" of pink might be understating things somewhat – the cushions, the pillows, the lights around the pool table, the microphone heads on the in-house karaoke system (which is itself a great idea), the basketball ring above the swimming pool (which is also a great idea, especially after a drink or two)... everything's pink or pink-fringed, and the pool itself sometimes glows pink in the evening. The rooms are comfortable, and the atmosphere cordial – a great find. $\overline{\text{PP}}$

Viet Ville 13 Santa Lourdes ⌨ facebook.com/VietVille Restaurant. Located on the way from Puerto Princesa up to Honda Bay, this traditional Vietnamese restaurant is one of the few that remain near the city, situated in a former refugee village created when many fled here in the 1970s and 1980s. The menu includes *chao long* (Palawan's answer to Vietnamese *pho*), and delights such as shrimp in tamarind sauce. A few veggie dishes are also available. $\overline{\text{PP}}$

Sabang

The jumping-off point for the Underground River is **SABANG**, a small village and laidback beach resort some 78km and two hours north of Puerto Princesa by road. The Underground River aside, Sabang's main appeal is its lovely white, palm-fringed sand **beach** facing St Paul's Bay. Many people just come here for the day to see the Underground River, but it's well worth staying for a couple of nights. As well as sunbathing and swimming (pay attention to the flags, though, as currents can be strong), there's an 800m **zipline** at the far eastern end of the beach, and the promise of **jungle trekking** (see page 363). You could also simply settle down in one of the numerous **massage shacks** dotted along the beach.

ARRIVAL AND INFORMATION   SABANG

By bus, jeepney and van There are daily morning buses to Sabang (2–3hr) from the San José terminal near Puerto Princesa. Most visitors, however, either come on rented wheels, or else catch one of the daily vans from Puerto Princesa – your accommodation can book a seat for you, and you'll be picked up from your door. You can also catch a jeepney to the junction at Salvacion (4 daily; 1hr) and change there. For Port Barton, there are similar "tourist" vans to those from Puerto Princesa (4 daily; 3hr 30min). You can buy van seats in advance at the stand near the wharf.

By boat There were once unscheduled bangkas doing the Sabang–Port Barton route, though the authorities have clamped down on this practice.

Information and tours There are a number of tour companies along the beachfront. All can assist with everything from bangkas and buses to motorbike rental, as well as Underground River permits and Port Barton boats. They can also help arrange a host of local activities from ATV rides and jungle trekking to mangrove boat rides.

ACCOMMODATION

Most places to **stay** on Sabang are aimed at backpackers, with cold showers and electricity cuts fairly common, though things continue to improve.

Dabdab Tourist Inn ⌨ 0949 469 9421. Pleasant little place near the beach, with extremely imaginatively decorated rooms – one has been painted with a psychedelic image of the cosmos, while another boasts bright and bold rainbow stripes. There's a small terrace and garden to relax in. $\overline{\text{PP}}$

★ **Daluyon Beach and Mountain Resort** ⌨ daluyon beachandmountainresort.com. Tucked away at the eastern end of the beach, these attractive two-storey cottages have thatched roofs and luxurious rooms that open out to the sea. There's an attractive pool, 24hr power and a restaurant and bar (see page 364). **PPP**

Four Points by Sheraton ⓦ marriott.com. Ultra-posh (and expensive) hotel, right in the middle of the beach, with well-designed, modern rooms, a huge pool, a good fitness centre and a host of extras, plus a good restaurant (see below). Pick-ups from Princesa available. **PPPP**

Hill Myna Beach Resort ⓦ facebook.com/hillmyna puertoprincesa. A popular choice, with private nipa huts right on the beachfront. All have a fan, mosquito nets and charming wooden balcony. There's also an attached restaurant

serving grilled fish, sandwiches, pastas and meat dishes. **PP**

Ocean Green Eco Resort Almost halfway to Sabang from the highway turn-off ⓦ oceangreepalawan. com. Something a bit different, and not in Sabang at all, but on the way here from Puerto Princesa. Though it's a bit inconveniently located if you're intending to race around seeing stuff, this eco resort makes a great choice for those who just want to kick back and enjoy some calm – from their little infinity pool, you've a great view of trees, sea, sky and little else. Accommodation is in bamboo huts (sturdy, but don't bring food in unless you want plenty of insect lodgers). **PP**

EATING AND DRINKING

Evolution Four Points by Sheraton ⓦ marriott.com. A decent range of local and international dishes served at tables looking over the beach. The native chicken *tinola* (with green papaya, chilli and pepper) is good. This is also the best place in Sabang for a coffee. **PPPP**

Pawikan Restaurant Daluyon Beach Resort ⓦ daluyon beachandmountainresort.com. This refined resort

restaurant makes for a quiet evening, with frozen margaritas, pizza and pasta and excellent Filipino dishes on offer. **PPPP**

Wegers La Casa Daluyon Beach Resort. The most popular place to eat in Sabang, thanks to a friendly welcome, and a wide-ranging menu featuring everything from seafood to grilled fare, via *sisig*, noodle dishes and German bratwurst. **PPP**

DRINKING

Sunken Pool Bar Daluyon Beach Resort ⓦ daluyon beachandmountainresort.com. Resort bar by the pool,

which prides itself on using Filipino ingredients wherever possible in its cocktails – reason enough to swing by.

The Underground River

Recognized by UNESCO as a World Heritage Site and voted as one of the "new Seven Wonders of Nature" in 2012, the **Underground River**, officially **Puerto Princesa Subterranean River National Park**, is a unique underwater river system that cuts through the limestone hills for 8.2km before emptying out into the South China Sea. The **caves** are completely natural and unlit, ranging from low-lying passages to vast, cathedral-like caverns. Because of the site's popularity and fragile ecosystem, visitor numbers are restricted to a daily quota of nine hundred visitors, which is reached every day during peak season (Nov–May); make sure you book your visit ahead of time.

Visiting the Underground River
Charge

After sorting out your permit (see page 365), you take a twenty-minute bangka from Sabang to the next bay along. Languid **monitor lizards** often congregate near the rangers' hut here, while macaque monkeys hang out in the trees, looking to grab any loose snacks – don't feed them (or the lizards). After showing your pass and getting your audioguide at the rangers' hut, you take a 150m hike through the forest to the river mouth, where boats depart. The audioguide commentary gives the low-down on the history and ecology of the caves, as well as singling out interesting rock formations inside, including the 62m high "**Cathedral**", a vast chamber that soars into the darkness and contains stalactites that resemble Mary, Jesus and friends; there's also one named "Sharon Stone" for the actress's infamous pose in the movie *Basic Instinct*. There are also more than four thousand bats living in the caves and numerous swallows.

Visitors get to see just 1.5km of the caves on the regular 45-minute tours; you can travel up to 4.3km into the system, but you'll need to arrange a special permit at least three days in advance. Afterwards, if you're feeling energetic, you can hike back from the mouth of the river to Sabang, a 5km trip through lush scenery, though this is steep and sometimes slippery, especially after rain.

| ARRIVAL AND INFORMATION | THE UNDERGROUND RIVER |

Permits Permits can be arranged at the park office in the City Coliseum in San Pedro, Puerto Princesa (☎ 048 433 4297; see page 357), at least one day in advance. It's best to secure a permit for 8am–9am (before the day-trippers arrive), but even if you're issued a different time you can just turn up at the wharf, show your permit and pay the terminal fee – they'll probably put you on the next boat that has space. If you haven't pre-organized a permit in Puerto Princesa, local agents in Sabang can make the necessary arrangements the day before you want to go. If you join an organized tour (see page 357), permits will be arranged for you.

By boat Your permit will specify the time you need to report to Sabang wharf for the 20min bangka ride to the cave.

By van Renting a whole van for a day-trip to the Underground River is a plausible but relatively pricey option.

Tours Day-tours (see page 357) from Puerto Princesa to the Underground River include all fees, permits and a basic lunch buffet. If you want to stay on in Sabang they'll drop you off after the tour.

Port Barton and around

On the northwest coast of Palawan, roughly halfway between Puerto Princesa and El Nido, **PORT BARTON** is far less developed than its busier neighbours, and more peaceful, too. The streets are still mostly dirt tracks (though new segments get a concrete makeover each year), there are no day-trippers, and the rhythms of Filipino life continue alongside the groups of backpackers lounging around in the increasing number of budget beach hotels. The hotels face crescent-shaped **Pagdanan Bay**, with its magical sunset views. **Port Barton Beach** itself, a gorgeous strip of sugary sand, is great for sunset strolls, but less great for swimming thanks to the presence of box jellyfish – locals tend to know when it's safer to get in (any time you see a load of schoolchildren in the water, it's probably safe), but many of them also bear distinctively tentacle-shaped scars.

Minutes away, however are safer waters surrounding fourteen pristine white-sand islands, and a number of top-notch dive and snorkelling sites in **Port Barton Marine Park**; you'll have to pay an environmental fee if headed out this way, and take it with you on subsequent tours too.

Pagdanan Bay

You can rent a bangka from Port Barton for a day of island-hopping in **Pagdanan Bay**, aka Port Barton Marine Park. Popular targets include the spectacular coral at **Twin Reef** and **Aquarium Reef** (both a few minutes' ride from Port Barton); the former in particular offers vast banks of hard coral, including plenty of spiny staghorn, and hordes of tropical fish. There are also certain places where you can spot sea turtles. The bay islands themselves are traditional desert island types where you can swim or just chill out. Most trips take in the beach at **Exotic Island**, which has the odd monkey and a number of thatched beach huts for relaxing. You can wade across the narrow sandbar to **Albaguen Island**, which also has accommodation. Most tours stop for lunch at lush **Paradise Island**.

| ARRIVAL AND DEPARTURE | PORT BARTON AND AROUND |

By bus, jeepney and van From Puerto Princesa you can take a minivan to Port Barton (6 daily; 3hr); book via your accommodation and you'll probably be picked up at the door. There are also similar minivans from Sabang (2 daily; 3hr 30min) and El Nido (3 daily; 4hr). Alternatively, take the daily bus (3hr 30min) from the San José terminal (see page 355) in Puerto Princesa. The last 22km from the turn-off near Roxas (from which you could, at a push, charter a motorbike or tricycle) is pretty bumpy whichever method of transport you take; all buses and vans arrive in Port Barton at a small station near the top of town, close enough to the beach and the town centre.

By boat By far the most appealing way to reach Port Barton is by boat. Bangkas are no longer allowed to do the Sabang–Port Barton route, after a few notable sinkings, though some run to and from San Vicente in the mornings (often connected to flights schedules from its airport), or you can charter one at any time of day.

TOURS AND ACTIVITIES

Boat tours Any agency in town can get you on group tours to the islands in Pagdanan Bay, and your accommodation will almost certainly be able to do likewise.

Massage There are plenty of places for a massage, both at the resorts and along the beach.

Scuba diving Sunset Divers Palawan (⊕ diveportbarton.com), inconveniently located up near the bus station, offer three-dive trips, PADI courses and the like.

ACCOMMODATION

Buses and boats arriving in Port Barton are met by staff from any number of **hotels**; take a look before making a choice. High season runs from mid-November to May – you'll get much cheaper deals outside this period.

PORT BARTON, SEE MAP PAGE 366

Aquarius Rizal St ⊕ aquariusportbarton.com. You'll find homely and comfortable rooms in this friendly hotel, just a few minutes' walk from the beach. Breakfast is good, and evening meals are available, and if you're looking for something to do in the daytime, there are kayaks for hire. P̄P̄

Ausan Beach Front Cottages Beachfront ⊕ ausanbeachfront.com. This place has cottages and basic nipa huts, some with colourful murals on the walls and balconies. The treehouse room is particularly popular. P̄P̄

CocoRico Hostel Rizal St ⊕ instagram.com/cocoricohostels. Palawan's most popular hostel – not so much thanks to its rooms (which are fine), but to its status as the town centre's nightlife spot of choice (see opposite). P̄

★**Ferranco Tourist Inn** Lona St ⊕ 0918 693 7198. An excellent budget choice, since a range of rooms – the cheapest have no a/c – upstairs in the main building, and on two levels out back. A simple breakfast awaits guests in the morning, and coffee (of the granulated kind) and tea are available through the day. P̄

★**Greenviews Resort** Beachfront ⊕ palawandg.clara.net. At the far northern end of the beach, offering spotless nipa huts with fans and bathrooms (cold showers only) within a lush garden that attracts giant birdwing butterflies, sunbirds and the odd monitor lizard. The owners are extremely helpful, and give great advice for onward travel. They also have a separate outdoor bar area (away from the cottages) with occasional live bands. P̄P̄

Holiday Suites Rizal St ⊕ portbarton.holidaysuites.ph. Although it's overpriced, for sure, this makes for one of the most comfortable stays in town. Rooms – which are pretty, if a little small – lead on to a popular pool area, which sees a breakfast spread laid out every morning, and live music (of a more refined and calming ilk to that of most resorts

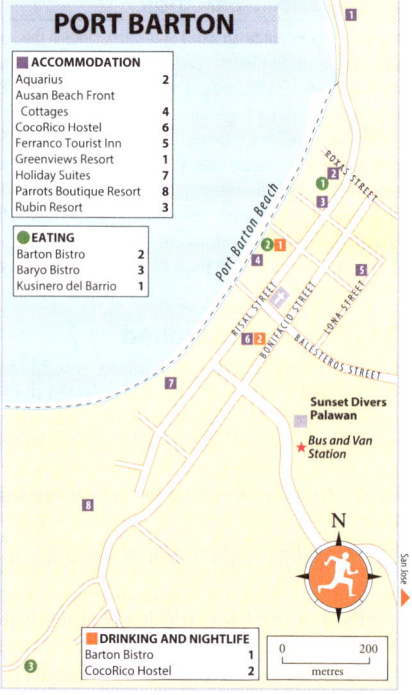

PORT BARTON

ACCOMMODATION	
Aquarius	2
Ausan Beach Front Cottages	4
CocoRico Hostel	6
Ferranco Tourist Inn	5
Greenviews Resort	1
Holiday Suites	7
Parrots Boutique Resort	8
Rubin Resort	3

EATING	
Barton Bistro	2
Baryo Bistro	3
Kusinero del Barrio	1

Sunset Divers Palawan

★ **Bus and Van Station**

N

DRINKING AND NIGHTLIFE	
Barton Bistro	1
CocoRico Hostel	2

0   200
metres

hereabouts) in the evenings. P̄P̄P̄

Parrots Boutique Resort Bonifacio St ⊕ parrots portbarton.com. A short walk from the beach, Parrots is a friendly and welcoming hotel with gorgeously quirky architecture – there are few right angles here, just flowing corners and curves in a creamy-white colour scheme. There's a pool in the courtyard, and the home-cooked food is excellent. P̄P̄P̄

Rubin Resort Rizal St ⊕ rubin-resort.com. Simple and clean – if perhaps a tad overpriced – rooms in villas set around a garden area with a pool. There's a bar on-site, and the friendly staff can help with arranging tours and activities around Port Barton. P̄P̄P̄

PAGDANAN BAY ISLANDS

Coconut Garden Island Resort Cacnipa Island ⊕ coconutgardenislandresort.com. Wonderfully remote spot with attractive A-frame huts and cheaper rooms in a block at the back. It's a lovely place to while away the days, but there are also a host of activities on offer from volleyball to kayaking. The resort can arrange bangka pick-up from Port Barton or San Vicente for an extra charge. Limited wi-fi. P̄P̄

EATING

Most of the **restaurants** in Port Barton are at the resorts,

SEE MAP PAGE 366

but independent places – so few in number until recently –

are starting to proliferate.

★ **Barton Bistro** Beachfront ⓦ facebook.com/Barton Bistro. The undisputed king of the beach strip, even though most places have similar offerings – here they're done well, and they take card, plus there are some quirkier bonus dishes such as beer-battered fish tacos (which are really good, and quite filling), pulled pork sliders, crispy chips, and even good gelato. The coffee is also excellent, and it's no wonder that the beach bean bags most customers use for seating are full through the day, and into evening – just watch everyone run like mad for the covered upstairs terrace when it starts to rain. PPP

Baryo Bistro Uphill at the southern edge of town

☎ 0912 360 0433. If you fancy a little hike before your meal, head on out to this place on the very periphery of town. Fish curry, laksa and adobo chicken are the standouts, but there's more besides, and the views out over the surrounding countryside are just stupendous. PP

Kusinero del Barrio Rizal St ☎ 0920 152 4301. Good Filipino standards (as evidenced by the fact that there are often more locals than tourists here) in a pretty setting, as well as a somewhat unexpected but not unwelcome sideline in French-style crepes. There are a couple of decent vegetarian choices on the menu too, but the standout dish may actually be the *chao long* (Palawan's answer to Vietnamese pho), which is fantastic. PP

DRINKING

SEE MAP PAGE 366

Nightlife is not a major part of Port Barton's appeal – bar a couple of notable spots, everything tends to shut down by 10pm, even on the beach, though even this stands in stark contrast to the pre-Covid years, when there was only one bar in town. All in all, this is one of those places where you may choose to grab a tiny bottle of local rum from a shop, find someone to cut you open a coconut, and saunter down to the beach to pour one into the other, and then the resulting mix into yourself, looking out at the sea.

Barton Bistro Beachfront ⓦ facebook.com/Barton Bistro. This excellent restaurant also makes a good place to

drink – most of ites tables end up sporting umpteen beer bottles or cocktail glasses, in any case.

★ **CocoRico Hostel** Rizal St ⓦ instagram.com/cocorico hostels. Each evening, vehicle after vehicle arrives to disgorge young folk into this hostel; some are staying here, and others are simply coming along to join the party. They have cheap drinks, and live music most nights; bands appear to have been instructed only to play songs that stand a chance of turning into a mass singalong (which happens with pleasing regularity). Great fun.

San Vicente

About 15km north of Port Barton is the sleepy fishing village of **SAN VICENTE**, accessible by bangka or a bone-shaking jeepney ride from Princesa. It has a small market, a petrol station and a couple of snack stalls but little else; it does offer an alternative to taking longer bangka rides between Port Barton and El Nido however, as it has road links to the north coast and Taytay.

The only reason to linger around here is **Long Beach**, a so-far undeveloped 14km stretch of sand south of town that ranks as one of the most extraordinary beaches in the country – you can see both ends only on a brilliantly clear day. Enjoy its unspoilt feel while you can, as the opening of an airport here in 2017 has already prompted the development of large resorts, and it is only a matter of time before the beach is "discovered" by package tours.

ARRIVAL AND DEPARTURE

SAN VICENTE

By plane San Vicente airport, about 3km east of town, offers no facilities whatsoever; there have, in the past, been flights to Manila and Puerto Princesa, though at the time of writing your only choice was Cebu (3 weekly; 1hr 45min) with Cebgo.

By bus, van and jeepney From Princesa there are buses (4–5hr) and vans (4 daily). For moving on, you can either wait for a bus or van, or locals should be able to rustle up a

driver; it's a rough and bumpy 2hr 30min ride to Taytay (only the main highway between Roxas and Taytay is surfaced).

By boat A bangka leaves for Port Barton at 8am, otherwise you can charter a boat for the 45min journey.

By motorcycle To get to Long Beach, you will need to catch a lift on a motorcycle from San Vicente's market, near the pier.

ACCOMMODATION

Foxy's Beach Resort ⓦ facebook.com/foxysbeach resort. A resort, yes, but a very small one. Some of their rooms are on the wee side, too, though others are quite

palatial; the swimming pool is something to behold, and the beach is mere steps away. PPP

Picardal Lodge ⓦ facebook.com/picardallodge. A

8

short walk from the pier, this simple, friendly place has half-decent rooms and cottages set amid greenery. They can assist with island-hopping. Wi-fi is limited to common areas. $\overline{PP}$

Taytay

On the northeast coast of Palawan, about 140km north of Port Barton by road and 50km south of El Nido, the quaint and friendly town of **TAYTAY** ("tie-tie") was capital of Palawan from the earliest days of Spanish conquest in the seventeenth century until Princesa assumed the role in 1903. Today there's little to show of this history save the impressive **Fuerza de Santa Isabel** (daily 9am–5pm; charge), the squat stone fortress built by the Spanish between 1667 and 1738. As with many places in Palawan, the main attractions lie **offshore** – you can tour the wonderfully untouched islands in the bay by chartering a bangka for the day from the harbour. **Elephant Island** is best known for its hidden lagoon: it's a wonderful place to swim, with a natural skylight in the rock which acts like a roof.

ARRIVAL AND INFORMATION TAYTAY

By bus, van and jeepney All transport from Puerto Princesa and El Nido will drop you at the bus terminal on the edge of town; tricycles should shuttle you to the harbour for tours of the bay.

Services There are a couple of banks in Taytay, but neither have ATMs – if you need money, you may be able to get a cash advance with your credit card at Palawan Bank in an emergency, or head up to El Nido.

ACCOMMODATION AND EATING

TAYTAY TOWN

Casa Rosa ☎ 0920 895 0092. Pleasant little resort on a hill behind the town hall, with clean, good-value rooms plus cottages set in attractive gardens. The excellent café offers spectacular fort and ocean views and serves delicious home-cooked pizzas, fish and grilled chicken, as well as sandwiches. They can also offer tours including kayaking, dolphin-watching, birdwatching and waterfall trips. $\overline{PP}$

Pem's Pension House and Restaurant Rizal St ☎ 0917 158 3916. Located near the fort, and offering single rooms with a shared bathroom, plus charming wooden cottages with private bathrooms, either with fan or a/c. $\overline{P}$

TAYTAY BAY ISLANDS

Apulit Island Resort Apulit Island ⓦ elnidoresorts. com. Run by *El Nido Resorts*, this swish hideaway is close to Taytay town and offers accommodation in luxury cottages built on stilts over the water; you can spot baby sharks from your balcony. The resort has various bars and restaurants, including a lovely little bar high on a rocky cliff at the back of the beach, reached by 109 steps. $\overline{PPPP}$

★ Flower Island Resort Flower Island ⓦ flower islandresort.com. This idyllic, eco-friendly, all-inclusive resort features romantic and attractively furnished nipa huts scattered along the shore, equipped with bathrooms, fans (some have a/c) and verandas with hammocks. The restaurant serves buffet meals. $\overline{PPPP}$

El Nido and the Bacuit archipelago

With its scruffy beach, narrow, tricycle-choked streets and unplanned rows of concrete hotels, the small but booming resort town of **EL NIDO**, in the far northwest of Palawan, comes as quite a surprise for somewhere that's marketed as paradise. But though the town makes a poor first impression, El Nido's **surroundings** are jaw-dropping, hemmed in between spectacular jagged cliffs and an iridescent bay littered with jungle-smothered limestone outcrops. One of the most popular tourist hubs in Palawan, El Nido is becoming increasingly crowded and expensive. You can still find good-value options compared to some other places in the Philippines, but many visitors are now looking to the nearby beaches of **Corong-Corong** and **Caalan** to escape the noise and crowds of El Nido.

The town is the departure point for trips to the mesmerizing **Bacuit archipelago**, where the **El Nido marine sanctuary** is the largest such reserve in the Philippines. The archipelago's striking beauty has not gone unnoticed by developers, who have established a number of **exclusive resorts** on some of the islands. Rates for this taste of

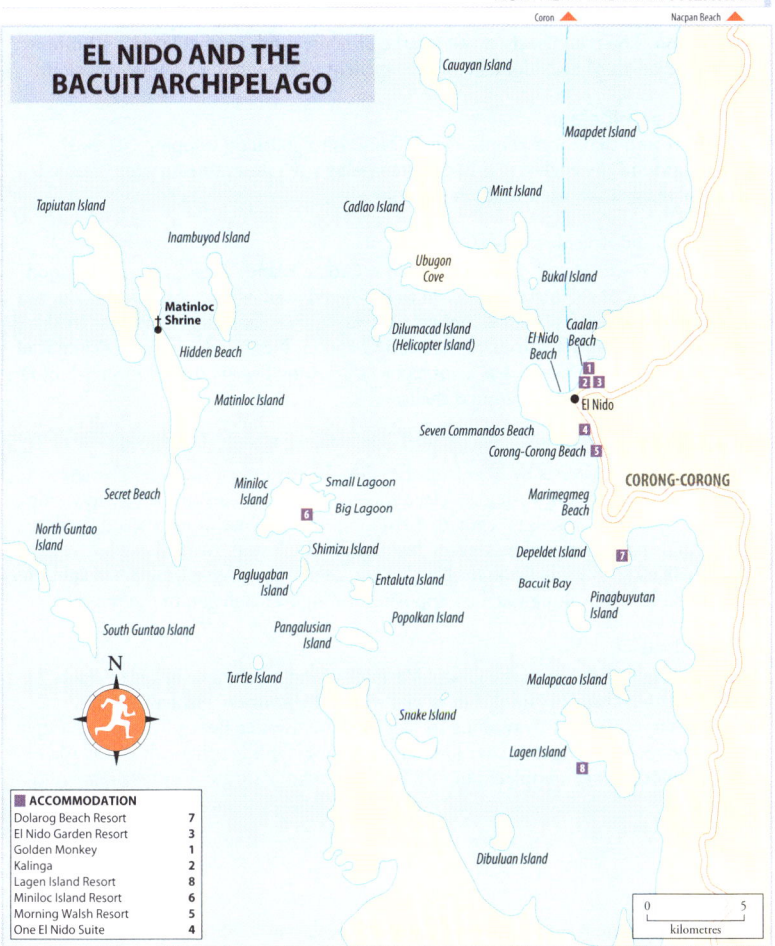

EL NIDO AND THE
BACUIT ARCHIPELAGO

ACCOMMODATION

Dolarog Beach Resort	7
El Nido Garden Resort	3
Golden Monkey	1
Kalinga	2
Lagen Island Resort	8
Miniloc Island Resort	6
Morning Walsh Resort	5
One El Nido Suite	4

paradise are high, though, so the budget-conscious may wish to stay on the mainland and island-hop by day. Note that El Nido has 24hr electricity, although blackouts (or brown-outs, as locals call them) are still common.

El Nido Taraw Via Ferrata

Brgy Maligaya Zone 1 • Charge; tickets are sold from the office at the start of the climb • ☎ 0977 171 4960

Don't miss the climb to the top of the marble cliffs of **Mount Taraw**, the ridge that backs the town, via the **El Nido Taraw Via Ferrata** canopy walk. It's a strenuous haul, via a series of rope bridges and metal staircases (a harness keeps you hooked to the metal guide ropes), but the views are magnificent. A guide is mandatory.

El Nido beaches

The El Nido bayfront has ravishing views, but the **beach** itself is average and not especially attractive for swimming thanks to the heavy bangka traffic. **Caalan** or **Corong-Corong**, just a short walk north and south of town respectively, are much quieter, although still not great for swimming – Caalan is full of rocks and coral. A better option is **Nacpan Beach**, a vast swathe of white sand, reachable via a 40-minute tricycle ride north of El Nido; take insect repellent as the sandflies can be voracious.

The Bacuit archipelago

The main reason that most people visit El Nido is to go **island-hopping** (see box opposite) around the enchanting **Bacuit archipelago**, 45 limestone outcrops riddled with karst cliffs, sinkholes and idyllic lagoons.

Cadlao Island and Helicopter Island

The dramatic tower of rock just off El Nido is **Cadlao Island**. The star here is **Ubugon Cove** at the back of the island, hemmed in by jagged rock, where you can snorkel, but this is also one of the few islands that you can explore on land, too: one-hour trekking tours take in the unusual saltwater Makaamo Lagoon. Near Cadlao Island, **Dilumacad Island** (aka **Helicopter Island**) has a gorgeous 300m-long beach covered in shards of rare blue coral and lots of multicoloured shells.

Miniloc Island

Miniloc Island, 45 minutes by boat from El Nido, boasts one of the area's greatest treasures, the **Big Lagoon**, with glass-clear aquamarine water surrounded by towering limestone cliffs that look like a cathedral rising up from below. Tours aboard small bangkas take a spin around the lagoon, but usually don't stop, while those on larger bangkas will have to wade through. Nearby, the similarly awe-inspiring **Small Lagoon** is only accessible by kayaking (see box opposite) through a small gap in the rocks.

Matinloc Island

One of the largest islands in the group, **Matinloc Island** takes a bit longer to reach (around an hour from El Nido), but is well worth the journey, and has several intriguing targets tucked away along its jagged shore. **Hidden Beach** lies around a tight bend in the rocks, a gorgeous cove hidden from view. On the other side of the island is the **Matinloc Shrine**, completed in 1993 – this Catholic shrine is usually quiet and

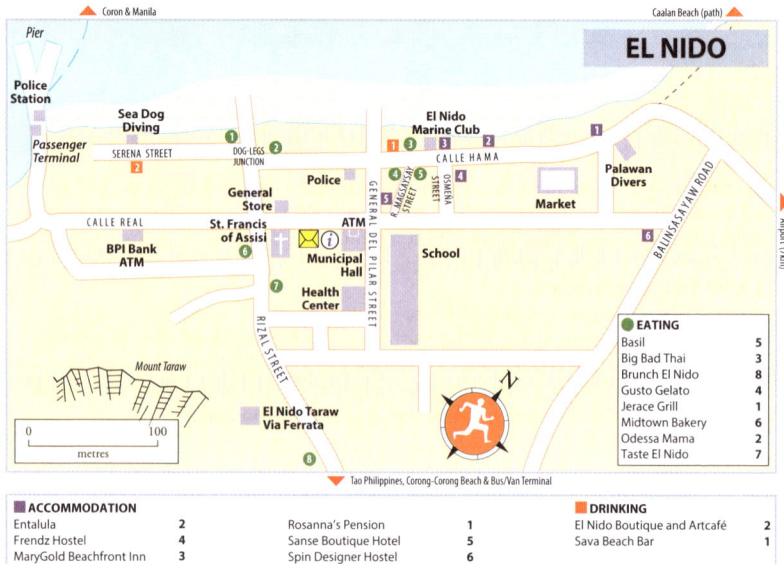

EL NIDO

EATING	
Basil	5
Big Bad Thai	3
Brunch El Nido	8
Gusto Gelato	4
Jerace Grill	1
Midtown Bakery	6
Odessa Mama	2
Taste El Nido	7

■ ACCOMMODATION				■ DRINKING	
Entalula	2	Rosanna's Pension	1	El Nido Boutique and Artcafé	2
Frendz Hostel	4	Sanse Boutique Hotel	5	Sava Beach Bar	1
MaryGold Beachfront Inn	3	Spin Designer Hostel	6		

ISLAND-HOPPING IN THE BACUIT ARCHIPELAGO

Bacuit archipelago **tours** (generally 9am–4pm) have been standardized into packages, and prices are set by the local government. Costs depend on the islands visited and usually include lunch, and there's also an ecotourism development fee valid for ten days. Numerous places offer trips; one of the best options is *El Nido Boutique and Artcafé* on Serena St in El Nido (welnidoboutiqueandartcafe.com). **Tour A** takes in the attractions of Miniloc and Shimizu islands; **Tour B** goes to Snake Island, Cudugnon Cave and points south; **Tour C** goes to Matinloc's Secret and Hidden beaches; and **Tour D** takes in Cadlao Island and Ipil Beach, among others. The highlights are scattered throughout each itinerary, to encourage several days of touring, but you can also choose a combo tour, taking in the highlights of A and B or A and C, for example.

If time is short you can **charter your own boat**, taking in all the best locations. Another option is a **kayak tour**, bookable via *El Nido Boutique and Artcafé* or Northern Hope Tours on Calle Real (wnorthernhopetours.com): trips to Cadlao and Miniloc are both viable options. If you simply want to stay put on a **beach** for a few hours and do some snorkelling, you can charter a boat to Seven Commandos Beach on the mainland, which has a small bar behind a lovely strip of sand.

windswept other than on May 31, when it's mobbed by believers for the Feast of the Lady of Matinloc.

Matinloc's main draw is **Secret Beach**, reached by a tiny gap you can swim through; on the other side is a spellbinding cove facing a white-sand beach surrounded by steep rock walls. Tours also usually stop in the Tapiutan Strait off Matinloc for the chance to see **turtles**, but it depends on weather conditions.

8

Southern islands

The main attractions in the southern archipelago include **Snake Island**, a serpentine sandbar lapped by crystal-clear waters, making it a great spot for sunbathing and a dip at low tide; and **Pangalusian Island** with its long, palm-fringed, white-sand beach, perfect for swimming and snorkelling at any time.

ARRIVAL AND DEPARTURE

By plane El Nido centre is a 6km tricycle ride from El Nido airport, also called Lio Airport.
Destinations Busuanga (1 daily; 40min); Caticlan (for Boracay; 1 daily; 1hr); Clark (1 daily; 1hr 30min); Cebu (1 daily; 1hr 40min); Manila (7 daily; 1hr 15min).
By boat Daily fast ferries (4hr), operated by Montenegro Lines, leave for Coron at 6am; there are onward ferries to Manila from Coron. Arrange your ticket at least one day in advance online, from one of the many tour operators in town, or *El Nido Boutique and Artcafé*, which can also arrange tickets for all other boats. There are also daily bangkas to Coron leaving at 8am (8–9hr), but as they are

EL NIDO AND THE BACUIT ARCHIPELAGO

slower, less comfortable and more vulnerable to weather-related delays, the ferry is a much better choice – though the bangkas do include lunch.
By bus and van The bus and van "terminal" is in Corong-Corong, a 10–15min walk or short tricycle ride from El Nido town. Regular and a/c buses run till 6pm to Puerto Princesa (via Taytay and Roxas); they take around 8hr. More expensive, but faster and more convenient (and offering hotel pick-ups), vans to Puerto Princesa (10 daily; 6hr) and Port Barton (3 daily; 4hr) also leave throughout the day; try Alpha Sierra Transport Services (☎0998 433 9714).

INFORMATION

Tourist office Inside the DENR building near the town hall on Calle Real in El Nido, one block inland from the beach (daily 8am–8pm; ☎0917 841 7771).
El Nido Boutique and Artcafé The travel centre (daily

7am–8pm; welnidoboutiqueandartcafe.com) of this café on Serena St (see page 373) is a good source of up-to-date local information. You can book tours, boats and ferries, and change money. Credit cards accepted.

ACCOMMODATION

You should book ahead (especially at Christmas and Chinese New Year) for El Nido town's **budget accommodation**;

TAO PHILIPPINES

Tao Philippines (W taophilippines.com) offer a unique way to travel between El Nido and the Calamian islands. Five-day (and four-night) tours aboard a traditional Paraw sailing boat explore the remote string of jewel-like islands between El Nido and Coron Town on Busuanga. Guests live like locals, camping and sleeping in native villages along the way. Trips run from October to early June.

rates are a bit higher at quieter and prettier **Corong-Corong** or **Caalan** beaches.

EL NIDO, SEE MAP PAGE 370

Entalula Calle Hama W entalula.com. Elegant beachfront option with standard a/c rooms beautifully crafted from wood and nipa; there are also four fan-cooled cabañas; all have hot water and sea-view verandas. PPP

Frendz Hostel Osmeña St W frendzresorthostels.com. If you're looking for an excellent budget option in El Nido, Frendz will probably tick your boxes. Beds in the mixed and female-only dorms are among the cheapest to be found in town, and there are private family rooms too. There's a swimming pool on the roof, offering great views across the bay. PP

MaryGold Beachfront Inn Calle Hama W mgelnido. com. Charming beachfront accommodation with spotless country-cottage and seaside-themed rooms. The more expensive are at the front, with sea views and balconies. PP

Rosanna's Pension Calle Hama ☎ 0920 605 4631. Formerly a top budget choice, *Rosanna's* has moved a little upmarket, but still offers friendly service and beachfront rooms, these days with a/c and solar-powered hot water. PP

Sanse Boutique Hotel Real St W facebook.com/sanseboutiquehotelelnido. Well-located hotel, with quirky but not overwhelming decoration – think plants, treated floorboards and freestanding bathtubs. PPP

★ **Spin Designer Hostel** Balinsasayaw Rd at Calle Real W spinhostel.com. Trendy backpacker hostel with mixed dorms, female dorms and single or twin private doubles. There's also a lounge area with cable TV, basic kitchen equipment for use, self-service laundry and free breakfast. PP

CAALAN BEACH, SEE MAP PAGE 369

El Nido Garden Resort Calle Hama W elnidogardenph. com. Upmarket resort at the north end of Caalan Beach, with accommodation in individual villas set around a lovely pool, with views over the bay beyond. Facilities include a spa, a restaurant and a bar. Not cheap but not a bad choice for a splash. PPP

Golden Monkey ☎ 0929 206 4352. Peaceful little resort with well-constructed garden and smart rooms with views

in the main block, as well as beachfront huts. They also have kayaks for rent. PP

Kalinga ☎ 0928 393 2620. One of the cheaper options on peaceful Caalan Beach. There are a variety of attractive rooms and huts set in a garden just back from the sand, all of which have TV and hot water. Rooms with a/c are a little pricier. PP

CORONG-CORONG, SEE MAP PAGE 369

Dolarog Beach Resort Dolarog Beach W dolarogresort. com. Peaceful beachside accommodation with thatched cottages and rooms in a grassy coconut grove on a quiet and rather isolated stretch of private beach, 4km south of Corong-Corong. The resort is well run, serves excellent meals and is easy enough to reach from town by tricycle or bangka. You can also arrange for staff to meet you at the airport. PPPP

★ **Morning Walsh Resort** ☎ 0999 548 4336. A private home, owned by the lovely Nelma, in the middle of laidback Corong-Corong Beach, with ten spacious rooms, individually decorated and with beautifully carved wooden furniture, private bathrooms and a/c. There's also a large garden filled with quirky sculptures, beachside massage huts and kayaks for rent. PPP

One El Nido Suite Opposite the bus terminal ☎ 0917 137 4566. Comfortable and clean rooms, in a convenient location just a few minutes' walk to the beach. Staff are very friendly and helpful, and the breakfast buffet is extensive. P

BACUIT ARCHIPELAGO, SEE MAP PAGE 369

★ **Lagen Island Resort** Lagen Island W elnidoresorts. com. Operated by *El Nido Resorts*, this private island paradise has superb beaches and diving, with stylish tropical accommodation in fan-cooled or a/c cottages. Package rates include meals and watersports. PPPP

★ **Miniloc Island Resort** Miniloc Island W elnido resorts.com. Another *El Nido* resort, *Miniloc* offers a coastal village vibe, with beautifully stylish native-style cottages. At the reef, just offshore, guests get the chance to swim with huge 1.5m jackfish. PPPP

EATING

SEE MAP PAGE 370

Basil Calle Hama ☎ 0916 264 3989. This friendly and atmospheric restaurant serves up some of El Nido's best

pizza, which is stonebaked in a traditional brick oven. The truffle pizza is the most popular choice on the menu, and

DIVING AND SNORKELLING AROUND EL NIDO

The waters off El Nido are popular with **divers**, especially those looking to do a PADI course. **Snorkelling** is good, too, though much of the reef system has been killed off over the years due to crown-of-thorns starfish, bleaching and dynamite fishing. There are a few reliable **dive operators** in El Nido, who can also advise about trips to the Tubbataha Reef (see page 358) and Apo Reef (see page 241).

DIVE OPERATORS
Adventure Scuba Dive Center ⓦelnidoadventurescuba.com.

Palawan Divers Calle Hama ⓦpalawan-divers.org.
Submariner Diving Center ⓦsubmarinerdiving.com.

with good reason. $\overline{PPP}$

Big Bad Thai Calle Hama ⓦbigbadthai.com. If you're looking for authentic Thai food, this is the best place in El Nido to find it – the massaman curry is perfect, and the stir fries are excellent too. Try to snag a seat on the balcony to enjoy the marvellous view as you eat. $\overline{PPP}$

★ **Brunch El Nido** Rizal St ⓦfaebook.com. You have to admire a place that focuses squarely on one particular mealtime – and one that isn't really a mealtime at all (although it is kind of two mealtimes, which probably explains things). Anyway, head here any time you like for eggs benedict/royale, English breakfasts, Filipino *silog* breakfasts, waffles, crepes, panini, overnight oats and more – oh, and good coffee. No wonder it's so popular. $\overline{PP}$

★ **Gusto Gelato** Calle Hama ☎0905 572 3524. Probably the best place to get a decent espresso coffee in El Nido, this small spot is also extremely popular for its excellent ice cream, which comes in a huge range of flavours. $\overline{P}$

Jerace Grill Rizal St ⓦjaracegrill.com. Right on the beachfront, this loud and lively restaurant is popular with both locals and travellers, and serves up classic Filipino dishes, as well as excellent fresh seafood. Choose your "catch of the day", and it'll be grilled right in front of you on the shore, and served with rice and vegetables. $\overline{PPP}$

Midtown Bakery Rizal St. The best bakery in town, with the usual buttery buns, white bread and *pandesal* (bread rolls), plus a tempting array of cakes such as the delicious egg-custard tart, all for a few pesos – plenty of budget travellers load up here. $\overline{P}$

Odessa Mama Calle Hama ☎0927 655 0360. This Ukrainian restaurant is an unexpected find in El Nido, offering delicious home cooking that's popular with travellers, as evidenced by the notes scrawled across the walls. Try the *varenyky* (dumplings stuffed with cottage cheese and honey) and classic borsch (beetroot soup). Also, a good place for a beer. $\overline{PPP}$

Taste El Nido Rizal St ☎0915 317 6724. Without a doubt the best place in El Nido to get vegan food – the main choices are the smoothie bowls, but there are a few main meal options too. The coffee is great as well. $\overline{PPP}$

8

DRINKING

SEE MAP PAGE 370

El Nido Boutique and Artcafé Serena St, Calan Beach ⓦelnidoboutiqueandartcafe.com. The heart of El Nido's visitor scene, thanks to its excellent travel centre. The food at the café isn't great, so it's better to just go for a drink at the bar and enjoy the live music.

Sava Beach Bar Calle Hama ⓦfacebook.com/SAVA BeachBar. This stylish bar, with chairs and loungers out on the sand, is one of liveliest on El Nido beachfront. The tunes are just as good as the colourful cocktails and usually have everyone up and dancing.

DIRECTORY

Banks and exchange There are a few ATMs in El Nido: there's a good one outside the Municipal Hall, and another on Calle Real.

The Calamian Islands

The island-hopping, kayaking, diving and trekking in the **Calamian Islands**, north of mainland Palawan, in many ways trumps that in the parent island, especially when it comes to its world-famous **wreck-diving**. From the main settlement of **Coron Town** on the largest island, **Busuanga**, you can explore the awe-inspiring islands and reefs of Coron Bay, beginning with the lagoons and coves hidden among the staggering limestone cliffs of **Coron Island**. Southwest is **Culion Island**, an intriguing former leper colony. The waters

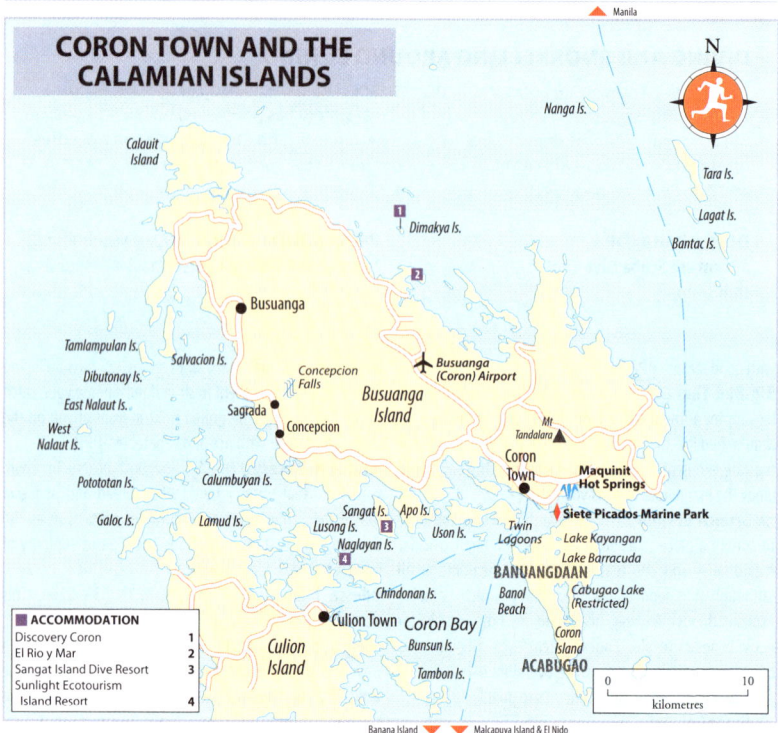

around the Calamians are also feeding grounds for the endangered **dugong** – the best tours to see them are arranged by *Club Paradise* on Dimakya Island.

Busuanga Island

Busuanga is the largest island in the Calamian group, but is mostly wild and undeveloped, with little to see beyond the lively fishing community of **Coron Town** on the south coast and its hinterlands. Coron Town is the main base for exploring the **shipwrecks** in adjacent **Coron Bay**, but non-divers will find the pristine snorkelling, swimming and hiking trails nearby just as enticing.

Coron Town and around

With its narrow streets and ramshackle wharf, **CORON TOWN** retains an old-fashioned provincial charm, although like most Filipino towns its roads are congested with an ever-growing number of tricycles. Refreshingly, you won't see any fast-food chains here, and there are a good number of restaurants and accommodation options. Coron Town is a major resort-in-the-making, with regular flights from Manila helping to ramp up development and ambitious land-reclamation projects in the pipeline. The phenomenal views across the bay to Coron Island never get old; these are best appreciated from the top of **Mount Tapyas**, a steep 30 to 45-minute hike along a trail which starts at the end of San Augustin Street.

Maquinit Hot Springs

7km east of Coron Town • Charge • Accessible by tricycle from Coron Town (including a usual 2 hr wait) or by private minivan rental; some boat tours of Coron Bay include the springs

Facing Coron Bay, the **Maquinit Hot Springs** comprise a series of enticing open pools of spring water that feed into each other before cascading into the sea; the springs are 36°C, making it best to visit during rain or the cool of the evening.

ARRIVAL AND DEPARTURE

By plane Flights arrive at Busuanga (Coron) Airport, with its small terminal building and handful of sari-sari stores (30min by van/jeepney from Coron Town). There's a tourist information counter next to the baggage claim (☎ 0918 725 4665), but no ATM. All the airlines have offices in town, and tickets can also be booked through Calamian Islands Travel and Tours (🖥 coron-travel.com) on Rosario St.
Destinations Cebu (3 daily; 1hr 30min); Clark (4 daily; 1hr 15min); El Nido (1 daily; 40min); Manila (6 daily; 1hr 15min).

BUSUANGA ISLAND

By boat The 2GO Manila–Coron ferry service hits Busuanga once a week from Manila (14hr) on its way to Puerto Princesa (14hr), and vice versa. For El Nido, Montenegro Lines operate a daily fast ferry (4hr). There are also daily morning bangkas to Coron (8–9 hr), but as they are slower, less comfortable and more vulnerable to weather-related delays, you're much better off taking the ferry. Both are bookable through any resort or guesthouse. Both ferries and bangkas arrive and depart from the public pier.

INFORMATION

Tourist information The helpful tourist centre in Coron Town faces the market (Mon–Fri 9am–noon & 1–5pm;   ☎ 0920 662 0057).

ACCOMMODATION

There are plenty of **places to stay** in Coron Town, and some of the best resorts in the Calamians lie off the **north coast of Busuanga**, a bus and boat ride from the airport and a 1hr drive from town.

CORON TOWN, SEE MAP PAGE 376

Corto del Mar Comiseria St 🖥 cortodelmar.com. Resembling a colonial-era Spanish building, the Corto del Mar is an elegant place on the seafront, with cleanly decorated rooms – some with sea views – surrounding a courtyard and pool. Staff are friendly and helpful, and there's a pretty good bar and restaurant on-site. $\overline{PPP}$

Darayonan Lodge 132 National Hwy 🖥 darayonan-coron.weebly.com. Rambling hotel with decent deluxe rooms in the newer wing; the older rooms at the front are a bit shabby and damp. The pool is a nice extra, as is the leafy garden. The alfresco restaurant serves good breakfast, lunch and dinner. $\overline{PP}$

The Funny Lion Sitio Jolo, Poblacion V 🖥 thefunnylion. com. This contemporary boutique resort is located just

north of the town and offers spectacular views of the bay. Rooms are sleek and well appointed, and there's a beautiful infinity pool and a good restaurant. $\overline{PPP}$

Hop Hostel Nueva St 🖥 hophostel.com.ph. Sleek hostel with all the things a modern backpacker might need – good dorm berths with privacy curtains, a chillout room full of beanbags, cooking facilities, and added to this a terrace with a view, which is perfect for the draining of an evening beer. $\overline{P}$

★ **KokosNuss Resort** National Hwy 🖥 kokosnuss. info. The first resort as you approach Coron Town from the airport, 1km north of town. Accommodation is set around a lovely garden area with hammocks and a small pool. Rooms range from quaint thatched bungalows with a/c to eco-rooms with solar-heated showers and cave-style rooms with fans. $\overline{PP}$

THE NORTH COAST, SEE MAP PAGE 374

Discovery Coron Dimakya Island 🖥 discoverycoron. com. Slick place with cosy, modern a/c cottages a stone's

8

CORON TOWN TOUR OPERATORS

Most hotels can arrange various **tours** of the islands and attractions near Coron Town, but it's worth shopping around as itineraries and prices vary. The following **operators** are recommended.

Calamian Islands Travel & Tours 🖥 coron-travel. com. This basic outfit has its own fixed prices for island-hopping, and runs regular tours to surrounding islands and places of interest.

Calamianes Expeditions 11 San Augustin St 🖥 calamianes.com. An excellent, eco-friendly budget

choice. They need a minimum of five people to run tours, but will pair you with other groups to make up the numbers. Check what each tour includes: Coron Island trips, for example, include lunch but exclude snorkel gear and entrance to Kayangan Lake.

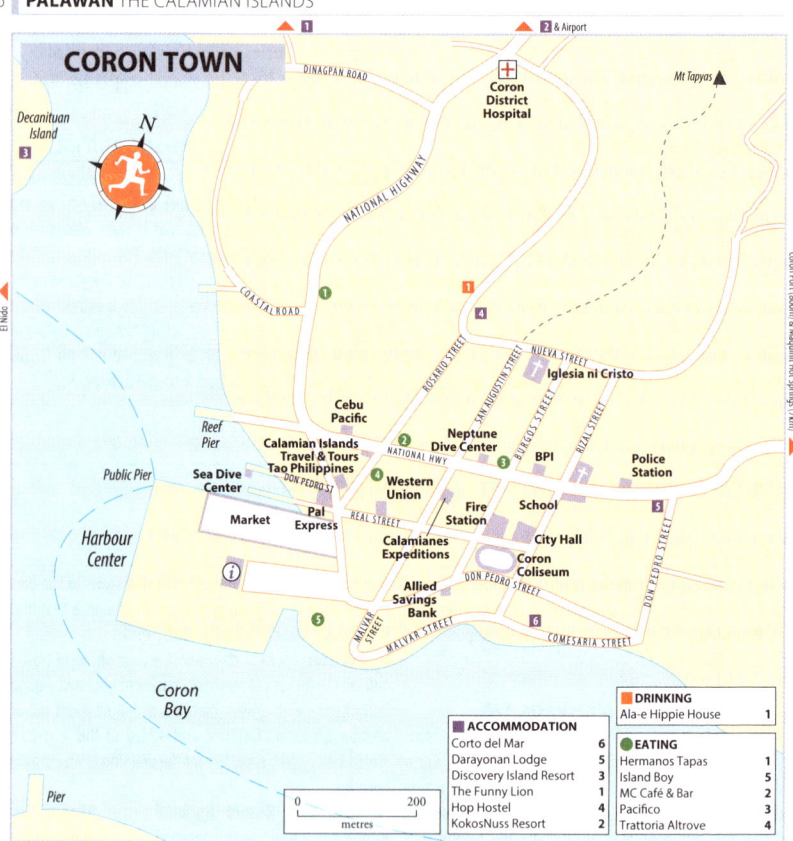

CORON TOWN

ACCOMMODATION	
Corto del Mar	6
Darayonan Lodge	5
Discovery Island Resort	3
The Funny Lion	1
Hop Hostel	4
KokosNuss Resort	2

DRINKING	
Ala-e Hippie House	1

EATING	
Hermanos Tapas	1
Island Boy	5
MC Café & Bar	2
Pacifico	3
Trattoria Altrove	4

throw from the beach and a fabulous reef just offshore, where turtles and dugongs are regularly sighted. Rates include full board. **PPPP**

El Rio y Mar Port Caltom, San José ⓦelrioymar.com. Set on a 500m-stretch of beach facing a lagoon (it's on a promontory, not an island), with an infinity pool. The spotless, beautifully maintained native or cedar cabañas all have hot water, TV and wi-fi. The many activities, including kayaking, sailing, fishing and snorkelling, cost extra, as do diving and tours. **PPPP**

EATING

SEE MAP PAGE 376

CORON TOWN

★ **Hermanos Tapas** National Hwy ⓦfacebook.com/ HermanosTapas. Popular central spot offering a good range of authentically Spanish tapas – the tiger prawns are excellent, as are the Spanish omelette, the patatas bravas and the meatballs. Make sure to leave room for the churros for dessert. **PP**

Island Boy Reef pier ☎0927 418 2195. To some extent, you're paying for the location on the pier, but the seafood and grills on offer at Island Boy aren't half bad. Later in the evening, when the place is lit up in zany style, it often gets quite lively with live band performances. **PP**

MC Café & Bar National Hwy ⓦfacebook.com/ bluemoonrestobar. A café-bar and restaurant serving international dishes such as pizzas, burgers (recommended), Philly cheese steak, Western and Filipino brunches, and good coffee. Also, a decent place to repair to for a drink. **PPP**

Pacifico National Hwy ⓦfacebook.com/PacifiCoron. On the main street running through Coron Town, Pacifico has the feel of an American diner, both in ambience and in the options on the menu, which include burgers, sandwiches and pizzas, alongside a few Filipino and Thai choices. It's a great place for a beer or cocktail too. **PP**

★ **Trattoria Altrove** Rosario St ☎0917 888 0793. This breezy top-floor restaurant has a romantic air and some of the best Italian food you'll find anywhere in Palawan. The giant thin-crust pizzas are particularly popular, and are topped with authentic ingredients. $\overline{PP}$

DRINKING

SEE MAP PAGE 376

Ala-e Hippie House 5 Nueva St ☎ 0927 947 4500. This reggae-loving hippy bar is hidden high on a hill above Coron Town and offers spectacular sunset views from its balcony, as well as live reggae music. Covered in posters, artwork and tie-dye wall hangings, seats are on cushions on the floor. You'll be treated like a good friend, but may have to put up with warm beers. $\overline{P}$

DIRECTORY

Banks and exchange There are several banks in Coron Town, most of which have ATMs that accept foreign cards.

Coron Bay Islands

The primary reason to stay in Coron Town is to explore the spellbinding islands and coves scattered around **Coron Bay** – also a fantastic destination for **wreck-diving** (see box, page 378). Bangka trips are easy to arrange, but it's worth comparing the various packages on offer (see box, opposite). **Coron Island** is the most popular destination, but you should also try to spend some time on the smaller, less-visited islands.

Coron Island

Agencies offer day-trips for a bangka of up to four people; prices do not usually include the various admission fees, and lunch is usually extra too

Most hotels and tour operators in Coron Town offer day-trips to **Coron Island**, an enchanting cluster of jagged limestone cliffs and peaks just fifteen minutes across the bay. The island offers truly spectacular landscapes and some rich snorkelling sites, though visitors are confined to the northern coast; Coron is the traditional home of the **Tagbanua** people and the rest of the island is strictly off limits to outsiders. The Tagbanua in the two main east-coast communities of **Banuangdaan** (Old Coron Town) and **Acabugaonow** make most of their income from charging admission fees to the island's various attractions; this supplements their traditional sources of livelihood, fishing and bird's-nest collecting.

   Tours involve plenty of snorkelling and swimming. In between Coron Island and Coron Town you'll typically stop at **Lake Kayangan** (see page 377) and **Siete Picados Marine Park** (charge), which offers a relatively rich spread of coral and marine life (sea snakes, sea fans, clownfish and whale sharks are sometimes spotted on the deeper side of the reef).

Lake Kayangan
Charge

To visit volcanic **Lake Kayangan**, boats dock at a gorgeous lagoon rimmed with coral and turquoise waters – here the Tagbanua have a small hut with basic information about the island and the Indigenous people, with staff on hand to answer any questions. The lake itself is reached by climbing up a steep flight of steps – at the top, turn left along a narrow path to tiny **Kayangan Cave** for awe-inspiring views of the lagoon below. The main path continues down to the lake, where you can snorkel in the warm waters and spy schools of odd-looking needlefish and plunging cathedral-like rock formations.

The rest of the island
Lake Barracuda (charge) is encircled by jagged limestone outcrops that give way to lush jungle, but is only really worth the additional entrance fee if you are on a **dive trip**; on the surface the water is the usual temperature, but 18m down it heats up so much that you can drift along on hot thermals. To the west are the **Twin Lagoons** (charge), hemmed in by jagged pillars of limestone towering over the water like abstract

8

WRECK-DIVING IN CORON BAY

Most divers come to the Coron area for the World War II **Japanese shipwrecks**. There are 24 wrecks in all, all sunk in one massive attack by US aircraft on September 24, 1944. Among the most interesting are:

Akitsushima A big ship lying on her side with a crane once used for hoisting a seaplane. Between Culion and Busuanga islands, near Manglet Island, the wreck attracts huge schools of giant batfish and barracuda.

Irako The best of the wrecks and still almost intact; it's home to turtles and enormous groupers, who hang in the water and eyeball you as you float past. A swim through the engine room reveals a network of pipes and valves inhabited by moray eels and lionfish, which have spines that deliver a hefty dose of poison.

Morazan Maru Japanese freighter sitting upright at 28m. Large shoals of banana fish, giant batfish and pufferfish the size of footballs can be seen, especially around the mast, bow and stern. It's easy to get into the cargo holds, making this a good wreck-dive for beginners.

Taiei Maru Japanese tanker covered with beautiful corals and a large variety of marine life. The deck is relatively shallow at between 10m and 16m deep, and is well suited to wreck-dive beginners.

DIVE OPERATORS

There are a dozen or so dive operators in Coron Town. The following are reliable.

Freediving Coron Real St ⓦ freediving-coron.com.   **Neptune Dive Center** National Hwy ⓦ neptune divecenter.com.

sculptures. Boats dock at the end of the first lagoon, where you can swim through a low-lying water tunnel into the second one, a tranquil and very deep inlet. Odd coral formations cling to the sides of the lagoon, looking like a sunken city under the surface. A little further along the coast is **Skeleton Wreck** (charge), a sunken Japanese fishing vessel easily viewed by snorkellers, and a series of narrow **beaches** backed by sheer cliffs. Tours usually stop for lunch on one of these (Banol Beach is the most popular), but each one charges a fee.

The southern islands

Calamianes Expeditions (see box, above) run tours

One hour south of Coron Town lies the enticing trio of **Malcapuya Island** (charge), **Banana Island** (charge) and **Bolog Island** (charge), classic desert islands where the main activity is lounging on the beach. Malcapuya has monkeys inland, while Bolog features alluring **Malaroyroy Beach**, a curving bar of silky white sand.

Sangat Island

Calamianes Expeditions (see box, above) and other agencies run trips

Sangat Island, west of Coron Town (1hr 30min by boat), is yet another craggy, picture-perfect tropical island. As well as plenty of coral gardens laced with tropical fish, the island is close to eleven World War II shipwrecks, some of which can be explored by snorkellers at low tide.

ACCOMMODATION   CORON BAY ISLANDS, SEE MAPS PAGES 374 AND 376

★ **Discovery Island Resort** Decanituan Island ⓦ discoverydiversresort.com. Popular, laidback resort, a 10min bangka ride from Coron Town, with a 24hr shuttle service back and forth. The seventeen bungalows all have private bathrooms and terraces with fine views of the bay. Staff are friendly and there's a good restaurant. The beach

here is nothing special, but there are kayaks available, with which you can get to nicer ones nearby. P̲P̲P̲

★ **Sangat Island Dive Resort** Sangat Island ⓦ sangat.com.ph. Established by a British expat in 1994 on a gorgeous island – 30min from Coron Town – with a giddy interior of cliffs and jungle and a shore of coves and coral reefs. Accommodation is in thirteen native-style beachfront and hillside cottages (with fans), and they specialize in diving courses. PPPP

★ **Sunlight Ecotourism Island Resort** Naglayan Island ⓦsunlighthotelsandresorts.com. A gorgeous taste of paradise on a privately owned island a 45-minute boat ride from Coron Town. The accommodation consists of 55 separate villas, which come with sea views as standard, and many also include a variety of features, such as balconies, jacuzzi baths, and even glass floors to view the marine life below. There are two beautiful beaches close by, with diving equipment available to hire, as well as facilities including a pool, gym and spa. PPPP

Culion Island

Few travellers make it to the curious island of **Culion**, around two hours south of Coron Town by boat. In 1904 the Americans decided to create an isolated but self-sufficient leper colony here – it became the world's largest **leprosarium**, a place that inspired fear and often revulsion. Today the leper colony has all but been erased, but haunting monuments of the island's past remain, as well as some untouched, empty beaches. Like Busuanga, Culion is quite large and undeveloped, but the main attractions lie in the pretty little capital, **Culion Town**. The approach to town is dominated by the striking coral-walled **La Inmaculada Concepción Church**, which was rebuilt in 1933 on the site of an older fortified Spanish chapel, completed in 1740. Beside it is the old lighthouse, with tremendous views north to Coron Town.

Culion Museum

Culion Sanatorium and General Hospital compound • Mon–Fri 9am–11am & 1–4pm • Charge

The intriguing **Culion Museum**, housed in the island's former leprosy research lab (built in 1930), details the history of the colony. Featuring medical relics and photographs from the early twentieth century, with a vast archive of patient records that you can browse, it also maintains the rooms where doctors worked, complete with original, rather frightening-looking equipment.

8

ARRIVAL AND INFORMATION

CULION ISLAND

By boat Culion can only be reached by bangka from Coron Town; a large outrigger leaves daily from Coron Town (1hr 30min). Boats return the next morning – so you'll have to stay overnight unless you rent a private bangka from the Calamian Tourist Boat Association for a return trip (2hr one-way), or join the tour with Calamianes Expeditions (see box, page 375).

Tourist information Inside the town hall (Mon–Fri 9am–5pm; ☎0917 552 2277).

Services There are no banks or ATMs, and credit cards are rarely accepted, so bring enough cash for your stay.

ACCOMMODATION AND EATING

Hotel Maya Culion Town ⓦfacebook.com/hotelmaya-culion. Next to La Inmaculada Concepción Church, Culion's best hotel is actually a teaching hotel operated by the Jesuit-run Loyola College of Culion. Rooms are spacious and comfortable and service is friendly. Single rooms are available. PP

Tabing Dagat Lodging House Culion Town ☎0921 653 1470. A 5min walk from the port, opposite the local government offices, this is a comfy option offering doubles with shared bathrooms or larger a/c en-suites with balconies. There's also a decent Filipino restaurant. Credit cards accepted. P

Mindanao

GUYAM ISLAND

9

Mindanao

Mindanao, the massive island at the foot of the Philippine archipelago, is in many ways the cultural heart of the country, a place where Indigenous people still farm their ancient homelands and Christians live alongside Muslims who first settled here in the fourteenth century. Spanish rule came late to much of Mindanao, and was tenuous at best throughout the nineteenth century; when the Americans occupied the islands, it was here they met their most bitter resistance. Today, the island remains a conflict zone: in spite of a peace pact between the Moro Islamic Liberation Front (MILF) rebels and the government early in 2014, the island has become mired in anti-government insurgencies, terrorist attacks and tourist kidnappings. With the exception of the islands of Camiguin and Siargao, caution is advised against travel anywhere on the island, and certain parts should be avoided altogether (essentially the western half, and the Sulu Islands). In 2017, Mindanao was placed under martial law following the Islamist-militant attack on the city of Marawi in the BARMM (see box, page 385), which led to a five-month long conflict culminating in the governmental recovery of Marawi. Martial law was lifted at the end of 2019.

North Mindanao, which sees the most tourist activity, is comparatively safe and accessible, although the lively gateway city of **Cagayan de Oro** (CDO) was the site of a number of roadside explosions and grenade blasts in 2016. From the north coast, most visitors make a beeline for the pint-sized island of **Camiguin**, one of the country's most appealing tourist spots and an island with more volcanoes per square mile than anywhere else in the world. Elsewhere, northeast Mindanao is rich in ecotourism potential and offshore islands. Highlights include the ancient wooden boat discovered at **Butuan**, the spellbinding **Enchanted River** and the surfing and backpacker hotspot of **Siargao**.

The **southeast** is home to Mindanao's largest city, **Davao**, a diverse and friendly place best known for its fresh fruit. Davao itself is not a city of legendary sights, but the nearby countryside and coast offer plenty of attractions, from **Samal Island** to the **Philippine Eagle Center**. Davao is also the gateway to **Mount Apo**, the nation's highest peak and a magnet for trekkers and climbers.

Much of western Mindanao is part of the **Bangsamoro Autonomous Region in Muslim Mindanao** (BARMM), an area of huge tourism potential, but where the security situation is in a state of flux (see box, page 410). We have removed most of our coverage of the region; check the current **security** situation before considering a visit.

Cagayan de Oro and around

Sprawled along the north coast of Mindanao, the city of **CAGAYAN DE ORO** (CDO) makes an ideal introduction to the island, with its smattering of sights and fine restaurants, and a handful of enticing attractions in the mountains beyond, including **whitewater rafting** on the Cagayan de Oro River (see box, page 387). Sitting on the eastern bank of the river, the city stretches from **Vicente de Lara Park** in the north, with

Highlights

❶ Whitewater rafting on the Cagayan de Oro River Shoot the rapids near the city of Cagayan de Oro; the full 15km course offers four hours of thrills in a beautiful setting. See page 387

❷ Lanzones festival, Camiguin Visit this dazzling little island in October, when the colourful four-day Lanzones festival is held. See page 390

❸ Enchanted River This magical, remote lagoon is a deep cove of crystalline water crammed with colourful tropical fish – a visual delight. See page 395

❹ Siargao Island With tranquil resorts, powdery beaches, top-notch surfing and laidback nightlife, Siargao is a backpacker's dream. See page 397

HIGHLIGHTS ARE MARKED ON THE MAP ON PAGE 384

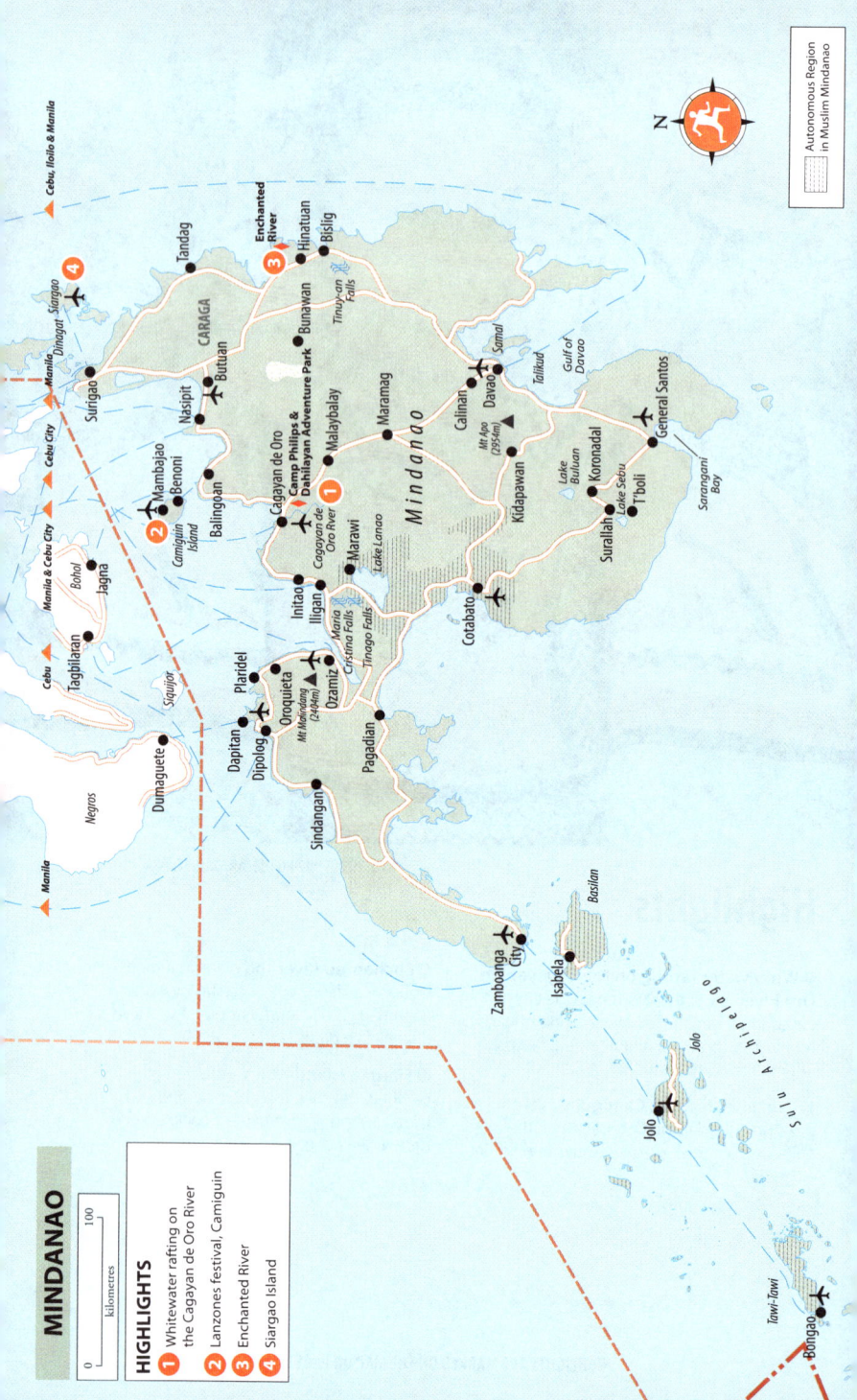

MINDANAO

kilometres

0   100

HIGHLIGHTS

1 Whitewater rafting on
the Cagayan de Oro River

2 Lanzones festival, Camiguin

3 Enchanted River

4 Siargao Island

Autonomous Region
in Muslim Mindanao

N

Cebu, Iloilo & Manila

Manila

Cebu City

Manila & Cebu City

Cebu

Manila

Tandag

Enchanted
River

Hinatuan

Bislig

Surigao

Dinagat

Siargao

CARAGA

Bunawan

Tinuy-an
Falls

Butuan

Nasipit

Cagayan de Oro

**Camp Philips &
Dahilayan Adventure Park**

Malaybalay

Maramag

Calinan

Davao

Samal

Talikud

Gulf of
Davao

General Santos

Mambajao

Benoni

Camiguin
Island

Balingoan

Cagayan de
Oro River

Marawi

Lake Lanao

Mt Apo
(2954m)

Kidapawan

Lake
Buluan

Koronadal

Lake Sebu

T'boli

Surallah

Sarangani
Bay

Jagna

Bohol

Tagbilaran

Siquijor

Dumaguete

Negros

Initao

Iligan

Maria
Cristina Falls

Tinago Falls

Cotabato

Plaridel

Oroquieta

Ozamiz

Mt Malindang
(2404m)

Dapitan

Dipolog

Pagadian

Sindangan

Zamboanga
City

Isabela

Basilan

Jolo

Jolo

Sulu Archipelago

Tawi-Tawi

Bongao

Mindanao

its age-old mahogany trees, to circular **Gaston Park** in the south, once the site of city executions, bullfights and parades.

Southwest of the park, you'll find the **San Augustine Cathedral**, a dour off-white stone edifice, with immense stained-glass windows, rebuilt in the 1950s. A couple of kilometres northeast of **Xavier University**, the hip, modern heart of the city revolves around the **Limketkai Center**, an upscale mall, and the adjacent **Rosario Strip**. At weekends, locals can also be found flooding into outposts of the city's two largest shopping mall chains, **Centrio Ayala Mall** and **SM City Mall.**

Museum of Three Cultures

Capitol University, Corrales Ave, 2km north of Plaza Divisoria • Charge • ⓦ cu.edu.ph/museum-of-three-cultures

THE MINDANAO PROBLEM

Because of its volatile political situation, advice from Western governments is to avoid all but essential travel to western and central Mindanao and the Sulu archipelago – excluding Camiguin and Siargao – you should always check the **current situation** before travelling. Politically, things are fluid and confusing; a number of factions and splinter groups are calling for varying degrees of autonomy from Manila.

The thorniest issue involves Mindanao's Muslims (known as Moros), who are seeking self-determination. The **Moro National Liberation Front** (MNLF) started a war for independence in the 1970s that lasted until 1987, when it signed an agreement accepting the government's offer of autonomy. As a result, the **Autonomous Region in Muslim Mindanao**, or ARMM, was created in 1990, covering the western provinces of Basilan, Lanao del Sur, Maguindanao, Sulu and Tawi-Tawi, plus Marawi City. The **Moro Islamic Liberation Front** (MILF) splintered from the MNLF in 1981 and refused to accept the accord. At the height of the fighting, more than 750,000 people were displaced and about four hundred people killed. In 2019, ARMM was replaced with BARMM (Bangsamoro Autonomous Region in Muslim Mindanao), and the transition process from the one to the other is due to continue until 2025.

Unfortunately, Mindanao's problems didn't end with MILF. In the early 1990s another disaffected group of fighters founded **Abu Sayyaf**, whose name translated means "Bearer of the Sword". Based on **Basilan Island**, off Mindanao's southern coast, Abu Sayyaf is said to have ties to a number of Islamic fundamentalist organizations, including al-Qaeda and Islamic State.

In November 2009, 57 people (including 34 journalists) were tortured and murdered in what was dubbed the **Maguindanao Massacre**, apparently for attempting to register a rival candidate for the upcoming elections; the perpetrators were a private militia controlled by the powerful Ampatuan clan, who were arrested and tried in 2010. Since the massacre, which led to the president declaring a state of emergency, numerous ceasefires between the government, military and various rebel groups have come and gone.

At least four Muslim rebel groups continue to operate on the island, and since 2015 there has been an increase in **bomb threats** and the **kidnapping** of foreign nationals and tourists. Abu Sayyaf beheaded two Canadian hostages in 2016, for example, and there were multiple attacks in November 2016, including some specifically targeting foreigners. In May 2017, the **Maute** rebel group, with the backing of Islamic State, attacked Marawi city in the ARMM and took several hostages. President Duterte declared martial law on Mindanao, and the incident developed into a five month long conflict which ended with the government's recovery of Marawi. Martial law on Mindanao continued until the end of 2019.

The current UK government advice, one echoed by the majority of Western nations, is to avoid **all but essential travel** to the eastern half of Mindanao – including Davao, Cagayan de Oro, Camiguin and Siargao – and avoid the rest of the island completely. In other words, making any trip at all to Mindanao could well **invalidate your travel insurance** – contact your provider to check.

9

CAGAYAN DE ORO

Macabalan Wharf (4km)

Eastbound Bus Terminal

& Limketkai Mall

Capitol University Medical Center; Centrio; Ayala Mall & Museum of Three Cultures

SM City Mall &

Airport; Great White Water Tours, CDO Buguay River Rafting,

MARCOS BRIDGE

N

Cagayan de Oro
River

M.H. DEL PILAR STREET

MACAHAMBUS STREET

KALAMBAGOHAN STREET

Iglesia ni
Cristo

MONTALBAN STREET

MABINI STREET

YACAPIN STREET

P. PACANA STREET

BORJA STREET

GOMEZ STREET

CRUZ TAAL STREET

BURGOS STREET

RIZAL STREET

Plaza
Divisoria

T. NERI STREET

ABEJUELA STREET

T. CHAVEZ STREET

City
Hall

PCMC
Hospital

HAYES STREET

GAERLAN STREET

Gaston
Park

SAN AGUSTIN STREET

San Augustine
Cathedral

DOLORES STREET

Tourism
Showcase

Cyberium

Police

Mercury
pharmacy

DBP

Domain

Xavier
University
Building

Viajero
Outdoor
Centre

Museo de Oro

XAVIER UNIVERSITY
CAMPUS

C.M. RECTO AVENUE

MAGSAYSAY STREET

Cagayan De Oro
Medical Center II

NACALABAN ST.

Provincial
Capitol

Vicente de
Lara Park

LUNA STREET

Land
Bank

GENERAL CAPISTRANO STREET

AKUT STREET

TIANO BROTHERS STREET

DON APOLINAR VELEZ STREET

PABAYO STREET

CORRALES AVENUE

Library

Kagay
Whitewater
Rafting

| 0 | 50 |
metres

● EATING

Apostrophe Café	2
Bigby's Café & Restaurant	1
Cucina Higala	3
Thai Me Up	5
Vjandep Bakeshop	4

■ DRINKING

The Oak Room	1

■ ACCOMMODATION

Budgetel	3
CDO Hotel Xentro	5
GC Suites	6
Limketkai Luxe	1
Red Planet	2
Seda Centrio	4

The **Museum of Three Cultures** is devoted to the Christians, Muslims and seven Indigenous traditions (or "Lumad") of northern Mindanao. The first gallery is dedicated to history, with exhibits on the Huluga Caves, early trade with China and the Butuan boats (see page 394). The most interesting section is dedicated to the M'ranao of Marawi, an area at the heart of the Moro dispute. Exhibits cover Islamic brass work, giant ceremonial swords and traditional *torogan*-style houses.

Museo de Oro

Xavier University, Corrales Ave • Charge • ⓦ xu.edu.ph

Part of Xavier University's campus, **Museo de Oro** (Museum of Gold) is one of the country's most important collections of folkloric artefacts. The museum is split into three exhibits: the ethnic history of Northern Mindanao, the ethnology of Mindanao, and the Francisco Demetrio SJ Gallery, which contains art and historical artefacts. The museum is an informative and useful introduction to Mindanao's complicated make-up, but don't come expecting any gold; despite the name, there's no haul of booty.

Dahilayan Adventure Park

40km southeast on the highway to Davao • Charge • ⓦ dahilayanadventurepark.com • Best reached by van from CDO

Billed as Mindanao's most extreme playground, the **Dahilayan Adventure Park** makes for an entertaining day out, primarily for its long **zipline** and refreshingly cool alpine location, in the hills some 1370m above sea level. The **Dahilayan Zip Zone** comprises three ziplines: an exhilarating 320m section, a tamer 150m segment, and the 840m finale, where you are chained into a full-body harness before hurtling down the mountain at 90km/hour. There's also whitewater rafting – either come with a group or call in advance and they should be able to place you in a boat (minimum six).

ARRIVAL AND DEPARTURE   CAGAYAN DE ORO AND AROUND

By plane Laguindingan International Airport is 33km northwest of the city – about an hour's drive. The airport is accessible by jeepney (first to the Laguindingan turn-off, then take the shuttle to the airport), but the most convenient transfers are with LAX Shuttle, which picks up at the Centrio Ayala Mall, or with Magnum Express, which leaves from Magnum Radio in CM Recto.
Destinations Cebu City (6–7 daily; 50min); Davao (1–2 daily; 55min); Iloilo (3 weekly; 1hr); Manila (12–13 daily;

1hr 30min).
By bus The Eastbound bus terminal is near the Limketkai Center, 3km east of the centre (off Recto Ave), while the Westbound Bus and Jeepney Station lies 6km west of the centre on the Iligan road. From either, you can take a jeepney or a taxi into town.
Destinations from Eastbound terminal Balingoan (for Camiguin; every 45min till 5pm; 1hr 45min); Butuan (every 45min till 5pm; 4hr); Davao (every 30min; 6–8hr); Surigao

RAFTING THE CAGAYAN DE ORO RIVER

Whitewater rafting along the fourteen major rapids of the Cagayan de Oro River gained popularity after former president Gloria Macapagal-Arroyo took a ride here in 2002. The jumping-off point is at the barangay of **Mambuaya**, a thirty- to forty-minute ride from the city proper. The wet months (Sept and Oct) are best for intermediate and professional levels (when the rapids range from class 3 to 4), while the rest of the year is more suitable for beginners.

RAFTING OPERATORS

CDO Bugsay River Rafting ⓦ cdorafting.com. Reliable operator offering a variety of packages for beginner through to advanced paddlers.
Great White Water Tours ⓦ riverraftingcdo.com. This decent company offers half- or full-day tours. Rates

include transfers, guides, equipment, snacks and meals.
Kagay Whitewater Rafting ⓦ facebook.com/kagay.whitewater.rafting/. The most popular outfit in the city offers 2–4hr trips on the upper, mid and lower levels of the river.

9

(2 daily; 6hr).

Destinations from Westbound terminal Dipolog (2 daily; 6–7hr); Iligan (hourly; 1hr 30min); Marawi (hourly; 3hr); Ozamiz (hourly; 4hr); Zamboanga (hourly; 12hr).

By boat Macabalan Wharf is 4km north of the centre; regular jeepneys make the journey back and forth. 2GO (w travel.2go.com.ph), Trans-Asia (w transasiashipping.

com) and Lite Shipping (w liteferries.com.ph) have services to Cebu; the latter also sail to Dumaguete, and Jagna on Bohol.

Destinations Bacolod (weekly; 21hr); Cebu City (1–2 daily; 10hr); Dumaguete (3 weekly; 7hr); Iloilo (3 weekly; 14hr); Jagna (4 weekly; 6–7hr); Manila (daily; 35hr); and Tagbilaran (3 weekly; 10hr).

GETTING AROUND

By tricycle Most locals use tricycles to get around the city (6am–10pm).

By jeepney Jeepneys are easy to pick up.

INFORMATION AND ACTIVITIES

Tourist office The Cagayan De Oro Tourism Showcase is on Don Apolinar Velez St (Mon–Fri 8am–noon & 1–5pm).

Viajero Outdoor Centre This is a one-stop hub for those seeking camping, caving and mountaineering excursions across northern Mindanao. The owners rent out ropes, tents, safety gear and more. They're also an excellent source of local information, and can arrange all kinds of trips into the

jungle (47B Domingo Velez, Aguinaldo St; w facebook.com/ viajerocdo).

Hospitals and clinics The Capitol University Medical Center is on Iligan Rd east of the city centre (T 082 856 4730). The Cagayan De Oro Medical Center II is on Nacalaban St (T 088 2271 1874).

ACCOMMODATION

SEE MAP PAGE 386

Budgetel Corrales Ave, north of C.M. Recto T 0917 794 1010. Handy for the Eastbound bus terminal, this hotel is the city's cheapest deal. It offers 34 en-suite a/c singles, twins and doubles, as well as enormous sixteen- and eighteen-bed dorms with shared bathrooms. There's a laundry, too. P̄

CDO Hotel Xentro Corrales Ave, behind Peleaz Sports Center T 0917 723 0861. This hotel offers great-value deals for single travellers. The pros are that it's bright, clean and modern, and there's a range of rooms from seven-bed dorms to deluxe suites; the downside is that its popular with groups, so can get noisy. If you fancy a massage, try the spa on the ground floor. P̄P̄

★ **GC Suites** 4th Floor, Grand Central Building, Hayes St w facebook.com/gcsuitescdo. The closest this city has to a boutique hotel, GC Suites offers a variety of a/c single and double rooms decorated in homage to musical icons such as The Beatles and Bob Marley, and with TVs and clean en-suite bathrooms. Guests are given a voucher for a free

meal, redeemable at one of six restaurants in the same complex. P̄P̄

★ **Limketkai Luxe** Limketkai Dr w limketkailuxe. com. You can't miss this place – a gleaming gold monolith, sticking out of the city like a sore (and bejeweled) thumb. The rooms are suitably opulent, and the chic, tree-fringed swimming pool would look quite at home in a boutique Mediterranean resort. An excellent choice. P̄P̄P̄

Red Planet C.M. Recto Ave w redplanethotels.com. Between Centrio Ayala Mall and the Limketkai Center, this candy-cane-coloured hotel is as switched-on to traveller needs as Cagayan De Oro gets. All rooms have a/c, a power shower, and a flat-screen TV. P̄P̄

Seda Centrio C.M. Recto Ave w sedahotels.com. Sharing a roof with the Centrio Ayala Mall (where it seems half of the city spends half of their lives), this business hotel, spread over six floors, is a functional stopover. Rooms are clean and comfy, and fitted with all mod cons. It's popular with out-of-town shoppers, hence the inflated prices. P̄P̄P̄P̄

EATING

SEE MAP PAGE 386

Cagayan de Oro is the best place to eat in northern Mindanao, with a range of affordable **restaurants**. The centre of the action is where A. Velez crosses Hayes and Chavez streets, while a couple of kilometres east, the **Limketkai Center** mall also has a good mix of restaurants.

Apostrophe Café Centrio Ayala Mall w facebook.com/ ApostropheCafe. Yeah, so it's in a mall, but that doesn't stop this being a pretty and relaxing spot for coffee, of which plenty of styles are available. Also has a good cake selection. P̄

Bigby's Café & Restaurant Centrio Ayala Mall

w bigbyscafe.com. Local chain offering a fusion of Western and Filipino dishes, from "Rack a Bye Baby" and pork chops to burgers. Don't miss the Midnight Dream Cake. Also, one at SM City CDO. P̄P̄P̄

★ **Cucina Higala** 222 Capistrano St w facebook.com/pg/ CucinaHigala. This Filipino restaurant combines traditional Mindanaoan recipes with modern techniques. Try its *sinuglaw* (seafood ceviche with grilled pork) or *humba* (braised pork belly stew) prepared sous-vide-style. P̄P̄P̄

Thai Me Up Masterson Ave w facebook.com/ thaimeupuptown. Not a fetish club, but a superb Thai restaurant, with an odd dining area modelled like a market from a children's film. Expect the usual dishes – tom yung, pad thai and *som tam* (papaya salad) – but also the odd Filipino dish that's sneaked its way onto the menu. The bad news – formerly located in the centre, they're now 6km away to the south, so a taxi ride may be in order. P̄P̄P̄

Vjandep Bakeshop 78 Tiano Brothers St Ⓦvjandep. com. Locals say you haven't been to Cagayan de Oro if you haven't eaten at *Vjandep Bakeshop*, the city's most popular bakery. Its especially popular for its *pastels*, bread buns filled with custard; other fillings include pineapple, jackfruit and mango. P̄

DRINKING

SEE MAP PAGE 386

The Oak Room Gateway Park, Limketkai Dr Ⓦfacebook.com/TheOakRoomCDO. Cool but friendly bar that offers Cagayan de Oro's best cocktails, as well as a very fine selection of whiskies and a not half-bad wine list. Also does decent bar food. P̄P̄

Iligan and around

Some 90km west of Cagayan de Oro, the port city of **ILIGAN** is served by regular ferries from Manila and Cebu, making it an alternative gateway to Mindanao if you're travelling on a budget. Little more than a village in the early 1900s, it boomed as an industrial centre after the creation of a hydroelectric power scheme in the 1950s, but was almost completely rebuilt after a devastating fire in 1957. Famed for its **waterfalls**, it's a friendly, laidback place with a population of around 365,000. The best cluster of cascades lies on the west side, on the highway towards Ozamiz and Zamboanga.

Maria Cristina Falls

8.5km southwest of Iligan on the highway to Ozamiz and Zamboanga • Charge, extra for zipline • ☎ 063 221 3988 • It's 150m to the park entrance from the main road jeepney stop; walking to the falls from the entrance takes 20min (800m), or you can take the park shuttle (charge)

The most impressive cascade in the region, and located within the **NPC Nature Park**, the **Maria Cristina Falls** serves as the main source of power for much of Mindanao. The twin falls (named after two heartbroken girls who are supposed to have jumped from the top), plunge 100m into the torrential Agus River, and are at their best on Saturday and Sunday at 11am, when the Agus VI Hydroelectric Plant upstream releases the most water. There is a zipline here, too.

Timoga Springs and Macaraeg-Macapagal House

9.5km west of Iligan on the highway to Ozamiz and Zamboanga • **Timoga Springs** Charge • **Macaraeg-Macapagal House** Free • ☎ 063 223 6992

Just 1km beyond the Maria Cristina Falls, the ice-cold, crystal-clear **Timoga Springs** flow freely to a collection of privately owned swimming pools and resorts that can all get very crowded in summer.

Next door to the springs, right on the highway, is the **Macaraeg-Macapagal House**, sometime home to both Diosdado Macapagal, the ninth president of the Philippines, and Gloria Macapagal-Arroyo, the fourteenth president. As a child, Gloria spent many happy days in this house, which was built in 1950 by her maternal grandfather, and the handsome property has been well maintained, preserved as it would have looked in the 1950s. There's not much inside other than family portraits, including a sultry study of the ex-president from 1983, and a statue of Gloria as a child outside, playing on a swing.

Tinago Falls

15km southwest of Iligan, off the Zamboanga road • Charge • Jeepneys will drop you off on the highway, from where you can hike or take a habal-habal to the falls (make sure to arrange a return pick-up)

9

The **Tinago Falls**, a beautiful ribbon of water cascading 73m into a deep-blue pool, get their name from their location, nestled in a dramatic ravine (*tinago* means hidden). They became locally famous when they featured in the 2011 Pinoy movie *Forever and a Day*. From the top it's a tough walk down four hundred or more steps into the ravine; take plenty of care if it's raining.

ARRIVAL AND DEPARTURE

By bus The northbound bus terminal, off Bonifacio Ave, 3km north of the centre, serves Cagayan de Oro. The southbound terminal off Roxas Ave, just south of the centre, serves western and southern destinations. Jeepneys and taxis are usually easy to find near both terminals.
Destinations from northbound terminal Cagayan de Oro (hourly; 1hr 30min).

ILIGAN AND AROUND

Destinations from southbound terminal Dapitan (several daily; 4hr) Marawi (hourly; 2hr); Ozamiz (hourly; 2hr); Zamboanga (8 hourly; 10hr).
By boat Ferries from Cebu and Manila dock on the edge of the downtown area. If you walk towards the first traffic circle, you'll find plenty of taxis and jeepneys.
Destinations Cebu (7 weekly; 13hr); Manila (3 weekly; 34hr).

GETTING AROUND AND INFORMATION

By jeepney Jeepney rides around town are easy to find.
By taxi A/C taxis can take you around town or on tours of the waterfalls. There are also non-a/c "PU" taxis which run fixed routes for a set rate.

Tourist information The tourist office (Mon–Fri 8am–5pm; ☎ 063 221 3426) is at Bahay Salakot on leafy Buhanginan Hill, next to City Hall at the far eastern end of Quezon Ave; take a taxi or jeepney here from downtown.

ACCOMMODATION AND EATING

Cheradel Suites Bro. Raymond Jeffrey Rd ☎ 063 221 4926. Kitschy collection of rooms and suites in a six-building complex around a small pool. Rooms are modern and comfortable and have a/c and cable TV; the biggest Presidential Suite has three bedrooms plus a kitchen. P̄P̄
Go Hotel 158 Macapagal Ave ⊛ gohotels.ph. Iligan's branch of this reliable national chain is conveniently located by the river and shopping mall, and offers decently priced if unimaginative rooms. It's unlikely to be the standout

accommodation of your trip, but it's handy in a pinch. P̄P̄
Mariano's Home Cooked Specialities Meadow Lark St ⊛ facebook.com/MarianosHCS. The Mariano family know how to cook up a storm. They offer an exciting range of Filipino-European creations in their fine-dining restaurant, where dishes range from pan-seared snapper with clams to herb-roasted chicken with pumpkin mash and beef short rib. P̄P̄

Camiguin Island

Around 20km off the north coast of mainland Mindanao, little **Camiguin Island** ("cam-ee-*geen*") is one of the country's most appealing tourist spots, offering ivory beaches, iridescent lagoons and jagged mountain scenery. There's no shortage of adventure here, with reasonable scuba diving and tremendous trekking and climbing in the rugged interior, especially on volcanic **Mount Hibok-Hibok**.

Another major tourist draw is the annual **Lanzones festival**, held in the fourth week of October. Lanzones are a type of fruit that taste a bit like a grapefruit only less bitter. Revellers dressed only in lanzones leaves stomp and dance in the streets as a tribute to the humble fruit, one of the island's major sources of income.

The beauty of Camiguin is that it doesn't really matter where you stay, as you can visit all the sights easily from anywhere. The **coastal road** is only 64 km long, making it entirely feasible to circle the island in a day. If you don't want to depend on public transport, consider renting a motorbike for day-trips.

Mambajao and around

There's no reason to hang around in **MAMBAJAO** ("mah-bow-ha"), the island's capital, other than to sort out the practicalities of your stay. Of the nearby beaches, **Cabua-an Beach**, to the east, near the barangay of Balbagon, is marginally the closest, with some nice coral close to the shore and half a dozen decent resorts. **Agoho Beach**, 7km west of Mambajao, is wider and sandier, with many resorts – an ideal place to base yourself for all sorts of activities, including scuba diving and volcano climbing.

Katibawasan Falls

Charge • Take a tricycle or minivan to the falls from Mambajao

Easily accessible by road – or you can trek along a marked trail from Balbagon (2hr) – the impressive **Katibawasan Falls** is a narrow, 70m-high cascade with a crystal-clear plunge pool at the bottom, perfect for a chilly swim. A number of souvenir stalls also congregate at the base of the falls.

Ardent Hot Springs

Charge

Some 3km inland from the barangay of Tagdo, **Ardent Hot Springs** can be reached in about an hour on foot from either Mambajao or Agoho Beach. The water in these pools, which lie in a developed park in a jungle valley, is warmed by the volcanic interior of Mount Hibok-Hibok and can reach 40°C. The best time to visit is from late afternoon or after dark, when you can sit in a pool with a cold drink and gaze at the stars. There's a little restaurant, a coffee shop and accommodation in a number of simple cottages.

CAMIGUIN

Jagna (Bohol)

■ ACCOMMODATION	
Balai sa Babai	1
Camiguin Volcano Houses	7
Casa Roca Inn	6
Kurrma	3
Nypa Style Resort	2
Paras Beach Resort	4
Seaside Travellers Inn	8
Volcan Beach Eco Retreat & Dive Resort	5

White Island
Agoho Beach
Bug-ong
Mambajao
Cabu-an Beach
Agoho
Yumbing
Balgabon
Sunken Cemetery
Naasag
Old Camiguin Volcano
Philvocs
San Roque Church
Ardent Hot Springs
Katibawasan Falls
Tupsan
Bonbon
Mt Hibok-Hibok (1332m)
Mt Tres Marias
Tuasan Falls
Santo Niño Cold Springs
Mt Timpoong
Mahinog
Taguines Lagoon
Benoni
Catarman

● EATING	
The BeeHive Driftwood Café	5
Guerrera	3
Hayahay Café	2
J&A Fishpen	6
La Dolce Vita	1
Peninsular Kape Art	4

Cantaan
Cantaan Kaliba Giant Clam Sanctuary
Sagay
Guinsiliban
Moro Watchtower

0   5
kilometres

Balingoan

9

Mount Hibok-Hibok

Charge for a permit to climb the volcano • Most resorts can recommend a local guide (additional charge)

In the northwest of the island, Camiguin's only active volcano, **Mount Hibok-Hibok**, had its last major eruption in 1951, with tremors and landslides that killed five hundred people. At a relatively modest 1332m, it can be climbed in four to five hours, but the strenuous trail crosses some steep slopes and treacherous rocks, and the hike shouldn't be attempted alone. Along the way, you'll see steam vents and hot pools, and at the top there's a crater lake. Views from the summit are unforgettable.

Philvocs

Itum Rd

At **Philvocs**, an easy 3km trip inland from Mambajao by tricycle, volcanologists who monitor Mount Hibok-Hibok are happy to talk to visitors about their work, and have a number of spectacular photographs of past eruptions.

White Island

Charge • Visit via return pump-boat trips from the pier next to Paras Beach Resort in Yumbing

About halfway between Mambajao and Bonbon, off the island's northwest coast, lies one of Camiguin's most popular attractions, **White Island**, a dazzling serpentine ribbon of sand only visible at low tide and easily reached by bangka from Yumbing. The views and the water are gorgeous, but there's no shade, so make sure that you take lots of sunblock.

Bonbon

The small fishing town of **BONBON** on Camiguin's west coast has an attractive little plaza and a pretty, whitewashed church; it also lies a few kilometres south of the slopes of the **Old Camiguin Volcano**, which you can climb easily in an hour (entry charge). The path to the summit, from where the views are stunning, is marked by life-size alabaster statues representing the **Stations of the Cross**.

A little southwest of the old volcano you'll see a striking, enormous **white cross** floating on a pontoon in the bay. This marks the site of the **Sunken Cemetery**, which slipped into the sea during a volcanic eruption in 1871 – you can observe reef fish massing around the decaying tombs on a diving or snorkelling trip. The same eruption destroyed the seventeenth-century Spanish **San Roque Church** on the northern fringes of modern Bonbon; its brooding ruins still stand, with a memorial altar inside.

Catarman and around

There are some quiet stretches of sandy beach near the ramshackle little town of **CATARMAN**, 24km south of Mambajao, plus springs and falls, but there's no accommodation in the area. On the southern coast, hidden behind Guinsiliban Elementary School, fifteen minutes east by jeepney from Catarman, is a three-hundred-year-old **Moro Watchtower**.

Santo Niño Cold Springs and Tuasan Falls

Santo Niño Cold Springs; Tuasan Falls Charge • Visit by habal-habal round trip to both

Santo Niño Cold Springs lies some 6km north of Catarman, while further north on an island tour will bring you to **Tuasan Falls**. Both have deep pools that are good for swimming, but much to the chagrin of locals, the area surrounding the once-pristine cascades has been blighted by the building of a controversial cross-island highway.

Cantaan Kaliba Giant Clam Sanctuary

9

Just south of Benoni, at the end of the road past Cabu-an • Charge, including mini-tour of the rehabilitation tanks; extra fees for clams snorkelling, snorkel hire and picnicking

The family-run **Cantaan Kaliba Giant Clam Sanctuary** is home to about three thousand clams. Entry includes a short tour of the rehabilitation tanks, and grants you access to one of the island's most beautiful stretches of white-sand beach, as well as a coral reef that's good for snorkelling. Though the entry fee is reasonable, the extra charges for snorkelling are overpriced.

ARRIVAL AND DEPARTURE
CAMIGUIN ISLAND

By plane The airport, on the coast 1km west of Mambajao, sees daily flights to and from Cebu (1–2 daily; 50min). The airport charges a terminal fee.

By boat Ferries leave Balingoan on Mindanao for Benoni

on Camiguin's southeast coast roughly hourly (1hr). Super Shuttle Ferries leave from Benoni for Jagna on Bohol three times a week (3 weekly; 4hr 30min; ⚲ supershuttleroro. com).

GETTING AROUND AND INFORMATION

Island transport Transport rates to everywhere on the island are fixed by the tourist office, and displayed on a board at the Benoni pier.

Tourist information The tourist office (Mon–Fri 8am–5pm; ☏ 088 387 1097) is in the Provincial Capitol building,

a short tricycle ride from the centre of Mambajao. As well as accommodation suggestions, they can advise on activities, including climbing Hibok-Hibok.

Services In Mambajao there are branches of PNB and Landbank, and plenty of ATMs.

ACCOMMODATION
SEE MAP PAGE 391

Most of the seaside accommodation in Camiguin is west of Mambajao on the beaches between the small towns of **Bug-ong** and **Naasag**. Resorts near the town of **Agoho**, a little west of Bug-ong, remain popular due to their easy access to White Island. East of Mambajao, around the village of **Balgabon**, you'll find more resorts, although the beach here isn't as good as at Agoho, Yumbing or Naasag.

★ **Balai sa Babai** Agoho ⚲ balaisababai.com. The most romantic place on the island, with plunge pools, private gardens and outdoor Bali-style outdoor bathrooms. Literally meaning "house by the beach", this chichi pad is run on solar power and is straight from the cover of an interior design magazine. The private villa is a stunner – as good as Filipino accommodation gets – while the a/c rooms are a lesson in textbook glamour. $\overline{PPP}$

Camiguin Volcano Houses Mambajao ⚲ facebook. com/camiguinvolcanohouses. Found a little way inland rather than by the shore, this isn't the place if you want sea views – instead, you'll get a room in a remarkable wood A-frame house set in a jungle clearing, with gorgeous traditional decoration and hammocks to relax in. Guests have the use of the kitchen to cook dinner. $\overline{PP}$

Casa Rocca Inn Naasag ☏ 0961 980 0935. Perched on a hillock on the far northwestern tip of the island, this heavenly three-room tranquil resort is a lovely place to wind-down for a few days. There are two standard rooms, and one veranda room with sweeping sunset views. Good restaurant offering steaks, salmon and crab dishes, too. $\overline{PP}$

Kurma Yumbing ⚲ kurmafreedive.com. Formerly known as *Secret Cove Beach Resort*, this place has boldly painted fan or a/c rooms, including two family rooms right on the

oceanfront. The resort is the HQ for the couple's highly recommended free-diving and yoga camps as well as the on-site, veg-friendly restaurant that specializes in fusion cuisine using local, organic produce. $\overline{PP}$

★ **Nypa Style Resort** 500m inland from Bug-ong ⚲ nypastyleresort.jimdo.com. Owned by the hospitable Elena, this gorgeous hilltop resort, centred around a beautiful Indian-almond tree, features six bungalows and a natural swimming pool. The emphasis here is on wellness and massage; the food is superb home-made Italian. Breakfast is additional, but worth it. $\overline{PP}$

Paras Beach Resort Yumbing ☏ 088 387 9081. In an enviable position on the shore, this was a private beach house belonging to the Paras family until they decided to add a whole range of a/c rooms with hot showers and cable TV, and open it to the public. Right in the thick of things. $\overline{PPP}$

Seaside Travellers Inn Bacnit ⚲ seasidetravelersinn. com. On the southwest side of the island, the Seaside Travellers Inn offers clean and comfortable rooms as well as a few beachfront villas. They can arrange tours, taking in the island's highlights, at very reasonable prices. $\overline{P}$

Volcan Beach Eco Retreat & Dive Resort Naasag ⚲ camiguinvolcanbeach.com. The highlights at this resort are the charming bungalows, the tropical garden strung with hammocks and the excellent dive centre. As if that's not enough, it's got its own reef on the doorstep, a bamboo deck for yoga and a wood-fired oven for home-made breads. It's the perfect place to watch the spectacular sunsets, too. The beach villas are among the loveliest on the island. $\overline{PP}$

9

Eating on Camiguin is mostly limited to the **resorts**, but a few new standout **restaurants** have opened in recent years. Like everywhere else in the Philippines, there's an inexplicable number of Italian pizzerias and restaurants, while in Mambajao, there's a cluster of cheap places to eat around the market area.

The BeeHive Driftwood Café On the Catibac beach road ⓦ beehivedriftwoodcafe.weebly.com. With conch shells swinging from the ceiling, driftwood tables, and an idyllic oceanfront setting, this outpost feels more like a castaway's shack than a café. Visitors are spoiled with fresh-brew coffee, honeycomb-shaped pizzas and souvenir pots of organic honey. Worth the journey just to see it. **PPP**

★ **Guerrera** Agoho Beach Rd ⓦ guerrera.ph. The street-food craze has reached Camiguin, and the location of this first-rate restaurant, set beside a beautiful rice paddy and organic garden, instantly transports you to rural Vietnam or Laos. Dishes such as pad thai, Vietnamese noodle salads and *bánh xèo* (savoury crispy pancakes) are all knockouts. Also has a couple of rooms. **PPPP**

Hayahay Café Agoho Beach Rd ⓦ hayahaycafe.com. Excellent spot for coffee or brunch fare, including smoothie bowls (really well presented), shakshuka (which always looks a bit of a mess, to be fair) and banana pancakes. They have heartier meals on offer for later in the day, including

plenty of veg choices, and an interesting "leftover pasta" dish. **PP**

J&A Fishpen Taguines Lagoon, Benoni ⦿ 088 387 4008. Though it's a trek to get to, this over-the-water seafood shack is an enjoyable place to kill time, particularly if you're getting a ferry to or from Benoni, or fancy trying the nearby zipline over the lagoon. The menu is as straightforward as they come: choose your fish or crabs from the water pens, and they'll cook it how you like. **PP**

La Dolce Vita Opposite the airport ⦿ 0998 945 6389. One of Camiguin's many high-quality Italian restaurants, *La Dolce Vita* may not have the ideal hilltop locations of its island rivals, but everything from its al dente pastas and pizzas to pesto is home-made and delicious. The Italian owner imports many of the ingredients from his homeland. The restaurant also has a pleasant outdoor deck – good for watching the locals buzz between Mambajao and Yumbing. **PPP**

Peninsular Kape Art Next to Paros Beach Hotel, Yumbing ⓦ facebook.com/PeninsularKapeArt. This Spanish-run tapas restaurant and handicraft store is a breath of fresh air, providing something entirely different from the usual Italian places. Paellas, spicy mussels or *gambas ajillo* are on offer in the garden, while local Pinikas artwork, jewellery, and woven bags are for sale inside. Free wi-fi. **PPPP**

Butuan and the east

The bustling capital of Agusan del Norte province, **BUTUAN** lies around 200km east of Cagayan de Oro. Butuan is thought to have been the first coastal trading settlement in the Philippines; in 1976 a carefully crafted and ornate oceangoing outrigger (*balangay*) was unearthed on the banks of the Agusan River and carbon-dated, astonishingly, to 320 AD. Of nine boats since discovered in the mud, two more have been excavated, dating from 1215 and 1250 and adding to the growing wealth of evidence that the Philippines was actively trading with Asia long before the Spanish arrived.

Butuan also acts as a hub for visits to sights on and around the east coast, which include the Enchanted River (one of the island's best spots for wild swimming) and the picturesque, Niagara-like Tinuy-An Falls.

Balangay Shrine

City Hall compound, 1km north of the city centre • Free

The original "Butuan boat" is now in the small **Balangay Shrine**, around 5km west of the city, along with the remains of a number of other ancient boats and ethnological treasures such as ceramics and coffins.

Butuan National Museum

City Hall compound, 1km north of the city centre • Free • ⓦ nationalmuseum.gov.ph

The **Butuan National Museum** is home to a small but intriguing collection including cooking implements and jewellery from pre-Hispanic Butuan. There are two galleries: the Archeological Hall, which exhibits stone crafts, metal objects, pots, gold and burial coffins; and the Ethnological Hall, which focuses on the culture of the Manobo, Mamanua, Higaonon and lowland Butuanons.

ARRIVAL AND INFORMATION
BUTUAN

By plane Butuan's Bancasi airport is 10km west of the city. Taxis and tricycles are on hand to take you into town.
Destinations Cebu (4 daily; 50min); Manila (7 daily; 1hr 45min).
By bus The terminal is 3.5km north of Butuan off Montilla Blvd.
Destinations Cagayan de Oro (hourly; 4hr); Davao (every 20min; 5–6hr); Surigao (hourly; 2hr).
By boat Ferries dock at the port town of Nasipit, 24km

west of Butuan, from where it's a 30min jeepney ride into the city. 2GO (ⓦtravel.2go.com.ph) has one weekly service to Cebu (9hr), while Cokaliong Shipping Lines (ⓦcokaliongshipping.com) has a weekly service to Jagna on Bohol (5hr). The same operator also has a route to Cebu (4 weekly).
Tourist information The provincial Department of Tourism office is at the Grateful Realty Corp Building, on Pili Drive (Mon–Fri 8am–5pm; ☎085 341 8413).

ACCOMMODATION AND EATING

Almont Inland Resort San José St, Rizal Park ⓦalmont.com.ph. This 56-room resort with pool and man-made lake has a range of spacious rooms and suites, all with a/c, private bathroom and cable TV. To stay closer to the city bustle at a lower price, check out its dependable sister, the *Almont City Hotel* next to the Agusan River. $\overline{PPP}$
Go Hotels J.C. Aquino Ave ⓦgohotels.ph. Value chain hotel with a hundred a/c box-size rooms with hot and cold shower, in-room safe, and cable TV. Charges for luggage storage. $\overline{P}$
Ocean Bloom Boutique Beach Resort 5km from Butuan in Manapa ⓦfacebook.com/OceanBloomPH. This family-run beach hotel is a relaxing place to chill out for a few days. There are a variety of rooms, including deluxe a/c and family rooms, while the courtyard offers simpler four- and six-bed dorms. The resort accepts no walk-ins, so book in advance. $\overline{PP}$
★ **Project Brew** Jose Rosales Ave ⓦfacebook.com/

ProjectBrewBXU. Professional café that focuses on the beans – with its minimalist appearance and smattering of tables, this isn't the sort of place in which you can get in a day's laptop work, but for a cuppa it's just the trick. $\overline{PP}$
★ **Watergate** Jose Rosales Ave ⓦwatergatehotel butuan.ph. Boutique hotel aimed at the flashpacker and business market, with a design supposedly inspired by the nearby Agusan River. All rooms come with bouncy mattresses, fancy toiletries and power showers, while the excellent service and free pick-ups from the airport underline its status as the best accommodation in the city; just make sure that the phones haven't been tapped. $\overline{PPP}$
Y Hotel South Montilla Blvd ⓦfacebook.com/yhotel butuan. Promising the most modern atmosphere in the city, *Y Hotel*'s a/c rooms are clean and equipped with comfy beds and fridges. The staff couldn't be more personable. There's a coffee shop next door. $\overline{PP}$

The Enchanted River

At the end of a 12km dirt road, just beyond the fishing village of Talisay • Charge; additional fee for lifejacket rental • The turning to the river and Talisay is signposted 2km north of Hinatuan on the main coast road, 150km south of Butuan; the main road is served by frequent buses between Butuan and Mangagoy – without your own transport it's a very long walk or habal-habal ride from Hinatuan

Swimming in the **Enchanted River** is one of the highlights of a trip to Mindanao. The accessible part of the river is more like a narrow saltwater lagoon that ends at an underwater cave and ravine crammed with all sorts of tropical fish that get fed every day at noon. The colours are mesmerizing; the water glows like liquid sapphire, surrounded by dense jungle and karst outcrops.

The site is managed as a small park, but it's well off the beaten path, and few foreign tourists make it this far. Crowds of locals descend at weekends, so it's highly recommended to go during the week.

Tinuy-An Falls

15km west of Bislig • Charge; additional fee for bamboo raft • Most people hire a minivan and driver in Butuan, but you can take a bus to Bislig or Mangagoy (5hr) and then a habal-habal to the falls (40min)

Around 160km south of Butuan, near the port town of **Bislig**, a dirt road leads some 15km to the astounding **Tinuy-An Falls**, a thunderous, multi-tiered 95m cascade that's like Niagara Falls reimagined in the heart of jungle. Get here early

9

and it's a magical place, with lush foilage, durian trees and giant ferns drooping over the river – you can lounge on the bank and enjoy the views or clamber up to the higher levels and paddle or swim in the pools, where a bamboo raft takes you closer in to get thoroughly soaked. Come in the morning to see the falls' most spectacular rainbows.

Surigao City

The bustling, ramshackle capital of the province of Surigao del Norte, **SURIGAO CITY**, some 120km north of Butuan, is essentially just a place to pass through on the way to the picture-postcard island of Siargao. It's a compact place and easy to get around on foot, but there's just not that much to do here: if you find yourself with time on your hands it's worth a trip up to the pretty pebble beach at **Mabua**, 12km north.

ARRIVAL AND DEPARTURE   SURIGAO CITY

By plane The airport, 5km outside the city on the road to Butuan, sees daily flights to and from Cebu (2 daily; 45min). Tricycles can be picked up to take you into the centre of town.

By bus, jeepney and multicab Buses arrive at the terminal 4km west of the city centre, with town accessible by jeepney and multi-cab. To head to Cagayan de Oro or Balingoan (for Camiguin) you'll need to change in Butuan. Destinations Butuan (hourly; 2hr); Davao (hourly; 8hr).

By boat The Eva M. Macapagal Passenger Terminal is on the harbour; you can walk or take a tricycle from here to the city centre. There's a terminal fee for all departures. Coming from the Visayas, Cokaliong Shipping Lines (ⓦcokaliongshipping.com) serves Cebu (6 weekly; 9hr 30min, sometimes via Maasin). Heading to Siargao, there are a variety of options, from fast, cramped outriggers (2–3hr) to slower, more spacious and safer RORO boats (3–4hr). Montenegro Lines (ⓦmontenegrolines.com.ph) runs a daily service (3hr 30min). All of these boats leave Surigao for Dapa on Siargao before noon, so it's best to arrive in town early, or accept that you'll have to spend a night in the city.

INFORMATION

Tourist information Near Luneta Park, City Hall is home to the Department of Tourism (☏ 086 826 8064) and offers information about accommodation and ferries.

ACCOMMODATION

Almont Beach Resort Lipata ⓦalmont.com.ph. For a bit of luxury, 15min drive from the port, the *Almont* offers good rooms with sensational views of the bay. There's also a decent pool and a good on-site café. P̄P̄

Le Chard Place 4km south on National Hwy ⓦfacebook.com/LechardPlace. With a fair amount of designer swagger to it – rooms are painted bold orange, green and purple, and the walls are covered in pop art – this conveniently located B&B manages to squeeze in plenty of goodies. They offer free breakfast and free airport transfers, as well as 24hr security, parking and there's a back-up generator for those all-too-common blackouts. P̄

One Hive Hotel & Suites Rizal St ☏086 232 0065. Across the road from the Surigao Provincial Sports Complex, this affordable business hotel has a variety of clean, a/c, bee-themed rooms, such as "queen bee", "bumble bee", "hive room" and so on. Breakfast is included, while downstairs the café-restaurant serves quick bites and fusion cuisine. P̄P̄

Tavern Borromeo St ⓦhoteltavern.com. Not far from the ferry terminal, this place has smart modern rooms in the newer west wing, and comfy cheaper rooms in the older east building. Sea views and balconies are available for a little more. Good breakfast buffet and free pick-up both included. P̄P̄P̄

EATING AND DRINKING

EJ's Garden Café Borromeo St ⓦfacebook.com/EJsCafeSurigao. In addition to great coffee, milkshakes, frappes, cold-brew teas and beers, *EJ's Café* pulls in the crowds for its imaginative, if scattershot, menu, including the likes of burgers, poutine, empanadas, fettucine and roast-beef sandwiches. If you're waiting for the next ferry, pull up a chair for some people-watching and try the Willy Wonka-esque chocolate bomb frappe. The café is near the *Hotel Tavern* compound. It occasionally hosts musical performances. P̄

Harborside Resto & Grill City Blvd ⓦfeedmehealthy. ph. Seafront restaurant decked out in slightly nightmarish red and black, though serving excellent seafood, including their hugely popular *kinilaw* (ceviche). There's plenty of non-fishy fare, too, including cheap rice and noodle mains, and BBQ items by the stick. **PPP**

Manzanitas City Blvd ☎ 0930 812 5140. This small restaurant on the seafront serves up a good selection of meals, skewing towards Filipino classics rather than international. The seafood is delicious, and the pork dinakdakan salad has a great chilli kick to it. It's also a pleasant place to relax with a cold beer. **PP**

Siargao Island

Off the northeastern tip of Mindanao lies the teardrop-shaped island of **SIARGAO**, a largely undeveloped backwater with languid beaches, dramatic coves and lagoons battered by the Pacific Ocean. Some of the first tourists here were **surfers**, who discovered a Pacific reef break at Tuason Point – so good, they called it **Cloud 9**. Though old-timers now dub it "Crowd 9" because of its popularity, there is a friendly, welcoming surfing scene here, and Siargao gives Malapascua and Panglao a run for their money as the backpacker capital of the southern Philippines. The annual **International Surfing Cup**, usually held in late September or early October, attracts international competitors from Australia, the US and Europe, as well as from around the Philippines. The 2022 edition was cancelled (as were the two events previous, thanks to Covid) due to major damage caused by Typhoon Odette at the tail end of 2021; thankfully, Siargao wasted little time getting back on its feet.

SURIGAO, SIARGAO ISLAND AND DINAGAT

9

General Luna (GL)

Most visitors arrive at **Sayak Airport**, near Del Carmen, 30km from the surf resorts and honeymoon hideaways around the island's friendly little capital of **GENERAL LUNA**, known as **GL**, on the east coast. Resorts line the coast north from here, and though there are only small patches of decent beach, it's a lush, laidback strip, with swathes of coconut palms, beach bars and surf shops. While surfing has grabbed the headlines, **kitesurfing** has made its mark too (see page 399).

Cloud 9 (Tuason Point)

A 30min walk from GL, or quick ride on a habal-habal

Sleep, eat, surf: that's the mantra 2km further north from GL at **Cloud 9**, the world-renowned break at **Tuason Point**. On most days, from sunrise to sundown, you'll find surfers in action: beach bums previously watched from the multi-storey **wooden viewing pavilion** in front of the break, and will no doubt do so again once it is rebuilt following its destruction in Typhoon Odette. The peak **surf season** is September and October, lasting until early December before things slow down at the end of the year; beginners will find the weaker surf from April to July more manageable.

Magpupungko Beach

Charge; extra fees for parking and entry to the Fri night beach parties • Motorbike from GL takes around 1hr via a bumpy road, or hire a bangka from Cloud 9

Travelling 35km north of GL, mostly via dirt road, brings you to **PILAR**, a village of traditional wooden stilt houses on the edge of the mangroves. It's best known for **Magpupungko Beach**, 2km further north, the site of sporadic Friday night beach parties. The sandy beach is one of the island's best, but the highlight is the giant natural swimming pool that forms to the far left of the beach at low tide. The water is beautifully clear and inviting – assuming the weather cooperates.

Sohoton Cove and Lagoon

Bucas Grande • Cave and lagoon entry charge • Reached by Bangka from Siargao

The enticing island of **Bucas Grande** lies between Siargao and Mindanao proper, with mushroom-shaped limestone rocks sprouting from its shimmering waters. The inland **Sohoton Cove and Lagoon** on the east side of the island is the must-do excursion from Siargao – but it takes two hours each way, so you'll need most of a day to do it justice. The best time to visit is between March and July, when the weather and the sea crossing are at their calmest.

Once at the cove, you'll have to sign in and get a short briefing about the site; you then transfer into another boat that will take you through the cave entrance into the enchanting lagoon, a cavernous space hemmed in by soaring vine-smothered cliffs and home to giant non-stinging jellyfish. It's a phenomenal sight and worth the journey and expense, assuming the weather is good. There are several other caves here that your *banquero* should be able to guide you to with no extra charge: if you are brave and can hold your breath for long enough (unless it's low tide when there is a small gap), you can swim through a short tunnel into **Hagukan Cave** where there are strange fish, stalactites, rock oysters and wild orchids.

ARRIVAL AND DEPARTURE

SIARGAO ISLAND

By plane The tiny airport is in, and named after, the barangay of Sayak on the west coast; minivans and habal-habals will run to GL and Cloud 9 – check with your accommodation in advance about potential free pick-ups.

The airport charges a terminal fee.
Destinations Cebu (8 daily; 1hr); Clark (4 daily; 2hr 30min); Davao (4 weekly; 1hr 10min); Manila (2 daily; 2hr).
By boat A number of companies, including Evaristo and

SIARGAO ISLAND-HOPPING

The seas around Siargao are littered with unspoilt and rarely visited **islands**. The easiest to reach are the three islands just off the coast of GL (around 30min by bangka): most resorts can fix you up with local bangka operators for half-day trips to all three.

Naked Island is little more than a giant sandbar, and perfect for lounging in the sun. **Dako Island** is the largest of the three, smothered in coconut palms and home to a small fishing community. The villagers will happily serve you fresh coconut or barbecue chicken, and you can even rent out the basic beach cottages for the day or overnight. Tiny **Guyam Island** comes closest to the stereotype of a classic desert island: a circular clump of sand dotted with palm trees ideal for picnics, swimming or sunbathing. The island caretaker usually charges a small fee per person. **Snorkelling** isn't much good from any of these islands – the best reefs lie in between them, so ask your boat to make an extra stop.

If you're keen to escape the crowds and head a little further ahead, you can give Corregidor Island (not the one near Manila, of course) a try; it's about 45min away by boat, and has a modest peak that you can scale for views of the sea and its confetti of islands. Even more distant, Mam-On Island (about 1hr away from GL) has a truly unspoiled beach.

Sons (℡ facebook.com/evaristoandsonsseatransportcorp) and Montenegro Shipping Lines (℡ montenegrolines. com.ph), operate ferries from Surigao to Dapa, 16km from GL on the south coast. There's a choice of slow ferries (3hr 30min–4hr) or faster outriggers (2hr 30min). Most boats in either direction leave in the morning, often at early hours for the faster services. You must pay a terminal fee to board the boats.

INFORMATION AND ACTIVITIES

Services There's a post office in Dapa, as well as plenty of ATMs, though most places accept credit cards.

Surfing Leading the pack of highly recommended surf schools is *Buddha Resort* (see page 399), while *Kermit Surf Resort* (see page 400) offers a full range of rentals and classes.

Kitesurfing There are plenty of kitesurfing camps, offering lessons, rental and full beginner courses. Two to try are Sea Breeze Kite Club (℡ seabreezekiteclub.com) and *Viento Del Mar* (℡ vientodelmar.com), both located on the beachfront just north of GL.

GETTING AROUND

By habal-habal Choices for getting around the island are fairly limited. Most locals use the habal-habals, good for up to two people and light luggage; the vehicles are customized with retro-fitted carry racks for long- and shortboards. Rates are fixed, so you shouldn't need to negotiate.

Motorbike rental If you intend to do a lot of roaming around, having your own wheels is definitely recommended. Ask your accommodation about renting a motorcycle. There is no hospital on the island, so take care if driving: accidents are common, especially at night after the bars close.

Tricycles and minivans Tricycles will often quote high charges for the trip between Dapa and GL, so ask around and be prepared to haggle.

ACCOMMODATION

Siargao accommodation ranges from low-budget surf lodges to upmarket tropical resorts. Most places are a short distance from GL or Cloud 9, and the best can help arrange motorbike rentals, bangka trips and all kinds of tours.

Bravo Beach Resort North of GL ✪ bravosiargao.com. If any sign were needed that Siargao is going upmarket, this lovely beach resort is it. Rooms have comfy queen beds, safes, wardrobes and convertible sofas for extra guests. On site is an oceanfront Spanish-fusion restaurant – one of the island's prettiest places to while away a hot afternoon. Despite the frills, it also has a cheapie eight-bed dorm. <u>PPP</u>

★ **Buddha Resort** At the northern edge of GL ℡ buddhasiargao.com. On some nights, this fabulously funky surfers' retreat may resemble an overflowing beer garden, due to its deservedly popular acoustic gigs and burger nights. *Buddha's* is the beating heart of GL's surf scene, with thatched-roof a/c privates and suites kitted out with in-room water coolers and inviting balconies. For all manner of lessons and rentals, you really don't need to look further. <u>PP</u>

Harana Surf Resort Midway between GL and Cloud 9 ℡ haranasurf.com. One of the newest surf camps, with a confident open-plan design, beachfront deck and bespoke surf art. The rooms come in a variety of doubles or sprawling family rooms, while the twelve-bed dorm – or community hut – is the nicest on the island. To top it all off, there are

9

appealing hammocks, relaxing beanbags and a great cocktail bar. Wi-fi in the restaurant. **PPP**

Kalinaw Resort Midway between GL and Cloud 9 ⓦ kalinawresort.com. The most luxurious (and expensive) option on the island, facing the loveliest stretch of beach in the area. The five immaculate wooden villas have gorgeous minimalist interiors, balconies and satellite TV, while the pool villa has its own private infinity tub. There's also a top-notch French restaurant with dishes such as truffle risotto and croque-monsieurs. **PPPP**

Kermit Surf Resort 300m off the main GL beach road ⓦ kermitsiargao.com. In a head-to-head competition with *Buddha's* for the best flashpackers in town, this well-run place has a/c and fan cottages, as well as dorms with shared bathroom. The real draw is its hangout area, though, with hammocks, ping-pong table, library and sociable bar. **PP**

Siargao Island Villas Opposite Buddha's Surf Resort ⓦ siargaoislandvillas.com. Large and modern rooms await at Siargao Island Villas, where you'll also find a pool in a relaxing leafy garden. There's a good restaurant offering Indonesian cuisine, and the friendly staff can arrange tours and watersports activities. **PPPP**

Three Little Birds Surf Hostel 200m from Kermit Surf Resort Cloud 9 ⓦ instagram.com/3littlebirds_siargao. One of the only genuine budget deals in town, this sociable hostel is justifiably popular with surfers for its free-to-use kitchen, lockers, and hangout area. The bunk beds each have their own little fan (a great idea), and all toilet and showers are shared. Minimum three-night stay in high season. **P**

Tropical Temple Siargao Resort Tourism Rd, GL ⓦ instagram.com/tropicaltemple. The stylish architecture at this resort combines jungle huts with modern aesthetics, producing a memorable design – the main building looks a little bit like a church on a tropical holiday. The room interiors are less exciting, though still very comfortable. For those on a budget, there are dorm rooms here too. **PP**

EATING

Most of the best places to eat and drink are in the **resorts**, but a number of independent places have opened over the past few years.

Fin & Fin ⓦ facebook.com. Inspired by the cuisine of the American Gulf Coast, a simple spot where fried stuff (seafood, chips etc) is served in trays on blue-and-white chequered grease paper. The DIY seafood platter is a good choice – load your plate up with fried fish, calamari or chicken (or all three; why not?), then get sides such as mac and cheese or cornmeal fritters dolloped on too. **PP**

★ **Kawayan Villa** Just south of Cloud 9 ⓦ kawayan villasiargao.com. Accessed along a leafy garden path, this dimly lit, all-wood bar-restaurant has a Thai lounge feel. There are pool tables, cheap happy-hour beers and a cracking French-Moroccan-Filipino menu. Choose from the likes of tropical ceviche and a delicious tagine, accompanied by imported French wines. Also has two lovely cottages for rent out the back. **PPP**

L'Osteria Tuason Point, GL ⓦ facebook.com/losteria. siargao. An excellent Italian restaurant, with great pasta and meat dishes, though the real stars of the show are the excellent pizzas, cooked in a proper brick oven. They also have an attractive villa with pool available for rent. **PPPP**

Mama's Grill On the beach road north of GL. This no-nonsense street-side BBQ shack is a hit with surfers and locals alike. Regulars come here nightly for the chicken and seafood kebabs, perfectly cooked on the charcoal-stoked grill, and washed down with a cold San Miguel or two. **P**

Shaka Next to Kawayan Siarago Resort ⓦ facebook. com/ShakaSiargao. Great organic café specializing in healthy shakes, juices and fresh-fruit power bowls made with granola; you can pocket a few raw, vegan energy balls for the day of surfing ahead. The mini gallery of surf prints for sale on the wall adds to the laidback island atmosphere. **PP**

The Smoking Joint BBQ Tourism Rd, GL ⓦ facebook. com/TheSmokingJointBBQSiargao. One of the many barbecue places to be found in GL, the Smoking Joint stands out for its relaxed beachside location and – perhaps more importantly – the excellent dishes on offer. The pulled pork and ribs are divine, and the mac and cheese is extremely popular too. **PPP**

EATING AND DRINKING

Everywhere is lively during peak season, particularly during the International Surfing Cup, when various places on Cloud 9 put on live music.

Kanaloa Beach Bar Doot Beach ⓦ instagram.com/ kanaloasiargao. Bar right on one of the more relaxed beaches in the area – great for a cold one and some grilled seafood, then paddle through the nearby mangroves on a stand-up paddleboard.

Mama Coco On the beach road north of GL ⓦ instagram. com/mamacoco.siargao. Friendly bar which offers cold beer and great cocktails, as well as frequent entertainment which may range from live music to fire dancing. One of the most popular night spots in GL.

Manu Purok 2, GL ⓦ instagram.com/manusiargaoofficial. Lovely, relaxed bar decked out with wicker chairs and polished wood tables, where you'll find some of the best cocktails in Siargao. All the classics are here, as well as a fine selection of home-grown recipes – one of the best selling of which is the typhoon-defying F*ck Odette.

Dinagat Island

There are several morning bangkas from Surigao to San José (4hr), from where bangkas can take you virtually anywhere along the coast of Dinagat

Just a short bangka ride from Surigao, wild and undeveloped **Dinagat Island**, around 60km from tip to toe, is an adventure paradise-in-waiting. Its rugged coastline has tantalizing **islets**, beautiful sugary-sand **beaches** and sheer cliffs that are attracting an increasing number of **rock climbers**. The main drawback is the lack of **accommodation**: there are basic beach huts on the southwest coast around the town of Dinagat, but not much else. Only a handful of travellers make it this far.

The best way to get an overview of what Dinagat has to offer is to rent a bangka in San José, where ferries arrive from Surigao. On the west-coast islet of **Unib** you'll find unspoilt Bitaug Beach and several immense, largely unexplored caves. The waters of this area are fringed by good coral and deep sea walls, but there's no equipment for rent so you'll have to bring whatever you need, including snorkelling gear. In the same area, the uninhabited islet of **Hagakhak** is another beauty, with scintillating above- and underwater rock formations.

Davao

Known as the **durian** capital of the Philippines, and the de facto capital of Mindanao, **DAVAO**, in Mindanao's southeast, is a relaxed city with a reputation for delicious seafood. There are a couple of things to see in the city itself – and in the barangay of **Lanang**, 6km north along the coast – but mostly Davao makes a good base for exploring the surrounding area. That said, the city's formidable line-up of **annual festivals** is certainly worth attending, especially **Kadayawan**, a harvest festival held annually during the third week of August, which focuses on flamboyant tribal dance parades and a beauty pageant.

Despite the obvious pride locals have for the city, Davao remains caught in a violent tug-of-war between the authorities and terrorist groups such as militant Islamic group Abu Sayyaf (see box, page 385). On September 2, 2016, a bomb rocked a Davao night market, causing at least fifteen deaths and injuring seventy people. President Duterte described the attack as an act of **terrorism**, declaring "a state of lawlessness". Abu Sayyaf initially claimed responsibility for the blast, before apportioning blame to one of its allies. The UK's FCDO continues to advise against all but essential travel to the region (and, indeed, all of the relatively "good" bits of Mindanao), which remains under a heightened security alert; any visit to Davao should be **approached with caution**.

People's Park

J. Camus St • Free

A welcome slice of green in the heart of the city, liberally sprinkled with sculptures representing southern Mindanao's Indigenous groups, **People's Park** is especially lively at weekends when there's an evening fountain show, and in the early mornings when it's popular with joggers.

National Museum

Palma Gil St • Free • Ⓦ nationalmuseum.gov.ph

Set in People's Park is the city's latest attraction – the National Museum, housed in a building that's supposed to look something like a durian (some people might associate the design with Minecraft instead, but it does look pretty cool). Exhibits include segments featuring natural history, cultural and historical artifacts, the

9

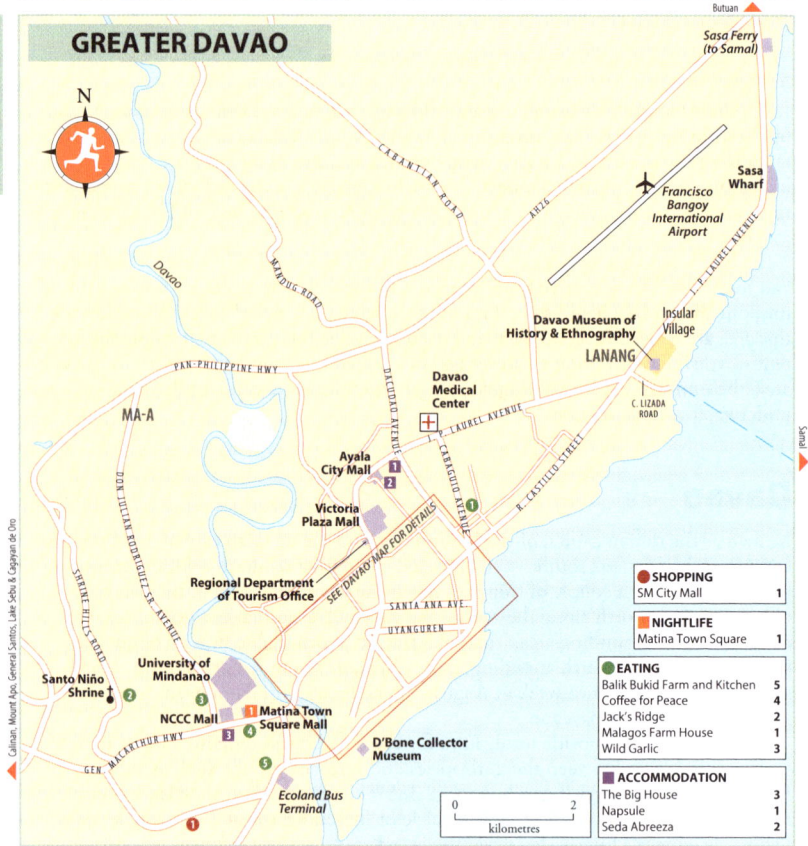

GREATER DAVAO

N

Butuan

Sasa Ferry
(to Samal)

Sasa
Wharf

Francisco
Bangoy
International
Airport

Insular
Village

Davao Museum of
History & Ethnography

LANANG

Davao
Medical
Center

Ayala
City Mall

Victoria
Plaza Mall

SEE DAVAO MAP FOR DETAILS

Regional Department
of Tourism Office

SANTA ANA AVE.

UYANGUREN

University of
Mindanao

Santo Niño
Shrine

NCCC Mall

Matina Town
Square Mall

D'Bone Collector
Museum

Ecoland Bus
Terminal

MA-A

CABANTIAN ROAD

MADUG ROAD

Davao

PAN-PHILIPPINE HWY

DACUDAO AVENUE

C.M. RECTO AVENUE

J. P. LAUREL AVENUE

CARAGUIO AVENUE

R. CASTILLO STREET

C. LIZADA
ROAD

J. P. LAUREL AVENUE

DON JULIAN RODRIGUEZ SR. AVENUE

SHRINE HILLS ROAD

GEN. MACARTHUR HWY.

Calinan, Mount Apo, General Santos, Lake Sebu & Cagayan de Oro

Samal

● SHOPPING	
SM City Mall	1

■ NIGHTLIFE	
Matina Town Square	1

● EATING	
Balik Bukid Farm and Kitchen	5
Coffee for Peace	4
Jack's Ridge	2
Malagos Farm House	1
Wild Garlic	3

■ ACCOMMODATION	
The Big House	3
Napsule	1
Seda Abreeza	2

0   2
kilometres

artistry of Indigenous textiles in Mindanao, and artwork by artists hailing from Davao.

San Pedro Cathedral

San Pedro St at C.M. Recto St • Open during Mass only • Free

The bizarre giant concrete bowl that is **San Pedro Cathedral** began life as a simple nipa chapel in 1848. A more solid structure went up in 1886, but the whole thing was rebuilt in the current Modernist style in the 1970s.

Museo Dabawenyo

Pichon St • Free • Ⓦ facebook.com/museodabawenyo

For an overview of Davao's turbulent and complex history and its ethnic make-up, visit the **Museo Dabawenyo**, housed in the restored court building opposite Osmeña Park. It's small but well presented, and though there are fewer objects on display than at the Davao Museum (see page 405), it is easier to reach. Indigenous people are described in detail, as is the fateful struggle between Datu Bago and conquistador Don José Uyanguren in the 1840s. Panels also throw light on the American occupation boom years in the early twentieth century, the massive migrations that took place from the Visayas thereafter and the arrival of Japanese settlers in the 1930s – hard to believe this was once "Little Tokyo".

D'Bone Collector Museum

San Pedro St • Charge • Ⓦ bone.museum

FORMER PRESIDENT DUTERTE

The Philippines has a long and colourful history of controversial leaders. The Ilocos Norte-born politician **Ferdinand Marcos**, who ruled the country from 1965 to 1986, governed the archipelago with an iron fist. Keeping the country under martial law from 1972 until 1981, he ruled as a dictator, before being run out of office after accusations of mass cheating, political turmoil and a series of human rights abuses. Nonetheless, Ferdinand Marcos has nothing on **Rodrigo Roa Duterte**, "The Punisher". The Philippines' former president and military Commander in Chief, Duterte was so ruthless and unpredictable that he became known as "Duterte Harry" (after the Clint Eastwood character, Dirty Harry).

At the centre of world debate since he took office in June 2016, Duterte was rarely out of the headlines – from rolling back on a diplomatic promise to China over the territorial dispute of an ocean region off the country's northeastern coast, to calling former US President Barack Obama a "son of a whore". Not only has he made the extrajudicial killing of drug dealers and – even more controversially – drug users the cornerstone of his domestic policy, but as the former **mayor of Davao** and the first ever Mindanaoan to hold office, he threatened to impose martial law nationwide if peace and order fails to become the daily norm. That he openly stood up to America, Japan and China, publically swore at press conferences, and had a reputation for frank – and frankly offensive – speechmaking, only adds to his anti-establishment credentials. (While discussing his war on drugs he said, "Hitler massacred three million Jews. Now, there is three million drug addicts – I'd be happy to slaughter them.") This hard-knock reputation and the surrounding mythology has helped him succeed and to swell his grassroots support.

Behind the bluster, Duterte is an ambitious lawyer-turned-politician, with a track record of getting results, even if he splits opinion like an axe. While Mayor of Davao from 2013 to 2016, he vowed to clean up the city's endemic **corruption** and notorious **crime levels** that were the highest in the Philippines. At the time, it was widely alleged that he sanctioned **death squads** who targeted petty criminals, drug dealers and street children. Duterte, many say, appointed himself judge, jury and executioner by rubber-stamping hundreds of extrajudicial killings. The result? Davao's per capita crime rate plummeted to the lowest in the country, and the turnaround helped determine Duterte's political future. Though he is the son of a former provincial governor, he is not a member of the ruling political elite; this has struck a powerful chord with the people of Davao. In 2016, he ran a cleverly marketed election campaign using the slogan Du30 (a shorthand nickname for the politician, which went viral on social media), in which he promised to fight crime and narcotics, and to **eradicate illicit drugs** within six months. Soon after, he was handed the keys to the most important office in the country.

Throughout his tenure as president, Duterte's brash and abrasive approach divided international opinion. In their human rights report from January 2017, Amnesty International claimed that Filipino police paid officers to kill alleged drug offenders, and planted evidence on vulnerable victims as part of what they call Duterte's "murderous war on the poor". The president shrugged off the criticism, saying it would not dissuade him. "I do not give a sh*t," he said. "I have a duty to do, and I will do it." Limited to a single term by the constitution, Duterte was ineligible to run for re-election, and his presidency came to an end in June 2022; this hasn't stopped him from politicking, and in 2024 he stirred things up by calling for Mindanao to secede from the rest of the Philippines.

9

DAVAO

Francisco Bangoy International Airport

Regional Department of Tourism, Victoria Plaza Mall & Ayala Mall

Davao Museum of History & Ethnography & Sasa Wharf (7km)

Samal & Talikud

ACCOMMODATION
Apo View	2
The Bourke	3
Green Windows	1
Dormitel	1
My Hotel	4

EATING
Basement 2D Restaurant	3
Bondi&Bourke	1
Naty's Lechon House	2

SHOPPING
Aldevinco Shopping Center	1

DRINKING
Botanica	2
The Grid at the Alley	1

N

500
0   metres

Santa Ana Wharf

Magsaysay Park

Medical Mission Hospital

LEON GARCIA STREET

LAPU-LAPU STREET

Allied Bank

Agdao Market

CHINATOWN

Immigration Office

STA. ANA AVENUE

MONTEVERDE STREET

SALES ST

R. MAGSAYSAY AVENUE

J. LUNA ST

University of Southeastern Philippines

Brick Lane Square

San Pedro Hospital

Gaisano Mall

J. P. LAUREL AVENUE

D. SUAZO ST

CHAVEZ ST

GUERRERO ST

PONCE STREET

AURORA QUEZON ST

QUEZON BOULEVARD

Ateneo de Davao University

Philippines Airlines

E. JACINTO STREET

ROXAS AVENUE

MABINI STREET

ARTIAGA ST

S. DE JESUS STREET

University Mall

Aldevinco Shopping Center

Citibank

Central Bank

HSBC

Davao City High School

E. TORRES STREET

XVANCERA ST

ARAULLO ST

V. MAPA ST

A. MABINI ST

KRELLANO ST

ARTIONKO AVENUE

PARDO DE TAVERA ST

MT APO ST

PLDT & SMART

C. BANGOY STREET

People's Park

School

National Museum

University of Mindanao

PALMA GIL STREET

C. M. RECTO STREET

BONIFACIO ST

RIZAL STREET

BOLTON STREET

INIGO STREET

San Pedro Cathedral

Davao Doctors' Hospital

Calinan Bus Station

GEN MALVAR ST

E. QUIRINO AVENUE

I. CAMUS ST

GEN. LUNA ST

GOV. DUTERTE ST

V. TIUSTRE ST

PELAYO ST

Gaisano
Citimall
Citibank

RIZAL PROMENADE

SAN PEDRO STREET

Rizal Park

City Hall

Osmeña Park

Museo Dabawenyo

PICHON ST (MAGELLANES)

Bankerohan Market

DAVAO River

Ecoland Bus Terminal

D'Bone Collector Museum

9

Though it sounds more like a relic from a horror film, the award-winning **D'Bone Collector Museum** exhibits a myriad of animal and reptile skeletons. While there are bones of all shapes and sizes, and terrific displays of invertebrates hanging ominously from the ceiling, the focus is firmly on **educating** visitors about animal conservation. Visits are by hourly tour only.

Davao Museum of History & Ethnography

Insular Village 1, J.P Laurel Ave, Lanang • ☎ 082 233 1734 • Lanang is reached via jeepney (marked "Sasa") or by taxi; sign in at the gate and then turn right, from where it's a 5min walk

You'll find the small but enlightening **Davao Museum of History & Ethnography** tucked away at the back of a gated community in the barangay of Lanang, 4km north of Magsaysay Park. On the ground floor, a detailed timeline describes the city's key events, with temporary exhibits such as rare sculptures on display. Upstairs there's a decent introduction to Davao's fifteen Indigenous groups, including the Bagobos, with displays of ancient weaponry, betel nut boxes, jewellery (including a wildcat tooth necklace) and fancy brass work.

ARRIVAL AND DEPARTURE

DAVAO

BY PLANE

Davao International Airport The modern and spacious Francisco Bangoy International Airport lies 12km northwest of the city centre. Ignore taxi touts with their inflated quotes for a ride into the city, and head for the rank where drivers offer metered fares – or, of course, book a Grab cab.
Routes Davao airport has handy air links to a host of destinations in the Philippines. For all domestic flights, you'll have to pay a terminal fee before departure, though this is often included in the price of tickets. As well as the domestic destinations listed here, the airport also hosts flights from Singapore, Hong Kong, Thailand and even far-away Qatar.
Destinations Bacolod (2 weekly; 1hr 10min); Cagayan de Oro (1–2 daily; 1hr); Caticlan (2 weekly; 1hr 35min); Cebu (5–7 daily; 1hr); Angeles (3 weekly; 1hr 50min); Iloilo (1–2 daily; 1hr 10min); Manila (1–3 hourly; 1hr 50min); Panglao (Bohol; 1 daily; 1hr); Puerto Princesa (3 weekly; 1hr 45min); Siargao (4 weekly; 1hr 10min); Tacloban (3 weekly; 1hr 10min); Zamboanga (1 daily; 1hr).

BY BUS

Terminal Calinan is served by frequent bus and jeepneys

from the Calinan Bus Terminal (aka Annil transport terminal) on San Pedro, just north of E. Quirino Ave. All other buses depart the Ecoland terminal on Quimpo Blvd, across the Davao River from the city centre.
Operators and routes Bus operators, all based at the Ecoland terminal, include Bachelor Express (☏facebook. com/YGBCDavao), Mindanao Star (☏facebook.com/ msbti), Philtranco (☏philtranco.net) and Rural Transit (☏facebook.com/YGBCDipolog).
Destinations Butuan (every 20min; 5–6hr); Cagayan de Oro (every 30min; 7hr 30min); Cotabato (every 25min; 6hr); General Santos (every 30min; 3hr 15min); Kidapawan, for Mt Apo (every 25min; 2hr 30min); Surigao (daily; 9hr).

BY BOAT

Ferries Ferries arrive at and leave from Sasa wharf, 8km northeast along the coast, although aside from bus-ferry connections on the RORO ferry across to Samal, there aren't any destinations of use from here. To take a passenger ferry to Manila, Iloilo, Bacolod, Cebu City or Bohol, you'll need to travel north to Cagayan de Oro.

INFORMATION

Tourist information The tourist office on the south side of Magsaysay Park (Mon–Fri 8am–5pm; ☎ 082 221 6276) offers basic maps and leaflets. The Regional Department of

Tourism is on the fifth floor of the Landco Pacific Building, J.P. Laurel Ave, near Victoria Plaza (Mon–Fri 8am–5pm; ☎ 082 221 6955).

GETTING AROUND

By taxi It's cheap and easy to get around Davao by taxi; you can hail them in the street, though check the meter is turned on. They can also be hired out for day-trips, but make sure you clearly establish the price and what it entails. The Grab ride-hailing app is widely used here, too, and should

save money versus regular taxi fares.
By jeepney Jeepneys run back and forth along all major thoroughfares with their destinations pasted on the side – it's just a question of flagging one down and hopping on.
By tricycle Tricycles offer trips within the city – this

includes Santa Ana wharf, Ecoland bus terminal, and north as far as Victoria Plaza.

ACCOMMODATION SEE MAPS PAGES 402 AND 404

Apo View 150 J. Camus St ⓦapoviewhotel.com. The oldest upmarket hotel in Davao, with big, comfortable a/c rooms – it can't compete with *Seda Abreeza* for luxury, but it has a certain old-fashioned charm, despite having now seen better days. You don't always get a view of Mt Apo, although on a clear day you can see it from the top-floor restaurant. $\overline{\text{PPP}}$

The Big House 12 Juna Ave, Matina ⓦfacebook.com/ thebighousedavao. This two-storey, 1950s-era heritage house is one of the oldest in the city and is decorated with family pictures and memorabilia that give it a homely touch. There's a range of eleven rooms, from economy twins to queen doubles, all with wood-frame beds and lamps. The hotel also has a lovely garden and spacious veranda, and breakfast is included. $\overline{\text{PP}}$

The Bourke 115 Pelayo St ⓦthebourke.com. Smart and elegant rooms await inside the attractive Bourke Hotel, found in the heart of the city in easy walking distance from the People's Park. Breakfast comes from the award-winning Bondi&Bourke restaurant downstairs (see page 406), and is delicious. $\overline{\text{PPP}}$

Green Windows Dormitel 1034 Mt Apo St ⓦgreen windowsdormitel.com. Davao's best option for shoestring travellers. The value-for-money a/c backpacker dorm comes with personal wardrobes and hot and cold shower, while doubles and triples are a reliable option for those in need of more privacy. $\overline{\text{P}}$

My Hotel San Pedro St, Polblacion ☎082 300 4040. The tiny, clean fan rooms here, with communal bathrooms, are among the best bargains in the city, while the a/c rooms are more spacious and have cable TV. Downstairs, there are friendly staff and excellent value at *My Café*. $\overline{\text{PP}}$

Napsule JP Laurel Ave, Polblacion ☎0933 825 0057. Bargain hunters rejoice – this is one of the cheapest acceptable places in Davao to lay your head. The small, clean and slightly space-age units contain a bed and nothing else, so you'll probably not want to spend loads of time here, but for a cheap overnight stay it ticks all the boxes. If the capsule-style beds don't appeal, there are slightly more expensive double rooms with shared bathrooms. $\overline{\text{P}}$

Seda Abreeza Abreeza Ayala Business Park ⓦseda hotels.com. Gleaming multi-storey tower overlooking the Ayala Mall, and home to the most luxurious hotel in the city. The large deluxe rooms come with mini-bars and big, bouncy beds, as well as eye-popping views of the Davao Gulf. If you fancy an upgrade to a Club Room you'll gain access to the Executive Lounge, where you'll be treated to free-flowing wine. $\overline{\text{PPPP}}$

EATING SEE MAPS PAGES 402 AND 404

Davao's best **restaurants** are scattered all over the city, but the safest bet for a cheap meal are the **food courts** located in or around the shopping malls. Durian fruit is a big deal in Davao, and is available in every form, from durian ice cream to durian-flavoured cappuccino. The best season for the fruit is Sept–Dec.

★ **Balik Bukid Farm and Kitchen** Quimpo Blvd, Ecoland ⓦfacebook.com/BalikBukiDako. Organic farm-to-fork family restaurant that specializes in wholesome, healthy and fresh food straight from the garden. Vegans are well catered for with salads and rice dishes, while carnivores can go wild over the traditional pork, chicken and river fish. Also makes cheese and delicious home-made chocolate ice cream. $\overline{\text{PPP}}$

Basement 2D Restaurant 329A Bonifacio St, ⓦinstagram.com/thebasementdc. Proudly proclaiming itself to be the first 2D restaurant in Davao, Basement is decorated with a monochrome cartoon mural of a kitchen covering the walls, and a black and white striped floor. The effect is rather like being inside a visual illusion. The menu consists largely of grilled meat and fried chicken, and is tasty (if not as imaginative) as the décor. $\overline{\text{PPP}}$

★ **Bondi&Bourke** 115 Pelayo St ⓦbondiandbourke. com. Award-winning restaurant in the centre of town, offering up a largely meat-focused menu, with American steak and New Zealand lamb chops being particularly fine choices. There's absolutely divine seafood too, and an excellent dessert menu, but very little concession made to vegetarians. $\overline{\text{PPPP}}$

Coffee for Peace Frederic Building, MacArthur Hwy ⓦcoffeeforpeace.com. As well as serving up the freshest Arabica bean brews in Davao, this collective of big-hearted coffee advocates works closely with farmers, exporters and NGOs for the benefit of the entire community. Well worth a visit to learn more about its backstory. $\overline{\text{P}}$

Jack's Ridge Shrine Hills, Matina ⓦjacksridgedavao. com. Just across from the Santo Niño shrine, this complex is all about the views and cool breezes. The Filipino food in the main *Taklobo Restaurant* is delicious: the *sinigang*, *lechon*, grilled tuna and BBQ chicken are all superb. Take a taxi from town. $\overline{\text{PP}}$

★ **Malagos Farm House** Bolcan Street, Agdao ⓦmalagosfarmhouse.com. Quality cheese in the Philippines – this is a real one-off. Making several delicious varieties of artisan feta, blue and goat cheese, this farm-to-fork fromagerie serves up bite-size pieces, raclette and toasties. Don't miss the insightful sample tastings, which take place a couple of times daily. $\overline{\text{PPP}}$

Naty's Lechon House 836 Chavez St ☎082 221 8570. There are several places along this street serving lechon (roast suckling pig), but Naty's is the best – the meat is absolutely delicious, and the staff are extremely friendly. Make sure you're hungry when you arrive. $\overline{\text{PP}}$

Wild Garlic 497 South St ⓦfacebook.com/WildGarlic Davao. Filipino delicacies dominate the menu at this lovely, rustic café with a classic deli vibe and wooden tables and chairs. Try the tuna *panga* stewed in *bagoong* (fish paste), a local favourite such as *kinilaw*, or the house speciality of wild garlic chicken. $\overline{\text{PP}}$

DRINKING AND NIGHTLIFE

SEE MAPS PAGES 402 AND 404

It may not be as avant-garde as Manila, but there's some entertaining **nightlife** in Davao, with cosy live-music venues, karaoke bars and discos. You'll find a cluster of bars and clubs around *Brick Lane Square*, a restaurant and bar quadrangle just south of the University of the Southeastern Philippines.

Botanica Esquina de Tavera, Tavera St. The most attractive cocktail bar in town, which may not be saying too much, but there are indeed other choices. As you might expect with such a name, they're sweet on their gins, and there's tasty food on offer too.

The Grid at the Alley Gil St ☎0969 071 6081. In the popular drinking area south of the University of the Southeastern Philippines, this popular pub offers live music sessions, full-on club nights, and acceptably cheap drinks. Should it get too crowded, you won't be short of other bar options nearby.

Matina Town Square MacArthur Hwy ⓦfacebook. com/matinatownsquare. Davao's premier cultural hub, showcasing a variety of nightclubs, low-key food and drink spots, as well as more refined restaurants. It's a fun place to wander, while they sometimes host a free Indigenous music show on the outdoor stage.

SHOPPING

SEE MAPS PAGES 402 AND 404

Aldevinco Shopping Center Between C.M. Recto Ave and Roxas Ave. For souvenirs and handicrafts, head to this maze of small shops selling tribal artefacts and cheap batik clothes. Enjoy bargaining for a sarong or statues and masks.

SM City Mall Quimpo Blvd, Ecoland ⓦsmsupermalls. com. Home to dozens of local and international brands, as well as a multiplex cinema and entertainment centre. The mall was subject to a terrorist bombing in September 2013.

DIRECTORY

Hospitals The city's major hospital is the Davao Doctors' Hospital (☎082 222 8000, ⓦddh.com.ph) on General Malvar St.

Around Davao

For many visitors, Davao acts as a springboard for a series of trips beyond the city limits to see southern Mindanao at its finest. Head north to **Calinan** and you'll be in the company of majestic eagles at the **Philippine Eagle Center** and in touching distance of **Mount Apo**, the highest mountain in the archipelago. Venture east and you'll find yourself on the deserted white-sand beaches of **Samal and Talikud Islands**. Both are ripe to be explored.

Samal Island

Just across the narrow Pakiputan Strait from Davao, **Samal Island** is graced with lovely coves, beaches, excellent scuba diving and huge bat caves – there are also plenty of resorts to choose from. Most tourists visit Samal on organized tours but it's also easy to arrange a trip independently. You can spend time at one of the resorts (most of which allow day guests for a fee), or jump on a habal-habal and tour the island by motorbike. Samal is bigger than it seems, with an area of more than 300 square kilometres and nearly 100,000 permanent residents. Of the many beaches, it's worth taking the bumpy, hour-long ride across the island to **Canibad Beach Cove**, a pristine, untouched swathe of sand with little more than a sari-sari store selling soft drinks.

Note that over the 2010s, Samal became increasingly prone to **terrorist activity** and **kidnapping**. Alongside a number of locals and other holidaymakers, Canadians John Ridsdel and Robert Hall were abducted and taken by armed Abu Sayyaf gunmen while

9

staying on the island in September 2015. Despite the story going viral around the world, efforts to rescue them failed and they were both beheaded the following year. The remaining hostages were later freed, and there have been no subsequent hostage crises, though obviously it's a good idea to check the current safety situation before heading to this area.

Monfort Bat Sanctuary

Sitio Dunggas, Barangay Tambo • Charge • ⓦ facebook.com/MonfortBatSanctuary

Don't miss the **Monfort Bat Sanctuary** in the northern part of the island, a vast cavern jam-packed with around 1.8 million of the nocturnal creatures – the world's largest known population of Geoffrey's Rousette fruit bats. They usually hang in the cave during the day, but come sundown they flood the skies like a diffusing dark cloud – it's a chilling experience.

ARRIVAL AND DEPARTURE   SAMAL ISLAND

By private boat Getting to Samal from Davao is relatively straightforward. Most resorts on the island have private boats that zip guests across the Pakiputan Strait direct to the hotel grounds, and some of these – notably *Pearl Farm Resort* (see page 408) – also take day-trippers, for a fee.

By ferry Three main ferry companies make the journey to Samal: Babak, Caliclic and Kaputian ferries.

On a tour Most hotels in Davao will arrange day-tours to the island.

GETTING AROUND

By habal-habal No matter which port you arrive at, if you want to get beyond the resorts you can choose from the many habal-habal riders offering personalized tours – it's a good idea to hire one for the whole or half-day rather than trying to get separate lifts.

Tricycles and minivans Tricycles and minivans are available, but unless you have a group, these are much more expensive than habal-habals.

ACCOMMODATION

Most reasonably priced **resorts** on Samal are on the northwest coast, south of the barangay of Caliclic. From the wharf at Babak you can walk to many of these resorts, or hop on a tricycle. All the major resorts have private boats for guests – these depart from piers off R. Castillo St north of the city.

Chema's By The Sea Brgy Limao ⓦ chemasbythesea. com.ph. With a collection of handsome exposed-brick cabanas and bungalows that fuse Balinese and Spanish design, this tropical oasis is only 10min from Davao, yet seems to have stepped out of Boracay. Expect white sands, acres of tropical forest to explore and impressive views of Davao in the distance. Day visitors are welcome for a charge. **PPP**

Paradise Island Park & Beach Resort Caliclic ⓦ facebook.com/paradiseislanddavao.This eighty-room resort can get busy at weekends with day-trippers escaping the city, but has attractive a/c cottages under shady trees in landscaped gardens, a convivial native-style restaurant, and scuba diving. Day guests may visit for a charge. **PPP**

★ **Pearl Farm Resort** Lizada Village, Lanang ⓦ pearl farmresort.com. Situated on the west coast, this is the island's classiest and most expensive resort, with more than seventy native-style cottages either on a hillside overlooking the bay or perched on stilts in the sea. For even more luxury, there are also seven secluded villas on beautiful little Malipano Island, a short hop from the main resort. **PPPP**

Talikud

Talikud Island, off the southwest coast of Samal, is even more torpid than its big brother, making it a perfect place to escape Davao's crowds. On the west coast there's good, easy diving and snorkelling in an area known as Coral Gardens, and a couple of more demanding drop-off dives dot the north coast.

ARRIVAL AND DEPARTURE   TALIKUD

By boat Outrigger ferries regularly chug between Santa Ana wharf, near Magsaysay Park in Davao, and Santa Cruz on Talikud (6 daily; 1hr). Boats leave from the second pier, left of the wharf entrance; just jump on and pay. For day-trippers, the last boat from Santa Cruz wharf to Santa Ana leaves at 3pm.

ACCOMMODATION

Isla Reta ⓦfacebook.com/IslaReta.Beach. Popular if fairly basic resort, with simple rooms and dorms on the beachfront on the eastern side of the island. If you aren't staying here, it's possible to pay for day entry. P̱

Calinan

The small but lively town of **CALINAN**, 45km northwest of Davao on the main highway to Cagayan de Oro, became a major Japanese farming community in the 1930s. Though there's little evidence of this today, the period is commemorated at the **Philippine-Japanese Historical Museum**, and there are a few attractions nearby. It's worth coming here during the week to avoid the crowds, but if you find yourself in Calinan on a Sunday you could head for the *Malagos Garden Resort* free-flight bird show, daily at 10.30am (charge; see below). The resort is also responsible for the fabulous *Malagos Farmhouse* in Davao, and has opened the country's first **chocolate museum** and interactive bean-to-bar laboratory.

Philippine-Japanese Historical Museum

De Lara St, in the Durian Village section of Calinan • Charge • ☎ 082 295 0221 • It's hard to find, so take a habal-habal

Calinan's curious and largely forgotten Japanese history is remembered through a collection of old photos and the fascinating written testimonies of Japanese settlers in the **Philippine-Japanese Historical Museum**. Also on display are sepia pictures of the many memorials to Japanese people killed during World War II in the area.

Philippine Eagle Center

Malagos • Charge for both Eagle Center and Philippines Water Authority Park • ⓦ philippineeaglefoundation.org • Many hotels in Davao offer day-trips

The **Philippine Eagle Center**, 5km west of Calinan, is known for its excellent work breeding and rehabilitating the Philippine eagle, a majestic creature with a fearsome beak, distinctive frilly head feathers and a 2m wingspan. Sadly, the eagle is now officially on the endangered species list, with only a maximum of four hundred believed to be living in the wilds of Mindanao, Samar and Leyte. While the centre's captive breeding programme focuses on developing a viable gene pool, the goal is to reintroduce the birds into their natural habitat. The first captive-bred bird, Pag-aso (meaning "Hope"), was born here in 1992 and the centre is now home to dozens of Philippine eagles, many of which are captive-bred.

To get to the centre, you first walk through the Philippines Water Authority Grounds before reaching the entrance proper and a pleasant café overlooking a lily pond. In addition to the large aviaries containing the big eagles, there are plenty of other birds of prey on display, from grass owls and kites to screeching fish eagles. Note that the centre is a bit like an old-fashioned zoo – there are compounds for the Philippine brown deer, warty pig, long-tailed macaques and even a giant crocodile – and some of the cages are very small and dirty. It can be uncomfortably busy at weekends, so try to schedule your visit for a weekday.

ARRIVAL AND DEPARTURE   CALINAN

By jeepney or bus From Davao, take one of the frequent a/c jeepneys or buses to Calinan (45min) from the Calinan Bus Terminal on San Pedro St, just north of E. Quirino Ave. Once there, you can take a habal-habal for the last 5km.

By car You can rent a vehicle from your Davao hotel for the trip, or negotiate directly with a taxi driver for a one-way fare or a day-trip including waiting time.

ACCOMMODATION

Malagos Garden Resort Brgy Malagos, Baguio District ⓦmalagos.com. A hub of activity, this slightly faded garden resort with comfortable, if worn, wood cabins is where Davaoan families come to play at the weekend. It offers horseriding, has a skate park and staff can organize a number of outdoor adventures, including the Skywalker

THE BANGSAMORO AUTONOMOUS REGION IN MUSLIM MINDANAO

While it is potentially one of the most beguiling areas of the Philippines, the **Bangsamoro Autonomous Region in Muslim Mindanao (BARMM)**, a patchwork of several predominantly Muslim provinces in the western part of the island, is not safe to visit. Created in 1989 as the Autonomous Region in Muslim Mindanao, and revamping itself as BARMM in 2019, the regional government (based in Cotabato) has the power to levy taxes and apply Shariah law to Muslims. Despite this autonomy, the region remains extremely poor and the epicentre for anti-government protest, though the situation has improved since the establishment of BARMM.

The US, UK and Australian governments (and most Filipinos) usually advise foreigners to **avoid BARMM** entirely. Especially in light of recent violent incidents (see box, page 385), we recommend that you do not visit this region until the situation has calmed down. Check the latest government travel advice for updates.

high-wires course, while the extensive grounds hide family cottages that can sleep four to six. In addition to all that, there's a pool, an aviary, a butterfly enclosure and an interactive chocolate museum and laboratory where you can make your own cocoa creation. Day entry charge. **PPP**

Mount Apo

Looming over all Davao, **Mount Apo** (2954m) is the highest mountain in the country: the name Apo means "grandfather of all mountains". Apo is actually a volcano, but is certified inactive and has no recorded eruptions. What it does have is enough flora and fauna to make your head spin – the national park has thundering waterfalls, rapids, lakes, geysers, sulphur pillars, primeval trees, endangered plant and animal species and a steaming blue lake. Then there are exotic ferns, carnivorous pitcher plants and the queen of Philippine orchids, the *waling-waling*. The local people, the Bagobos, believe the gods Apo and Mandaragan inhabit Apo's upper slopes; they revere it as a sacred mountain, calling it Sandawa or "Mountain of Sulphur".

On March 26, 2016, 115 hectares of the mountain's grasslands were razed in a **wildfire** believed to have been started by trekkers who left a campfire unattended. The fire started near the peak, and quickly spread down the slopes to Lake Venado and Kidapawan; it took 28 days for firefighters to contain. With government agencies keen to preserve and rehabilitate the area, it was several years before trekkers were allowed back. It is now open to climbers for nine months each year: check with tour operators such as Mt Apo Adventures (see page 410) exactly when the mountain is open.

Climbing Mount Apo

The summit is approached via one of two main routes: the **Kidapawan Trail** on the Cotabato side features hot springs, river crossings and a steep forested trail that leads to the peak via swampy Lake Venado; and the tougher **Kapatagan Trail** on the Davao side that cuts through more stereotypically volcanic terrain, culminating in a boulder-strewn slope up to the crater. Most operators recommend a three- to four-day expedition, but experienced tropical climbers will be able to summit faster.

INFORMATION   MOUNT APO

Tourist offices The Kidapawan Tourist Center (☎ 0930 620 8602) is next to city hall, while the Kapatagan registration office (no phone) is in the small settlement of Kapatagan.

Tours Mt Apo Adventures (🌐 mtapoadventures.com) is a small-scale trekking organization that can arrange all elements of the climb. Another highly recommended outfit is Trail Adventours (⊙trailadventours.com), which as well as organizing four-day hikes up the Kapatagan route, arranges multi-day treks and summit ascents across the Philippines.

ACCOMMODATION

Mt Apo Highland Resort Lake Agko ☎0927 701 8773. Right on the lake, this place is ideal for whiling away a few days. It has a scattering of rustic cottages on concrete stilts, as well as plenty of pitches for camping. The views of Mt Apo are astounding. $\overline{P}$

FERDINAND MAGELLAN'S DEATH IN THE PHILIPPINES, 1521

Contexts

History

Philippine history is frequently dismissed as "beginning with the Spanish and ending with the Americans", yet the modern country is a result of many diverse influences – Malay, Chinese, Spanish and American – that have collided in the archipelago down the centuries. While the influence of Spain and the US is significant, recent scholarship has thrown light on the native and Islamic civilizations that flourished here before Magellan's arrival in 1521, and – thanks to new archeological discoveries – their highly developed trade links with the rest of Asia. Today one issue looms over all others: in 1960 the population of the Philippines was just 27 million; in 2022 it was estimated to have topped 115 million. Such explosive growth has meant that real economic gains made in the last few generations have had a negligible effect on poverty; though the birth rate has now gone back down towards nuclear, said poverty remains, along with corruption, one of the country's biggest problems.

Prehistory

Human fossil remains found in Palawan suggest that humans first migrated to the Philippines across land bridges from Borneo during the Ice Age, some fifty thousand years ago. Carbon dating of fossilized human remains discovered at the Tabon Caves in Palawan showed so-called "**Tabon Man**" was living in the cave about 22,000 years ago. Deeper excavations of the caves indicated humans were in the area from 45,000 to 50,000 years ago.

The **Aeta** or Negritos, the country's Indigenous people, are said to be descended from these first migrants. Successive migrations populated the islands through the centuries. **Malays** from Indonesia and the Malay peninsula streamed into the archipelago more than two thousand years ago, sailing across the Sulu Sea and settling first in the Visayas and southwestern Luzon. Their outrigger boats, equipped with lateen sails, each carried a family or clans led by a chief. Once ashore, they remained together in villages – known as barangays, after the name for their boats (*balangays*). The bulk of Filipinos today, at least in the Visayas and Mindanao, are descended from these Malay settlers.

Hindu kingdoms and Islamic sultanates

The early Malay communities gradually developed into a complex patchwork of kingdoms such as the Rajahnates of Butuan and Cebu, influenced by the powerful **Hindu empires** in Java and Sumatra. Several archeological finds hint at the sophistication and wealth of these early civilizations: the Laguna Copperplate

900–1535	1380	1475
So-called "Classical States" period; the archipelago ruled by Hindu-influenced kingdoms	Karim ul' Makdum establishes the Islamic Sultanate of Sulu	Shariff Mohammed Kabungsuwan establishes the Islamic Sultanate of Maguindanao

Inscription, the earliest writing found in the Philippines, dates from around 900 AD and concerns a debt of gold in the Hindu-Malay state of Tondo, around today's Manila Bay. Equally enlightening is the Surigao Treasure, a trove of sensational gold objects dug up by accident in Mindanao in 1981 and dating from the tenth to thirteenth centuries. Chinese shipwrecks loaded with porcelain prove that trade ties with **China** and the rest of Asia were extensive by the tenth century.

Contact with Arab traders, which reached its peak in the twelfth century, drew Sufis and missionaries who began the propagation of **Islam** in the Philippines. In 1380, the Arab scholar Karim ul' Makdum arrived in Jolo and established the Sultanate of Sulu. In 1475 Shariff Mohammed Kabungsuwan of Johor (Malaysia), married a native princess and established the Sultanate of Maguindanao, ruling large parts of Mindanao. During the reign of Sultan Bolkiah (1485–1521), the Sultanate of Brunei absorbed Tondo; by the time the Spanish arrived, Islam was established as far north as Luzon, where a great Muslim monarch, Rajah Sulaiman II, ruled Manila.

Spanish rule

The archipelago's turbulent relationship with Spain began on April 24, 1521 when **Ferdinand Magellan** arrived in Cebu. Magellan planted a wooden cross to claim the islands for Spain, baptizing a local king, Raja Humabon. **Lapu-Lapu** (1491–1542), a chief on the nearby island of Mactan, and Humabon's traditional enemy, resisted; in the subsequent Battle of Mactan (see box, page 314), Magellan was killed and Spain's conquest of the Philippines was put on hold. Lapu-Lapu is now regarded as a Filipino hero.

Spanish conquistador Ruy López de Villalobos tried once again to claim the islands for Spain in 1543, but was driven out by the natives a year later – though not before naming the islands the Philippines, in honour of the future King Philip II. In 1564 **Miguel López de Legazpi** (1502–72), a minor Basque aristocrat, was chosen to lead a hazardous expedition to establish a permanent base in the Philippines, which the Spanish hoped would act as a wedge between Portugal and China. Legazpi sailed to the Philippines on board the *Capitana*, established a colony in Bohol in 1565 and then moved on to Cebu where he erected the first Spanish fort in the Philippines. But a series of misunderstandings – one involving the gift of a concubine that Legazpi piously refused – made the situation in Cebu perilous, and Legazpi looked for a more solid base.

In 1570 a Spanish expedition defeated Rajah Sulaiman III, and a year later Legazpi occupied his former base; a new Spanish capital – **Manila** – was established on the site of Sulaiman's old Islamic kingdom. Spanish conquistadors and friars zealously set about propagating **Catholicism**, building churches and bringing rural folk *debajo de las compañas* ("under the bells") into organized Spanish *pueblos*, establishing many of the country's towns and cities. They imposed a **feudal system**, concentrating populations under their control into new towns and estates, and resulting in numerous small revolts. Most of the Philippines, however, remained beyond the pale of the colonial authorities.

The Friarocracy

The islands were administered from the Spanish colony of **Mexico**, and its Spanish residents, especially those in Manila, grew prosperous from the galleon trade, exporting Chinese goods from Manila to Mexico. The Church, dreading change, did nothing to

1485–1521	1521	1565	1571
The Sultanate of Brunei extends Islamic rule as far as modern-day Manila	Ferdinand Magellan arrives in Cebu; killed fighting local chief Lapu-Lapu	Miguel López de Legazpi founds permanent Spanish settlement on Bohol	Legazpi founds Manila; formal Spanish control over the islands begins

improve the subsistence economy, while in the capital, according to an early diarist, "the rich spend ten months of the year with nothing to do".

In theory, the Philippines was ruled by civil and military representatives of the King of Spain, but in practice it was the Catholic **friars** who ran the show. They derived their power from the enormous influence of the monastic orders – Augustinian, Dominican and Franciscan – which spanned the world like global corporations. Secular officials came and went, but the clergy stayed. Many friars ignored their vows of celibacy and sired children with local women. They exercised their power through a number of administrative functions, including setting budgets, conducting the parish census, screening recruits for the military and presiding over the police. There were cosmetic local administrations, but they could not act without the friars' consent.

It wasn't until the late eighteenth century that the ossification of the colonial regime eased in the face of external shocks. Attempts by the Dutch, Portuguese and Chinese to establish a presence in the archipelago were repelled, but the **British** occupied Manila in 1762, in a sideshow to the **Seven Years' War**. They handed it back to Spain under the 1763 Treaty of Paris, but their easy victory served notice that the Philippines was vulnerable. In 1821 Mexico became independent and the galleon trade ended, after which the Philippines were administered directly from Madrid, ushering in a period of relatively enlightened colonial rule and prosperity.

The independence movement

The Spanish began to establish a free public school system in the Philippines in 1863, increasing the number of educated and Spanish-speaking Filipinos. The opening of the Suez Canal in 1869 (combined with the increasing use of steam power) cut travel times between Spain and the Philippines to weeks rather than months, and many of this new generation were able to continue their studies in Europe. They frequently returned with liberal ideas and talk of freedom.

A small **revolt** in Cavite in 1872 was quickly put down, but the anger and frustration Filipinos felt about colonial rule would not go away. Intellectuals such as Marcelo H. Del Pilar and Juan Luna were the spiritual founders of the independence movement, but it was the writings of a diminutive young doctor from Laguna province, **José Rizal** (1861–96), that provided the spark for the flame. His novel *Noli Me Tángere* was written while he was studying in Spain in the 1880s, and portrayed colonial rule as a cancer and the Spanish friars as fat, pompous fools. It was promptly banned by the Spanish, but distributed underground along with other inflammatory essays by Rizal and, later, his second novel, *El Filibusterismo*.

In 1892, Rizal returned to Manila and founded the movement La Liga Filipina, which espoused moderate reform, though never revolution. Its members swore oaths and took part in blood rites, and, innocuous as the movement was, the friars smelled sedition. Rizal was arrested and exiled to Dapitan on Mindanao. **Andrés Bonifacio** (1863–97) took over the reins by establishing the secret society known as the Katipunan or KKK (its full name was Kataastaasan, Kagalanggalang na Katipunan nang mga Anak ng Bayan, which means "Honorable, respectable sons and daughters of the nation"). In August 1896, an armed struggle for independence broke out, and Rizal was accused of masterminding it. Rizal had, in fact, called the revolution "absurd and savage" and had earlier turned down an invitation from Bonifacio to participate. His trial lasted a day, one of the seven military

1570–1890s	1762	1821	1872
The "Friarocracy" controls the Philippines during the colonial Spanish period; the Manila galleon trade links Asia with Spanish Mexico	British occupy Manila during the Seven Years' War	Mexico becomes independent; the Manila galleon trade ends	Cavite Revolt

judges concluding that Rizal's being a native must be considered "an aggravating factor". Rizal's Spanish military lawyer did little for him so he finally rose to defend himself. "I have sought political liberty," he said, "but never the freedom to rebel." He was duly found guilty and executed by firing squad in Manila in what is now known as Rizal Park on December 30, 1896. The night before he died he wrote *Mi Último Adiós*, a farewell poem to the country he loved (see page 68).

The Philippine Revolution

News of Rizal's martyrdom inflamed the uprising ignited by Bonifacio. Spanish officials deluded themselves, blaming it on a few troublemakers, but by now Bonifacio had decided violence was the only option and, with his young firebrand general, **Emilio Aguinaldo** (1869–1964), he called openly for a government "like that of the United States". Aguinaldo, a local government official from Cavite, had joined the Katipunan in 1894 and once the fighting started swiftly became the rebels' most successful commander. At the **Tejeros Convention** in 1897 Aguinaldo was elected president of the new Republic of the Philippines by his fellow *katipuneros* – when Bonifacio was offered a far lower position, he declared the election void in a fit of rage. Soon after, Aguinaldo had Bonifacio and his brothers arrested, sentenced in a mock trial and executed. At the end of 1897, the Spanish finalized a truce with Aguinaldo, the **Pact of Biak-na-Bato**: the Spanish would pay the rebels 800,000 pesos, half immediately, a quarter when they laid down their arms and the rest after a Te Deum to mark the armistice was chanted in Manila Cathedral. In exchange Aguinaldo agreed to go abroad. A cheque in his pocket, he sailed for Hong Kong, disavowing his rebellion.

However, in 1898, as a result of a dispute over Cuba, war broke out between the **United States** and Spain, and as an extension of it the US decided to expel Spain from the Philippines. The Spanish fleet was soundly beaten in Manila Bay by ships under the command of George Dewey, who on the morning of April 30, 1898, gave the famous order to his captain, "You may fire when you are ready, Gridley." The Filipinos fought on the side of the US, and when the battle was over General Aguinaldo, now back from Hong Kong having disavowed his disavowal of the rebellion, declared the Philippines independent; the First **Philippine Republic** was formally established by the **Malolos Constitution** in January 1899, with Aguinaldo as first president. The US, however, had other ideas and paid Spain US$20 million for its former possession. Having got rid of one colonizing power, the Filipinos were now answerable to another.

American rule

After the Spanish left the country, the Filipinos continued to fight for independence in what's known as the **Philippine–American War**, a savage conflict that is virtually forgotten in the US today. Fighting began in early 1899 and lasted for three years, although skirmishes continued for another seven years, especially in Mindanao. US troops used tactics to pacify locals that they would later employ in Vietnam, such as strategic hamleting and scorched earth, and by the end of February, Manila was ablaze as American troops took charge of the city. But crushing the Filipinos was not easy. The US forces, for all their superior firepower, were nagged by relentless heat, torrential rain and pervasive disease. Aguinaldo still commanded Filipino forces, though the intensity of the Manila assault had

1887	1892	1896	1897
José Rizal's novel *Noli Me Tángere* published in Berlin	Andrés Bonifacio founds the Katipunan to fight for independence from Spain	José Rizal executed by the Spanish in Manila; the Philippine Revolution breaks out	Bonifacio is executed by rival rebel leader Emilio Aguinaldo

shocked him. Malolos, to the north of Manila, the seat of his revolutionary government, was overrun, but by June 1899 the Americans had become bogged down and controlled territory no more than 40km from Manila. The war degenerated into a **manhunt** for Aguinaldo, and when he was finally captured in March 1902 in Palanan on Luzon's east coast, the war ended officially three months later. After a brief internment, the wily general took an oath of allegiance to the US, was granted a pension from the US government and retired from public life until 1935 (see below). The war had resulted in the death of at least 600,000 Filipinos and 4234 Americans; exact records were not kept of Filipino casualties.

Benevolent assimilation

When the Philippine–American War ended, American teachers fanned out across the country to begin President McKinley's policy of "**benevolent assimilation**". They were known as Thomasites, as the first group arrived on a ship called the *Thomas*. The Thomasites took to their task with apostolic fervour and Filipinos quickly achieved the highest literacy rate in Southeast Asia.

The American administration in the Philippines sought to inculcate Filipinos with American ethics, to turn the Philippines into a stable, prosperous democracy. Filipinos learned to behave, dress and eat like Americans, sing American songs and speak American English. American educators decided that teaching Filipinos in their many local languages would require too many textbooks, so English became the lingua franca. Meanwhile in Washington, debate raged over what form of government the Philippines should have. It wasn't until 1935 that a bill was passed in Washington allowing President Roosevelt to recognize a new Philippine constitution and the ten-year transition status of "**Commonwealth of the Philippines**" – autonomous but not completely independent. Presidential elections were held in September of that year and won by **Manuel Quezon** (1878–1944), the leading light among a new breed of postwar politicians, beating Aguinaldo, who had come out of retirement. (Aguinaldo was to cooperate with the Japanese in World War II, but after briefly being jailed by the Americans a second time, lived to see Philippine independence.)

World War II

Quezon realized how vulnerable the archipelago was and invited the US commander of the country, **General Douglas MacArthur**, to become military adviser to the autonomous regime. MacArthur accepted, demanding US$33,000 a year and an air-conditioned suite in the *Manila Hotel*.

Within minutes of the December 1941 attack on **Pearl Harbor**, Japanese bombers hit military bases in Cavite and at Clark. MacArthur appealed for help from Washington, but it never came. He declared Manila an open city in order to save its population and prepared for a tactical retreat to Corregidor, the island at the mouth of Manila Bay, from where he would supervise the defence of the strategic Bataan peninsula. Quezon, now increasingly frail from tuberculosis, went with him.

The Philippines underwent heavy **bombardment** during World War II and casualties were high. Japanese troops occupied Manila on January 2, 1942. MacArthur and Quezon abandoned Corregidor when it became clear that the situation was hopeless, but arriving in Darwin, Australia, MacArthur promised Filipinos, "I shall return."

1898	1899	1899–1902	1935
Spanish–American War; the US navy destroys the Spanish fleet in Manila Bay	Philippine Republic proclaimed with Emilio Aguinaldo president, but Spain cedes the Philippines to the US	Philippine–American War; US introduces "benevolent assimilation"	The Commonwealth of the Philippines is established: Manuel Quezon is the first president

MacArthur left behind soldiers engaged in a protracted and bloody struggle for **Bataan**. When it fell to Japanese forces, they then launched an all-out assault on Corregidor. The island, defended by starving and demoralized troops huddled in damp tunnels, capitulated in days. On the notorious **Bataan Death March** that followed, some ten thousand Americans and Filipinos died from disease, malnutrition and wanton brutality.

Two years of **Japanese military rule** followed. Unable to quell popular opposition and a nascent guerrilla movement, the Japanese turned increasingly to brutality, beheading innocent victims and displaying their bodies as an example. The guerrillas multiplied, however, until their various movements comprised two hundred thousand men. The strongest force was the People's Anti-Japanese Army, the Hukbalahap in Tagalog or the **Huks** for short, most of them poor sharecroppers and farm workers. MacArthur, meanwhile, kept his promise to return. On October 19, 1944, with Quezon at his side, he waded ashore at Leyte, forcing a showdown with the Japanese and driving across the island to the port of Ormoc. The Huks helped the US liberate Luzon, acting as guides in the push towards Manila and freeing Americans from Japanese prison camps. None exploited their wartime adventures more than **Ferdinand Marcos**, an ambitious young lawyer from Ilocos who now set his sights on entering politics.

The Marcos years

The Philippines received full **independence** from the US on July 4, 1946, when **Manuel Roxas**, an experienced politician from Panay, was sworn in as the first President of the Republic. His government marred by corruption and conflict with the now outlawed Huks, Roxas died of a heart attack in 1948 and was replaced by his Ilocano vice president Elpidio Quirino. The 1950s were something of a golden age for the Philippines, with the presidency of Ramón Magsaysay (1953–57) considered a high point: politics was largely corruption-free, trade and industry boomed and the country was ranked Asia's second cleanest and best governed after Japan. In the early 1960s, however, the Liberal government of Diosdado Macapagal was crippled by Nacionalista Party opposition in Congress. It was in these years that **Ferdinand Marcos** came to power, promoting himself as a force for unification and reform.

Marcos (1917–89) was born in Sarrat, Ilocos Norte. A brilliant young lawyer who had successfully defended himself against a murder charge, he was elected to the Philippine House of Representatives in 1949, to the Senate in 1959 and became president in 1965 on the Nacionalista Party ticket, defeating incumbent Macapagal. Marcos's first term as president was innovative and inspirational. He invigorated both populace and bureaucracy, embarking on a huge **infrastructure** programme and unifying scattered islands with a network of roads, bridges, railways and ports. During these early years of the Marcos presidency, before the madness of martial law, **First Lady Imelda** (see box, page 419) busied herself with social welfare and cultural projects that complemented Marcos's work in economics and foreign affairs.

Martial law

In 1969 Marcos became the first Filipino president to be re-elected for a **second term**. The country's problems, however, were grave. Poverty, social inequality and rural stagnation were rife. Marcos was trapped between the entrenched oligarchy,

1942	1944	1946	1965
Japan defeats US forces in the Philippines in World War II	US forces retake the Philippines	Republic of the Philippines becomes fully independent; Manuel Roxas first president	Ferdinand Marcos becomes president

THE IRON BUTTERFLY

Imelda Remedios Visitación was born on July 2, 1929, in the little town of Tolosa in Leyte. Her youth was troubled, her father jobless. At 23 she left Leyte for Manila with just five pesos in her purse, seeking her fortune. Her break came in 1953, when a magazine editor featured her face on his cover; she then entered a beauty contest and won the title of **Miss Manila**. Ferdinand Marcos later recounted that he saw the magazine picture and told friends, "I'm getting married." He arranged an introduction and, after an eleven-day courtship, proposed.

Following his 1965 election victory, Marcos said of Imelda, "She was worth a million votes." In fact, Imelda had cleverly cajoled tycoon Fernando Lopez into standing as Marcos's vice president, bringing with him his family's immeasurable fortune. Once the election was won, Imelda announced she would be "more than a mere decorative figure", and in 1966 made her international debut when she sang to Lyndon Johnson at a White House dinner. "A blessing not only to her country, but also to the world", gushed a US newspaper columnist.

Imelda laid on lavish fiestas for every visiting dignitary. She posed as a patron of the arts, flying in international stars such as Margot Fonteyn. Her husband later made her **governor of Manila** with a brief to turn the city into a showpiece. She set about the task with gusto, spending P37 million on the Coconut Palace (see page 73) and at least P100 million on the Manila Film Center (see box, page 73). As well as a patron of the arts, the First Lady also appointed herself the country's roving envoy, relentlessly roaming the world on jumbo jets "borrowed" from Philippine Airlines to meet the likes of Fidel Castro, Emperor Hirohito and Chairman Mao. A prodigious social climber, she pursued Rockefellers and Fords, and dreamed of betrothing her daughter Imee to Prince Charles.

Throughout much of the 1980s Imelda went on notoriously profligate **shopping binges** to New York and Los Angeles, spending millions of dollars on grotesque art, jewellery and the occasional apartment. In Geneva, another favourite haunt, she spent US$12 million in jewellery in a single day. After her husband's downfall in 1986, Imelda became deeply upset at reports that three thousand pairs of **shoes** had been found inside the Malacañang Palace, claiming that she had only accumulated them in order to promote the Philippine shoe industry in her trips abroad. The shoes became the most potent symbol of her mad spending.

Imelda returned to Manila in 1991, still popular in some quarters. In 1995 she was elected **Congresswoman** for her home province of Leyte, and in 2010 she was elected to represent the second district of Ilocos Norte, replacing her son Ferdinand Marcos, Jr (who was elected to the Senate). She was re-elected to the same post twice, in 2013 and 2016. Various corruption cases against Imelda have dragged on over the years, but her nickname – the **Iron Butterfly**, for her thick-skinned bravura – is surely well deserved.

which controlled Congress, and a rising communist insurgency that traced its roots back to the Huks (see page 418), fuelled mostly by landless, frustrated peasants led by the articulate and patriarchal José Maria Sison (b.1939), who lives today in exile in the Netherlands. The country was roiled by student, labour and peasant unrest, much of it stoked by communists and their fledgling military wing, the **New People's Army**. On September 21, 1972, Marcos declared **martial law**, arresting **Benigno "Ninoy" Aquino** (1932–83) and other opposition leaders. A curfew was imposed and Congress suspended. Marcos announced he was pioneering a Third World approach to

1969	1972	1981	1983
Marcos is re-elected amid allegations of electoral fraud	Marcos declares martial law	Martial law is lifted; Marcos wins presidential elections again	Benigno Aquino returns to the Philippines, but is assassinated as he leaves his plane

democracy through his "New Society" and his new political party the New Society Movement. His regime became a byword for profligacy, corruption and repression.

The **Mindanao** problem also festered. After the Jabidah Massacre in 1968, when Filipino troops executed 28 Muslim recruits who refused to take part in a hopelessly misconceived invasion of Sabah, Muslims took up arms against the government, forming the **Moro National Liberation Front** (MNLF; see box, page 385). Marcos made few real efforts to quell the insurgency, knowing it would give him another excuse for martial law. The US worried that the longer Marcos's excesses continued the faster the communist insurgency would spread, threatening their military bases in the islands.

The People Power Revolution (EDSA)

Ninoy Aquino, who by the spring of 1980 had been languishing in jail for seven years, was released on condition that he went into exile in the US. In 1983 he decided to return, but when he emerged from his plane at Manila airport on August 21, 1983, he was assassinated. The country was outraged. In a snap election called in panic by Marcos on February 7, 1986, the opposition united behind Aquino's widow, **Corazón Aquino** (1933–2009), and her running mate Salvador Laurel. On February 25, both Marcos and Aquino claimed victory and were sworn in at separate ceremonies. Aquino, known by the people as Cory, became a rallying point for change and was backed by the Catholic Church in the form of **Archbishop Cardinal Jaime Sin** (1928–2005), who urged people to take to the streets in a **People Power Revolution**, known as the EDSA Revolution.

When Marcos's key allies saw which way the wind was blowing and deserted him, the game was up. Defence Minister Juan Ponce Enrile and Deputy Chief of Staff of the Armed Forces, General **Fidel Ramos** (b.1928), later to become president, announced a coup d'état. The US prevaricated, but eventually told Marcos to "cut and cut cleanly". Ferdinand and Imelda fled into exile in Hawaii, where Ferdinand died in 1989. Conservative estimates of their plunder put the figure at US\$10 billion, US\$600 million of it spirited into Swiss bank accounts – rumours persist that Marcos had also appropriated a hoard of Japanese war loot dubbed "Yamashita's Gold", though this has never been proven.

The return of democracy

Hopes were high for the presidency of **Cory Aquino**, but she never managed to bring the powerful feudal families or the armed forces under her control. **Land reform** was eagerly awaited by the country's landless masses, but when Aquino realized that reform would also involve her own family's haciendas in Tarlac, she quietly shelved the idea: most of the country's farmers remain beholden to landlords today. Aquino survived seven coup attempts and made little headway in improving life for most Filipinos, who remained below the poverty line. The communist New People's Army (NPA) emerged once again as a threat, and human rights abuses continued.

Aquino also had to deal with another thorny issue: the presence of **US military bases** in the country, Clark Air Base and Subic Naval Base. Public opinion had been turning against the bases for some time, with many seeing them as a colonial imposition. In 1987 Congress voted not to renew the bases treaty and the US withdrawal, set for 1991, was hastened by the portentous eruption of **Mount Pinatubo** (see box, page 117), which scattered ash over both Clark and Subic, causing millions of dollars of

1986	1989	1991
People Power Revolution (aka EDSA Revolution) sees Marcos flee the country; Corazón Aquino becomes president	Ferdinand Marcos dies in exile in Hawaii	The US abandons Clark Air Base after the Mount Pinatubo eruption smothers it with ash; Imelda Marcos returns to the Philippines

damage to US aircraft and ships. The withdrawal made jobless six hundred thousand Filipinos who had depended on the bases for employment either directly or indirectly.

In **Mindanao**, the **Moro National Liberation Front** had started a war for independence in the 1970s that dragged on until 1987, when it accepted the offer of autonomy. The Autonomous Region in Muslim Mindanao, or ARMM, was created in 1990 (see box, page 385), but the more radical **Moro Islamic Liberation Front** (MILF) refused to accept the 1987 accord and continued fighting.

Ultimately, Aquino's only legacy was that she maintained some semblance of a democracy, which was something for her successor, **Fidel Ramos**, to build on. Ramos took office on July 1, 1992, announcing plans to create jobs, revitalize the economy and reduce the US$32 billion foreign debt. First, he had to establish a reliable electricity supply: the country was being paralysed for hours every day by **power cuts**, and no multinational companies wanted to invest under such conditions. Ramos's success in sorting this out – at least in Manila and many cities – led to a moderate influx of foreign investment, for industrial parks and new manufacturing facilities. The economy picked up, but foreign debt was crippling and tax collection was so lax that the government had nothing in the coffers to fall back on. Infrastructure improved marginally and new roads and transit systems began to take shape. Ramos also liberalized the banking sector and travelled extensively to promote the Philippines abroad. Most Filipinos view his years in office as a success, although when he stepped down at the end of his six-year term, poverty and crime were still rife.

Erap

Ramos's successor, former vice president **Joseph Estrada** (b.1937), was a former tough-guy film actor with pomaded hair and a cowboy swagger, known universally as **Erap**, a play on the slang word *pare*, which means friend or buddy. Estrada's folksy, macho charm appealed to the masses and in 1998 he was elected president against politicians of greater stature on a **pro-poor** platform. His rallying cry was *Erap para sa mahirap*, or "Erap for the poor". He promised food security, jobs, mass housing, education and health for all, but the media was soon accusing him of lacking direction and of returning to the **cronyism** of the Marcos years. The **economy** floundered, and every day there was some new allegation of mismanagement, favours for friends or plain incompetence.

In 2000, the Philippine Center for Investigative Journalism (PCIJ) began to research Estrada's wealth. Its report listed seventeen pieces of **real estate** worth P2 billion acquired by Estrada and his family members since 1998. Some, it was alleged, were for his favourite mistress, former actress Laarni Enriquez. Later in 2000, Luis Singson, governor of Ilocos Sur, alleged that Estrada had received P500 million in **gambling payoffs** from an illegal numbers game known as *jueteng* (pronounced "wet-eng"). On November 13, 2000, Estrada became the first president to be **impeached**, setting the stage for a Senate trial that would grip the nation for weeks. When the Senate let him off, people gathered in the streets to demand his resignation. The Church and its leader, Cardinal Jaime Sin, again became involved and urged Estrada to step down. Half a million people gathered at the EDSA shrine in Ortigas in scenes reminiscent of those before the downfall of Marcos – the four-day demonstrations were later dubbed **EDSA II**. On the evening of Friday January 19, 2001, cabinet members saw that the cause was lost and began to defect.

1992	1996	1998	2001
Fidel Ramos becomes president; US naval base at Subic Bay closed	Peace agreement reached with Muslim separatist group, the Moro National Liberation Front	Joseph Estrada elected president	EDSA II: Estrada is replaced by his vice president, Gloria Macapagal-Arroyo

The decisive blow came when the **military** announced it had withdrawn its support for Estrada. The next morning he was ushered ignominiously from the Malacañang Palace and vice president Gloria Macapagal-Arroyo was promptly sworn in as the fourteenth President of the Republic of the Philippines. Anti-Erap forces hailed what they deemed a noble moral victory. But a nagging question remained: Estrada had been voted into office by a landslide of 10.7 million people and removed by a predominantly middle-class movement of five hundred thousand who took to the streets. His impeachment trial had been aborted and he had been found guilty of nothing.

Macapagal-Arroyo

Gloria Macapagal-Arroyo (b.1947) proved slightly less dramatic as president than her predecessors, but just as divisive. The first years of her presidency were solid if unspectacular, her main priority simply to survive and bring some level of stability. The House of Representatives and Senate were bitterly divided along pro- and anti-Estrada lines. In 2007, Estrada was finally found guilty of plunder; a month later, he was pardoned by the president.

After winning her second term in 2004, things started to unravel for Macapagal-Arroyo; she was accused of vote rigging, though two attempts to impeach her failed. In 2006 an army plot led to a state of emergency across the country. On the economy, the president had some success, with GDP growth rates the strongest in decades, though critics disputed the figures, which in any case failed to improve the lives of the poor.

In Mindanao, things looked even worse. A new terrorist organization, **Abu Sayyaf**, emerged on Basilan Island, thought to be responsible for the February 2004 bombing of *Superferry 14*, which sank with 116 dead. The Moro Islamic Liberation Front launched new attacks on government troops in 2008 after the Supreme Court ruled unconstitutional a deal offering them large areas of the south. In 2009, 57 people (including 34 journalists) were murdered in the **Maguindanao Massacre**, part of a local election-time "clan" war.

Macapagal-Arroyo's term finished in 2010, marred by claims of cronyism, extrajudicial killings, torture and illegal arrests; corruption still ran unchecked, and the gap between the impoverished and a thin layer of super-wealthy had grown ever wider, with the dirt-poor growing in numbers and wretchedness, accounting probably for sixty percent of the population of nearly one hundred million. After standing down as president, Macapagal-Arroyo defied convention and stayed in politics, and, after a brief period of retirement from 2019 until 2022, continues to sit in the House of Representatives today.

The return of the Aquinos

The presidential election of 2010 was typically dramatic. In 2009, Cory Aquino died from colon cancer, aged 76, sending the country into a five-day period of deep mourning – the former president was genuinely loved. Following her funeral many voters appealed to Cory's son, senator **Benigno Aquino III** ("Noynoy Aquino" or just "PNoy"; b.1960), to stand for president; the "Noynoy Phenomenon" posed a special dilemma because Aquino's Liberal Party had already chosen a candidate for the presidency, Manuel "Mar" Roxas (grandson of the first president), and the former leader's son had until then not

2009	2010	2012
Maguindanao massacre; 57 people killed in Mindanao	Benigno "Noynoy" Aquino becomes president; Imelda Marcos is elected to Congress	Peace plan signed with the Muslim rebel Moro Islamic Liberation Front

THE GREATEST AND THE PACMAN

Boxing has been a Filipino passion for over one hundred years. Ferdinand Marcos capitalized on the nation's love of the sport by using government money to finance the "**Thrilla in Manila**" in 1975, a notoriously brutal encounter between Muhammad Ali and Joe Frazier often ranked as one of the greatest fights of twentieth-century boxing. Fought at the Araneta Coliseum in Quezon City, Ali won in the 15th and final round. The beneficent Marcos even stumped up the cash for the fight's multimillion-dollar purse.

Filipinos have never made it in the high-profile heavyweight game, but in the lighter divisions they've excelled. In recent years, one name stands out in particular: **Manny "the Pacman" Pacquiao** (b.1978), the poor boy from Mindanao who became world super featherweight champion, made a movie, made millions, and was the first boxer in history to win ten world titles in eight different weight divisions (he's current super welterweight champ). In probably his most famous bout, he defeated Oscar De La Hoya in Las Vegas in 2008, in what was dubbed the "Dream Match". In 2010 Pacquiao was elected to the House of Representatives, representing the province of Sarangani, and subsequently was elected to the Senate in 2016, before making an unsuccessful run for president in 2022.

been expected to run. Driven by nostalgia as much as politics, support for Benigno Aquino grew so fierce that Roxas withdrew from the race. Aquino's rival in the election was none other than ex-president Joseph Estrada. After a keenly fought campaign, Aquino won with 42.08 percent of the vote to Estrada's 26.25 percent.

Benigno Aquino, respected for his family connections and obsessed over in the tabloids for his love life, was a teetotaller and self-styled fighter of corruption. He abolished lunchtime closing in government offices, and his "no *wang-wang*" policy cut the use of sirens by official vehicles to get through traffic. He made some progress in Mindanao – generally peaceful since 2010 – and signed a **peace deal** with the MILF in 2014, promising a new Muslim autonomous entity called **Bangsamoro** to replace the Autonomous Region of Muslim Mindanao.

Aquino was heavily criticized for his administration's slow reaction to November 2013's Typhoon Haiyan (known as **Yolanda** in the Philippines), which particularly devastated the Visayas, killing at least 6268 people. He also took a lot of flak for the January 2015 **Mamasapano massacre**, when an operation to capture two jihadist bomb-makers in Mindanao was successful but cost the lives of 44 police officers; in the aftermath, Congress halted passage of the Bangsamoro autonomy bill.

Aquino's opponents accused him of laziness, and coined the term **noynoying** to describe his supposed indolence. One big success he had was to push through a 2012 **Reproductive Health Act** in the teeth of strong clerical opposition, guaranteeing free access to contraception for everybody.

Rodrigo Duterte

Having served six years, Aquino was ineligible to run in the 2016 election, which was won for the PDP–Laban by Davao's outspoken and controversial mayor, **Rodrigo Duterte** (see box page 403), running on a law-and-order ticket. The first Filipino

2013	2016	2017
Typhoon Yolanda devastates the central part of the country, killing over six thousand	Rodrigo Duterte elected sixteenth president of the Philippines	Islamic militant groups capture the city of Marawi in Mindanao; it is retaken after five months

president to hail from Mindanao, Duterte took office promising to transform the Philippines into a **federal country**, in which Bangsamoro would gain its promised autonomy. As he did in Davao, Duterte instituted a policy of **killing suspected drug dealers** extrajudicially, which met with condemnation from human rights groups, but won much support domestically. In **foreign policy**, Duterte distanced himself from the US (in typical style, he called US president Barrack Obama a "son of a whore"), and moved closer to China and Russia. In particular, he backed off from territorial disputes with China over islands in the South China Sea.

Duterte was also conciliatory over Muslim autonomy in **Mindanao**, promising federal statehood for Bangsamoro, and creation of the Bangsamoro Autonomous Region in any event, even if his aim of federalism nationwide is not achieved. As a sign of his commitment, in November 2016, he expanded the Bangsamoro Transition Commission and made a speech reiterating his support for the peace process. However, after Islamist militants and government forces clashed in Marawi City in May 2017, Duterte introduced **martial law** on Mindanao, which remained in place until the end of 2019. The Bangsamoro Autonomous Region is under transition, with the process expected to have reached completion by the time you read this.

Despite criticism from human rights organizations and notwithstanding his willingness to court controversy and to ignore convention, Duterte remained extremely popular throughout his tenure. *Shabu* (methamphetamine) addiction was undoubtedly a serious problem in the Philippines, and the president's policy of extrajudicial killing certainly reduced it, whatever the collateral damage and killings of the innocent that may have accompanied this strategy. His 2016 decision to allow Ferdinand Marcos's burial in Manila's Heroes' Cemetery shocked many, and appeared to suggest some endorsement of the former president's contempt for democracy. The February 2017 arrest of his staunchest critic, Liberal senator Leila de Lima, for supposed involvement in drug trafficking, also sounded alarm bells – Amnesty International called it "a blatant attempt ... to silence criticism." However, in other fields Duterte was keen to expand democratic rights, and to tackle corruption. His July 2016 **Freedom of Information Order**, for example, has increased government transparency, guaranteeing citizens the right to examine all official transactions except for those affecting national security. As for corruption, in typical Duterte style, he threatened to throw corrupt officials out of helicopters.

Duterte's tenure as president saw the outbreak of the Covid-19 pandemic: by March Duterte had declared a state of medical emergency, and banned the arrival of foreign tourists. Partial lockdowns and quarantines were imposed across the country, and Duterte promised to shoot quarantine violators.

Duterte stood down as president in June 2022 after his term was complete; his successor was Ferdinand Marcos Jr, the son of Ferdinand and Imelda, who goes by the affectionate nickname of Bongbong. His vice-president was Sara Duterte, a daughter of Rodrigo, who found herself impeached in 2025 on several charges, including plotting to kill the president, as well as graft and corruption; at the time of writing Duterte was still in office, pending a final Senate verdict. Their policies were considered a continuation of those of Duterte, and though they enjoyed considerable popular support, opposition parties made considerable ground during the general elections that followed the impeachment.

2020	2022	2025
Covid-19 pandemic arrives in the Philippines; the country remains closed to foreign tourists until February 2022	Ferdinand 'Bongbong' Marcos Jr elected seventeenth president of the Philippines	Vice-president Sara Duterte impeached after charges of corruption, involvement in extrajudicial killings, and plotting to assassinate the president

Religious beliefs

Religious belief – among Muslims as well as Christians – is genuine and deeply held all over the Philippines. Though the nation remains predominantly Roman Catholic, parts of Mindanao are one hundred percent Islamic, and even traditional Catholic communities have been shaken up by new Catholic movements such as El Shaddai. Perhaps most surprising has been the success of Protestant churches such as Iglesia ni Cristo, which has branches all over the archipelago.

Catholicism

The Philippines is one of only two **predominantly Catholic** nations in Asia (the other being East Timor) – more than eighty percent of the population is Roman Catholic, with around ten percent Protestant. In addition to the Christian majority, there is a Muslim minority of between five and ten percent, concentrated on the southern islands of Mindanao and Sulu.

Yet to describe the Philippines as a Roman Catholic country is an over-simplification. Elements of Indigenous belief absorbed into Catholicism have resulted in a form of "**folk Catholicism**" that manifests itself in various homespun observances – a folk healer might use Catholic liturgy mixed with native rituals, or suited entrepreneurs might be seen scattering rice around their premises to ensure that their ventures are profitable. There's also the infamous **re-enactments of the Crucifixion** held near San Fernando, Pampanga, every year (see box, page 115), which are frowned upon by the official Church. The **Chinese** minority, too, has been influential in colouring Filipino Catholicism with the beliefs and practices of Buddhism, Confucianism and Taoism; many Catholic Filipinos believe in the balance of *yin* and *yang*, and that time is cyclical in nature.

The new Catholic movements

Today, the supremacy of the Catholic Church in the Philippines is being challenged by a variety of Christian sects. The largest of these is **El Shaddai**, established by lay preacher Mike Velarde on his weekly Bible-quoting radio show in the 1980s. Known to his followers as Brother Mike, Velarde captured the imagination of poor Catholics, many of whom feel isolated from the mainstream Church. Velarde started preaching in colloquial and heavily accented Tagalog at huge open-air gatherings every weekend on Roxas Boulevard – the movement moved into a purpose-built "House of Prayer" in Paranaque, Metro Manila, in 2009. Velarde tends to wear screamingly loud, made-to-measure suits and outrageous bow ties, but his message is straightforward: give to the Lord and He will return it to you tenfold. El Shaddai now has over eight million followers, most of whom suffer from *sakit sa bulsa*, or "ailment of the pocket", but are nevertheless happy to pay ten percent of their income to become card-carrying members of the flock. Brother Mike's relationship with the mainstream Catholic Church is uneasy. His relationship with politicians is not. With so many followers hanging on his every word, Brother Mike is a potent political ally and few candidates for high office are willing to upset him. In the 1998 elections, Brother Mike backed Joseph Estrada, which was a significant factor in the former movie actor's initial success. The **Neocatechumenal Way**, a Catholic movement that started in Spain in the 1960s, also has a very large and expanding presence in the Philippines.

THE ASWANG WHO CAME TO DINNER

Heard the one about the pretty young housewife in a remote Visayan village who was possessed by the spirit of a jealous witch? Or the poor woman from a Manila shanty town who had taken to flying through the barangay, terrorizing her neighbours? These are stories from the pages of Manila's daily tabloid newspapers, reported as if they actually happened. Foreign visitors greet news of the latest barangay haunting with healthy cynicism, but when you are lying in your creaking nipa hut in the pitch dark of a moonless evening, it's not hard to see why so many Filipinos grow up embracing strange stories about creatures that inhabit the night. Even urbane professionals, when returning to the barangay of their childhood on holiday, can be heard muttering the incantation *tabi tabi lang-po* as they walk through paddy field or forest. Meaning "please let us pass safely", it's a request to the spirits and dwarves that might be lying in wait.

Most Filipino **spirits** are not the abstract souls of Western folklore who live in a netherworld; they are corporeal entities who live in trees or hang around the jeepney station, waiting to inflict unspeakable horrors on those who offend them. The most feared and widely talked about creature of Philippine folklore is the **aswang**; hundreds of cheesy films have been made about the havoc they wreak and hundreds of *aswang* sightings have been carried by the tabloid press. By day the *aswang* is a beautiful woman. The only way to identify her is by looking into her eyes at night, when they turn red. The *aswang* kills her victims as they sleep; threading her long tongue through the gaps in the floor or walls and inserting it into one of the body's orifices to suck out the internal organs.

Other creatures on the bogeyman list include the arboreal *tikbalang*, which has the head of a nag and the body of a man, and specializes in the abduction of virgins. Then there's the *duwende*, an elderly, grizzled dwarf who lurks in the forest and can predict the future, and the *engkanto*, who hides in trees and throws dust in the faces of passers-by, giving them permanently twisted lips.

Protestantism and the new religious movements

Some of the fastest-growing religious movements in the Philippines are actually Protestant. Eddie Villanueva, one of the candidates in the 2004 and 2010 presidential elections (he had very little success on either occasion, though did make it into congress in 2019), established the charismatic **Jesus is Lord Church** in 1978, which he claims has some six million members, with branches in Asia, Europe and North America.

You'll see the distinctive fairy-tale spires of **Iglesia ni Cristo** churches throughout the Philippines, an independent, purely Filipino movement founded by Felix Manalo in 1914 (the movement is currently run by his grandson, Eduardo V. Manalo). Iglesia ni Cristo is explicitly anti-Catholic in its beliefs (the doctrine of the Trinity is rejected, for example) and is very influential during elections. Membership is estimated to be over three million but is probably much higher.

One of the churches most successful at expanding overseas is the **Pentecostal Missionary Church of Christ**, founded in 1973 and based in Marikina City. **The United Methodist Church** in the Philippines is an umbrella group for around one million Methodists in the country, while there are about twenty different **Baptist** groups in the islands, at least half a million **Mormons**, and half a million **Seventh-Day Adventists**.

Another well-known loose affiliation of groups, the **Rizalistas**, have only a tenuous connection with standard Christian doctrine. All regard José Rizal (see page 415) as the second son of God and a reincarnation of Christ, and some hold Mount Banahaw (see page 187) in Quezon province to be sacred, regularly attending pilgrimages to the mountain.

Islam

Islam spread north to the Philippines from Indonesia and Malaysia in the fourteenth century, and by the time the Spanish arrived it was firmly established on Mindanao and Sulu, with outposts on Cebu and Luzon.

Islam remains a very dominant influence in the southern Philippines (25 percent of Mindanao's population is Muslim), and Muslims have added cultural character to the nation, with Filipino Christians expressing admiration over their warlike defiance of colonization. However, many Muslims feel they have become strangers in their own country, ignored by the Manila-centric government and marginalized by people resettled in Mindanao from Luzon; the **Autonomous Region in Muslim Mindanao** was established in 1990, the only region that has its own government (see boxes, page 385 and 410).

While all Filipino Muslims follow the basic tenets of Islam, their religion has absorbed a number of Indigenous elements, such as making offerings to spirits known as **diwatas**. Many native Muslim people believe in a spirit known as **Bal-Bal**; with the body of a man and the wings of a bird, Bal-Bal is credited with the habit of eating out the livers of unburied bodies. In Jolo and Tawi-Tawi, Muslims use mediums to contact the dead, while many Muslim groups trade amulets, wearing them as necklaces to ward off ill fortune.

Muslim **women** are freer in the Philippines than in many Islamic countries, and have traditionally played a prominent role in everything from war to ceremonies. "The women of Jolo", wrote a Spanish infantryman in the eighteenth century, "prepare for combat in the same manner as their husbands and brothers and are more desperate and determined than the men. With her child suspended to her breast or slung across her back, the Moro woman enters the fight with the ferocity of a panther."

Filipino arts and culture

In *El Filibusterismo*, José Rizal worried that Filipinos would become "a people without a soul". It's a theme that has been much developed by travel writers ever since, from Pico Iyer's description of "lush sentimentality" and Filipina "obsession" with high-school romance and pageants in *Video Night in Kathmandu*, to Michael Palin observing that American interest in the country is "unashamedly obvious" in *Full Circle*. Yet there is a lot more to Philippine culture than cover bands, go-go bars and endless beauty pageants. Over the years Filipino writers, rappers, film-makers and artists have developed distinctive styles that incorporate elements of all the nation's disparate cultural elements.

Fine arts

Classical painting in the Philippines goes back to the Spanish period, but there are two acknowledged Filipino masters: **Juan Luna** (1859–99) and **Félix Hidalgo** (1855–1913). Both artists helped shine attention on the Philippines after submitting paintings to the 1884 Exposición General de Bellas Artes in Madrid. Luna's huge and drama-laced *Spolarium* (1884) is perhaps the most famous painting in the Philippines (on display at the National Art Gallery), while his equally admired *The Blood Compact* graces the Malacañang Palace. Luna spent most of his career in Europe and died in Hong Kong, and he's best known today for painting literary and historical scenes. Hidalgo also spent much of his career in Europe and died in Spain, creating haunting works such as *Las Virgenes Cristianas Expuestas al Populacho* ("The Christian Virgins Exposed to the Populace") and *Laguna Estigia* ("The Styx").

With the end of Spanish rule and a growing sense of independence in the twentieth century, Filipino painters were more content to develop their craft at home. **Fernando Amorsolo** (1892–1972) studied at the University of the Philippines' School of Fine Arts and gained prominence during the 1920s and 1930s for popularizing images of Philippine landscapes and demure rural Filipinas; his *Rice Planting* (1922) became one of the most popular images of the American period, and he became the first "National Artist" in 1972. Meanwhile, **Victorio Edades** (1895–1985) introduced Modernism to the Philippines with *The Builders* (1928), a style he'd developed in the US in direct contrast to Amorsolo. He went on to establish the UST College of Fine Arts in the 1930s, a bastion of avant-garde art.

World War II changed the way artists saw the world: Amorsolo's pastoral scenes gave way to the grimmer, urban images of **Vicente Manansala** (1910–82), as portrayed in works like *Jeepneys* (1951). Other notable late twentieth-century painters include **José T. Joya** (1931–95), the Filipino abstract artist, and **Fernando Zóbel de Ayala y Montojo** (1924–84), a Modernist painter who also developed his craft in the US.

The **contemporary art scene** in the Philippines is dynamic and eclectic, fed in part by exceptionally good art schools in the capital, with popular current forms and styles covering everything from installation art and video to realism and street art. One of the most highly acclaimed contemporary artists is **Ronald Ventura**, whose *Grayground Painting* fetched almost P47 million at auction in 2011, making it the most expensive Philippine painting ever sold, until *Space Transfiguration* by abstract artist Jose Goya went for over P112 million in 2018. Pilipinas Street Plan (🄸instagram.com/pilipinas_ street_plan) and Ili-Likha (🄸ililikhaartistswateringhole)are **art communities** that showcase street art, graffiti, posters, stickers and installations. One of the hottest visual artists today is **Maya Muñoz**, whose work is often displayed in Manila's galleries.

Film

Although film-making has a distinguished history in the Philippines, and locally made movies (and their stars) remain popular, they remain a long way behind their Hollywood counterparts in terms of audience and income.

Early movies arrived in the Philippines in the late 1890s, but the first genuinely Filipino film is credited to **Jose Nepumuceno**, the "Father of Philippine Movies", who made a version of a popular play, *Dalagang Bukid* (Country Maiden), in 1919. The domestic film industry didn't really get going until the 1950s, when four big studios (Sampaguita, LVN, Premiere and Lebran) churned out hundreds of movies such as Gerardo de Leon's *Ifugao* (1954) and Manuel Conde's *Genghis Khan* (1952). Despite Gerardo de Leon's lauded adaptations of the Rizal novels *Noli Me Tángere* (1961) and *El Filibusterismo* (1962), the following decade was much poorer creatively and all four studios eventually closed.

Despite censorship during the Marcos years, **avant-garde** movie-making flourished in the 1970s, with Lino Brocka's *The Claws of Light* (1975) considered by many critics to be the greatest Philippine film ever made, and Kidlat Tahimik's *Mababangong Bangungot* (Perfumed Nightmare) winning the International Critic's Prize at the Berlin Film Festival of 1977. Brocka's *This Is My Country*, which tackles the issue of labour union control under Marcos, was entered into the 1984 Cannes Film Festival.

The late 1980s and 1990s is regarded as a weaker period, but since the turn of the century **independent Filipino movies** have been undergoing something of a renaissance, in part thanks to digital technology. In 2003 Mark Meily scored a big hit with the comedy *Crying Ladies*, about three Filipinas working as professional mourners in Manila's Chinatown, while *Ang Pagdadalaga ni Maximo Oliveros* (The Blossoming of Maximo Oliveros; 2005) by Auraeus Solito and *Kubrador* (The Bet Collector; 2006) by Jeffrey Jeturian were internationally acclaimed. Filipinos have also excelled in other formats: Carlo Ledesma won best short film at the Cannes Film Festival in 2007 for *The Haircut*. In 2008, Brillante Mendoza's *Serbis* (Service) became the first full-length Filipino film to compete at Cannes since 1984; the account of a day in the life of a family running a porno film theatre in Angeles City is bawdy and brutally realistic. Mendoza's *Kinatay* (Butchered) competed at Cannes the following year.

Lavish historical drama *El Presidente* (2012), another film directed by Mark Meily, is the nation's most expensive movie to date, starring several acting heavyweights and exploring the life of Emilio Aguinaldo. The **Metro Manila Film Festival** showcases the latest Filipino films over the Christmas period every year, not all of them arthouse material. To get a feel for what Filipinos like to watch today – from kitsch and campy romantic comedies to fantasy romps – see *Enteng Ng Ina Mo* (Your Monther Enteng; 2011), a fantasy parody; *Hello, Love,* Goodbye (2018), a romantic drama that holds the current record for greatest takings at the Filipino box office; *Sisterakas* (2012), a contemporary slapstick comedy starring vet Vice Ganda (the name is a play on Sister Act); and blockbuster *The Unkabogable: Praybeyt Benjamin* (Private Benjamin; 2011), an action comedy also starring Ganda as a reluctant soldier – the name is a loose reference to the 1980 Goldie Hawn movie, but the slapstick and sexual themes are very different. 2016 was a big year for local cinema on the international festival circuit, with *Die Beautiful* by Jun Lana winning in Tokyo, and Lav Diaz winning both in Berlin for *A Lullaby to the Sorrowful Mystery – and* Venice for *The Woman Who Left*.

Music

Any Friday night in Manila (and all over Asia), countless Filipino **showbands** can be seen in countless hotel lobbies performing accomplished cover versions of Western classics. While there's no doubt that when Filipinos mimic they do it exceedingly well, **Indigenous music** does survive. Filipino pop and rap artists and to a lesser extent rock groups have all been making a comeback in recent years, part of a slow but discernible trend away from the adulation of solely American pop stars and celebrities.

Traditional music

Folk songs and stories, handed down orally, are still sung at gatherings and ceremonies among Indigenous peoples. Among the ethnic and Indigenous groups of Mindanao and the Sulu archipelago there's a sophisticated musical genre called **kulintang**, in which the main instruments are bossed gongs similar to the Indonesian gamelan. *Kulintang* is commonly performed by small ensembles playing instruments that include the *kulintang* itself (a series of small gongs for the melody), the *agung* (large gongs for the lower tones) and the *gandingan* (four large vertical gongs used as a secondary melodic instrument). *Kulintang* music serves as a means of entertainment and a demonstration of hospitality; it's used at weddings, festivals, coronations, to entertain visiting dignitaries and to honour those heading off on or coming back from a pilgrimage. It is also used to accompany healing ceremonies and, up to the beginning of the twentieth century, was a form of communication, using goatskin drums to beat messages across the valleys.

The Manila Sound

The "**Manila Sound**" was the sound of the 1970s in the Philippines. Against a backdrop of student riots and martial law, some audiences found comfort with bell-bottom-wearing bands, like **The Hotdogs** and **The Boyfriends**, who set romantic novelty lyrics to catchy melodic hooks. Some sneered at the frivolity of it all, but the Manila Sound was as big as disco. Today it's effectively extinct, but it gave rise to a number of major stars who evolved and are still going strong. The most well known is indefatigable diva **Sharon Cuneta**, who is known throughout the country by the modest moniker "The Megastar". She first appeared in the Philippine pop charts at the age of 12 singing the disco tune *Mr. D.J.* and has since released numerous albums including one of duets with other apparently ageless Filipina singers such as Pops Fernandez (the "Concert Queen") and Sunshine Cruz.

The folkies

In the 1970s the only truly original artists performing in Manila were folksy beatniks such as singer-songwriters **Joey Ayala** and **Freddie Aguilar**. In the 1980s, Aguilar wrote a popular ballad called **Anak** and found himself a fan in First Lady Imelda Marcos who, ever eager to bathe herself in the reflected glory of Manila's celebs, invited him to Malacañang Palace so they could sing the song together at banquets. Aguilar was appalled by the excesses he saw inside the palace and never went back.

As the anti-Marcos movement grew, so did the popularity of *Anak*. Aguilar, by now something of a talisman for left-wing groups opposing martial law, took the opportunity to become even more political, recording a heartfelt version of *Bayan Ko* (My Country), a patriotic anthem that now took on extraordinary political significance.

One of the most well-known groups of the new generation was **APO Hiking Society**, a foursome from Ateneo University whose anthem *Handog ng Pilipino sa Mundo* (A New And Better Way) has been covered by numerous Filipino artists. Its lyrics are carved on the wall of Manila's Our Lady of EDSA Shrine, traditionally a focal point of protests and revolutions.

Tribal-pop and OPM (Original Pilipino Music)

In the 1990s – largely as a reaction to the decline of the protest movement and the creeping Americanization of Filipino music – a roots movement emerged that took the traditional rhythms and chants of tribal music such as *kulintang* and merged them with contemporary instruments and production techniques. One of the chief exponents of so-called tribal-pop (the term **Original Pilipino Music** or Original Pinoy Music was coined in the late 1980s) was **Grace Nono**. She never quite cracked the big time, but cleared the path for others, including **Pinikpikan**, the most successful tribal-pop band in the country (the band reformed as **Kalayo** in 2007). Over the last few years the term OPM has become diluted, and now encompasses the young stars of the twenty-first century, most of whom have modelled themselves on Celine Dion and Michael Bublé, not the revolutionary Manila singers of the Marcos years. This new generation includes **Kyla**, **Erik Santos**, **Sarah Geronimo** and **Christian Bautista**.

The mainstream: Filipino pop, rock and alternative music

Any consideration of mainstream popular **rock music** in the Philippines won't get off the ground without reference to the irreverent **Eraserheads**. After more than a decade at the top they disbanded in 2003, but remain the most popular Filipino band ever, a position only cemented by their subsequently reunion in 2012. Many current popular groups have been inspired by their infectious blend of irony and irresistibly melodic pop, including **Rivermaya**, still producing platinum-selling albums at a rate of knots, and **Parokya ni Edgar**, one of the few bands that have come close to equalling the Eraserheads; their 1996 debut album, *Khangkhungkherrnitz*, features a tribute to the nation's favourite food: instant noodles. Today Filipino pop, rock and alternative music is flourishing; 21st-century success stories have included **6cyclemind**, **Alamat**, **Ben&Ben**, **Chicosci**, **Sponge Cola** and **Sandwich**.

Despite the proliferation of progressive acts, the popular Philippine music scene has become dominated in recent years by comely solo performers singing plaintive **ballads** in the style of Whitney Houston or Mariah Carey. In the hierarchy of balladeers, Regine Velasquez and Martin Nievera are at the top. **Regine Velasquez**'s story is the quintessential Filipino movie script: a beautiful girl from the sticks – she grew up in Leyte in the 1970s – wins a singing contest in 1989 (with a performance of *You'll Never Walk Alone* in Hong Kong) and heads off to Manila. Her repertoire is typical of the Filipina diva canon, comprising misty-eyed love songs such as *Could It Be?*, *What You Are to Me* and *Long For Him*. Velasquez follows in the tradition of Sharon Cuneta, Pops Fernandez and Kuh Ledesma, who at one time or another have all been dubbed the country's "concert queen" by the media. **Martin Nievera** puts his success – he's been recording since 1982 – down to the fact that Filipinos love a good drama. His songs are indeed melodramatic, his album *Forever, Forever* being an open book about his high-profile marital break-up with singer-actress Pops Fernandez.

Filipino hip-hop

Filipino hip-hop or **Pinoy rap** emerged in the 1980s, with tracks by **Dyords Javier** and **Vincent Dafalong**. The genre hit the mainstream with **Francis Magalona**'s debut album, *Yo!* in 1990, which included the nationalistic hit *Mga Kababayan* ("My Countrymen"), a call to political arms that bore the hallmarks of Freddie Aguilar. In 1994, Death Threat released the first Filipino gangsta rap album *Gusto Kong Bumaet* ("I Want to be Good"). Since 2004 the **Philippine Hip-Hop Music Awards** has been held annually in Metro Manila and the genre remains incredibly popular throughout the country; current stars include **Gloc-9** (former member of Death Threat), **Abra** and **Pikaso**. The most successful Filipino-American rapper is the Black Eyed Peas' **apl.de.ap**, who was born in Angeles City in 1974 and moved to Los Angeles at the age of 14.

P-pop

The global success of Korean pop was not lost on the Philippines, which has spun out its own clones – and more interesting tweaks – in a genre inevitably known as P-pop. Girl-group BINI have arguably been the most successful product, with (Korean-produced) SB19 a male equivalent, while Sarah Geronimo has followed the well-trodden path from singing to acting to talent-show-judging.

DISCOGRAPHY

FOLK

Freddie Aguilar *Collection* (1985). A mixture of studio and live recordings featuring most of the folk hero's greatest songs, including *Trabaho* and a cover version of Joey Ayala's

Mindanao. *Pinoy* is a dark, but melodic exposition of the average Filipino's lot, while the lyrical *Magdalena* was based on conversations Aguilar had with Manila prostitutes, all of whom desperately wanted to escape the life. There's no *Anak*, but there are plenty of other Freddie Aguilar collections that feature it.

TRIBAL-POP

Cynthia Alexander *Insomnia and Other Lullabyes* (1996). Introspective but affecting collection of progressive/tribal ballads from Joey Ayala's talented little sister. The navel-gazing becomes wearisome at times, but there are also some memorable moments, including *No Umbrella*, a pleading love song with sonorous strings and plaintive fretless bass.

Barbie's Cradle *Music from the Buffet Table* (1999). Their semi-acoustic sound dominated by the frail but evocative voice of Barbie Almalbis, Barbie's Cradle injected a new note of realism into OPM songwriting, with lyrics – in both English and Filipino – that spoke not of love and happiness, but of vulnerability and dysfunction. Highlights include *Money for Food*, a musical poem about poverty, and *It's Dark and I Am Lonely*, a personal and frank assessment of modern life for young people.

Grace Nono *Isang Buhay* (1997). Quintessential Nono, this is an album of sometimes strident but hypnotic rhythms and original traditional songs blended with additional lyrics drawing attention to the plight of Indigenous people, the environment and the avarice of the country's rulers. *Isang Buhay* means one house; the title track is Nono's plea for unity.

Pinikpikan *Kaamulan* (2003). Psychedelia meets tribal tradition on this, Pinikpikan's third album, released in 2003. The band's influences are eclectic and worn on the sleeve, from the Hindu overtones on *Child* to the flute solos – inspired by the wooden-flute music of the Manobo people of Mindanao – on *Butanding*, a haunting stream-of-consciousness piece about the endangered whale shark.

ROCK, POP AND HIP-HOP

6cyclemind *Project 6 Cyclemind* (2009). The last album by the popular alt-rockers before the controversial departure of lead singer Ney Dimaculangan is primarily a collection of thoughtful tunes and ballads, though the band still gets to rock out on tracks such as *Mahiwagang Pag-ibig*.

Abra *Abra* (2012). First solo album from the gifted rapper of Pinoy hip-hop group, Lyrically Deranged Poets, his trademark lyrical style and humorous raps in full effect – the smooth R&B-inspired hit *Gayuma* (featuring the son of Freddie Aguilar) has millions of hits on YouTube.

Bamboo *Tomorrow Becomes Yesterday* (2008). Bamboo's fourth, final and best album: intelligent and thoughtful indie rock in Filipino and English, with everything from acoustic ballads to hard rock anthems.

BINI *Feel Good* (2022). The girl group's second album, which enjoyed great online success (and not only in the Philippines) during the Covid years, provides a good example of what has become known as P-pop.

Eraserheads *Ultraelectromagneticpop* (1993). Thoroughly enjoyable debut album featuring spirited Beatles-inspired pop, novelty pieces that poke fun at everyone and everything, and the brilliant *Pare Ko* ("My Friend"), which had the establishment in a spin because it contained a couple of swear words and gay references. The band matured after this and even got better – their second album, *Circus*, includes the track *Butterscotch* which takes a not so gentle dig at the Catholic Church ("Father Markus said to me/Just confess and you'll be free/Sit yer down upon me lap/And tell me all yer sins") – but *Ultraelectromagneticpop* will always be special because it blazed a trail.

Gloc-9 *Liham at Lihim* (2013). The seventh album ("Letter and Secret") from current godfather of Filipino rap sees speed-rapper Gloc-9 collaborating with Rico Blanco and even veteran chanteuse Regine Velasquez.

Kamikazee *Romantico* (2012). If you want to get a taste of current Filipino indie rock this is for you, with the catchy riffs and jangling guitars on the Manila punk band's fourth album reminiscent of Green Day.

Kitchie Nadal *Kitchie Nadal* (2004). The debut album of the soulful Filipino singer-songwriter Nadal, featuring the award-winning *Wag na Wag Mong Sasabihin*, an indie anthem worthy of Coldplay.

Martin Nievera *Live with the Philippine Philharmonic Orchestra* (2000). Two-disc set recorded in Manila that captures some of the energy of Nievera live, when he's a much greater force than on many of his overly sentimental studio recordings. A master of patter and performance, Nievera sings in English, in Filipino, on his own, and with guests including the popular Filipina singing sisters Dessa and Cris Villonco – and his dad, Bert. The highlight is a mammoth montage of Broadway hits from *Carousel*, *West Side Story* and *Evita*, the nadir a self-indulgent spoken preamble to one of his signature songs, *Before You Say Goodbye*.

Rivermaya *It's Not Easy Being Green* (1999). Rivermaya's audience is unashamedly middle of the road and so is their music, an amiable blend of guitar-driven pop and laidback love songs for twenty-somethings. This album is typical, suffused with British influences ranging from the Beatles to Belle and Sebastian. The highpoint, however, is Pure Pinoy, the ironic ballad *Grounded ang Girlfriend Ko* ("My Girlfriend's Grounded Me"), which owes more to Eraserheads than Britpop.

Sponge Cola *Ultrablessed* (2014). Fifth studio album of the award-winning Pinoy rock band and the much-awaited follow up to 2011's bestselling *Araw Oras Tagpuan*. It includes the single *Anting-Anting*, featuring Gloc-9, and plenty of the band's trademark smooth pop-rock.

Regine Velasquez *Unsolo* (2000). This was the album that marked the beginning of Velasquez's attempts to become an international star, or at least a pan-Asian one, raising her profile with duets featuring the likes of David Hasselhoff – for a syrupy rendition of *More Than Words Can Say* – and Jacky Cheung. There's only one song in Filipino.

Books

The Philippines hasn't been as well documented in fiction or non-fiction as many of its Asian neighbours. There are, however, a number of good investigative accounts of two subjects – American involvement in the Philippines and the excesses of the Marcoses. Some of the books reviewed below are published in the Philippines, and are unlikely to be on sale in bookshops outside the country; you should have more luck online.

HISTORY AND POLITICS

Alan Berlow *Dead Season: A Story of Murder and Revenge*. This brilliantly atmospheric work is the story of three murders that took place in the 1970s on Negros, against the backdrop of communist guerrilla activity and appeals for land reform. It's impossible to read without feeling intense despair for a country where humble, peaceful people have often become pawns in a game of power and money played out around them. Cory Aquino comes out of it badly – the Church asked her to investigate the murders but she refused, fearful that this might entail treading on too many toes.

Raymond Bonner *Waltzing with a Dictator*. Former *New York Times* correspondent Bonner reports on the complex twenty-year US relationship with the Marcos regime and how Washington kept Marcos in power long after his sell-by date: US bases in the country needed a patron and Marcos was the right man. Marcos cleverly played up the threat of a communist insurgency in the Philippines, making it seem to Washington that he was their only hope of stability.

Patricia Evangelista *Some People Need Killing*. A local journalist's memoirs about her time reporting on Duterte's war on drugs, this scooped a few awards, as well as being listed as one of the *New York Times'* top ten books of 2023 (and *Time* magazine's top hundred).

Luis Francia *History of the Philippines: From Indios Bravos to Filipinos*. A welcome history of the archipelago offering the perfect introduction to the country and plenty of new insights about the Spanish and American periods in particular.

★ **James Hamilton-Paterson** *America's Boy: The Rise and Fall of Ferdinand Marcos and Other Misadventures of US Colonialism in the Philippines*. A controversial narrative history of the US-supported dictatorship that came to define the Philippines. The author makes the very plausible claim that the Marcoses were merely the latest in a long line of corrupt Filipino leaders in a country which had historically been ruled by oligarchies, and gathers first-hand information from senators, cronies, rivals and Marcos family members, including Imelda.

★ **James D. Hornfischer** *The Last Stand of the Tin Can Sailors*. Gripping and in parts harrowing narrative of the battle between the Americans and Japanese off Samar in October 1944, and the larger battle of Leyte Gulf that followed, the

beginning of the American liberation of the Philippines. Hornfischer also intelligently provides a Japanese perspective to the battle. Well written and easy to read.

★ **Stanley Karnow** *In Our Image: America's Empire in the Philippines*. This Pulitzer Prize-winning effort is really a book about America, not about the Philippines. The Philippines is the landscape, but the story is of America going abroad for the first time in its history at the turn of the last century. The book examines how the US sought to remake the Philippines as a clone of itself, an experiment marked from the outset by blundering, ignorance and mutual misunderstanding.

Eric Morris *Corregidor*. Intimate account of the defence of the island fortress, based on interviews with more than forty Filipinos and Americans who battled hunger, dysentery and malaria in the run-up to the critical battle with Japanese forces. As the book explains, the poorly equipped Allied troops, abandoned by General MacArthur and almost forgotten by military strategists in Washington, had little chance of winning, though against all the odds Corregidor held out for six months.

Ambeth Ocampo *Rizal without the Overcoat*. This collection of essays and musings (originally a column in the *Philippine Daily Globe*) offers entertaining and easily digested insights into the great Filipino hero. It's become almost as common in schools as Rizal's *Noli* (see page 435).

Vicente L. Rafael *The Sovereign Trickster*. Delving into the rule of Rodrigo Duterte, with particular emphasis on his methods and how they fit within the global context. It's heavy going, but fascinating and very well-researched.

Beth Day Romulo *Inside the Palace: The Rise and Fall of Ferdinand and Imelda Marcos*. Beth Day Romulo, wife of Ferdinand Marcos's foreign minister Carlos Romulo, was among those who enjoyed the privileges of being a Malacañang insider, something she feels the need to excuse and justify on almost every page. Her book borders on being a Marcos hagiography – she clearly didn't want to upset her old friend Imelda too much – and is gossipy more than investigative, but does nevertheless offer some insight into Imelda's lavish and frivolous lifestyle, and the disintegration of the regime.

William Henry Scott *Barangay: Sixteenth-Century*

Philippine Culture and Society. This lucid account of life in the Philippines during the century the Spanish arrived is the best there is of the period. The author's love for the Philippines and his deep knowledge of its customs are reflected in this scholarly but accessible investigation into Hispanic-era society, the country's elite, its Indigenous people and their customs – everything from that most quotidian of rituals, taking a bath, to the once common practice of penis piercing.

Hampton Sides *Ghost Soldiers: The Epic Account of World War II's Greatest Rescue Mission*. Recounts the astonishing and mostly forgotten story of the combined US Ranger and Filipino guerrilla force that managed to free hundreds of POWs from behind Japanese lines in 1944.

CULTURE AND SOCIETY

Sheila Coronel (ed) *Pork and Other Perks*. Comprising nine case studies by some of the country's foremost investigative journalists, this pioneering work uncovers the many forms corruption takes in the Philippines and points fingers at those responsible. The book is concerned mainly with what happens to "pork", the budget allocated annually to every senator and congressman. It's thought that much of the money goes towards hiring corrupt contractors who use below-par materials on infrastructure projects, with the politicians themselves benefiting from the discrepancy between the official and actual cost of the projects concerned.

★ **James Hamilton-Paterson** *Playing With Water: Passion and Solitude on a Philippine Island*. "No money, no honey," says one of the characters in Hamilton-Paterson's lyrical account of several seasons spent among the impoverished fishermen of Marinduque. This is a rich and original book, which by turns warms you and disturbs you. The author's love of the Philippine landscape and the people – many of whom think he must be related to US actor George Hamilton – is stunningly rendered. The diving accounts will stay with you forever, as will the episode in which H-P discovers he has worms.

★ **F. Sionil José** *We Filipinos: Our Moral Malaise, Our Heroic Heritage*. Deeply cynical and incredibly patriotic in equal measure, this collection of essays from the nation's pre-eminent writer is required reading for anyone wanting to get under the skin of Philippine culture.

★ **Manny Pacquiao** *Pacman: My Story of Hope, Resilience, and Never-Say-Never Determination*. Ghost-written? Certainly. Full of corny sentiment? Perhaps. But Pacquiao's story is so remarkable that it's hard to put this "autobiography" down, charting the tenacious fighter's rise from the backstreets of Mindanao to boxing champion of the world and multimillionaire. Inspirational stuff.

Earl K. Wilkinson *The Philippines: Damaged Culture?* Written by a long-time expat, this book explores the underlying reasons for the many maladies affecting the country. *Damaged Culture* is never pontificating or presumptuous, but it is sometimes shocking in its revelations of corruption in high places, highlighting a number of travesties of justice which the author campaigned to put right. He also offers solutions, arguing that the nation's entrenched elite could start the recovery ball rolling by abandoning its traditional antipathy towards free-market competition.

ARCHITECTURE

Pedro Galende *San Agustin*. An evocative tribute to the first Spanish stone church to be built in the Philippines, San Agustin in Intramuros. The first part of the book is a detailed account of the church's history, while the second is a walking tour, illustrated with photographs, through the church and the neighbouring monastery.

Pedro Galende & Rene Javelana *Great Churches of the Philippines*. Coffee-table book full of beautiful colour photographs of most of the country's notable Spanish-era churches. The accompanying text explains the evolution of the unique "earthquake Baroque" style developed to protect stone structures against earthquakes. The style typifies Philippine churches and provides a reminder that many of these stunning buildings are in a perilous state, with little money available to guarantee their upkeep and survival.

THE ENVIRONMENT

Robin Broad et al. *Plundering Paradise: The Struggle for the Environment in the Philippines*. Disturbing but often inspiring account of how livelihoods and habitats are disappearing throughout the Philippines as big business harvests everything from fish to trees, turned into packaging for multinational companies.

Gutsy Tuason and Eduardo Cu *Anilao*. Winner of the Palme d'Or at the World Festival of Underwater Images in Antibes, France, this hard-to-get but stunning coffee-table collection of colour photographs were all taken around Anilao, Batangas, one of the country's most popular diving areas. What's remarkable about the book is the way it makes you take notice of the small marine life many divers ignore.

FOOD

Reynaldo Alejandro et al. *The Food of the Philippines*. Proof that there's so much more to Filipino cuisine than adobo and rice. The recipes range from classics such as chilli crab simmered in coconut milk to a fail-safe method for that trickiest of desserts, *leche* flan. Every recipe details how to find the right ingredients and what to use as a substitute if you can't. There's also a revealing history of Filipino food.

Glenda Rosales-Barretto *Flavors of the Philippines*. Rosales-Barretto is chief executive officer of the popular *Via Mare* restaurant chain in Manila, and what she doesn't know about Filipino food isn't worth knowing. This lavishly illustrated hardback highlights recipes region by region. There's a classic Bicol Express, with lots of spices and fish paste, but many of the recipes here are far from standard – instead, modern variations feature, such as fresh vegetarian pancake rolls with peanut sauce and roast chicken with passionfruit.

FICTION

Cecilia Manguerra Brainard *When the Rainbow Goddess Wept*. The moving story of Yvonne Macaraig, a young Filipina during the Japanese invasion of the Philippines in World War II; the myths and legends of Philippine folklore sustain her despite the carnage all around. Though some of Brainard's character development and language is uneven, it's this connection with the rural, pre-Hispanic Philippines that makes the book so memorable. Brainard was born in Cebu but emigrated to the US in 1968.

Jessica Hagedorn (ed) *Manila Noir*. This project forms part of New York-based Akashic Books' *Noir* series, a collection of compelling short stories with Manila as a focus for Gothic, supernatural and crime genres. The plots might be fictional but up-and-coming writers such as Gina Apostol and Budjette Tan portray the city with uncanny realism.

F. Sionil José *Dusk*. This is the fifth book in the author's acclaimed saga of the landowning Rosales family at the end of the nineteenth century. It wouldn't be a quintessential Filipino novel if it didn't touch on the themes of poverty, corruption, tyranny and love; all are on display here, presented through the tale of one man, a common peasant, and his search for contentment. *Dusk* has been published in the US in paperback, though you can always buy it from José's bookshop, Solidaridad, in Manila (see page 95).

★ **F. Sionil José** *Ermita*. Eminently readable novella that atmospherically evokes the Philippines from World War II until the 1960s and stands as a potent allegory of the nation's ills. The Ermita of the title, apart from being the *mise en scène*, is also a girl, the unwanted child of a rich Filipina raped in her own home by a drunken Japanese soldier. The story follows young Ermita, abandoned in an orphanage, as she tries to trace her mother and then sets about exacting revenge on those she feels have wronged her.

★ **José Rizal** *Noli Me Tángere*. Published in 1886 (and banned by the Spanish), this is a passionate exposure of the double standards and the rank injustice of colonial rule; it's still required reading for every Filipino schoolchild. It tells the story of Crisostomo Ibarra's love for the beautiful Maria Clara, infusing it with tragedy and significance of almost Shakespearean proportions.

Ninotchka Rosca *State of War*. Considered a Filipino classic, this allegorical novel presents the history and culture of the Philippines through the eyes of three different characters, each with a very different viewpoint.

Miguel Syjuco *Ilustrado*. Winner of the 2008 Man Asian Literary Prize, this gripping saga takes over 150 years of Philippine history, as well as offering a scathing indictment of corruption and inequity among the Filipino ruling classes. Syjuco is a Filipino writer now based in Montreal.

THE PHILIPPINES IN FOREIGN LITERATURE

William Boyd *The Blue Afternoon*. Boyd has never been to the Philippines, but spent hours researching the country from England. In flashbacks, the novel moves from 1930s Hollywood to the exotic, violent world of the Philippines in 1902, recounting a tale of medicine, the murder of American soldiers and the creation of a magical flying machine.

Alex Garland *The Tesseract*. Alex Garland loves the Philippines, so it's hardly surprising that the follow-up to *The Beach* is set there. Garland may get most of his Fiipino wrong, but his prose captures perfectly the marginal existence of his characters. The story involves a foreigner abroad, a villainous tycoon called Don Pepe, some urchins and a beautiful girl. The characters may be clichéd, but Garland's plot is so intriguing that it's impossible not to be swept along by the baleful atmosphere the book creates.

Jessica Hagedorn *Dogeaters*. Filipino-American Jessica Hagedorn assembles a cast of diverse and dubious characters that comes as close to encapsulating the mania of life in Manila as any writer has ever come. Urchins, pimps, seedy tycoons and corpulent politicos are brought together in a brutal but beautiful narrative that serves as a jolting reminder of all the country's frailties and woes.

★ **James Hamilton-Paterson** *Ghosts of Manila*. Hamilton-Paterson's excoriating novel is haunting, powerful and for the most part alarmingly accurate. Much of it is taken from real life: the extrajudicial "salvagings" of suspected criminals, the corruption and the abhorrent saga of Imelda Marcos's infamous film centre. From the despair and detritus, the author conjures up a lucid story that is thriller, morality play and documentary in one.

Timothy Mo *Brownout on Breadfruit Boulevard*. Mo wrote this blunt satire of cultural and imperial domination in 1995 when he'd fallen out with his publisher, and his career subsequently fell off a cliff; the novel starts with a now infamous sex scene involving excrement. This story is much better than its sales (and the first page) suggested, though, set in the fictional town of Gobernador de Leon and following a motley bunch of locals and foreigners attending a conference.

Language

English is widely spoken in the Philippines, a legacy of the country's time under US rule. Most everyday transactions – checking into a hotel, ordering a meal, buying a ferry ticket – can be carried out in English, and most people working in tourism speak it reasonably well. Even off the beaten track, many Filipinos understand enough to help with basics such as accommodation and directions. However, it's worth learning a few words of Filipino, the standardized form of the Tagalog dialect. You will be a source of amusement if you try, even though the response will most likely come in English. The Filipino language has assimilated many Spanish words, such as *mesa* (table) and *cuarto* (bedroom, written *kuwarto* in Filipino), though few Filipinos can speak Spanish today. Cebuano (or "Visayan") spoken in the south of the archipelago uses even more Spanish – including all the numbers.

Filipino

The structure of the language is simple, though the **word order** is different from English; as an example, take *kumain ng mangga ang bata*, which literally translates as "ate a mango the child". For **plurals**, the word *mga* is used – hence *bahay/mga bahay* for house/houses – although in many cases Filipinos simply state the actual number of objects or use *marami* (several) before the noun.

Consonants and vowels

The language sounds staccato to the foreign ear, with clipped vowels and **consonants**. The **p**, **t** and **k** sounds are never aspirated and sound a little gentler than in English. The **g** is always hard, as in **g**et. The letter **c** seldom crops up in Filipino and where it does – in names such as Boracay and Bulacan, for example – it's pronounced like *k*. The hardest sound to master for most beginners is the **ng** sound as in the English word "si**ng**ing" (with the *g* gently nasalized, not hard); in Filipino this sound can occur at the beginning of a word, eg in **ng**ayon (now). The **mg** combination in words such as *mga* looks tricky but is in fact straightforward to pronounce, as *mang*.

As for **vowels and diphthongs** (vowel combinations):

a is pronounced as in **a**pple

e as in m**e**ss

i as in d**i**tto, though a little more elongated than in English

o as in b**o**re

u as in p**u**t

ay as in b**uy**

aw in m**ou**nt

iw is a sound that simply doesn't exist in English; it's close to the *ieu* sound in "lieu", but with greater separation between the vowels (almost as in "lee-you")

oy as in n**oise**

uw as in q**uar**ter

uy produced making the sound oo and continuing it to the i sound in "ditto".

Vowels that fall consecutively in a word are always pronounced individually, as is every syllable, adding to the choppy nature of the language; for example, *tao* meaning person or people is pronounced "ta-o", while *oo* for yes is pronounced "o-o" (with each vowel closer to the *o* in "show" than in "bore").

Stress

Most words are spoken as they are written, though working out which syllable to **stress** is tricky. In words of two syllables the first syllable tends to be stressed, while in words of three or more syllables the stress is almost always on the final or penultimate syllable.

In the vocabulary lists that follow, stressed syllables are indicated in **bold** text except where the term in question is obviously an English loan word. Note that English loan words may be rendered a little differently in Filipino, in line with the rules mentioned above; thus "bus" for instance has the vowel sound of the English word "put".

USEFUL WORDS AND PHRASES

GREETINGS AND CIVILITIES
hello/how are you? kamus**ta**
Fine, thanks ma**bu**ti, sa**la**mat (*formal*) okay lang (*informal*)
Goodbye bye
good morning magan**dang** u**ma**ga
good afternoon magan**dang** ha**pon**
good evening/good night magan**dang** gabi
please ... paki ...(before a request)
thank you sa**la**mat
excuse me (to say sorry) ipagpau**man**hin mo ak
excuse me (to get past) makiki**ra**an lang **po**/pasensiya ka na
sorry sorry
what's your name? anong pa**nga**lan mo?
my name is ... ang pa**nga**lan ko ay ...
do you speak English? ma**ru**nong ka bang mag-Ingles?
I (don't) understand (hindi) ko naiintindi**han**
could you repeat that? paki-**u**lit?
where are you from? **ta**ga sa**an** ka?
I am from ... **ta**ga ... ako (most countries are rendered as in English)
I don't know ew**an** (used to avoid confrontation)
okay?/is that okay? puwe**de**?/puwe**de** ba? (*informal*)
mate, buddy pa**re**

COMMON TERMS
Yes oo
No hin**di**
Maybe si**gu**ro
good/bad ma**ga**ling/ma**sa**ma
big/small ma**la**ki/ma**liit**
easy/difficult ma**da**li/ma**hi**rap
open/closed bu**kas**/sa**ra**do

hot/cold ma**init**/ma**la**mig
cheap/expensive mu**ra**/ma**hal**
a lot/a little ma**da**mi/**kon**ti
one more/another... isa pa ...
beautiful magan**da**
hungry gu**tom**
thirsty na**uu**haw
very ... (followed by **tu**nay ...adjective)
with/without ... me**ron**/wa**la** ...
watch out! ingat!
who? sino?
what? ano?
why? ba**kit**?
when? kai**lan**?
how? paano?

GETTING AROUND
Airport airport
bus/train station ista**syon** ng bus/tren
pier pier
aeroplane ero**pla**no
ferry barco (*for large vessels – "ferry" will also do*)
boat (outrigger) bang**ka**
taxi taxi
bicycle bisik**le**ta
car kot**se**
where do I/we catch the ...to ... ? saan puwe**de**ng ku**mu**ha ng ... pa**pun**tang ...?
when does the ... for ... leave? kailan a**a**lis ang ... pa**pun**tang ...?
when does the next ... leave? anong oras ho a**a**lis ang ...?
Ticket tiket
can I/we book a seat puwe**de**ng bu**mi**li kaa**gad** ng ticket **pa**ra i-reser**ba** ang upu**an**

FORMAL LANGUAGE: THE USE OF "PO"
Filipino has formal and informal **forms of address**, the formal usually reserved for people who are significantly older. The "po" suffix indicates respect and can be added to almost any word or phrase: *o-po* is a respectful "yes" and it's common to hear Filipinos say *sorry-po* for "sorry". Even the lowliest beggar is given esteem by language: the standard reply to beggars is *patawarin-po*, literally, "forgive me, sir". First names are fine for people of your own generation; for your elders, use Mr or Mrs (if you know a woman is married) before the surname. It's common to use *manong/manang* (uncle/aunt) and *kuya* (brother/sister) to address superiors informally, even if they are not blood relatives (eg *manong* Jun, *kuya*).

I'd/we'd like to go to the … please gusto naming pumunta sa …

[I'd like to] pay bayad po (*to a jeepney or tricycle driver*)

how long does it take? gaano katagal?

how many kilometres is it to …? ilang kilometro papunta sa …?

please stop here paki-tigil ditto or para

I'm in a hurry nagmamadali ako

DIRECTIONS

where is the …? saan ang …?

bank banko

beach beach

church simbahan

cinema sinehan

filling station gasolinahan

hotel hotel

market palengke

moneychanger taga-palit ng pera (*or just "money-changer"*)

pharmacy botika

post office koreo (*or post office*)

town hall town hall

left kaliwa

right kanan

straight on derecho/diretso

opposite katapat ng

in front of sa harap ng

behind sa likod ng

near/far malapit/malayo

north hilaga

south timog

east silangan

west kanluran

ACCOMMODATION

do you have any rooms? meron pa kayong kuwarto?

could I have the bill please? puwedeng kunin ang check?

Bathroom CR (*comfort room*) or banyo

room with a private bathroom kuwarto na may sariling banyo

EMERGENCIES

fire! sunog!

help! saklolo!

there's been an accident may aksidente

please call a doctor paki-tawag ng duktor

ill may sakit

hospital ospital

police station istasyon ng pulis

---

single room kuwarto para sa isa

double room kuwarto para sa dalawang tao

clean/dirty malinis/marumi

air-conditioner aircon

fan elektrik fan

key susi

telephone telepono

mobile phone/cellphone cellphone or cell

laundry labahan

passport pasaporte

SHOPPING

do you have …? meron kang …?

[we have] none wala

Money pera

how much? magkano?

it's too expensive masyadong mahal or sobra (*too much*)

I'll take this one kukunin ko ito

cigarettes sigarilyo

matches posporo

soap sabon

toilet paper tisyu

NUMBERS

Filipinos often resort to Spanish numbers, spelt as they are pronounced, especially when telling the time.

Tagalog/Filipino Spanish

0 zero sero

1 isa uno

2 dalawa dos

3 tatlo tres

4 apat kuwatro

5 lima singko

6 anim seis

7 pito siyete

8 walo otso

9 siyam nuwebe

10 sampu dyis

11 labing isa onse

12 labing dalawa dose

13 labing tatlo trese

20 dalawampu bente

21 dalawampu't benteuno isa

22 dalawampu't bentedos dalawa

30 tatlumpu trenta

40 apatnapu kwarenta

50 limampu singkwenta

60 animnapu sesenta

70 pitumpu setenta

80 walampu otsenta

90 siyamnapu nobenta

100 sandaan syen

1000 isang libo mil

1,000,000 isang milyun un miyon
a half kalahati medio/a

TIMES AND DATES

Days of the week and months of the year are mostly derived from Spanish.

what's the time? anong oras na?
9 o'clock alas nuwebe
10.30 alas diyes y media
morning umaga
noon tanghali
afternoon hapon
evening/night gabi
midnight hating-gabi
minute minuto
hour oras
day araw
week linggo
month buwan
year taon
today/now ngayon

tomorrow bukas
yesterday kahapon
Monday Lunes
Tuesday Martes
Wednesday Miyerkoles
Thursday Huwebes
Friday Biyernes
Saturday Sabado
Sunday Linggo
January Enero
February Pebrero
March Marso
April Abril
May Mayo
June Hunyo
July Hulyo
August Agosto
September Setyembre
October Oktubre
November Nobyembre
December Disyembre

FOOD AND DRINK TERMS

Most menus in the Philippines are in English, although in places that specialize in Filipino cuisine you'll see Filipino on the menu, usually with an explanation in English below. For foods that arrived in the Philippines comparatively recently there often isn't an equivalent Filipino word, so to have cake, for example, you ask for cake. Even in the provinces waiters and waitresses tend to speak enough English to understand what you're after.

GENERAL TERMS

can I see the menu? patingin ng menu?
I would like … gusto ko …
Delicious sarap
hot (spicy) maanghang
can I have the bill please? puwede kunin ang check?
I'm vegetarian vegetarian ako or gulay lang ang
  kinakain ko (literally "I only eat vegetables")
Breakfast almusal
lunch tanghalian
dinner hapunan (rare) or dinner
fork tinidor
knife kutsilyo
plate plato
spoon kutsara
glass baso

STAPLES AND COMMON INGREDIENTS

bread tinapay
bread rolls pan de sal
butter mantikilya
cheese keso

chillies sili
coconut milk gata
egg itlog
fermented fish/shrimp paste bagoong
fish sauce patis
garlic bawang
ginger luya
noodles pancit
onion sibuyas
pepper paminta
rice bigas (the uncooked grain) or kanin (cooked rice)
salt asin
soy sauce toyo
sugar asukal
tomato kamatis
vegetables gulay

MEAT (KARNE) AND POULTRY

baboy pork
baka beef
crispy pata deep-fried pig's knuckle
kambing goat
kordero/karnero lamb
lengua tongue
manok chicken
pato duck
pugo quail
tenga ng baboy pig's ears

COMMON MEAT DISHES

asado roast meat

A glossary of **Filipino fruits** is given in Basics (see box, page 35).

adobo chicken and/or pork simmered in soy sauce and vinegar with pepper and garlic

beef tapa beef marinated in vinegar, sugar and garlic, then dried in the sun and fried

Bicol Express fiery dish of pork ribs cooked in coconut milk, soy sauce, vinegar, *bagoong* and hot chillies

bistek tagalog beef tenderloin with lime and onion

bulalo beef shank in onion broth

dinuguan pork cubes simmered in pig's blood with garlic, onion and laurel leaves

ginisang monggo any combination of pork, vegetables or shrimp sautéed with mung beans

kaldereta spicy mutton stew

kare-kare rich oxtail stew with aubergine, peanut and *puso ng saging* (banana flower)

lechon (de leche) roast whole (suckling) pig, dipped in a liver paste sauce

longganisa/longganiza small beef or pork sausages, with a lot of garlic

longsilog longganisa with garlic rice and fried egg

mechado braised beef

puchero boiled beef and vegetables

sinigang sour fish, pork, beef, shrimp or chicken soup or stew flavoured with tamarind

sisig fried chopped pork (usually including pig's head), liver and onions

tapsilog beef tapa with garlic rice and fried egg

tinola tangy soup with chicken, papaya and ginger

tocino marinated fried pork

tosilog marinated fried pork with garlic rice and fried egg

FISH (ISDA) AND SEAFOOD

alimango crab

bangus milkfish

hipon shrimps

hito catfish

lapu-lapu grouper

panga ng tuna tuna jaw

posit squid

sugpo prawns

tahong mussels

talaba oysters

tanguingue popular and affordable sea fish, not unlike tuna in flavour

COMMON SEAFOOD DISHES

daing na bangus milkfish marinated in vinegar and spices, then fried

gambas shrimps sautéed in chilli and garlic sauce

pinaksiw na lapu-lapu grouper marinated in vinegar and spices, served cold

rellenong bangus stuffed milkfish

SNACKS (MERIENDA) AND STREET FOOD

Adidas chicken feet served on a stick with a choice of sauces for dipping

arroz caldo rice porridge with chicken

balut raw, half-formed duck embryo

camote sweet potato fried with brown sugar, or boiled and served with a pat of butter

chicharron fried pork skin, served with a vinegar dip

dilis dried anchovies, eaten whole and dipped in vinegar as a bar snack or added to vegetable stews

ensaimada sweet cheese rolls

fishballs, squidballs mashed fish or squid blended with wheat flour and deep-fried; served on a stick with a sweet sauce

goto rice porridge often containing pork and garlic

isaw grilled chicken or pig's intestines served with a cup of vinegar for dipping

lugaw plain rice porridge

lumpia fried spring rolls (from Hokkien)

mami noodle soup

mais steamed corn-on-the-cob

pugo hard-boiled quail's eggs, sold in packets of fifteen to twenty

pulutan general term for snacks or finger food

puto rice muffins

sinangag garlic fried rice

siopao Chinese buns filled with spicy pork

sorbetes ice cream

DESSERTS

Bibingka cake made of ground rice, sugar and coconut milk, baked in a clay stove and served hot with fresh, salted duck's eggs on top

bilo-bilo glutinous rice and small pieces of tapioca in coconut milk

brazos meringues, often with cashew-nut filling

cassava cake dark, sticky cake with a fudge-like consistency

champorado chocolate rice pudding

guinatan chocolate pudding served with lashings of coconut cream

halo-halo sweet concoction made from ice cream, shaved ice, jelly, beans and tinned milk; the name literally means "mix-mix"

kutsinta brown rice cake with coconut shavings

leche flan caramel custard

maja blanca blancmange of corn and coconut cream

polvoron sweets made from butter, sugar and toasted flour, pale in colour with a crumbly texture

puto bumbong glutinous rice steamed in a bamboo tube, infusing it with a delicate, woody taste

sago at nata de coco blend of sago and coconut served cold in a glass

suman sweet and sticky rice cake served inside a banana leaf

turon banana and jackfruit in a fried spring roll

DRINKS (INUMIN)

(merong/walang) yelo (with/without) ice

(merong/walang) asukal (with/without) sugar

Alak wine (in practice, everyone just says "wine")

beer beer

buko juice coconut water

calamansi juice/soda calamansi juice (see box, page 35), made into a cold drink by adding soda or a hot one with boiled water and a touch of honey

chocolate-eh thick hot chocolate

gatas milk

ginebra gin

juice juice

kape coffee

lambanog alcoholic drink made from fermented fruit and available in a range of flavours

mineral mineral water

rum rum (the popular Tanduay brand has become almost synonymous with rum)

tapuy rice wine

tsa tea

tubig water

tubo juice sugar-cane juice

Glossary

amihan the northwest monsoon from November to April (dry season)

bahay house

bahay kubo wooden house

bahay na bato house built of stone

bangka boat carved from wood, with stabilizing outriggers made from bamboo; the so-called "big bangkas" are used as ferries and often feature cabins

barangay the smallest political voting unit, whose residents elect "barangay captains" to represent their views to the mayor; barangays take different forms, ranging from part of a village through a whole village to a district of a town or city. In the Guide barangay is used more generally to mean "village".

barong or **barong tagalog** formal shirt worn by men, woven from fine fabric such as *piña* and worn hanging outside the trousers

barrio village

bulol rice god carved from wood, used by many northern hill Indigenous people in religious rituals

buri type of palm used to make mats and rugs

butanding whale shark

capiz a white seashell that's almost translucent when flattened and is used to make windows and screens

carabao water buffalo

carinderia canteen where food is presented in pots on a counter-top

chinito a Filipino/Filipina who looks Chinese

chinoy slang for Filipino/Filipina Chinese

cogon/kogon wild grass that is often used as thatch on provincial homes and beach cottages

CR toilet ("comfort room")

DoT Department of Tourism

earthquake Baroque style of church architecture typical of Spanish churches in the Philippines, which were built with thick buttresses to protect them from earthquakes and a separate bell tower that wouldn't hit the main church if the tower collapsed

GRO guest relations officer; waitress or hostess in a bar who receives a cut of the payment for the drinks a customer buys her; often a euphemism for sex worker

habagat southwest monsoon from May to October (wet season)

ilustrado the wealthy elite

isla island

kalesa or **calesa** horse-drawn carriage, still seen in some areas including Chinatown in Manila and Vigan

kalye street

kuweba cave

mabuhay literally, "long live". Used most often at toasts, at rallies, or to welcome guests (and in tourism campaigns)

malong tube-like woven garment worn by many Muslims in Mindanao, similar to a sarong

Moro Muslim

narra the national tree, whose wood is considered best for furniture

nipa short, sturdy palm that is dried and used for building houses

nito native vine woven into hats, mats and decorative items such as lampshades

pasalubong The (almost mandatory) Filipino tradition of bringing back gifts, usually food items, for friends and family from abroad – one which serves tourist shops well

Pilipino Filipino; also means Tagalog

piña fibre taken from the outside of the pineapple and woven into fine, shiny cloth

Pinoy/Pinay slang for Filipino/Filipina

poblacion town centre

rugby boys street children, named after the "Rugby" brand of glue they are often addicted to sniffing

sabong cockfighting

sala living room

santo saint; also small statues of the saints found in churches and sold in antique shops

Santo Niño the Christ Child; patron of many communities, revered by Christian Filipinos

sari-sari store small store, often no more than a hut, selling essentials such as matches, snacks, shampoo and toothpaste

sikat native grass woven into various items, especially rugs

sitio small village or outpost, often consisting of no more than a few houses

tamaraw dwarf water buffalo, an endangered species found only on Mindoro

terno classic Filipino formal gown popularized by Imelda Marcos, with high butterfly sleeves and low, square-cut neckline

tinikling folk dance in which participants hop adeptly between heavy bamboo poles as they are struck together at shin height, at increasing speed

Tsinoy slang for Filipino/Filipina Chinese

Small print and index

A ROUGH GUIDE TO ROUGH GUIDES

Published in 1982, the first Rough Guide – to Greece – was a student scheme that became a publishing phenomenon. Mark Ellingham, a recent graduate in English from Bristol University, had been travelling in Greece the previous summer and couldn't find the right guidebook. With a small group of friends he wrote his own guide, combining a contemporary, journalistic style with a thoroughly practical approach to travellers' needs.

The immediate success of the book spawned a series that rapidly covered dozens of destinations. And, in addition to impecunious backpackers, Rough Guides soon acquired a much broader readership that relished the guides' wit and inquisitiveness as much as their enthusiastic, critical approach and value-for-money ethos. These days, Rough Guides include recommendations from budget to luxury and cover more than 120 destinations around the globe, from Amsterdam to Zanzibar, all regularly updated by our team of roaming writers.

Browse all our latest guides, read inspirational features and book your trip at **roughguides.com**.

Rough Guide credits

Editor: Beth Williams
Cartography: Carte
Picture Manager: Tom Smyth
Layout: Pradeep Thapliyal
Publishing Technology Manager: Rebeka Davies
Production Operations Manager: Katie Bennett
Head of Publishing: Sarah Clark

Publishing information

Seventh Edition 2026

Distribution

UK, Ireland and Europe
Apa Publications (UK) Ltd; mail@roughguides.com
United States and Canada
Two Rivers; ips@ingramcontent.com
Australia and New Zealand
Woodslane; info@woodslane.com.au
Worldwide
Apa Publications (UK) Ltd; mail@roughguides.com

Special Sales, Content Licensing and CoPublishing

Rough Guides can be purchased in bulk quantities
at discounted prices. We can create special editions,
personalized jackets and corporate imprints tailored to
your needs. mail@roughguides.com

roughguides.com

EU Representative

LOGOS EUROPE, 9 rue Nicolas Poussin, 17000,
LA ROCHELLE, France; Contact@logoseurope.eu;
+33 (0) 667937378

Printed by Finidr in Czech Republic

ISBN: 9781835293904

This book was produced using **Typefi** automated
publishing software.

A catalogue record for this book is available from the
British Library.

Every effort has been made to ensure that this publication
is accurate, free from safety risks, and provides accurate
information. However, changes and errors are inevitable.
The publisher is not responsible for any resulting loss,
inconvenience, injury or safety concerns arising from the
use of this book.

Help us update

We've gone to a lot of effort to ensure that this edition of
The Rough Guide to Philippines is accurate and up-to-
date. However, things change – places get "discovered",
transport routes are altered, restaurants and hotels raise
prices or lower standards, and businesses cease trading. If
you feel we've got it wrong or left something out, we'd like
to know, and if you can direct us to the web address, so
much the better.

Please send your comments with the subject line
"Rough Guide Philippines Update" to mail@roughguides.
com. We'll send a copy of the next edition (or any other
Rough Guide if you prefer) for the very best emails.

Acknowledgements

Martin would like to thank the rolling cast of characters he met during his time in the Philippines, including Rolyn in
Palawan, Christopher Wegener in Makati, and Kharla Maria in Ortigas. He would also like to thank Marie Patricia Mendoza,
Crystel Joyce Lapuz and the rest of the Astoria team for their assistance in Ortigas and beyond.

ABOUT THE AUTHOR

Martin Zatko has clocked up over a half-century of Rough Guides since his first effort in
2008, including guides to Korea, Japan, China, Taiwan, Vietnam, Malaysia, Australia, Fiji, India,
Turkey, Greece, Morocco and Egypt. When not assignment, he usually finds himself doing
pretty much the same thing, except taking fewer notes and staying in weirder places.

Photo credits
(Key: T-top; C-centre; B-bottom; L-left; R-right)

All images **Shutterstock**

Cover: Aerial View of Lagoon with Kayaks, El Nido, Palawan **iStock**

Index

Map symbols

The symbols below are used on maps throughout the book

—··—	International boundary	🕘	Telephone office	⛪	Monastery	Cliff	Cliff
—··—	State/province boundary	ⓘ	Tourist office	✷	Dive site	Reef	Reef
———	Chapter-division boundary	✚	Hospital/clinic	🏛	Monument	Beach	Beach
	Road	✉	Post office	⚶	Spring/spa	Lighthouse	Lighthouse
	Unpaved road	P	Parking	⊤	Gardens	Fuel station	Fuel station
	Railway	E	Embassy/consulate		Waterfall	Market	Market
	Steps	⊠	Gate	🍷	Museum	Building	Building
	Ferry route	♦	Point of interest	⌣	Bridge	Church (town maps)	Church (town maps)
- - - - -	Footpath	∴	Ruin	▲	Mountain peak	Stadium	Stadium
✈	Airport	⛳	Golf course	⋀⋀	Mountain range	Beach	Beach
★	Transport stop	⊙	Statue	◠	Cave	Park	Park
Ⓛ	LRT	♱	Church (regional)	✿	Turtle nesting site	Cemetery	Cemetery
Ⓜ	MRT	♟	Mosque	✹	Shipwreck		
Ⓟ	Philippines national railway	🏯	Chinese temple	卅	Picnic area		

Listings key

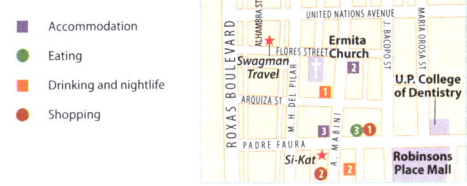

- 🟪 Accommodation
- 🟢 Eating
- 🟧 Drinking and nightlife
- 🔴 Shopping

ECODIVER

samsonite.co.uk